THE
COMPLETE
ESSAYS OF
PLUTARCH

ROYAL

CLASSICS

The Complete Essays of Plutarch
Plutarch 46 AD – 119
Text © 2020 Royal Classics
Design © 2020 Royal Classics

Mailing address:
Royal Classics
PO BOX 4608
Main Station Terminal
349 West Georgia Street
Vancouver, BC
Canada, V6B 4A1

Cover design by: A.R. Roumanis

Text set in Minion Pro. Chapter headings
set in News Gothic Standard.

ISBN: 978-1-77437-609-6

FIRST EDITION / FIRST PRINTING

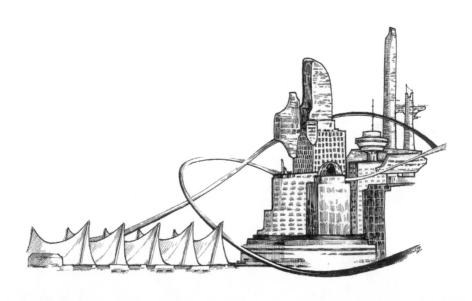

THE COMPLETE ESSAYS OF PLUTARCH

PLUTARCH

VANCOUVER:
ROYAL CLASSICS
2020

CONTENTS

That it is not possible to live pleasurably according to the Doctrine of Epicurus. Plutarch, Zeuxippus, Theon, Aristodemus

EPICURUS'S GREAT CONFIDANT AND familiar, Colotes, set forth a book with this title to it, that according to the tenets of the other philosophers it is impossible to live. Now what occurred to me then to say against him, in the defence of those philosophers, hath been already put into writing by me. But since upon breaking up of our lecture several things have happened to be spoken afterwards in the walks in further opposition to his party, I thought it not amiss to recollect them also, if for no other reason, yet for this one, that those who will needs be contradicting other men may see that they ought not to run cursorily over the discourses and writings of those they would disprove, nor by tearing out one word here and another there, or by falling foul upon particular passages without the books, to impose upon the ignorant and unlearned.

Now as we were leaving the school to take a walk (as our manner is) in the gymnasium, Zeuxippus began to us: In my opinion, said he, the debate was managed on our side with more softness and less freedom than was fitting. I am sure, Heraclides went away disgusted with us, for handling Epicurus and Aletrodorus more roughly than they deserved. Yet you may remember, replied Theon, how you told them that Colotes himself, compared with the rhetoric of those two gentlemen, would appear the complaisantest man alive; for when they have raked together the lewdest terms of ignominy the tongue of man ever used, as buffooneries, trollings, arrogancies, whorings, assassinations, whining counterfeits, black-guards, and blockheads, they faintly throw them in the faces of Aristotle, Socrates, Pythagoras, Protagoras, Theophrastus, Heraclides, Hipparchus, and which not, even of the best and most celebrated authorities. So that, should they pass for very knowing men upon all other accounts, yet their very calumnies and reviling language would bespeak them at the greatest distance from philosophy imaginable. For emulation can never enter that godlike consort, nor such fretfulness as wants resolution to conceal its own resentments. Aristodemus then subjoined: Heraclides, you know, is a great philologist; and that may be the reason why he made Epicurus those amends for the poetic din (so, that party style poetry) and for the fooleries of Homer; or else, it may be, it was because Metrodorus had libelled that poet in so many books. But let us let these gentlemen pass at present, Zeuxippus, and rather return to what was charged upon the philosophers in the beginning of our discourse, that it is impossible to live according to their tenets. And I see not why we two may not despatch this affair betwixt us, with the good assistance of Theon; for I find this gentleman (meaning me) is already tired. Then Theon said to him,

Our fellows have that garland from us won;

therefore, if you please,

Let's fix another goal, and at that run.

("Odyssey," xxii, 6)

We will even prosecute them at the suit of the philosophers, in the following form: We'll prove, if we can, that it is impossible to live a pleasurable life according to their tenets. Bless me! said I to him, smiling, you seem to me to level your foot at the very bellies of the men, and to design to enter the list with them for their lives, whilst you go about to rob them thus of their pleasure, and they cry out to you,

"Forbear, we're no good boxers, sir;

no, nor good pleaders, nor good senators, nor good magistrates either;

"Our proper talent is to eat and drink."

("Odyssey," viii, 246, 248)

and to excite such tender and delicate motions in our bodies as may chafe our imaginations to some jolly delight or gayety." And therefore you seem to me not so much to take off (as I may say) the pleasurable part, as to deprive the men of their very lives, while you will not leave them to live pleasurably. Nay then, said Theon, if you approve so highly of this subject, why do you not set in hand to it? By all means, said I, I am for this, and shall not only hear but answer you too, if you shall insist. But I must leave it to you to take the lead.

Then, after Theon had spoken something to excuse himself, Aristodemus said: When we had so short and fair a cut to our design, how have you blocked up the way before us, by preventing us from joining issue with the faction at the very first upon the single point of propriety! For you must grant, it can be no easy matter to drive men already possessed that pleasure is their utmost good yet to believe a life of pleasure impossible to be attained. But now the truth is, that when they failed of living becomingly they failed also of living pleasurably; for to live pleasurably without living becomingly is even by themselves allowed inconsistent.

Theon then said: We may probably resume the consideration of that in the process of our discourse; in the interim we will make use of their concessions. Now they suppose their last good to lie about the belly and such other conveyances of the body as let in pleasure and not pain; and are of opinion, that all the brave and ingenious inventions that ever have been were contrived at first for the pleasure of the belly, or the good hope of compassing such pleasure,–as the sage Metrodorus informs us. By which, my good friend, it is very plain, they found their pleasure in a poor, rotten, and unsure thing, and one that is equally perforated for pains, by the very passages they receive their pleasures by; or rather indeed, that admits pleasure but by a few, but pain by all its parts. For the whole of pleasure is in a manner in the joints, nerves, feet, and hands; and these are oft the seats of very grievous and lamentable distempers, as gouts, corroding rheums, gangrenes, and putrid ulcers. And if you apply to yourself the exquisitest of perfumes or gusts, you will find but some one small part of your body is finely and delicately touched, while the rest are many times filled with anguish and complaints. Besides, there is no part of us proof against fire, sword, teeth, or scourges, or insensible of dolors and aches; yea, heats, colds, and fevers sink into all our parts alike. But pleasures, like gales of soft wind, move simpering, one towards one extreme of the body and another towards another, and then go off in a vapor. Nor are they of any long durance, but, as so many glancing meteors, they are no sooner kindled in the body than they are quenched by it. As to pain, Aeschylus's Philoctetes affords us a sufficient testimony:–

The cruel viper ne'er will quit my foot;
Her dire envenomed teeth have there ta'en root.

For pain will not troll off as pleasure doth, nor imitate it in its pleasing and tickling touches. But as the clover twists its perplexed and winding roots into the earth, and through its coarseness abides there a long time; so pain disperses and entangles its hooks and roots in the body, and continues there, not for a day or a night, but for several seasons of years, if not for some revolutions of Olympiads, nor scarce ever departs unless struck out by other pains, as by stronger nails. For who ever drank so long as those that are in a fever are a-dry? Or who was ever so long eating as those that are besieged suffer hunger? Or where are there any that are so long solaced with the conversation of friends as tyrants are racking and tormenting? Now all this is owing to the baseness of the body and its natural incapacity for a pleasurable life; for it bears pains better than it doth pleasures, and with respect to those is firm and hardy, but with respect to these is feeble and soon palled. To which add, that if we are minded to discourse on a life of pleasure, these men won't give us leave to go on, but will presently confess themselves that the pleasures of the body are but short, or rather indeed but of a moment's continuance; if they do not design to banter us or else speak out of vanity, when Metrodorus tells us, We many times spit at the pleasures of the body, and Epicurus saith, A wise man, when he is sick, many times laughs in the very extremity of his distemper.

For Ithaca is no fit place
For mettled steeds to run a race.
("Odyssey," iv. 605.)

Neither can the joys of our poor bodies be smooth and equal; but on the contrary they must be coarse and harsh, and immixed with much that is displeasing and inflamed.

Zeuxippus then said: And do you not think then they take the right course to begin at the body, where they observe pleasure to have its first rise, and thence to pass to the mind as the more stable and sure part, there to complete and crown the whole?

They do, by Jove, I said; and if, after removing thither they have indeed found something more consummate than before, a course too as well agreeing with nature as becoming men adorned with both contemplative and civil knowledge. But if after all this you still hear them cry out, and protest that the mind of man can receive no satisfaction or tranquillity from anything under Heaven but the pleasures of the body either in possession or expectance, and that these are its proper and only good, can you forbear thinking they make use of the soul but as a funnel for the body, while they mellow their pleasure by shifting it from one vessel to another, as they rack wine out of an old and leaky vessel into a new one and there let it grow old, and then imagine they have performed some extraordinary and very fine thing? True indeed, a fresh pipe may both keep and recover wine that hath thus been drawn off; but the mind, receiving but the remembrance only of past pleasure, like a kind of scent, retains that and no more. For as soon as it hath given one hiss in the body, it immediately expires, and that little of it that stays behind in the memory is but flat and like a queasy fume: as if a man should lay up and treasure in his fancy what he either ate or drank yesterday, that he may have recourse to that when he wants fresh fare. See now how much more temperate the Cyrenaics are, who, though they have drunk out of the same bottle with Epicurus, yet will not allow men so much as to practise their amours by candlelight, but only under the covert of the dark, for fear seeing should fasten too quick an impression of the images of such actions upon the fancy and thereby too frequently inflame the desire. But these gentlemen account it the highest accomplishment of a philosopher to have a clear and retentive memory of all the various figures, passions, and touches of past pleasure. We will not now say, they present us with nothing worthy the name of philosophy, while they leave the refuse of pleasure in their wise man's mind, as if it could be a lodging for bodies; but that it is impossible such things as these should make a man live pleasurably, I think is abundantly manifest from hence.

For it will not perhaps seem strange if I assert, that the memory of pleasure past brings no pleasure with it if it appeared but little in the very enjoyment, or to men of such abstinence as to account it for their benefit to retire from its first approaches; when even the most amazed and sensual admirers of corporeal delights remain no longer in their gaudy and pleasant humor than their pleasure lasts them. What remains is but an empty shadow and dream of that pleasure that hath now taken wing and is fled from them, and that serves but for fuel to foment their untamed desires. Like as in those that dream they are a-dry or in love, their unaccomplished pleasures and enjoyments do but excite the inclination to a greater keenness. Nor indeed can the remembrance of past enjoyments afford them any real contentment at all, but must serve only, with the help of a quick desire, to raise up very much of outrage and stinging pain out of the remains of a feeble and befooling pleasure. Neither doth it befit men of continence and sobriety to exercise their thoughts about such poor things, or to do what one twitted Carneades with, to reckon, as out of a diurnal, how oft they have lain with Hedia or Leontion, or where they last drank Thasian wine, or at what twentieth-day feast they had a costly supper. For such transport and captivatedness of the mind to its own remembrances as this is would show a detestable and bestial restlessness and raving towards the present and hoped-for acts of pleasure. And therefore I cannot but look upon the sense of these inconveniences as the true cause of their retiring at last to a freedom from pain and a firm state of body; as if living pleasurably could lie in bare imagining this either past or future to some persons. True indeed it is, "that a sound state of body and a good assurance of its continuing must needs afford a most transcending and solid satisfaction to all men capable of reasoning."

But yet look first what work they make, while they course this same thing–whether it be pleasure, exemption from pain, or good health–up and down, first from the body to the mind, and then back again from the mind to the body, being compelled to return it to its first origin, lest it should run out and so give them the slip. Thus they place the pleasure of the body (as Epicurus says) upon the complacent joy in the mind, and yet conclude again with the good hopes that complacent joy hath in bodily pleasure. Indeed what wonder is it if, when the foundation shakes, the superstructure totter? Or that there should be no sure hope nor unshaken joy in a matter that suffers so great concussion and changes as continually attend a body exposed to so many violences and strokes from without, and having within it the origins of such evils as human reason cannot avert? For if it could, no understanding man would ever fall under stranguries, gripes, consumptions, or dropsies; with some of which Epicurus himself did conflict and Polyaenus with others, while others of them were the deaths of Neocles and Agathobulus. And this we mention not to disparage them, knowing very well that Pherecydes and Heraclitus, both very excellent persons, labored under very uncouth and calamitous distempers. We only beg of them, if they will own their own diseases and not by noisy rants and popular harangues incur the imputation of false bravery, either not to take the health of the whole body for the ground of their content, or else not to say that men under the extremities of dolors and diseases can yet rally and be pleasant. For a sound and hale constitution of body is indeed a thing that often happens, but a firm and steadfast assurance of its continuance can never befall an intelligent mind. But as at sea (according to Aeschylus)

Night to the ablest pilot trouble brings,
(Aechylus, "Suppliants," 770.)

and so will a calm too, for no man knows what will be,–so likewise is it impossible for a soul that dwells in a healthful body, and that places her good in the hopes she hath of that body, to perfect her voyage here without frights or waves. For man's mind hath not, like the sea, its tempests and storms only from without it, but it also raises up from within far more and greater disturbances. And a man may with more reason look for constant fair weather in the midst of winter than for perpetual exemption from afflictions in his body. For what else hath given the poets occasion to term us ephemeral creatures, uncertain and unfixed, and to liken our lives to leaves that both spring and fall in the lapse of a summer, but the unhappy, calamitous, and sickly condition of the body, whose very utmost good we are warned to dread and prevent? For an exquisite habit, Hippocrates saith, is slippery and hazardous. And

> *He that but now looked jolly, plump, and stout,*
> *Like a star shot by Jove, is now gone out;*

as it is in Euripides. And it is a vulgar persuasion, that very handsome persons, when looked upon, oft suffer damage by envy and an evil eye; for a body at its utmost vigor will through delicacy very soon admit of changes.

But now that these men are miserably unprovided for an undisturbed life, you may discern even from what they themselves advance against others. For they say that those who commit wickedness and incur the displeasure of the laws live in constant misery and fear, for, though they may perhaps attain to privacy, yet it is impossible they should ever be well assured of that privacy; whence the ever impending fear of the future will not permit them to have either complacency or assurance in their present circumstances. But they consider not how they speak all this against themselves. For a sound and healthy state of body they may indeed oftentimes possess, but that they should ever be well assured of its continuance is impossible; and they must of necessity be in constant disquiet and pain for the body with respect to futurity, never being able to reach that firm and steadfast assurance which they expect. But to do no wickedness will contribute nothing to our assurance; for it is not suffering unjustly but suffering in itself that is dismaying. Nor can it be a matter of trouble to be engaged in villanies one's self, and not afflictive to suffer by the villanies of others. Neither can it be said that the tyranny of Lachares was less, if it was not more, calamitous to the Athenians, and that of Dionysius to the Syracusans, than they were to the tyrants themselves; for it was disturbing that made them be disturbed; and their first oppressing and pestering of others gave them occasion to expect to suffer ill themselves. Why should a man recount the outrages of rabbles, the barbarities of thieves, or the villanies of inheritors, or yet the contagions of airs and the concursions of seas, by which Epicurus (as himself writeth) was in his voyage to Lampsacus within very little of drowning? The very composition of the body–it containing in it the matter of all diseases, and (to use a pleasantry of the vulgar) cutting thongs for the beast out of its own hide, I mean pains out of the body–is sufficient to make life perilous and uneasy, and that to the good as well as to the bad, if they have learned to set their complacence and assurance in the body and the hopes they have of it, and in nothing else; as Epicurus hath written, as well in many other of his discourses as in that of Man's End.

They therefore assign not only a treacherous and unsure ground of their pleasurable living, but also one in all respects despicable and little, if the escaping of evils be the matter of their complacence and last good. But now they tell us, nothing else can be so much as imagined, and nature hath no other place to bestow her good in but only that out of which her evil hath been driven; as Metrodorus speaks in his book against the Sophists. So that this single thing, to escape evil, he says, is the supreme good; for there is no room to lodge this good in where no more of what is painful and afflicting goes out. Like unto this is that of Epicurus, where he saith: The very essence of good arises from the escaping of bad, and a man's recollecting, considering, and rejoicing within himself that this hath befallen him. For what occasions transcending joy (he saith) is some great impending evil escaped; and in this lies the very nature and essence of good, if a man consider it aright, and contain himself when he hath done, and not ramble and prate idly about it. Oh, the rare satisfaction and felicity these men enjoy, that can thus rejoice for having undergone no evil and endured neither sorrow nor pain! Have they not reason, think you, to value themselves for such things as these, and to speak as they are wont when they style themselves immortals and equals to gods?–and when, through the excessiveness and transcendency of the blessed things they enjoy, they rave even to the degree of whooping and hollowing for very satisfaction that, to the shame of all mortals, they have been the only men that could find out this celestial and divine good that lies in an exemption from all evil? So that their beatitude differs little from that of swine and sheep, while they place it in a mere tolerable and contented state, either of the body, or of the mind upon the body's account. For even the more prudent and more ingenious sort of brutes do not esteem escaping of evil their last end; but when they have taken their repast, they are disposed next by fullness to singing, and they divert themselves with swimming and flying; and their gayety and sprightliness prompt them to entertain themselves with attempting to counterfeit all sorts of voices and notes; and then they make their caresses to one another, by skipping and dancing one towards another; nature inciting them, after they have escaped evil, to look after some good, or rather to shake off what they find uneasy and disagreeing, as an impediment to their pursuit of something better and more congenial.

For what we cannot be without deserves not the name of good; but that which claims our desire and preference must be something beyond a bare escape from evil. And so, by Jove, must that be too that is either agreeing or congenial to us, according to Plato, who will not allow us to give the name of pleasures to the bare departures of sorrows and pains, but would have us look upon them rather as obscure draughts and mixtures of agreeing and disagreeing, as of black and white, while the extremes would advance themselves to a middle temperament. But oftentimes unskilfulness and ignorance of the true nature of extreme occasions some to mistake the middle temperament for the extreme and outmost part. Thus do Epicurus and Metrodorus, while they make avoiding of evil to be the very essence and consummation of good, and so receive but as it were the satisfaction of slaves or of rogues newly discharged the jail, who are well enough contented if they may but wash and supple their sores and the stripes they received by whipping, but never in their lives had one taste or sight of a generous, clean, unmixed and unulcerated joy. For it follows not that, if it be vexatious to have one's body itch or one's eyes to run, it must be therefore a blessing to scratch one's self, and to wipe one's eye with a rag; nor that, if it be bad to be dejected or dismayed at divine matters or to be discomposed with the relations of hell, therefore the bare avoiding of all this must be some happy and amiable thing. The truth is, these men's opinion, though it pretends so far to outgo that of the vulgar, allows their joy but a straight and narrow compass to toss and tumble in, while it extends it but to an exemption from the fear of hell, and so makes that the top of acquired wisdom which is doubtless natural to the brutes. For if freedom from bodily pain be still the same, whether it come by endeavor or by nature, neither then is an undisturbed state of mind the greater for being attained to by industry than if it came by nature. Though a man may with good reason maintain that to be the more confirmed habit of the mind which naturally admits of no disorder, than that which by application and judgment eschews it.

But let us suppose them both equal; they will yet appear not one jot superior to the beasts for being unconcerned at the stories of hell and the legends of the gods, and for not expecting endless sorrows and everlasting torments hereafter. For it is Epicurus himself that tells us that, had our surmises about heavenly phenomena and our foolish apprehensions of death and the pains that ensue it given us no disquiet, we had not then needed to contemplate nature for our relief. For neither have the brutes any weak surmises of the gods or fond opinion about things after death to disorder themselves with; nor have they as much as imagination or notion that there is anything in these to be dreaded. I confess, had they left us the benign providence of God as a presumption, wise men might then seem, by reason of their good hopes from thence, to have something towards a pleasurable life that beasts have not. But now, since they have made it the scope of all their discourses of God that they may not fear him, but may be eased of all concern about him, I much question whether those that never thought at all of him have not this in a more confirmed degree than they that have learned to think he can do no harm. For if they were never freed from superstition, they never fell into it; and if they never laid aside a disturbing conceit of God, they never took one up. The like may be said as to hell and the future state. For though neither the Epicurean nor the brute can hope for any good thence; yet such as have no forethought of death at all cannot but be less amused and scared with what comes after it than they that betake themselves to the principle that death is nothing to us. But something to them it must be, at least so far as they concern themselves to reason about it and contemplate it; but the beasts are wholly exempted from thinking of what appertains not to them; and if they fly from blows, wounds, and slaughters, they fear no more in death than is dismaying to the Epicurean himself.

Such then are the things they boast to have attained by their philosophy. Let us now see what those are they deprive themselves of and chase away from them. For those diffusions of the mind that arise from the body, and the pleasing condition of the body, if they be but moderate, appear to have nothing in them that is either great or considerable; but if they be excessive, besides their being vain and uncertain, they are also importune and petulant; nor should a man term them either mental satisfactions or gayeties, but rather corporeal gratifications, they being at best but the simperings and effeminacies of the mind. But now such as justly deserve the names of complacencies and joys are wholly refined from their contraries, and are immixed with neither vexation, remorse, nor repentance; and their good is congenial to the mind and truly mental and genuine, and not superinduced. Nor is it devoid of reason, but most rational, as springing either from that in the mind that is contemplative and inquiring, or else from that part of it that is active and heroic. How many and how great satisfactions either of these affords us, no one can ever relate. But to hint briefly at some of them. We have the historians before us, which, though they find us many and delightful exercises, still leave our desire after truth insatiate and uncloyed with pleasure, through which even lies are not without their grace. Yea, tales and poetic fictions, while they cannot gain upon our belief, have something in them that is charming to us.

For do but think with yourself, with what a sting we read Plato's "Atlantic" and the conclusion of the "Iliad," and how we hanker and gape after the rest of the tale, as when some beautiful temple or theatre is shut up. But now the informing of ourselves with the truth herself is a thing so delectable and lovely as if our very life and being were for the sake of knowing. And the darkest and grimmest things in death are its oblivion, ignorance, and obscurity. Whence, by Jove, it is that almost all mankind encounter with those that would destroy the sense of the departed, as placing the very whole of their life, being, and satisfaction solely in the sensible and knowing part of the mind. For even the things that grieve and afflict us yet afford us a sort of pleasure in the hearing. And it is often seen that those that are disordered by what is told them, even to the degree of weeping, notwithstanding require the telling of it. So he in the tragedy who is told,

Alas I now the very worst must tell,
replies,
I dread to hear it too, but I must hear.
(Sophocles, "Pedipus Tyrannus," 1169, 1170.)

But this may seem perhaps a sort of intemperateness of delight in knowing everything, and as it were a stream violently bearing down the reasoning faculty. But now, when a story that hath in it nothing that is troubling and afflictive treats of great and heroic enterprises with a potency and grace of style such as we find in Herodotus's Grecian and in Xenophon's Persian history, or in what,

Inspired by heavenly gods, sage Homer sung,

or in the Travels of Euxodus, the Foundations and Republics of Aristotle, and the Lives of Famous Men compiled by Aristoxenus; these will not only bring us exceeding much and great contentment, but such also as is clean and secure from repentance. And who could take greater satisfaction either in eating when a-hungry or drinking when a-dry amongst the Phaeacians, than in going over Ulysses's relation of his own voyage and rambles? And what man could be better pleased with the embraces of the most exquisite beauty, than with sitting up all night to read over what Xenophon hath written of Panthea, or Aristobulus of Timoclea, or Theopompus of Thebe?

But now these appertain all solely to the mind. But they chase away from them the delights that accrue from the mathematics also. Though the satisfactions we receive from history have in them something simple and equal; but those that come from geometry, astronomy, and music inveigle and allure us with a sort of nimbleness and variety, and want nothing that is tempting and engaging; their figures attracting us as so many charms, whereof whoever hath once tasted, if he be but competently skilled, will run about chanting that in Sophocles,

I'm mad; the Muses with new rage inspire me.
I'll mount the hill; my lyre, my numbers fire me.
(From the "Thamyras" of Sophocles, Frag. 225)

Nor doth Thamyras break out into poetic raptures upon any other score; nor, by Jove, Euxodus, Aristarchus, or Archimedes. And when the lovers of the art of painting are so enamoured with the charmingness of their own performances, that Nicias, as he was drawing the Evocation of Ghosts in Homer, often asked his servants whether he had dined or no, and when King Ptolemy had sent him threescore talents for his piece, after it was finished, he neither would accept the money nor part with his work; what and how great satisfactions may we then suppose to have been reaped from geometry and astronomy by Euclid when he wrote his Dioptrics, by Philippus when he had perfected his demonstration of the figure of the moon, by Archimedes when with the help of a certain angle he had found the sun's diameter to make the same part of the largest circle that that angle made of four right angles, and by Apollonius and Aristarchus who were the inventors of some other things of the like nature? The bare contemplating and comprehending of all these now engender in the learners both unspeakable delights and a marvellous height of spirit. And it doth in no wise beseem me, by comparing with these the fulsome debauchees of victualling-houses and stews, to contaminate Helicon and the Muses,–

Where swain his flock ne'er fed,
Nor tree by hatchet bled.
(Euripides, "Hippolytus," 75.)

But these are the verdant and untrampled pastures of ingenious bees; but those are more like the mange of lecherous boars and he-goats. And though a voluptuous temper of mind be naturally erratic and precipitate, yet never any yet sacrificed an ox for joy that he had gained his will of his mistress; nor did any ever wish to die immediately, might he but once satiate himself with the costly dishes and comfits at the table of his prince. But now Eudoxus wished he might stand by the sun, and inform himself of the figure, magnitude, and beauty of that luminary,

though he were, like Phaethon, consumed by it. And Pythagoras offered an ox in sacrifice for having completed the lines of a certain geo-
metric diagram; as Apollodotus tells us,

> *When the famed lines Pythagoras devised,*
> *For which a splendid ox he sacrificed.*

Whether it was that by which he showed that the line that regards
the right angle in a triangle is equivalent to the two lines that contain
that angle, or the problem about the area of the parabolic section of a
cone. And Archimedes's servants were forced to hale him away from
his draughts, to be anointed in the bath; but he notwithstanding drew
the lines upon his belly with his strigil. And when, as he was washing (as the story goes of him), he thought of a manner of computing
the proportion of gold in King Hiero's crown by seeing the water flowing over the bathing-stool, he leaped up as one possessed or inspired,
crying, "I have found it;" which after he had several times repeated,
he went his way. But we never yet heard of a glutton that exclaimed
with such vehemence, "I have eaten," or of an amorous gallant that ever
cried, "I have kissed," among the many millions of dissolute debauchees
that both this and preceding ages have produced. Yea, we abominate
those that make mention of their great suppers with too luscious a gust,
as men overmuch taken with mean and abject delights. But we find
ourselves in one and the same ecstasy with Eudoxus, Archimedes, and
Hipparchus; and we readily give assent to Plato when he saith of the
mathematics, that while ignorance and unskilledness make men despise them, they still thrive notwithstanding by reason of their charmingness, in despite of contempt.

These then so great and so many pleasures, that run like perpetual
springs and rills, these men decline and avoid; nor will they permit
those that put in among them so much as to take a taste of them, but
bid them hoist up the little sails of their paltry cock-boats and fly from
them. Nay, they all, both he and she philosophers, beg and entreat Pythocles, for dear Epicurus's sake, not to affect or make such account
of the sciences called liberal. And when they cry up and defend one
Apelles, they write of him that he kept himself clean by refraining himself all along from the mathematics. But as to history–to pass over their
aversedness to other kinds of compositions–I shall only present you
with the words of Metrodorus, who in his treatise of the Poets writes
thus: Wherefore let it never disturb you, if you know not either what
side Hector was of, or the first verses in Homer's Poem, or again what
is in its middle. But that the pleasures of the body spend themselves
like the winds called Etesian or Anniversary, and utterly determine

when once age is past its vigor, Epicurus himself was not insensible; and therefore he makes it a problematic question, whether a sage philosopher, when he is an old man and disabled for enjoyment, may not still be recreated with having handsome girls to feel and grope him, being not, it seems, of the mind of old Sophocles, who thanked God he had at length escaped from this kind of pleasure, as from an untamed and furious master. But, in my opinion, it would be more advisable for these sensual lechers, when they see that age will dry up so many of their pleasures, and that, as Euripides saith,

> Dame Venus is to ancient men a foe,
> (Euripides, "Aeolus," Frag. 23.)

in the first place to collect and lay up in store, as against a siege, these other pleasures, as a sort of provision that will not impair and decay; that then, after they have celebrated the venereal festivals of life, they may spend a cleanly after-feast in reading over the historians and poets, or else in problems of music and geometry. For it would never have come into their minds so much as to think of these purblind and toothless gropings and spurtings of lechery, had they but learned, if nothing more, to write comments upon Homer or Euripides, as Aristotle, Heraclides, and Dicaerchus did. But I verily persuade myself that their neglecting to take care for such provisions as these, and finding all the other things they employed themselves in (as they use to say of virtue) but insipid and dry, and being wholly set upon pleasure, and the body no longer supplying them with it, give them occasion to stoop to do things both mean and shameful in themselves and unbecoming their age; as well when they refresh their memories with their former pleasures and serve themselves of old ones (as it were) long since dead and laid up in pickle for the purpose, when they cannot have fresh ones, as when again they offer violence to nature by suscitating and inflaming in their decayed bodies, as in cold embers, other new ones equally senseless, they having not, it seems, their minds stored with any congenial pleasure that is worth the rejoicing at.

As to the other delights of the mind, we have already treated of them, as they occurred to us. But their aversedness and dislike to music, that affords us so great delights and such charming satisfactions, a man could not forget if he would, by reason of the inconsistency of what Epicurus saith, when he pronounceth in his book called his Doubts that his wise man ought to be a lover of public spectacles and to delight above any other man in the music and shows of the Bacchanals; and yet he will not admit of music problems or of the critical inquiries of philologists, no, not so much as at a compotation. Yea, he advises such princes as are lovers of the Muses rather to entertain themselves at their feasts either with some narration of military adventures or with the importune scurrilities of drolls and buffoons, than to engage in disputes about music or in questions of poetry. For this very thing he had the face to write in his treatise of Monarchy, as if he were writing to Sardanapalus, or to Nanarus ruler of Babylon. For neither would a Hiero nor an Attalus nor an Archelaus be persuaded to make a Euripides, a Simonides, a Melanippides, a Crates, or a Diodotus rise up from their tables, and to place such scaramuchios in their rooms as a Cardax, an Agrias, or a Callias, or fellows like Thrasonides and Thrasyleon, to make people disorder the house with hollowing and clapping. Had the great Ptolemy, who was the first that formed a consort of musicians, but met with these excellent and royal admonitions, would he not, think you, have thus addressed himself to the Samians:–

O Muse, whence art thou thus maligned?

For certainly it can never belong to any Athenian to be in such enmity and hostility with the Muses. But

No animal accurst by Jove
Music's sweet charms can ever love.
(Pindar, "Pythian," i. 25.)

What sayest thou now, Epicurus? Wilt thou get thee up betimes in the morning, and go to the theatre to hear the harpers and flutists play? But if a Theophrastus discourse at the table of Concords, or an Aristoxenus of Varieties, or if an Aristophanes play the critic upon Homer, wilt thou presently, for very dislike and abhorrence, clap both thy hands upon thy ears? And do they not hereby make the Scythian king Ateas more musical than this comes to, who, when he heard that admirable flutist Ismenias, detained then by him as a prisoner of war, playing upon the flute at a compotation, swore he had rather hear his own horse neigh? And do they not also profess themselves to stand at an implacable and irreconcilable defiance with whatever is generous and becoming? And indeed what do they ever embrace or affect that is either genteel or regardable, when it hath nothing of pleasure to accompany it? And would it not far less affect a pleasurable way of living, to abhor perfumes and odors, like beetles and vultures, than to shun and abhor the conversation of learned, critics and musicians? For what flute or harp ready tuned for a lesson, or

What sweetest concerts e'er with artful noise,
Warbled by softest tongue and best tuned voice,

ever gave Epicurus and Metrodorus such content as the disputes and precepts about concerts gave Aristotle, Theophrastus, Hieronymus, and Dicaerchus? And also the problems about flutes, rhythms, and harmonies; as, for instance, why the longer of two flutes of the same longitude should speak flatter?–why, if you raise the pipe, will all its notes be sharp; and flat again, if you depress it?–and why, when clapped to another, will it sound flatter; and sharper again, when taken from it?–why also, if you scatter chaff or dust about the orchestra of a theatre, will the sound be deadened?–and why, when one would have set up a bronze Alexander for a frontispiece to a stage at Pella, did the architect advise to the contrary, because it would spoil the actors' voices? and why, of the several kinds of music, will the chromatic diffuse and the harmonic compose the mind? But now the several humors of poets, their differing turns and forms of style, and the solutions of their difficult places, have conjoined with a sort of dignity and politeness somewhat also that is extremely agreeable and charming; insomuch that to me they seem to do what was once said by Xenophon, to make a man even forget the joys of love, so powerful and overcoming is the pleasure they bring us.

In this investigation these gentlemen have not the least share, nor do they so much as pretend or desire to have any. But while they are sinking and depressing their contemplative part into the body, and dragging it down by their sensual and intemperate appetites, as by so many weights of lead, they make themselves appear little better than hostlers or graziers that still ply their cattle with hay, straw, or grass, looking upon such provender as the properest and meetest food for them. And is it not even thus they would swill the mind with the pleasures of the body, as hogherds do their swine, while they will not allow it can be gay any longer than it is hoping, experiencing, or remembering something that refers to the body; but will not have it either to receive or seek for any congenial joy or satisfaction from within itself? Though what can be more absurd and unreasonable than–when there are two things that go to make up the man, a body and a soul, and the soul besides hath the perogative of governing–that the body should have its peculiar, natural, and proper good, and the soul none at all, but must sit gazing at the body and simper at its passions, as if she were pleased and affected with them, though indeed she be all the while wholly untouched and unconcerned, as having nothing of her own to choose, desire, or take delight in? For they should either pull off the vizor quite, and say plainly that man is all body (as some of them do, that take away all mental being), or, if they will allow us to have two distinct natures, they should then leave to each its proper good and evil, agreeable and disagreeable; as we find it to be with our senses, each of which is peculiarly adapted to its own sensible, though they all very strangely intercommune one with another. Now the intellect is the proper sense of the mind; and therefore that it should have no congenial speculation, movement, or affection of its own, the attaining to which should be matter of complacency to it, is the most irrational thing in the world, if I have not, by Jove, unwittingly done the men wrong, and been myself imposed upon by some that may perhaps have calumniated them.

Then I said to him: If we may be your judges, you have not; yea, we must acquit you of having offered them the least indignity; and therefore pray despatch the rest of your discourse with assurance. How! said I, and shall not Aristodemus then succeed me, if you are tired out yourself? Aristodemus said: With all my heart, when you are as much tired as he is; but since you are yet in your vigor, pray make use of yourself, my noble friend, and don't think to pretend weariness. Theon then replied: What is yet behind, I must confess, is very easy; it being but to go over the several pleasures contained in that part of life that consists in action. Now themselves somewhere say that there is far more satisfaction in doing than in receiving good; and good may be done many times, it is true, by words, but the most and greatest part of good consists in action, as the very name of beneficence tells us and they themselves also attest. For you may remember, continued he, we heard this gentleman tell us but now what words Epicurus uttered, and what letters he sent to his friends, applauding and magnifying Metrodorus,–how bravely and like a spark he quitted the city and went down to the port to relieve Mithrus the Syrian,–and this, though Metrodorus did not then do anything at all. What and how great then may we presume the pleasures of Plato to have been, when Dion by the measures he gave him deposed the tyrant Dionysius and set Sicily at liberty? And what the pleasures of Aristotle, when he rebuilt his native city Stagira, then levelled with the ground, and brought back its exiled inhabitants? And what the pleasures of Theophrastus and of Phidias, when they cut off the tyrants of their respective countries? For what need a man recount to you, who so well know it, how many particular persons they relieved, not by sending them a little wheat or a measure of meal (as Epicurus did to some of his friends), but by procuring restoration to the banished, liberty to the imprisoned, and restitution of wives and children to those that had been bereft of them? But a man could not, if he were willing, pass by the sottish stupidity of the man who, though he tramples under foot and vilifies the great and generous actions of Themistocles and Miltiades, yet writes these very words to his friends about himself: "You have given a very gallant and noble testimony of your care of me in the provision of corn you have made for me, and have declared your affection to me by signs that mount to the very skies." So that, should a man but take that poor parcel of corn out of the great philosopher's epistle, it might seem to be the recital of some letter of thanks for the delivery or preservation of all Greece or of the commons of Athens.

We will now forbear to mention that Nature requires very large and chargeable provisions to be made for accomplishing the pleasures of the body; nor can the height of delicacy be had in black bread and lentil pottage. But voluptuous and sensual appetites expect costly dishes, Thasian wines, perfumed unguents, and varieties of pastry works,

> And cakes by female hands wrought artfully,
> Well steep'd in th' liquor of the gold-wing'd bee;

and besides all this, handsome young lassies too, such as Leontion, Boidion, Hedia, and Nicedion, that were wont to roam about in Epicurus's philosophic garden. But now such joys as suit the mind must undoubtedly be grounded upon a grandeur of actions and a splendor of worthy deeds, if men would not seem little, ungenerous, and puerile, but on the contrary, bulky, firm, and brave. But for a man to be elated by happiness, as Epicurus is, like sailors upon the festivals of Venus, and to vaunt himself that, when he was sick of an ascites, he notwithstanding called his friends together to certain collations and grudged not his dropsy the addition of good liquor, and that, when he called to remembrance the last words of Neocles, he was melted with a peculiar sort of joy intermixed with tears,–no man in his right senses would call these true joys or satisfactions. Nay, I will be bold to say that, if such a thing as that they call a sardonic or grinning laughter can happen to the mind, it is to be found in these artificial and crying laughters. But if any will needs have them still called by the name of joys and satisfactions, let him but yet think how far they are exceeded by the pleasures that here ensue:–

> Our counsels have proud Sparta's glory clipt; and Stranger, this is his country Rome's great star;

and again this,

> I know not which to guess thee, man or god.

Now when I set before my eyes the brave achievements of Thrasybulus and Pelopidas, of Aristides engaged at Platea and Miltiades at Marathon, I am here constrained with Herodotus to declare it my opinion, that in an active state of life the pleasure far exceeds the glory. And Epaminondas herein bears me witness also, when he saith (as is reported of him), that the greatest satisfaction he ever received in his life was that his father and mother had lived to see the trophy set up at Leuctra when himself was general. Let us then compare with Epaminondas's Epicurus's mother, rejoicing that she had lived to see her son cooping himself up in a little garden, and getting children in common with Polyaenus upon the strumpet of Cyzicus. As for Metrodorus's mother and sister, how extravagantly rejoiced they were at his nuptials appears by the letters he wrote to his brother in answer to his; that is, out of his own books. Nay, they tell us bellowing that they have not only lived a life of pleasure, but also exult and sing hymns in the praise of their own living. Though, when our servants celebrate the festivals of Saturn or go in procession at the time of the rural bacchanals, you would scarcely brook the hollowing and din they make, if the intemperateness of their joy and their insensibleness of decorum should make them act and speak such things as these:–

Lean down, boy! why dost sit I let's tope like mad!
Here's belly-timber store; ne'er spare it, lad.
Straight these huzza like wild. One fills up drink;
Another plaits a wreath, and crowns the brink
O' th' teeming bowl. Then to the verdant bays
All chant rude carols in Apollo's praise;
While one the door with drunken fury smites,
Till he from bed his loving consort frights.

And are not Metrodorus's words something like to these when he writes to his brother thus: It is none of our business to preserve the Greeks, or to get them to bestow garlands upon us for our wit, but to eat well and drink good wine, Timocrates, so as not to offend but pleasure our stomachs. And he saith again, in some other place in the same epistles: How gay and how assured was I, when I had once learned of Epicurus the true way of gratifying my stomach; for, believe me, philosopher Timocrates, our prime good lies at the stomach.

In brief, these men draw out the dimensions of their pleasures like a circle, about the stomach as a centre. And the truth is, it is impossible for those men ever to participate of generous and princely joy, such as enkindles a height of spirit in us and sends forth to all mankind an unmade hilarity and calm serenity, that have taken up a sort of life that is confined, unsocial, inhuman, and uninspired towards the esteem of the world and the love of mankind. For the soul of man is not an abject, little, and ungenerous thing, nor doth it extend its desires (as polyps do their claws) unto eatables only,–yea, these are in an instant of time taken off by the least plenitude, but when its efforts towards what is brave and generous and the honors and caresses that accrue therefrom are now in their consummate vigor this life's duration cannot limit them, but the desire of glory and the love of mankind grasp at whole eternity, and wrestle with such actions and charms as bring with them an ineffable pleasure, and such as good men, though never so fain, cannot decline, they meeting and accosting them on all sides and surrounding them about, while their being beneficial to many occasions joy to themselves.

> *As he passes through the throngs in the city,*
> *All gaze upon him as some deity.*
> ("Odyssey," viii. 173.)

For he that can so affect and move other men as to fill them with joy and rapture, and to make them long to touch him and salute him, cannot but appear even to a blind man to possess and enjoy very extraordinary satisfactions in himself. And hence it comes that such men are both indefatigable and undaunted in serving the public, and we still hear some such words from them

> *Thy father got thee for the common good;*

and

> *Let's not give off to benefit mankind.*

But what need I instance in those that are consummately good? For if to one of the middling rank of bad men, when he is just a-dying, he that hath the power over him (whether his god or prince) should but allow one hour more, upon condition that, after he hath spent that either in some generous action or in sensual enjoyment, he should then presently die, who would in this time choose rather to accompany with Lais or drink Ariusion wine, than to despatch Archias and restore the Athenians to their liberties? For my part I believe none would. For I see that even common sword-players, if they are not utter brutes and savages, but Greek born, when they are to enter the list, though there be many and very costly dishes set before them, yet take more content in employing their time in commanding their poor wives to some of their friends, yea, and in conferring freedom on their slaves, than in gratifying their stomachs. But should the pleasures of the body be allowed to have some extraordinary matter in them, this would yet be common to men of action and business.

> *For they can eat good meat, and red wine drink,* (See "Iliad," v. 341.)

aye, and entertain themselves with their friends, and perhaps with a greater relish too, after their engagements and hard services,–as did Alexander and Agesilaus, and (by Jove) Phocion and Epaminondas too,–than these gentlemen who anoint themselves by the fireside, and are gingerly rocked about the streets in sedans. Yea, those make but small account of such pleasures as these, as being comprised in those greater ones. For why should a man mention Epaminondas's denying to sup with one, when he saw the preparations made were above the man's estate, but frankly saying to his friend, "I thought you had intended a sacrifice and not a debauch," when Alexander himself refused Queen Ada's cooks, telling her he had better ones of his own, to wit, travelling by night for his dinner, and a light dinner for his supper, and when Philoxenus writing to him about some handsome boys, and desiring to know of him whether he would have him buy them for him, was within a small matter of being discharged his office for it? And yet who might better have them than he? But as Hippocrates saith that of two pains the lesser is forgot in the greater, so the pleasures that accrue from action and the love of glory, while they cheer and refresh the mind, do by their transcendency and grandeur obliterate and extinguish the inferior satisfactions of the body.

If, then, the remembering of former good things (as they affirm) be that which most contributes to a pleasurable living, not one of us will then credit Epicurus when he, tells us that, while he was dying away in the midst of the strongest agonies and distempers, he yet bore himself up with the memory of the pleasures he formerly enjoyed. For a man may better see the resemblance of his own face in a troubled deep or a storm, than a smooth and smiling remembrance of past pleasure in a body tortured with such lancing and rending pains. But now the memories of past actions no man can put from him that would. For did Alexander, think you, (or indeed could he possibly) forget the fight at Arbela? Or Pelopidas the tyrant Leontiadas? Or Themistocles the engagement at Salamis? For the Athenians to this very day keep an annual festival for the battle at Marathon, and the Thebans for that at Leuctra; and so, by Jove, do we ourselves (as you very well know) for that which Daiphantus gained at Hyampolis, and all Phocis is filled with sacrifices and public honors. Nor is there any of us that is better satisfied with what himself hath either eaten or drunk than he is with what they have achieved. It is very easy then to imagine what great content, satisfaction, and joy accompanied the authors of these actions in their lifetime, when the very memory of them hath not yet after five hundred years and more lost its rejoicing power. The truth is, Epicurus himself allows there are some pleasures derived from fame. And indeed why should he not, when he himself had such a furious lechery and wriggling after glory as made him not only to disown his masters and scuffle about syllables and accents with his fellow-pedant Democritus (whose principles he stole verbatim), and to tell his disciples there never was a wise man in the world besides himself, but also to put it in writing how Colotes performed adoration to him, as he was one day philosophizing, by touching his knees, and that his own brother Neocles was used from a child to say, "There neither is, nor ever was in the world, a wiser man than Epicurus," and that his mother had just so many atoms within her as, when coming together, must have produced a complete wise man? May not a man then–as Callicratidas once said of the Athenian admiral Conon, that he whored the sea as well say of Epicurus that he basely and covertly forces and ravishes Fame, by not enjoying her publicly but ruffling and debauching her in a corner? For as men's bodies are oft necessitated by famine, for want of other food, to prey against nature upon themselves, a like mischief to this does vainglory create in men's minds, forcing them, when they hunger after praise and cannot obtain it from other men, at last to commend themselves.

And do not they then that stand so well affected towards applause and fame themselves own they cast away very extraordinary pleasures, when they decline, magistrature, public offices, and the favor and confidences of princes, from whom Democritus once said the grandest blessings of human life are derived? For he will never induce any mortal to believe, that he that could so highly value and please himself with the attestation of his brother Neocles and the adoration of his friend Colotes would not, were he clapped by all the Greeks at the Olympiads, go quite out of his wits and even hollow for joy, or rather indeed be elated in the manner spoken of by Sophocles,

Puffed like the down of a gray-headed thistle.

If it be a pleasing thing then to be of a good fame, it is on the contrary afflictive to be of an ill one; and it is most certain that nothing in the world can be more infamous than want of friendship, idleness, atheism, debauchery, and negligence. Now these are looked upon by all men except themselves as inseparable companions of their party. But unjustly, some one may say. Be it so then; for we consider not now the truth of the charge, but what fame and reputation they are of in the world. And we shall forbear at present to mention the many books that have been written to defame them, and the blackening decrees made against them by several republics; for that would look like bitterness. But if the answers of oracles, the providence of the gods, and the tenderness and affection of parents to their issue,–if civil policy, military order, and the office of magistracy be things to be looked upon as deservedly esteemed and celebrated, it must of necessity then be allowed also, that they that tell us it is none of their business to preserve the Greeks, but they must eat and drink so as not to offend but pleasure their stomachs, are base and ignominious persons, and that their being reputed such must needs extremely humble them and make their lives untoward to them, if they take honor and a good name for any part of their satisfaction.

When Theon had thus spoken, we thought good to break up our walk to rest us awhile (as we were wont to do) upon the benches. Nor did we continue any long space in our silence at what was spoken; for Zeuxippus, taking his hint from what had been said, spake to us: Who will make up that of the discourse which is yet behind? For it hath not yet received its due conclusion; and this gentleman, by mentioning divination and providence, did in my opinion suggest as much to us; for these people boast that these very things contribute in no way to the providing of their lives with pleasure, serenity, and assurance; so that there must be something said to these too. Aristodemus subjoined then and said: As to pleasure, I think there hath been enough said already to evince that, supposing their doctrine to be successful and to attain its own design, it yet doth but ease us of fear and a certain superstitious persuasion but helps us not to any comfort or joy from the gods at all; nay, while it brings us to such a state as to be neither disquieted nor pleased with them, it doth but render us in the same manner affected towards them as we are towards the Scythians or Hyrcanians, from whom we look for neither good nor harm. But if something more must be added to what hath been already spoken, I think I may very well take it from themselves. And in the first place, they quarrel extremely with those that would take away all sorrowing, weeping, and sighing for the death of friends, and tell them that such unconcernedness as arrives to an insensibility proceeds from some other worse cause, to wit, inhumanity, excessive vainglory, or prodigious fierceness, and that therefore it would be better to be a little concerned and affected, yea, and to liquor one's eyes and be melted, with other pretty things of the like kind, which they use artificially to affect and counterfeit, that they may be thought tender and loving-hearted people. For just in this manner Epicurus expressed himself upon the occasion of the death of Hegesianax, when he wrote to Dositheus the father and to Pyrson the brother of the deceased person; for I fortuned very lately to run over his epistles. And I say, in imitation of them, that atheism is no less an evil than inhumanity and vainglory, and into this they would lead us who take away with God's anger the comfort we might derive from him. For it would be much better for us to have something of the unsuiting passion of dauntedness and fear conjoined and intermixed with our sentiments of a deity, than while we fly from it, to leave ourselves neither hope, content, nor assurance in the enjoyment of our good things nor any recourse to God in our adversity and misfortunes.

We ought, it is true, to remove superstition from the persuasion we have of the gods, as we would the gum from our eyes; but if that be impossible, we must not root out and extinguish with it the belief which the most have of the gods; nor is that a dismaying and sour one either, as these gentlemen feign, while they libel and abuse the blessed Providence, representing her as a witch or as some fell and tragic fury. Yea, I must tell you, there are some in the world that fear God in an excess, for whom yet it would not be better not so to fear him. For, while they dread him as a governor that is gentle to the good and severe to the bad, and are by this one fear, which makes them not to need many others, freed from doing ill and brought to keep their wickedness with them in quiet and (as it were) in an enfeebled languor, they come hereby to have less disquiet than those that indulge the practice of it and are rash and daring in it, and then presently after fear and repent of it. Now that disposition of mind which the greater and ignorant part of mankind, that are not utterly bad, are of towards God, hath, it is very true, conjoined with the regard and honor they pay him, a kind of anguish and astonished dread, which is also called superstition; but ten thousand times more and greater is the good hope, the true joy, that attend it, which both implore and receive the whole benefit of prosperity and good success from the gods only. And this is manifest by the greatest tokens that can be; for neither do the discourses of those that wait at the temples, nor the good times of our solemn festivals, nor any other actions or sights more recreate and delight us than what we see and do about the gods ourselves, while we assist at the public ceremonies, and join in the sacred balls, and attend at the sacrifices and initiations. For the mind is not then sorrowful depressed, and heavy, as if she were approaching certain tyrants or cruel torturers; but on the contrary, where she is most apprehensive and fullest persuaded the divinity is present, there she most of all throws off sorrows, tears, and pensiveness, and lets herself loose to what is pleasing and agreeable, to the very degree of tipsiness, frolic, and laughter. In amorous concerns, as the poet said once,

> When old man and old wife think of love's fires,
> Their frozen breasts will swell with new desires;

but now in the public processions and sacrifices not only the old man and the old wife, nor yet the poor and mean man only, but also

> The dusty thick-legged drab that turns the mill,

and household-slaves and day-laborers, are strangely elevated and transported with mirth and joviality. Rich men as well as princes are used at certain times to make public entertainments and to keep open houses; but the feasts they make at the solemnities and sacrifices, when they now apprehend their minds to approach nearest the divinity, have conjoined with the honor and veneration they pay him a much more transcending pleasure and satisfaction. Of this, he that hath renounced God's providence hath not the least share; for what recreates and cheers us at the festivals is not the store of good wine and roast meat, but the good hope and persuasion that God is there present and propitious to us, and kindly accepts of what we do. From some of our festivals we exclude the flute and garland; but if God be not present at the sacrifice, as the solemnity of the banquet, the rest is but unhallowed, unfeast-like, and uninspired. Indeed the whole is but ungrateful and irksome to such a man; for he asks for nothing at all, but only acts his prayers and adorations for fear of the public, and utters expressions contradictory to his philosophy. And when he sacrifices, he stands by and looks upon the priest as he kills the offering but as he doth upon a butcher; and when he hath done, he goes his way, saying with Menander,

> To bribe the gods I sacrificed my best,
> But they ne'er minded me nor my request.

For so Epicurus would have us arrange ourselves, and neither to envy nor to incur the hatred of the common herd by doing ourselves with disgust what others do with delight. For, as Evenus saith,

> No man can love what he is made to do.

For which very reason they think the superstitious are not pleased in their minds but in fear while they attend at the sacrifices and mysteries; though they themselves are in no better condition, if they do the same things our of fear, and partake not either of as great good hope as the others do, but are only fearful and uneasy lest they should come to be discovered as cheating and abusing the public, upon whose account it is that they compose the books they write about the gods and the divine nature,

> Involved, with nothing truly said.
> But all around enveloped;

hiding out of fear the real opinions they contain.

And now, after the two former ranks of ill and common men, we will in the third place consider the best sort and most beloved of the gods, and what great satisfactions they receive from their clean and generous sentiments of the deity, to wit, that he is the prince of all good things and the parent of all things brave, and can no more do an unworthy thing than he can be made to suffer it. For he is good, and he that is good can upon no account fall into envy, fear, anger, or hatred; neither is it proper to a hot thing to cool, but to heat; nor to a good thing to do harm. Now anger is by nature at the farthest distance imaginable from complacency, and spleenishness from placidness, and animosity and turbulence from humanity and kindness. For the latter of these proceed from generosity and fortitude, but the former from impotency and baseness. The deity is not therefore constrained by either anger or kindnesses; but that is because it is natural to it to be kind and aiding, and unnatural to be angry and hurtful. But the great Jove, whose mansion is in heaven, is the first that descends downwards and orders all things and takes the care of them. But of the other gods one is surnamed the Distributor, and another the Mild, and a third the Averter of Evil. And according to Pindar,

> Phoebus was by mighty Jove designed
> Of all the gods to be to man most kind.

And Diogenes saith, that all things are the gods', and friends have all things common, and good men are the gods' friends; and therefore it is impossible either that a man beloved of the gods should not be happy, or that a wise and a just man should not be beloved of the gods. Can you think then that they that take away Providence need any other chastisement, or that they have not a sufficient one already, when they root out of themselves such vast satisfaction and joy as we that stand thus affected towards the deity have? Metrodorus, Polyaenus, and Aristobulus were the confidence and rejoicing of Epicurus; the better part of whom he all his lifetime either attended upon in their sicknesses or lamented at their deaths. As did Lycurgus, when he was saluted by the Delphic prophetess,

> Dear friend to heavenly Jove and all the gods.

And did Socrates when he believed that a certain divinity was used out of kindness to discourse him, and Pindar when he heard Pan sing one of the sonnets he had composed, but a little rejoice, think you? Or Phormio, when he thought he had treated Castor and Pollux at his house? Or Sophocles, when he entertained Aesculapius, as both he himself believed, and others too, that thought the same with him by reason of the apparition that then happened? What opinion Hermogenes had of the gods is well worth the recounting in his very own words. "For these gods," saith he, "who know all things and can do all things, are so friendly and loving to me that, because they take care of me, I never escape them either by night or by day, wherever I go or whatever I am about. And because they know beforehand what issue everything will have, they signify it to me by sending angels, voices, dreams, and presages."

Very amiable things must those be that come to us from the gods; but when these very things come by the gods too, this is what occasions vast satisfaction and unspeakable assurance, a sublimity of mind and a joy that, like a smiling brightness, doth as it were gild over our good things with a glory. But now those that are persuaded otherwise obstruct the very sweetest part of their prosperity, and leave themselves nothing to turn to in their adversity; but when they are in distress, look only to this one refuge and port, dissolution and insensibility; just as if in a storm or tempest at sea, some one should, to hearten the rest, stand up and say to them: Gentlemen, the ship hath never a pilot in it, nor will Castor and Pollux come themselves to assuage the violence of the beating waves or to lay the swift careers of the winds; yet I can assure you there is nothing at all to be dreaded in all this, for the vessel will be immediately swallowed up by the sea, or else will very quickly fall off and be dashed in pieces against the rocks. For this is Epicurus's way of discourse to persons under grievous distempers and excessive pains. Dost thou hope for any good from the gods for thy piety? It is thy vanity; for the blessed and incorruptible Being is not constrained by either angers or kindnesses. Dost thou fancy something better after this life than what thou hast here? Thou dost but deceive thyself; for what is dissolved hath no sense, and that which hath no sense is nothing to us. Aye; but how comes it then, my good friend, that you bid me eat and be merry? Why, by Jove, because he that is in a great storm cannot be far off a shipwreck; and your extreme danger will soon land you upon Death's strand. Though yet a passenger at sea, when he is got off from a shattered ship, will still buoy himself up with some little hope that he may drive his body to some shore and get out by swimming; but now the poor soul, according to these men's philosophy,

Is ne'er more seen without the hoary main.

("Odyssey," v. 410.)

Yea, she presently evaporates, disperses, and perishes, even before the body itself; so that it seems her great and excessive rejoicing must be only for having learned this one sage and divine maxim, that all her misfortunes will at last determine in her own destruction, dissolution, and annihilation.

But (said he, looking upon me) I should be impertinent, should I say anything upon this subject, when we have heard you but now discourse so fully against those that would persuade us that Epicurus's doctrine about the soul renders men more disposed and better pleased to die than Plato's doth. Zeuxippus therefore subjoined and said: And must our present debate be left then unfinished because of that? Or shall we be afraid to oppose that divine oracle to Epicurus? No, by no means, I said; and Empedocles tells us that

What's very good claims to be heard twice.

Therefore we must apply ourselves again to Theon; for I think he was present at our former discourse; and besides, he is a young man, and needs not fear being charged by these young gentlemen with having a bad memory.

Then Theon, like one constrained, said: Well then, if you will needs have me to go on with the discourse, I will not do as you did, Aristodemus. For you were shy of repeating what this gentleman spoke, but I shall not scruple to make use of what you have said; for I think indeed you did very well divide mankind into three ranks; the first of wicked and very bad men, the second of the vulgar and common sort, and the third of good and wise men. The wicked and bad sort then, while they dread any kind of divine vengeance and punishment at all, and are by this deterred from doing mischief, and thereby enjoy the greater quiet, will live both in more pleasure and in less disturbance for it. And Epicurus is of opinion that the only proper means to keep men from doing ill is the fear of punishments. So that we should cram them with more and more superstition still, and raise up against them terrors, chasms, frights, and surmises, both from heaven and earth, if their being amazed with such things as these will make them become the more tame and gentle. For it is more for their benefit to be restrained from criminal actions by the fear of what comes after death, than to commit them and then to live in perpetual danger and fear.

As to the vulgar sort, besides their fear of what is in hell, the hope they have conceived of an eternity from the tales and fictions of the ancients, and their great desire of being, which is both the first and the strongest of all, exceed in pleasure and sweet content of mind that childish dread. And therefore, when they lose their children, wives, or friends, they would rather have them be somewhere and still remain, though in misery, than that they should be quite destroyed, dissolved, and reduced to nothing. And they are pleased when they hear it said of a dying person, that he goes away or departs, and such other words as intimate death to be the soul's remove and not destruction. And they sometimes speak thus:

But I'll even there think on my dearest friend;

("Iliad," xxii. 390.)

and thus:–

What's your command to Hector? Let me know;

And to your dear old Priam shall I go?
(Euripides, "Hecuba," 422.)

And (there arising hereupon an erroneous deviation) they are the better pleased when they bury with their departed friends such arms, implements, or clothes as were most familiar to them in their lifetime; as Minos did the Cretan flutes with Glaucus,

Made of the shanks of a dead brindled fawn.

And if they do but imagine they either ask or desire anything of them, they are glad when they give it them. Thus Periander burnt his queen's attire with her, because he thought she had asked for it and complained she was a-cold. Nor doth an Aeacus, an Ascalaphus, or an Acheron much disorder them whom they have often gratified with balls, shows, and music of every sort. But now all men shrink from that face of death which carries with it insensibility, oblivion, and extinction of knowledge, as being dismal, grim, and dark. And they are discomposed when they hear it said of any one, he is perished, or he is gone or he is no more; and they show great uneasiness when they hear such words as these:–

Go to the wood-clad earth he must,
And there lie shrivelled into dust,
And ne'er more laugh or drink, or hear
The charming sounds of flute or lyre;

and these:–

But from our lips the vital spirit fled
Returns no more to wake the silent dead.
("Iliad," ix. 408.)

Wherefore they must needs cut the very throats of them that shall with Epicurus tell them, We men were born once for all, and we cannot be born twice, but our not being must last forever. For this will bring them to slight their present good as little, or rather indeed as nothing at all compared with everlastingness, and therefore to let it pass unenjoyed and to become wholly negligent of virtue and action, as men disheartened and brought to a contempt of themselves, as being but as it were of one day's continuance and uncertain, and born for no considerable purpose. For insensibility, dissolution, and the conceit that what hath no sense is nothing to us, do not at all abate the fear of death, but rather help to confirm it; for this very thing is it that nature most dreads,–

But may you all return to mould and wet,
(Ibid. vii. 99.)

to wit, the dissolution of the soul into what is without knowledge or sense. Now, while Epicurus would have this to be a separation into atoms and void, he doth but further cut off all hope of immortality; to compass which (I can scarce refrain from saying) all men and women would be well contented to be worried by Cerberus, and to carry water into the tub full of holes, so they might but continue in being and not be exterminated. Though (as I said before) there are not very many that stand in fear of these things, they being but the tenets of old women and the fabulous stories of mothers and nurses,–and even they that do fear them yet believe that certain rites of initiation and purgation will relieve them, by which after they are cleansed they shall play and dance in hell forever, in company with those that have the privilege of a bright light, clear air, and the use of speech,–yet to be deprived of living disturbs all both young and old. We

> *Impatient love the light that shines on earth,*
> *(Euripides, "Hippolytus," 193)*

as Euripides saith. Nor are we easy or without regret when we hear this:–

> *Him speaking thus th' eternal brightness leaves,*
> *Where night the wearied steeds of day receives.*

And therefore it is very plain that with the belief of immortality they take away the sweetest and greatest hopes the vulgar sort have. And what shall we then think they take away from the good and those that have led pious and just lives, who expect no ill after dying, but on the contrary most glorious and divine things? For, in the first place, athletes are not used to receive the garland before they have performed their exercises, but after they have contested and proved victorious; in like manner is it with those that are persuaded that good men have the prize of their conquests after this life is ended; it is marvellous to think to what a pitch of grandeur their virtue raises their spirits upon the contemplation of those hopes, among the which this is one, that they shall one day see those men that are now insolent by reason of their wealth and power, and that foolishly flout at their betters, undergo just punishment. In the next place, none of the lovers of truth and the contemplation of being have here their fill of them; they having but a watery and puddled reason to speculate with, as it were, through the fog and mist of the body; and yet they still look upwards like birds, as ready to take their flight to the spacious and bright region, and endeavor to make their souls expedite and light from things mortal, using philosophy as a study for death. Thus I account death a truly great and accomplished good thing; the soul being to live there a real life, which here lives not a waking life, but suffers things most resembling dreams. If then (as Epicurus saith) the remembrance of a dead friend be a thing every way complacent; we may easily from thence imagine how great a joy they deprive themselves of who think they do but embrace and pursue the phantoms and shades of their deceased familiars, that have in them neither knowledge nor sense, but who never expect to be with them again, or to see their dear father and dear mother and sweet wife, nor have any hopes of that familiarity and dear converse they have that think of the soul with Pythagoras, Plato, and Homer. Now what their sort of passion is like to was hinted at by Homer, when he threw into the midst of the soldiers, as they were engaged, the shade of Aeneas, as if he had been dead, and afterwards again presented his friends with him himself,

    Coming alive and well, as brisk as ever;
at which, he saith,
    They all were overjoyed.
    ("Iliad," v. 514 and 515)

And should not we then,–when reason shows us that a real converse with persons departed this life may be had, and that he that loves may both feel and be with the party that affects and loves him,– relinquish these men that cannot so much as cast off all those airy shades and outside barks for which they are all their time in lamentation and fresh afflictions?

Moreover, they that look upon death as the commencement of another and better life, if they enjoy good things, are the better pleased with them, as expecting much greater hereafter; but if they have not things here to their minds, they do not much grumble at it, but the hopes of those good and excellent things that are after death contain in them such ineffable pleasures and expectances, that they wipe off and wholly obliterate every defect and every offence from the mind, which, as on a road or rather indeed in a short deviation out of the road, bears whatever befalls it with great ease and indifference. But now, as to those to whom life ends in insensibility and dissolution,–death brings to them no removal of evils, though it is afflicting in both conditions, yet is it more so to those that live prosperously than to such as undergo adversity? For it cuts the latter but from an uncertain hope of doing better hereafter; but it deprives the former of a certain good, to wit, their pleasurable living. And as those medicinal potions that are not grateful to the palate but yet necessary give sick men ease, but rake and hurt the well; just so, in my opinion, doth the philosophy of Epicurus; it promises to those that live miserably no happiness in death, and to those that do well an utter extinction and dissolution of the mind, while it quite obstructs the comfort and solace of the grave and wise and those that abound with good things, by throwing them down from a happy living into a deprivation of both life and being. From hence then it is manifest, that the contemplation of the loss of good things will afflict us in as great a measure as either the firm hope or present enjoyment of them delights us.

Yea, themselves tell us, that the thought of future dissolution leaves them one most assured and complacent good, freedom from anxious surmises of incessant and endless evils, and that Epicurus's doctrine effects this by stopping the fear of death through the soul's dissolution. If then deliverance from the expectation of infinite evils be a matter of greatest complacence, how comes it not to be afflictive to be bereft of eternal good things and to miss of the highest and most consummate felicity? For not to be can be good for neither condition, but is on the contrary both against nature and ungrateful to all that have a being. But those being eased of the evils of life through the evils of death have, it is very true, the want of sense to comfort them, while they, as it were, make their escape from life. But, on the other hand, they that change from good things to nothing seem to me to have the most dismaying end of all, it putting a period to their happiness. For Nature doth not fear insensibility as the entrance upon some new thing, but because it is the privation of our present good things. For to declare that the destruction of all that we call ours toucheth us not is untrue for it toucheth us already by the very anticipation. And insensibility afflicts not those that are not, but those that are, when they think what damage they shall sustain by it in the loss of their being and in being suffered never to emerge from nothingness. Wherefore it is neither the dog Cerberus nor the river Cocytus that has made our fear of death boundless; but the threatened danger of not being, representing it as impossible for such as are once extinct to shift back again into being. For we cannot be born twice, and our not being must last forever; as Epicurus speaks. For if our end be in not being, and that be infinite and unalterable, then hath privation of good found out an eternal evil, to wit, a never ending insensibleness. Herodotus was much wiser, when he said that God, having given men a taste of the delights of life, seems to be envious, (Herodotus, vii. 46) and especially to those that conceit themselves happy, to whom pleasure is but a bait for sorrow, they being but permitted to taste of what they must be deprived of. For what solace or fruition or exultation would not the perpetual injected thought of the soul's being dispersed into infinity, as into a certain huge and vast ocean, extinguish and quell in those that found their amiable good and beatitude in pleasure? But if it be true (as Epicurus thinks it is) that most men die in very acute pain, then is the fear of death in all respects inconsolable; it bringing us through evils unto a deprivation of good.

And yet they are never wearied with their brawling and dunning of all persons to take the escape of evil for a good, no longer to repute privation of good for an evil. But they still confess what we have asserted, that death hath in it nothing of either good hope or solace, but that all that is complacent and good is then wholly extinguished; at which time those men look for many amiable, great, and divine things, that conceive the minds of men to be unperishable and immortal, or at least to go about in certain long revolutions of times, being one while upon earth and another while in heaven, until they are at last dissolved with the universe and then, together with the sun and moon, sublimed into an intellective fire. So large a field and one of so great pleasures Epicurus wholly cuts off, when he destroys (as hath been said) the hopes and graces we should derive from the gods, and by that extinguishes both in our speculative capacity the desire of knowledge, and in our active the love of glory, and confines and abases our nature to a poor narrow thing, and that not cleanly neither, to wit, the content the mind receives by the body, as if it were capable of no higher good than the escape of evil.

That a Philosopher Ought Chiefly to Converse with Great Men

THE RESOLUTION WHICH YOU have taken to enter into the friendship and familiarity of Sorcanus, that by the frequent opportunities of conversing with him you may cultivate and improve a soil which gives such early promises of a plentiful harvest, is an undertaking which will not only oblige his relations and friends, but rebound very much to the advantage of the public; and (notwithstanding the peevish censures of some morose or ignorant people) it is so far from being an argument of an aspiring vainglorious temper, that it shows you to be a lover of virtue and good manners, and a zealous promoter of the common interest of mankind.

They themselves are rather to be accused of an indirect but more vehement sort of ambition, who would not upon any terms be found in the company or so much as be seen to give a civil salute to a person of quality. For how unreasonable would it be to enforce a well-disposed young gentleman, and one who needs the direction of a wise governor, to such complaints as these: "Would that I might become from a Pericles or a Cato to a cobbler like Simon or a grammarian like Dionysius, that I might like them talk with such a man as Socrates, and sit by him."

So far, I am sure, was Aristo of Chios from being of their humor, that when he was censured for exposing and prostituting the dignity of philosophy by his freedom to all comers, he answered, that he could wish that Nature had given understanding to wild beasts, that they too might be capable of being his hearers. Shall we then deny that privilege to men of interest and power, which this good man would have communicated (if it had been possible) to the brute beasts? But these men have taken a false notion of philosophy, they make it much like the art of statuary, whose business it is to carve out a lifeless image in the most exact figure and proportion, and then to raise it upon its pedestal, where it is to continue forever. The true philosophy is of a quite different nature; it is a spring and principle of motion wherever it comes; it makes men active and industrious, it sets every wheel and faculty a-going, it stores our minds with axioms and rules by which to make a sound judgment, it determines the will to the choice of what is honorable and just; and it wings all our faculties to the swiftest prosecution of it. It is accompanied with an elevation and nobleness of mind, joined with a coolness and sweetness of behavior, and backed with a becoming assurance and inflexible resolution. And from this diffusiveness of the nature of good it follows, that the best and most accomplished men are inclined to converse with persons of the highest condition. Indeed a physician if he have any good nature and sense of honor, would be more ready to cure an eye which is to see and to watch for a great many thousands, than that of a private person; how much more then ought a philosopher to form and fashion, to rectify and cure the soul of such a one, who is (if I may so express it) to inform the body politic,–who is to think and understand for so many others, to be in so great measure the rule of reason, the standard of law, and model of behavior, by which all the rest will square and direct their actions? Suppose a man to have a talent at finding out springs and contriving of aqueducts (a piece of skill for which Hercules and other of the ancients are much celebrated in history), surely he could not so satisfactorily employ himself in sinking a well or deriving water to some private seat or contemptible cottage, as in supplying conduits to some fair and populous city, in relieving an army just perishing with thirst, or in refreshing and adorning with fountains and cool streams the beautiful gardens of some glorious monarch. There is a passage of Homer very pertinent to this purpose, in which he calls Minos [Greek text], which, as Plato interprets it, signifies THE DISCIPLE AND COMPANION OF JUPITER. For it were beneath his dignity indeed to teach private men, such as care only for a family or indulge their useless speculations; but kings are scholars worthy the tuition of a god, who, when they are well advised, just, good, and magnanimous, never fail to procure the peace and prosperity of all their subjects. The naturalists tell us that the eryngium hath such a property with it, that if one of the flock do but taste it, all the rest will stand stock still in the same place till the shepherd hath taken it out of its mouth. Such swiftness of action does it have, pervading and inserting itself in everything near it, as if it were fire. The effects of philosophy, however, are different according to the difference of inclinations in men. If indeed it lights on one who loves a dull and inactive sort of life, that makes himself the centre and the little conveniences of life the circumference of all his thoughts, such a one does contract the sphere of her activity, so that having only made easy and comfortable the life of a single person, it fails and dies with him; but when it finds a man of a ruling genius, one fitted for conversation and able to grapple with the difficulties of public business, if it once possess him with principles of honesty, honor, and religion, it takes a compendious method, by doing good to one, to oblige a great part of mankind. Such was the effect of the intercourse of Anaxagoras with Pericles, of Plato with Dion, and of Pythagoras with the principal statesmen of all Italy. Cato himself took a voyage, when he had the concern of an expedition lying upon him, to see and hear Athenodorus; and Scipio sent for Panaetius, when he was commissioned by the senate "to take a survey alike of the habits of men good and bad," ("Odyssey," xvii. 487.) as Posidonius says. Now what a pretty sort of return would it have been in Panaetius to send word back,–"If indeed you were in a private capacity, John a Nokes or John a Stiles, that had a mind to get into some obscure corner or cell, to state cases and resolve syllogisms, I should very gladly have accepted your invitation; but now, because you are the son of Paulus AEmilius who was twice consul, and grandson of that Scipio who was surnamed from his conquest of Hannibal and Africa, I cannot with honor hold any conversation with you!"

The objections which they bring from the two kinds of discourse, one of which is mental, the other like the gift of Mercury expressed in words or interpretative of the former, are so frivolous, that they are best answered by laughter or silence; and we may quote the old saying, "I knew this before Theognis arose." However, thus much shall be added, that the end of them both is friendship,–in the first case with ourselves, in the second with another. For he that hath attained to virtue by the methods of philosophy hath his mind all in tune and good temper; he is not struck with those reproaches of conscience, which cause the acutest sense of pain and are the natural punishments of our follies; but he enjoys (the great prerogative of a good man) to be always easy and in amity with himself.

> *No factious lusts reason's just power control,*
> *Nor kindle civil discord in his soul.*

His passion does not stand in defiance to his reason, nor do his reasonings cross and thwart one the other, but he is always consistent with himself. But the very joys of wicked men are tumultuary and confused, like those who dwell in the borders of two great empires at variance, always

insecure, and in perpetual alarms; whilst a good man enjoys an uninterrupted peace and serenity of mind, which excels the other not only in
duration, but in sense of pleasure too. As for the other sort of converse,
that which consists in expression of itself to others, Pindar says very well,
that it was not mercenary in old time, nor indeed is it so now; but by the
baseness and ambition of a few it is made use of to serve their poor secu-
lar interests. For if the poets represent Venus herself as much offended
with those who make a trade and traffic of the passion of love, how much
more reasonably may we suppose that Urania and Clio and Calliope have
an indignation against those who set learning and philosophy to sale?
Certainly the gifts and endowments of the Muses should be privileged
from such mean considerations.

If indeed some have made fame and reputation one of the ends of
their studies, they used it only as an instrument to get friends; since we
find by common observation that men only praise those whom they
love. If they sought its own praise, they were as much mistaken as Ixion when he embraced a cloud instead of Juno; for there is nothing so
fleeting, so changeable, and so inconstant as popular applause; it is but
a pompous shadow, and hath no manner of solidity and duration in it.
But a wise man, if he design to engage in business and matters of state,
will so far aim at fame and popularity as that he may be better enabled
to benefit others; for it is a difficult and very unpleasant task to do good
to those who are disaffected to our persons. It is the good opinion men
have of us which disposes men to give credit to our doctrine. As light
is a greater good to those who see others by it than to those who only
are seen, so is honor of a greater benefit to those who are sensible of
it than to those whose glory is admired. But even one who withdraws
himself from the noise of the world, who loves privacy and indulges his
own thoughts, will show that respect to the good word of the people
which Hippolytus did to Venus,–though he abstain from her mysteries,
he will pay his devotions at a distance; (Euripides, "Hippolytus," 102.)
but he will not be so cynical and sullen as not to hear with gladness the
commendations of virtuous men like himself; he will neither engage
himself in a restless pursuit of wealth, interest, or honor, nor will he
on the other hand be so rustic and insensible as to refuse them in a
moderate degree, when they fairly come in his way; in like manner he
will not court and follow handsome and beautiful youth, but will rather choose such as are of a teachable disposition, of a gentle behavior,
and lovers of learning. The charms and graces of youth will not make a
philosopher shy of their conversation, when the endowments of their
minds are answerable to the features of their bodies. The case is the

same when greatness of place and fortune concur with a well disposed person; he will not therefore forbear loving and respecting such a one, nor be afraid of the name of a courtier, nor think it a curse that such attendance and dependence should be his fate.

> *They that try most Dame Venus to despise*
>> *Do sin as much as they who her most prize.*   (From the "Veiled Hippolytus" of Euripides, Frag. 431.)

The application is easy to the matter in hand.

A philosopher therefore, if he is of a retired humor, will not avoid such persons; while one who generously designs his studies for the public advantage will cheerfully embrace their advances of friendship, will not bore them to hear him, will lay aside his sophistic terms and distinctions, and will rejoice to discourse and pass his time with them when they are disposed.

> *I plough the wide Berecynthian fields,*
> *Full six days' journey long,*
> (From the "Niobe" of Aechylus, Frag. 153.)

says one boastingly in the poet; the same man, if he were as much a lover of mankind as of husbandry, would much rather bestow his pains on such a farm, the fruits of which would serve a great number, than to be always dressing the olive-yard of some cynical malcontent, which, when all was done, would scarce yield oil enough to dress a salad or to supply his lamp in the long winter evenings. Epicurus himself, who places happiness in the profoundest quiet and sluggish inactivity, as the only secure harbor from the storms of this troublesome world, could not but confess that it is both more noble and delightful to do than to receive a kindness; (Almost the same words with those of our Saviour, It is more blessed to give than to receive. So that a man can scarcely be a true Epicurean without practising some of the maxims of Christianity.) for there is nothing which produces so humane and genuine a sort of pleasure as that of doing good. He who gave the names to the three Graces was intelligent, for they all mean delectation and joy, (Aglaia, Euphrosyne, and Thalia.) and these feelings surely are far greater and purer in the giver. This is so evidently true, that we all receive good turns blushing and with some confusion, but we are always gay and well pleased when we are conferring one.

If then it is so pleasant to do good to a few, how are their hearts dilated with joy who are benefactors to whole cities, provinces, and kingdoms? And such benefactors are they who instil good principles into those upon whom so many millions do depend. On the other hand, those who debauch the minds of great men—as sycophants, false informers, and flatterers worse than both, manifestly do–are the centre of all the curses of a nation, as men not only infuse deadly poison into the cistern of a private house, but into the public springs of which so many thousands are to drink. The people therefore laughed at the parasites of Callias, whom, as Eupolis says, neither with fire nor brass nor steel could prevent from supping with him; but as for the favorites of those execrable tyrants Apollodorus, Phalaris, and Dionysius, they racked them, they flayed them alive, they roasted them at slow fires, looked on them as the very pests of society and disgraces of human nature; for to debauch a simple person is indeed an ill thing, but to corrupt a prince is an infinite mischief. In like manner, he who instructs an ordinary man makes him to pass his life decently and with comfort; but he who instructs a prince, by correcting his errors and clearing his understanding, is a philosopher for the public, by rectifying the very mould and model by which whole nations are formed and regulated. It is the custom of all nations to pay a peculiar honor and deference to their priests; and the reason of it is, because they do not only pray for good things for themselves, their own families and friends, but for whole communities, for the whole state of mankind. Yet we are not so fond as to think that the priests make the gods to be givers of good things, or inspire a vein of beneficence into them; but they only make their supplications to a being which of itself is inclinable to answer their requests. But in this a good tutor hath the privilege above the priests,–he effectually renders a prince more disposed to actions of justice, of moderation, and mercy, and therefore hath a greater satisfaction of mind when he reflects upon it.

For my own part, I cannot but think that an ordinary mechanic–for instance, a maker of musical instruments–would be much more attentive and pleased at his work, and if his harp would be touched by the famous Amphion, and in his hand to serve for the builder of Thebes, or if that Thales had bespoke it, who was so great a master by the force of his music he pacified a popular tumult amongst the Lacedaemonians. A good-natured shipwright would ply his work more heartily, if he were constructing the rudder for the admiral galley of Themistocles when he fought for the liberty of Greece, or of Pompey when he went on his expedition against the pirates: what ecstasy of delight then must a philosopher be in, when he reflects that his scholar is a man of authority, a prince or great potentate, that he is employed in so public a work, giving laws to him who is to give laws to a whole nation, who is to punish vice, and to reward the virtuous with riches and honor? The builder of the ARGO certainly would have been mightily pleased, if he had known what noble mariners were to row in his ship, and that at last she should be translated into heaven; and a carpenter would not be half so much pleased to make a chariot or plough, as to cut the tablets on which Solon's laws were to be engraved. In like manner the discourses and rules of philosophy, being once deeply stamped and imprinted on the minds of great personages, will stick so close, that the prince shall seem no other than justice incarnate and animated law. This was the design of Plato's voyage into Sicily,–he hoped that the lectures of his philosophy would serve for laws to Dionysius, and bring his affairs again into a good posture. But the soul of that unfortunate prince was like paper scribbled all over with the characters of vice; its piercing and corroding quality had stained quite through, and sunk into the very substance of his soul. Whereas, such persons must be taken when they are on the run, if they are to absorb useful discourses.

Sentiments Concerning Nature
with which Philosophers were
Delighted

Book One

IT BEING OUR DETERMINATION to discourse of Natural Philosophy, we judge it necessary, in the first place and chiefly, to divide the body of philosophy into its proper members, so that we may know what is that which is called philosophy, and what part of it is physical, or the explanation of natural things. The Stoics affirm that wisdom is the knowledge of things human and divine; that philosophy is the pursuit of that art which is convenient to this knowledge; that virtue is the sole and sovereign art which is thus convenient; and this distributes itself into three general parts–natural, moral, and logical. By which just reason (they say) philosophy is tripartite; of which one natural, the other moral, the third logical. The natural when our inquiries are concerning the world and all things contained in it; the ethical is the employment of our minds in those things which concern the manners of man's life; the logical (which they also call dialectical) regulates our conversation with others in speaking. Aristotle, Theophrastus, and after them almost all the Peripatetics give the same division of philosophy. It is absolutely requisite that the complete person he contemplator of things which have a being, and the practiser of those thing which are decent; and this easily appears by the following instances. If the question be proposed, whether the sun, which is so conspicuous to us, be informed of a soul or inanimate, he that makes this disquisition is the thinking man; for he proceeds no farther than to consider the nature of that thing which is proposed. Likewise, if the question be propounded, whether the world be infinite, or whether beyond the system of this world there is any real being, all these things are the objects about which the understanding of man is conversant.

But if these be the questions,–what measures must be taken to compose the well-ordered life of man, what are the best methods to govern and educate children, or what are the exact rules whereby sovereigns may command and establish laws,–all these queries are proposed for the sole end of action, and the man skilled therein is the moral and practical man.

CHAPTER I.

WHAT IS NATURE?

Since we have undertaken to make a diligent search into Nature, I cannot but conclude it necessary to declare what Nature is. It is very absurd to attempt a discourse of the essence of natural things, and not to understand what is the power and sphere of Nature. If Aristotle be credited, Nature is the principle of motion and rest, in that thing in which it exists as a principle and not by accident. For all things that are conspicuous to our eyes, which are neither fortuitous nor necessary, nor have a divine original, nor acknowledge any such like cause, are called natural and enjoy their proper nature. Of this sort are earth, fire, water, air, plants, animals; to these may be added all things produced from them, such as showers, hail, thunders, hurricanes, and winds. All these confess they had a beginning, none of these were from eternity, but had something as the origin of them; and likewise animals and plants have a principle whence they are produced. But Nature, which in all these things hath the priority, is not only the principle of motion but of repose; whatsoever enjoys the principle of motion, the same has a possibility to find a dissolution. Therefore on this account it is that Nature is the principle of motion and rest.

CHAPTER II.

WHAT IS THE DIFFERENCE BETWEEN A PRINCIPLE

AND AN ELEMENT?

THE FOLLOWERS OF ARISTOTLE and Plato conclude that elements are discriminated from principles. Thales the Milesian supposeth that a principle and the elements are one and the same thing, but it is evident that they vastly differ one from another. For the elements are things compounded; but we do pronounce that principles admit not of a composition, nor are the effects of any other being. Those which we call elements are earth, water, air, and fire. But we call those principles which have nothing prior to them out of which they are produced; for otherwise not these themselves, but rather those things whereof they are produced, would be the principles. Now there are some things which have a pre-existence to earth and water, from which they are begotten; to wit, matter, which is without form or shape; then form, which we call [Greek omitted] (actuality); and lastly, privation. Thales therefore is most in error, by affirming that water is both an element and a principle.

CHAPTER III.

WHAT ARE PRINCIPLES?

THALES THE MILESIAN DOTH affirm that water is the principle from whence all things in the universe spring. This person appears to be the first of philosophers; from him the Ionic sect took its denomination, for there are many families and successions amongst philosophers. After he had professed philosophy in Egypt, when he was very old, he returned to Miletus. He pronounced, that all things had their original from water, and into water all things are resolved. His first ground was, that whatsoever was the prolific seed of all animals was a principle, and that is moist; so that it is probable that all things receive their original from humidity. His second reason was, that all plants are nourished and fructified by that thing which is moist, of which being deprived they wither away. Thirdly, that that fire of which the sun and stars are made is nourished by watery exhalations,–yea, and the world itself; which moved Homer to sing that the generation of it was from water:–

The ocean is
Of all things the kind genesis.
(Iliad, xiv. 246.)

Anaximander, who himself was a Milesian, assigns the principle of all things to the Infinite, from whence all things flow, and into the same are corrupted; hence it is that infinite worlds are framed, and those dissolve again into that whence they have their origin. And thus he farther proceeds, For what other reason is there of an Infinite but this, that there may be nothing deficient as to the generation or subsistence of what is in Nature? There is his error, that he doth not acquaint us what this Infinite is, whether it be air, or water, or earth, or any other such like body. Besides he is mistaken, in that, giving us the material cause, he is silent as to the efficient cause of beings; for this thing which he makes his Infinite can be nothing but matter; but operation cannot come about in the sphere of matter, except an efficient cause be annexed.

Anaximenes his fellow-citizen pronounceth, that air is the principle of all beings; from it all receive their original, and into it all return. He affirms that our soul is nothing but air; it is that which constitutes and preserves; the whole world is invested with spirit and air. For spirit and air are synonymous. This person is in this deficient, in that he concludes that of pure air, which is a simple body and is made of one only form, all animals are composed. It is not possible to think that a single principle should be the matter of all things, from whence they receive their subsistence; besides this there must be an operating cause. Silver (for example) is not of itself sufficient to frame a drinking cup; an operator also is required, which is the silversmith. The like may be applied to vessels made of wood, brass, or any other material.

Anaxagoras the Clazomenian asserted Homoeomeries (or parts similar or homogeneous) to be the original cause of all beings; it seemed to him impossible that anything could arise of nothing or be dissolved into nothing. Let us therefore instance in nourishment, which appears simple and uniform, such as bread which we owe to Ceres and water which we drink. Of this very nutriment, our hair, our veins, our arteries, nerves, bones, and all our other parts are nourished. These things thus being performed, it must be granted that the nourishment which is received by us contains all those things by which these of us are produced. In it there are those particles which are producers of blood, bones, nerves, and all other parts; these particles (he thought) reason discovers for us. For it is not necessary that we should reduce all things under the objects of sense; for bread and water are fitted to the senses, yet in them there are those particles latent which are discoverable only by reason. It being therefore plain that there are particles in the nourishment similar to what is produced by it, he terms these homogeneous parts, averring that they are the principles of beings. Matter is according to him these similar parts, and the efficient cause is a Mind, which orders all things that have an existence. Thus he begins his discourse: "All things were confused one among another; but Mind divided and brought them to order." In this he is to be commended, that he yokes together matter and an intellectual agent.

Archelaus the son of Apollodorus, the Athenian, pronounceth, that the principles of all things have their origin from an infinite air rarefied or condensed. Air rarefied is fire, condensed is water.

These philosophers, the followers of Thales, succeeding one another, made up that sect which takes to itself the denomination of the Ionic.

Pythagoras the Samian, the son of Mnesarchus, from another origin deduces the principles of all things; it was he who first called philosophy by its name. He thought the first principles to be numbers, and those symmetries in them which he styles harmonies; and the composition of both he terms elements, called geometrical. Again, he places unity and the indefinite binary number amongst the principles. One of these principles ends in an efficient and forming cause, which is Mind, and that is God; the other to the passive and material part, and that is the visible world. Moreover, the nature of number (he saith) consists in the ten; for all people, whether Grecians or barbarians, reckon from one to ten, and thence return to one again. Farther he avers the virtue of ten consists in the quaternion; the reason whereof is this,–if any person start from one, and add numbers so as to take in the quaternary, he shall complete the number ten; if he passes the four, he shall go beyond the ten; for one, two, three, and four being added up together make ten. The nature of numbers, therefore, if we regard the units, abideth in the ten; but if we regard its power, in the four. Therefore the Pythagoreans say that their most sacred oath is by that god who delivered to them the quaternary.

> By th' founder of the sacred number four,
> Eternal Nature's font and source, they swore.

Of this number the soul of man is composed; for mind, knowledge, opinion, and sense are the four that complete the soul, from which all sciences, all arts, all rational faculties derive themselves. For what our mind perceives, it perceives after the manner of a thing that is one, the soul itself being a unity; as for instance, a multitude of persons are not the object of our sense nor are comprehended by us, for they are infinite; our understanding gives the general concept of A MAN, in which all individuals agree. The number of individuals is infinite; the generic or specific nature of all being is a unit, or to be apprehended as one only thing; from this one conception we give the genuine measures of all existence, and therefore we affirm that a certain class of beings are rational and discoursive. But when we come to give the nature of a horse, it is that animal which neighs; and this being common to all horses, it is manifest that the understanding, which hath such like conceptions, is in its nature unity. It follows that the number called the infinite binary must be science; in every demonstration or belief belonging to science, and in every syllogism, we draw that conclusion which is in dispute from those propositions which are by all granted, by which means another proposition is obtained from the premises. The comprehension of these we call knowledge; for which reason science is the binary number. But opinion is the ternary; for that rationally follows from comprehension. The objects of opinion are many things, and the ternary number denotes a multitude, as "Thrice happy Grecians"; for which reason Pythagoras admits the ternary. This sect of philosophers is called the Italic, by reason Pythagoras started his school in Italy; his hatred of the tyranny of Polycrates enforced him to abandon his native country Samos.

Heraclitus and Hippasus of Metapontum suppose that fire gives the origination to all beings, that they all flow from fire, and in fire they all conclude; for of fire when first quenched the world was constituted. The first part of the world, being most condensed and contracted within itself, made the earth; but part of that earth being loosened and made thin by fire, water was produced; afterwards this water being exhaled and rarefied into vapors became air; after all this the world itself, and all other corporeal beings, shall be dissolved by fire in the universal conflagration. By them therefore it appears that fire is what gives beginning to all things, and is that in which all things receive their period.

Epicurus the son of Neocles, the Athenian, his philosophical sentiments being the same with those of Democritus, affirms that the principles of all being are bodies which are only perceptible by reason; they admit not of a vacuity, nor of any original, but being of a self-existence are eternal and incorruptible; they are not liable to any diminution, they are indestructible, nor is it possible for them to receive any transformation of parts, or admit of any alterations; of these reason is only the discoverer; they are in a perpetual motion in vacuity, and by means of the empty space; for the vacuum itself is infinite, and the bodies that move in it are infinite. Those bodies acknowledge these three accidents, figure, magnitude, and gravity. Democritus acknowledged but two, magnitude and figure. Epicurus added the third, to wit, gravity; for he pronounced that it is necessary that bodies receive their motion from that impression which springs from gravity, otherwise they could not be moved. The figures of atoms cannot be incomprehensible, but they are not infinite. These figures are neither hooked nor trident-shaped nor ring-shaped, such figures as these being exposed to collision; but the atoms are impassible, impenetrable; they have indeed figures of their own, which are conceived only by reason. It is called an atom, by reason not of its smallness but of its indivisibility; in it no vacuity, no possible affection is to be found. And that there is an atom is perfectly clear; for there are elements which have a perpetual duration, and there are animals which admit of a vacuity, and there is a unity.

Empedocles the Agrigentine, the son of Meton, affirms that there are four elements, fire, air, earth, and water, and two powers which bear the greatest command in nature, concord and discord, of which one is the union, the other the division of beings. Thus he sings,

> *Hear first the four roots of all created things:–*
> *Bright shining Jove, Juno that beareth life,*
> *Pluto beneath the earth, and Nestis who*
> *Doth with her tears water the human fount.*

By Jupiter he understands fire and ether, by Juno that gives life he means the air, by Pluto the earth, by Nestis and the spring of all mortals (as it were) seed and water.

Socrates the son of Sophroniscus, and Plato son of Ariston, both natives of Athens, entertain the same opinion concerning the universe; for they suppose three principles, God, matter, and the idea. God is the universal understanding; matter is that which is the first substratum, accommodated for the generation and corruption of beings; the idea is an incorporeal essence, existing in the cogitations and apprehensions of God; for God is the soul and mind of the world.

Aristotle the son of Nichomachus, the Stagirite, constitutes three principles; Entelecheia (which is the same with form), matter, and privation. He acknowledges four elements, and adds a certain fifth body, which is ethereal and not obnoxious to mutation.

Zeno son of Mnaseas, the native of Citium, avers these to be principles, God and matter, the first of which is the efficient cause, the other the passible and receptive. Four more elements he likewise confesses.

CHAPTER IV.

HOW WAS THIS WORLD COMPOSED IN THAT

ORDER AND AFTER THAT MANNER IT IS?

THE WORLD BEING BROKEN and confused, after this manner it was reduced into figure and composure as now it is. The insectible bodies or
atoms, by a wild and fortuitous motion, without any governing power,
incessantly and swiftly were hurried one amongst another, many bodies being jumbled together; upon this account they have a diversity in
the figures and magnitude. These therefore being so jumbled together,
those bodies which were the greatest and heaviest sank into the lowest place; they that were of a lesser magnitude, being round, smooth,
and slippery, these meeting with those heavier bodies were easily broken into pieces, and were carried into higher places. But when that
force whereby these variously particles figured particles fought with
and struck one another, and forced the lighter upwards, did cease, and
there was no farther power left to drive them into superior regions,
yet they were wholly hindered from descending downwards, and were
compelled to reside in those places capable to receive them; and these
were the heavenly spaces, unto which a multitude of these small bodies were hurled, and these being thus shivered fell into coherence and
mutual embraces, and by this means the heaven was produced. Then
a various and great multitude of atoms enjoying the same nature, as it
is before asserted, being hurried aloft, did form the stars. The multitude of these exhaled bodies, having struck and broke the air in shivers,
forced a passage through it; this being turned into wind invested the
stars, as it moved, and whirled them about, by which means to this
present time that circulary motion which these stars have in the heavens is maintained. Much after the same manner the earth was made;
for by those little particles whose gravity made them to reside in the
lower places the earth was formed. The heaven, fire, and air were constituted of those particles which were carried aloft. But a great deal of
matter remaining in the earth, this being condensed by the driving of
the winds and the air from the stars, every little part and form of it was
compressed, which created the element of water; but this being fluidly
disposed did run into those places which were hollow, and these places
were those that were capable to receive and protect it; or the water,
subsisting by itself, did make the lower places hollow. After this manner
the principal parts of the world were constituted.

CHAPTER V.

WHETHER THE UNIVERSE IS ONE SINGLE THING.

THE STOICS PRONOUNCE that the world is one thing, and this they say is the universe and is corporeal.

But Empedocles's opinion is, that the world is one; yet by no means the system of this world must be styled the universe, but that it is a small part of it, and the remainder is inactive matter.

What to Plato seems the truest he thus declares, that there is one world, and that world is the universe; and this he endeavors to evince by three arguments. First, that the world could not be complete and perfect, if it did not within itself include all beings. Secondly, nor could it give the true resemblance of its original and exemplar, if it were not the one only begotten thing. Thirdly, it could not be incorruptible, if there were any being out of its compass to whose power it might be obnoxious. But to Plato it may be thus returned. First, that the world is not complete and perfect, nor doth it contain all things within itself. And if man is a perfect being, yet he doth not encompass all things. Secondly, that there are many exemplars and originals of statues, houses, and pictures. Thirdly, how is the world perfect, if anything beyond it is possible to be moved about it? But the world is not incorruptible, nor can it be so conceived, because it had an original.

To Metrodorus it seems absurd, that in a large field one only stalk should grow, and in an infinite space one only world exist; and that this universe is infinite is manifest by this, that there is an infinity of causes. Now if this world be finite and the causes producing it infinite, it follows that the worlds likewise be infinite; for where all causes concur, there the effects also must appear, let the causes be what they will, either atoms or elements.

CHAPTER VI.

WHENCE DID MEN OBTAIN THE KNOWLEDGE OF

THE EXISTENCE AND ESSENCE OF A DEITY?

THE STOICS THUS DEFINE the essence of a god. It is a spirit intellectual and fiery, which acknowledges no shape, but is continually changed into what it pleases, and assimilates itself to all things. The knowledge of this deity they first received from the pulchritude of those things which so visibly appeared to us; for they concluded that nothing beauteous could casually or fortuitously be formed, but that it was framed from the art of a great understanding that produced the world. That the world is very resplendent is made perspicuous from the figure, the color, the magnitude of it, and likewise from the wonderful variety of those stars which adorn this world. The world is spherical; the orbicular hath the pre-eminence above all other figures, for being round itself it hath its parts like itself. (On this account, according to Plato, the understanding, which is the most sacred part of man, is in the head.) The color of it is most beauteous; for it is painted with blue; which, though little blacker than purple, yet hath such a shining quality, that by reason of the vehement efficacy of its color it cuts through such a space of air; whence it is that at so great a distance the heavens are to be contemplated. And in this very greatness of the world the beauty of it appears. View all things: that which contains the rest carries a beauty with it, as an animal or a tree. Also things which are visible to us accomplish the beauty of the world. The oblique circle called the Zodiac in heaven is with different images painted and distinguished:–

> There's Cancer, Leo, Virgo, and the Claws;
> Scorpio, Arcitenens, and Capricorn;
> Amphora, Pisces, then the Ram, and Bull;
> The lovely pair of Brothers next succeed.   (From Aratus.)

There are a thousand others that give us the suitable reflections of the beauty of the world. Thus Euripides:–

> The starry splendor of the skies,
> The beautiful and varied work of that wise
> Creator, Time.

From this the knowledge of a god is conveyed to man; that the sun, the moon, and the rest of the stars, being carried under the earth, rise again in their proper color, magnitude, place, and times. Therefore they who by tradition delivered to us the knowledge and veneration of the gods did it by these three manner of ways:–first, from Nature; secondly, from fables; thirdly, from the testimony supplied by the laws of commonwealths. Philosophers taught the natural way; poets, the fabulous; and the political way is to be had from the constitutions of each commonwealth. All sorts of this learning are distinguished into these seven parts. The first is from things that are conspicuous, and the observation of those bodies which are in places superior to us. To men the heavenly bodies that are so visible did give the knowledge of the deity; when they contemplated that they are the causes of so great an harmony, that they regulate day and night, winter and summer, by their rising and setting, and likewise considered those things which by their influences in the earth do receive a being and do likewise fructify. It was manifest to men that the Heaven was the father of those things, and the Earth the mother; that the Heaven was the father is clear, since from the heavens there is the pouring down of waters, which have their spermatic faculty; the Earth the mother, because she receives them and brings forth. Likewise men considering that the stars are running (Greek omitted) in a perpetual motion, that the sun and moon give us the stimulus to view and contemplate (Greek omitted), they call them all gods (Greek omitted).

In the second and third place, they thus distinguished the deities into those which are beneficial and those that are injurious to mankind. Those which are beneficial they call Jupiter, Juno, Mercury, Ceres; those who are mischievous the Dirae, Furies, and Mars. These, which threaten dangers and violence, men endeavor to appease and conciliate by sacred rites. The fourth and the fifth order of gods they assign to things and passions; to passions, Love, Venus, and Desire; the deities that preside over things, Hope, Justice, and Eunomia.

The sixth order of deities are the ones made by the poets; Hesiod, willing to find out a father for those gods that acknowledge an original, invented their progenitors,–

Hyperion, Coeus, and Iapetus,
With Creius:
(Hesiod, "Theogony," 134.)

upon which account this is called the fabulous. The seventh rank of the deities added to the rest are those which, by their beneficence to mankind, were honored with a divine worship, though they were born of mortal race; of this sort were Hercules, Castor and Pollux, and Bacchus. These are reputed to be of a human species; for of all beings that which is divine is most excellent, and man amongst all animals is adorned with the greatest beauty, is also the best, being adorned by virtue above the rest because of the gift of intellect: therefore it was thought that those who were admirable for excellence should resemble that which is the best and most beautiful.

CHAPTER VII.

WHAT IS GOD?

SOME OF THE PHILOSOPHERS, such as Diagoras the Melian, Theodorus the Cyrenean, and Euemerus the Tegeatan, did deny unanimously that there were any gods; and Callimachus the Cyrenean discovered his mind concerning Euemerus in these Iambic verses, thus writing:–

To th' ante-mural temple flock apace,
Where he that long ago composed of brass
Great Jupiter, Thrasonic old bald pate,
Now scribbles impious books,–a boastful ass!

meaning books which prove there are no gods. Euripides the tragedian durst not openly declare his sentiment; the court of Areopagus terrified him. Yet he sufficiently manifested his thoughts by this method. He presented in his tragedy Sisyphus, the first and great patron of this opinion, and introduced himself as one agreeing with him:–

Disorder in those days did domineer,
And brutal power kept the world in fear.

Afterwards by the sanction of laws wickedness was suppressed; but by reason that laws could prohibit only public villanies, yet could not hinder many persons from acting secret impieties, some wise persons gave this advice, that we ought to blind truth with lying disguises, and persuade men that there is a God:–

There's an eternal God does hear and see
And understand every impiety;
Though it in dark recess or thought committed be.

But this poetical fable ought to be rejected, he thought, along with Callimachus, who thus saith:–

If you believe a God, it must be meant
That you conceive this God omnipotent.

But God cannot do everything; for, if it were so, then a God could make snow black, and the fire cold, and him that is in a posture of sitting to be upright, and so on the contrary. The brave-speaking Plato pronounceth that God formed the world after his own image; but this smells rank of the old dotages, old comic writers would say; for how did God, casting his eye upon himself, frame this universe? Or how can God be spherical, and be inferior to man?

Anaxagoras avers that bodies did consist from all eternity, but the divine intellect did reduce them into their proper orders, and effected the origination of all beings. But Plato did not suppose that the primary bodies had their consistence and repose, but that they were moved confusedly and in disorder; but God, knowing that order was better than confusion, did digest them into the best methods. Both these were equally peccant; for both suppose God to be the great moderator of human affairs and for that cause to have formed this present world; when it is apparent that an immortal and blessed being, replenished with all his glorious excellencies, and not at all obnoxious to any sort of evil, but being wholly occupied with his own felicity and immortality, would not employ himself with the concerns of men; for certainly miserable is the being which, like a laborer or artificer, is molested by the troubles and cares which the forming and governing of this world must give him. Add to this, that the God whom these men profess was either not at all existing before this present world (when bodies were either reposed or in a disordered motion), or that at that time God did either sleep, or else was in a constant watchfulness, or that he did neither of these. Now neither the first nor the second can be entertained, because they suppose God to be eternal; if God from eternity was in a continual sleep, he was in an eternal death,—and what is death but an eternal sleep?—but no sleep can affect a deity, for the immortality of God and alliance to death are vastly different. But if God was in a continual vigilance, either there was something wanting to make him happy, or else his beatitude was perfectly complete; but according to neither of these can God be said to be blessed; not according to the first, for if there be any deficiency there is no perfect bliss; not according to the second, for, if there be nothing wanting to the felicity of God, it must be a needless enterprise for him to busy himself in human affairs. And how can it be supposed that God administers by his own providence human concerns, when to vain and trifling persons prosperous things happen, to great and high adverse? Agamemnon was both

> *A virtuous prince, for warlike acts renowned,*
>
> *("Iliad," iii. 179.)*

and by an adulterer and adulteress was vanquished and perfidiously slain. Hercules, after he had freed the life of man from many things that were pernicious to it, perished by the witchcraft and poison of Deianira.

Thales said that the intelligence of the world was God.

Anaximander concluded that the stars were heavenly deities.

Democritus said that God, being a globe of fire, is the intelligence and the soul of the world.

Pythagoras says that, of his principles, unity is God; and the good, which is indeed the nature of a unity, is mind itself; but the binary number, which is infinite, is a daemon, and evil,–about which the multitude of material beings and this visible world are related.

Socrates and Plato agree that God is that which is one, hath its original from its own self, is of a singular subsistence, is one only being perfectly good; all these various names signifying goodness do all centre in mind; hence God is to be understood as that mind and intellect, which is a separate idea, that is to say, pure and unmixed of all matter, and not mingled with anything subject to passions.

Aristotle's sentiment is, that God hath his residence in superior regions, and hath placed his throne in the sphere of the universe, and is a separate idea; which sphere is an ethereal body, which is by him styled the fifth essence or quintessence. For there is a division of the universe into spheres, which are contiguous by their nature but appear to reason to be separated; and he concludes that each of the spheres is an animal, composed of a body and soul; the body of them is ethereal, moved orbicularly, the soul is the rational form, which is unmoved, and yet is the cause that the sphere is in motion.

The Stoics affirm that God is a thing more common and obvious, and is a mechanic fire which every way spreads itself to produce the world; it contains in itself all seminal virtues, and by this means all things by a fatal necessity were produced. This spirit, passing through the whole world, received different names from the mutations in the matter through which it ran in its journey. God therefore is the world, the stars, the earth, and (highest of all) the mind in the heavens. In the judgment of Epicurus all the gods are anthropomorphites, or have the shape of men; but they are perceptible only by reason, for their nature admits of no other manner of being apprehended, their parts being so small and fine that they give no corporeal representations. The same Epicurus asserts that there are four other natural beings which are immortal: of this sort are atoms, the vacuum, the infinite, and the similar parts; and these last are called Homoeomeries and likewise elements.

CHAPTER VIII.

OF THOSE THAT ARE CALLED GENIUSES AND HEROES

HAVING TREATED OF THE essence of the deities in a just order, it follows that we discourse of daemons and heroes. Thales, Pythagoras, Plato, and the Stoics do conclude that daemons are essences endowed with souls;

that the heroes are the souls separated from their bodies, some are good, some are bad; the good are those whose souls are good, the evil those whose souls are wicked. All this is rejected by Epicurus.

CHAPTER IX.

OF MATTER.

MATTER IS THAT FIRST being which is substrate for generation, corruption, and all other alterations.

The disciples of Thales and Pythagoras, with the Stoics, are of opinion that matter is changeable, mutable, convertible, and sliding through all things.

The followers of Democritus aver that the vacuum, the atom, and the incorporeal substance are the first beings, and not obnoxious to passions.

Aristotle and Plato affirm that matter is of that species which is corporeal, void of any form, species, figure, and quality, but apt to receive all forms, that she may be the nurse, the mother, and origin of all other beings. But they that do say that water, earth, air, and fire are matter do likewise say that matter cannot be without form, but conclude it is a body; but they that say that individual particles and atoms are matter do say that matter is without form.

CHAPTER X.

OF IDEAS.

AN IDEA IS A being incorporeal, not subsisting by itself, but gives figure unto shapeless matter, and becomes the cause of its phenomena.

Socrates and Plato conjecture that these ideas are beings separate from matter, subsisting in the understanding and imagination of the deity, that is, of mind.

Aristotle accepted forms and ideas; but he doth not believe them separated from matter, or patterns of the things God has made.

Those Stoics, that are of the school of Zeno, profess that ideas are nothing else but the conceptions of our own mind.

CHAPTER XI.

OF CAUSES.

A CAUSE IS THAT by which anything is produced, or by which anything is effected.

Plato gives this triple division of causes,–the material, the efficient, and the final cause; the principal cause he judges to be the efficient, which is the mind and intellect.

Pythagoras and Aristotle judge the first causes are incorporeal beings, but those that are causes by accident or participation become corporeal substances; by this means the world is corporeal.

The Stoics grant that all causes are corporeal, inasmuch as they are physical.

CHAPTER XII.

OF BODIES.

A BODY IS THAT being which hath these three dimensions, breadth, depth, and length;–or a bulk which makes a sensible resistance;–or whatsoever of its own nature possesseth a place.

Plato saith that it is neither heavy nor light in its own nature, when it exists in its own place; but being in the place where another should be, then it has an inclination by which it tends to gravity or levity.

Aristotle saith that, if we simply consider things in their own nature, the earth only is to be judged heavy, and fire light; but air and water are on occasions heavy and at other times light.

The Stoics think that of the four elements two are light, fire and air; two ponderous, earth and water; that which is naturally light doth by its own nature, not by any inclination, recede from its own centre; but that which is heavy doth by its own nature tend to its centre; for the centre is not a heavy thing in itself.

Epicurus thinks that bodies are not limited; but the first bodies, which are simple bodies, and all those composed of them, all acknowledge gravity; that all atoms are moved, some perpendicularly, some obliquely; some are carried aloft either by immediate impulse or with vibrations.

CHAPTER XIII.

OF THOSE THINGS THAT ARE LEAST IN NATURE.

EMPEDOCLES, BEFORE THE four elements, introduceth the most minute bodies which resemble elements; but they did exist before the elements, having similar parts and orbicular.

Heraclitus brings in the smallest fragments, and those indivisible.

CHAPTER XIV.

OF FIGURES.

A FIGURE IS THE exterior appearance, the circumscription, and the boundary of a body.

The Pythagoreans say that the bodies of the four elements are spherical, fire being in the supremest place only excepted, whose figure is conical.

CHAPTER XV.

OF COLORS.

COLOR IS THE visible quality of a body.

The Pythagoreans called color the external appearance of a body. Empedocles, that which is consentaneous to the passages of the eye. Plato, that they are fires emitted from bodies, which have parts harmonious for the sight. Zeno the Stoic, that colors are the first figurations of matter. The Pythagoreans, that colors are of four sorts, white and black, red and pale; and they derive the variety of colors from the mixtures of the elements, and that seen in animals also from the variety of food and the air.

CHAPTER XVI.

OF THE DIVISION OF BODIES.

THE DISCIPLES OF THALES and Pythagoras grant that all bodies are passible and divisible into infinity. Others hold that atoms and indivisible parts are there fixed, and admit not of a division into infinity. Aristotle, that all bodies are potentially but not actually divisible into infinity.

CHAPTER XVII.

HOW BODIES ARE MIXED AND CONTEMPERATED

ONE WITH ANOTHER.

THE ANCIENT PHILOSOPHERS held that the mixture of elements proceeded from the alteration of qualities; but the disciples of Anaxagoras and Democritus say it is done by apposition. Empedocles composes the elements of still minuter bulks, those which are the most minute and may be termed the element of elements. Plato assigns three bodies (but he will not allow these to be elements, nor properly so called), air, fire, and water, which are mutable into one another; but the earth is mutable into none of these.

CHAPTER XVIII.

OF A VACUUM.

ALL THE NATURAL PHILOSOPHERS from Thales to Plato rejected a vacuum. Empedocles says that there is nothing of a vacuity in Nature, nor anything superabundant. Leucippus, Democritus, Demetrius, Metrodorus, Epicurus, that the atoms are in number infinite; and that a vacuum is infinite in magnitude. The Stoics, that within the compass of the world there is no vacuum, but beyond it the vacuum is infinite. Aristotle, that the vacuum beyond the world is so great that the heaven has liberty to breathe into it, for the heaven is fiery.

CHAPTER XIX.

OF PLACE.

PLATO, TO DEFINE PLACE, calls it that thing which in its own bosom receives forms and ideas; by which metaphor he denotes matter, being (as it were) a nurse or receptacle of beings. Aristotle, that it is the ultimate superficies of the circumambient body, contiguous to that which it doth encompass.

CHAPTER XX.

OF SPACE.

THE STOICS AND EPICUREANS make a place, a vacuum, and space to differ. A vacuum is that which is void of anything that may be called a body; place is that which is possessed by a body; a space that which is partly filled with a body, as a cask with wine.

CHAPTER XXI.

OF TIME.

IN THE SENSE OF Pythagoras, time is that sphere which encompasses the world. Plato says that it is a movable image of eternity, or the interval of the world's motion.

Eratosthenes, that it is the solar motion.

CHAPTER XXII.

OF THE SUBSTANCE AND NATURE OF TIME.

PLATO SAYS THAT THE heavenly motion is time. Most of the Stoics that motion is time. Most philosophers think that time had no commencement; Plato, that time had only in intelligence a beginning.

CHAPTER XXIII.

OF MOTION.

PLATO AND PYTHAGORAS SAY that motion is a difference and alteration in matter. Aristotle, that it is the actual operation of that which may be moved. Democritus, that there is but one sort of motion, and it is that which is vibratory. Epicurus, that there are two species of motion, one perpendicular, and the other oblique. Herophilus, that one species of motion is obvious only to reason, the other to sense. Heraclitus utterly denies that there is anything of quiet or repose in nature; for that is the state of the dead; one sort of motion is eternal, which he assigns to beings eternal, the other perishable, to those things which are perishable.

CHAPTER XXIV.

OF GENERATION AND CORRUPTION.

PARMENIDES MELISSUS, and Zeno deny that there are any such things as generation and corruption, for they suppose that the universe is unmovable. Empedocles, Epicurus, and other philosophers that combine in this, that the world is framed of small corporeal particles meeting together, affirm that corruption and generation are not so properly to be accepted; but there are conjunctions and separations, which do not consist in any distinction according to their qualities, but are made according to quantity by coalition or disjunction. Pythagoras, and all those who take for granted that matter is subject to mutation, say that generation and corruption are to be accepted in their proper sense, and that they are accomplished by the alteration, mutation, and dissolution of elements.

CHAPTER XXV.

OF NECESSITY.

THALES SAYS THAT NECESSITY is omnipotent, and that it exerciseth an empire over everything. Pythagoras, that the world is invested by necessity. Parmenides and Democritus, that there is nothing in the world but what is necessary, and that this same necessity is otherwise called fate, justice, providence, and the architect of the world.

CHAPTER XXVI.

OF THE NATURE OF NECESSITY.

BUT PLATO DISTINGUISHETH AND refers some things to Providence, others to necessity. Empedocles makes the nature of necessity to be that cause which employs principles and elements. Democritus makes it to be a resistance, impulse, and force of matter. Plato sometimes says that necessity is matter; at other times, that it is the habitude or respect of the efficient cause towards matter.

CHAPTER XXVII.

OF DESTINY OR FATE.

HERACLITUS, WHO ATTRIBUTES all things to fate, makes necessity to be the same thing with it. Plato admits of a necessity in the minds and the acts of men, but yet he introduceth a cause which flows from ourselves. The Stoics, in this agreeing with Plato, say that necessity is a cause invincible and violent; that fate is the ordered complication of causes, in which there is an intexture of those things which proceed from our own determination, so that certain things are to be attributed to fate, others not.

CHAPTER XXVIII.

OF THE NATURE OF FATE.

ACCORDING TO HERACLITUS, the essence of fate is a certain reason which penetrates the substance of all being; and this is an ethereal body, containing in itself that seminal faculty which gives an original to every being in the universe. Plato affirms that it is the eternal reason and the eternal law of the nature of the world. Chrysippus, that it is a spiritual faculty, which in due order doth manage and rule the universe. Again, in his book styled the "Definitions," that fate is the reason of the world, or that it is that law whereby Providence rules and administers everything that is in the world; or it is that reason by which all things have been, all things are, and all things will be produced. The Stoics say that it is a chain of causes, that is, it is an order and connection of causes which cannot be resisted. Posidonius, that it is a being the third in degree from Jupiter; the first of beings is Jupiter, the second Nature, and the third Fate.

CHAPTER XXIX.

OF FORTUNE.

PLATO SAYS, THAT IT is an accidental cause and a casual consequence in things which proceed from the election and counsel of men. Aristotle, that it is an accidental cause in those things done by an impulse for a certain end; and this cause is uncertain and unstable: there is a great deal of difference betwixt that which flows from chance and that which falls out by Fortune; for that which is fortuitous allows also chance, and belongs to things practical; but what is by chance cannot be also by Fortune, for it belongs to things without action: Fortune, moreover, pertains to rational beings, but chance to rational and irrational beings alike, and even to inanimate things. Epicurus, that it is a cause not always consistent, but various as to persons, times, and manners. Anaxagoras and the Stoics, that it is that cause which human reason cannot comprehend; for there are some things which proceed from necessity, some things from Fate, some from choice and free-will, some from Fortune, some from chance.

CHAPTER XXX.

OF NATURE.

EMPEDOCLES AFFIRMS THAT Nature is nothing else but the mixture and separation of the elements; for thus he writes in the first book of his natural philosophy:–
> *Nature gives neither life nor death,*
> *Mutation makes us die or breathe.*
> *The elements first are mixed, then each*
> *Do part: this Nature is in mortal speech.*

Anaxagoras is of the same opinion, that Nature is coalition and separation, that is, generation and corruption.

Book Two

HAVING FINISHED MY DISSERTATION concerning principles and elements and those things which chiefly appertain to them, I will turn my pen to discourse of those things which are produced by them, and will take my beginning from the world, which contains and encompasseth all beings.

CHAPTER I.

OF THE WORLD.

PYTHAGORAS WAS THE FIRST philosopher that called the world [Greek omitted], from the order and beauty of it; for so that word signifies. Thales and his followers say the world is one. Democritus, Epicurus, and their scholar Metrodorus affirm that there are infinite worlds in an infinite space, for that infinite vacuum in its whole extent contains them. Empedocles, that the circle which the sun makes in its motion circumscribes the world, and that circle is the utmost bound of the world. Seleucus, that the world knows no limits. Diogenes, that the universe is infinite, but this world is finite. The Stoics make a difference between that which is called the universe, and that which is called the whole world;–the universe is the infinite space considered with the vacuum, the vacuity being removed gives the right conception of the world; so that the universe and the world are not the same thing.

CHAPTER II.

OF THE FIGURE OF THE WORLD.

THE STOICS SAY THAT the figure of the world is spherical, others that it is conical, others oval. Epicurus, that the figure of the world may be globular, or that it may admit of other shapes.

CHAPTER III.

WHETHER THE WORLD BE AN ANIMAL.

DEMOCRITUS, EPICURUS, and those philosophers who introduced atoms and a vacuum, affirm that the world is not an animal, nor governed by any wise Providence, but that it is managed by a nature which is void of reason. All the other philosophers affirm that the world is informed with a soul, and governed by reason and Providence. Aristotle is excepted, who is somewhat different; he is of opinion, that the whole world is not acted by a soul in every part of it, nor hath it any sensitive, rational, or intellectual faculties, nor is it directed by reason and Providence in every part of it; of all which the heavenly bodies are made partakers, for the circumambient spheres are animated and are living beings; but those things which are about the earth are void of those endowments; and though those terrestrial bodies are of an orderly disposition, yet that is casual and not primogenial.

CHAPTER IV.

WHETHER THE WORLD IS ETERNAL

AND INCORRUPTIBLE.

PYTHAGORAS [AND PLATO], agreeing with the Stoics, affirm that the world was framed by God, and being corporeal is obvious to the senses, and in its own nature is obnoxious to destruction; but it shall never perish, it being preserved by the providence of God. Epicurus, that the world had a beginning, and so shall have an end, as plants and animals have. Xenophanes, that the world never had a beginning, is eternal and incorruptible. Aristotle, that the part of the world which is sublunary is subject to change, and there terrestrial beings find a decay.

CHAPTER V.

WHENCE DOES THE WORLD RECEIVE

ITS NUTRIMENT?

ARISTOTLE SAYS THAT, if the world be nourished, it will likewise be dissolved; but it requires no aliment, and will therefore be eternal. Plato, that this very world prepares for itself a nutriment, by the alteration of those things which are corruptible in it. Philolaus affirms that a destruction happens to the world in two ways; either by fire failing from heaven, or by the sublunary water being poured down through the whirling of the air; and the exhalations proceeding from thence are aliment of the world.

CHAPTER VI.

FROM WHAT ELEMENT GOD DID BEGIN TO RAISE

THE FABRIC OF THE WORLD.

THE NATURAL PHILOSOPHERS pronounce that the forming of this world took its original from the earth, it being its centre, for the centre is the principal part of the globe. Pythagoras, from the fire and the fifth element. Empedocles determines, that the first and principal element distinct from the rest was the aether, then fire, after that the earth, which earth being strongly compacted by the force of a potent revolution, water springs from it, the exhalations of which water produce the air; the heaven took its origin from the aether, and fire gave a being to the sun; those things nearest to the earth are condensed from the remainders. Plato, that the visible world was framed after the exemplar of the intellectual world; the soul of the visible world was first produced, then the corporeal figure, first that which proceeded from fire and earth, then that which came from air and water. Pythagoras, that the world was formed of five solid figures which are called mathematical; the earth was produced by the cube, the fire by the pyramid, the air by the octahedron, the water by the icosahedron, and the globe of the universe by the dodecahedron. In all these Plato hath the same sentiments with Pythagoras.

CHAPTER VII.

IN WHAT FORM AND ORDER THE WORLD

WAS COMPOSED.

Parmenides maintains that there are small coronets alternately twisted one within another, some made up of a thin, others of a condensed, matter; and there are others between mixed mutually together of light and of darkness, and around them all there is a solid substance, which like a firm wall surrounds these coronets. Leucippus and Democritus cover the world round about, as with a garment and membrane. Epicurus says that that which abounds some worlds is thin, and that which limits others is gross and condensed; and of these spheres some are in motion, others are fixed. Plato, that fire takes the first place in the world, the second the aether, after that the air, under that the water; the last place the earth possesseth: sometimes he puts the aether and the fire in the same place. Aristotle gives the first place to the aether, as that which is impassible, it being a kind of a fifth body after which he placeth those that are passible, fire, air, and water, and last of all the earth. To those bodies that are accounted celestial he assigns a motion that is circular, but to those that are seated under them, if they be light bodies, an ascending, if heavy, a descending motion. Empedocles, that the places of the elements are not always fixed and determined, but they all succeed one another in their respective stations.

CHAPTER VIII.

WHAT IS THE CAUSE OF THE WORLD'S INCLINATION.

Diogenes and Anaxagoras state that, after the world was composed and had produced living creatures, the world out of its own propensity made an inclination toward the south. Perhaps this may be attributed to a wise Providence (they affirm), that thereby some parts of the world may be habitable, others uninhabitable, according as the various climates are affected with a rigorous cold, or a scorching heat, or a just temperament of cold and heat. Empedocles, that the air yielding to the impetuous force of the solar rays, the poles received an inclination; whereby the northern parts were exalted and the southern depressed, by which means the whole world received its inclination.

CHAPTER IX.

OF THAT THING WHICH IS BEYOND THE WORLD,

AND WHETHER IT BE A VACUUM OR NOT.

PYTHAGORAS AND HIS followers say that beyond the world there is a vacuum, into which and out of which the world hath its respiration. The Stoics, that there is a vacuum into which infinite space by a conflagration shall be dissolved. Posidonius, not an infinite vacuum, but as much as suffices for the dissolution of the world; and this he asserts in his first book concerning the Vacuum. Aristotle affirms, that a vacuum does not exist. Plato concludes that neither within nor without the world there is any vacuum.

CHAPTER X.

WHAT PARTS OF THE WORLD ARE ON THE RIGHT

HAND, AND WHAT ON THE LEFT.

PYTHAGORAS, PLATO, and Aristotle declare that the eastern parts of the world, from whence motion commences, are of the right, those of the western are of the left hand of the world. Empedocles, that those that are of the right hand face the summer solstice, those of the left the winter solstice.

CHAPTER XI.

OF HEAVEN, WHAT IS ITS NATURE AND ESSENCE.

ANAXIMENES AFFIRMS THAT the circumference of heaven makes the limit of the earth's revolution. Empedocles, that the heaven is a solid substance, and hath the form and hardness of crystal, it being composed of the air compacted by fire, and that in both hemispheres it invests the elements of air and fire. Aristotle, that it is formed by the fifth body, and by the mixture of extreme heat and cold.

CHAPTER XII.

INTO HOW MANY CIRCLES IS THE HEAVEN

DISTINGUISHED; OR, OF THE DIVISION OF HEAVEN.

THALES, PYTHAGORAS, and the followers of Pythagoras do distribute the universal globe of heaven into five circles, which they denominate zones; one of which is called the arctic circle, which is always conspicuous to us, another is the summer tropic, another is the solstice, another is the winter tropic, another is the antarctic circle, which is always out of sight. The circle called the zodiac is placed under the three that are in the midst, and is oblique, gently touching them all. Likewise, they are all divided in right angles by the meridian, which goes from pole to pole. It is supposed that Pythagoras made the first discovery of the obliquity of the zodiac, but one Oenopides of Chios challenges to himself the invention of it.

CHAPTER XIII.

WHAT IS THE ESSENCE OF THE STARS, AND HOW

THEY ARE COMPOSED.

THALES AFFIRMS THAT THEY are globes of earth set on fire. Empedocles, that they are fiery bodies arising from that fire which the aether embraced within itself, and did shatter in pieces when the elements were first separated one from another. Anaxagoras, that the circumambient aether is of a fiery substance, which, by a vehement force in its whirling about, did tear stones from the earth, and by its own power set them on fire, and establish them as stars in the heavens. Diogenes thinks they resemble pumice stones, and that they are the breathings of the world; again he supposeth that there are some invisible stones, which fall sometimes from heaven upon the earth, and are there quenched; as it happened at Aegos-potami, where a stony star resembling fire did fall. Empedocles, that the fixed stars fastened to the crystal, but the planets are loosened. Plato, that the stars for the most part are of a fiery nature, but they are made partakers of another element, with they are mixed after the resemblance of glue. Zenophanes, that they are composed of inflamed clouds, which in the daytime are quenched, and in the night are kindled again. The like we see in coals; for the rising and setting of the stars is nothing else but the quenching and kindling of them. Heraclitus and the Pythagoreans, that every star is a world in an infinite aether, and encompasseth air, earth, and aether; this opinion is current among the disciples of Orpheus, for they suppose that each of the stars does make a world. Epicurus condemns none of these opinions, for he embraces anything that is possible.

CHAPTER XIV.

OF WHAT FIGURE THE STARS ARE.

THE STOICS SAY THAT the stars are of a circular form, like as the sun, the moon, and the world. Cleanthes, that they are of a conical figure. Anaximenes, that they are fastened as nails in the crystalline firmament; some others, that they are fiery plates of gold, resembling pictures.

CHAPTER XV.

OF THE ORDER AND PLACE OF THE STARS.

XENOCRATES SAYS THAT THE stars are moved in one and the same superficies. The other Stoics say that they are moved in various superficies, some being superior, others inferior. Democritus, that the fixed stars are in the highest place; after those the planets; after these the sun, Venus, and the moon, in order. Plato, that the first after the fixed stars that makes its appearance is Phaenon, the star of Saturn; the second Phaeton, the star of Jupiter; the third the fiery, which is the star of Mars; the fourth the morning star, which is the star of Venus; the fifth the shining star, and that is the star of Mercury; in the sixth place is the sun, in the seventh the moon. Plato and some of the mathematicians conspire in the same opinion; others place the sun as the centre of the planets. Anaximander, Metrodorus of Chios, and Crates assign to the sun the superior place, after him the moon, after them the fixed stars and planets.

CHAPTER XVI.

OF THE MOTION AND CIRCULATION OF THE STARS.

ANAXAGORAS, DEMOCRITUS, and Cleanthes say that all the stars have their motion from east to west. Alcmaeon and the mathematicians, that the planets have a contrary motion to the fixed stars, and in opposition to them are carried from the west to the east. Anaximander, that they are carried by those circles and spheres on which they are placed. Anaximenes, that they are turned under and about the earth. Plato and the mathematicians, that the sun, Venus, and Mercury hold equal measures in their motions.

CHAPTER XVII.

WHENCE DO THE STARS RECEIVE THEIR LIGHT?

METRODORUS SAYS THAT ALL the fixed stars derive their light from the sun. Heraclitus and the Stoics, that earthly exhalations are those by which the stars are nourished. Aristotle, that the heavenly bodies require no nutriment, for they being eternal cannot be obnoxious to corruption. Plato and the Stoics, that the whole world and the stars are fed by the same things.

CHAPTER XVIII.

WHAT ARE THOSE STARS WHICH ARE CALLED THE

DIOSCURI, THE TWINS, OR CASTOR AND POLLUX?

XENOPHANES SAYS THAT THOSE which appear as stars in the tops of ships are little clouds brilliant by their peculiar motion. Metrodorus, that the eyes of frighted and astonished people emit those lights which are called the Twins.

CHAPTER XIX.

HOW STARS PROGNOSTICATE, AND WHAT IS THE CAUSE OF WINTER AND SUMMER.

PLATO SAYS THAT THE summer and winter indications proceed from the rising and setting of the stars, that is, from the rising and setting of the sun, the moon, and the fixed stars. Anaximenes, that the rest in this are not at all concerned, but that it is wholly performed by the sun. Eudoxus and Aratus assign it in common to all the stars, for thus Aratus says:–

> *Thund'ring Jove stars in heaven hath fixed,*
> *And them in such beauteous order mixed,*
> *Which yearly future things predict.*

CHAPTER XX.

OF THE ESSENCE OF THE SUN.

ANAXIMANDER SAYS, that the sun is a circle eight and twenty times bigger than the earth, and has a circumference very much like that of a chariot-wheel, which is hollow and full of fire; the fire of which appears to us through its mouth, as by an aperture in a pipe; and this is the sun. Xenophanes, that the sun is constituted of small bodies of fire compacted together and raised from a moist exhalation, which condensed make the body of the sun; or that it is a cloud enfired. The Stoics, that it is an intelligent flame proceeding from the sea. Plato, that it is composed of abundance of fire. Anaxagoras, Democritus, and Metrodorus, that it is an enfired stone, or a burning body. Aristotle, that it is a sphere formed out of the fifth body. Philolaus the Pythagorean, that the sun shines as crystal, which receives its splendor from the fire of the world and so reflecteth its light upon us; so that first, the body of fire which is celestial is in the sun; and secondly, the fiery reflection that comes from it, in the form of a mirror; and lastly, the rays spread upon us by way of reflection from that mirror; and this last we call the sun, which is (as it were) an image of an image. Empedocles, that there are two suns; the one the prototype, which is a fire placed in the other hemisphere, which it totally fills, and is always ordered in a direct opposition to the reflection of its own light; and the sun which is visible to us, formed by the reflection of that splendor in the other hemisphere (which is filled with air mixed with heat), the light reflected from the circular sun in the opposite hemisphere falling upon the crystalline sun; and this reflection is borne round with the motion of the fiery sun. To give briefly the full sense, the sun is nothing else but the light and brightness of that fire which encompasseth the earth. Epicurus, that it is an earthy bulk well compacted, with ores like a pumice-stone or a sponge, kindled by fire.

CHAPTER XXI.

OF THE MAGNITUDE OF THE SUN.

Anaximander says, that the sun itself in greatness is equal to the earth, but that the circle from whence it receives its respiration and in which it is moved is seven and twenty times larger than the earth. Anaxagoras, that it is far greater than Peloponnesus. Heraclitus, that it is no broader than a man's foot. Epicurus, that he equally embraceth all the foresaid opinions,—that the sun may be of magnitude as it appears, or it may be somewhat greater or somewhat less.

CHAPTER XXII.

WHAT IS THE FIGURE OR SHAPE OF THE SUN.

ANAXIMENES AFFIRMS that in its dilatation it resembles a leaf. Heraclitus, that it hath the shape of a boat, and is somewhat crooked. The Stoics, that it is spherical, and it is of the same figure with the world and the stars. Epicurus, that the recited dogmas may be defended.

Book Two

CHAPTER XXIII.

OF THE TURNING AND RETURNING OF THE STARS, OR THE SUMMER AND WINTER SOLSTICE.

ANAXIMENES BELIEVES THAT the stars are forced by a condensed and resisting air. Anaxagoras, by the repelling force of the northern air, which is violently pushed on by the sun, and thus rendered more condensed and powerful. Empedocles, that the sun is hindered from a continual direct course by its spherical vehicle and by the two circular tropics. Diogenes, that the sun, when it comes to its utmost declination, is extinguished, a rigorous cold damping the heat. The Stoics, that the sun maintains its course only through that space in which its sustenance is seated, let it be the ocean or the earth; by the exhalations proceeding from these it is nourished. Plato, Pythagoras, and Aristotle, that the sun receives a transverse motion from the obliquity of the zodiac, which is guarded by the tropics; all these the globe clearly manifests.

CHAPTER XXIV.

OF THE ECLIPSE OF THE SUN.

THALES WAS THE FIRST who affirmed that the eclipse of the sun was caused by the moon's running in a perpendicular line between it and the world; for the moon in its own nature is terrestrial. And by mirrors it is made perspicuous that, when the sun is eclipsed, the moon is in a direct line below it. Anaximander, that the sun is eclipsed when the fiery mouth of it is stopped and hindered from respiration. Heraclitus, that it is after the manner of the turning of a boat, when the concave seems uppermost to our sight, and the convex nethermost. Xenophanes, that the sun is eclipsed when it is extinguished; and that a new sun is created and rises in the east. He gives a farther account of an eclipse of the sun which remained for a whole month, and again of an eclipse which changed the day into night. Some declare that the cause of an eclipse is the invisible concourse of condensed clouds which cover the orb of the sun. Aristarchus placeth the sun amongst the fixed stars, and believeth that the earth [the moon?] is moved about the sun, and that by its inclination and vergency it intercepts its light and shadows its orb. Xenophanes, that there are many suns and many moons, according as the earth is distinguished by climates, circles, and zones. At some certain times the orb of the sun, falling upon some part of the world which is untenanted, wanders in a vacuum and becomes eclipsed. The same person affirms that the sun proceeding in its motion in the infinite space, appears to us to move orbicularly, taking that representation from its infinite distance from us.

CHAPTER XXV.

OF THE ESSENCE OF THE MOON.

ANAXIMANDER AFFIRMS THAT THE circle of the moon is nineteen times bigger than the earth, and resembles the sun, its orb being full of fire; and it suffers an eclipse when the wheel makes a revolution,–which he describes by the divers turnings of a chariot-wheel, in the midst of it there being a hollow nave replenished with fire, which hath but one way of expiration. Xenophanes, that it is a condensed cloud. The Stoics, that it is mixed of fire and air. Plato, that it is a body of the greatest part fiery. Anaxagoras and Democritus, that it is a solid, condensed, and fiery body, in which there are flat countries, mountains, and valleys. Heraclitus, that it is an earth covered with a bright cloud. Pythagoras, that the body of the moon was of a nature resembling a mirror.

CHAPTER XXVI.

OF THE SIZE OF THE MOON.

THE STOICS DECLARE, that in magnitude it exceeds the earth, just as the sun itself doth. Parmenides, that it is equal to the sun, from whom it receives its light.

CHAPTER XXVII.

OF THE FIGURE OF THE MOON.

THE STOICS BELIEVE THAT it is of the same figure with the sun, spherical. Empedocles, that the figure of it resembles a quoit. Heraclitus, a boat. Others, a cylinder.

CHAPTER XXVIII.

FROM WHENCE IS IT THAT THE MOON RECEIVES

HER LIGHT?

ANAXIMANDER THINKS THAT she gives light to herself, but it is very slender and faint. Antiphon, that the moon shines by its own proper light; but when it absconds itself, the solar beams darting on it obscure it. Thus it naturally happens, that a more vehement light puts out a weaker; the same is seen in other stars. Thales and his followers, that the moon borrows all her light of the sun. Heraclitus, that the sun and moon are after the same manner affected; in their configurations both are shaped like boats, and are made conspicuous to us by receiving their light from moist exhalations. The sun appears to us more refulgent, by reason it is moved in a clearer and purer air; the moon appears more duskish, it being carried in an air more troubled and gross.

CHAPTER XXIX.

OF THE ECLIPSE OF THE MOON.

ANAXIMENES BELIEVES THAT the mouth of the wheel, about which the moon is turned, being stopped is the cause of an eclipse. Berasus, that it proceeds from the turning of the dark side of the lunar orb towards us. Heraclitus, that it is performed just after the manner of a boat turned upside downwards. Some of the Pythagoreans say, that the splendor arises from the earth, its obstruction from the Antichthon (or counter-earth). Some of the later philosophers, that there is such a distribution of the lunar flame, that it gradually and in a just order burns until it be full moon; in like manner, that this fire decays by degrees, until its conjunction with the sun totally extinguisheth it. Plato, Aristotle, the Stoics, and all the mathematicians agree, that the obscurity with which the moon is every month affected ariseth from a conjunction with the sun, by whose more resplendent beams she is darkened; and the moon is then eclipsed when she falls upon the shadow of the earth, the earth interposing between the sun and moon, or (to speak more properly) the earth intercepting the light of the moon.

CHAPTER XXX.

OF THE PHASES OF THE MOON, OR THE LUNAR ASPECTS; OR HOW IT COMES TO PASS THAT THE MOON APPEARS TO US TERRESTRIAL.

THE PYTHAGOREANS SAY, that the moon appears to us terraneous, by reason it is inhabited as our earth is, and in it there are animals of a larger size and plants of a rarer beauty than our globe affords; that the animals in their virtue and energy are fifteen degrees superior to ours; that they emit nothing excrementitious; and that the days are fifteen times longer. Anaxagoras, that the reason of the inequality ariseth from the commixture of things earthy and cold; and that fiery and caliginous matter is jumbled together, whereby the moon is said to be a star of a counterfeit aspect. The Stoics, that on account of the diversity of her substance the composition of her body is subject to corruption.

CHAPTER XXXI.

HOW FAR THE MOON IS REMOVED FROM THE SUN.

EMPEDOCLES DECLARES, that the distance of the moon from the sun is double her remoteness from the earth. The mathematicians, that her distance from the sun is eighteen times her distance from the earth. Eratosthenes, that the sun is remote from the earth seven hundred and eighteen thousand furlongs.

CHAPTER XXXII.

OF THE YEAR, AND HOW MANY CIRCULATIONS MAKE UP THE GREAT YEAR OF EVERY PLANET.

THE YEAR OF SATURN is completed when he has had his circulation in the space of thirty solar years; of Jupiter in twelve; of Mars in two, of the sun in twelve months; in so many Mercury and Venus, the spaces of their circulation being equal; of the moon in thirty days, in which time her course from her prime to her conjunction is finished. As to the great year, some make it to consist of eight years solar, some of nineteen, others of fifty-nine. Heraclitus, of eighteen thousand. Diogenes, of three hundred and sixty-five such years as Heraclitus assigns. Others there are who lengthen it to seven thousand seven hundred and seventy-seven years.

Book Three

IN MY TWO PRECEDENT treatises having in due order taken a compendious view and given an account of the celestial bodies, and of the moon which stands between them and the terrestrial, I must now convert my pen to discourse in this third book of Meteors, which are beings above the earth and below the moon, and are extended to the site and situation of the earth, which is supposed to be the centre of the sphere of this world; and from thence will I take my beginning.

CHAPTER I.

OF THE GALAXY, OR THE MILKY WAY.

IT IS A CLOUDY CIRCLE, which continually appears in the air, and by reason of the whiteness of its colors is called the galaxy, or the milky way. Some of the Pythagoreans say that, when Phaeton set the world on fire, a star falling from its own place in its circular passage through the region caused an inflammation. Others say that originally it was the first course of the sun; others, that it is an image as in a looking-glass, occasioned by the sun's reflecting its beams towards the heavens, and this appears in the clouds and in the rainbow. Metrodorus, that it is merely the solar course, or the motion of the sun in its own circle. Parmenides, that the mixture of a thick and thin substance gives it a color which resembles milk. Anaxagoras, that the sun moving under the earth and not being able to enlighten every place, the shadow of the earth, being cast upon the part of the heavens, makes the galaxy. Democritus, that it is the splendor which ariseth from the coalition of many small bodies, which, being firmly united amongst themselves, do mutually enlighten one another. Aristotle, that it is the inflammation of dry, copious, and coherent vapor, by which the fiery mane, whose seat is beneath the aether and the planets, is produced. Posidonius, that it is a combination of fire, of finer substance than the stars, but denser than light.

CHAPTER II.

OF COMETS AND SHOOTING FIRES, AND THOSE

WHICH RESEMBLE BEAMS.

SOME OF THE PYTHAGOREANS say, that a comet is one of those stars which do not always appear, but after they have run through their determined course, they then rise and are visible to us. Others, that it is the reflection of our sight upon the sun, which gives the resemblance of comets much after the same manner as images are reflected in mirrors. Anaxagoras and Democritus, that two or more stars being in conjunction by their united light make a comet. Aristotle, that it is a fiery coalition of dry exhalations. Strato, that it is the light of the star darting through a thick cloud that hath invested it; this is seen in light shining through lanterns. Heraclides, native of Pontus, that it is a lofty cloud inflamed by a sublime fire. The like causes he assigns to the bearded comet, to those circles that are seen about the sun or stars, or those meteors which resemble pillars or beams, and all others which are of this kind. This way unanimously go all the Peripatetics, holding that these meteors, being formed by the clouds, do differ according to their various configurations. Epigenes, that a comet arises from a rising of spirit or wind, mixed with an earthy substance and set on fire. Boethus, that it is a phantasy presented to us by fiery air. Diogenes, that comets are stars. Anaxagoras, that those styled shooting stars descend from the aether like sparks, and therefore are soon extinguished. Metrodorus, that it is a forcible illapse of the sun upon clouds which makes them to sparkle as fire. Xenophanes, that all such fiery meteors are nothing else but the conglomeration of the enfired clouds, and the flashing motions of them.

CHAPTER III.

OF VIOLENT ERUPTION OF FIRE OUT OF THE

CLOUDS. OF LIGHTNING. OF THUNDER. OF

HURRICANES. OF WHIRLWINDS.

Anaximander affirms that all these are produced by the wind after this manner: the wind being enclosed by condensed clouds, on account of its minuteness and lightness violently endeavors to make a passage; and in breaking through the cloud gives noise; and the tearing the cloud, because of the blackness of it, gives a resplendent flame. Metrodorus, that when the wind falls upon a cloud whose densing firmly compacts it, by breaking the cloud it causeth a great noise, and by striking and rending the cloud it gives the flame; and in the swiftness of its motion, the sun imparting heat to it, it throws out the bolt. The weak declining of the thunderbolt ends in a violent tempest. Anaxagoras, that when heat and cold meet and are mixed together (that is, ethereal parts with airy), thereby a great noise of thunder is produced, and the color observed against the blackness of the cloud occasions the flashing of fire; the full and great splendor is lightning, the more enlarged and embodied fire becomes a whirlwind, the cloudiness of it gives the hurricane. The Stoics, that thunder is the clashing of clouds one upon another, the flash of lightning is their fiery inflammation; their more rapid splendor is the thunderbolt, the faint and weak the whirlwind. Aristotle, that all these proceed from dry exhalations, which, if they meet with moist vapors, forcing their passage, the breaking of them gives the noise of thunder; they, being very dry, take fire and make lightning; tempests and hurricanes arise from the plenitude of matter which each draw to themselves, the hotter parts attracted make the whirlwinds, the duller the tempests.

CHAPTER IV.

OF CLOUDS, RAIN, SNOW, AND HAIL.

Anaximenes thinks that the air by being very much condensed clouds are formed; this air being more compacted, rain is compressed through it; when water in its falling down freezeth, then snow is generated; when it is encompassed with a moist air, it is hail. Metrodorus, that a cloud is composed of a watery exhalation carried into a higher place. Epicurus, that they are made of vapors; and that hail and snow are formed in a round figure, being in their long descent pressed upon by the circumambient air.

CHAPTER V.

OF THE RAINBOW.

THOSE THINGS WHICH AFFECT the air in the superior places of it are of two sorts. Some have a real subsistence, such are rain and hail; others not. Those which enjoy not a proper subsistence are only in appearance; of this sort is the rainbow. Thus the continent to us that sail seems to be in motion.

Plato says, that men admiring it feigned that it took origination from one Thaumas, which word signifies admiration. Homer sings:–

Jove paints the rainbow with a purple dye,
Alluring man to cast his wandering eye.
(Iliad, xvii. 547.)

Others therefore fabled that the bow hath a head like a bull, by which it swallows up rivers.

But what is the cause of the rainbow? It is evident that what apparent things we see come to our eyes in right or in crooked lines, or by refraction: these are incorporeal and to sense obscure, but to reason they are obvious. Those which are seen in right lines are those which we see through the air or horn or transparent stones, for all the parts of these things are very fine and tenuous; but those which appear in crooked lines are in water, the thickness of the water presenting them bended to our sight. This is the reason that oars in themselves straight, when put into the sea, appear to us crooked. The third manner of our seeing is by refraction, and this is perspicuous in mirrors. After this third sort the rainbow is affected. We conceive it is a moist exhalation converted into a cloud, and in a short space it is dissolved into small and moist drops. The sun declining towards the west, it will necessarily follow that the whole bow is seen opposite to the sun; for the eye being directed to those drops receives a refraction, and by this means the bow is formed. The eye doth not consider the figure and form, but the color of these drops; the first of which colors is a shining red, the second a purple, the third is blue and green. Let us consider whether the reason of this red shining color be the splendor of the sun falling upon these small drops, the whole body of light being refracted, by which this bright red color is produced; the second part being troubled and the light languishing in the drops, the color becomes purple (for the purple is the faint red); but the third part, being more and more troubled, is changed into the green color. And this is proved by other effects of Nature; if any one shall put water in his mouth and spit it out so opposite to the sun, that its rays may be refracted on the drops, he shall see the resemblance of a rainbow; the same appears to men that are blear-eyed, when they fix their watery eyes upon a candle.

Anaximenes thinks the bow is thus formed; the sun casting its splendor upon a thick, black, and gross cloud, and the rays not being in a capacity to penetrate beyond the superficies. Anaxagoras, that, the solar rays being reflected from a condensed cloud, the sun being placed directly opposite to it forms the bow after the mode of the repercussion of a mirror; after the same manner he assigns the natural cause of the Parhelia or mock-suns, which are often seen in Pontus. Metrodorus, that when the sun casts its splendor through a cloud, the cloud gives itself a blue, and the light a red color.

CHAPTER VI.

OF METEORS WHICH RESEMBLE RODS, OR OF

RODS.

THESE RODS AND THE mock-suns are constituted of a double nature, a real subsistence, and a mere appearance;–of a real subsistence, because the clouds are the object of our eyes; of a mere appearance, for their proper color is not seen, but that which is adventitious. The like affections, natural and adventitious, in all such things do happen.

CHAPTER VII.

OF WINDS.

ANAXIMANDER BELIEVES THAT WIND is a fluid air, the sun putting into motion or melting the moist subtle parts of it. The Stoics, that all winds are a flowing air, and from the diversity of the regions whence they have their origin receive their denomination; as, from darkness and the west the western wind; from the sun and its rising the eastern; from the north the northern, and from the south the southern winds. Metrodorus, that moist vapors heated by the sun are the cause of the impetuousness of violent winds. The Etesian, or those winds which annually commence about the rising of the Little Dog, the air about the northern pole being more compacted, blow violently following the sun when it returns from the summer solstice.

CHAPTER VIII.

OF WINTER AND SUMMER.

EMPEDOCLES AND THE STOICS believe that winter is caused by the thickness of the air prevailing and mounting upwards; and summer by fire, it falling downwards.

This description being given by me of Meteors, or those things that are above us, I must pass to those things which are terrestrial.

CHAPTER IX.

OF THE EARTH, WHAT IS ITS NATURE

AND MAGNITUDE.

THALES AND HIS FOLLOWERS say that there is but one earth. Hicetes the Pythagorean, that there are two earths, this and the Antichthon, or the earth opposite to it. The Stoics, that this earth is one, and that finite and limited. Xenophanes, that the earth, being compacted of fire and air, in its lowest parts hath laid a foundation in an infinite depth. Metrodorus, that the earth is mere sediment and dregs of water, as the sun is of the air.

CHAPTER X.

OF THE FIGURE OF THE EARTH.

THALES, THE STOICS, and their followers say that the earth is globular. Anaximander, that it resembles a smooth stony pillar. Anaximenes, that it hath the shape of a table. Leucippus, of a drum. Democritus, that it is like a quoit externally, and hollow in the middle.

CHAPTER XI.

OF THE SITE AND POSITION OF THE EARTH.

THE DISCIPLES OF THALES say that the earth is the centre of the universe. Xenophanes, that it is first, being rooted in the infinite space. Philolaus the Pythagorean gives to fire the middle place, and this is the source fire of the universe; the second place to the Antichthon; the third to that earth which we inhabit, which is placed in opposition unto and whirled about the opposite,–which is the reason that those which inhabit that earth cannot be seen by us. Parmenides was the first that confined the habitable world to the two solstitial (or temperate) zones.

CHAPTER XII.

OF THE INCLINATION OF THE EARTH.

LEUCIPPUS AFFIRMS THAT THE earth vergeth towards the southern parts, by reason of the thinness and fineness that is in the south; the northern parts are more compacted, they being congealed by a rigorous cold, but those parts of the world that are opposite are enfired. Democritus, because, the southern parts of the air being the weaker, the earth as it enlarges bends towards the south; the northern parts are of an unequal, the southern of an equal temperament; and this is the reason that the earth bends towards those parts where the earth is laden with fruits and its own increase.

CHAPTER XIII.

OF THE MOTION OF THE EARTH.

MOST OF THE PHILOSOPHERS say that the earth remains fixed in the same place. Philolaus the Pythagorean, that it is moved about the element of fire, in an oblique circle, after the same manner of motion that the sun and moon have. Heraclides of Pontus and Ecphantus the Pythagorean assign a motion to the earth, but not progressive, but after the manner of a wheel being carried on its own axis; thus the earth (they say) turns itself upon its own centre from west to east. Democritus, that when the earth was first formed it had a motion, the parts of it being small and light; but in process of time the parts of it were condensed, so that by its own weight it was poised and fixed.

CHAPTER XIV.

INTO HOW MANY ZONES IS THE EARTH DIVIDED?

PYTHAGORAS SAYS THAT, as the celestial sphere is distributed into five zones, into the same number is the terrestrial; which zones are the arctic and antarctic, the summer and winter tropics (or temperate zones), and the equinoctial; the middle of which zones equally divides the earth and constitutes the torrid zone; but that portion which is in between the summer and winter tropics is habitable, by reason the air is there temperate.

CHAPTER XV.

OF EARTHQUAKES.

THALES AND DEMOCRITUS ASSIGN the cause of earthquakes to water. The Stoics say that it is a moist vapor contained in the earth, making an irruption into the air, that causes the earthquake. Anaximenes, that the dryness and rarity of the earth are the cause of earthquakes, the one of which is produced by extreme drought, the other by immoderate showers. Anaxagoras, that the air endeavoring to make a passage out of the earth, meeting with a thick superficies, is not able to force its way, and so shakes the circumambient earth with a trembling. Aristotle, that a cold vapor encompassing every part of the earth prohibits the evacuation of vapors; for those which are hot, being in themselves light, endeavor to force a passage upwards, by which means the dry exhalations, being left in the earth, use their utmost endeavor to make a passage out, and being wedged in, they suffer various circumvolutions and shake the earth. Metrodorus, that whatsoever is in its own place is incapable of motion, except it be pressed upon or drawn by the operation of another body; the earth being so seated cannot naturally be moved, yet divers parts and places of the earth may move one upon another. Parmenides and Democritus, that the earth being so equally poised hath no sufficient ground why it should incline more to one side than to the other; so that it may be shaken, but cannot be removed. Anaximenes, that the earth by reason of its latitude is borne upon by the air which presseth upon it. Others opine that the earth swims upon the waters, as boards and broad planks, and by that reason is moved. Plato, that motion is by six manner of ways, upwards, downwards, on the right hand and on the left, behind and before; therefore it is not possible that the earth should be moved in any of these modes, for it is altogether seated in the lowest place; it therefore cannot receive a motion, since there is nothing about it so peculiar as to cause it to incline any way; but some parts of it are so rare and thin that they are capable of motion. Epicurus, that the possibility of the earth's motion ariseth from a thick and aqueous air under the earth, that may, by moving or pushing it, be capable of quaking; or that being so compassed, and having many passages, it is shaken by the wind which is dispersed through the hollow dens of it.

CHAPTER XVI.

OF THE SEA, AND HOW IT IS COMPOSED, AND

HOW IT BECOMES TO THE TASTE BITTER.

ANAXIMANDER AFFIRMS THAT the sea is the remainder of the primogenial humidity, the greatest part of which being dried up by the fire, the influence of the great heat altered its quality. Anaxagoras that in the beginning water did not flow, but was as a standing pool; and that it was burnt by the movement of the sun about it, by which the oily part of the water being exhaled, the residue became salt. Empedocles, that the sea is the sweat of the earth heated by the sun. Antiphon, that the sweat of that which was hot was separated from the rest which were moist; these by seething and boiling became bitter, as happens in all sweats. Metrodorus, that the sea was strained through the earth, and retained some part of its density; the same is observed in all those things which are strained through ashes. The schools of Plato, that the element of water being compacted by the rigor of the air became sweet, but that part which was expired from the earth, being enfired, became of a brackish taste.

CHAPTER XVII.

OF TIDES, OR OF THE EBBING AND FLOWING

OF THE SEA.

ARISTOTLE AND HERACLIDES SAY, they proceed from the sun, which moves and whirls about the winds; and these falling with a violence upon the Atlantic, it is pressed and swells by them, by which means the sea flows; and their impression ceasing, the sea retracts, hence they ebb. Pytheas the Massilian, that the fulness of the moon gives the flow, the wane the ebb. Plato attributes it all to a certain balance of the sea, which by means of a mouth or orifice causes the tide; and by this means the seas do rise and flow alternately. Timaeus believes that those rivers which fall from the mountains of the Celtic Gaul into the Atlantic produce a tide. For upon their entering upon that sea, they violently press upon it, and so cause the flow; but they disemboguing themselves, there is a cessation of the impetuousness, by which means the ebb is produced. Seleucus the mathematician attributes a motion to the earth; and thus he pronounceth that the moon in its circumlation meets and repels the earth in its motion; between these two, the earth and the moon, there is a vehement wind raised and intercepted, which rushes upon the Atlantic Ocean, and gives us a probable argument that it is the cause the sea is troubled and moved.

CHAPTER XVIII.

OF THE AUREA, OR A CIRCLE ABOUT A STAR.

THE AUREA OR CIRCLE is thus formed. A thick and dark air intervening between the moon or any other star and our eye, by which means our sight is dilated and reflected, when now our sight falls upon the outward circumference of the orb of that star, there presently seems a circle to appear. This circle thus appearing is called the [Greek omitted] or halo; and there is constantly such a circle seen by us, when such a density of sight happens.

Book Four

HAVING TAKEN A SURVEY of the general parts of the world, I will take a view of the particular members of it.

CHAPTER I.

OF THE OVERFLOWING OF THE NILE.

THALES CONJECTURES THAT the Etesian or anniversary northern winds blowing strongly against Egypt heighten the swelling of the Nile, the mouth of that river being obstructed by the force of the sea rushing into it. Euthymenes the Massilian concludes that the Nile is filled by the ocean and that sea which is outward from it, the last being naturally sweet. Anaxagoras, that the snow in Ethiopia which is frozen in winter is melted in summer, and this makes the inundation. Democritus, that the snows which are in the northern climates when the sun enters the summer solstice are dissolved and diffused; from those vapors clouds are compacted, and these are forcibly driven by the Etesian winds into the southern parts and into Egypt, from whence violent showers are poured; and by this means the fens of Egypt are filled with water, and the river Nile hath its inundation. Herodotus the historian, that the waters of the Nile receive from their fountain an equal portion of water in winter and in summer; but in winter the water appears less, because the sun, making its approach nearer to Egypt, draws up the rivers of that country into exhalation. Ephorus the historiographer, that in summer all Egypt seems to be melted and sweats itself into water, to which the thin and sandy soils of Arabia and Lybia contribute. Eudoxus relates that the Egyptian priests affirm that, when it is summer to us who dwell under the northern tropic, it is winter with them that inhabit under the southern tropic; by this means there is a various contrariety and opposition of the seasons in the year, which cause such showers to fall as make the water to overflow the banks of the Nile and diffuse itself throughout all Egypt.

CHAPTER II.

OF THE SOUL.

THALES FIRST PRONOUNCED that the soul is that being which is in a perpetual motion, or that whose motion proceeds from itself. Pythagoras, that it is a number moving itself; he takes a number to be the same thing with a mind. Plato, that it is an intellectual substance moving itself, and that motion is in a numerical harmony. Aristotle, that it is the first actuality [Greek ommitted] of a natural organical body which has life potentially; and this actuality must be understood to be the same thing with energy or operation. Dicaearchus, that it is the harmony of the four elements. Asclepiades the physician, that it is the concurrent exercitation of the senses.

CHAPTER III.

WHETHER THE SOUL BE A BODY, AND WHAT IS

THE NATURE AND ESSENCE OF IT.

ALL THOSE NAMED BY me do affirm that the soul itself is incorporeal, and by its own nature is in a motion, and in its own self is an intelligent substance, and the living actuality of a natural organical body. The followers of Anaxagoras, that it is airy and a body. The Stoics, that it is a hot exhalation. Democritus, that it is a fiery composition of things which are perceptible by reason alone, the same having their forms spherical and without an inflaming faculty; and it is a body. Epicurus, that it is constituted of four qualities, of a fiery quality, of an aerial quality, a pneumatical, and of a fourth quality which hath no name, but it contains the virtue of the sense. Heraclitus, that the soul of the world is the exhalation which proceeds from the moist parts of it; but the soul of animals, arising from exhalations that are exterior and from those that are within them, is homogeneous to it.

CHAPTER IV.

OF THE PARTS OF THE SOUL.

PLATO AND PYTHAGORAS, according to their first account, distribute the soul into two parts, the rational and irrational. By a more accurate and strict account the soul is branched into three parts; they divide the unreasonable part into the concupiscible and the irascible. The Stoics say the soul is constituted of eight parts; five of which are the senses, hearing, seeing, tasting, touching, smelling, the sixth is the faculty of speaking, the seventh of generating, the eighth of commanding; this is the principal of all, by which all the other are guided and ordered in their proper organs, as we see the eight arms of a polypus aptly disposed. Democritus and Epicurus divide the soul into two parts, the one rational, which bath its residence in the breast, and the irrational, which is diffused through the whole structure of the body. Democritus, that the quality of the soul is communicated to everything, yea, to the dead corpses; for they are partakers of heat and some sense, when the most of both is expired out of them.

CHAPTER V.

WHAT IS THE PRINCIPAL PART OF THE SOUL, AND

IN WHAT PART OF THE BODY IT RESIDES.

PLATO AND DEMOCRITUS PLACE its residence in the whole head. Strato, in that part of the forehead where the eyebrows are separated. Erasiatratus, in the Epikranis, or membrane which involves the brain. Herophilus, in that sinus of the brain which is the basis of it. Parmenides, in the breast; which opinion is embraced by Epicurus. The Stoics are generally of this opinion, that the seat of the soul is throughout the heart, or in the spirit about it. Diogenes, in the arterial ventricle of the heart, which is also full of vital spirit. Empedocles, in the mass of the blood. There are that say it is in the neck of the heart, others in the pericardium, others in the midriff. Certain of the Neoterics, that the seat of the soul is extended from the head to the diaphragm. Pythagoras, that the animal part of the soul resides in the heart, the intellectual in the head.

CHAPTER VI.

OF THE MOTION OF THE SOUL.

PLATO BELIEVES THAT THE soul is in perpetual motion, but that it is immovable as regards motion from place to place. Aristotle, that the soul is not naturally moved, but its motion is accidental, resembling that which is in the forms of bodies.

CHAPTER VII.

OF THE SOUL'S IMMORTALITY.

PLATO AND PYTHAGORAS say that the soul is immortal; when it departs out of the body, it retreats to the soul of the world, which is a being of the same nature with it. The Stoics, when the souls leave the bodies, they are carried to divers places; the souls of the unlearned and ignorant descend to the coagmentation of earthly things, but the learned and vigorous last till the general fire. Epicurus and Democritus, the soul is mortal, and it perisheth with the body. Plato and Pythagoras, that part of the soul of man which is rational is eternal; for though it be not God, yet it is the product of an eternal deity; but that part of the soul which is divested of reason dies.

CHAPTER VIII.

OF THE SENSES, AND OF THOSE THINGS WHICH

ARE OBJECTS OF THE SENSES,

THE STOICS GIVE THIS definition of sense: Sense is the Apprehension or comprehension of an object by means of an organ of sensation. There are several ways of expressing what sense is; it is either a habit, a faculty, an operation, or an imagination which apprehends by means of an organ of sense,–and also the eighth principal thing, from whence the senses originate. The instruments of sense are intelligent exhalations, which from the said commanding part extend unto all the organs of the body. Epicurus, that sense is a faculty, and that which is perceived by the sense is the product of it; so that sense hath a double acceptation,–sense which is the faculty, and the thing received by the sense, which is the effect. Plato, that sense is that commerce which the soul and body have with those things that are exterior to them; the power of which is from the soul, the organ by which is from the body; but both of them apprehend external objects by means of the imagination. Leucippus and Democritus, that sense and intelligence arise from external images; so neither of them can operate without the assistance of image falling upon us.

CHAPTER IX.

WHETHER WHAT APPEARS TO OUR SENSES AND

IMAGINATIONS BE TRUE OR NOT.

THE STOICS SAY THAT what the senses represent is true; what the imagination, is partly false, partly true. Epicurus that every impression of the sense or imagination is true, but of those things that fall under the head of opinion, some are true, some false: sense gives us a false presentation of those things only which are the objects of our understanding; but the imagination gives us a double error, both of things sensible and things intellectual. Empedocles and Heraclides, that the senses act by a just accommodation of the pores in every case; everything that is perceived by the sense being congruously adapted to its proper organ.

CHAPTER X.

HOW MANY SENSES ARE THERE?

THE STOICS SAY THAT there are five senses properly so called, seeing, hearing, smelling, tasting, and touching. Aristotle indeed doth not add a sixth sense; but he assigns a common sense, which is the judge of all compounded species; into this each sense casts its proper representation, in which is discovered a transition of one thing into another, like as we see in figure and motion where there is a change of one into another. Democritus, that there are divers species of senses, which appertain to beings destitute of reason, to the gods, and to wise men.

CHAPTER XI.

HOW THE ACTIONS OF THE SENSES, THE CONCEPTIONS OF OUR MINDS, AND THE HABIT OF OUR REASON ARE FORMED.

THE STOICS AFFIRM THAT every man, as soon as he is born, has a principal and commanding part of his soul, which is in him like a sheet of writing-paper, to which he commits all his notions. The first manner of his inscribing is by denoting those notions which flow from the senses. Suppose it be of a thing that is white; when the present sense of it is vanished, there is yet retained the remembrance; when many memorative notions of the same similitude do concur, then he is said to have an experience; for experience is nothing more than the abundance of notions that are of the same form met together. Some of these notions are naturally begotten according to the aforesaid manner, without the assistance of art; the others are produced by discipline, learning, and industry; these only are justly called notions, the others are prenotions. But reason, which gives us the denomination of rational, is completed by prenotions in the first seven years. The conception of the mind is the vision that the intelligence of a rational animal hath received; when that vision falls upon the rational soul, then it is called the conception of the mind, for it hath derived its name from the mind [Greek omitted] from [Greek omitted]. Therefore these visions are not to be found in any other animals; they only are appropriated to gods and to us men. If these we consider generally, they are phantasms; if specifically, they are notions. As pence or staters, if you consider them according to their own value, are simply pence and staters; but if you give them as a price for a naval voyage, they are called not merely pence, etc., but your freight.

CHAPTER XII. WHAT IS THE DIFFERENCE BETWEEN IMAGINATION [GREEK OMITTED], THE IMAGINABLE [GREEK OMITTED], FANCY [GREEK OMITTED], AND PHANTOM [GREEK OMITTED]?

CHRYSIPPUS AFFIRMS, these four are different one from another. Imagination is that passion raised in the soul which discovers itself and that which was the efficient of it; to use example, after the eye hath looked upon a thing that is white, the sight of which produceth in the mind a certain impression, this gives us reason to conclude that the object of this impression is white, which affecteth us. So with touching and smelling Phantasy or imagination is denominated from [Greek omitted] which denotes light; for as light discovers itself and all other things which it illuminates, so this imagination discovers itself and that which is the cause of it. The imaginable is the efficient cause of imagination; as anything that is white, or anything that is cold, or everything that may make an impression upon the imagination. Fancy is a vain impulse upon the mind of man, proceeding from nothing which is really conceivable; this is experienced in those that whirl about their idle hand and fight with shadows; for to the imagination there is always some real imaginable thing presented, which is the efficient cause of it; but to the fancy nothing. A phantom is that to which we are brought by such a fanciful and vain attraction; this is to be seen in melancholy and distracted persons. Of this sort was Orestes in the tragedy, pronouncing these words:

> *Mother, these maids with horror me affright;*
> *Oh bring them not, I pray, into my sight!*
> *They're smeared with blood, and cruel, dragon-like,*
> *Skipping about with deadly fury strike.*

These rave as frantic persons, they see nothing, and yet imagine they see. Thence Electra thus returns to him:

> *O wretched man, securely sleep in bed;*
> *Nothing thou seest, thy fancy's vainly led.*
> *(Euripides, "Orestes", 255.)*

After the same manner Theoclymenus in Homer.

CHAPTER XIII.

OF OUR SIGHT, AND BY WHAT MEANS WE SEE.

DEMOCRITUS AND EPICURUS suppose that sight is caused by the insertion of little images into the visive organ, and by the reception of certain rays which return to the eye after meeting the object. Empedocles supposes that images are mixed with the rays of the eye; these he styles the rays of images. Hipparchus, that the visual rays extend from both the eyes to the superficies of bodies, and give to the sight the apprehension of those same bodies, after the same manner in which the hand touching the extremity of bodies gives the sense of feeling. Plato, that the sight is the splendor of united rays; there is a light which reaches some distance from the eyes into a cognate air, and there is likewise a light shed from bodies, which meets and joins with the fiery visual light in the intermediate air (which is liquid and mutable); and the union of these rays gives the sense of seeing. This is Plato's corradiancy, or splendor of united rays.

CHAPTER XIV.

OF THOSE IMAGES WHICH ARE PRESENTED TO

OUR EYES IN MIRRORS.

EMPEDOCLES SAYS THAT these images are caused by certain effluxes which, meeting together and resting upon the superficies of the mirror, are perfected by that fiery element emitted by the said mirror, which transforms withal the air that surrounds it. Democritus and Epicurus, that the specular appearances are made by the subsistence of the images which flow from our eyes; these fall upon the mirror and remain, while the light returns to the eye. The followers of Pythagoras explain it by the reflection of the sight; for our sight being extended (as it were) to the brass, and meeting with the smooth dense surface thereof it is forced back, and caused to return upon itself: the same takes place in the hand, when it is stretched out and then brought back again to the shoulder. Any one may use these instances to explain the manner of seeing.

CHAPTER XV.

WHETHER DARKNESS CAN BE VISIBLE TO US.

THE STOICS SAY THAT darkness is seen by us, for out of our eyes there issues out some light into it; and our eyes do not impose upon us, for they really perceive there is darkness. Chrysippus says that we see darkness by the striking of the intermediate air; for the visual spirits which proceed from the principal part of the soul and reach to the ball of the eye pierce this air, which, after they have made those strokes upon it, extend conically on the surrounding air, where this is homogeneous in quality. For from the eyes those rays are poured forth which are neither black nor cloudy. Upon this account darkness is visible to us.

CHAPTER XVI.

OF HEARING.

EMPEDOCLES SAYS THAT hearing is formed by the insidency of the air upon the cochlea, which it is said hangs within the ear as a bell, and is beat upon by the air. Alcmaeon, that the vacuity that is within the ear makes us to have the sense of hearing, for the air forcing a vacuum gives the sound; every inanity affords a ringing. Diogenes the air which exists in the head, being struck upon by the voice gives the hearing. Plato and his followers, the air which exists in the head being struck upon, is reflected to the principal part of the soul, and this causeth the sense of hearing.

CHAPTER XVII.

OF SMELLING.

ALCMAEON BELIEVES THAT the principal part of the soul, residing in the brain, draws to itself odors by respiration. Empedocles, that scents insert themselves into the breathing of the lungs; for, when there is a great difficulty in breathing, odors are not perceived by reason of the sharpness; and this we experience in those who have the defluxion of rheum.

CHAPTER XVIII.

OF TASTE.

ALCMAEON SAYS THAT A moist warmth in the tongue, joined with the softness of it, gives the difference of taste. Diogenes, that by the softness and sponginess of the tongue, and because the veins of the body are joined in it, tastes are diffused by the tongue; for they are attracted from it to that sense and to the commanding part of the soul, as from a sponge.

CHAPTER XIX.

OF THE VOICE.

PLATO THUS DEFINES A voice,–that it is a breath drawn by the mind through the mouth, and a blow impressed on the air and through the ear, brain, and blood transmitted to the soul. Voice is abusively attributed to irrational and inanimate beings; thus we improperly call the neighing of horses or any other sound by the name of voice. But properly a voice [Greek omitted] is an articulate sound, which illustrates [Greek omitted] the understanding of man. Epicurus says that it is an efflux emitted from things that are vocal, or that give sounds or great noises; this is broken into those fragments which are after the same configuration. Like figures are round figures with round, and irregular and triangular with those of the same kind. These falling upon the ears produce the sense of hearing. This is seen in leaking vessels, and in fullers when they fan or blow their cloths.

Democritus, that the air is broken into bodies of similar configuration, and these are rolled up and down with the fragments of the voice; as it is proverbially said, One daw lights with another, or, God always brings like to like. Thus we see upon the seashore, that stones like to one another are found in the same place, in one place the long-shaped, in another the round are seen. So in sieves, things of the same form meet together, but those that are different are divided; as pulse and beans falling from the same sieve are separated one from another. To this it may be objected: How can some fragments of air fill a theatre in which there is an infinite company of persons. The Stoics, that the air is not composed of small fragments, but is a continued body and nowhere admits a vacuum; and being struck with the air, it is infinitely moved in waves and in right circles, until it fill that air which surrounds it; as we see in a fish-pool which we smite by a falling stone cast upon it; yet the air is moved spherically, the water orbicularly. Anaxagoras says a voice is then formed when upon a solid air the breath is incident, which being repercussed is carried to the ears; after the same manner the echo is produced.

CHAPTER XX.

WHETHER THE VOICE IS INCORPOREAL. WHAT IS

IT THAT THE GIVES ECHO?

PYTHAGORAS, PLATO, and Aristotle declare that the voice is incorporeal; for it is not the air that causes the voice, but the figure which compasseth the air and its superficies having received a stroke, give the voice. But every superficies of itself is incorporeal. It is true that it move with the body but itself it hath no body; as we observe in a staff that is bended, the matter only admits of an inflection, while the superficies doth not. According to the Stoics a voice is corporeal since everything that is an agent or operates is a body; a voice acts and operates, for we hear it and are sensible of it; for it falls and makes an impression on the ear, as a seal of a ring gives its similitude upon the wax. Besides, everything that creates a delight or injury is a body; harmonious music affects with delight, but discord is tiresome. And everything that moved is a body; and the voice moves, and having its illapse upon smooth places is reflected, as when a ball is cast against a wall it rebounds. A voice spoken in the Egyptian pyramids is so broken, that it gives four or five echoes.

CHAPTER XXI.

BY WHAT MEANS THE SOUL IS SENSIBLE, AND WHAT

IS THE PRINCIPAL AND COMMANDING PART OF IT.

THE STOICS SAY THAT the highest part of the soul is the commanding part of it: this is the cause of sense, fancy, consents, and desires; and this we call the rational part. From this principal and commander there are produced seven parts of the soul, which are spread through the body, as the seven arms in a polypus. Of these seven parts, five are assigned to the senses, seeing, hearing, smelling, tasting, touching. Sight is a spirit which is extended from the commanding part of the eyes; hearing is that spirit which from the principle reacheth to the ears; smelling a spirit drawn from the principal to the nostrils; tasting a spirit extended from the principle to the tongue; touching is a spirit which from the principal is drawn to the extremity of those bodies which are obnoxious to a sensible touch. Of the rest, the one called the spermatical is a spirit which reacheth from the principal to the generating vessels; the other, which is the vocal and termed the voice, is a spirit extended from the principal to the throat, tongue, and other proper organs of speaking. And this principal part itself hath that place in our spherical head which God hath in the world.

CHAPTER XXII.

OF RESPIRATION OR BREATHING.

EMPEDOCLES THINKS, that the first breath the first animal drew was when the moisture in the embryo was separated, and by that means an entrance was given to the external air into the gaping vessels, the moisture in them being evacuated. After this the natural heat, in a violent force pressing upon the external air for a passage, begets an expiration; but this heat returning to the inward parts, and the air giving way to it, causeth a respiration. The respiration that now is arises when the blood is borne to the exterior surface, and by this movement drives the airy substance through the nostrils; thus in its recess it causeth expiration, but the air being again forced into those places which are emptied of blood, it causeth an inspiration. To explain which, he proposeth the instance of a water-clock, which gives the account of time by the running of water.

Asclepiades supposeth the lungs to be in the manner of a funnel, and the cause of breathing to be the fineness of the inward parts of the breast; for thither the outward air which is more gross hastens, but is forced backward, the breast not being capable either to receive or want it. But there being always some of the more tenuous parts of the air left, so that all of it is not exploded, to that which there remains the more ponderous external air with equal violence is forced; and this he compares to cupping-glasses. All spontaneous breathings are formed by the contracting of the smaller pores of the lungs, and to the closing of the pipe in the neck; for these are at our command.

Herophilus attributes a moving faculty to the nerves, arteries, and muscles, but thinks that the lungs are affected only with a natural desire of enlarging and contracting themselves. Farther, there is the first operation of the lungs by attraction of the outward air, which is drawn in because of the abundance of the external air. Next to this, there is a second natural appetite of the lungs; the breast, pouring in upon itself the breath, and being filled, is no longer able to make an attraction, and throws the superfluity of it upon the lungs, whereby it is then sent forth in expiration; the parts of the body mutually concurring to this function by the alternate participation of fulness and emptiness. So that to lungs pertain four motions–first, when the lungs receive the outward air; secondly, when the outward air thus entertained is transmitted to the breast; thirdly, when the lungs again receive that air which they imparted to the breast; fourthly, when this air then received from the breast is thrown outwards. Of these four processes two are dilatations, one when the lungs attract the air, another when the breast dischargeth itself of it upon the lungs; two are contractions, one when the breast draws into itself the air, the second when it expels this which was insinuated into it. The breast admits only of two motions–of dilatation, when it draws from the lungs the breath, and of contraction, when it returns what it did receive.

CHAPTER XXIII.

OF THE PASSIONS OF THE BODY, AND WHETHER THE SOUL HATH A SYMPATHETICAL CONDOLENCY WITH IT.

THE STOICS SAY THAT all the passions are seated in those parts of the body which are affected, the senses have their residence in the commanding part of the soul. Epicurus, that all the passions and all the senses are in those parts which are affected, but the commanding part is subject to no passion. Strato, that all the passions and senses of the soul are in the rational or commanding part of it, and are not fixed in those places which are affected; for in this place patience takes its residence, and this is apparent in terrible and dolorous things, as also in timorous and valiant individuals.

Book Five

CHAPTER I.

OF DIVINATION.

PLATO AND THE STOICS introduce divination as a godlike enthusiasm, the soul itself being of a divine constitution, and this prophetic faculty being inspiration, or an illapse of the divine knowledge into man; and so likewise they account for interpretation by dreams. And these same allow many divisions of the art of divination. Xenophanes and Epicurus utterly refuse any such art of foretelling future contingencies. Pythagoras rejects all manner of divination which is by sacrifices. Aristotle and Dicaearchus admit only these two kinds of it, a fury by a divine inspiration, and dreams; they deny the immortality of the soul, yet they affirm that the mind of man hath a participation of something that is divine.

CHAPTER II.

WHENCE DREAMS DO ARISE.

DEMOCRITUS SAYS THAT DREAMS are formed by the illapse of adventitious representations. Strato, that the irrational part of the soul in sleep becoming more sensible is moved by the rational part of it. Herophilus, that dreams which are caused by divine instinct have a necessary cause; but dreams which have their origin from a natural cause arise from the soul's forming within itself the images of those things which are convenient for it, and which will happen; those dreams which are of a constitution mixed of both these have their origin from the fortuitous appulse of images, as when we see those things which please us; thus it happens many times to those persons who in their sleep imagine they embrace their mistresses.

CHAPTER III.

OF THE NATURE OF GENERATIVE SEED.

Aristotle says, that seed is that thing which contains in itself a power of moving, whereby it is enabled to produce a being like unto that from whence it was emitted. Pythagoras, that seed is the sediment of that which nourisheth us, the froth of the purest blood, of the same nature of the blood and marrow of our bodies. Alcmaeon, that it is part of the brain. Plato, that it is the deflux of the spinal marrow. Epicurus, that it is a fragment torn from the body and soul. Democritus, that it proceeds from all the parts of the body, and chiefly from the principal parts, as the tissues and muscles.

CHAPTER IV.

WHETHER THE SPERM BE A BODY.

Leucippus and Zeno say, that it is a body and a fragment of the soul. Pythagoras, Plato, and Aristotle, that the spermatic faculty is incorporeal, as the mind is which moves the body; but the effused matter is corporeal. Strato and Democritus, that the essential power is a body; for it is like spirit.

CHAPTER V.

WHETHER WOMEN DO GIVE A SPERMATIC

EMISSION AS MEN DO.

Pythagoras, Epicurus, and Democritus say, that women have a seminal projection, but their spermatic vessels are inverted; and it is this that makes them have a venereal appetite. Aristotle and Plato, that they emit a material moisture, as sweat we see produced by exercise and labor; but that moisture has no spermatic power. Hippo, that women have a seminal emission, but not after the mode of men; it contributes nothing to generation, for it falls outside of the matrix; and therefore some women without coition, especially widows, give the seed. They also assert that from men the bones, from women the flesh proceed.

CHAPTER VI.

HOW IT IS THAT CONCEPTIONS ARE MADE.

ARISTOTLE SAYS, that conception takes place when the womb is drawn down by the natural purgation, and the monthly terms attract from the whole mass part of the purest blood, and this is met by the seed of man. On the contrary, there is a failure by the impurity and inflation of the womb, by fear and grief, by the weakness of women, or the decline of strength in men.

CHAPTER VII.

AFTER WHAT MANNER MALES AND FEMALES

ARE GENERATED.

EMPEDOCLES AFFIRMS, that heat and cold give the difference in the generation of males and females. Hence is it, as histories acquaint us, that the first men originated from the earth in the eastern and southern parts, and the first females in the northern parts. Parmenides is of opinion perfectly contrariant. He affirms that men first sprouted out of the northern earth, for their bodies are more dense; women out of the southern, for theirs are more rare and fine. Hippo, that the more compacted and strong sperm, and the more fluid and weak, discriminate the sexes. Anaxagoras and Parmenides, that the seed of the man is naturally cast from his right side into the right side of the womb, or from the left side of the man into the left side of the womb; there is an alteration in this course of nature when females are generated. Cleophanes, whom Aristotle makes mention of, assigns the generation of men to the right testicle, of women to the left. Leucippus gives the reason of it to the alteration or diversity of parts, according to which the man hath a yard, the female the matrix; as to any other reason he is silent. Democritus, that the parts common to both sexes are engendered indifferently; but the peculiar parts by the one that is more powerful. Hippo, that if the spermatic faculty be more effectual, the male, if the nutritive aliment, the female is generated.

CHAPTER VIII.

BY WHAT MEANS IT IS THAT MONSTROUS BIRTHS

ARE EFFECTED.

EMPEDOCLES BELIEVES THAT monsters receive their origination from the abundance or defect of seed, or from its division into parts which are superabundant, or from some disturbance in the motion, or else that there is an error by a lapse into an unsuitable receptacle; and thus he presumes he hath given all the causes of monstrous conceptions. Strato, that it comes through addition, subtraction, or transposition of the seed, or the distension or inflation of the matrix. And some physicians say that the matrix suffers distortion, being distended with wind.

CHAPTER IX.

HOW IT COMES TO PASS THAT A WOMAN'S TOO

FREQUENT CONVERSATION WITH A MAN

HINDERS CONCEPTION.

DIOCLES THE PHYSICIAN SAYS that either no genital sperm is projected, or, if there be, it is in a less quantity than nature requires, or there is no prolific faculty in it; or there is a deficiency of a due proportion of heat, cold, moisture, and dryness; or there is a resolution of the generative parts. The Stoics attribute sterility to the obliquity of the yard, by which means it is not able to ejaculate in a due manner, or to the unproportionable magnitude of the parts, the matrix being so contracted as not to have a capacity to receive. Erasistratus assigns it to the womb's being more callous or more carneous, thinner or smaller, than nature does require.

CHAPTER X.

WHENCE IT IS THAT ONE BIRTH GIVES TWO OR THREE CHILDREN.

EMPEDOCLES AFFIRMS, that the superabundance of sperm and the division of it causes the bringing forth of two or three infants. Asclepiades, that it is performed from the excellent quality of the sperm, after the manner that from the root of one barleycorn two or three stalks do grow; sperm that is of this quality is the most prolific. Erasistratus, that superfetation may happen to women as to irrational creatures; for, if the womb be well purged and very clean, then there can be divers births. The Stoics, that it ariseth from the various receptacles that are in the womb: when the seed illapses into the first and second of them at once, then there are conceptions upon conception; and so two or three infants are born.

CHAPTER XI.

WHENCE IT IS THAT CHILDREN REPRESENT THEIR PARENTS AND PROGENITORS.

EMPEDOCLES SAYS, that the similitude of children to their parents proceeds from the vigorous prevalency of the generating sperm; the dissimilitude from the evaporation of the natural heat it contains. Parmenides, that when the sperm falls on the right side of the womb, then the infant gives the resemblance of the father; if from the left, it is stamped with the similitude of the mother. The Stoics, that the whole body and soul give the sperm; and hence arise the likenesses in the characters and faces of the children, as a painter in his copy imitates the colors in a picture before him. Women have a concurrent emission of seed; if the feminine seed have the predominancy, the child resembles the mother; if the masculine, the father.

CHAPTER XII.

HOW IT COMES TO PASS THAT CHILDREN HAVE A GREATER SIMILITUDE WITH STRANGERS THAN WITH THEIR PARENTS.

THE GREATEST PART OF physicians affirm, that this happens casually and fortuitously; for, when the sperm of the man and woman is too much refrigerated, then children carry a dissimilitude to their parents. Empedocles, that a woman's imagination in conception impresses a shape upon the infant; for women have been enamoured with images and statues, and the children which were born of them gave their similitudes. The Stoics, that the resemblances flow from the sympathy and consent of minds, through the insertion of effluvias and rays, not of images or pictures.

CHAPTER XIII.

WHENCE ARISETH BARRENNESS IN WOMEN, AND IMPOTENCY IN MEN?

THE PHYSICIANS MAINTAIN, that sterility in women can arise from the womb; for if it be after any ways thus affected, there will be a barrenness,–if it be more condensed, or more thin, or more hardened, or more callous, or more carneous; or it may be from languor, or from an atrophy or vicious condition of body; or, lastly, it may arise from a twisted or distorted position. Diocles holds that the sterility in men ariseth from some of these causes,–either that they cannot at all ejaculate any sperm, or if they do, it is less than nature doth require, or else there is no generative faculty in the sperm, or the genital members are flagging; or from the obliquity of the yard. The Stoics attribute the cause of sterility to the contrariant qualities and dispositions of those who lie with one another; but if it chance that these persons are separated, and there happen a conjunction of those who are of a suitable temperament, then there is a commixture according to nature, and by this means an infant is formed.

CHAPTER XIV. HOW IT ARISES THAT MULES

ARE BARREN.

ALCMAEON SAYS, that the barrenness of the male mules ariseth from the thinness of the genital sperm, that is, the seed is too chill; the female mules are barren, because the womb does not open its mouth (as he expresses it). Empedocles, the matrix of the mule is so small, so depressed, so narrow, so invertedly growing to the belly, that the sperm cannot be regularly ejaculated into it, and if it could, there would be no capacity to receive it. Diocles concurs in this opinion with him; for, saith he, in our anatomical dissection of mules we have seen that their matrices are of such configurations; and it is possible that there may be the same reason why some women are barren.

CHAPTER XV.

WHETHER THE INFANT IN THE MOTHER'S

WOMB BE AN ANIMAL.

PLATO SAYS, THAT THE embryo is an animal; for, being contained in the mother's womb, motion and aliment are imparted to it. The Stoics say that it is not an animal, but to be accounted part of the mother's belly; like as we see the fruit of trees is esteemed part of the trees, until it be full ripe; then it falls and ceaseth to belong to the tree; thus it is with the embryo. Empedocles, that the embryo is not an animal, yet whilst it remains in the belly it breathes. The first breath that it draws as an animal is when the infant is newly born; then the child having its moisture separated, the extraneous air making an entrance into the empty places, a respiration is caused in the infant by the empty vessels receiving of it. Diogenes, that infants are nurtured in the matrix inanimate, yet they have a natural heat; but presently, when the infant is cast into the open air, its heat brings air into the lungs, and so it becomes an animal. Herophilus acknowledgeth that a natural, but not an animal motion, and that the nerves are the cause of that motion; that then they become animals, when being first born they suck in something of the air.

CHAPTER XVI.

HOW EMBRYOS ARE NOURISHED, OR HOW THE

INFANT IN THE BELLY RECEIVES ITS ALIMENT.

DEMOCRITUS AND EPICURUS SAY, that the embryos in the womb receive their aliment by the mouth, for we perceive, as soon as ever the infant is born, it applies its mouth to the breast; in the wombs of women (our understanding concludes) there are little dugs, and the embryos have small mouths by which they receive their nutriment. The Stoics, that by the secundines and navel they partake of aliment, and therefore the midwife instantly after their birth ties the navel, and opens the infant's mouth, that it may receive another sort of aliment. Alcmaeon, that they receive their nourishment from every part of the body; as a sponge sucks in water.

CHAPTER XVII.

WHAT PART OF THE BODY IS FIRST FORMED

IN THE WOMB.

THE STOICS BELIEVE THAT the whole is formed at the same time. Aristotle, as the keel of a ship is first made, so the first part that is formed is the loins. Alcmaeon, the head, for that is the commanding and the principal part of the body. The physicians, the heart, in which are the veins and arteries. Some think the great toe is first formed; others affirm the navel.

CHAPTER XVIII.

WHENCE IS IT THAT INFANTS BORN IN THE

SEVENTH MONTH ARE BORN ALIVE.

EMPEDOCLES SAYS, that when the human race took first its original from the earth, the sun was so slow in its motion that then one day in its length was equal to ten months, as now they are; in process of time one day became as long as seven months are; and there is the reason that those infants which are born at the end of seven months or ten months are born alive, the course of nature so disposing that the infant shall be brought to maturity in one day after that night in which it is begotten. Timaeus says, that we count not ten months but nine, by reason that we reckon the first conception from the stoppage of the menstruas; and so it may generally pass for seven months when really there are not seven; for it sometimes occurs that even after conception a woman is purged to some extent. Polybus, Diocles, and the Empirics, acknowledge that the eighth month gives a vital birth to the infant, though the life of it is more faint and languid; many therefore we see born in that month die out of mere weakness. Though we see many born in that month arrive at the state of man, yet (they affirm) if children be born in that month, none wish to rear them.

Aristotle and Hippocrates, that if the womb is full in seven months, then the child falls from the mother and is born alive, but if it falls from her but is not nourished, the navel being weak on account of the weight of the infant, then it doth not thrive; but if the infant continues nine months in the womb, and then comes forth from the woman, it is entire and perfect. Polybus, that a hundred and eighty-two days and a half suffice for the bringing forth of a living child; that is, six months, in which space of time the sun moves from one tropic to the other; and this is called seven months, for the days which are over plus in the sixth are accounted to give the seventh month. Those children which are born in the eighth month cannot live, for, the infant then falling from the womb, the navel, which is the cause of nourishment, is thereby too much wrenched; and is the reason that the infant languishes and hath an atrophy. The astrologers, that eight months are enemies to every birth, seven are friends and kind to it. The signs of the zodiac are then enemies, when they fall upon those stars which are lords of houses; whatever infant is then born will have a life short and unfortunate. Those signs of the zodiac which are malevolent and injurious to generation are those pairs of which the final is reckoned the eighth from the first, as the first and the eighth, the second and the ninth, etc; so is the Ram unsociable with Scorpio, the Bull with Sagittarius, the Twins with the Goat, the Crab with Aquarius, the Lion with Pisces, the Virgin with the Ram. Upon this reason those infants that are born in the seventh or tenth months are like to live, but those in the eighth month will die.

CHAPTER XIX.

OF THE GENERATION OF ANIMALS, HOW ANIMALS

ARE BEGOTTEN, AND WHETHER THEY ARE

OBNOXIOUS TO CORRUPTION.

THOSE PHILOSOPHERS WHO entertain the opinion that the world had an original do likewise assert that all animals are generated and corruptible. The followers of Epicurus, who gives an eternity to the world, affirm the generation of animals ariseth from the various permutation of parts mutually among themselves, for they are parts of this world. With them Anaxagoras and Euripides concur:

Nothing dies,
Different changes give their various forms.

Anaximander's opinion is, that the first animals were generated in moisture, and were enclosed in bark on which thorns grew; but in process of time they came upon dry land, and this thorny bark with which they were covered being broken, they lived only for a short space of time. Empedocles says, that the first generation of animals and plants was by no means completed, for the parts were disjoined and would not admit of a union; the second preparation and for their being generated was when their parts were united and appeared in the form of images; the third preparation for generation was when their parts mutually amongst themselves gave a being to one another; the fourth, when there was no longer a mixture of like elements (as earth and water), but a union of animals among themselves,–in some the nourishment being made dense, in others female beauty provoking a desire of spermatic motion. All sorts of animals are discriminated by their proper temperament and constitution; some are carried by a proper appetite and inclination to water, some, which partake of a more fiery quality, to live in the air those that are heavier incline to the earth; but those animals whose parts are of a just temperament are fitted equally for all places.

CHAPTER XX.

HOW MANY SPECIES OF ANIMALS THERE ARE, AND WHETHER ALL ANIMALS HAVE THE ENDOWMENTS OF SENSE AND REASON.

THERE IS A CERTAIN treatise of Aristotle, in which animals are distributed into four kinds, terrestrial, aqueous, fowl, and heavenly; and he calls the stars and the world too animals, yea, and God himself he posits to be an animal gifted with reason and immortal. Democritus and Epicurus consider all animals rational which have their residence in the heavens. Anaxagoras says that animals have only that reason which is operative, but not that which is passive, which is justly styled the interpreter of the mind, and is like the mind itself. Pythagoras and Plato, that the souls of all those who are styled brutes are rational; but by the evil constitution of their bodies, and because they have a want of a discursive faculty, they do not conduct themselves rationally. This is manifested in apes and dogs, which have inarticulate voice but not speech. Diogenes, that this sort of animals are partakers of intelligence and air, but by reason of the density in some parts of them, and by the superfluity of moisture in others, they neither enjoy understanding nor sense; but they are affected as madmen are, the commanding rational part being defectuous and injured.

CHAPTER XXI.

WHAT TIME IS REQUIRED TO SHAPE THE PARTS OF ANIMALS IN THE WOMB.

EMPEDOCLES BELIEVES, that the joints of men begin to be formed from the thirty-sixth day, and their shape is completed in the nine and fortieth. Asclepiades, that male embryos, by reason of a greater natural heat, have their joints begun to be formed in the twenty-sixth day,–many even sooner,–and that they are completed in all their parts on the fiftieth day; the parts of the females are articulated in two months, but by the defect of heat are not consummated till the fourth; but the members of brutes are completed at various times, according to the commixture of the elements of which they consist.

CHAPTER XXII.

OF WHAT ELEMENTS EACH OF THE MEMBERS OF

US MEN IS COMPOSED.

EMPEDOCLES SAYS, that the fleshy parts of us are constituted by the contemperation of the four elements in us; earth and fire mixed with a double proportion of water make nerves; but when it happens that the nerves are refrigerated where they come in contact with the air, then the nails are made; the bones are produced by two parts of water and the same of air, with four parts of fire and the same of earth, mixed together; sweat and tears flow from liquefaction of bodies.

CHAPTER XXIII.

WHAT ARE THE CAUSES OF SLEEP AND DEATH?

ALCMAEON SAYS, that sleep is caused when the blood retreats to the concourse of the veins, but when the blood diffuses itself then we awake and when there is a total retirement of the blood, then men die. Empedocles, that a moderate cooling of the blood causeth sleep, but a total remotion of heat from blood causeth death. Diogenes, that when all the blood is so diffused as that it fills all the veins, and forces the air contained in them to the back and to the belly that is below it, the breast being thereby more heated, thence sleep arises, but if everything that is airy in the breast forsakes the veins, then death succeeds. Plato and the Stoics, that sleep ariseth from the relaxation of the sensitive spirit, it not receiving such total relaxing as if it fell to the earth, but so that that spirit is carried about the intestine, parts of the eyebrows, in which the principal part has its residence; but when there is a total relaxing of the sensitive spirit, death ensues.

CHAPTER XXIV.

WHEN AND FROM WHENCE THE PERFECTION OF A MAN COMMENCES.

HERACLITUS AND THE STOICS say, that men begin their completeness when the second septenary of years begins, about which time the seminal serum is emitted. Trees first begin their perfection when they give their seeds; till then they are immature, imperfect, and unfruitful. After the same manner a man is completed in the second septenary of years, and is capable of learning what is good and evil, and of discipline therein.

CHAPTER XXV.

WHETHER SLEEP OR DEATH APPERTAINS TO THE SOUL OR BODY.

ARISTOTLE'S OPINION IS, that both the soul and body sleep; and this proceeds from the evaporation in the breast, which doth steam and arise into the head, and from the aliment in the stomach, whose proper heat is cooled in the heart. Death is the perfect refrigeration of all heat in body; but death is only of the body, and not of the soul, for the soul is immortal. Anaxagoras thinks, that sleep makes the operations of the body to cease; it is a corporeal passion and affects not the soul. Death is the separation of the soul from the body. Leucippus, that sleep is only of the body; but when the smaller particles cause excessive evaporation from the soul's heat, this makes death; but these affections of death and sleep are of the body, not of the soul. Empedocles, that death is nothing else but separation of those fiery parts by which man is composed, and according to this sentiment both body and soul die; but sleep is only a smaller separation of the fiery qualities.

CHAPTER XXVI.

HOW PLANTS INCREASE.

PLATO AND EMPEDOCLES believe, that plants are animals, and are informed with a soul; of this there are clear arguments, for they have tossing and shaking, and their branches are extended; when the woodmen bend them they yield, but they return to their former straightness and strength again when they are let loose, and even carry up weights that are laid upon them. Aristotle doth grant that they live, but not that they are animals; for animals are affected with appetite, sense, and reason. The Stoics and Epicureans deny that they are informed with a soul; by reason that all sorts of animals have either sense, appetite, or reason; but plants act fortuitously, and not by means of any soul. Empedocles, that the first of all animals were trees, and they sprang from the earth before the sun in its motion enriched the world, and before day and night were distinguished; but by the harmony which is in their constitution they partake of a masculine and feminine nature; and they increase by that heat which is exalted out of the earth, so that they are parts belonging to it, as embryos in the womb are parts of the womb. Fruits in plants are excrescences proceeding from water and fire; but the plants which lack water, when this is dried up by the heat of summer, shed their leaves; whereas they that have plenty thereof keep their leaves on, as the olive, laurel, and palm. The differences of their moisture and juice arise from the difference of particles and various other causes, and they are discriminated by the various particles that feed them. And this is apparent in vines for the excellence of wine flows not from the difference in the vines, but from the soil from whence they receive their nutriment.

CHAPTER XXVII.

OF NUTRITION AND GROWTH.

EMPEDOCLES BELIEVES, that animals are nourished by the remaining in them of that which is proper to their own nature; they are augmented by the application of heat; and the subtraction of either of these makes them to languish and decay. The stature of men in this present age, if compared with the magnitude of those men which were first produced, is only a mere infancy.

CHAPTER XXVIII.

WHENCE IT IS THAT IN ANIMALS THERE ARE APPETITES AND PLEASURES.

EMPEDOCLES SAYS THAT the want of those elements which compose animals gives to them appetite, and pleasures spring from humidity. As to the motions of dangers and such like things as perturbations, etc....

CHAPTER XXIX.

WHAT IS THE CAUSE OF A FEVER, OR WHETHER IT IS AN AFFECTION OF THE BODY ANNEXED TO A PRIMARY PASSION

ERASISTRATUS GIVES THIS definition of a fever: A fever is a quick motion of blood, not produced by our consent, which enters into the vessels, the seat of the vital spirits. This we see in the sea; it is in a serene calm when nothing disturbs it, but is in motion when a violent preternatural wind blows upon it, and then it rageth and is circled with waves. After this manner it is in the body of man; when the blood is in a nimble agitation, then it falls upon those vessels in which the spirits are, and there being in an extraordinary heat, it fires the whole body. The opinion that a fever is an appendix to a preceding affection pleaseth him. Diocles proceeds after this manner: Those things which are internal and latent are manifested by those which externally break forth and appear; and it is clear to us that a fever is annexed to certain outward affections, for example, to wounds, inflaming tumors, inguinary abscesses.

CHAPTER XXX.

OF HEALTH, SICKNESS, AND OLD AGE.

ALCMAEON SAYS THAT THE preserver of health is an equal proportion of the qualities of heat, moisture, cold, dryness, bitterness, sweetness, and the other qualities; on the contrary, the prevailing empire of one above the rest is the cause of diseases and author of destruction. The direct cause of disease is the excess of heat or cold, the formal cause is excess or defect, the place is the blood or brain. But health is the harmonious commixture of the elements. Diocles, that sickness for the most part proceeds from the irregular disposition of the elements in the body, for that makes an ill habit or constitution of it. Erasistratus, that sickness is caused by the excess of nourishment, indigestion, and corruptions; on the contrary, health is the moderation of the diet, and the taking that which is convenient and sufficient for us. It is the unanimous opinion of the Stoics that the want of heat brings old age, for (they say) those persons in whom heat more abounds live the longer. Asclepiades, that the Ethiopians soon grow old, and at thirty years of age are ancient men, their bodies being excessively heated and scorched by the sun; in Britain persons live a hundred and twenty years, on account of the coldness of the country, and because the people keep the fiery element within their bodies; the bodies of the Ethiopians are more fine and thin, because they are relaxed by the sun's heat, while they who live in northern countries are condensed and robust, and by consequence are more long lived.

Abstract of a Discourse Showing that the Stoics Speak Greater Improbabilities than the Poets

PINDER'S CAENEUS HATH been taken to task by several, for being improbably feigned, impenetrable by steel and impassible in his body, and so

> Descending, into hell without a wound.
> And with sound foot parting in two the ground.

But the Stoics' Lapithes, as if they had carved him out of the very adamantine matter of impassibility itself, though he is not invulnerable, nor exempt from either sickness or pain, yet remains fearless, regretless, invincible, and unconstrainable in the midst of wounds, dolors, and torments, and in the very subversions of the walls of his native city, and other such like great calamities. Again, Pindar's Caeneus is not wounded when struck; but the Stoics' wise man is not detained when shut up in a prison, suffers no compulsion by being thrown down a precipice, is not tortured when on the rack, takes no hurt by being maimed, and when he catches a fall in wrestling he is still unconquered; when he is encompassed with a vampire, he is not besieged; and when sold by his enemies, he is still not made a prisoner. The wonderful man is like to those ships that have inscribed upon them A PROSPEROUS VOYAGE, OR PROTECTING PROVIDENCE, or A PRESERVATIVE AGAINST DANGERS, and yet for all that endure storms, and are miserably shattered and overturned.

Euripides's Iolaus of a feeble, superannuated old man, by means of a certain prayer, became on a sudden youthful and strong for battle; but the Stoics wise man was yesterday most detestable and the worst of villains, but today is changed on a sudden into a state of virtue, and is become of a wrinkled, pale fellow, and as Aeschylus speaks,

Of an old sickly wretch with stitch in 's back,
Distent with rending pains as on a rack,
a gallant, godlike, and beauteous person.

The goddess Minerva took from Ulysses his wrinkles, baldness, and deformity, to make him appear a handsome man. But these men's wise man, though old age quits not his body, but contrariwise still lays on and heaps more upon it, though he remains (for instance) humpbacked, toothless, one-eyed, is yet neither deformed, disfigured, nor ill-favored. For as beetles are said to relinquish perfumes and to pursue after ill scents; so Stoical love, having used itself to the most foul and deformed persons, if by means of philosophy they change into good form and comeliness, becomes presently disgusted.

He that in the Stoics' account was in the forenoon (for example) the worst man in the world is in the afternoon the best of men; and he that falls asleep a very sot, dunce, miscreant, and brute, nay, by Jove, a slave and a beggar to boot, rises up the same day a prince, a rich and a happy man, and (which is yet more) a continent, just, determined, and unprepossessed person;–not by shooting forth out of a young and tender body a downy beard or the sprouting tokens of mature youth, but by having in a feeble, soft, unmanful, and undetermined mind, a perfect intellect, a consummate prudence, a godlike disposition, an unprejudiced science, and an unalterable habit. All this time his viciousness gives not the least ground in order to it, but he becomes in an instant, I had almost said, of the vilest brute, a sort of hero, genius, or god. For he that receives his virtue from the Stoics portico may say,

Ask what thou wilt, it shall be granted thee.

(From Menander)

It brings wealth along with it, it contains kingship in it, it confers fortune; it renders men prosperous, and makes them to want nothing and to have a sufficiency of everything, though they have not one drachm of silver in the house.

The fabular relations of the poets are so careful of decorum, that they never leave a Hercules destitute of necessaries; but those still spring, as out of some fountain, as well for him as for his companions. But he that hath received of the Stoics Amalthaea becomes indeed a rich man, but he begs his victuals of other men; he is a king, but resolves syllogisms for hire; he is the only man that hath all things, but yet he pays rent for the house he lives in, and oftentimes buys bread with borrowed money, or else begs it of those that have nothing themselves.

The king of Ithaca begs with a design that none may know who he is, and makes himself

> *As like a dirty sorry beggar*
> *("Odyssey," xvi. 273.)*

as he can. But he that is of the Portico, while he bawls and cries out, It is I only that am a king, It is I only that am a rich man, is yet many times seen at other people's doors saying:–

> *On poor Hipponax, pray, some pity take,*
> *Bestow an old cast coat for heaven's sake;*
> *I'm well-nigh dead with cold, and all o'er quake.*

Symposiacs

Book One

SOME, MY DEAR SOSSIUS Senecio imagine that this sentence, [Greek omitted] was principally designed against the stewards of a feast, who are usually troublesome and press liquor too much upon the guests. For the Dorians in Sicily (as I am informed) called the steward, [Greek omitted] a REMEMBRANCER. Others think that this proverb admonisheth the guests to forget everything that is spoken or done in company; and agreeably to this, the ancients used to consecrate forgetfulness with a ferula to Bacchus, thereby intimating that we should either not remember any irregularity committed in mirth and company, or apply a gentle and childish correction to the faults. But because you are of opinion (as Euripides says) that to forget absurdities is indeed a piece of wisdom, but to deliver over to oblivion all sort of discourse that merry meetings do usually produce is not only repugnant to that endearing quality that most allow to an entertainment, but against the known practice of the greatest philosophers (for Plato, Xenophon, Aristotle, Speusippus, Epicurus, Prytanis, Hieronymus, Dion the Academic, have thought it a worthy and noble employment to deliver down to us those discourses they had at table), and since it is your pleasure that I should gather up the chiefest of those scattered topics which both at Rome and Greece amidst our cups and feasting we have disputed on, in obedience to your commands I have sent three books, each containing ten problems; and the rest shall quickly follow, if these find good acceptance and do not seem altogether foolish and impertinent.

QUESTION I. WHETHER AT TABLE IT IS ALLOWABLE TO PHI-
LOSOPHIZE? SOSSIUS, SENECIO, ARISTO, PLUTARCH, CRATO,
AND OTHERS.

The first question is, Whether at table it is allowable to philosophize? For I remember at a supper at Athens this doubt was started, whether at a merry meeting it was fit to use philosophical discourse, and how far it might be used? And Aristo presently cried out: What then, for heaven's sake, are there any that banish philosophy from company and wine? And I replied: Yes, sir, there are, and such as with a grave scoff tell us that philosophy, like the matron of the house, should never be heard at a merry entertainment; and commend the custom of the Persians, who never let their wives appear, but drink, dance, and wanton with their whores. This they propose for us to imitate; they permit us to have mimics and music at our feasts, but forbid philosophy; she, forsooth, being very unfit to be wanton with us, and we in a bad condition to be serious. Isocrates the rhetorician, when at a drinking bout some begged him to make a speech, only returned: With those things in which I have skill the time doth not suit; and in those things with which the time suits I have no skill.

And Crato cried out: By Bacchus, he was right to forswear talk, if he designed to make such long-winded discourses as would have spoiled all mirth and conversation; but I do not think there is the same reason to forbid philosophy as to take away rhetoric from our feasts. For phi-losophy is quite of another nature; it is an art of living, and therefore must be admitted into every part of our conversation, into all our gay humors and our pleasures, to regulate and adjust them, to proportion the time, and keep them from excess; unless, perchance, upon the same scoffing pretence of gravity, they would banish temperance, justice, and moderation. It is true, were we to feast before a court, as those that entertained Orestes, and were silence enjoined by law, that might prove no mean cloak of our ignorance; but if Bacchus is really [Greek omitted] (A LOOSER of everything), and chiefly takes off all restraints and bridles from the tongue, and gives the voice the greatest freedom, I think it is foolish and absurd to deprive that time in which we are usu-ally most talkative of the most useful and profitable discourse; and in our schools to dispute of the offices of company, in what consists the excellence of a guest, how mirth, feasting, and wine are to be used and yet deny philosophy a place in these feasts, as if not able to confirm by practice what by precepts it instructs.

And when you affirmed that none ought to oppose what Crato said, but determine what sorts of philosophical topics were to be admitted as fit companions at a feast, and so avoid that just and pleasant taunt put upon the wrangling disputers of the age,

Come now to supper, that we may contend;

and when you seemed concerned and urged us to speak to that head, I first replied: Sir, we must consider what company we have; for if the greater part of the guests are learned men,–as for instance, at Agatho's entertainment, characters like Socrates, Phaedrus, Pausanias, Euryximachus; or at Callias's board, Charmides, Antisthenes, Hermogenes, and the like,–we will permit them to philosohize, and to mix Bacchus with the Muses as well as with the Nymphs; for the latter make him wholesome and gentle to the body, and the other pleasant and agreeable to the soul. And if there are some few illiterate persons present, they, as consonants with vowels, in the midst of the other learned, will participate not altogether inarticulately and insignificantly. But if the greater part consists of such who can better endure the noise of any bird, fiddle-string, or piece of wood than the voice of a philosopher, Pisistratus hath shown us what to do; for being at difference with his sons, when he heard his enemies rejoiced at it, in a full assembly he declared that he had endeavored to persuade his sons to submit to him, but since he found them obstinate, he was resolved to yield and submit to their humors. So a philosopher, midst those companions that slight his excellent discourse, will lay aside his gravity, follow them, and comply with their humor as far as decency will permit; knowing very well that men cannot exercise their rhetoric unless they speak, but may their philosophy even whilst they are silent or jest merrily, nay, whilst they are piqued upon or repartee. For it is not only (as Plato says) the highest degree of injustice not to be just and yet seem so; but it is the top of wisdom to philosophize, yet not appear to do it; and in mirth to do the same with those that are serious, and still seem in earnest. For as in Euripides, the Bacchae, though unprovided of iron weapons and unarmed, wounded their invaders with their boughs, thus the very jests and merry talk of true philosophers move those that are not altogether insensible.

I think there are topics fit to be used at table, some of which reading and study give us, others the present occasion; some to incite to study, others to piety and great and noble actions, others to make us rivals of the bountiful and kind; which if a man cunningly and without any apparent design inserts for the instruction of the rest, he will free these entertainments from many of those considerable evils which usually attend them. Some that put borage into the wine, or sprinkle the floor with water in which verbena and maiden-hair have been steeped, as good raise mirth and jollity in the guests (in imitation of Homer's Helen, who with some medicament diluted the pure wine she had prepared), do not understand that that fable, coming from round Egypt, after a long way ends at last in easy and fit discourse. For whilst they were drinking Helen relates the story of Ulysses,

> How Fortune's spite the hero did control,
> And bore his troubles with a manly soul.
> ("Odyssey," iv. 242.)

For that, in my opinion, was the Nepenthe, the care-dissolving medicament, viz, that story exactly fitted to the then disasters and juncture of affairs. The pleasing men, though they designedly and apparently instruct, draw on their maxims rather with persuasive and smooth arguments, than the violent force of demonstrations. You see that even Plato in his Symposium, where he disputes of the chief end, the chief good, and is altogether on subjects theological, doth not lay down strong and close demonstrations; he doth not make himself ready for the contest (as he is wont) like a wrestler, that he may take the firmer hold of his adversary and be sure of giving him the trip; but draws men on by more soft and pliable attacks, by pleasant fictions and pat examples.

Besides the questions should be easy, the problems known, the interrogations plain, familiar, and not intricate and dark that they might neither vex the unlearned, nor fright them from the disquisition. For–as it is allowable to dissolve our entertainment into a dance, but if we force our guests to toss quoits or play at cudgels, we shall not only make our feast unpleasant, but hurtful and unnatural–thus light and easy disquisitions do pleasantly and profitably excite us, but we must forbear all contentions and (to use Democritus's word) wrangling disputes, which perplex the proposers with intricate and inexplicable doubts, and trouble all the others that are present. Our discourse should be like our wine, common to all, and of which every one may equally partake; and they that propose hard problems seem no better fitted for society than Aesop's fox and crane. For the fox vexed the crane with thin broth poured out upon a plain table, and laughed at her when he saw her, by reason of the narrowness of her bill and the thinness of the broth, incapable of partaking what he had prepared; and the crane, in requital, inviting the fox to supper, brought forth her dainties in a pot with a long and narrow neck, into which she could conveniently thrust her bill, whilst the fox could not reach one bit. Just so, when philosophers midst their cups dive into minute and logical disputes, they are very troublesome to those that cannot follow them through the same depths; and those that bring in idle songs, trifling disquisitions, common talk, and mechanical discourse destroy the very end of conversation and merry entertainments, and abuse Bacchus. Therefore, as when Phrynichus and Aeschylus brought tragedy to discourse of fictions and misfortunes, it was asked, What is this to Bacchus?–so methinks, when I hear some pedantically drawing a syllogism into table-talk, I have reason to cry out, Sir, what is this to Bacchus? Perchance one, the great bowl standing in the midst, and the chaplets given round, which the god in token of the liberty he bestows sets on every head, sings one of those songs called [Greek omitted] (CROOKED OR OBSCURE); this is not fit nor agreeable to a feast. Though some say these songs were not dark and intricate composures; but that the guests sang the first song all together, praising Bacchus and describing the power of the god; and the second each man sang singly in his turn, a myrtle bough being delivered to every one in order, which they call an [Greek omitted] because he that received it was obliged [Greek omitted] to sing; and after this a harp being carried round the company, the skilful took it, and fitted the music to the song; this when the unskilful could not perform, the song was called [Greek omitted] because hard to them, and one in which they could not bear a part. Others say this myrtle bough was not delivered in order, but from bed to bed; and when the uppermost of the first table had sung, he sent it to the uppermost of the second, and he to the uppermost of the third; and so the second in like manner to the second; and from these many windings and this circuit it was called [Greek omitted] CROOKED.

QUESTION II. WHETHER THE ENTERTAINER SHOULD SEAT THE GUESTS, OR LET EVERY MAN TAKE HIS OWN PLACE. TIMON, A GUEST, PLUTARCH, PLUTARCH'S FATHER, LAMPRIAS, AND OTHERS.

My brother Timon, making a great entertainment, desired the guests as they came to seat themselves; for he had invited strangers and citizens, neighbors and acquaintance, and all sorts of persons to the feast. A great many being already come, a certain stranger at last appeared, dressed as fine as hands could make him, his clothes rich, and an unseemly train of foot-boys at his heels; he walking up to the parlor-door, and, staring round upon those that were already seated, turned his back and scornfully retired; and when a great many stepped after him and begged him to return, he said, I see no fit place left for me. At that, the other guests (for the glasses had gone round) laughed abundantly, and desired his room rather than his company.

But after supper, my father addressing himself to me, who sat at another quarter of the table,–Timon, said he, and I have a dispute, and you are to be judge, for I have been upon his skirts already about that stranger; for if according to my directions he had seated every man in his proper place, we had never been thought unskilful in this matter, by one

Whose art is great in ordering horse and foot.

("Iliad," ii 554.)

And story says that Paulus Aemilius, after he had conquered Perseus the king of Macedon, making an entertainment besides his costly furniture and extraordinary provision, was very critical in the order of his feast; saying, It is the same man's task to order a terrible battle and a pleasing, entertainment, for both of them require skill in the art of disposing right, and Homer often calls the stoutest and the greatest princes [Greek omitted] disposers of the people; and you use to say that the great Creator, by this art of disposing, turned disorder into beauty, and neither taking away nor adding any new being, but setting everything in its proper place, out of the most uncomely figure and confused chaos produced this beauteous, this surprising face of nature that appears. In these great and noble doctrines indeed you instruct us; but our own observation sufficiently assures us, that the greatest profuseness in a feast appears neither delightful nor genteel, unless beautified by order. And therefore it is absurd that cooks and waiters should be solicitous what dish must be brought first, what next, what placed in the middle, and what last; and that the garlands, and ointment, and music (if they have any) should have a proper place and order assigned, and yet that the guests should be seated promiscuously, and no respect be had to age, honor, or the like; no distinguishing order by which the man in dignity might be honored, the inferior learn to give place, and the disposer be exercised in distinguishing what is proper and convenient. For it is not rational that, when we walk or sit down to discourse, the best man should have the best place, and not the same order be observed at table; or that the entertainer should in civility drink to one before another, and yet make no difference in their seats, at the first dash making the whole company one Myconus (as they say), a hodge-podge and confusion. This my father brought for his opinion.

And my brother said: I am not so much wiser than Bias, that, since he refused to be arbitrator between two only of his friends, I should pretend to be a judge between so many strangers and acquaintance; especially since it is not a money matter, but about precedence and dignity, as if I invited my friends not to treat them kindly, but to abuse them.

Menelaus is accounted absurd and passed into a proverb, for pretending to advise when unasked; and sure he would be more ridiculous that instead of an entertainer should set up for a judge, when nobody requests him or submits to his determination which is the best and which the worst man in the company; for the guests do not come to contend about precedency, but to feast and be merry. Besides, it is no easy task to distinguish for some claim respect by reason of their age, others–from their familiarity and acquaintance; and, as those that make declamations consisting of comparisons, he must have Aristotle's [Greek omitted] and Thrasymachus's [Greek omitted] (books that furnish him with heads of argument) at his fingers' ends; and all this to no good purpose or profitable effect but to bring vanity from the bar and the theatre into our feasts and entertainments, and, whilst by good fellowship endeavor to remit all other passions, especially pride and arrogance, from which, in my opinion we should be more careful to cleanse our souls than to wash our feet from dirt, that our conversation be free, simple, and full of mirth. And while by such meetings we strive to end all differences that have at any time risen amongst the invited, we should make them flame anew, and kindle them again by emulation, by thus humbling some and puffing up others. And if, according as we seat them, we should drink oftener and discourse more with some than others and set daintier dishes before them, instead of being friendly we should be lordly in our feasts. And if in other things we treat them all equally, why should we not begin at the first part, and bring it into fashion for all to take their seats promiscuously, without ceremony or pride, and to let them see, as soon as they enter, that they are invited to a dinner whose order is free and democratical, and not, as particular chosen men to the government of a city where aristocracy is the form; since the richest and the poorest sit promiscuously together.

When this had been offered on both sides, and all present required my determination, I said: Being an arbitrator and not a judge, I shall close strictly with neither side, but go indifferently in the middle between both. If a man invites young men, citizens, or acquaintance, they should (as Timon says) be accustomed to be content with any place, without ceremony or concernment; and this good nature and unconcernedness would be an excellent means to preserve and increase friendship. But if we use the same method to strangers, magistrates, or old men, I have just reason to fear that, whilst we seem to thrust our pride at the fore-door, we bring it in again at the back, together with a great deal of indifferency and disrespect. But in this, custom and the established rules of decency must guide; or else let us abolish all those modes of respect expressed by drinking to or saluting first; which we do not use promiscuously to all the company but according to their worth we honor every one

With better places, meat, and larger cups,
("Iliad," xii. 311.)

as Agamemnon says, naming the place first, as the chiefest sign of honor. And we commend Alcinous for placing his guest next himself:–

He stout Laomedon his son removed,
Who sat next him, for him he dearly loved;
("Iliad," xx. 15.)

for to place a suppliant stranger in the seat of his beloved son was wonderful kind, and extreme courteous. Nay even amongst the gods themselves this distinction is observed; for Neptune, though he came last into the assembly,

sat in the middle seat,
("Odyssey," vii. 170.)

as if that was his proper place. And Minerva seems to have that assigned her which is next Jupiter himself; and this the poet intimates, when speaking of Thetis he says,

She sat next Jove, Minerva giving Place.
(Ibid. xxiv. 100.)

And Pindar plainly says,

She sits just next the thunder-breathing flames.

Indeed Timon urges, we ought not to rob many to honor one, which he seems to do himself, even more than others; for he robs that which makes something that is individual common; and suitable honor to his worth is each man's possession. And he gives that preeminence to running fast and making haste, which belongs to virtue, kindred, magistracies, and such other qualities; and whilst he endeavors not to affront his guests, he necessarily falls into that very inconvenience; for he must affront every one by defrauding them of their proper honor. Besides, in my opinion it is no hard matter to make this distinction, and seat our guests according to their quality; for first, it very seldom happens that many of equal honor are invited to the same banquet; and then, since there are many honorable places, you have room enough to dispose them according to content, if you can but guess that this man must be seated uppermost, that in the middle, another next to yourself, friend, acquaintance, tutor, or the like, appointing every one some place of honor; and as for the rest, I would supply their want of honor with some little presents, affability, and kind discourse. But if their qualities are not easy to be distinguished, and the men themselves hard to be pleased, see what device I have in that case; for I seat in the most honorable place my father, if invited; if not my grandfather, father-in-law, uncle, or somebody whom the entertainer hath a more particular reason to esteem. And this is one of the many rules of decency that we have from Homer; for in his poem, when Achilles saw Menelaus and Antilochus contending about the second prize of the horse-race, fearing that their strife and fury would increase, he gave the prize to another, under pretence of comforting and honoring Eumelus, but indeed to take away the cause of their contention.

When I had said this, Lamprias, sitting (as he always doth) upon a low bed, cried out: Sirs, will you give me leave to correct this sottish judge? And the company bidding him speak freely and tell me roundly of my faults, and not spare, he said: And who can forbear that philosopher who disposes of places at a feast according to the birth, wealth, or offices of the guests, as if they were in a theatre or the Council House, so that pride and arrogance must be admitted even into our mirth and entertainments? In seating our guests we should not have any respect to honor, but mirth and conversation; not look after every man's quality, but their agreement and harmony with one another, as those do that join several different things in one composure. Thus a mason doth not set an Athenian or a Spartan stone, because formed in a more noble country, before an Asian or a Spanish; nor a painter give the most costly color the chiefest place; nor a shipwright the Corinthian fir or Cretan cypress; but so distribute them as they will best serve to the common end, and make the whole composure strong, beautiful, and fit for use. Nay, you see even the deity himself (by our Pindar named the most skilful artificer) doth not everywhere place the fire above and the earth below; but, as Empedocles hath it,

The Oysters Coverings do directly prove,
That heavy Earth is sometimes rais'd above;

not having that place that Nature appoints, but that which is necessary to compound bodies and serviceable to the common end, the preservation of the whole. Disorder is in everything an evil; but then its badness is principally discovered, when it is amongst men whilst they are making merry; for then it breeds contentions and a thousand unspeakable mischiefs, which to foresee and hinder shows a man well skilled in good order and disposing right.

We all agreed that he had said well, but asked him why he would not instruct us how to order things aright, and communicate his skill. I am content, says he, to instruct you, if you will permit me to change the present order of the feast, and will yield as ready obedience to me as the Thebans to Epaminondas when he altered the order of their battle. We gave him full power; and he, having turned all the servants out, looked round upon every one, and said: Hear (for I will tell you first) how I design to order you together. In my mind, the Theban Pammenes justly taxeth Homer as unskilful in love matters, for setting together, in his description of an army, tribe and tribe, family and family; for he should have joined the lover and the beloved, so that the whole body being united in their minds might perfectly agree. This rule will I follow, not set one rich man by another, a youth by a youth, a magistrate by a magistrate, and a friend by a friend; for such an order is of no force, either to beget or increase friendship and good-will. But fitting that which wants with something that is able to supply it, next one that is willing to instruct I will place one that is as desirous to be instructed; next a morose, one good-natured; next a talkative old man a youth patient and eager for a story; next a boaster, a jeering smooth companion; and next an angry man, a quiet one. If I see a wealthy fellow bountiful and kind, I will take some poor honest man from his obscure place, and set him next, that something may run out of that full vessel to the other empty one. A sophister I will forbid to sit by a sophister, and one poet by another;

> For beggars beggars, poets envy poets.
> (Hesiod, "Work and Days," 26)

I separate the clamorous scoffers and the testy, by putting some good-nature between them, so they cannot jostle so roughly on one another; wrestlers, hunters, and farmers I put in one company. For some of the same nature, when put together, fight as cocks; others are very sociable as daws. Drinkers and lovers I set together, not only those who (as Sophocles says) feel the sting of masculine love, but those that are mad after virgins or married women; for they being warmed with the like fire, as two pieces of iron to be joined, will more readily agree; unless perhaps they both fancy the same person.

QUESTION III. UPON WHAT ACCOUNT IS THE PLACE AT THE TABLE CALLED CONSULAR ESTEEMED HONORABLE. THE SAME.

This raised a dispute about the dignity of places, for the same seat is not accounted honorable amongst all nations; in Persia the midst, for that is the place proper to the king himself; in Greece the uppermost; at Rome the lowermost of the middle bed, and this is called the consular; the Greeks about Pontus, and those of Heraclea, reckon the uppermost of the middle bed to be the chief. But we were most puzzled about the place called consular; for though it is esteemed most honorable, yet it is not because it is either the first or the midst; and its other circumstances are either not proper to that alone, or very frivolous. Though I confess three of the reasons alleged seemed to have something in them. The first, that the consuls, having dissolved the monarchy and reduced everything to a more equal level and popular estate, left the middle, the kingly place, and sat in a lower seat; that by this means their power and authority might be less subject to envy, and not so grievous to their fellow-citizens. The second, that, two beds being appointed for the invited guests, the third–and the first place in it–is most convenient for the master of the feast, from whence like a pilot, he can guide and order everything, and readily overlook the management of the whole affair. Besides, he is not so far removed that he can easily discourse, talk to, and compliment his guests; for next below him his wife and children usually are placed; next above him the most honorable of the invited, that being the most proper place, as near the master of the feast. The third reason was, that it is peculiar to the this place to be most convenient for the despatch of any sudden business; for the Roman consul will not as Archias, the governor of Thebes, say, when letters of importance are brought to him at dinner, "serious things to-morrow" and then throw aside the packet and take the great bowl; but he will be careful, circumspect, and mind it at that very instant. For not only (as the common saying hath it)

Each throw doth make the dicer fear,

but even midst his feasting and his pleasure a magistrate should be intent on intervening business; and he hath this place appointed, as the most convenient for him to receive any message, answer it, or sign a bill; for there the second bed joining with the third, the turning at the corner leaves a vacant space, so that a notary, servant, guard, or a messenger from the army might approach, deliver the message, and receive orders; and the consul, having room enough to speak or use his hand, neither troubles any one, nor is hindered by any the guests.

QUESTION IV. WHAT MANNER OF MAN SHOULD A DIRECTOR OF A FEAST BE? CRATO, THEON, PLUTARCH, AND OTHERS.

Crato my relative, and Theon my acquaintance, at a certain banquet, where the glasses had gone round freely, and a little stir arose but was suddenly appeased, began to discourse of the office of the steward of a feast; declaring that it was my duty to wear the chaplet, assert the decaying privilege, and restore that office which should take care for the decency and good order of the banquet. This proposal pleased every one, and they were all an end begging me to do it. Well then, said I, since you will have it so, I make myself steward and director of you all, command the rest to drink every one what he will but Crato and Theon, the first proposers and authors of this decree, I enjoin to declare in short what qualifications fit a man for this office, what he should principally aim at and how behave himself towards those under his command. This is the subject, and let them agree amongst themselves which head each shall manage.

They made some slight excuse at first; but the whole company urging them to obey, Crato began thus. A captain of a watch (as Plato says) ought to be most watchful and diligent himself, and the director of merry companions ought to be the best. And such a one he is, that will not be easily overtaken or apt to refuse a glass; but as Cyrus in his epistle to the Spartans says, that in many other things he was more fit than his brother to be a king, and chiefly because he could bear abundance of wine. For one that is drunk must have an ill carriage and be apt to affront; and he that is perfectly sober must be unpleasant, and fitter to be a governor of a school than of a feast. Pericles as often as he was chosen general, when he put on his cloak, used to say to himself, as it were to refresh his memory, Take heed, Pericles, thou dost govern freemen, thou dost govern Greeks, thou dost govern Athenians. So let our director say privately to himself, Thou art a governor over friends, that he may remember to neither suffer them to be debauched nor stint their mirth. Besides he ought to have some skill in the serious studies of the guests and not be altogether ignorant of mirth and humor yet I would have him (as pleasant wine ought to be) a little severe and rough, for the liquor will soften and smooth him, and make his temper pleasant and agreeable. For as Xenophon says, that Clearchus's rustic and morose humor in a battle, by reason of his bravery and heat, seemed pleasant and surprising; thus one that is not of a very sour nature, but grave and severe, being softened by a chirping cup becomes more pleasant and complaisant. But chiefly he should be acquainted with every one of the guests' humors, what alteration the liquor makes in him, what passion he is most subject to, and what quantity he can bear; for it is not to be supposed different sorts of water bear various proportions to different sorts of wine (which kings' cup-bearers understanding sometimes pour in more, sometimes less), and that man hath no such relation to them. This our director ought to know, and knowing, punctually observe; so that like a good musician, screwing up one and letting down another, he may make between these different natures a pleasing harmony and agreement; so that he shall not proportion his wine by measure, but give every one what was proper and agreeable, according to the present circumstances of time and strength of body. But if this is too difficult a task, yet it is necessary that a steward should know the common accidents of age and nature, such as these,–that an old man will be sooner overtaken than a youth, one that leaps about or talks than he that is silent or sits still, the thoughtful and melancholy than the cheerful and the brisk. And he that understands these things is much more able to preserve quietness and order, than one that is perfectly ignorant and unskilful. Besides, I think none will doubt but that the steward ought to be a friend, and have no pique at any of the guests; for otherwise in his injunctions he will be intolerable, in his distributions unequal, in his jests apt to scoff and give offence. Such a figure, Theon, as out of wax, hath my discourse framed for the steward of a feast; and now I deliver him to you.

And Theon replied: He is welcome,–a very well-shaped gentleman, and fitted for the office; but whether I shall not spoil him in my particular application, I cannot tell. In my opinion he seems such a one as will keep an entertainment to its primitive institution, and not suffer it to be changed, sometimes into a mooting hall, sometimes a school of rhetoric, now and then a dicing room, a playhouse, or a stage. For do not you observe some making fine orations and putting cases at a supper, others declaiming or reading some of their own compositions, and others proposing prizes to dancers and mimics? Alcibiades and Theodorus turned Polition's banquet into a temple of initiation, representing there the sacred procession and mysteries of Ceres; now such things as these, in my opinion, ought not to be suffered by a steward, but he must permit such discourse only, such shows, such merriment, as promote the particular end and design of such entertainments; and that is, by pleasant conversation either to beget or maintain friendship and good-will among the guests; for an entertainment is only a pastime table with a glass of wine, ending in friendship through mutual goodwill.

But now because things pure and unmixed are usually surfeiting and odious, and the very mixture itself, unless the simples be well proportioned and opportunely put together, spoils the sweetness and goodness of the composition; it is evident that there ought to be a director to take care that the mirth and jollity of the guests be exactly and opportunely tempered. It is a common saying that a voyage near the land and a walk near the sea are the best recreation. Thus our steward should place seriousness and gravity next jollity and humor; that when they are merry, they should be on the very borders of gravity itself, and when grave and serious, they might be refreshed as sea-sick persons having an easy and short prospect to the mirth and jollity on land. For mirth may be exceeding useful, and make our grave discourses smooth and pleasant,–

As near the bramble oft the lily grows,
And neighboring rue commands the blushing rose.

But against vain and empty tempers, that wantonly break in upon our feasts, like henbane mixed with the wine, he must advise the guests, lest scoffing and affronts creep in under these, lest in their questions or commands they grow scurrilous and abuse, as for instance by enjoining stutterers to sing, bald-pates to comb their heads, or a cripple to rise and dance. As the company abused Agapestor the Academic, one of whose legs was lame and withered, when in a ridiculing frolic they ordained that every man should stand upon his right leg and take off his glass, or pay a fine; and he, when it was his turn to command, enjoined the company to follow his example drink as he did, and having a narrow earthen pitcher brought in, he put his withered leg into it, and drank his glass and every one in the company, after a fruitless endeavor to imitate, paid his forfeit. It was a good humor of Agapestor's and thus every little merry abuse must be as merrily revenged. Besides he must give such commands as will both please and profit, putting such as are familiar and easy to the person, and when performed will be for his credit and reputation. A songster must be enjoined to sing, an orator to speak, a philosopher to solve a problem, and a poet to make a song; for every one very readily and willingly undertakes that

In which he may outdo himself.

An Assyrian king by public proclamation promised a reward to him that would find out any new sort of luxury and pleasure. And let the governor, the king of an entertainments propose some pleasant reward for any one that introduceth inoffensive merriment, profitable delight and laughter, not such as attends scoffs and abusive jests, but kindness, pleasant humor, and goodwill; for these matters not being well looked after and observed spoil and ruin most of our entertainments. It is the office of a prudent man to hinder all sort of anger and contention; in the exchange, that which springs from covetousness; in the fencing and wrestling schools, from emulation; in offices and state affairs, from ambition; and in a feast or entertainment, from pleasantness and joke.

QUESTION V. WHY IT IS COMMONLY SAID THAT LOVE MAKES A MAN A POET. SOSSIUS, PLUTARCH, AND OTHERS.

One day when Sossius entertained us, upon singing some Sapphic verses, this question was started, how it could be true

That love in all doth vigorous thoughts inspire,
And teaches ignorants to tune the lyre?

Since Philoxenus, on the contrary, asserts, that the Cyclops

With sweet-tongued Muses cured his love.

Some said that love was bold and daring, venturing at new contrivances, and eager to accomplish, upon which account Plato calls it the enterpriser of everything; for it makes the reserved man talkative, the modest complimental, the negligent and sluggish industrious and observant; and, what is the greatest wonder, a close, hard, and covetous fellow, if he happens to be in love, as iron in fire, becomes pliable and soft, easy, good-natured, and very pleasant; as if there were something in that common jest. A lover's purse is tied with the blade of a leek. Others said that love was like drunkenness; it makes men warm, merry, and dilated; and, when in that condition, they naturally slide down to songs and words in measure; and it is reported of Aeschylus, that he wrote tragedies after he was heated with a glass of wine; and my grandfather Lamprias in his cups seemed to outdo himself in starting questions and smart disputing, and usually said that, like frankincense, he exhaled more freely after he was warmed. And as lovers are extremely pleased with the sight of their beloved, so they praise with as much satisfaction as they behold; and as love is talkative in everything, so more especially in commendation; for lovers themselves believe, and would have all others think, that the object of their passion is pleasing and excellent; and this made Candaules the Lydian force Gyges into his chamber to behold the beauty of his naked wife. For they delight in the testimony of others, and therefore in all composures upon the lovely they adorn them with songs and verses, as we dress images with gold, that more may hear of them and that they may be remembered the more. For if they present a cock, horse, or any other thing to the beloved, it is neatly trimmed and set off with all the ornaments of art; and therefore, when they would present a compliment, they would have it curious, pleasing, as verse usually appears.

Sossius applauding these discourses added: Perhaps we may make a probable conjecture from Theophrastus's discourse of Music, for I have lately read the book. Theophrastus lays down three causes of music,–grief, pleasure and enthusiasm; for each of these changes the usual tone, and makes the voice slide into a cadence; for deep sorrow has something tunable in its groans, and therefore we perceive our orators in their conclusions, and actors in their complaints, are somewhat melodious, and insensibly fall into a tune. Excess of joy provokes the more airy men to frisk and dance and keep their steps, though unskilful in the art; and, as Pindar hath it,

They shout, and roar, and wildly toss their heads.

But the graver sort are excited only to sing, raise their voice, and tune their words into a sonnet. But enthusiasm quite changes the body and the voice, and makes it far different from its usual constitution. Hence the very Bacchae use measure, and the inspired give their oracles in measure. And we shall see very few madmen but are frantic in rhyme and rave in verse. This being certain, if you will but anatomize love a little, and look narrowly into it, it will appear that no passion in the world is attended with more violent grief, more excessive joy, or greater ecstasies and fury; a lover's soul looks like Sophocles's city:–

At once 'tis full of sacrifice,
Of joyful songs, of groans and cries.'
(Sophocles, "Oedipus Tyrannus," 4.)

And therefore it is no wonder, that since love contains all the causes of music,–grief, pleasure, and enthusiasm,–and is besides industrious and talkative, it should incline us more than any other passion to poetry and songs.

QUESTION VI. WHETHER ALEXANDER WAS A GREAT DRINKER. PHILINUS, PLUTARCH, AND OTHERS.

Some said that Alexander did not drink much, but sat long in company, discoursing with his friends; but Philinus showed this to be an error from the king's diary, where it was very often registered that such a day, and sometimes two days together, the king slept after a debauch; and this course of life made him cold in love, but passionate and angry, which argues a hot constitution. And some report his sweat was fragrant and perfumed his clothes; which is another argument of heat, as we see the hottest and driest climates bear frankincense and cassia; for a fragrant smell, as Theophrastus thinks, proceeds from a due concoction of the humors, when the noxious moisture is conquered by the heat. And it is thought probable, that he took a pique at Calisthenes for avoiding his table because of the hard drinking, and refusing the great bowl called Alexander's in his turn, adding, I will not drink of Alexander's bowl, to stand in need of Aesculapius's. And thus much of Alexander's drinking.

Story tells us, that Mithridates, the famous enemy of the Romans, among other trials of skill that he instituted, proposed a reward to the greatest eater and the stoutest drinker in his kingdom. He won both the prizes himself; he outdrank every man living, and for his excellency that way was called Bacchus. But this reason for his surname is a vain fancy and an idle story; for whilst he was an infant a flash of lightning burnt his cradle, but did his body no harm, and only left a little mark on his forehead, which his hair covered when he was grown a boy; and after he came to be a man, another flash broke into his bedchambers, and burnt the arrows in a quiver that was hanging under him; from whence his diviners presaged, that archers and light-armed men should win him considerable victories in his wars; and the vulgar gave him this name, because in those many dangers by lightning he bore some resemblance to the Theban Bacchus.

From hence great drinkers were the subject of our discourse; and the wrestler Heraclides (or, as the Alexandrians mince it, Heraclus), who lived but in the last age, was accounted one. He, when he could get none to hold out with him, invited some to take their morning's draught, others to dinner, to supper others, and others after, to take a merry glass of wine; so that as the first went off, the second came, and the third and fourth company and he all the while without any intermission took his glass round, and outsat all the four companies.

Amongst the retainers to Drusus, the Emperor Tiberus's son, was a physician that drank down all the court; he, before he sat down, would usually take five or six bitter almonds to prevent the operation of the wine; but whenever he was forbidden that, he knocked under presently, and a single glass dozed him. Some think these almonds have a penetrating, abstersive quality, are able to cleanse the face, and clear it from the common freckles; and therefore, when they are eaten, by their bitterness vellicate and fret the pores, and by that means draw down the ascending vapors from the head. But, in my opinion, a bitter quality is a drier, and consumes moisture; and therefore a bitter taste is the most unpleasant. For, as Plato says, dryness, being an enemy to moisture, unnaturally contracts the spongy and tender nerves of the tongue. And green ulcers are usually drained by bitter injections. Thus Homer:–

He squeezed his herbs, and bitter juice applied;
And straight the blood was stanched, the sore was dried.
("*Iliad*," xi. 846.)

And he guesses well, that what is bitter to the taste is a drier. Besides, the powders women use to dry up their sweat are bitter, and by reason of that quality astringent. This then being certain, it is no wonder that the bitterness of the almonds hinders the operation of the wine, since it dries the inside of the body and keeps the veins from being overcharged; for from their distention and disturbance they say drunkenness proceeds. And this conjecture is much confirmed from that which usually happens to a fox; for if he eats bitter almonds without drinking, his moisture suddenly fails, and it is present death.

QUESTION VII. WHY OLD MEN LOVE PURE WINE. PLUTARCH AND OTHERS.

It was debated why old men loved the strongest liquors. Some, fancying that their natural heat decayed and their constitution grew cold, said such liquors were most necessary and agreeable to their age; but this was mean and the obvious, and besides, neither a sufficient nor a true reason; for the like happens to all their other senses. For they are not easily moved or wrought on by any qualities, unless they are in intense degrees and make a vigorous impression; but the reason is the laxity of the habit of their body, for that, being grown lax and weak, loves a smart stroke. Thus their taste is pleased most with strong sapors, their smelling with brisk odors; for strong and unalloyed qualities make a more pleasing impression on the sense. Their touch is almost senseless to a sore, and a wound generally raises no sharp pain. The like also in their hearing may be observed; for old musicians play louder and sharper than others, that they may move their own dull tympanum with the sound. For what steel is to the edge in a knife, that spirit is to the sense in the body; and therefore, when the spirits fail, the sense grows dull and stupid, and cannot be raised, unless by something, such as strong wine, that makes a vigorous impression.

QUESTION VIII. WHY OLD MEN READ BEST AT A DISTANCE. PLUTARCH, LAMPRIAS, AND OTHERS.

To my discourse in the former problem some objection may be drawn from the sense of seeing in old men; for, if they hold a book at a distance, they will read pretty well, nearer they cannot see a letter and this Aeschylus means by these verses:–

Behold from far; for near thou canst not see;
A good old scribe thou mayst much sooner be.

And Sophocles more plainly:–

Old men are slow in talk, they hardly hear;
Far off they see; but all are blind when near.

And therefore, if old men's organs are more obedient to strong and intense qualities, why, when they read, do they not take the reflection near at hand, but, holding the book a good way off, mix and weaken it by the intervening air, as wine by water?

Some answered, that they did not remove the book to lessen the light, but to receive more rays, and let all the space between the letters and their eyes be filled with lightsome air. Others agreed with those that imagine the rays of vision mix with one another; for since there is a cone stretched between each eye and the object, whose point is in the eye and whose basis is the object, it is probable that for some way each cone extends apart and by itself; but, when the distance increases, they mix and make but one common light; and therefore every object appears single and not two, though it is seen by both eyes at once; for the conjunction of the cones makes these two appearances but one. These things supposed, when old men hold the letters close to their eyes, the cones not being joined, but each apart and by itself, their sight is weak; but when they remove it farther, the two lights being mingled and increased, see better, as a man with both hands can hold that for which either singly is too weak.

But my brother Lamprias, though unacquainted with Hieronymus's notions, gave us another reason. We see, said he, some species that come from the object to the eye, which at their first rise are thick and great; and therefore when near disturb old men, whose eyes are stiff and not easily penetrated; but when they are separated and diffused into the air, the thick obstructing parts are easily removed, and the subtile remainders coming to the eye gently and easily slide into the pores; and so the disturbance being less, the sight is more vigorous and clear. Thus a rose smells most fragrant at a distance; but if you bring it near the nose, it is not so pure and delightful; and the reason is this,–many earthy disturbing particles are carried with the smell, and spoil the fragrancy when near, but in a longer passage those are lost, and the pure brisk odor, by reason of its subtility, reaches and acts upon the sense.

But we, according to Plato's opinion, assert that a bright spirit darted from the eye mixes with the light about the object, and those two are perfectly blended into one similar body; now these must be joined in due proportion one to another; for one part ought not wholly to prevail on the other, but both, being proportionally and amicably joined, should agree in one third common power. Now this (whether flux, illuminated spirit, or ray) in old men being very weak, there can be no combination, no mixture with the light about the object; but it must be wholly consumed, unless, by removing the letters from their eyes, they lessen the brightness of the light, so that it comes to the sight not too strong or unmixed, but well proportioned and blended with the other. And this explains that common affection of creatures seeing in the dark; for their eyesight being weak is overcome and darkened by the splendor of the day; because the little light that flows from their eyes cannot be proportionably mixed with the stronger and more numerous beams; but it is proportionable and sufficient for the feeble splendor of the stars, and so can join with it, and cooperate to move the sense.

QUESTION IX. WHY FRESH WATER WASHES CLOTHES BETTER THAN SALT. THEON, THEMISTOCLES, METRIUS, FLORUS, PLUTARCH; AND OTHERS.

Theon the grammarian, when Metrius Florus gave us an entertainment, asked Themistocles the Stoic, why Chrysippus, though he frequently mentioned some strange phenomena in nature (as that salt meat soaked in salt water grows fresher than before; fleeces of wool are more easily separated by a gentle than a quick and violent force, and men that are fasting eat slower than those who took a breakfast), yet never gave any reason for the appearance. And Themistocles replied, that Chrysippus only proposed such things by the by, as instances to correct us, who easily assent and without any reason to what seems likely, and disbelieve everything that seems unlikely at the first sight. But why, sir, are you concerned at this? For if you are speculative and would inquire into the causes of things you need not want subjects in your own profession; but pray tell me why Homer makes Nausicaa wash in the river rather than the sea, though it was near, and in all likelihood hotter, clearer, and fitter to wash with than that?

And Theon replied: Aristotle hath already given an account for this from the grossness of the sea water; for in this an abundance of rough earthy particles is mixed, and those make it salt; and upon this account swimmers or any other weights sink not so much in sea water as in fresh for the latter, being thin and weak, yields to every pressure and is easily divided, because it is pure and unmixed and by reason of this subtility of parts it penetrates better than salt water, and so looseneth from the clothes the sticking particles of the spot. And is not this discourse of Aristotle very probable?

Probable indeed, I replied, but not true; for I have observed that with ashes, gravel, or, if these are not to be gotten, with dust itself they usually thicken the water, as if the earthy particles being rough would scour better than fair water, whose thinness makes it weak and ineffectual. And therefore he is mistaken when he says the thickness of the sea water hinders the effect, since the sharpness of the mixed particles very much conduces to make it cleansing; for that open the pores, and draws out the stain. But since all oily matter is most difficult to be washed out and spots a cloth, and the sea is oily, that is the reason why it doth not scour as well as fresh and that it is oily, even Aristotle himself asserts, for salt in his opinion hath some oil in it, and therefore makes candles, when sprinkled on them, burn the better and clearer than before. And sea water sprinkled on a flame increaseth it, and it more easily kindled than any other; in my opinion, makes it hotter than the fresh. And besides, I may urge another cause; for the end of washing is drying, and that seems cleanest which is driest; and the moisture that scours (as hellebore, with the humors that it purges) ought to fly away quickly together with the stain. The sun quickly draws out the fresh water, because it is so light but the salt water being rough lodges in the pores, and therefore is not easily dried.

And Theon replied: You say just nothing, sir; for Aristotle in the same book affirms that those that wash in the sea, if they stand in sun, are sooner dried than those that wash in the fresh streams. If it is true, I am answered, he says so; but I hope that Homer asserting the contrary will, by you especially, be more easily believed; for Ulysses (as he writes) after his shipwreck meeting Nausicaa,

> *A frightful sight, and with the salt besmeared* said to her maidens,
> *Retire a while, till I have washed my skin,*

And when he had leaped into the river,

> *He from his head did scour the foaming sea.*
> *(See "Odyssey," vi. 137, 218, 226.)*

The poet knew very well what happens in such a case; for when those that come wet out of the sea stand in the sun, the subtilest and lightest parts suddenly exhale, but the salt and rough particles stick upon the body in a crust, till they are washed away by the fresh water of a spring.

QUESTION X. WHY AT ATHENS THE CHORUS OF THE TRIBE AEANTIS WAS NEVER DETERMINED TO BE THE LAST. PHILOPAPPUS, MARCUS, MILO, GLAUCIAS, PLUTARCH, AND OTHERS.

When we were feasting at Serapion's, who gave an entertainment after the tribe Leontis under his order and direction had won the prize (for we were citizens and free of that tribe), a very pertinent discourse, and proper to the then occasion, happened. It had been a very notable trial of skill, the king Philopappus being very generous and magnificent in his rewards, and defraying the expenses of all the tribes. He was at the same feast with us and being a very good-humored man and eager for instruction, he would now and then freely discourse of ancient customs, and as freely hear.

Marcus the grammarian began thus: Neanthes the Cyzicenian, in his book called the "Fabulous Narrations of the City," affirms that it was a privilege of the tribe Aeantis that their chorus should never be determined to be the last. It is true, he brings some stories for confirmation of what he says; but if he falsifies, the matter is open, and let us all inquire after the reason of the thing. But, says Milo, suppose it be a mere tale. It is no strange thing replied Philopappus, if in our disquisitions after truth we meet now and then with such a thing as Democritus the philosopher did; for he one day eating a cucumber, and finding it of a honey taste, asked his maid where she bought it; and she telling him in such a garden, he rose from table and bade her direct him to the place. The maid surprised asked him what he meant; and he replied, I must search after the cause of the sweetness of the fruit, and shall find it the sooner if I see the place. The maid with a smile replied, Sit still, pray, sir, for I unwittingly put it into a honey barrel. And he, as it were discontented, cried out, Shame take thee, yet I will pursue my purpose, and seek after the cause, as if this sweetness were a taste natural and proper to the fruit. Therefore neither will we admit Neanthes's credulity and inadvertency in some stories as an excuse and a good reason for avoiding this disquisition; for we shall exercise our thoughts by it, though no other advantage rises from that inquiry.

Presently every one poured out something in commendation of that tribe, mentioning every matter that made for its credit and reputation. Marathon was brought in as belonging to it, and Harmodius with his associates, by birth Aphidneans, were also produced as glorious members of that tribe. The orator Glaucias proved that that tribe made up the right wing in the battle at Marathon, from the elegies of Aeschylus, who had himself fought valiantly in the same encounter; and farther evinced that Callimachus the field marshal was of that tribe, who behaved himself very bravely, and was the principal cause next to Miltiades, with whose opinion he concurred, that that battle was fought. To this discourse of Glaucias I added, that the edict which impowered Miltiades to lead forth the Athenians, was made when the tribe Aeantis was chief of the assembly, and that in the battle of Plataea the same tribe won the greatest glory; and upon that account, as the oracle directed, that tribe offered a sacrifice for this victory to the nymphs Sphragitides, the city providing a victim and all other necessaries belonging to it. But you may observe (I continued) that other tribes likewise have their peculiar glories; and you know that mine, the tribe Leontids, yields to none in any point of reputation. Besides, consider whether it is not more probable that this was granted out of a particular respect, and to please Ajax, from whom this tribe received its name; for we know he could not endure to be outdone, but was easily hurried on to the greatest enormities by his contentious and passionate humor; and therefore to comply with him and afford him some comfort in his disasters, they secured him from the most vexing grievance that follows the misfortune of the conquered, by ordering that his tribe should never be determined to be last.

Book Two

OF THE SEVERAL THINGS that are provided for an entertainment, some, my Sossius Senecio, are absolutely necessary; such are wine, bread, meat, lounges, and tables. Others are brought in, not for necessity, but pleasure; such are songs, shows, mimics, and buffoons; which, when present, delight indeed, but when absent, are not eagerly desired; nor is the entertainment looked upon as mean because such things are wanting. Just so of discourses; some the sober men admit as necessary to a banquet, and others for their pretty nice speculations, as more profitable and agreeable than the fiddle and the pipe. My former book gives you examples of both sorts. Of the first are these, Whether we should philosophize at table?–Whether the entertainer should appoint proper seats, or leave the guests to agree upon there own? Of the second, Why lovers are inclined to poetry? And the question about the tribe of Aeantis. The former I call properly [Greek omitted] but both together I comprehend under the general name of Symposiacs. They are promiscuously set down, not in the exact method, but as each singly occurred to memory. And let not my readers wonder that I dedicate these collections to you, which I have received from others or your own mouth; for if all learning is not bare remembrance, yet to learn and to remember are very commonly one and the same.

QUESTION I WHAT, AS XENOPHON INTIMATES, ARE THE MOST AGREEABLE QUESTIONS AND MOST PLEASANT RAILLERY AT AN ENTERTAINMENT? SOSSIUS, SENECIO, AND PLUTARCH.

Now each book being divided into ten questions, that shall make the first in this, which Socratial Xenophon hath as it were proposed; for he tells that, Gobryas banqueting with Cyrus, amongst other things he found admirable in the Persians, was surprised to hear them ask one another such questions that it was more pleasant to be interrogated than to be let alone, and pass such jests on one another that it was more pleasant to be jested on than not. For if some, even whilst they praise, offend, why should not their polite and neat facetiousness be admired, whose very raillery is delightful and pleasant to him that is the subject of it? Once you said: I wish I could learn what kind of questions those are; for to be skilled in and make right use of apposite questions and pleasant raillery, I think is no small part of conversation.

A considerable one, I replied; but pray observe whether Xenophon himself, in his descriptions of Socrates's and the Persian entertainments, hath not sufficiently explained them. But if you would have my thoughts, first, men are pleased to be asked those questions to which they have an answer ready; such are those in which the persons asked have some skill and competent knowledge; for when the inquiry is above their reach, those that can return nothing are troubled, as if requested to give something beyond their power; and those that do answer, producing some crude and insufficient demonstration, must needs be very much concerned, and apt to blunder on the wrong. Now, if the answer not only is easy but hath something not common, it is more pleasing to them that make it; and this happens, when their knowledge is greater than that of the vulgar, as suppose they are well skilled in points of astrology or logic. For not only in action and serious matters, but also in discourse, every one hath a natural disposition to be pleased (as Euripides hath it)

To seem far to outdo himself.

And all are delighted when men put such questions as they understand, and would have others know that they are acquainted with; and therefore travellers and merchants are most satisfied when their company is inquisitive about other countries, the unknown ocean, and the laws and manners of the barbarians; they are very ready to inform them, and describe the countries and the creeks, imagining this to be some recompense for their toil, some comfort for the dangers they have passed. In short, whatever though unrequested, we are wont to discourse of, we are desirous to be asked; because then we seem to gratify those whom otherwise our prattle would disturb and force from our conversation. And this is the common disease of travellers. But more genteel and modest men love to be asked about those things which they have bravely and successfully performed, and which modesty will not permit to be spoken by themselves before company; and therefore Nestor did well when, being acquainted with Ulysses's desire of reputation, he said,

Tell, brave Ulysses, glory of the Greeks,
How you the horses seized.
("*Iliad,*" x. 544.)

For man cannot endure the insolence of those who praise themselves and repeat their own exploits, unless the company desires it and they are forced to a relation; therefore it tickles them to be asked about their embassies and administrations of the commonwealth, if they have done anything notable in either. And upon this account the envious and ill-natured start very few questions of that they sort; that thwart and hinder all such kind of motions, being very unwilling to give any occasion or opportunity for that discourse which shall tend to the advantage of the relater. In short, we please those to whom we put them, when we start questions about those matters which their enemies hate to hear.

Ulysses says to Alcinous,
You bid me tell what various ills I bore,
That the sad tale might make me grieve the more.
(Sophocles, "Oedipus at Colonus," 510.)
And Oedipus says to the chorus,
'Tis pain to raise again a buried grief.
("Odyssey," ix. 12.)
But Euripides on the contrary,
How sweet it is, when we are lulled in ease,
To think of toils!–when well, of a disease!
(Euripides, "Andromeda," Frag. 131.)

True indeed, but not to those that are still tossed, still under a misfortune. Therefore be sure never ask a man about his own calamities; it is irksome to relate his losses of children or estate, or any unprosperous adventure by sea or land; but ask a man how he carried the cause, how he was caressed by the king, how he escaped such a storm, such an assault, thieves, and the like; this pleaseth him, he seems to enjoy it over again in his relation, and is never weary of the topic. Besides, men love to be asked about their happy friends, or children that have made good progress in philosophy or the law, or are great at court; as also about the disgrace and open conviction of their enemies; or of such matters they are most eager to discourse, yet are cautious of beginning it themselves, lest they should seem to insult over and rejoice at the misery of others. You please a hunter if you ask him about dogs, a wrestler about exercise, and an amorous man about beauties; the ceremonious and superstitious man discourses about dreams, and what success he hath had by following the directions of omens or sacrifices, and by the kindness of the gods; and some questions concerning those things will extremely please him. He that inquires anything of an old man, though the story doth not at all concern him, wins his heart, and urges one that is very willing to discourse:–

Nelides Nestor, faithfully relate
How great Atrides died, what sort of fate;
And where was Menelaus largely tell?
Did Argos hold him when the hero fell?
("Odyssey," iii. 247.)

Here is a multitude of questions and variety of subjects; which is much better than to confine and cramp his answers, and so deprive the old man of the most pleasant enjoyment he can have. In short, they that had rather please than distaste will still propose such questions, the answers to which shall rather get the praise and good-will than the contempt and hatred of the hearers. And so much of questions.

As for raillery, those that cannot use it cautiously with art, and time it well, should never venture at it. For as in a slippery place, if you but just touch a man as you pass by, you throw him down; so when we are in drink, we are in danger of tripping at every little word that is not spoken with due address. And we are more apt to be offended with a joke than a plain and scurrilous abuse; for we see the latter often slip from a man unwittingly in passion, but consider the former as a thing voluntary, proceeding from malice and ill-nature; and therefore we are generally more offended at a sharp jeerer than a whistling snarler. Such a jest has indeed something designedly malicious about it, and often seems to be an insult skilfully devised and prepared. For instance, he that calls thee salt-fish monger plainly and openly abuseth; but he that says, I remember when you wiped your nose upon your sleeve, maliciously jeers. Such was Cicero's to Octavius, who was thought to be descended from an African slave; for when Cicero spoke something, and Octavius said he did not hear him, Cicero rejoined, Remarkable, for you have a hole through your ear. And Melanthius, when he was ridiculed by a comedian, said, You pay me now something that you do not owe me. And upon this account jeers vex more; for like bearded arrows they stick a long while, and gall the wounded sufferer. Their smartness is pleasant, and delights the company; and those that are pleased with the saving seem to believe the detracting speaker. For according to Theophrastus, a jeer is a figurative reproach for some fault or misdemeanor; and therefore he that hears it supplies the concealed part, as if he knew and gave credit to the thing. For he that laughs and is tickled at what Theocritus said to one whom he suspected of a design upon his clothes, and who asked him if he went to supper at such a place,–Yes, he replied, I go, but shall likewise lodge there all night,–doth, as it were, confirm the accusation, and believe the fellow was a thief. And therefore an impertinent jeerer makes the whole company seem ill-natured and abusive, as being pleased with and consenting to the scurrility of the jeer. It was one of the excellent laws in Sparta, that none should be bitter in their jests, and the jeered should patiently endure; but if he took offence, the other was to forbear, and pursue the frolic no farther. How is it possible therefore to determine such raillery as shall delight and please the person that is jested on, when to be smart without offence is no mean piece of cunning and address?

First then, such as will vex and gall the conscious must please those that are clean, innocent, and not suspected of the matter. Such a joke is Xenophon's, when he pleasantly brings in a very ugly ill-looking fellow, and is smart upon him for being Sambaulas's minion. Such was that of Aufidius Modestus, who, when our friend Quinitus in an ague complained his hands were cold, replied, Sir, you brought them warm from your province; for this made Quintius laugh, and extremely pleased him; yet it had been a reproach and abuse to a covetous and oppressing governor. Thus Socrates, pretending to compare faces with the beauteous Critobulus, rallied only, and not abused. And Alcibiades again was smart on Socrates, as his rival in Agatho's affection. Kings are pleased when jests are put upon them as if they were private and poor men. Such was the flatterer's to Philip, who chided him: Sir, don't I keep you? For those that mention faults of which the persons are not really guilty intimate those virtues with which they are really adorned. But then it is requisite that those virtues should be evident and certainly belong to them; otherwise the discourse will breed disturbance and suspicion. He that tells a very rich man that he will procure him a sum of money,–a temperate sober man, and one that drinks water only, that he is foxed, or hath taken a cup too much,–a hospitable, generous, good-humored man, that he is a niggard and pinch-penny,–or threatens an excellent lawyer to meet him at the bar,–must make the persons smile and please the company. Thus Cyrus was very obliging and complaisant, when he challenged his playfellows at those sports in which he was sure to be overcome. And Ismenias piping at a sacrifice, when no good omens appeared, the man that hired him snatched the pipe, and played very ridiculously himself; and when all found fault, he said: To play satisfactorily is the gift of Heaven. And Ismenias with a smile replied: Whilst I played, the gods were so well pleased that they were careless of the sacrifice; but to be rid of thy noise they presently received it.

But more, those that jocosely put scandalous names upon things commendable, if it be opportunely done, please more than he that plainly and openly commends; for those that cover a reproach under fair and respectful words (as he that calls an unjust man Aristides, a coward Achilles) gall more than those that openly abuse. Such is that of Oedipus, in Sophocles,–

The faithful Creon, my most constant friend.
(Sophocles, "Oedipus Tyrannus," 385.)

The familiar irony in commendations answers to this on the other side. Such Socrates used, when he called the kind endeavor and industry of Antisthenes to make men friends pimping, bawds-craft, and allurement; and others that called Crates the philosopher, who wherever he went was caressed and honored, the door-opener.

Again, a complaint that implies thankfulness for a received favor is pleasant raillery. Thus Diogenes of his master Antisthenes:–

That man that made me leave my precious ore,
Clothed me with rags, and forced me to be poor;
That man that made me wander, beg my bread,
And scorn to have a house to hide my head.

For it had not been half so pleasant to have said, that man that made me wise, content, and happy. And a Spartan, making as if he would find fault with the master of the exercises for giving him wood that would not smoke, said, He will not permit us even to shed a tear. And he calls a hospitable man, and one that treats often, a kidnapper, and a tyrant who for a long time would not permit him to see his own table; and he whom the king hath raised and enriched, that says he had a design upon him and robbed him of his sleep and quiet. So if he that hath an excellent vintage should complain of Aeschlus's Cabeiri for making him want vinegar, as they haul jocosely threatened. For such as these have a pungent pleasantness, so that the praised are not offended nor take it ill.

Besides, he that would be civilly facetious must know the difference between a vice and a commendable study or recreation; for instance, between the love of money or contention and of music or hunting; for men are grieved if twitted with the former, but take it very well if they are laughed at for the latter. Thus Demosthenes the Mitylenean was pleasant enough when, knocking at a man's door that was much given to singing and playing on the harp, and being bid come in, he said, I will, if you will tie up your harp. But the flatterer of Lysimachus was offensive; for being frighted at a wooden scorpion that the king threw into his lap, and leaping out of his seat, he said after he knew the humor, And I'll fright your majesty too; give me a talent.

In several things about the body too the like caution is to be observed. Thus he that is jested on for a flat or hooked nose usually laughs at the jest. Thus Cassander's friend was not at all displeased when Theophrastus said to him, 'Tis strange, sir, that your eyes don't play, since your nose is so near and so well fitted for a pipe to give them the tune; and Cyrus commanded a long hawk-nosed fellow to marry a flat-nosed girl, for then they would very well agree. But a jest on any for his stinking breath or filthy nose is irksome; for baldness it may be borne, but for blindness or infirmity in the eyes it is intolerable. It is true, Antigonus would joke upon himself, and once, receiving a petition written in great letters, he said, This a man may read if he were stark blind. But he killed Theocritus the Chian for saying,–wh Byzantine to Pasiades saying, Sir, your eyes upbraid me with this infirmity, not considering that thy son carries the vengeance of Heaven on his back: now Pasiades's son was hunch-backed. And Archippus the popular Athenian was much displeased with Melanthius for being smart on his crooked back; for Melanthius had said that he did not stand at the head of the state but bowed down before it. It is true, some are not much concerned at such jeers. Thus Antigonus's friend, when he had begged a talent and was denied, desired a guard, lest somebody should rob him of that talent he was now to carry home. Different tempers make men differently affected, and that which troubles one is not regarded by another. Epaminondas feasting with his fellow-magistrates drank vinegar; and some asking if it was good for his health, he replied, I cannot tell that, but I know it makes me remember what I drink at home. Therefore it becomes every man that would rally, to look into the humors of his company, and take heed to converse without offence.

Love, as in most things else, so in this matter causes different effects; for some lovers are pleased and some displeased at a merry jest. Therefore in this case a fit time must be accurately observed; for as a blast of wind puffs out a fire whilst it is weak and little, but when thoroughly kindled strengthens and increaseth it; so love, before it is evident and confessed, is displeased at a discoverer, but when it breaks forth and blazes in everybody's eyes, then it is delighted and gathers strength by the frequent blasts of joke and raillery. When their beloved is present it will gratify them most to pass a jest upon their passion, but to fall on any other subject will be counted an abuse. If they are remarkably loving to their own wives, or entertain a generous affection for a hopeful youth, then are they proud, then tickled when jeered for such a love. And therefore Arcesilaus, when an amorous man in his school laid down this proposition, in my opinion one thing cannot touch another, replied, Sir you touch this person, pointing to a lovely boy that sat near him.

Besides, the company must be considered; for what a man will only laugh at when mentioned amongst his friends and familiar acquaintance, he will not endure to be told of before his wife, father, or his tutor, unless perhaps it be something that will please those too; as for instance, if before a philosopher one should jeer a man for going barefoot or studying all night; or before his father, for carefulness and thrift; or in the presence of his wife, for being cold to his companions and doting upon her. Thus Tigranes, when Cyrus asked him, What will your wife say when she hears that you are put to servile offices? replied, Sir, she will not hear it, but be present herself and see it.

Again, those jokes are accounted less affronting which reflect somewhat also on the man that makes them; as when one poor man, baseborn fellow, or lover jokes upon another. For whatever comes from one in the same circumstances looks more like a piece of mirth than a designed affront; but otherwise it must needs be irksome and distasteful. Upon this account, when a slave whom the king had lately freed and enriched behaved himself very impertinently in the company of some philosophers, asking them, how it came to pass that the broth of beans whether white or black, was always green, Aridices putting another question, why, let the whips be white or not, the wales and marks they made were still red, displeased him extremely, and made him rise from the table in a great rage and discontent. But Amphias the Tarsian, who was supposed to be sprung from a gardener, joking upon the governor's friend for his obscure and mean birth, and presently subjoining, But 'tis true, I sprung from the same seed, caused much mirth and laughter. And the harper very facetiously put a cheek to Philip's ignorance and impertinence; for when Philip pretended to correct him, he cried out, God forbid, sir, that ever you should be brought so low as to understand these things better than I. For by this seeming joke he instructed him without giving any offence. And therefore some of the comedians seem to lay aside their bitterness in every jest that may reflect upon themselves; as Aristophanes, when he is merry upon a baldpate; and Cratinus in his play "Pytine" upon drunkenness and excess.

Besides, you must be very careful that the jest should seem to be extempore, taken from some present question or merry humor; not far-fetched, as if premeditate and designed. For as men are not much concerned at the anger and disputes among themselves at table while they are drinking, but if any stranger should come in and offer abuse, they would hate and look upon him as an enemy; so they will easily pardon and indulge a jest if undesignedly taken from any present circumstance; but if it is nothing to the matter in hand but fetched from another thing, it must look like a design and be resented as an affront. Such was that of Timagenes to the husband of a woman that often vomited,–"Thou beginnest thy troubles by bringing home this vomiting woman," saying [Greek omitted] (this vomiting woman), when the poet had written [Greek omitted] (this Muse); and also his question to Athenodorus the philosopher,–Is affection to our children natural? For when the raillery is not founded on some present circumstance, it is an argument of ill-nature and a mischievous temper; and such as these do often for a mere word, the lightest thing in the world (as Plato says), suffer the heaviest punishment. But those that know how to time and apply a jest confirm Plato's opinion, that to rally pleasantly and facetiously is the business of a scholar and a wit.

QUESTION II. WHY IN AUTUMN MEN HAVE BETTER STOMACHS THAN IN OTHER SEASONS OF THE YEAR. GLAUCLAS, XENOCLES, LAMPRIAS, PLUTARCH, AND OTHERS.

In Eleusis, after the solemn celebration of the sacred mysteries, Glaucias the orator entertained us at a feast; where after the rest had done, Xenocles of Delphi, as his humor is, began to be smart upon my brother Lamprias for his good Boeotian stomach. I in his defence opposing Xenocles, who was an Epicurean, said, Pray, sir, do not all place the very substance of pleasure in privation of pain and suffering? But Lamprias, who prefers the Lyceum before the Garden, ought by his practice to confirm Aristotle's doctrine; for he affirms that every man hath a better stomach in the autumn than in other seasons of the year, and gives the reason, which I cannot remember at present. So much the better (says Glaucias), for when supper is done, we will endeavor to discover it ourselves. That being over, Glaucias and Xenocles drew the autumnal fruit. One said that it scoured the body, and by this evacuation continually raised new appetites. Xenocles affirmed, that ripe fruit had usually a pleasing, vellicating sapor, and thereby provoked the appetite better than sauces or sweetmeats; for sick men of a vitiated stomach usually recover it by eating fruit. But Lamprias said, that our natural heat, the principal instrument of nutrition, in the midst of summer is scattered and becomes rare and weak, but when autumn comes it unites again and gathers strength, being shut in by the ambient cold and contraction of the pores, and I for my part said: In summer we are more thirsty and use more moisture than in other seasons; and therefore Nature, observing the same method in all her operations, at this change of seasons employs the contrary and makes us hungry; and to maintain an equal temper in the body, she gives us dry food to countervail the moisture taken in the summer. Yet none can deny but that the food itself is a partial cause; for not only new fruit, bread, or corn, but flesh of the same year, is better tasted than that of the former, more forcibly provokes the guests, and enticeth them to eat on.

QUESTION III. WHICH WAS FIRST THE BIRD OR THE EGG? PLUTARCH, ALEXANDER, SYLLA, FIRMUS, SOSSIUS SENECIO, AND OTHERS.

When upon a dream I had forborne eggs a long time, on purpose that in an egg (as in a heart) I might make experiment of a notable vision that often troubled me; some at Sossius Senecio's table suspected that I was tainted with Orpheus's or Pythagoras's opinions, and refused to eat an egg (as some do the heart and brain) imagining it to be the principle of generation. And Alexander the Epicurean ridiculingly repeated,

To feed on beans and parents' heads
Is equal sin;

As if the Pythagoreans meant eggs by the word [Greek omitted] (BEANS), deriving it from [Greek omitted](TO CONCEIVE), and thought it as unlawful to feed on eggs as on the animals that lay them. Now to pretend a dream for the cause of my abstaining, to an Epicurean, had been a defence more irrational than the cause itself; and therefore I suffered jocose Alexander to enjoy his opinion, for he was a pleasant man and an excellent scholar.

Soon after he proposed that perplexed question, that plague of the inquisitive, Which was first, the bird or the egg? And my friend Sylla, saying that with this little question, as with an engine, we shook the great and weighty problem (whether the world had a beginning), declared his dislike of such questions. But Alexander deriding the question as slight and impertinent, my relation Firmus said:. Well, sir, at present your atoms will do me some service; for if we suppose that small things must be the principles of greater, it is likely that the egg was before the bird; for an egg amongst sensible things is very simple, and the bird is more mixed, and contains a greater variety of parts. It is universally true that a principle is before that whose principle it is; now the seed is a principle, and the egg is somewhat more than the seed and less than the bird for as a disposition or a progress in goodness is something between a tractable mind and a habit of virtue, so an egg is as it were a progress of Nature tending from the seed to a perfect animal. And as in an animal they say the veins and arteries are formed first, upon the same account the egg should be before the bird, as the thing containing before the thing contained. Thus art first makes rude and ill-shapen figures and afterwards perfects everything with its proper form; and it was for this that the statuary Polycletus said, Then our work is most difficult, when the clay comes to be fashioned by the fingers. So it is probable that matter, not readily obeying the slow motions of contriving Nature, at first frames rude and indefinite masses, as the egg, and of these moulded anew, and joined in better order, the animal afterward is formed. As the canker is first, and then growing dry and cleaving lets forth a winged animal, called psyche; so the egg is first as it were the subject-matter of the generation. For it is certain that, in every change, that out of which the thing changes must be before the thing changing. Observe how worms and caterpillars are bred in trees from the moisture corrupted or concocted; now none can say but that the engendering moisture is naturally before all these. For (as Plato says) matter is as a mother or nurse in respect of the bodies that are formed, and we call that matter out of which anything that is made. And with a smile continued he, I speak to those that are acquainted with the mystical and sacred discourse of Orpheus, who not only affirms the egg to be before the bird, but makes it the first being in the whole world. The other parts, because deep mysteries, we shall now pass by; but let us look upon the various kinds of animals, and we shall find almost every one beginning from an egg,–fowls and fishes; land animals, as lizards; amphibious, as crocodiles; some with two legs, as a cock; some without any, as a snake; and some with many, as a locust. And therefore in the solemn feast of Bacchus it is very well done to dedicate an egg, as the emblem of that which begets and contains everything in itself.

To this discourse of Firmus, Senecio replied: Sir, your last similitude contradicts your first, and you have unwittingly opened the world (instead of the door, as the proverb goes) against yourself. For the world was before all, being the most perfect; and it is rational that the perfect in Nature should be before the imperfect, as the sound before the maimed, and the whole before the part. For it is absurd that there should be a part when there is nothing whose part it is; and therefore nobody says the seed's man or egg's hen, but the man's seed and hen's egg; because those being after these and formed in them, pay as it were a debt to Nature, by bringing forth another. For they are not in themselves perfect, and therefore have a natural appetite to produce such a thing as that out of which they were first formed; and therefore seed is defined as a thing produced that is to be perfected by another production. Now nothing can be perfected by or want that which as yet is not.

Everybody sees that eggs have the nature of a concretion or consistence in some animal or other, but want those organs, veins, and muscles which animals enjoy. And therefore no story delivers that ever any egg was formed immediately from earth; and the poets themselves tell us, that the egg out of which came the Tyndaridae fell down from heaven. But even till this time the earth produceth some perfect and organized animals, as mice in Egypt, and snakes, frogs, and grasshoppers almost everywhere, some external and invigorating principle assisting in the production. And in Sicily, where in the servile war much blood was shed, and many carcasses rotted on the ground, whole swarms of locusts were produced, and spoiled the corn over the whole isle. Such spring from and are nourished by the earth; and seed being formed in them, pleasure and titillation provoke them to mix, upon which some lay eggs, and some bring forth their young alive; and this evidently proves that animals first sprang from earth, and afterwards by copulation, after different ways, propagated their several kinds. In short, it is the same thing as if you said the womb was before the woman; for as the womb is to the egg, the egg is to the chick that is formed in it; so that he that inquires how birds should be when there were no eggs, might ask as well how men and women could be before any organs of generation were formed. Parts generally have their subsistence together with the whole; particular powers follow particular members, and operations those Powers, and effects those operations. Now the effect of the generative power is the seed and egg; so that these must be after the formation of the whole. Therefore consider, as there can be no digestion of food before the animal is formed, so there can be no seed nor egg; for those, it is likely, are made by some digestion and alterations; nor can it be that, before the animal is, the superfluous parts of the food of the animal should have a being. Besides, though seed may perhaps pretend to be a principle, the egg cannot; for it doth not subsist first, nor hath it the nature of a whole, for it is imperfect. Therefore we do not affirm that the animal is produced without a principle of its being; but we call the principle that power which changes, mixes, and tempers the matter, so that a living creature is regularly produced; but the egg is an after-production, as the blood or milk of an animal after the taking in and digestion of the food. For we never see an egg formed immediately of mud, for it is produced in the bodies of animals alone; but a thousand living creatures rise from the mud. What need of many instances? None ever found the spawn or egg of an eel; yet if you empty a pit and take out all the mud, as soon as other water settles in it, eels likewise are presently produced. Now that must exist first which hath no need of any other thing that it may exist, and that after, which cannot be without the concurrence of another thing. And of this priority is our present discourse. Besides, birds build nests before they lay their eggs; and women provide cradles, swaddling cloths and the like; yet who says that the nest is before the egg, or the swaddling cloths before the infant. For the earth (as Plato says doth not imitate a woman, but a woman, and so likewise all other females, the earth.) Moreover, it is probable that the first production out of the earth, which was then vigorous and perfect, was self-sufficient and entire, nor stood in need of those secundines, membranes, and vessels, which now Nature forms to help the weakness and supply the defects of breeders.

QUESTION IV. WHETHER OR NO WRESTLING IS THE OLDEST EXERCISE. SOSICLES, LYSIMACHUS, PLUTARCH, PHILINUS.

Sosicles of Coronea having at the Pythian games won the prize from all the poets, gave us an entertainment. And the time for running, cuffing, wrestling, and the like drawing on, there was a great talk of the wrestlers; for there were many and very famous men, who came to try their skill. Lysimachus, one of the company, a procurator of the Amphictyons, said he heard a grammarian lately affirm that wrestling was the most ancient exercise of all, as even the very name witnessed; for some modern things have the names of more ancient transferred to them; thus to tune a pipe is called fitting it, and playing on it is called striking; both these names being transferred to it from the harp. Thus all places of exercise they call wrestling schools, wrestling being the oldest exercise, and therefore giving its name to the newer sorts. That, said I, is no good argument, for these palaestras or wrestling schools are called so from wrestling [Greek omitted] not because it is the most ancient exercise, but because it is the only sort in which they use clay [Greek omitted] dust, and oil; for in these there is neither racing nor cuffing, but wrestling only, and that feature of the pancratium in which they struggle on the ground,–for the pancratium comprises both wrestling and cuffing. Besides, it is unlikely that wrestling, being more artificial and methodical than any other sort of exercise, should likewise be the most ancient; for mere want or necessity putting us upon new inventions, produces simple and inartificial things first, and such as have more of force in them than sleight and skill. This ended, Sosicles said: You speak right, and I will confirm your discourse from the very name; for, in my opinion, [Greek omitted] wrestling, is derived from [Greek omitted] i.e. to throw down by sleight and artifice. And Philinus said, it seems to me to be derived from [Greek omitted] the palm of the hand, for wrestlers use that part most, as cuffers do the [Greek omitted] fist; and hence both these sorts of exercises have their proper names, the one [Greek omitted] the other [Greek omitted]. Besides, since the poets use the word [Greek omitted] for [Greek omitted] and [Greek omitted], to sprinkle, and this action is most frequent amongst wrestlers, this exercise [Greek omitted] may receive its name from that word. But more, consider that racers strive to be distant from one another; cuffers, by the judges of the field, are not permitted to take hold; and none but wrestlers come up breast to breast, and clasp one another round the waist, and most of their turnings, liftings, lockings bring them very close. It is probable that this exercise is called [Greek omitted] from [Greek omitted] or [Greek omitted] to come up close or to be near together.

QUESTION V. WHY, IN RECKONING UP DIFFERENT KINDS OF EXERCISES, HOMER PUTS CUFFING FIRST, WRESTLING NEXT, AND RACING LAST. LYSIMACHUS, CRATES, TIMON, PLUTARCH.

This discourse being ended, and Philinus hummed, Lysimachus began again, What sort of exercise then shall we imagine to be first? Racing, as at the Olympian games? For here in the Pythian, as every exercise comes on, all the contenders are brought in, the boy wrestlers first, then the men, and the same method is observed when the cuffers and fencers are to exercise; but there the boys perform all first, and then the men. But, says Timon interposing, pray consider whether Homer hath not determined this matter; for in his poems cuffing is always put in the first place, wrestling next, and racing last. At this Menecrates the Thessalian surprised cried out, Good God, what things we skip over! But, pray sir, if you remember any of his verses to that purpose, do us the favor to repeat them. And Timon replied: That the funeral solemnities of Patroclus had this order I think every one hath heard; but the poet, all along observing the same order, brings in Achilles speaking to Nestor thus:

With this reward I Nestor freely grace,
Unfit for cuffing, wrestling, or the race.

And in his answer he makes the old man impertinently brag:–

I cuffing conquered Oinop's famous son,
With Anceus wrestled, and the garland won,
And outran Iphiclus.
("Iliad," xxiii. 620 and 634.)

And again he brings in Ulysses challenging the Phaeacians
To cuff, to wrestle, or to run the race;
and Alcinous answers:
Neither in cuffing nor in wrestling strong
But swift of foot are we.
("Odyssey" viii. 206 and 246.)

So that he doth not carelessly confound the order, and, according to the present occasion, now place one sort first and now another; but he follows the then custom and practice and is constant in the same. And this was so as long as the ancient order was observed.

To this discourse of my brother's I subjoined, that I liked what he said, but could not see the reason of this order. And some of the company, thinking it unlikely that cuffing or wrestling should be a more ancient exercise than racing, they desired me to search farther into the matter; and thus I spake upon the sudden. All these exercises seem to me to be representations of feats of arms and training therein; for after all, a man armed at all points is brought in to show that that is the end at which all these exercises and trainings end. And the privilege granted to the conquerors, viz., as they rode into the city, to throw down some part of the wall–hath this meaning; that walls are but a small advantage to that city which hath men able to fight and overcome. In Sparta those that were victors in any of the crowned games had an honorable place in the army and were to fight near the king's person. Of all other creatures a horse only can have a part in these games and win the crown, for that alone is designed by nature to be trained to war, and to prove assisting in a battle. If these things seem probable, let us consider farther, that it is the first work of a fighter to strike his enemy and ward the other's blows; the second, when they come up close and lay hold of one another, to trip and overturn him; and in this, they say, our countrymen being better wrestlers very much distressed the Spartans at the battle of Leuctra. And Aeschylus describes a warrior thus,–
One stout, and skilled to wrestle in his arms;
and Sophocles somewhere says of the Trojans,–
They rid the horse, they could the bow command
And wrestle with a rattling shield in hand.

But it is the third and last, either when conquered to fly, when conquerors to pursue. And therefore it is likely that cuffing is set first, wrestling next, and racing last; for the first bears the resemblance of charging or warding the blows; the second, of close fighting and repelling; the third, of flying a victorious, or pursuing a routed enemy.

QUESTION VI. WHY FIR-TREES, PINE-TREES, AND THE LIKE WILL NOT BE GRAFTED UPON. SOCLARUS, CRATO, PHILO.

Soclarus entertaining us in his gardens, round which the river Cephissus runs, showed us several trees strangely varied by the different grafts upon their stocks. We saw an olive upon a juniper, a peach upon a myrtle, pear grafts on an oak, apple upon a plane, a mulberry on a fig and a great many such like, which were grown strong enough to bear. Some joked on Soclarus as nourishing stranger kinds of things than the poets' Sphinxes or Chimaeras, but Crato set us to inquire why those stocks only that are of an oily nature will not admit such mixtures for we never see a pine, fir, or cypress bear a graft of another kind.

And Philo subjoined: There is, Crato, a reason for this amongst the philosophers, which the gardeners confirm and strengthen. For they say, oil is very hurtful to all plants, and any plant dipped in it like a bee, will soon die. Now these trees are of a fat and oily nature, insomuch that they weep pitch and rosin; and, if you cut then gore (as it were) appears presently in the wound. Besides, a torch made of them sends forth an oily smoke, and the brightness of the flame shows it to be fat; and upon this account these trees are as great enemies to all other kinds of grafts as oil itself. To this Crato added, that the bark was a partial cause; for that, being rare and dry, could not afford either convenient room or sufficient nourishment to the grafts; but when the bark is moist, it quickly joins with those grafts that are let into the body of the tree.

Then Soclarus added: This too ought to be considered, that that which receives a graft of another kind ought to be easy to be changed, that the graft may prevail, and make the sap in the stock fit and natural to itself. Thus we break up the ground and soften it, that being thus broken it may more easily be wrought upon, and applied to what we plant in it; for things that are hard and rigid cannot be so quickly wrought upon nor so easily changed. Now those trees, being of very light wood, do not mix well with the grafts, because they are very hard either to be changed or overcome. But more, it is manifest that the stock which receives the graft should be instead of a soil to it, and a soil should have a breeding faculty; and therefore we choose the most fruitful stocks to graft on, as women that are full of milk, when we would put out a child to nurse. But everybody knows that the fir, cypress, and the like are no great bearers. For as men very fat have few children (for, the whole nourishment being employed in the body, there remains no overplus to make seed), so these trees, spending all their sap in their own stock, flourish indeed and grow great; but as for fruit, some bear none at all, some very little, and that too slowly ripens; therefore it is no wonder that they will not nourish another's fruit, when they are so very sparing to their own.

QUESTION VII. ABOUT THE FISH CALLED REMORA OR ECH-ENEIS. CHAEREMONIANUS, PLUTARCH, AND OTHERS.

Chaeremonianus the Trallian, when we were at a very noble fish dinner, pointing to a little, long, sharp-headed fish, said the echeneis (ship-stopper) was like that, for he had often seen it as he sailed in the Sicilian sea, and wondered at its strange force; for it stopped the ship when under full sail, till one of the seamen perceived it sticking to the outside of the ship, and took it off. Some laughed at Chaeremonianus for believing such an incredible and unlikely story. Others on this occasion talked very much of antipathies, and produced a thousand instances of such strange effects; for example, the sight of a ram quiets an enraged elephant; a viper lies stock-still, if touched with a beechen leaf; a wild bull grows tame, if bound with the twigs of a fig-tree; and amber draws all light things to it, except basil and such as are dipped in oil; and a loadstone will not draw a piece of iron that is rubbed with onion. Now all these, as to matter of fact, are very evident; but it is hard, if not altogether impossible, to find the cause.

Then said I: This is a mere shift and avoiding of the question, rather than a declaration of the cause; but if we please to consider, we shall find a great many accidents that are only consequents of the effect to be unjustly esteemed the causes of it; as for instance, if we should fancy that by the blossoming of the chaste-tree the fruit of the vine is ripened; because this is a common saying,–

The chaste-tree blossoms, and the grapes grow ripe;

Or that the little protuberances in the candle-snuff thicken the air and make it cloudy; or the hookedness of the nails is the cause and not an accident consequential to an ulcer. Therefore as those things mentioned are but consequents to the effect, though proceeding from one and the same cause, so one and the same cause stops the ship, and joins the echeneis to it; for the ship continuing dry, not yet made heavy by the moisture soaking into the wood, it is probable that it lightly glides, and as long as it is clean, easily cuts the waves; but when it is thoroughly soaked, when weeds, ooze, and filth stick upon its sides, the stroke of the ship is more obtuse and weak; and the water, coming upon this clammy matter, doth not so easily part from it; and this is the reason why they usually calk their ships. Now it is likely that the echeneis in this case, sticking upon the clammy matter, is not thought an accidental consequent to this cause, but the very cause itself.

QUESTION VIII. WHY THEY SAY THOSE HORSES CALLED [GREEK OMITTED] ARE VERY METTLESOME. PLUTARCH, HIS FATHER, AND OTHERS.

Some say the horses called [Greek omitted] received that name from the fashion of their bridles (called [Greek omitted]), that had prickles like the teeth on the wolf's jaw; for being fiery and hard-mouthed, the riders used such to tame them. But my father, who seldom speaks but on good reason, and breeds excellent horses, said, those that were set upon by wolves when colts, if they escaped, grew swift and mettlesome, and were called [Greek omitted] Many agreeing to what he said, it began to be inquired why such an accident as that should make them more mettlesome and fierce; and many of the company thought that, from such an assault, fear and not courage was produced; and that thence growing fearful and apt to start at everything, their motions became more quick and vigorous, as they are in wild beasts when entangled in a net. But, said I, it ought to be considered whether the contrary be not more probable; for the colts do not become more swift by escaping the assault of a wild beast, but they had never escaped unless they had been swift and mettlesome before. As Ulysses was not made wise by escaping from the Cyclops, but by being wise before he escaped.

QUESTION IX. WHY THE FLESH OF SHEEP BITTEN BY WOLVES IS SWEETER THAN THAT OF OTHERS, AND THE WOOL MORE APT TO BREED LICE. PATROCLIAS, THE SAME.

After the former discourse, mention was made of those sheep that wolves have bitten; for it is commonly said of them, that their flesh is very sweet, and their wool breeds lice. My relative Patroclias seemed to be pretty happy in his reasoning upon the first part, saying, that the beast by biting it did mollify the flesh; for wolves' spirits are so hot and fiery, that they soften and digest the hardest bones and for the same reason things bitten by wolves rot sooner than others. But concerning the wool we could not agree, being not fully resolved whether it breeds those lice, or only opens a passage for them, separating the flesh by its fretting roughness or proper warmth; and appeared that this power proceeded from the bite of wolf, which alters even the very hair of the creature that it kills. And this some particular instances seem to confirm; for we know some huntsmen and cooks will kill a beast with one stroke, so that it never breathes after, whilst others repeat their blows, and scarce do it with a great deal of trouble. But (what is more strange) some, as they kill it, infuse such a quality that the flesh rots presently and cannot be kept sweet above a day; yet others that despatch it as soon find no such alteration, but the flesh will keep sweet a long while. And that by the manner of killing a great alteration is made even in the skins, nails, and hair of a beast, Homer seems to witness, when, speaking of a good hide, he says,–

An ox's hide that fell by violent blows;
("Iliad," iii. 375.)

for not those that fell by a disease or old age, but by a violent death, leave us tough and strong hides; but after they are bitten by wild beasts, their hoofs grow black, their hair falls, their skins putrefy and are good for nothing.

QUESTION X. WHETHER THE ANCIENTS, BY PROVIDING EVERY ONE HIS MESS, DID BEST OR WE, WHO SET MANY TO THE SAME DISH. PLUTARCH, HAGIAS.

When I was chief magistrate, most of the suppers consisted of distinct messes, where every particular guest had his portion of the sacrifice allowed him. Some were wonderfully well pleased with this order; others blamed it as unsociable and ungenteel, and were of the opinion that, as soon as I was out of my office, the manner of entertainments ought to be reformed; for, says Hagias, we invite one another not barely to eat and drink, but to eat and drink together. Now this division into messes takes away all society, makes many suppers, and many eaters, but no one sups with another; but every man takes his pound of beef, as from the meat shop, sets it before himself, and falls on. And is it not the same thing to provide a different cup and different table for every guest (as the Demophontidae treated Orestes), as now to set each man his loaf of bread and mess of meat, and feed him, as it were, out of his own proper manger? Only, it is true, we are not (as those that treated Orestes were) obliged to be silent and not discourse. Besides, that all the guests should have a share in everything, we may draw an argument from hence;–the same discourse is common to us all, the same songstress sings, and the same musician plays to all. So, when the same cup is set in the midst, not appropriated to any, it is a large spring of good fellowship, and each man may take as much as his appetite requires; not like this most unjust distribution of bread and meat, which prides itself forsooth in being equal to all, though unequal, stomachs; for the same share to a man of a small appetite is too much; to one of a greater, too little. And, sir, as he that administers the very same dose of physic to all sorts of patients must be very ridiculous; so likewise must that entertainer who, inviting a great many guests that can neither eat nor drink alike, sets before every one an equal mess, and measures what is

just and fit by an arithmetical not geometrical proportion. When we go to a shop to buy, we all use, it is true, one and the same public measure; but to an entertainment each man brings his own belly, which is satisfied with a portion, not because it is equal to that which others have, but because it is sufficient for itself. Those entertainments where every one had his single mess Homer mentions amongst soldiers and in the camp, which we ought not to bring into fashion amongst us; but rather imitate the good friendship of the ancients, who, to show what reverence they had for all kinds of societies, not only respected those that lived with them or under the same roof, but also those that drank out of the same cup or ate out of the same dish. Let us never mind Homer's entertainments; they were good for nothing but to starve a man, and the makers of them were kings more stingy and observant than the Italian cooks; insomuch that in the midst of a battle, whilst they were at handy-blows with their enemies, they could exactly reckon up how many glasses each man drank at his table. But those that Pindar describes are much better,–
  Where heroes mixed sat round the noble board,
because they maintained society and good fellowship; for the latter truly mixed and joined friends, but our modern system divides and asperses them as persons who, though seemingly very good friends, cannot so much as eat with one another out of the same dish.

To this polite discourse of Hagias they urged me to reply. And I said: Hagias, it is true, hath reason to be troubled at this unusual disappointment, because having so great a belly (for he was an excellent trencherman) he had no larger mess than others; for in a fish eaten together Democritus says, there are no bones. But that very thing is likely to increase our share beyond our own proper allowance. For it is equality, as the old woman in Euripides hath it,
  That fastens towns to towns, and friends to friends;
  (Euripides, "Phoenissae," 536.)
and entertainments chiefly stand in need of this. The necessity is from nature as well as custom, and is not lately introduced or founded only on opinion. For when the same dish lies in common before all, the man that is slow and eats little must be offended at the other that is too quick for him, as a slow ship at the swift sailor. Besides, snatching, contention, shoving, and the like, are not, in my mind, neighborly beginnings of mirth and jollity; but they are absurd, doggish, and often end in anger or reproaches, not only against one another, but also against the entertainer himself or the carvers of the feast. But as long as Moera and Lachesis (DIVISION AND DISTRIBUTION) maintained equality in

feasts, nothing uncivil or disorderly was seen, and they called the feasts [Greek omitted], DISTRIBUTIONS, the entertained [Greek omitted], and the carvers [Greek omitted], DISTRIBUTERS, from dividing and distributing to every man his proper mess. The Lacedaemonians had officers called distributers of the flesh, no mean men, but the chief of the city; for Lysander himself by king Agesilaus was constituted one of these in Asia. But when luxury crept into our feasts, distributing was thrown out; for I suppose they had not leisure to divide these numerous tarts, cheese-cakes, pies, and other delicate varieties; but, surprised with the pleasantness of the taste and tired with the variety, they left off cutting it into portions, and left all in common. And this is confirmed from the present practice; for in our religious or public feasts, where the food is simple and inartificial, each man hath his mess assigned him; so that he that endeavors to retrieve the ancient custom will likewise recover thrift and almost lost frugality again. But, you object, where only property is, community is lost. True indeed, where equality is not; for not the possession of what is proper and our own, but the taking away of another's and coveting that which is common, is the cause of all injury and contention; and the laws, restraining and confining these within the proper bounds, receive their name from their office, being a power distributing equally to every one in order to the common good. Thus every one is not to be honored by the entertainer with the garland or the chiefest place; but if any one brings with him his sweetheart or a singing girl, they must be common to him and his friends, that all possessions may be brought together, as Anaxagoras would have it. Now if propriety in these things doth not in the least hinder but that things of greater moment, and the only considerable, as discourse and civility, may be still common, let us leave off abasing distributions or the lot, the son of Fortune (as Euripides hath it), which hath no respect either to riches or honor, but in its inconsiderate wheel now and then raiseth up the humble and the poor, and makes him master of himself, and, by accustoming the great and rich to endure and not be offended at equality, pleasingly instructs.

Book Three

SIMONIDES THE POET, my Sossius Senecio, seeing one of the company sit silent and discourse nobody, said: Sir, if you are fool, it is wisely done; if a wise man, very foolishly. It is good to conceal a man's folly (but as Heraclitus says) it is very hard to do it over a glass of wine,–

Which doth the gravest men to mirth advance,
And let them loose to sing, to laugh, and dance,
And speak what had been better unsaid.
("Odyssey," xiv. 464.)

In which lines the poet in my mind shows the difference between being a little heated and downright drunk; for to sing, laugh, and dance may agree very well with those that have gone no farther than the merry cup; but to prattle, and speak what had been better left unsaid, argues a man to be quite gone. And therefore Plato thinks that wine is the must ingenious discoverer of men's humors; and Homer, when he says,–

At feasts they had not known each other's minds,
(Ibid. xxi. 35.)

evidently shows that he knew wine was powerful to open men's thoughts, and was full of new discoveries. It is true from the bare eating and drinking, if they say nothing we can give no guess at the tempers of the men; but because drinking leads them into discourse, and discourse lays a great many things open and naked which were secret and hid before, therefore to sport a glass of wine together lets us into one another's humors. And therefore a man may reasonably fall foul on Aesop: Why sir, would you have a window in every man's breast, through which we may look in upon his thoughts? Wine opens and exposes all, it will not suffer us to be silent, but takes off all mask and visor, and makes us regardless of the severe precepts of decency and custom. Thus Aesop or Plato, or any other that designs to look into a man, may have his desires satisfied by the assistance of a bottle; but those that are not solicitous to pump one another, but to be sociable and pleasant, discourse of such matters and handle such questions as make no discovery of the bad parts of the soul, but such as comfort the good, and, by the help of neat and polite learning, lead the intelligent part into an agreeable pasture and garden of delight This made me collect and dedicate the first to you this third dedication of table discourses, the first of which is about chaplets made of flowers.

QUESTION I. WHETHER IT IS FITTING TO WEAR CHAPLETS OF FLOWERS AT TABLE. ERATO, AMMONIUS, TRYPHO, PLUTAR-CH, AND OTHERS.

At Athens Erato the musician keeping a solemn feast to the Muses, and inviting a great many to the treat, the company was full of talk, and the subject of the discourse garlands. For after supper many of all sorts of flowers being presented to the guests, Ammonius began to jeer me for choosing a rose chaplet before a laurel, saying that those made of flowers were effeminate, and fitted toyish girls and women more than grave philosophers and men of music. And I admire that our friend Erato, that abominates all flourishing in songs, and blames good Agatho, who first in his tragedy of the Mysians ventured to introduce the chromatic airs, should himself fill his entertainment with such various and such florid colors; yet, while he shuts out all the soft delights that through the ears can enter to the soul, he should introduce others through the eyes and through the nose, and make these garlands, instead of signs of piety, to be instruments of pleasure. For it must be confessed that this ointment gives a better smell than those trifling flowers, which wither even in the hands of those that wreathe them. Besides, all pleasure must be banished the company of philosophers, unless it is of some use or desired by natural appetite; for as those that are carried to a banquet by some of their invited friends (as, for instance, Socrates carried Aristodemus to Agatho's table) are as civilly entertained as the bidden guests, but he that goes on his own account is shut out of doors; thus the pleasures of eating and drinking, being invited by natural appetite, should have admission; but all the others which come on no account and have only luxury to introduce them, ought in reason to be denied.

At this some young men, not thoroughly acquainted with Ammonius's humor, being abashed, privately tore their chaplets; but I, perceiving that Ammonius proposed this only for discourse and disputation's sake, applying myself to Trypho the physician, said: Sir, you must put off that sparkling rosy chaplet as well as we, or declare, as I have often heard you, what excellent preservatives these flowery garlands are against the strength of liquor. But here Erato putting in said: What, is it decreed that no pleasure must be admitted without profit? And must we be angry with our delight, unless hired to endure it? Perhaps we may have reason to be ashamed of ointments and purple vests, because so costly and expensive, and to look upon them as (in the barbarian's phrase) treacherous garments and deceitful odors; but these natural smells and colors are pure and simple as fruits themselves, and without expense or the curiosity of art. And I appeal to any one, whether it is not absurd to receive the pleasant savors Nature gives us, and enjoy and reject those smells and colors that the seasons afford us, because forsooth they blossom with delight, if they have no other external profit or advantage. Besides, we have an axiom against you, for if (as you affirm) Nature makes nothing in vain, those things that have no other use were designed on purpose to please and to delight. Besides, observe that to thriving trees Nature hath given leaves, both for the preservation of the fruit and of the stock itself; for those sometimes warming, sometimes cooling it, the seasons creep on by degrees, and do not assault it with all their violence at once. But now the flower, whilst it is on the plant, is of no profit at all, unless we use it to delight our nose with the admirable smell, and to please our eyes when it opens that inimitable variety of colors. And therefore, when the leaves are plucked off, the plants as it were suffer injury and grief. There is a kind of an ulcer raised, and an unbecoming nakedness attends them; and we must not only (as Empedocles says)

> *By all means spare the leaves that grace the palm,*

but likewise of all other trees, and not injuriously against Nature robbing them of their leaves, bring deformity on them to adorn ourselves. But to pluck the flowers doth no injury at all. It is like gathering of grapes at the time of vintage; unless plucked when ripe, they wither of themselves and fall. And therefore, like the barbarians who clothe themselves with the skins more commonly than with the wool of sheep, those that wreathe leaves rather than flowers into garlands seem to me to use the plants neither according to the dictates of reason nor the design of Nature. And thus much I say in defence of those who sell chaplets of flowers; for I am not grammarian enough to remember those poems which tell us that the old conquerors in the sacred games were crowned with flowers. Yet, now I think of it, there is a story of a rosy crown that belongs to the Muses; Sappho mentions it in a copy of verses to a woman unlearned and unacquainted with the Muses:–

> *Thou shalt unregarded lie*
> *Cause ne'er acquainted with the Muses' Rose.*
> *(From Sappho, Frag. 68.)*

But if Trypho can produce anything to our advantage from physic, pray let us have it.

Then Trypho taking the discourse said: The ancients were very curious and well acquainted with all these things, because plants were the chief ingredients of their physic. And of this some signs remain till now; for the Tyrians offer to Agenor, and the Magnesians to Chiron, the first supposed practitioners of physic, as the first fruits, the roots of those plants which have been successful on a patient. And Bacchus was not only counted a physician for finding wine, the most pleasing and most potent remedy, but for bringing ivy, the greatest opposite imaginable to wine, into reputation, and for teaching his drunken followers to wear garlands of it, that by that means they might be secured against the violence of a debauch, the heat of the liquor being remitted by the coldness of the ivy. Besides, the names of several plants sufficiently evidence the ancients curiosity in this matter; for they named the walnut-tree [Greek omitted], because it sends forth a heavy and [Greek omitted] drowsy spirit, which affects their heads who sleep beneath it; and the daffodil, [Greek omitted], because it benumbs the nerves and causes a stupid narcotic heaviness in the limbs, and therefore Sophocles calls it the ancient garland flower of the great (that is, the earthy) gods. And some say rue was called [Greek omitted] from its astringent quality; for, by its dryness preceding from its heat, it fixes [Greek omitted] or dries the seed, and is very hurtful to great-bellied women. But those that imagine the herb amethyst [Greek omitted], and the precious stone of the same name, are called so because powerful against the force of wine are much mistaken; for both receive there names from their color; for its leaf is not of the color of strong wine, but resembles that of weak diluted liquor. And indeed I could mention a great many which have their names from their proper virtues. But the care and the experience of the ancients sufficiently appears in those of which they made their garlands when they designed to be merry and frolic over a glass of wine; for wine, especially when it seizes on the head, and weakens the body just at the very spring and origin of the sense, disturbs the whole man. Now the effluvia of flowers are an admirable preservative against this, they secure the brain, as it were a citadel, against the effects of drunkenness; for those that are hot upon the pores and give the fumes free passage to exhale, and those moderately cold repel and keep down the ascending vapors. Such are the violet and rose; for the odors of both these are prevalent against any ache and heaviness in the head. The flowers of the privet and crocus bring those that have drunk freely into a gentle sleep; for they send forth a smooth and gentle effluvia, which softly takes off all asperities that arise in the body of the drunken; and so all things being quiet and composed, the violence on the noxious humor is abated and thrown off. The smells of some flowers being received into the brain cleanse the organs and instruments of sense, and gently by their heat, without any violence or force, dissolve the humors, and warm and cherish the brain itself, which is naturally cold. And upon this account, they call those little posies they hang about their necks [Greek omitted], and anointed their breasts with the oils that were squeezed from them; and of this Alcaeus is a witness, when he bids his friends,

> Pour ointments o'er his laboring temples, pressed
> With various cares, and o'er his aged breast.

For the warm odors shoot upward into the very brain, being drawn up by the nostrils. For they did not call those garlands hung about the neck [Greek omitted] because they thought the heart was the seat and citadel of the mind [Greek omitted], for on that account they should rather have called them [Greek omitted], but, as I said before, from their vapor and exhalation. Besides, it is no strange thing that these smells of garlands should be of so considerable a virtue; for some tell us that the shadow of the yew, especially when it blossoms, kills those that sleep under it; and a subtle spirit ariseth from pressed poppy, which suddenly overcomes the unwary squeezers. And there is an herb called alyssus, which to some that take it in their hands, to others that do but look on it, is found a present remedy against the hiccough; and some affirm that planted near the stalls it preserves sheep and goats from the rot and mange. And the rose is called [Greek omitted], probably because it sends forth a stream [Greek omitted] of odors; and for that reason it withers presently. It is a cooler, yet fiery to look upon; and no wonder, for upon the surface a subtile heat, being driven out by the inward heat, looks vivid and appears.

QUESTION II. WHETHER IVY IS OF A HOT OR COLD NATURE. AMMONIUS, TRYPHO, ERATO.

Upon this discourse, when we all hummed Trypho, Ammonius with a smile said: It is not decent by any contradiction to pull in pieces, like a chaplet, this various and florid discourse of Trypho's. Yet methinks the ivy is a little oddly interwoven, and unjustly said by its cold powers to temper the heat of strong wine; for it is rather fiery and hot, and its berries steeped in wine make the liquor more apt to inebriate and inflame. And from this cause, as in sticks warped by the fire, proceeds the crookedness of the boughs. And snow, that for many days will lie on other trees, presently melts from the branches of the ivy, and wastes all around, as far as the warmth reaches. But the greatest evidence is this. Theophrastus tells us, that when Alexander commanded Harpalus to plant some Grecian trees in the Babylonian gardens, and–because the climate is very hot and the sun violent–such as were leafy, thick, and fit to make a shade, the ivy only would not grow; though all art and diligence possible were used, it withered and died. For being hot itself, it could not agree with the fiery nature of the soil; for excess in similar qualities is destructive, and therefore we see everything as it were affects its contrary; a cold plant flourishes in a hot ground, and a hot plant is delighted with a cold. Upon which account it is that bleak mountains, exposed to cold winds and snow, bear firs, pines, and the like, full of pitch, fiery, and excellent to make a torch. But besides, Trypho, trees of a cold nature, their little feeble heat not being able to diffuse itself but retiring to the heart, shed their leaves; but their natural oiliness and warmth preserve the laurel, olive, and cypress always green; and the like too in the ivy may be observed. And therefore it is not likely our dear friend Bacchus, who called wine [Greek omitted] intoxicating and himself [Greek omitted], should bring ivy into reputation for being a preservative against drunkenness and an enemy to wine. But in my opinion, as lovers of wine, when they have not any juice of the grape ready, drink ale, mead, cider, or the like; thus he that in winter would have a vine-garland on his head, and finding the vine naked and without leaves, used the ivy that is like it; for its boughs are twisted and irregular, its leaves moist and disorderly confused, but chiefly the berries, like ripening clusters, make an exact representation of the vine. But grant the ivy to be a preservative against drunkenness,–that to please you, Trypho, we may name Bachus a physician,–still I affirm that power to proceed from its heat, which either opens the pores or helps to digest the wine.

Upon this Trypho sat silent, studying for an answer. Erato addressing himself to us youths, said: Trypho wants your assistance; help him in this dispute about the garlands, or be content to sit without any. Ammonius too bade us not be afraid, for he would not reply to any of our discourses; and Trypho likewise urging me to propose something, I said: To demonstrate that the ivy is cold is not so proper a task for me as Trypho, for he often useth coolers and binders; but that proposition, that wine in which ivy berries have been is more inebriating, is not true; for that disturbance which it raiseth in those that drink it is not so properly called drunkenness as alienation of mind or madness, such as hyoscyamus and a thousand other things that set men beside themselves usually produce. The crookedness of the bough is no argument at all, for such violent and unnatural effects cannot be supposed to proceed from any natural quality or power. Now sticks are bent by the fire, because that draws the moisture, and so the crookedness is a violent distortion; but the natural heat nourishes and preserves the body. Consider, therefore, whether it is not the weakness and coldness of the body that makes it wind, bend, and creep upon the ground; for those qualities check its rise, and depress it in its ascent, and render it like a weak traveller, that often sits down and then goes on again. And therefore the ivy requires something to twine about, and needs a prop; for it is not able to sustain and direct its own branches, because it wants heat, which naturally tends upward. The snow is melted by the wetness of the leaf, for water destroys it easily, passing through the thin contexture, it being nothing but a congeries of small bubbles; and therefore in very cold but moist places the snow melts as soon as in hot. That it is continually green doth not proceed from its heat, for to shed its leaves doth not argue the coldness of a tree. Thus the myrtle and well fern, though not hot, but confessedly cold, are green all the year. Some imagine this comes from the equal and duly proportioned mixture of the qualities in the leaf, to which Empedocles hath added a certain aptness of pores, through which the nourishing juice is orderly transmitted, so that there is still supply sufficient. But now it is otherwise in trees whose leaves fall, by reason of the wideness of their higher and narrowness of their lower pores; for the latter do not send juice enough, nor do the former keep it, but as soon as a small stock is received pour it out. This may be illustrated from the usual watering of our gardens; for when the distribution is unequal, the plants that are always watered have nourishment enough, seldom wither, and look always green. But you further argue, that being planted in Babylon it would not grow. It was well done of the plant, methinks, being a particular friend and familiar of the Boeotian god, to scorn to live amongst the barbarians, or imitate Alexander in following the manners of those nations; but it was not its heat but cold that was the cause of this aversion, for that could not agree with the contrary quality. For one similar quality doth not destroy but cherish another. Thus dry ground bears thyme, though it is naturally hot. Now at Babylon they say the air is so suffocating, so intolerably hot, that many of the more prosperous sleep upon skins full of water, that they may lie cool.

QUESTION III. WHY WOMEN ARE HARDLY, OLD MEN EASILY,
FOXED. FLORUS, SYLLA.

Florus thought it strange that Aristotle in his discourse of Drunkenness, affirming that old men are easily, women hardly, overtaken, did
not assign the cause, since he seldom failed on such occasions. Therefore he proposed it to us (we were a great many acquaintance met at
supper) as a fit subject for our inquiry. Sylla began: One part will conduce to the discovery of the other; and if we rightly hit the cause in
relation to the women, the difficulty, as it concerns the old men, will be
easily despatched; for their two natures are quite contrary. Moistness,
smoothness, and softness belong to the one; and dryness, roughness,
and hardness are the accidents of the other. As for women, I think the
principal cause is the moistness of their temper; this produceth a softness in the flesh, a shining smoothness, and their usual purgations. Now
when wine is mixed with a great deal of weak liquor, it is overpowered
by that, loses its strength, and becomes flat and waterish. Some reason
likewise may be drawn from Aristotle himself; for he affirms that those
that drink fast, and take a large draught without drawing breath, are
seldom overtaken, because the wine doth not stay long in their bodies,
but having acquired an impetus by this greedy drinking, suddenly runs
through; and women are generally observed to drink after that manner. Besides, it is probable that their bodies, by reason of the continual
deduction of the moisture in order to their usual purgations, are very
porous, and divided as it were into many little pipes and conduits; into
which when the wine falls, it is quickly conveyed away, and doth not
lie and fret the principal parts, from whose disturbance drunkenness
proceeds. But that old men want the natural moisture, even the name
[Greek omitted], in my opinion, intimates; for that name was given them
not as stooping to the earth [Greek omitted] but as being in the habit of
their body [Greek omitted] and [Greek omitted], earthlike and earthy.
Besides, the stiffness and roughness prove the dryness of their nature.
Therefore it is probable that, when they drink, their body, being grown
spongy by the dryness of its nature, soaks up the wine, and that lying in
the vessels it affects the senses and prevents the natural motions. For as
floods of water glide over the close grounds, nor make them slabby, but
quickly sink into the open and chapped fields; thus wine, being sucked
in by the dry parts, lies and works in the bodies of old men. But besides,
it is easy to observe, that age of itself hath all the symptoms of drunkenness. These symptoms everybody knows; viz., shaking of the joints,
faltering of the tongue, babbling, passion, forgetfulness, and distraction
of the mind; many of which being incident to old men, even whilst they

are well and in perfect health, are heightened by any little irregularity and accidental debauch. So that drunkenness doth not beget in old men any new and proper symptoms, but only intend and increase the common ones. And an evident sign of this is, that nothing is so like an old man as a young man drunk.

QUESTION IV. WHETHER THE TEMPER OF WOMEN IS COLDER OR HOTTER THAN THAT OF MEN. APOLLONIDES, ATHRYILATUS.

Thus Sylla said, and Apollonides the marshal subjoined: Sir, what you discoursed of old men I willingly admit; but in my opinion you have omitted a considerable reason in relation to the women, viz., the coldness of their temper, which quencheth the heat of the strongest wine, and makes it lose all its destructive force and fire. This reflection seeming reasonable, Athryilatus the Thasian, a physician, kept us from a hasty conclusion in this matter, by saying that some supposed the female sex was not cold, but hotter than the male; and others thought wine rather cold than hot.

When Florus seemed surprised at this discourse, Athryilatus continued: Sir, what I mention about wine I shall leave to this man to make out (pointing to me, for a few days before we had handled the same matter). But that women are of a hot constitution, some suppose, may be proved, first, from their smoothness, for their heat wastes all the superfluous nourishment which breeds hair; secondly from their abundance of blood, which seems to be the fountain and source of all the heat that is in the body;–now this abounds so much in females, that they would be all on fire, unless relieved by frequent and sudden evacuations. Thirdly, from a usual practice of the sextons in burning the bodies of the dead, it is evident that females are hotter than males; for the bedsmen are wont to put one female body with ten males upon the same pile, for that contains some inflammable and oily parts, and serves for fuel to the rest. Besides, if that that is soonest fit for generation is hottest, and a maid begins to be furious sooner than a boy, this is a strong proof of the hotness of the female sex. But a more convincing proof follows: women endure cold better than men, they are not so sensible of the sharpness of the weather, and are contented with a few clothes.

And Florus replied: Methinks, sir, from the same topics I could draw conclusions against your assertion. For, first, they endure cold better, because one similar quality doth not so readily act upon another; and then again, their seed is not active in generation, but passive matter and nourishment to that which the male injects. But more, women grow effete sooner than men; that they burn better than the males proceeds from their fat, which is the coldest part of the body; and young men, or such as use exercise, have but little fat. Their monthly purgations do not prove the abundance, but the corruption and badness, of their blood; for being the superfluous and undigested part, and having no convenient vessel in the body it flows out, and appears languid and feculent, by reason of the weakness of its heat. And the shivering that seizes them at the time of their purgations sufficiently proves that which flows from them is cold and undigested. And who will believe their smoothness to be an effect of heat rather than cold, when everybody knows that the hottest parts of a body are the most hairy? For all such excrements are thrust out by the heat, which opens and makes passages through the skin; but smoothness is a consequent of that closeness of the superficies which proceeds from condensing cold. And that the flesh of women is closer than that of men, you may be informed by those that lie with women that have anointed themselves with oil or other perfumes; for though they do not touch the women, yet they find themselves perfumed, their bodies by reason of their heat and rarity drawing the odor to them. But I think we have disputed plausibly and sufficiently of this matter....

QUESTION V. WHETHER WINE IS POTENTIALLY COLD. ATHRYILATUS, PLUTARCH.

But now I would fain know upon what account you can imagine that wine is cold. Then, said I, do you believe this to be my opinion? Yes, said he, whose else? And I replied: I remember a good while ago I met with a discourse of Aristotle's upon this very question. And Epicurus, in his Banquet, hath a long discourse, the sum of which is that wine of itself is not hot, but that it contains some atoms that cause heat, and others that cause cold; now, when it is taken into the body, it loses one sort of particles and takes the other out of the body itself, as it agrees with one's nature and constitution; so that some when they are drunk are very hot, and others very cold.

This way of talking, said Florus, leads us by Protagoras directly to Pyrrho; for it is evident that, suppose we were to discourse of oil, milk, honey, or the like, we shall avoid all inquiry into their particular natures by saying that things are so and so by their mutual mixture with one another. But how do you prove that wine is cold? And I, being forced to speak extempore, replied: By two arguments. The first I draw from the practice of physicians, for when their patients' stomachs grow very weak, they prescribe no hot things, and yet give them wine as an excellent remedy. Besides, they stop looseness and immoderate sweating by wine; and this shows that they think it more binding and constipating than snow itself. Now if it were potentially hot, I should think it as wise a thing to apply fire to snow as wine to the stomach.

Again, most teach that sleep proceeds from the coolness of the parts; and most of the narcotic medicines, as mandrake and opium, are coolers. Those indeed work violently, and forcibly condense, but wine cools by degrees; it gently stops the motion, according as it hath more or less of such narcotic qualities. Besides, heat has a generative power; for owing to heat the fluid flows easily and the vital spirit gets vigor and a stimulating force. Now the great drinkers are very dull, inactive fellows, no women's men at all; they eject nothing strong, vigorous, and fit for generation, but are weak and unperforming, by reason of the bad digestion and coldness of their seed. And it is farther observable that the effects of cold and drunkenness upon men's bodies are the same,–trembling, heaviness, paleness, shivering, faltering of tongue, numbness, and cramps. In many, a debauch ends in a dead palsy, when the wine stupefies and extinguisheth all the heat. And the physicians use this method in curing the qualms and diseases gotten by debauch; at night they cover them well and keep them warm; and at day they annoint and bathe, and give them such food as shall not disturb, but by degrees recover the heat which the wine hath scattered and driven out of the body. Thus, I added, in these appearances we trace obscure qualities and powers; but as for drunkenness, it is easily known what it is. For, in my opinion, as I hinted before, those that are drunk are very much like old men; and therefore great drinkers grow old soonest, and they are commonly bald and gray before their time; and all these accidents certainly proceed from want of heat. But mere vinegar is of a vinous nature, and nothing quenches fire so soon as that; its extreme coldness overcomes and kills the flame presently. And of all fruits physicians use the vinous as the greatest coolers, as pomegranates and apples. Besides, do they not make wine by mixing honey with rain-water or snow; for the cold, because those two qualities are near akin, if it prevails, changes the luscious into a poignant taste? And did not the ancients of all the creeping beasts consecrate the snake to Bacchus, and of all the plants the ivy, because they were of a cold and frozen nature? Now, lest any one should think this is a proof of its heat, that if a man takes juice of hemlock, a large dose of wine cures him, I shall, on the contrary affirm that wine and hemlock juice mixed is an incurable poison, and kills him that drinks it presently. So that we can no more conclude it to be hot because it resists, than to be cold because it assists, the poison. For cold is the only quality by which hemlock juice works and kills.

QUESTION VI. WHICH IS THE FITTEST TIME FOR A MAN TO KNOW HIS WIFE? YOUTHS, ZOPYRUS, OLYMPICHUS, SOCLARUS.

Some young students, that had not gone far in the learning of the ancients, inveighed against Epicurus for bringing in, in his Svmposium, an impertinent and unseemly discourse, about what time was best to lie with a woman; for an old man at supper in the company of youths to talk of such a subject, and dispute whether after or before supper was the most convenient time, argued him to be a very loose and debauched man. To this some said that Xenophon, after his entertainment was ended, sent all his guests home on horseback, to lie with their wives. But Zopyrus the physician, a man very well read in Epicurus, said, that they had not duly weighed that piece; for he did not propose that question first, and then discuss that matter on purpose; but after supper he desired the young men to take a walk, and he then discoursed on it, that he might persuade them to continence, and to abate their desires and restrain their appetites; showing them that it was very dangerous at all times, but especially after they had been eating or making merry. But suppose he had proposed this as the chief topic for discourse, doth it never become a philosopher to inquire which is the convenient and proper time? Ought we not to time it well, and direct our embrace by reason? Or may such discourse be otherwise allowed, and must they be thought unseemly problems to be proposed at table? Indeed I am of another mind. It is true, I should blame a philosopher that in the middle of the day, in the schools, before all sorts of men, should discourse of such a subject; but over a glass of wine between friends and acquaintance, when it is necessary to propose something beside dull, serious discourse, why should it be a fault to hear or speak anything that may inform our judgments or direct our practice in such matters? And I protest I had rather that Zeno had inserted his loose topics in some merry discourses and agreeable table-talk, than in such a grave, serious piece as his politics.

The youth, startled at this free declaration, sat silent; and the rest of the company desired Zopyrus to deliver Epicurus's sentiment. He said: The particulars I cannot remember; but I believe he feared the violent agitations of such exercises, because the bodies employed in them are so violently disturbed. For it is certain that wine is a very great disturber, and puts the body out of its usual temper; and therefore, when thus disquieted, if quiet and sleep do not compose it but other agitations seize it, it is likely that those parts which knit and join the members may be loosened, and the whole frame be as it were unsettled from its foundation and overthrown. For then likewise the seed cannot freely pass, but is confusedly and forcibly thrown out, because the liquor hath filled the vessels of the body, and stopped its way. Therefore, says Epicurus, we must use those sports when the body is at quiet, when the meat hath been thoroughly digested, carried about and applied to several parts of the body, so that we begin to want a fresh supply of food. To this of Epicurus we might join an argument taken from physic. At daytime, while our digestion is performing, we are not so lusty nor eager to embrace; and presently after supper to endeavor it is dangerous, for the crudity of the stomach, the food being yet undigested, may be disorderly motion upon this crudity, and so the mischief be double. Olympicus, continuing the discourse, said: I very much like what Clinias the Pythagorean delivers. For the story goes that, being asked when a man should lie with a woman, he replied, when he hath a mind to receive the greatest mischief that he can. For Zopyrus's discourse seems rational, and other times as well as those he mentions have their peculiar inconveniences. And therefore,–as Thales the philosopher, to free himself from the pressing solicitations of his mother who advised him to marry, said at first, 'tis not yet time; and when, now he was growing old, she repeated her admonition, replied, nor is it now time,–so it is best for every man to have the same mind in relation to those sports of Venus; when he goes to bed, let him say, 'tis not yet time; and when he rises, 'tis not now time.

What you say, Olympicus, said Soclarus interposing, befits wrestlers indeed; it smells, methinks, of their meals of flesh and casks of wine, but is not suitable to the resent company, for there are some young married men here,

Whose duty 'tis to follow Venus' sports.

Nay, we ourselves seem to have some relation to Venus still, when in our hymns to the gods we pray thus to her,

Fair Venus, keep off feeble age.

But waiving this, let us inquire (if you think fit) whether Epicurus does well, when contrary to all right and equity he separates Venus and the Night, though Menander, a man well skilled in love matters, says that she likes her company better than that of any of the gods. For, in my opinion, night is a very convenient veil, spread over those that give themselves to that kind of pleasure; for it is not fit that day should be the time, lest modesty should be banished from our eyes, effeminacy grow bold, and such vigorous impressions on our memories be left, as might still possess us with the same fancies and raise new inclinations. For the sight (according to Plato) receives a more vigorous impression than any other bodily organ, and joining with the imagination, that lies near it, works presently upon the soul, and ever causes fresh desires by those images of pleasure which it brings. But the night, hiding many and the most furious of the actions, quiets and lulls nature, and doth not suffer it to be carried to intemperance by the eye. But besides this, how absurd is it, that a man returning from an entertainment merry perhaps and jocund, crowned and perfumed, should cover himself up, turn his back to his wife, and go to sleep; and then at day-time, in the midst of his business, send for her out of her apartment to serve his pleasure or in the morning, as a cock treads his hens. No, sir the evening is the end of our labor, and the morning the beginning. Bacchus the Loosener and Terpsichore and Thalia preside over the former; and the latter raiseth us up betimes to attend on Minerva the Work-mistress, and Mercury the merchandiser. And therefore songs, dances, and epithalamiums, merry-meetings, with balls and feasts, and sounds of pipes and flutes, are the entertainment of the one; but in the other, nothing but the noise of hammers and anvils, the scratching of saws, the city cries, citations to court or to attend this or that prince and magistrate are heard.

> *Then all the sports of pleasure disappear,*
> *Then Venus, then gay youth removes:*
> *No Thyrsus then which Bacchus loves;*
> *But all is clouded and o'erspread with care.*

Besides, Homer makes not one of the heroes lie with his wife or mistress in the day-time, but only Paris, who, having shamefully fled from the battle, sneaked into the embraces of his wife; intimating that such lasciviousness by day did not befit the sober temper of a man, but the mad lust of an adulterer. But, moreover, the body will not (as Epicurus fancies) be injured more after supper than at any other time, unless a man be drunk or overcharged,–for in those cases, no doubt, it is very dangerous and hurtful. But if a man is only raised and cheered, not overpowered by liquor, if his body is pliable, his mind agreeing, and then he sports, he need not fear any disturbance from the load he has within him; he need not fear catching cold, or too great a transportation of atoms, which Epicurus makes the cause of all the ensuing harm. For if he lies quiet he will quickly fill again, and new spirits will supply the vessels that are emptied.

But this is to be especially taken care of, that, the body being then in a ferment and disturbed, no cares of the soul, no business about necessary affairs, no labor, should distract and seize it, lest they should corrupt and sour its humors, Nature not having had time enough for settling what has been disturbed. For, sir, all men have not the command of that happy ease and tranquillity which Epicurus's philosophy procured him; for many great incumbrances seize almost upon every one every day, or at least some disquiets; and it is not safe to trust the body with any of these, when it is in such a condition and disturbance, presently after the fury and heat of the embrace is over. Let, according to his opinion, the happy and immortal deity sit at ease and never mind us; but if we regard the laws of our country, we must not dare to enter into the temple and offer sacrifice, if but a little before we have done any such thing. It is fit therefore to let night and sleep intervene, and after there is a sufficient space of time past between, to rise as it were pure and new, and (as Democritus was wont to say) "with new thoughts upon the new day."

QUESTION VII. WHY NEW WINE DOTH NOT INEBRIATE AS SOON AS OTHER. PLUTARCH, HIS FATHER, HAGIAS, ARISTAE-NETUS, AND OTHER YOUTH.

At Athens on the eleventh day of February (thence called [Greek omitted] THE BARREL-OPENING), they began to taste their new wine; and in old times (as it appears), before they drank, they offered some to the gods, and prayed that that cordial liquor might prove good and wholesome. By us Thebans the month is named [Greek omitted], and it is our custom upon the sixth day to sacrifice to our good Genius and then taste our new wine, after the zephyr has done blowing; for that wind makes wine ferment more than any other, and the liquor that can bear this fermentation is of a strong body and will keep well. My father offered the usual sacrifice, and when after supper the young men, my fellow-students, commended the wine, he started this question: Why does not new wine inebriate as soon as other? This seemed a paradox and incredible to most of us; but Hagias said, that luscious things were cloying and would presently satiate, and therefore few could drink enough to make them drunk; for when once the thirst is allayed, the appetite would be quickly palled by that unpleasant liquor; for that a luscious is different from a sweet taste, even the poet intimates, when he says,

With luscious wine, and with sweet milk and cheese.
("Odyssey, xx. 69.)

Wine at first is sweet; afterward, as it grows old, it ferments and begins to be pricked a little; then it gets a sweet taste.

Aristaenetus the Nicaean said, that he remembered he had read somewhere that sweet things mixed with wine make it less heady, and that some physicians prescribe to one that hath drunk freely, before he goes to bed, a crust of bread dipped in honey. And therefore, if sweet mixtures weaken strong wine, it is reasonable that wine should not be heady till it hath lost its sweetness.

We admired the acuteness of the young philosophers, and were well pleased to see them propose something out of the common road and give us their own sentiments on this matter. Now the common and obvious reason is the heaviness of new wine,–which (as Aristotle says) violently presseth the stomach,–or the abundance of airy and watery parts that lie in it; the former of which, as soon as they are pressed, fly out; and the watery parts are naturally fit to weaken the spirituous liquor. Now, when it grows old, the juice is improved, and though by the separation of the watery parts it loses in quantity, it gets in strength.

QUESTION VIII. WHY DO THOSE THAT ARE STARK DRUNK SEEM NOT SO MUCH DEBAUCHED AS THOSE THAT ARE BUT HALF FOXED? PLUTARCH, HIS FATHER.

Well then, said my father, since we have fallen upon Aristotle, I will endeavor to propose something of my own concerning those that are half drunk; for, in my mind, though he was a very acute man, he is not accurate enough in such matters. They usually say, I think, that a sober man's understanding apprehends things right and judges well; the sense of one quite drunk is weak and enfeebled; but of him that is half drunk the fancy is vigorous and the understanding weakened, and therefore, following their own fancies, they judge, but judge ill. But pray, sirs, what is your opinion in these matters?

This reason, I replied, would satisfy me upon a private disquisition; but if you will have my own sentiments, let us first consider, whether this difference doth not proceed from the different temper of the body. For of those that are only half drunk, the mind alone is disturbed, but the body not being quite overwhelmed is yet able to obey its motions; but when it is too much oppressed and the wine has overpowered it, it betrays and frustrates the motions of the mind, for men in such a condition never go so far as action. But those that are half drunk, having a body serviceable to the absurd motions of the mind, are rather to be thought to have greater ability to comply with those they have, than to have worse inclinations than the others. Now if, proceeding on another principle, we consider the strength of the wine itself, nothing hinders but that this may be different and changeable, according to the quantity that is drunk. As fire, when moderate, hardens a piece of clay, but if very strong, makes it brittle and crumble into pieces; and the heat of the spring fires our blood with fevers but as the summer comes on, the disease usually abates; what hinders then but that the mind, being naturally raised by the power of the wine, when it is come to a pitch, should by pouring on more be weakened again and its force abated? Thus hellebore, before it purges, disturbs the body; but if too small a dose be given, disturbs only and purges not at all; and some taking too little of an opiate are more restless than before; and some taking too much sleep well. Besides, it is probable that this disturbance into which those that are half drunk are put, when it comes to a pitch, leads to that decay. For a great quantity being taken inflames the body and consumes the frenzy of the mind; as a mournful song and melancholy music at a funeral raises grief at first and forces tears, but as it continues, by little and little it takes away all dismal apprehensions and consumes our sorrows. Thus wine, after it hath heated and disturbed, calms the mind again and quiets the frenzy; and when men are dead drunk, their passions are at rest.

QUESTION IX. WHAT IS THE MEANING OF THE SAYING: DRINK EITHER FIVE OR THREE, BUT NOT FOUR? ARISTO, PLUTARCH, PLUTARCH'S FATHER.

When I had said these things Aristo, as his habit was, cried out: A return has been decreed in banquets to a very popular and just standard, which, because it was driven away by unseasonable temperance as if by the act of a tyrant, has long remained in exile. For just as those trained in the canons of the lyre declare the sesquialter proportion produces the symphony diapente, the double proportion the diapason, the sesquiterte the diatessaron, the slowest of all, so the specialists in Bacchic harmonies have detected three accords between wine and water–Diapente, Diatrion, Diatessaron. For so they speak and sing, "drink five or three, but not four." For five have the sesquialter proportion, three cups of water being mixed in two of wine; three, the double proportion, two being mixed with one; four, the sesquiterce, three cups of water to one of wine, which is the epitrite proportion for those exercising their minds in the council-chamber or frowning over dialectics, when changes of speeches are expected,–a sober and mild mixture. But in regard to those proportions of two to one, that mixture gives the strength by which we are confused and made half drunk, "Exciting the chords of the soul never moved before." For it does not admit of sobriety, nor does it induce the senselessness of pure wine. The most harmonious is the proportion of two to three, provoking sleep, generating the forgetfulness of cares, and like that cornfield of Hesiod, "which mildly pacifieth children and heals injuries." It composes in us the harsh and irregular motions of the soul and secures deep peace for it. Against these sayings of Aristo no one had anything to offer in reply, since it was quite evident he was jesting. I suggested to him to take a cup and treat it as a lyre, tuning it to the harmony and order he praised. At the same time a slave came offering him pure wine. But he refused it, saying with a laugh that he was discussing logical not organic music. To what had been said before my father added that Jove seemed to have taken, according to the ancients, two nurses, Ite and Adrastea; Juno one, Euboea; Apollo also two, Truth and Corythalea; but Bacchus several, because he needed several measures of water to make him manageable, trained, milder, and more prudent.

QUESTION X. WHY FLESH STINKS SOONER WHEN EXPOSED TO THE MOON, THAN TO THE SUN. EUTHYDEMUS, SATYRUS.

Euthydemus of Sunium gave us at an entertainment a very large boar. The guests wondering at the bigness of the beast, he said that he had one a great deal larger, but in the carriage the moon had made it stink; he could not imagine how this should happen, for it was probable that the sun, being much hotter than the moon, should make it stink sooner. But, said Satyrus, this is not so strange as the common practice of the hunters; for, when they send a boar or a doe to a city some miles distant, they drive a brazen nail into it to keep it from stinking.

After supper Euthydemus bringing the question into play again, Moschio the physician said, that putrefaction was a colliquation of the flesh, and that everything that putrefied grew moister than before, and that all heat, if gentle, did stir the humors, though not force them out, but if strong, dry the flesh; and that from these considerations an answer to the question might be easily deduced. For the moon gently warming makes the body moist; but the sun by his violent beams dries rather, and draws all moisture from them. Thus Archilochus spoke like a naturalist,

I hope hot Sirius's beams will many drain,

And Homer more plainly concerning Hector, over whose body Apollo spread a thick cloud,

Lest the hot sun should scorch his naked limbs.
(Iliad, xxiii, 190.)

Now the moon's rays are weaker; for, as Ion says,
    They do not ripen well the clustered grapes.

When he had done, I said: The rest of the discourse I like very well, but I cannot consent when you ascribe this effect to the strength and degree of heat, and chiefly in the hot seasons; for in winter every one knows that the sun warms little, yet in summer it putrefies most. Now the contrary should happen, if the gentleness of the heat were the cause of putrefaction. And besides, the hotter the season is, so much the sooner meat stinks; and therefore this effect is not to be ascribed to the want of heat in the moon, but to some particular proper quality in her beams. For heat is not different only by degrees; but in fires there are some proper qualities very much unlike one another, as a thousand obvious instances will prove. Goldsmiths heat their gold in chaff fires; physicians use fires of vine-twigs in their distillations; and tamarisk is the best fuel for a glass-house. Olive-boughs in a chimney warm very well, but hurt other baths: they spoil the plastering, and weaken the foundation; and therefore the most skilful of the public officers forbid those that rent the baths to burn olive-tree wood, or throw darnel seed into the fire, because the fumes of it dizzy and bring the headache to those that bathe. Therefore it is no wonder that the moon differs in her qualities from the sun; and that the sun should shed some drying, and the moon some dissolving, influence upon flesh. And upon this account it is that nurses are very cautious of exposing their infants to the beams of the moon; for they being full of moisture, as green plants, are easily wrested and distorted. And everybody knows that those that sleep abroad under the beams of the moon are not easily waked, but seem stupid and senseless; for the moisture that the moon sheds upon them oppresses their faculty and disables their bodies. Besides, it is commonly said, that women brought to bed when the moon is a fort-night old, have easy labors; and for this reason I believe that Diana, which was the same with the moon, was called the goddess of child-birth. And Timotheus appositely says,
    By the blue heaven that wheels the stars,
    And by the moon that eases women's pains.

Even in inanimate bodies the power of the moon is very evident. For trees that are cut in the full of the moon carpenters refuse, as being soft, and, by reason of their moistness, subject to corruption; and in its wane farmers usually thresh their wheat, that being dry it may better endure the flail; for the corn in the full of the moon is moist, and commonly bruised in threshing. Besides, they say dough will be leavened sooner in the full, for then, though the leaven is scarce proportioned to the meal, yet it rarefies and leavens the whole lump. Now when flesh putrefies, the combining spirit is only changed into a moist consistence, and the parts of the body separate and dissolve. And this is evident in the very air itself, for when the moon is full, most dew falls; and this Alcman the poet intimates, when he somewhere calls dew the air's and moon's daughter, saying,

> See how the daughter of the Moon and Air
> Does nourish all things.

Thus a thousand instances do prove that the light of the moon is moist, and carries with it a softening and corrupting quality. Now the brazen nail that is driven through the flesh, if, as they say, it keeps the flesh from putrefying, doth it by an astringent quality proper to the brass. The rust of brass physicians use in astringent medicines, and they say those that dig brass ore have been cured of a rheum in their eyes, and that the hair upon their eyelids hath grown again; for the particles rising from the ore, being insensibly applied to the eyes, stops the rheum and dries up the humor, and upon this account, perhaps; Homer calls brass [Greek omitted] and [Greek omitted], and Aristotle says, that wounds made by a brazen dart or a brazen sword are less painful and sooner cured than those that are made of iron weapons, because brass hath something medicinal in itself, which in the very instant is applied to the wound. Now it is manifest that astringents are contrary to putrefying, and healing to corrupting qualities. Some perhaps may say, that the nail being driven through draws all the moisture to itself, for the humor still flows to the part that is hurt; and therefore it is said that by the nail there always appears some speck and tumor; and therefore it is rational that the other parts should remain sound, when all the corruption gathers about that.

Book Four

POLYBIUS, MY SOSSIUS Senecio, advised Scipio Africanus never to return from the Forum, where he was conversant about the affairs of
the city, before he had gained one new friend. Where I suppose the
word friend is not to be taken too nicely, to signify a lasting and unchangeable acquaintance; but, as it vulgarly means, a well-wisher, and
as Dicearchus takes it, when he says that we should endeavor to make
all men well-wishers, but only good men friends. For friendship is to
be acquired by time and virtue; but good-will is produced by a familiar
intercourse, or by mirth and trifling amongst civil and genteel men, especially if opportunity assists their natural inclinations to good-nature.
But consider whether this advice may not be accommodated to an entertainment as well as the Forum; so that we should not break up the
meeting before we had gained one of the company to be a well-wisher
and a friend. Other occasions draw men into the Forum, but men of
sense come to an entertainment as well to get new friends as to make
their old ones merry; indeed, to carry away anything else is sordid and
uncivil, but to depart with one friend more than we had is pleasing and
commendable. And so, on the contrary, he that doth not aim at this
renders the meeting useless and unpleasant to himself, and departs at
last, having been a partaker of an entertainment with his belly but not
with his mind. For he that makes one at a feast doth not come only to
enjoy the meat and drink, but likewise the discourse, mirth, and genteel
humor which ends at last in friendship and good-will. The wrestlers,
that they may hold fast and lock better, use dust; and so wine mixed
with discourse is of extraordinary use to make us hold fast of, and fasten upon, a friend. For wine tempered with discourse carries gentle and
kind affections out of the body into the mind; otherwise, it is scattered
through the limbs, and serves only to swell and disturb. Thus as a marble, by cooling red hot iron, takes away its softness and makes it hard,

fit to be wrought and receive impression; thus discourse at an entertainment doth not permit the men that are engaged to become altogether liquid by the wine, but confines and makes their jocund and obliging tempers very fit to receive an impression from the seal of friendship if dexterously applied.

QUESTION I. WHETHER DIFFERENT SORTS OF FOOD, OR ONE SINGLE DISH FED UPON AT ONCE, IS MORE EASILY DIGESTED. PHILO, PLUTARCH, MARCION.

The first question of my fourth decade of Table Discourses shall be concerning different sorts of food eaten at one meal. When we came to Hyampolis at the feast called Elaphebolia, Philo the physician gave us a very sumptuous entertainment; and seeing a boy who came with Philinus feeding upon dry bread and calling for nothing else, he cried out, O Hercules, well I see the proverb is verified,

They fought midst stones, but could not take up one,

and presently went out to fetch him some agreeable food. He stayed some time, and at last brought them dried figs and cheese; upon which I said: It is usually seen that those that provide costly and superfluous dainties neglect, or are not well furnished with, useful and necessary things. I protest, said Philo, I did not mind that Philinus designs to breed us a young Sosastrus, who (they say) never all his lifetime drank or ate anything beside milk, although it is probable that it was some change in his constitution that made him use this sort of diet; but our Chiron here,–quite contrary to the old one that bred Achilles from his very birth,–feeding his son with unbloody food, gives people reason to suspect that like a grasshopper he keeps him on dew and air. Indeed, said Philinus, I did not know that we were to meet with a supper of a hundred beasts, such as Aristomenes made for his friends; otherwise I had come with some poor and wholesome food about me, as a specific against such costly and unwholesome entertainments. For I have often heard that simple diet is not only more easily provided, but likewise more easily digested, than such variety. At this Marcion said to Philo: Philinus hath spoiled your whole provision by deterring guests from eating; but, if you desire it, I will be surety for you, that such variety is more easily digested than simple food, so that without fear or distrust they may feed heartily. Philo desired him to do so.

When after supper we begged Philinus to discover what he had to urge against variety of food, he thus began: I am not the author of this opinion, but our friend Philo here is ever now and then telling us, first, that wild beasts, feeding on one sort only and simple diet, are much more healthy than men are; and that those which are kept in pens are much more subject to diseases and crudities, by reason of the prepared variety we usually give them. Secondly, no physician is so daring, so venturous at new experiments, as to give a feverish patient different sorts of food at once. No, simple food, and without sauce, as more easy to be digested, is the only diet they allow. Now food must be wrought on and altered by our natural powers; in dyeing, cloth of the most simple color takes the tincture soonest; the most inodorous oil is soonest by perfumes changed into an essence; and simple diet is soonest changed, and soonest yields to the digesting power. For many and different qualities, having some contrariety, when they meet disagree and corrupt one another; as in a city, a mixed rout are not easily reduced into one body, nor brought to follow the same concerns; for each works according to its own nature, and is very hardly brought to side with another's quality. Now this is evident in wine; mixed wine inebriates very soon, and drunkenness is much like a crudity rising from undigested wine; and therefore the drinkers hate mixed liquors, and those that do mix them do it privately, as afraid to have their design upon the company discovered. Every change is disturbing and injurious, and therefore musicians are very careful how they strike many strings at once; though the mixture and variety of the notes would be the only harm that would follow. This I dare say, that belief and assent can be sooner procured by disagreeing arguments, than concoction by various and different qualities. But lest I should seem jocose, waiving this, I will return to Philo's observations again. We have often heard him declare that it is the quality that makes meat hard to be digested; that to mix many things together is hurtful, and begets unnatural qualities; and that every man should take that which by experience he finds most agreeable to his temper.

Now if nothing is by its own nature hard to be digested, but it is the quantity that disturbs and corrupts, I think we have still greater reason to forbear that variety with which Philo's cook, as it were in opposition to his master's practice, would draw us on to surfeits and diseases. For by the different sorts of food and new ways of dressing, he still keeps up the unwearied appetite, and leads it from one dish to another, till tasting of everything we take more than is sufficient and enough; as Hypsipyle's foster-son,

> *Who, in a garden placed, plucked up the flowers,*
> *One after one, and spent delightful hours;*
> *But still his greedy appetite goes on,*
> *And still he plucked till all the flowers were gone.*
> *(From the "Hypsipyle" of Euripides, Frag. 754.)*

But more, methinks, Socrates is here to be remembered, who adviseth us to forbear those junkets which provoke those that are not hungry to eat; as if by this he cautioned us to fly variety of meats. For it is variety that in everything draws us on to use more than bare necessity requires. This is manifest in all sorts of pleasures, either of the eye, ear, or touch; for it still proposeth new provocatives; but in simple pleasures, and such as are confined to one sort, the temptation never carries us beyond nature's wants. In short, in my opinion, we should more patie musician praise a disagreeing variety of notes, or a perfumer mixed ointments, than a physician commend the variety of dishes; for certainly such changes and turnings as must necessarily ensue will force us out of the right way of health.

Philinus having ended his discourse, Marcion said: In my opinion, not only those that separate profit from honesty are obnoxious to Socrates's curse, but those also that separate pleasure from health, as if it were its enemy and opposite, and not its great friend and promoter. Pain we use but seldom and unwillingly, as the most violent instrument. But from all things else, none, though he would willingly, can remove pleasure. It still attends when we eat, sleep, bathe, or anoint, and takes care of and nurses the diseased; dissipating all that is hurtful and disagreeable, by applying that which is proper, pleasing, and natural. For what pain, what want, what poison so quickly and so easily cures a disease as seasonable bathing? A glass of wine, when a man wants it, or a dish of palatable meat, presently frees us from all disturbing particles, and settles nature in its proper state, there being as it were a calm and serenity spread over the troubled humors. But those remedies that are painful do hardly and by little and little only promote the cure, every difficulty pushing on and forcing Nature. And therefore let not Philinus blame us, if we do not make all the sail we can to fly from pleasure, but more diligently endeavor to make pleasure and health, than other philosophers do to make pleasure and honesty, agree. Now, in my opinion, Philinus, you seem to be out in your first argument, where you suppose the beasts use more simple food and are more healthy than men; neither of which is true. The first the goats in Eupolis confute, for they extol their pasture as full of variety and all sorts of herbs, in this manner,

> We feed almost on every kind of trees,
> Young firs, the ilex, and the oak we crop:
> Sweet trefoil fragrant juniper, and yew,
> Wild olives, thyme,–all freely yield their store.

These that I have mentioned are very different in taste, smell, and other qualities, and he reckons more sorts which I have omitted. The second Homer skilfully refutes, when he tells us that the plague first began amongst the beasts. Besides, the shortness of their lives proves that they are very subject to diseases; for there is scarce any irrational creature long lived, besides the crow and the chough; and those two every one knows do not confine themselves to simple food, but eat anything. Besides, you take no good rule to judge what is easy and what is hard of digestion from the diet of those that are sick; for labor and exercise, and even to chew our meat well, contribute very much to digestion, neither of which can agree with a man in a fever. Again, that the variety of meats, by reason of the different qualities of the particulars, should disagree and spoil one another, you have no reason to fear. For if Nature takes from dissimilar bodies what is fit and agreeable, the diverse nourishment forces many and sundry qualities into the mass and bulk of the body, applying to every part that which is meet and fit; so that, as Empedocles words it,

> *The sweet runs to the sweet, the sour combines*
> *With sour, the sharp with sharp, the salt with salt;*

and after being mixed it is spread through the mass by the heat, the proper parts are separated and applied to the proper members. Indeed, it is very probable that such bodies as ours, consisting of parts of different natures, should be nourished and built up rather of various than of simple matter. But if by concoction there is an alteration made in the food, this will be more easily performed when there are different sorts of meat, than when there is only one, in the stomach; for similars cannot work upon similars and the very contrariety in the mixture considerably promotes the alteration of the weakened qualities. But if, Philinus, you are against all mixture, do not chide Philo only for the variety of his dishes and sauces, but also for using mixture in his sovereign antidotes, which Erasistratus calls the gods' hands. Convince him of absurdity and vanity, when he mixes herbs, metals, and animals, and things from sea and land, in one potion; and recommend him to neglect these, and to confine all physic to barley-broth, gourds, and oil mixed with water. But you urge farther, that variety enticeth the appetite that hath no command over itself. That is, good sir, cleanly, wholesome, sweet, palatable, pleasing diet makes us eat and drink more than ordinary. Why then, instead of fine flour, do not we thicken our broth with coarse bran? And instead of asparagus, why do we not dress nettle-tops and thistles; and leaving this fragrant and pleasant wine, drink sour, harsh liquor that gnats have been buzzing about a long while? Because, perhaps you may reply, wholesome feeding doth not consist in a perfect avoiding of all that is pleasing, but in moderating the appetite in that respect, and making it prefer profit before pleasure. But, sir, as a mariner has a thousand ways to avoid a stiff gale of wind, but when it is clear down and a perfect calm, cannot raise it again; thus to correct and restrain our extravagant appetite is no hard matter, but when it grows weak and faint, when it fails as to its proper objects, then to raise it and make it vigorous and active again is, sir, a very difficult and hard task. And therefore variety of viands is as much better than simple food, which is apt to satisfy by being but of one sort, as it is easier to stop Nature when she makes too much speed than to force her on when languishing and faint. Besides, what some say, that fullness is more to be avoided than emptiness, is not true; but, on the contrary, fullness then only hurts when it ends in a surfeit or disease; but emptiness, though it doth no other mischief, is of itself unnatural. And let this suffice as an answer to what you proposed. But you sparing men have forgot, that variety is sweeter and more desired by the appetite, unless too sweet. For, the sight preparing the way, it is soon assimilated to the eager receiving body; but that which is not desirable Nature either throws off again, or keeps it in for mere want. But pray observe this, that I do not plead for variety in tarts, cakes, or custards;– those are vain, insignificant, and superfluous things;–but even Plato allowed variety to those fine citizens of his, setting before them onions, olives, leeks, cheese, and all sorts of meat and fish, and besides these, allowed them some comfits.

QUESTION II. WHY MUSHROOMS ARE THOUGHT TO BE PRODUCED BY THUNDER, AND WHY IT IS BELIEVED THAT MEN ASLEEP ARE NEVER THUNDERSTRUCK. AGEMACHUS, PLUTARCH, DOROTHEUS.

At a supper in Elis, Agemachus set before us very large mushrooms. And when all admired at them, one with a smile said, These are worthy the late thunder, as it were deriding those who imagine mushrooms are produced by thunder. Some said that thunder did split the earth, using the air as a wedge for that purpose, and that by those chinks those that sought after mushrooms were directed where to find them; and thence it grew a common opinion, that thunder engenders mushrooms, and not only makes them a passage to appear; as if one should imagine that a shower of rain breeds snails, and not rather makes them creep forth and be seen abroad. Agemachus stood up stiffly for the received opinion, and told us, we should not disbelieve it only because it was strange, for there are a thousand other effects of thunder and lightning and a thousand omens deduced from them, whose causes it is very hard, if not impossible, to discover; for this laughed-at, this proverbial mushroom doth not escape the thunder because it is so little, but because it hath some antipathetical qualities that preserve it from blasting; as likewise a fig-tree, the skin of a sea-calf (as they say), and that of the hyena, with which sailors cover the ends of their sails. And husbandmen call thunder-showers nourishing, and think them to be so. Indeed, it is absurd to wonder at these things, when we see the most incredible things imaginable in thunder, as flame rising out of moist vapors, and from soft clouds such astonishing noises. Thus, he continued, I prattle, exhorting you to inquire after the cause; and I shall accept this as your club for these mushrooms.

Then I began: Agemachus himself helps us exceedingly towards this discovery; for nothing at the present seems more probable than that, together with the thunder, oftentimes generative waters fall, which take that quality from the heat mixed with them. For the piercing pure parts of the fire break away in lightning; but the grosser windy part, being wrapped up in cloud, changes it, taking away the coldness and heating the moisture, altering and being altered with it, affects it so that it is made fit to enter the pores of plants, and is easily assimilated to them. Besides, such rain gives those things which it waters a peculiar temperature and difference of juice. Thus dew makes the grass sweeter to the sheep, and the clouds from which a rainbow is reflected make those trees on which they fall fragrant. And our priests, distinguishing it by this, call the wood of those trees Iris-struck, fancying that Iris, or the rainbow, hath rested on them. Now it is probable that when these thunder and lightning showers with a great deal of warmth and spirit descend forcibly into the caverns of the earth, these are rolled around, and knobs and tumors are formed like those produced by heat and noxious humors in our bodies, which we call wens or kernels. For a mushroom is not like a plant, neither is it produced without rain; it hath no root nor sprouts, it depends on nothing, but is a being by itself, having its substance of the earth, a little changed and altered. If this discourse seems frivolous, I assure you that such are most of the effects of thunder and lightning which we see; and upon that account men think them to be immediately directed by Heaven, and not depending on natural causes.

Dorotheus the rhetorician, one of our company, said: You speak right, sir, for not only the vulgar and illiterate, but even some of the philosophers, have been of that opinion. I remember here in this town lightning broke into a house and did a great many strange things. It let the wine out of a vessel, though the earthen vessel remained whole; and falling upon a man asleep, it neither hurt him nor blasted his clothes, but melted certain pieces of silver that he had in his pocket, defaced them quite, and made them run into a lump. Upon this he went to a philosopher, a Pythagorean, that sojourned in the town, and asked the reason; the philosopher directed him to some expiating rites, and advised him to consider seriously with himself and go to prayers. And I have been told, upon a sentinel at Rome, as he stood to guard the temple, burned the latchet of his shoe, and did no other harm; and several silver candlesticks lying in wooden boxes, the silver was melted while the boxes lay untouched. These stories you may believe or not as you please. But that which is most wonderful, and which everybody knows, is this,–the bodies of those that are killed by thunderbolt never putrefy. For many neither burn nor bury such bodies, but let them lie above ground with a fence about them, so that every one may see the they remain uncorrupted, confuted by this Euripides's Clymene, who says thus of Phaeton,

> My best beloved, but now he lies
> And putrefies in some dark vale.

And I believe brimstone is called [Greek omitted] (DIVINE), because its smell is like that fiery offensive scent which rises from bodies that are thunderstruck. And I suppose that, because of this scent, dogs and birds will not prey on such carcasses. Thus far have I gone; let him proceed, since he hath been applauded for his discourse of mushrooms, lest the same jest might be put upon us that was upon Androcydes the painter. For when in his landscape of Scylla he painted fish the best and most to the life of anything in the whole draught, he was said to use his appetite more than his art, for he naturally loved fish. So some may say that we philosophize about mushrooms, the cause of whose production is confessedly doubtful, for the pleasure we take in eating them....

And when I put in my suggestion, saying that it was as seasonable to dispute about thunder and lightning amidst our banquets as it would be in a comedy to bring in machines to throw out lightning, the company agreed to omit all other questions relating to the subject, and desired me only to proceed on this head, Why men asleep are never struck with lightning. And I, though I knew I should get no great credit by proposing a cause whose reason was common to other things, said thus: Lightning is wonderfully piercing and subtile, partly because it rises from a very pure substance, and partly because by the swiftness of its motion it purges itself and throws off all gross earthy particles that are mixed with it. Nothing, says Democritus, is blasted with lightning, that cannot resist and stop the motion of the pure flame. Thus the close bodies, as brass, silver, and the like, which stop it, feel its force and are melted, because they resist; whilst rare, thin bodies, and such as are full of pores, are passed through and are not hurted, as clothes or dry wood. It blasts green wood or grass, the moisture within them being seized and kindled by the flame. Now if it is true that men asleep are never killed by lightning, from what we have proposed, and not from anything else, we must endeavor to draw the cause. Now the bodies of those that are awake are stiffer and more apt to resist, all the parts being full of spirits; which as it were in a harp, distending and screwing up the organs of sense, makes the body of the animal firm, close, and compacted. But when men are asleep, the organs are let down, and the body becomes rare, lax, and loose; and the spirits failing, it hath abundance of pores, through which small sounds and smells do flow insensibly. For in that case, there is nothing that can resist and by this resistance receive any sensible impression from any objects that are presented, much less from such as are so subtile and move so swiftly as lightning. Things that are weak Nature shields from harm, fencing them about with some hard, thick covering; but those things that cannot be resisted do less harm to the bodies that yield than to those that oppose their force. Besides, those that are asleep are not startled at the thunder; they have no consternation upon them, which kills a great many that are no otherwise hurt, and we know that thousands die with the very fear of being killed. Even shepherds teach their sheep to run together when it thunders, for whilst they lie scattered they die with fear; and we see thousands fall, which have no marks of any stroke or fire about them, their souls (as it seems), like birds, flying out of their bodies at the fright. For many, as Euripides says,

A clap hath killed, yet ne'er drew drop of blood.

For certainly the hearing is a sense that is soonest and most vigorously wrought upon, and the fear that is caused by an astonishing noise raiseth the greatest commotion and disturbance in the body; from all which men asleep, because insensible, are secure. But those that are awake are oftentimes killed with fear before they are touched; the fear contracts and condenses the body, so that the stroke must be strong, because there is so considerable a resistance.

QUESTION III. WHY MEN USUALLY INVITE MANY GUESTS TO A WEDDING SUPPER. SOSSIUS SENECIO, PLUTARCH, THEO.

At my son Autobulus's marriage, Sossius Senecio from Chaeronea and a great many other noble persons were present at the same feast; which gave occasion to this question (Senecio proposed it), why to a marriage feast more guests are usually invited than to any other. Nay even those law-givers that chiefly opposed luxury and profuseness have particularly confined marriage feasts to a set number. Indeed, in my opinion, he continued, Hecataeus the Abderite, one of the old philosophers, hath said nothing to the purpose in this matter, when he tells us that those that marry wives invite a great many to the entertainment, that many may see and be witnesses that they being born free take to themselves wives of the same condition. For, on the contrary, the comedians reflect on those who revel at their marriages, who make a great ado and are pompous in their feasts, as such who are taking wives with not much confidence and courage. Thus, in Menander, one replies to a bridegroom that bade him beset the house with dishes,...

Your words are great, but what's this to your bride?

But lest I should seem to find fault with those reasons others give, only because I have none of my own to produce, continued he, I will begin by declaring that there is no such evident or public notice given of any feast as there is of one at a marriage. For when we sacrifice to the gods, when we take leave of or receive a friend, a great many of our acquaintance need not know it. But a marriage dinner is proclaimed by the loud sound of the wedding song, by the torches and the music, which as Homer expresseth it,

The women stand before the doors to see and hear.

(Iliad, xviii. 495.)

And therefore when everybody knows it, the persons are ashamed to omit the formality of an invitation, and therefore entertain their friends and kindred, and every one that they are anyway acquainted with.

This being generally approved, Well, said Theo, speaking next, let it be so, for it looks like truth; but let this be added, if you please, that such entertainments are not only friendly, but also kindredly, the persons beginning to have a new relation to another family. But there is something more considerable, and that is this; since by this marriage two families join in one, the man thinks it his duty to be civil and obliging to the woman's friends, and the woman's friends think themselves obliged to return the same to him and his; and upon this account the company is doubled. And besides, since most of the little ceremonies belonging to the wedding are performed by women, it is necessary that, where they are entertained, their husbands should be likewise present.

QUESTION IV. WHETHER THE SEA OR LAND AFFORDS BETTER FOOD. CALLISTRATUS, SYMMACHUS, POLYCRATES.

Aedepsus in Euboea, where the baths are, is a place by nature every way fitted for free and gentle pleasures, and withal so beautified with stately edifices and dining rooms, that one would take it for no other than the common place of repast for all Greece. Here, though the earth and air yield plenty of creatures for the service of men, the sea no less furnisheth the table with variety of dishes, nourishing a store of delicious fish in its deep and clear waters. This place is especially frequented in the spring; for hither at this time of year abundance of people resort, solacing themselves in the mutual enjoyment of all those pleasures the place affords, and at spare hours pass away the time in many useful and edifying discourses. When Callistratus the Sophist lived here, it was a hard matter to dine at any place besides his house; for he was so extremely courteous and obliging, that no man whom he invited to dinner could have the face to say him nay. One of his best humors was to pick up all the pleasant fellows he could meet with, and put them in the same room. Sometimes he did, as Cimon one of the ancients used to do, and satisfactorily treated men of all sorts and fashions. But he always (so to speak) followed Celeus, who was the first man, it is said, that assembled daily a number of honorable persons of distinction, and called the place where they met the Prytaneum.

Several times at these public meetings divers agreeable discourses were raised; and it fell out that once a very splendid treat, adorned with all variety of dainties, gave occasion for inquiries concerning food, whether the land or sea yielded better. Here when a great part of the company were highly commanding the land, as abounding with many choice, nay, an infinite variety of all sorts of creatures, Polycrates calling to Symmachus, said to him: But you, sir, being an animal bred between two seas, and brought up among so many which surround your sacred Nicopolis, will not you stand up for Neptune? Yes, I will, replied Symmachus, and therefore command you to stand by me, who enjoy the most pleasant part of all the Achaean Sea. Well, says Polycrates, the beginning of my discourse shall be grounded upon custom; for as of a great number of poets we usually give one, who far excels the rest, the famous name of poet; so though there be many sorts of dainties, yet custom has so prevailed that the fish alone, or above all the rest, is called [Greek omitted], because it is more excellent than all others. For we do not call those gluttonous and great eaters who love beef as Hercules, who after flesh used to eat green figs; nor those that love figs, as Plato; nor lastly, those that are for grapes, as Arcesilaus; but those who frequent the fish-market, and soonest hear the market-bell. Thus when Demosthenes had told Philocrates that the gold he got by treachery was spent upon whores and fish, he upbraids him as a gluttonous and lascivious fellow. And Ctesiphon said pat enough, when a certain glutton cried aloud in company that he should burst asunder: No, by no means let us be baits for your fish! And what did he mean, do you think, who made this verse,

You capers gnaw, when you may sturgeon eat?

And what, for God's sake, do those men mean who, inviting one another to sumptuous collations, usually say: To-day we will dine upon the shore? Is it not that they suppose, what is certainly true, that a dinner upon the shore is of all others most delicious? Not by reason of the waves the sea-coast would be content to feed upon a pulse or a caper?—but because their table is furnished with plenty of fresh fish. Add to this, that sea-food is dearer than any other. Wherefore Cato inveighing against the luxury of the city, did not exceed the bounds of truth, when he said that at Rome a fish was sold for more than an ox. For they sell a small pot of fish for as much as a hecatomb of sheep and all the accessories of sacrifice. Besides, as the physician is the best judge of physic, and the musician of songs; so he is able to give the best account of the goodness of meat who is the greatest lover of it. For I will not make Pythagoras and Xenocrates arbitrators in this case; but Antagoras the poet, and Philoxenus the son of Eryxis, and Androcydes the painter, of whom it was reported that, when he drew a landscape of Scylla, he drew fish in a lively manner swimming round her, because he was a great lover of them. So Antigonus the king, surprising Antagoras the poet in the habit of a cook, broiling congers in his tent, said to him: Dost thou think that Homer was dressing congers when he writ Agamemnon's famous exploits? And he as smartly replied: Do you think that Agamemnon did so many famous exploits when he was inquiring who dressed congers in the camp? These arguments, says Polycrates, I have urged in behalf of fishmongers, drawing them from testimony and custom.

But, says Symmachus, I will go more seriously to work, and more like a logician. For if that may truly be said to be a relish which gives meat the best relish, it will evidently follow, that that is the best sort of relish which gets men the best stomach to their meat. Therefore, as those philosophers who were called Elpistics (from the Greek word signifying hope, which above all others they cried up) averred that there was nothing in the world which concurred more to the preservation of life than hope, without whose gracious influence life would be a burden and altogether intolerable; in the like manner that of all other things may be said to get us a stomach to our meat without which all meat would be unpalatable and nauseous. And among all those things the earth yields, we find no such things as salt, which we can only have from the sea. First of all, without salt, there would be nothing eatable which mixed with flour seasons bread also. Neptune and Ceres had both the same temple. Besides, salt is the most pleasant of all condiments. For those heroes who like athletes used themselves to a spare diet, banishing from their tables all vain and superfluous delicacies, to such a degree that when they encamped by the Hellespont they abstained from fish, yet for all this could not eat flesh without salt; which is a sufficient evidence that salt is the most desirable of all relishes. For as colors need light, so tastes require salt, that they may affect the sense, unless you would have them very nauseous and unpleasant. For, as Heraclitus used to say, a carcass is more abominable than dung. Now all flesh is dead and part of a lifeless carcass; but the virtue of salt, being added to it, like a soul, gives it a pleasing relish and a poignancy. Hence it comes to pass that before meat men use to take sharp things, and such as have much salt in them; for these beguile us into an appetite. And whoever has his stomach sharpened with these sets cheerfully and freshly upon all other sorts of meat. But if he begin with any other kind of food, all on a sudden his stomach grows dull and languid. And therefore salt doth not only make meat but drink palatable. For Homer's onion, which, he tells us, they were used to eat before they drank, was fitter for seamen and boatmen than kings. Things moderately salt, by being pleasing to the mouth, make all sorts of wine mild and palateable, and water itself of a pleasing taste. Besides, salt creates none of those troubles which an onion does, but digests all other kinds of meat, making them tender and fitter for concoction; so that at the same time it is sauce to the palate and physic to the body. But all other seafood, besides this pleasantness, is also very innocent for though it be fleshly, yet it does not load the stomach as all other flesh does, but is easily concocted and digested. This Zeno will avouch for me, and Crato too, who confine sick persons to a fish diet, as of all others the lightest sort of meat. And it stands with reason, that the sea should produce the most nourishing and wholesome food, seeing it yields us the most refined, the purest and therefore the most agreeable air.

You say right, says Lamprias, but let us think of something else to confirm what you have spoken. I remember my old grandfather was used to say in derision of the Jews, that they abstained from most lawful flesh; but we will say that that is the most lawful meat which comes from the sea. For we can claim no great right over land creatures, which are nourished with the same food, draw the same air, wash in and drink the same water, that we do ourselves; and when they are slaughtered, they make us ashamed of what we are doing, with their hideous cries; and then again, by living amongst us, they arrive at some degree of familiarity and intimacy with us. But sea creatures are altogether strangers to us, and are born and brought up as it were in another world; neither does their voice, look, or any service they have done us plead for their life. For this kind of creatures are of no use at all to us, nor is there any necessity that we should love them. But that place which we inhabit is hell to them, and as soon as ever they enter upon it they die.

QUESTION V. WHETHER THE JEWS ABSTAINED FROM SWINE'S FLESH BECAUSE THEY WORSHIPPED THAT CREATURE, OR BECAUSE THEY HAD AN ANTIPATHY AGAINST IT. CALLISTRATUS, POLYCRATES, LAMPRIAS.

After these things were spoken, and some in the company were minded to say something in defence of the contrary opinion, Callistratus interrupted their discourse and said: Sirs, what do you think of that which was spoken against the Jews, that they abstain from the most lawful flesh? Very well said, quoth Polycrates, for that is a thing I very much question, whether it was that the Jews abstained from swine's flesh because they conferred divine honor upon that creature, or because they had a natural aversion to it. For whatever we find in their own writings seems to be altogether fabulous, except they have some more solid reasons which they have no mind to discover.

Hence it is, says Callistratus, that I am of an opinion that this nation has that creature in some veneration; and though it be granted that the hog is an ugly and filthy creature, yet it is not quite so vile nor naturally stupid as a beetle, griffin, crocodile, or cat, most of which are worshipped as the most sacred things by some priests amongst the Egyptians. But the reason why the hog is had in so much honor and veneration amongst them is, because as the report goes, that creature breaking up the earth with its snout showed the way to tillage, and taught them how to use the ploughshare, which instrument for that very reason, as some say, was called HYNIS from [Greek omitted], A SWINE. Now the Egyptians inhabiting a country situated low and whose soil is naturally soft, have no need of the plough; but after the river Nile hath retired from the grounds it overflowed, they presently let in all their hogs into the fields, and they with their feet and snout break up the ground, and cover the sown seed. Nor ought this to seem strange to anyone, that there are in the world those that abstain from swine's flesh on such an account as this; when it is evident that in barbarous nations there are other animals had in greater honor and veneration for lesser reasons, if not altogether ridiculous.

For the field-mouse only for its blindness was worshipped as a god among the Egyptians, because they were of an opinion that darkness was before light and that the latter had its birth from mice about the fifth generation at the new moon; and moreover that the liver of this creature diminishes in the wane of the moon. But they consecrate the lion to the sun, because the lioness alone, of all clawed four-footed beasts, brings forth her young with their eyesight; for they sleep in a moment, and when they are asleep their eyes sparkle. Besides, they place gaping lions' heads for the spouts of their fountains, because Nilus overflows the Egyptian fields when the sign is Leo: they give it out that their bird ibis, as soon as hatched, weighs two drachms, which are of the same weight with the heart of a newborn infant; and that its legs being spread with the bill an exact equilateral triangle. And yet who can find fault with the Egyptians for these trifles, when it is left upon record that the Pythagoreans worshipped a white cock, and of sea creatures abstained especially from mullet and urtic. The Magi that descended from Zoroaster adored the land hedgehog above other creatures but had a deadly spite against water-rats, and thought that man was dear in the eyes of the gods who destroyed most of them. But I should think that if the Jews had such an antipathy against a hog, they would kill it as the magicians do mice; when, on the contrary, they are by their religion as much prohibited to kill as to eat it. And perhaps there may be some reason given for this; for as the ass is worshipped by them as the first discoverer of fountains, so perhaps the hog may be had in like veneration, which first taught them to sow and plough. Nay, some say that the Jews also abstain from hares, as abominable and unclean creatures.

They have reason for that, said Lamprias, because a hare is so like an ass which they detest; for in its color, ears, and the sparkling of its eyes, it is so like an ass, that I do not know any little creature that represents a great one so much as a hare doth an ass; except in this likewise imitating the Egyptians, they suppose that there is something of divinity in the swiftness of this creature, as also in its quickness of sense; for the eyes of hares are so unwearied that they sleep with them open. Besides, they seem to excel all other creatures in quickness of hearing; whence it was that the Egyptians painted a hare's ear amongst their other hieroglyphics, as an emblem of hearing. But the Jews do hate swine's flesh, because all the barbarians are naturally fearful of a scab and leprosy, which they presume comes by eating such kind of flesh. For we may observe that all pigs under the belly are overspread with a leprosy and scab; which may be supposed to proceed from an ill disposition of body and corruption within, which breaks out through the skin. Besides, swine's feeding is commonly so nasty and filthy, that it must of necessity cause corruptions and vicious humors; for, setting aside those creatures that are bred from and live upon dung, there is no other creature that takes so much delight to wallow in the mire and in other unclean and stinking places. Hogs' eyes are said to be so flattened and fixed upon the ground, that they see nothing above them, nor ever look up to the sky, except when turned upon their back they turn their eyes upwards contrary to nature. Therefore this creature, at other times most clamorous' when laid upon his back, is still, as astonished at the unusual sight of the heavens; while the greatness of the fear he is in (as it is supposed) is the cause of his silence. And if it be lawful to intermix our discourse with fables, it is said that Adonis was slain by a boar. Now Adonis is supposed to be the same with Bacchus; and there are a great many rites in both their sacrifices which confirm this opinion. Others will have Adonis to be Bacchus's paramour; and Phanocles an amorous love-poet writes thus,

> Bacchus on hills the fair Adonis saw,
> And ravished him, and reaped a wondrous joy.

QUESTION VI. WHAT GOD IS WORSHIPPED BY THE JEWS. SYMMACHUS, LAMPRIAS, MOERAGENES.

Here Symmachus, greatly wondering at what was spoken, says: What, Lamprias, will you permit our tutelar god, called Evius, the inciter of women, famous for the honors he has conferred upon him by madmen, to be inscribed and enrolled in the mysteries of the Jews? Or is there any solid reason that can be given to prove Adonis to be the same with Bacchus? Here Moeragenes interposing, said: Do not be so fierce upon him, for I who am an Athenian answer you, and tell you, in short, that these two are the very same. And no man is able or fit to bring the chief confirmation of this truth, but those amongst us who are initiated and skilled in the triennial [Greek omitted] or chief mysteries of the god. But what no religion forbids to speak of among friends, especially over wine, the gift of Bacchus, I am ready at the command of these gentlemen to disclose.

When all the company requested and earnestly begged it of him; first of all (says he), the time and manner of the greatest and most holy solemnity of the Jews is exactly agreeable to the holy rites of Bacchus; for that which they call the Fast they celebrate in the midst of the vintage, furnishing their tables with all sorts of fruits while they sit under tabernacles made of vines and ivy; and the day which immediately goes before this they call the day of Tabernacles. Within a few days after they celebrate another feast, not darkly but openly, dedicated to Bacchus, for they have a feast amongst them called Kradephoria, from carrying palm-trees, and Thyrsophoria, when they enter into the temple carrying thyrsi. What they do within I know not; but it is very probable that they perform the rites of Bacchus. First they have little trumpets, such as the Grecians used to have at their Bacchanalia to call upon their gods withal. Others go before them playing upon harps, which they call Levites, whether so named from Lusius or Evius,–either word agrees with Bacchus. And I suppose that their Sabbaths have some relation to Bacchus; for even now many call the Bacchi by the name of Sabbi, and they make use of that word at the celebration of Bacchus's orgies. And this may be discovered out of Demosthenes and Menander. Nor would it be out of place, were any one to say that the name Sabbath was given to this feast from the agitation and excitement [Greek omitted] which the priests of Bacchus display. The Jews themselves witness no less; for when they keep the Sabbath, they invite one another to drink till they are drunk; or if they chance to be hindered by some more weighty business, it is the fashion at least to taste the wine. Some perhaps may surmise that these are mere conjectures. But there are other arguments which will clearly evince the truth of what I assert. The first may be drawn from their High-priest, who on holidays enters their temple with his mitre on, arrayed in a skin of a hind embroidered with gold, wearing buskins, and a coat hanging down to his ankles; besides, he has a great many little bells depending from his garment which make a noise as he walks. So in the nocturnal ceremonies of Bacchus (as the fashion is amongst us), they make use of music, and call the god's nurses [Greek omitted]. High up on the wall of their temple is a representation of the thyrsus and timbrels, which surely suits no other god than Bacchus. Mor ancients were wont to make themselves drun And at this day barbarous people who want wine drink metheglin, allaying the sweetness of the honey by bitter roots, much of the taste of our wine. The Greeks offered to their gods these temperate offerings or honey-offerings, as they called them, because that honey was of a nature quite contrary to wine. But this is no inconsiderable argument that Bacchus was worshipped by the Jews, in that, amongst other kinds of punishment, that was most remarkably odious by which malefactors were forbid the use of wine for so long a time as the judge thought fit to prescribe. Those thus punished....

(The remainder of the Fourth Book is wanting.)

QUESTION VII. WHY THE DAYS WHICH HAVE THE NAMES OF THE PLANETS ARE NOT ARRANGED ACCORDING TO THE ORDER OF THE PLANETS, BUT THE CONTRARY. THERE IS ADDED A DISCOURSE ON THE POSITION OF THE SUN.

QUESTION VIII. WHY SIGNET-RINGS ARE WORN CHIEFLY ON THE FOURTH FINGER. QUESTION IX. WHETHER WE OUGHT TO CARRY IN OUR SEAL-RINGS EFFIGIES OF GODS, OR THOSE OF WISE PERSONAGES. QUESTION X. WHY WOMEN DO NOT EAT THE MIDDLE PART OF LETTUCE.

Book Five

What is your opinion at present, Sossius Senecio, of the pleasures of mind and body, is not evident to me;

> Because us two a thousand things divide,
> Vast shady hills, and the rough ocean's tide.
> ("Iliad" i. 156)

But formerly, I am sure, you did not lean to nor like their opinion, who will not allow the soul to have any proper agreeable pleasure, which without respect to the body she desires for herself; but define that she lives as a form assistant to the body, is directed by the passions of it, and, as that is affected, is either pleased or grieved, or, like a looking-glass, only receives the images of those sensible impressions made upon the body. This sordid and debasing opinion is especially confuted as follows; for at a feast, the genteel well-bred men after supper fall upon some topic or another as second course, and cheer one another by their pleasant talk. Now the body hath very little or no share in this; which evidently proves that this is a particular banquet for the soul, and that those pleasures are peculiar to her, and different from those which pass to her through the body and are vitiated thereby. Now, as nurses, when they feed children, taste a little of their pap, and have but little pleasure therefrom, but when the infants are satisfied, leave crying, and go to sleep, then being at their own disposal, they take such meat and drink as is agreeable to their own bodies; thus the soul partakes of the pleasures that arise from eating and drinking, like a nurse, being subservient to the appetites of the body, kindly yielding to its necessities and wants, and calming its desires; but when that is satisfied and at rest, then being free from her business and servile employment, she seeks her own proper pleasures, revels on discourse, problems, stories, curious questions, or subtle resolutions. Nay, what shall a man say, when he sees the dull unlearned fellows after supper minding such pleasures as have not the least relation to the body? They tell tales, propose riddles, or set one another a-guessing at names, comprised and hid under such and such numbers. Thus mimics, drolls, Menander and his actors were admitted into banquets, not because they can free the eye from any pain, or raise any tickling motion in the flesh; but because the soul, being naturally philosophical and a lover of instruction, covets its own proper pleasure and satisfaction, when it is free from the trouble of looking after the body.

QUESTION I. WHY WE TAKE DELIGHT IN HEARING THOSE THAT REPRESENT THE PASSIONS OF MEN ANGRY OR SORROWFUL, AND YET CANNOT WITHOUT CONCERN BEHOLD THOSE WHO ARE REALLY SO AFFECTED?

PLUTARCH, BOETHUS.

Of this we discoursed in your company at Athens, when Strato the comedian (for he was a man of great credit) flourished. For being entertained at supper by Boethus the Epicurean, with a great many more of the sect, as it usually happens when learned and inquisitive men meet together, the remembrance of the comedy led us to this inquiry,–Why we are disturbed at the real voices of men, either angry, pensive, or afraid, and yet are delighted to hear others represent them, and imitate their gestures, speeches, and exclamations. Every one in the company gave almost the same reason. For they said, he that only represents excels him that really feels, inasmuch as he doth not suffer the misfortunes; which we knowing are pleased and delighted on that account.

But I, though it was not properly my talent, said that we, being by nature rational and lovers of ingenuity, are delighted with and admire everything that is artificially and ingeniously contrived. For as a bee, naturally loving sweet things, seeks after and flies to anything that has any mixture of honey in it; so man, naturally loving ingenuity and elegancy, is very much inclined to accept and highly approve every word or action that is seasoned with wit and judgement. Thus, if any one offers a child a piece of bread, and at the same time, a little dog or ox made in paste, we shall see the boy run eagerly to the latter; so likewise if anyone, offers silver in the lump, and another a beast or a cup of the same metal, he will rather choose that in which he sees a mixture of art and reason. Upon the same account it is that a child is much in love with riddles, and such fooleries as are difficult and intricate; for whatever is curious and subtle doth attract and allure mankind, as antecedently to all instruction agreeable and proper to it. And therefore, because he that is really affected with grief or anger presents us with nothing but the common bare passion, but in the imitation some dexterity and persuasiveness appears, we are naturally inclined to be disturbed at the former, whilst the latter delights us. It is unpleasant to see a sick man, or one at his last gasp; yet with content we can look upon the picture of Philoctetes, or the statue of Jocasta, in whose face it is commonly said that the workmen mixed silver, so that the brass might depict the face and color of one ready to faint and expire. And this, said I, the Cyrenaics may use as a strong argument against you Epicureans, that all the sense of pleasure which arises from the working of any object on the ear or eye is not in those organs, but in the intellect itself. Thus the continual cackling of a hen or cawing of a crow is very ungrateful and disturbing; yet he that imitates those noises well pleases the hearers. Thus to behold a consumptive man is no delightful spectacle; yet with pleasure we can view the pictures and statues of such persons, because the very imitating hath something in it very agreeable to the mind, which allures and captivates its faculties. For upon what other account, for God's sake, from what external impression upon our organs, should men be moved to admire Parmeno's sow so much as to pass it into a proverb? Yet it is reported, that Parmeno being very famous for imitating the grunting of a pig, some endeavoured to rival and outdo him. And when the hearers, being prejudiced, cried out, Very well indeed, but nothing comparable to Parmeno's sow; one took a pig under his arm and came upon the stage. And when, though they heard the very pig, they still continued, This is nothing comparable to Parmeno's sow; he threw his pig amongst them, to show that they judged according to opinion and not truth. And hence it is very evident, that like motions of the sense do not always raise like affections in the mind, when there is not an opinion that the thing done was not neatly and ingeniously performed.

QUESTION II. THAT THE PRIZE FOR POETS AT THE GAMES WAS ANCIENT.

At the solemnity of the Pythian names, there was a consult about taking away all such sports as had lately crept in and were not of ancient institution. For after they had taken in the tragedy in addition to the three ancient, which were as old as the solemnity itself, the Pythian piper, the harper, and the singer to the harp, as if a large gate were opened, they could not keep out an infinite crowd of plays and musical entertainments of all sorts that rushed in after him. Which indeed made no unpleasant variety, and increased the company, but yet impaired the gravity and neatness of the solemnity. Besides it must create a great deal of trouble to the umpires, and considerable dissatisfaction to very many, since but few could obtain the prize. It was chiefly agreed upon, that the orators and poets should be removed; and this determination did not proceed from any hatred to learning, but forasmuch as such contenders are the most noted and worthiest men of all, therefore they reverence them, and were troubled that, when they must judge every one very deserving, they could not bestow the prize equally upon all. I, being present at this consult, dissuaded those who were for removing things from their present settled order, and who thought this variety as unsuitable to the solemnity as many strings and many notes to an instrument. And when at supper, Petraeus the president and director of the sports entertaining us, the same subject was discoursed on, I defended music, and maintained that poetry was no upstart intruder, but that it was time out of mind admitted into the sacred games, and crowns were given to the best performer. Some straight imagined that I intended to produce some old musty stories, like the funeral solemnities of Oeolycus the Thessalian or of Amphidamas the Chalcidean, in which they say Homer and Hesiod contended for the prize. But passing by these instances as the common theme of every grammarian, as likewise their criticisms who, in the description of Patroclus's obsequies in Homer, read [Greek omitted] ORATORS, and not [Greek omitted], DARTERS, ("Iliad," xxiii, 886.) as if Achilles had proposed a prize for the best speaker,–omitting all these, I said that Acastus at his father Pelias's funeral set a prize for contending poets, and Sibylla won it. At this, a great many demanding some authority for this unlikely and incredible relation, I happily recollecting myself produced Acesander, who in his description of Africa hath this relation; but I must confess this is no common book. But Polemo the Athenian's "Commentary of the Treasures of the City Delphi" I suppose most of you have diligently perused, he being a very learned man in the Greek Antiquities. In him you shall find that in the Sicyonian treasure there was a golden book dedicated to the god, with this inscription: Aristomache, the poetess of Erythraea, dedicated this after she had got the prize at the Isthmian games. Nor is there any reason, I continued, why we should so admire and reverence the Olympic games, as if, like Fate, they were unalterable, and never admitted any change since the first institution. For the Pythian, it is true, hath had three or four musical prizes added; but all the exercises of the body were for the most part the same from the beginning. But in the Olympian all beside racing are late additions. They instituted some, and abolished them again; such were the races of mules, either rode or in a chariot as likewise the crown appointed for boys that were victor's in the five contests. And, in short, a thousand things in those games are mere novelties. At Pisa they had a single combat, where he that yielded or was overcome was killed upon the place. But pray for the future require no author for my story, lest I may appear ridiculous if amidst my cups I should forget the name.

QUESTION III. WHY WAS THE PINE COUNTED SACRED TO NEPTUNE AND BACCHUS? AND WHY AT FIRST THE CONQUEROR IN THE ISTHMIAN GAMES WAS CROWNED WITH A GARLAND OF PINE, AFTERWARDS WITH PARSLEY, AND NOW AGAIN WITH PINE.

LUCANIUS, PRAXITELES.

This question was started, why the Isthmian garland was made of pine. We were then at supper in Corinth, in the time of the Isthmian games, with Lucanius the chief priest. Praxiteles the commentator brought this fable for a reason; it is said that the body of Melicertes was found fixed to a pine-tree by the sea; and not far from Megara, there is a place called the Race of a Fair Lady, through which the Megarians say that Ino, with her son Melicertes in her arms, ran to the sea. And when many put forth the common opinion, that the pine-tree garland peculiarly belongs to Neptune, Lucanius added that it is sacred to Bacchus too, but yet, for all that, it might also be appropriated to the honor of Melicertes; this started the question, why the ancients dedicated the pine to Neptune and Bacchus. As for my part, it did not seem incongruous to me, for both the gods seem to preside over the moist and generative principle; and almost all the Greeks sacrifice to Neptune the nourisher of plants, and to Bacchus the preserver of trees. Besides, it may be said that the pine peculiarly agrees to Neptune, not, as Apollodorus thinks, because it grows by the seaside, or because it loves a bleak place (for some give this reason), but because it is used in building ships; for it together with the like trees, as fir and cypress, affords the best and the lightest timber, and likewise pitch and rosin, without which the compacted planks would be altogether unserviceable at sea. To Bacchus they dedicate the pine, because it seasons wine, for among the pines they say the sweetest and most delicious grapes grow. The cause of this Theophrastus thinks to be the heat of the soil; for pines grow most in chalky grounds. Now chalk is hot, and therefore must very much conduce to the concoction of the wine; as a chalky spring affords the lightest and sweetest water; and if chalk is mixed with corn, by its heat it makes the grains swell, and considerably increases the heap. Besides, it is probable that the vine itself is bettered by the pine, for that contains several things which are good to preserve wine. All cover the insides of wine casks with rosin, and many mix rosin with wine, as the Euboeans in Greece, and in Italy those that live about the river Po. From the parts of Gaul about Vienna there is a sort of pitched wine brought, which the Romans value very much; for such things mixed with it do not only give it a good flavor, but make the wine generous, taking away by their gentle heat all the crude, watery, and undigested particles. When I had said thus much, a rhetorician in the company, a man well read in all sorts of polite learning, cried out: Good Gods! was it not but the other day that the Isthmian garland began to be made of pine? And was not the crown anciently of twined parsley? I am sure in a certain comedy a covetous man is brought in speaking thus:–

The Isthmian garland I will sell as cheap
As common wreaths of parsley may be sold.

And Timaeus the historian says that, when the Corinthians were marching to fight the Carthaginians in the defence of Sicily, some persons carrying parsley met them, and when several looked upon this as a bad omen,–because parsley is accounted unlucky, and those that are dangerously sick we usually say have need of parsley,–Timoleon encouraged them by putting them in mind of the Isthmian parsley garland with which the Corinthians used to crown the conquerors. And besides, the admiral-ship of Antigonus's navy, having by chance some parsley growing on its poop, was called Isthmia. Besides, a certain obscure epigram upon an earthen vessel stopped with parsley intimates the same thing. It runs thus:–

The Grecian earth, now hardened by the flame,
Holds in its hollow belly Bacchus blood;
And hath its mouth with Isthmian branches stopped.

Sure, he continued, they never read these authors, who cry up the pine as anciently wreathed in the Isthmian garlands, and would not have it some upstart intruder. The young men yielded presently to him, as being a man of various reading and very learned.

But Lucanius, with a smile looking upon me, cried out: Good God! here's a deal of learning. But others have taken advantage of our ignorance and unacquaintedness with such matters, and, on the contrary, persuaded us that the pine was the first garland, and that afterwards in honor of Hercules the parsley was received from the Nemean games, which in a little time prevailing, thrust out the pine, as if it were its right to be the wreath; but a little while after the pine recovered its ancient honor, and now flourishes in its glory. I was satisfied, and upon consideration found that I had run across a great many authorities for it. Thus Euphorion writes of Melicertes,

> *They mourned the youth, and him on pine boughs laid*
> *Of which the Isthmian victors' crowns are made.*
> *Fate had not yet seized beauteous Mene's son*
> *By smooth Asopus; since whose fall the crown*
> *Of parsley wreathed did grace the victor's brow.*

And Callimachus is plainer and more express, when he makes Hercules speak thus of parsley,

> *This at Isthmian sports*
> *To Neptune's glory now shall be the crown;*
> *The pine shall be disused, which heretofore*
> *In Corinth's fields successful victors wore.*

And besides, if I am not mistaken, in Procles's history of the Isthmian games I met with this passage; at first a pine garland crowned the conqueror, but when this game began to be reckoned amongst the sacred, then from the Nemean solemnity the parsley was received. And this Procles was one of Xenocrates's fellow-students at the Academy.

QUESTION IV. CONCERNING THAT EXPRESSION IN HOMER, [GREEK OMITTED] ("Iliad," ix. 203.)

NICERATUS, SOSICLES, ANTIPATER, PLUTARCH.

Some at the table were of opinion that Achilles talked nonsense when he bade Patroclus "mix the wine stronger," adding this reason,

> *For now I entertain my dearest friends.*

But Niceratus a Macedonian, my particular acquaintance, maintained that [Greek omitted] did not signify pure but hot wine; as if it were derived from [Greek omitted] and [Greek omitted] (LIFE-GIVING AND BOILING), and it were requisite at the coming of his friends to temper a fresh bowl, as every one of us in his offering at the altar pours out fresh wine. But Sosicles the poet, remembering a saying of Empedocles, that in the great universal change those things which before were [Greek omitted], UNMIXED, should then be [Greek omitted], affirmed that [Greek omitted] there signified [Greek omitted], WELL-TEMPERED, and that Achilles might with a great deal of reason bid Patroclus provide well-tempered wine for the entertainment of his friends; and it was absurd (he said) to use [Greek omitted] for [Greek omitted] any more than [Greek omitted] for [Greek omitted], or [Greek omitted] for [Greek omitted], for the comparatives are very properly put for the positives. My friend Antipater said that years were anciently called [Greek omitted], and that the particle [Greek omitted] in composition signified greatness; and therefore old wine, that had been kept for many years, was called by Achilles [Greek omitted].

I put them in mind that some imagine that [Greek omitted], hot, is signified by [Greek omitted], and that hotter means really faster, as when we command servants to move themselves more hotly or in hotter haste. But I must confess, your dispute is frivolous, since it is raised upon this supposition that if [Greek omitted], signifies more pure wine, Achilles's command would be absurd, as Zoilus of Amphipolis imagined. For first he did not consider that Achilles saw Phoenix and Ulysses to be old men, who are not pleased with diluted wine, and upon that account forbade any mixture. Besides, he having been Chiron's scholar, and from him having learned the rules of diet, he considered that weaker and more diluted liquors were fittest for those bodies that lay at ease, and were not employed in their customary exercise or labor. Thus with the other provender he gave his horses smallage, and this upon very good reason; for horses that lie still grow sore in their feet, and smallage is the best remedy in the world against that. And you will not find smallage or anything of the same nature given to any other horses in the whole "Iliad." Thus Achilles, being experienced in physic, provided suitable provender for his horses, and used the lightest diet himself, as the fittest whilst he lay at ease. But those that had been wearied all day in fight he did not think convenient to treat like those that had lain at ease, but commanded more pure and stronger wine to be prepared. Besides, Achilles doth not appear to be naturally addicted to drinking, but he was of a haughty, inexorable temper.

> No pleasant humor, no, soft mind he bore,
> But was all fire and rage.
> ("Iliad," xx. 467.)

And in another place very plainly Homer says, that

> Many a sleepless night he knew.
> ("Iliad," ix. 325.)

Now little sleep cannot content those that drink strong liquors; and in his railing at Agamemnon, the first ill name he gives him is drunkard, proposing his great drinking as the chiefest of his faults. And for these reasons it is likely that, when they came, he thought his usual mixture too weak and not convenient for them.

QUESTION V. CONCERNING THOSE THAT INVITE MANY TO A SUPPER. PLUTARCH, ONESICRATES, LAMPRIAS THE ELDER.

At my return from Alexandria all my friends by turns treated me, inviting all such too as were any way acquainted, so that our meetings were usually tumultuous and suddenly dissolved; which disorders gave occasion to discourses concerning the inconveniences that attend such crowded entertainments. But when Onesicrates the physician in his turn invited only the most familiar acquaintance, and men of the most agreeable temper, I thought that what Plato says concerning the increase of cities might be applied to entertainments. For there is a certain number which an entertainment may receive, and still be an entertainment; but if it exceeds that, so that by reason of the number there cannot be a mutual conversation amongst all, if they cannot know one another nor partake of the same jollity, it ceaseth to be such. For we should not want messengers there, as in a camp, or boatswains, as in a galley; but we ourselves should immediately converse with one another. As in a dance, so in an entertainment, the last man should be placed within hearing of the first.

As I was speaking, my grandfather Lamprias cried out: Then it seems there is need of temperance not only in our feasts, but also in our invitations. For methinks there is even an excess in kindness, when we pass by none of our friends, but draw them all in, as to see a sight or hear a play. And I think, it is not so great a disgrace for the entertainer not to have bread or wine enough for his, guests, as not to have room enough, with which he ought always to be provided, not only for invited guests, strangers and chance visitants. For suppose he hath not wine and bread enough, it may be imputed either to the carelessness or dishonesty of his servants; but the want of room must be imputed to the imprudence of the inviter. Hesiod is very much admired for beginning thus,

A vast chaos first was made.
(Hesiod, "Theogony," 116.)

For it was necessary that there should be first a place and room provided for the beings that were afterward to be produced; and not as was seen yesterday at my son's entertainment, according to Anaxagoras's saying,

All lay jumbled together.

But suppose a man hath room and provision enough, yet a large company itself is to be avoided for its own sake, as hindering all familiarity and conversation; and it is more tolerable to let the company have no wine, than to exclude all converse from a feast. And therefore

Theophrastus jocularly called the barbers' shops feasts without wine; because those that sit there usually prattle and discourse. But those that invite a crowd at once deprive all of free communication of discourse, or rather make them divide into cabals, so that two or three privately talk together, and neither know nor look on those that sit, as it were, half a mile distant.

> Some took this way to valiant Ajax's tent,
> And some the other to Achilles' went.
> ("Iliad," xi. 7.)

And therefore some rich men are foolishly profuse, who build rooms big enough for thirty tables or more at once; for such a preparation certainly is for unsociable and unfriendly entertainments, and such as are fit for a panegyriarch rather than a symposiarch to preside over. But this may be pardoned in those; for wealth would not he wealth, it would be really blind and imprisoned, unless it had witnesses, as tragedies would be devoid of spectators. Let us entertain few and often, and make that a remedy against having a crowd at once. For those that invite but seldom are forced to have all their friends, and all that upon any account they are acquainted with together; but those that invite frequently, and but three or four, render their entertainments like little barks, light and nimble. Besides, the very reason why we ask friends teaches us to select some out of the number. For as when we are in want we do not call all together, but only those that can best afford, help in that particular case,–when we would be advised, the wiser part; and when we are to have a trial, the best pleaders; and when we are to go a journey, those that can live pleasantly and are at leisure,–thus to our entertainments we should only call those that are at the present agreeable. Agreeable, for instance, to a prince's entertainment will be the magistrates, if they are his friends, or chiefest of the city; to marriage or birthday feasts, all their kindred, and such as are under the protection of the same Jupiter the guardian of consanguinity; and to such feasts and merry-makings as this those are to be invited whose tempers are most suitable to the occasion. When we offer sacrifice to one god, we do not worship all the others that belong to the same temple and altar at the same time; but suppose we have three bowls, out of the first we pour oblations to some, out of the second to others and out of the third to the rest, and none of the gods take distaste. And in this a company of friends may be likened to the company of gods; none takes distaste at the order of the invitation, if it be prudently managed and every one allowed a turn.

QUESTION VI. WHAT IS THE REASON THAT THE SAME ROOM WHICH AT THE BEGINNING OF A SUPPER SEEMS TOO NARROW APPEARS WIDE ENOUGH AFTERWARDS.

After this it was presently asked, why the room which at the beginning of supper seems too narrow for the guest is afterwards wide enough; when the contrary is most likely, after they are filled with the supper. Some said the posture of our sitting was the cause; for they sit when they eat, with their full breadth to the table, that they may command it with their right hand; but after they have supped, they sit more sideways, and make an acute figure with their bodies, and do not touch the place according to the superficies, if I may so say, but the line. Now as cockal bones do not take up as much room when they fall upon one end as when they fall flat, so every one of us at the beginning sitting broadwise, and with a full face to the table, afterwards changes the figure, and turns his depth, not his breadth, to the board. Some attribute it to the beds whereon we sat, for those when pressed stretch; as strait shoes after a little wearing have their pores widened, and grow fit for–sometimes too big for–the foot. An old man in the company merrily said, that the same feast had two very different presidents and directors; in the beginning, Hunger, that is not in the least skilled in ordering and disposing, but afterward Bacchus, whom all acknowledge to be the best orderer of an army in the world. As therefore Epaminondas, when the unskilful captains had led their forces into narrow disadvantageous straits, relieved the phalanx that was fallen foul on itself and all in disorder, and brought it into good rank and file again; thus we in the beginning, being like greedy hounds confused and disordered by hunger, the god (hence named the looser and the dancesetter) settles us in a friendly and agreeable order.

QUESTION VII. CONCERNING THOSE THAT ARE SAID TO BEWITCH. METRIUS FLORUS, PLUTARCH, SOCLARUS, PATROCLES, CAIUS.

A discourse happening at supper concerning those that are said to bewitch or have a bewitching eye, most of the company looked upon it as a whim, and laughed at it. But Metrius Florus, who then gave us a supper, said that the strange events wonderfully confirmed the report; and because we cannot give a reason for the thing, therefore to disbelieve the relation was absurd, since there are a thousand things which evidently are, the reasons of which we cannot readily assign. And, in short, he that requires everything should be probable destroys all wonder and admiration; and where the cause is not obvious, there we begin to doubt, that is, to philosophize. So that they who disbelieve all wonderful relations do in some measure take away all philosophy. The cause why anything is so, reason must find out; but that a thing is so, testimony is a sufficient evidence; and we have a thousand instances of this sort attested. We know that some men by looking upon young children hurt them very much, their weak and soft temperature being wrought upon and perverted, whilst those that are strong and firm are not so liable to be wrought upon. And Phylarchus tells us that the Thibians, the old inhabitants about Pontus, were destructive not only to little children, but to some also of riper years; for those upon whom they looked or breathed, or to whom they spake, would languish and grow sick. And this, likely, those of other countries perceived who bought slaves there. But perhaps this is not so much to be wondered at, for in touching and handling there is some apparent principle and cause of the effect. And as when you mix other birds' wings with the eagles', the plumes waste and suddenly consume; so there is no reason to the contrary, but that one man's touch may be good and advantageous, and another's hurtful and destructive. But that some, by being barely looked upon, are extremely prejudiced is certain; though the stories are disbelieved, because the reason is hard to be given.

True, said I, but methinks there is some small track to the cause of this effect, if you come to the effluvia of bodies. For smell, voice, breath, and the like, are effluvia from animal bodies, and material parts that move the senses, which are wrought upon by their impulse. Now it is very likely that such effluvia must continually part from animals, by reason of their heat and motion; for by that the spirits are agitated, and the body, being struck by those, must continually send forth effluvia. And it is probable that these pass chiefly through the eye. For the sight, being very vigorous and active, together with the spirit upon which it depends, sends forth a strange fiery power; so that by it men act and suffer very much, and are always proportionably pleased or displeased, according as the visible objects are agreeable or not. Love, that greatest and most violent passion of the soul, takes its beginning from the eye; so that a lover, when he looks upon the fair, flows out as it were, and seems to mix with her. And therefore why should any one, that believes men can be affected and prejudiced by the sight, imagine that they cannot act and hurt is well? For the mutual looks of mature beauties, and that which comes from the eye, whether light or a stream of spirits, melt and dissolve the lovers with a pleasing pain, which they call the bittersweet of love. For neither by touching or hearing the voice of their beloved are they so much wounded and wrought upon, as by looking and being looked upon again. There is such a communication, such a flame raised by one glance, that those must be altogether unacquainted with love that wonder at the Median naphtha, that takes fire at a distance from the flame. For the glances of a fair one, though at a great distance, quickly kindle a fire in the lover's breast. Besides every body knows the remedy for the jaundice; if they look upon the bird called charadrios they are cured. For that animal seems to be of that temperature and nature as to receive and draw away the disease, that like a stream flows out through the eyes; so that the charadrios will not look on one that hath the jaundice; he cannot endure it, but turns away his head and shuts his eyes, not envying (as some imagine) the cure he performs, but being really hurt by the effluvia of the patient. And of all diseases, soreness of the eyes is the most infectious; so strong and vigorous is the sight, and so easily does it cause infirmities in another.

Very right, said Patrocles, and you reason well as to changes wrought upon the body; but as to the soul, which in some measure exercises the power of witchcraft, how can this cause any disturbance by the eye? Sir, I replied, do not you consider that the soul, when affected, works upon the body? Ideas of love excite lust, and rage often blinds dogs as they fight with wild beasts. Sorrow, covetousness, or jealousy makes us change color, and destroys the habit of the body; and envy more than any passion, when fixed in the soul, fills the body full of ill humors, and makes it pale and ugly; which deformities good painters in their pictures of envy endeavor to represent. Now, when men thus perverted by envy fix their eyes upon another, and these, being nearest to the soul, easily draw the venom from it, and send out as it were poisoned darts, it is no wonder, in my mind, if he that is looked upon is hurt. Thus the biting of a dog when mad is most dangerous; and then the seed of a man is most prolific, when he embraces one that he loves; and in general the affections of the mind strengthen and invigorate the powers of the body. And therefore people imagine that those amulets that are preservative against witchcraft are likewise good and efficacious against envy; the sight by the strangeness of the spectacle being diverted, so that it cannot make so strong an impression upon the patient. This, Florus, is what I can say; and pray sir, accept it as my club for this entertainment.

Well, said Soclarus, but let us try whether the money be all good or no; for, in my mind some of it seems brass. But if we admit the general report about these matters to be true, you know very well that it is commonly supposed that some have friends, acquaintance, and even fathers, that have such evil eyes; so that the mothers will not show their children to them, nor for a long time suffer them to be looked upon by such; and how can the effects wrought by these proceed from envy? But what, for God's sake, wilt thou say to those that are reported to bewitch themselves?–for I am sure you have heard of such, or at least read these lines:–

Curls once on Eutel's head in order stood;
But when he viewed his figure in a flood,
He overlooked himself, and now they fall...

For they say that this Eutelidas, appearing very delicate and beauteous to himself, was affected with that sight and grew sick upon it, and lost his beauty and his health. Now, pray sir, what reason can you find for these wonderful effects?

At any other time, I replied, I question not but I shall give you full satisfaction. But now, sir, after such a large pot as you have seen me take, I boldly affirm, that all passions which have been fixed in the soul a long time raise ill humors in the body, which by continuance growing strong enough to be, as it were, a new nature, being excited by any intervening accident, force men, though unwilling, to their accustomed passions. Consider the timorous, they are afraid even of those things that preserve them. Consider the pettish, they are angry with their best and dearest friends. Consider the amorous and lascivious, in the height of their fury they dare violate a Vestal. For custom is very powerful to draw the temper of the body to anything that is suitable to it; and he that is apt to fall will stumble at everything that lies in his way. So it is no wonder that those that have raised in themselves an envious and bewitching habit, if according to the peculiarity of their passion they are carried on to suitable effects; for when they are once moved, they do that which the nature of the thing, not which their will, leads them to. For as a sphere must necessarily move spherically, and a cylinder cylindrically, according to the difference of their figures; thus his disposition makes an envious man move enviously to all things; and it is likely they should chiefly hurt their most familiar acquaintance and best beloved. And that fine fellow Eutelidas you mentioned, and the rest that are said to overlook themselves, may be easily and upon good rational grounds accounted for; for, according to Hippocrates, a good habit of body, when at height, is easily perverted, and bodies come to their full maturity do not stand at a stay there, but fall and waste down to the contrary extreme. And therefore when they are in very good plight, and see themselves look much better than they expected, they gaze and wonder; but then their body being nigh to change, and their habit declining into a worse condition, they overlook themselves. And this is done when the effluvia are stopped and reflected by the water rather than by any other reflecting body; for this exhales upon them whilst they look upon it, so that the very same particles which would hurt others must hurt themselves. And this perchance often happens to young children, and the cause of their diseases is falsely attributed to those that look upon them.

When I had done, Caius, Florus's son-in-law, said: Then it seems you make no more reckoning or account of Democritus's images, than of those of Aegium or Megara; for he delivers that the envious send out images which are not altogether void of sense or force, but full of the disturbing and poisonous qualities of those from whom they come. Now these being mixed with such qualities, and remaining with and abiding in those persons that injure them both in mind and body; for this, I think, is the meaning of that philosopher, a man in his opinion and expressions admirable and divine. Very true, said I, and I wonder that you did not observe that I took nothing from those effluvia and images but life and will; lest you should imagine that, now it is almost midnight, I brought in spectres and wise and understanding images to terrify and fright you; but in the morning, if you please, we will talk of those things.

QUESTION VIII. WHY HOMER CALLS THE APPLE-TREE [GREEK OMITTED], AND EMPEDOCLES CALLS APPLES [GREEK OMITTED]. PLUTARCH, TRYPHO, CERTAIN GRAMMARIANS, LAMPRIAS THE ELDER.

As we were at supper in Chaeronea, and had all sorts of fruit at the table, one of the company chanced to speak these verses,

The fig-trees sweet, the apple-trees that bear
Fair fruit, and olives green through all the year.
("Odyssey," vii. 115.)

Upon this there arose a question, why the poet calls apple-trees particularly [Greek omitted], BEARING FAIR FRUIT. Trypho the physician said that this epithet was given comparatively in respect of the tree, because, it being small and no goodly tree to look upon, bears fair and large fruit. Somebody else said, that the particular excellencies scattered amongst all other fruits are united in this alone. As to the touch, it is smooth and polished, so that it makes the hand that toucheth it odorous without defiling it; it is sweet to the taste, and to the smell and sight very pleasing; and therefore there is reason that it should be duly praised, as being that which congregates and allures all the senses together.

This discourse pleased us indifferently well. But whereas Empedocles has thus written,

Why pomegranates so late do thrive,
And apples give a lovely show [Greek omitted];

I guess the epithet to be given to pomegranates, because that at the end of autumn, and when the heats begin to decrease, they ripen the fruit; for the sun will not suffer the weak and thin moisture to thicken into a consistence until the air begins to wax colder; therefore, says Theophrastus, this only tree ripens its fruit best and soonest in the shade. But in what sense the philosopher gives the epithet [Greek omitted], to apples, I much question, since it is not his custom to try to adorn his verses with varieties of epithets, as with gay and florid colors. But in every verse he gives some description of the substance and virtue of the subject which he treats; as when he calls the body encircling the soul the mortal-surrounding earth; as also when he calls the air cloud-gathering, and the liver much blooded.

When now I had said these things myself, certain grammarians affirmed, that those apples were called [Greek omitted] by reason of their vigor and florid manner of growing; for to blossom and flourish after an extraordinary manner is by the poets expressed by the word [Greek omitted]. In this sense, Antimachus calls the city of Cadmeans flourishing with fruit; and Aratus, speaking of the dog-star Sirius, says that he

To some gave strength, but others did ruin,
Their bloom;

calling the greenness of the trees and the blossoming of the fruit by the name of [Greek omitted]. Nay, there are some of the Greeks also who sacrifice to Bacchus surnamed [Greek omitted]. And therefore, seeing the verdure and floridness chiefly recommend this fruit, philosophers call it [Greek omitted]. But Lamprias our grandfather used to say that the word [Greek omitted] did not only denote excess and vehemency, but external and supernal; thus we call the upper frame of a door [Greek omitted], and the upper portion of the house [Greek omitted]; and the poet calls the outward parts of the victim the upper-flesh, as he calls the entrails the inner-flesh. Let us see therefore, says he, whether Empedocles did not make use of this epithet in this sense, seeing that other fruits are encompassed with an outward rind and with certain coatings and membranes, but the only cortex rind that the apple has is a glutinous and smooth tunic (or core) containing the seed, so that the part which can be eaten, and lies without, was properly called [Greek omitted], that IS OVER or OUTSIDE OF THE HUSK.

QUESTION IX. WHAT IS THE REASON THAT THE FIG-TREE, BE-ING ITSELF OF A VERY SHARP AND BITTER TASTE, BEARS SO SWEET FRUIT? LAMPRIAS THE ELDER, AND OTHERS.

This discourse ended, the next question was about fig-trees, how so luscious and sweet fruit should come from so bitter a tree. For the leaf from its roughness is called [Greek omitted]. The wood of it is full of sap, and as it burns sends forth a very biting smoke; and the ashes of it thoroughly burnt are so acrimonious, that they make a lye extremely detersive. And, which is very strange, all other trees that bud and bear fruit put forth blossoms too; but the fig-tree never blossoms. And if (as some say) it is never thunderstruck, that likewise may be attributed to the sharp juices and bad temper of the stock; for such things are as secure from thunder as the skin of a sea calf or hyena. Then said the old man: It is no wonder that when all the sweetness is separated and employed in making the fruit, that which is left should be bitter and unsavory. For as the liver, all the gall being gathered in its proper place, is itself very sweet; so the fig-tree having parted with its oil and sweet particles to the fruit, reserves no portion for itself. For that this tree hath some good juice, I gather from what they say of rue, which grow-ing under a fig-tree is sweeter than usual, and hath a sweeter and more palatable juice, as if it drew some sweet particles from the tree which mollified its offensive and corroding qualities; unless perhaps, on the contrary, the fig-tree robbing it of its nourishment draws likewise some of its sharpness and bitterness away.

QUESTION X. WHAT ARE THOSE THAT ARE SAID TO BE [GREEK OMITTED], AND WHY HOMER CALLS SALT DIVINE? FLORUS, APOLLOPHANES, PLUTARCH, PHILINUS.

Florus, when we were entertained at his house, put this question, What are those in the proverb who are said to be about the salt and cummin? Apollophanes the grammarian presently satisfied him, say-ing, by that proverb were meant intimate acquaintance, who could sup together on salt and cummin. Thence we proceeded to inquire how salt should come to be so much honored as it is; for Homer plainly says,

> And after that he strewed his salt divine
> ("*Iliad*," ix. 214.)

and Plato delivers that by man's laws salt is to be accounted most sa-cred. And this difficulty was increased by the customs of the Egyptian priests, who professing chastity eat no salt, no, not so much as in their bread. For if it be divine and holy, why should they avoid it?

Florus bade us not mind the Egyptians, but speak according to the Grecian custom on the present subject. But I replied: The Egyptians are not contrary to the Greeks in this matter; for the profession of purity and chastity forbids getting children, laughter, wine, and many other very commendable and lawful things; and perhaps these priests avoid salt, as being, according to some men's opinions, by its heat provocative and apt to raise lust. Or they refuse it as the most pleasant of all sauces, for indeed salt may be called the sauce of all sauces; and therefore some call salt [Greek omitted]; because it makes food, which is necessary for life, to be relishing and pleasant.

What then, said Florus, shall we say that salt is termed divine for that reason? Indeed that is very considerable, for men for the most part deify those common things that are exceeding useful to their necessities and wants, as water, light, the seasons of the year; and the earth they do not only think to be divine, but a very god. Now salt is as useful as either of these, protecting in a way the food as it comes into the body, and making it palatable and agreeable to the appetite. But consider farther, whether its power of preserving dead bodies from rotting a long time be not a divine property, and opposite to death; since it preserves part, and will not suffer that which is mortal wholly to be destroyed. But as the soul, which is our diviner part, connects the limbs of animals, and keeps the composure from dissolution; thus salt applied to dead bodies, and imitating the work of the soul, stops those parts that were falling to corruption, binds and confines them, and so makes them keep their union and agreement with one another. And therefore some of the Stoics say, that swine's flesh then deserves the name of a body, when the soul like salt spreads through it and keeps the parts from dissolution. Besides, you know that we account lightning to be sacred and divine, because the bodies that are thunderstruck do not rot for a long time; what wonder is it then, that the ancients called salt as well as lightning divine, since it hath the same property and power?

I making no reply, Philinus subjoined: Do you not think that that which is generative is to be esteemed divine, seeing God is the principle of all things? And I assenting, he continued: Salt, in the opinion of some men, for instance the Egyptians you mentioned, is very operative that way; and those that breed dogs, when they find their bitches not apt to be hot, give them salt and seasoned flesh, to excite and arouse their sleeping lechery and vigor. Besides, the ships that carry salt breed abundance of mice; the females, as some imagine, conceiving without the help of the males, only by licking the salt. But it is most probable

that the salt raiseth an itching in animals, and so makes them sala-
cious and eager to couple. And perhaps for the same reason they call
a surprising and bewitching beauty, such as is apt to move and entice,
[Greek omitted], SALTISH. And I think the poets had a respect to this
generative power of salt in their fable of Venus springing from the sea.
And it may be farther observed, that they make all the sea gods very
fruitful, and give them large families. And besides, there are no land
animals so fruitful as the sea ones; agreeable to which observation is
that verse of Empedocles,

Leading the foolish race of fruitful fish.

Book Six

TIMOTHEUS THE SON OF Conon, Sossius Senecio, after a full enjoyment of luxurious campaign diet, being entertained by Plato
in his Academy, at a neat, homely, and (as Ion says) no surfeiting
feast (such an one as is constantly attended by sound sleep, and by
reason of the calm and pleasant state the body enjoys, rarely interrupted with dreams and apparitions), the next day, being sensible
of the difference, said that those that supped with Plato were well
treated, even the day after the feast. For such a temper of a body not
overcharged, but expedite and fitted for the ready execution of all its
enterprises, is without all doubt a great help for the more comfortable passing away of the day. But there is another benefit not inferior to the former, which does usually accrue to those that sup with
Plato, namely, the recollection of those points that were debated at
the table. For the remembrance of those pleasures which arise from
meat and drink is ungenteel, and short-lived withal, and nothing but
the remains of yesterday's smell. But the subjects of philosophical
queries and discourses, being always fresh after they are imparted,
are equally relished by all, as well by those that were absent as by
those that were present at them; insomuch that learned men even
now are as much partakers of Socrates's feasts as those who really
supped with him. But if things pertaining to the body had af discourse, but of the great variety of dishes, sauces, and other costly
compositions that were prepared in the houses of Callias and Agatho.
Yet there is not the least mention made of any such things, though
questionless they were as sumptuous as possible; but whatever things
were treated of and learnedly discussed by their guests were left
upon record and transmitted to posterity as precedents, not only for
discoursing at table, but also for remembering the things that were
handled at such meetings.

QUESTION I. WHAT IS THE REASON THAT THOSE THAT ARE FASTING ARE MORE THIRSTY THAN HUNGRY? PLUTARCH AND OTHERS.

I present you with this Sixth Book of Table Discourses, wherein the first thing that cometh to be discussed is an inquiry into the reason why those that are fasting are more inclinable to drink than to eat. For the assertion carries in it a repugnancy to the standing rules of reason; forasmuch as the decayed stock of dry nourishment seems more naturally to call for its proper supplies. Whereupon I told the company, that of those things whereof our bodies are composed, heat only–or, however, above all the rest–stands in continual need of such accessions; for the truth of which this may be urged as a convincing argument: neither air, water, nor earth requires any matter to feed upon, or devours whatsoever lies next it; but fire alone doth. Hence it comes to pass that young men, by reason of their greater share of natural heat, have commonly greater stomachs than old men; whereas on the contrary, old men can endure fasting much better, for this only reason, because their natural heat is grown weaker and decayed. Just so we see it fares with bloodless animals, which by reason of the want of heat require very little nourishment. Besides, every one of us finds by experience, that bodily exercises, clamors, and whatever other actions by violent motion occasion heat, commonly sharpen our stomachs and get us a better appetite. Now, as I take it, the most natural and principal nourishment of heat is moisture, as it evidently appears from flames, which increase by the pouring in of oil, and from ashes, which are of the driest things in nature; for after the humidity is consumed by the fire, the terrene and grosser parts remain without any moisture at all. Add to these, that fire separates and dissolves bodies by extracting that moisture which should keep them close and compact. Therefore, when we are fasting, the heat first of all forces the moisture out of the relics of the nourishment that remain in the body, and then, pursuing the other humid parts, preys upon the natural moisture of the flesh itself. Hence the body like clay becoming dry, wants drink more than meat; till the heat, receiving strength and vigor by our drinking, excites an appetite for more substantial food.

QUESTION II. WHETHER WANT OF NOURISHMENT CAUSETH HUNGER AND THIRST OR THE CHANGE IN THE FIGURES OF THE PORES. PHILO, PLUTARCH.

After these things were spoke, Philo the physician started the first question, asserting that thirst did not arise from the want of nourishment, but from the different transfiguration of certain passages. For, says he, this may be made evident, partly from what we see happens to those that thirst in the night, who, if sleep chance to steal upon them, though they did not drink before, are yet rid of their thirst; partly from persons in a fever, who, as soon as the disease abates or is removed, thirst no more. Nay, a great many men, after they have bathed or vomited, perceive presently that their thirst is gone; yet none of these add anything to their former moisture, but only the transfiguration of the pores causeth a new order and disposition. And this is more evident in hunger; for many sick persons, at the same time when they have the greatest need of meat, have no stomach. Others, after they have filled their bellies, have the same stomachs, and their appetites are rather increased than abated. There are a great many besides who loathe all sorts of diet, yet by taking of a pickled olive or caper recover and confirm their lost appetites. This doth clearly evince, that hunger proceeds from some change in the pores, and not from any want of sustenance, forasmuch as such kind of food lessens the defect by adding food, but increases the hunger; and the pleasing relish and poignancy of such pickles, by binding and straitening the mouth of the ventricle, and again by opening and loosening of it, beget in it a convenient disposition to receive meat, which we call by the name of appetite.

I must confess this discourse seemed to carry in it some shadow of reason and probability; but in the main it is directly repugnant to the chief end of nature, to which appetite directs every animal. For that makes it desire a supply of what they stand in need of, and avoid a defect of their proper food. For to deny what especially makes a living creature differ from an inanimate object as given to us for our preservation and conservation (being as it were the receiver of what supplements and agrees with the nature of our body) is the argument of one who takes no account of natural law, especially when he would add that the characteristic proceeds from the great or small size of the pores. Besides, it is absurd to think that a body through the want of natural heat should be chilled, and should not in like manner hunger and thirst through the want of natural moisture and nourishment. And yet this is more absurd, that Nature when overcharged should desire to disburden herself, and yet should not require to be supplied on account of emptiness, but on account of some condition or other, I know not what. Moreover, these needs and supplies in relation to animals have some resemblance to those we see in husbandry. There are a great many like qualities and like provisions on both sides. For in a drought we water our grounds, and in case of excessive heat, we frequently make use of moderate coolers; and when our fruits are too cold, we endeavor to preserve and cherish them, by covering and making fences about them. And for such things as are out of the reach of human power, we implore the assistance of the gods, that is, to send us softening dews, and sunshines qualified with moderate winds; that so Nature, being always desirous of a due mixture, may have her wants supplied. And for this reason I presume it was that nourishment is called [Greek omitted] (from [Greek omitted]), because it observes and preserves Nature. Now Nature is preserved in plants, which are destitute of sense, by the favorable influence of the circum-ambient air (as Empedocles says), moistening them in such a measure as is most agreeable to their nature. But as for us men, our appetites prompt us on to the chase and pursuance of whatsoever is wanting to our natural temperament.

But now let us pass to the examination of the truth of the arguments that seem to favor the contrary opinion. And for the first, I suppose that those meats that are palatable and of a quick and sharp taste do not beget in us an appetite, but rather bite and fret those parts that receive the nourishment, as we find that scratching the skin causes itching. And supposing we should grant that this affection or disposition is the very thing which we call the appetite, it is probable that, by the operation of such kind of food as this, the nourishment may be made small, and so much of it as is convenient for Nature severed from the rest, so that the indigency proceeds not from the transmutation, but from the evacuation and purgation of the passages. For sharp, tart, and salt things grate the inward matter, and by dispersing of it cause digestion, so that by the concoctions of the old there may arise an appetite for new. Nor does the cessation of thirst after bathing spring from the different position of the passages, but from a new supply of moisture received into the flesh, and conveyed from thence to them also. And vomiting, by throwing off whatever is disagreeable to Nature, puts her in a capacity of enjoying what is most suitable for her. For thirst does not call for a superfluity of moisture, but only for so much as sufficeth Nature; and therefore, though a man had plenty of disagreeable and unnatural moisture, yet he wants still, for that stops the course of the natural, which Nature is desirous of, and hinders a due mixture and temperament, till it be cast out and the pores receive what is most proper and convenient for them. Moreover, a fever forces all the moisture downward; and the middle parts being in combustion, it all retires thither, and there is shut up and forcibly detained. And therefore it is usual with a great many to vomit, by reason of the density of the inward parts squeezing out the moisture, and likewise to thirst, by reason of the poor and dry state the rest of the body is in. But after the violence of the distemper is once abated, and the raging heat hath left the middle parts, the moisture begins to disperse itself again; and according to its natural motion, by a speedy conveyance into all the parts, it refreshes the entrails, softens and makes tender the dry and parched flesh. Very often also it causes sweat, and then the defect which occasioned thirst ceases; for the moisture leaving that part of the body wherein it was forcibly detained, and out of which it hardly made an escape, retires to the place where it is wanted. For as it fares with a garden wherein there is a large well,–if nobody draw thereof and water it, the herbs must needs wither and die,–so it fares with a body; if all the moisture be contracted into one part, it is no wonder if the rest be in want and dry, till it is diffused again over the other limbs. Just so it happens to persons in a fever, after the heat of the disease is over, and likewise to those who go to sleep thirsty. For in these, sleep draws the moisture to the middle parts, and equally distributes it amongst the rest, satisfying them all. But, I pray, what kind of transfiguration of the passages is this which causes hunger and thirst? For my part, I know no other distinction of the pores but in respect of their number or that some of them are shut, others open. As for those that are shut, they can neither receive meat nor drink; and as for those that are open, they make an empty space, which is nothing but a want of that which Nature requires. Thus, sir, when men dye cloth, the liquor in which they dip it hath very sharp and abstersive particles; which, consuming and scouring off all the matter that filled the pores, make the cloth more apt to receive the dye, because its pores are empty and want something to fill them up.

QUESTION III. WHAT IS THE REASON THAT HUNGER IS ALLAYED BY DRINKING, BUT THIRST INCREASED BY EATING? THE HOST, PLUTARCH, AND OTHERS.

After we had gone thus far, the master of the feast told the company that the former points were reasonably well discussed; and waiving at present the discourse concerning the evacuation and repletion of the pores, he requested us to fall upon another question, that is, how it comes to pass that hunger is stayed by drinking, when, on the contrary, thirst is more violent after eating. Those who assign the reason to be in the pores seem with a great deal of ease and probability, though not with so much truth, to explain the thing. For seeing the pores in all bodies are of different sorts and sizes, the more capacious receive both dry and humid nourishment, the lesser take in drink, not meat; but the vacuity of the former causes hunger, of the latter thirst. Hence it is that men that thirst are never better after they have eaten, the pores by rea-

son of their straitness denying admittance to grosser nourishment, and
the want of suitable supply still remaining. But after hungry men have
drunk, the moisture enters the greater pores, fills the empty spaces, and
in part assuages the violence of the hunger.

Of this effect, said I, I do not in the least doubt, but I do not approve
of the reason they give for it. For if any one should admit these pores
(which some are so unreasonably fond of) to be in the flesh, he must
needs make it a very soft, loose, flabby substance; and that the same
parts do not receive the meat and drink, but that they run through different canals and strainers in them, seems to me to be a very strange
and unaccountable opinion. For the moisture mixes with the dry food,
and by the assistance of the natural heat and spirits cuts the nourishment far smaller than any cleaver or chopping-knife, to the end that
every part of it may be exactly fitted to each part of the body, not applied, as they would have it, to little vessels and pores, but united and
incorporated with the whole substance. And unless the thing were explained after this manner, the hardest knot in the question would still
remain unsolved. For a man that has a thirst upon him, supposing he
eats and doth not drink, is so far from quenching, that he does highly
increase it. This point is yet undiscussed. But mark, said I, whether the
positions on my side be clear and evident or not. In the first place, we
take it for granted that moisture is wasted and destroyed by heat, that
the drier parts of the nourishment qualified and softened by moisture,
are diffused and fly away in vapors. Secondly, we must by no means
suppose that all hunger is a total privation of dry, and thirst of humid nutriment, but only a moderate one, and such as is sufficient to
cause the one or the other; for whoever are wholly deprived of either
of these, they neither hunger nor thirst, but die instantly. These things
being laid down as a foundation, it will be no hard matter to find out
the cause. For thirst is increased by eating for this reason, because that
meat by its natural siccity contracts and destroys all that small quantity of moisture which remained scattered here and there through the
body; just as happens in things obvious to our senses; we see the earth,
dust, and the like presently suck in the moisture that is mixed with
them. Now, on the contrary, drink must of necessity assuage hunger;
for the moisture watering and diffusing itself through the dry and
parched relics of the meat we ate last, by turning them into thin juices,
conveys them through the whole body, and succors the indigent parts.
And therefore with very good reason Erasistratus called moisture the
vehicle of the meat; for as soon as this is mixed with things which by
reason of their dryness, or some other quality, are slow and heavy, it

raises them up and carries them aloft. Moreover, several men, when they have drunk nothing at all, but only washed themselves, all on a sudden are freed from a very violent hunger, because the extrinsic moisture entering the pores makes the meat within more succulent and of a more nourishing nature, so that the heat and fury of the hunger declines and abates; and therefore a great many of those who have a mind to starve themselves to death live a long time only by drinking water; that is, as long as the siccity does not quite consume whatever may be united to and nourish the body.

QUESTION IV. WHAT IS THE REASON THAT A BUCKET OF WATER DRAWN OUT OF A WELL, IF IT STANDS ALL NIGHT IN THE AIR THAT IS IN THE WELL, IS, MORE COLD IN THE MORNING THAN THE REST OF THE WATER?

A GUEST, PLUTARCH, AND OTHERS.
One of the strangers at the the table, who took wonderful great delight in drinking of cold water, had some brought to him by the servants, cooled after this manner; they had hung in the well a bucket full of the same water, so that it could not touch the sides of the well, and there let it remain, all night: the next day, when it was brought to table, it was colder than the water that was newdrawn. Now this gentleman was an indifferent good scholar, and therefore told the company that he had learned this from Aristotle, who gives the reason of it. The reason which he assigned was this. All water, when it hath been once hot, is afterwards more cold; as that which is prepared for kings, when it hath boiled a good while upon the fire, is afterwards put into a vessel set round with snow, and so made colder; just as we find our bodies more cool after we have bathed, because the body, after a short relaxation from heat, is rarefied and more porous, and therefore so much the more fitted to receive a larger quantity of air, which causes the alteration. Therefore the water, when it is drawn out of the well, being first warmed in the air, grows presently cold.

Whereupon we began to commend the man very highly for his happy memory; but we called in question the pretended reason. For if the air wherein the vessel hangs be cold, how, I pray, does it heat the water? If hot, how does it afterwards make it cold? For it is absurd to say, that the same thing is affected by the same thing with contrary qualities, no difference at all intervening. While the gentleman held his peace, as not knowing what to say; there is no cause, said I, that we should raise any scruple concerning the nature of the air, forasmuch as we are ascertained by sense that it is cold, especially in the bottom of a well; and therefore we can never imagine that it should make the water hot. But I should rather judge this to be the reason: the cold air, though it cannot cool the great quantity of water which is in the well, yet can easily cool each part of it, separate from the whole.

QUESTION V. WHAT IS THE REASON THAT PEBBLE STONES AND LEADEN BULLETS THROWN INTO THE WATER MAKE IT MORE COLD? A GUEST, PLUTARCH, AND OTHERS.

I suppose you may remember that what Aristotle says in his problems, of little stones and pieces of iron, how it hath been observed by some that being thrown into the water they temper and cool it. This is no more than barely asserted by him; but we will go farther and inquire into the reason of it, the discovery of which will be a matter of difficulty. Yes, says I, it will so, and it is much if we hit upon it; for do but consider, first of all, do not you suppose that the air which comes in from without cools the water? But now air has a great deal more power and force, when it beats against stones and pieces of iron. For they do not, like brazen and earthen vessels, suffer it to pass through; but, by reason of their solid bulk, beat it back and reflect it into the water, so that upon all parts the cold works very strongly. And hence it comes to pass that rivers in the winter are colder than the sea, because the cold air has a power over them, which by reason of its depth it has not over the sea, where it is scattered without any reflection. But it is probable that for another reason thinner waters may be made colder by the air than thicker, because they are not so strong to resist its force. Now whetstones and pebbles make the water thinner by drawing to them all the mud and other grosser substances that be mixed with it, that so by taking the strength from it may the more easily be wrought upon by the cold. But besides, lead is naturally cold, as that which, being dissolved in vinegar, makes the coldest of all poisons, called white-lead; and stones, by reason of their density, raise cold in the bottom of the water. For every stone is nothing else but a congealed lump of frozen earth, though some more or less than others; and therefore it is no absurdity to say that stones and lead, by reflecting the air, increase the coldness of the water.

QUESTION VI WHAT IS THE REASON THAT MEN PRESERVE SNOW BY COVERING IT WITH CHAFF AND CLOTHS? A GUEST, PLUTARCH.

Then the stranger, after he had made a little pause, said: Men in love are ambitious to be in company with their sweethearts; when that is denied them, they desire at least to talk of them. This is my case in relation to snow; and, because I cannot have it at present, I am desirous to learn the reason why it is commonly preserved by the hottest things. For, when covered with chaff and cloth that has never been at the fuller's, it is preserved a long time. Now it is strange that the coldest things should be preserved by the hottest.

Yes, said I, it is a very strange thing, if true. But it is not so; and we cozen ourselves by presently concluding a thing to be hot if it have a faculty of causing heat, when as yet we see that the same garment causes heat in winter, and cold in summer. Thus the nurse in the tragedy,

> In garments thin doth Niobe's children fold,
> And sometimes heats and sometimes cools the babes.

The Germans indeed make use of clothes only against the cold, the Ethiopians only against the heat; but they are useful to us upon both accounts. Why therefore should we rather say the clothes are hot, because they cause heat, than cold, because they cause cold? Nay, if we must be tried by sense, it will be found that they are more cold than hot. For at the first putting on of a coat it is cold, and so is our bed when we lie down; but afterwards they grow hot with the heat of our bodies, because they both keep in the heat and keep out the cold. Indeed, feverish persons and others that have a violent heat upon them often change their clothes, because they perceive that fresh ones at the first putting on are much colder; but within a very little time their bodies make them as hot as the others. In like manner, as a garment heated makes us hot, so a covering cooled keeps snow cold. Now that which causes this cold is the continual emanations of a subtile spirit the snow has in it, which spirit, as long as it remains in the snow, keeps it compact and close; but, after once it is gone, the snow melts and dissolves into water, and instantly loses its whiteness, occasioned by a mixture of this spirit with a frothy moisture. Therefore at the same time, by the help of these clothes, the cold is kept in, and the external air is shut out, lest it should thaw the concrete body of the snow. The reason why they make use of cloth that has not yet been at the fuller's is this, because that in such cloth the hair and coarse flocks keep it off from pressing too hard upon the snow, and bruising it. So chaff lying lightly upon it does not dissolve the body of the snow, besides the chaff lies close and shuts out the warm air, and keeps in the natural cold of the snow. Now that snow melts by the evaporating of this spirit, we are ascertained by sense; for when snow melts it raises a vapor.

QUESTION VII. WHETHER WINE OUGHT TO BE STRAINED OR NOT. NIGER, ARISTIO.

Niger, a citizen of ours, was lately come from school, after he had spent some time under the discipline of a celebrated philosopher, but had absorbed nothing but those faults by which his master was odious to others, especially his custom of reproving and of carping at whatever upon any occasion chanced to be discussed in company. And therefore, when we were at supper one time at Aristio's, not content to assume to himself a liberty to rail at all the rest of the preparations as too profuse and extravagant, he had a pique at the wine too, and said that it ought not to be brought to table strained, but that, observing Hesiod's rule, we ought to drink it new out of the vessel. Moreover, he added that this way of purging wine takes the strength from it, and robs it of its natural heat, which, when wine is poured out of one vessel into another, evaporates and dies. Besides he would needs persuade us that it showed too much of a vain curiosity, effeminacy, and luxury, to convert what is wholesome into that which is palatable. For as the riotous, not the temperate, use to cut cocks and geld pigs, to make their flesh tender and delicious, even against Nature; just so (if we may use a metaphor, says he) those that strain wine geld and emasculate it, whilst their squeamish stomachs will neither suffer them to drink pure wine, nor their intemperance to drink moderately. Therefore they make use of this expedient, to the end that it may render the desire they have of drinking plentifully more excusable. So they take all the strength from the wine, leaving the palatableness still: as we use to deal with those with whose constitution cold water does not agree, to boil it for them. For they certainly take off all the strength from the wine, by straining of it. And this is a great argument, that the wine deads, grows flat, and loses its virtue, when it is separated from the lees, as from its root and stock; for the ancients for very good reason called wine lees, as we use to signify a man by his head or soul, as the principal part of him. So in Greek, grape-gatherers are said [Greek omitted], the word being derived from [Greek omitted], which signifies lees; and Homer in one place calls the fruit of the wine [Greek omitted], and the wine itself high-colored and red,–not pale and yellow, such as Aristio gives us to supper, after all the goodness is purged out of it.

Then Aristio smiling presently replied: Sir, the wine I bring to table does not look so pale and lifeless as you would have it: but it appears only in the cup to be mild and well qualified. But for your part, you would glut yourself with night wine, which raises melancholy vapors; and upon this account you cry out against purgation, which, by carrying off whatever might cause melancholy or load men's stomachs, and make them drunk or sick, makes it mild and pleasant to those that drink it, such as heroes (as Homer tells us) were formerly wont to drink. And it was not dark wine which he called [Greek omitted], but clear and transparent; for otherwise he would never have named brass [Greek omitted], after characterizing it as man-exalting and resplendent. Therefore as the wise Anacharsis, discommending some things that the Grecians enjoined, commended their coals, because they leave the smoke without doors, and bring the fire into the house; so you judicious men might blame me for some other reason than this. But what hurt, I pray, have I done to the wine, by taking from it a turbulent and noisome quality, and giving it a better taste, though a paler color? Nor have I brought you wine to the table which, like a sword, hath lost its edge and vigorous relish, but such as is only purged of its dregs and filth. But you will say that wine not strained hath a great deal more strength. Why so, my friend? One that is frantic and distracted has more strength than a man in his wits; but when, by the help of hellebore or some other fit diet, he is come to himself, that rage and frenzy leave him and quite vanish, and the true use of his reason and health of body presently comes into its place. In like manner, purging of wine takes from it all the strength that inflames and enrages the mind, and gives it instead thereof a mild and wholesome temper; and I think there is a great deal of difference between gaudiness and cleanliness. For women, while they paint, perfume, and adorn themselves with jewels and purple robes, are accounted gaudy and profuse; yet nobody will find fault with them for washing their faces, anointing themselves, or platting their hair. Homer very neatly expresses the difference of these two habits, where he brings in Juno dressing herself:–

With sweet ambrosia first she washed her skin,
And after did anoint herself with oil.
("Iliad," xiv. 170.)

So much was allowable, being no more than a careful cleanliness. But when she comes to call for her golden buttons, her curiously wrought earrings, and last of all puts on her bewitching girdle, this appears to be an extravagant and idle curiosity, and betrays too much of wantonness, which by no means becomes a married woman. Just so they that sophisticate wine by mixing it with aloes, cinnamon, or saffron bring it to the table like a gorgeous-apparelled woman, and there prostitute it. But those that only take from it what is nasty and no way profitable do only purge it and improve it by their labor. Otherwise you may find fault with all things whatsoever as vain and extravagant, beginning at the house you live in. As first, you may say, why is it plastered? Why does it open especially on that side where it may have the best convenience for receiving the purest air, and the benefit of the evening sun? What is the reason that our cups are washed and made so clean that they shine and look bright? Now if a cup ought to have nothing that is nasty or loathsome in it, ought that which is drunk out of the cup to be full of dregs and filth? What need is there for mentioning anything else? The making corn into bread is a continual cleansing; and yet what a great ado there is before it is effected! There is not only threshing, winnowing, sifting, and separating the bran, but there must be kneading the dough to soften all parts alike, and a continual cleansing and working of the mass till all the parts become edible alike. What absurdity is it then by straining to separate the lees, as it were the filth of the wine, especially since the cleansing is no chargeable or painful operation?

QUESTION VIII. WHAT IS THE CAUSE OF BULIMY OR THE GREEDY DISEASE? PLUTARCH, SOCLARUS, CLEOMENES, AND OTHERS.

There is a certain sacrifice of very ancient institution, which the chief magistrate or archon performs always in the common-hall, and every private person in his own house. 'Tis called the driving out of bulimy; for they whip out of doors some one of their servants with a bunch of willow rods, repeating these words, Get out of doors, bulimy; and enter riches and health. Therefore in my year there was a great concourse of people present at the sacrifice; and, after all the rites and ceremonies of the sacrifice were over, when we had seated ourselves again at the table, there was an inquiry made first of all into the signification of the word bulimy, then into the meaning of the words which are repeated when the servant is turned out of doors. But the principal dispute was concerning the nature of it, and all its circumstances. First, as for the word bulimy, it was agreed upon by all to denote a great and public famine, especially among us who use the Aeolic dialect, putting [Greek omitted] for [Greek omitted]. For it was not called by the ancients [Greek omitted] but [Greek omitted], that is, [Greek omitted], much hunger. We concluded that it was not the same with the disease called Bubrostis, by an argument fetched out of Metrodorus's Ionics. For the said Metrodorus informs us that the Smyrnaeans, who were once Aeolians, sacrificed to Bubrostis a black bull cut into pieces with the skin on, and so burnt it. Now, forasmuch as every species of hunger resembles a disease, but more particularly Bulimy, which is occasioned by an unnatural disposition of the body, these two differ as riches and poverty, health and sickness. But as the word NAUSEATE [Greek omitted] first took its name from men who were sea-sick in a ship, and afterwards custom prevailed so far that the word was applied to all persons that were any way in like sort affected; so the word BULIMY, rising at first from hence, was at last extended to a more large and comprehensive signification. What has been hitherto said was a general club of the opinions of all those who were at table.

But after we began to inquire after the cause of this disease, the first thing that puzzled us was to find out the reason why bulimy seizes upon those that travel in the snow. As Brutus, one time marching from Dyrrachium to Apollonia in a deep snow, was endangered of his life by bulimy, whilst none of those that carried the provisions for the army followed him; just when the man was ready to faint and die, some of his soldiers were forced to run to the walls of the enemies' city, and beg a piece of bread of the sentinels, by the eating of which he was presently refreshed; for which cause, after Brutus had made himself master of the city, he treated all the inhabitants very mercifully. Asses and horses are frequently troubled with bulimy, especially when they are laden with dry figs and apples; and, which is yet more strange, of all things that are eaten, bread chiefly refreshes not only men but beasts; so that, by taking a little quantity of bread, they regain their strength and go forward on their journey.

After all were silent, I (who had observed that dull fellows and those of a less piercing judgment were satisfied with and did acquiesce in the reasons the ancients gave for bulimy, but to men of ingenuity and industry they only pointed out the way to a more clear discovery of the truth of the business) mentioned Aristotle's opinion, who says, that extreme cold without causes extreme heat and consumption within; which, if it fall into the legs, makes them lazy and heavy, but if it come to the fountain of motion and respiration, occasions faintings and weakness. When I had said that, some of the company opposed it, others held with me.

At length says Soclarus: I like the beginning of this reason very well, for the bodies of travellers in a great snow must of necessity be surrounded and condensed with cold; but that from the heat within there should arise such a consumption as invades the principle of respiration, I can no way imagine. I rather think, says he, that abundance of heat penned up in the body consumes the nourishment, and that failing, the fire as it were goes out. Here it comes to pass, that men troubled with this bulimy, when they are ready to starve with hunger, if they eat never so little meat, are presently refreshed. The reason is, because meat digested is like fuel for the heat to feed upon.

But Cleomenes the physician would have the word [Greek omitted] (which signifies hunger) to be added to the making up of the word [Greek omitted] without sufficient reason; as [Greek omitted], to drink, is added to [Greek omitted], to swallow; and [Greek omitted] to incline, into [Greek omitted] to raise the head. Nor is bulimy, as it seems, a kind of hunger, but an affection in the stomach causing a faintness on account of the concourse of heat. Therefore as things that have a good smell recall the spirits of those that are faint, so bread affects those that are almost overcome with a bulimy; not that they have any need of food (for the least piece of it restores them their strength), but the bread calls back their vigor and languishing spirits. Now that bulimy is not hunger but a faintness, is manifest from all laboring beasts, which are seized with it very often through the smell of dry figs and apples; for a smell does not cause any want of food, but rather a pain and agitation in the stomach.

These things seemed to be reasonably well urged; and yet it seemed that much might be said for the contrary opinion, and that it was possible enough to maintain that bulimy ariseth not from condensation but rarefication of the stomach. For the spirit which flows from the snow is nothing but the aether and finest fragment of the frozen substance, endued with a virtue of cutting and dividing not only the flesh, but also silver and brazen vessels; for we see that these are not able to keep in the snow, for it dissolves and evaporates, and glazes over the outmost superficies of the vessels with a thin dew, not unlike to ice, which this spirit leaves as it secretly passes through the pores. Therefore this piercing spirit, like a flame, seizing upon those that travel in the snow, seems to burn their outsides, and like fire to enter and penetrate the flesh. Hence it is that the flesh is more rarefied, and the heat is extinguished by the cold spirit that lies upon the superficies of the body; therefore the body evaporates a dewy thin sweat, which melts away and decays the strength. Now if a man should sit still at such a time, there would not much heat fly out of his body. But when the motion of the body doth quickly heat the nourishment, and that heat bursts through the thin skin, there must necessarily be a great loss of strength. Now we know by experience, that cold hath a virtue not only to condense but also to loosen bodies; for in extreme cold winters pieces of lead are found to sweat. And when we see that a bulimy happens where there is no hunger, we may conclude that at that time the body is rather in a fluid than condensed state. The reason that bodies are rarefied in winter is because of the subtility of the spirit; especially when the moving and tiring of the body stir the heat, which, as soon as it is subtilized and agitated, flies apace, and spreads itself through the whole body. Lastly, it is very possible that apples and dry figs exhale some such thing as this, which rarefies and attenuates the heat of the beasts; for some things have a natural tendency as well to weaken as to refresh different creatures.

QUESTION IX. WHY DOES HOMER APPROPRIATE A CERTAIN PECULIAR EPITHET TO EACH PARTICULAR LIQUID, AND CALL OIL ONLY LIQUID? PLUTARCH, AND OTHERS.

It was the subject once of a discourse, why, when there are several sorts of liquids, the poet should give every one of them a peculiar epithet, calling milk white, honey yellow, wine red, and yet for all this bestow no other upon oil but what it hath in common with all other liquids. To this it was answered that, as that is said to be most sweet which is perfectly sweet, and to be most white which is perfectly white (I mean here by perfectly that which hath nothing of a contrary quality mixed with it), so that ought to be called perfectly humid whereof never a part is dry; and this is proper to oil.

For first of all, its smoothness shows the evenness of its parts; for touch it where you please, it is all alike. Besides, you may see your face in it as perfectly as in a mirror; for there is nothing rough in it to hinder the reflection, but by reason of its humidity it reflects to the eye the least particle of light from every portion. As, on the contrary, milk, of all other liquids, does not return our images, because it hath too many terrene and gross parts mixed with it; again, oil of all other liquids makes the least noise when moved, for it is perfectly humid. When other liquids are moved or poured out, their hard and grosser parts fall and dash one against another, and so make a noise by reason of their roughness. Moreover, oil only is pure and unmixed; for it is of all other liquids most compact, nor has it any empty spaces and pores between the dry and earthy parts to receive what chances to fall upon it. Besides, because of the similitude of its parts, it is closely joined together, and unfit to be joined to anything else. When oil froths, it does not let any wind in, by reason of the contiguity and subtility of its parts; and this is also the cause why fire is nourished by it. For fire feeds upon nothing but what is moist, for nothing is combustible but what is so; for when the fire is kindled, the air turns to smoke, and the terrene and grosser parts remain in the ashes. Fire only preys upon the moisture, which is its natural nourishment. Indeed, water, wine, and other liquors, having abundance of earthy and heavy parts in them, by falling into fire part it, and by their roughness and weight smother and extinguish it. But oil, because purely liquid, by reason of its subtility, is overcome by the fire, and so changed into flame.

It is the greatest argument that can be of its humidity, that the least quantity of it spreads itself a great way; for so small a drop of honey, water, or any other liquid does not extend itself so far, but very often, by reason of the dry mixed parts, is presently wasted. Because oil is ductile and soft, men are wont to make use of it for anointing their bodies; for it runs along and spreads itself through all the parts, and sticks so firmly to them that it is not easily washed off. We find by experience, that a garment wet with water is presently dried again; but it is no easy matter to wash out the spots and stain of oil, for it enters deep, because of its most subtile and humid nature. Hence it is that Aristotle says, that the drops of diluted wine are the hardest to be got out of clothes, because they are most subtile, and run farther into the pores of the cloth.

QUESTION X. WHAT IS THE REASON THAT FLESH OF SACRI-FICED BEASTS, AFTER BEING HUNG A WHILE UPON A FIG-TREE IS MORE TENDER THAN BEFORE? ARISTIO, PLUTARCH, AND OTHERS.

At supper we were commanding Aristio's cook, who, amongst other dishes that he had dressed very curiously, brought a cock to table just killed as a sacrifice to Hercules, as tender as though it had been killed a day or two before. When Aristio told us that this was no wonder,–seeing such a thing might very easily be done, if the cock, as soon as he was killed, was hung upon a fig-tree,–we began to inquire into the reason of what he asserted. Indeed, I must confess, our eye assures us that a fig-tree sends out a fierce and strong spirit; which is yet more evident, from what we have heard said of bulls. That is, a bull, after he is tied to a fig-tree, though never so mad before, grows presently tame, and will suffer you to touch him, and on a sudden all his rage and fury cool and die. But the chiefest cause that works this change is the sharp acrimonious quality of the tree. For this tree is the fullest of sap, and so are its figs, wood, and bark; and hence it comes to pass, that the smoke of fig-wood is most offensive to the eyes; and when it is burned, its ashes make the best lye to scour withal. But all these effects proceed from heat. Now there are some that say, when the sap of this tree thrown into milk curds it, that this effect does not arise from the irregular figures of the parts of the milk, which the sap joins and (as it were) sticks together, the smooth and globose parts being squeezed out, but that by its heat it loosens the unstable and watery parts of the liquid body. And we may use as a proof the unprofitable-ness of the sap of this tree, which, though it is very sweet, yet makes the worst liquor in the world. For it is not the inequality in the parts that affects the smooth part, but what is cold and raw is stopped by heat. And salt help to do this; for it is hot, and works contrary to the uniting of the parts just mentioned, causing rather a dissolution; for to it, above all other things, Nature has given a dissolving faculty. Therefore the fig-tree sends forth a hot and sharp spirit, which cuts and boils the flesh of the bird. The very same thing may be effected by placing the flesh upon a heap of corn, or near nitre; the heat will produce the same that the fig-tree did. Now it may be made manifest that wheat is naturally hot, in that wine, put into a hogshead and placed among wheat, is presently consumed.

Book Seven

THE ROMANS, Sossius Senecio, remember a pretty saying of a pleasant man and good companion, who supping alone said that he had eaten to-day, but not supped; as if a supper always wanted company and agreement to make it palatable and pleasing. Evenus said that fire was the sweetest of all sauces in the world. And Homer calls salt [Greek omitted], divine; and most call it [Greek omitted], graces, because, mixed with most part of our food, it makes it palatable and agreeable to the taste. Now indeed the best and most divine sauce that can be at an entertainment or a supper is a familiar and pleasant friend; not because he eats and drinks with a man, but because he participates of and communicates discourse, especially if the talk be profitable, pertinent, and instructive. For commonly loose talk over a glass of wine raiseth passions and spoils company, and therefore it is fit that we should be as critical in examining what discourses as what friends are fit to be admitted to a supper; not following either the saying or opinion of the Spartans, who, when they entertained any young man or a stranger in their public halls, showed him the door, with these words, "No discourse goes out this way." What we use to talk of may be freely disclosed to everybody, because we have nothing in our discourses that tends to looseness, debauchery, debasing of ourselves, or back-biting others. Judge by the examples, of which this seventh book contains ten.

QUESTION I. AGAINST THOSE WHO FIND FAULT WITH PLATO FOR SAYING THAT DRINK PASSETH THROUGH THE LUNGS. NICIAS, PLUTARCH, PROTOGENES, FLORUS.

At a summer entertainment, one of the company pronounced that common verse,

Now drench thy lungs with wine, the Dog appears.

And Nicias of Nicopolis, a physician, presently subjoined: It is no wonder that Alcaeus, a poet, should be ignorant of that of which Plato the philosopher was. Though Alcaeus may be defended; for it is probable that the lungs, lying near the stomach, may participate of the steam of the liquor, and be drenched with it. But the philosopher, expressly delivering that most part of our drink passeth through the lungs, hath precluded all ways of excuse to those that would be willing to defend him. For it is a very great and complicated ignorance; for first, it being necessary that our liquid and dry food should be mixed, it is very probable that the stomach is the vessel for them both, which throws out the dry food after it is grown soft and moist into the guts. Besides, the lungs being a dense and compacted body, how is it possible that, when we sup gruel or the like, the thicker parts should pass through them? And this was the objection which Erasistratus rationally made against Plato. Besides, when he considered for what end every part of the body was made, and what use Nature designed in their contrivance, it was easy to perceive that the epiglottis was framed on purpose that when we drink the windpipe should be shut, and nothing be suffered to fall upon the lungs. For if anything by chance gets down that way, we are troubled with retching and coughing till it is thrown up again. And this epiglottis being framed so that it may fall on either side, whilst we speak it shuts the weasand, but when we eat or drink it falls upon the windpipe, and so secures the passage for our breath. Besides, we know that those who drink by little and little are looser than those who drink greedily and large draughts; for in the latter the very force drives it into their bladders, but in the former it stays, and by its stay is mixed with and moistens the meat thoroughly. Now this could not be, if in the very drinking the liquid was separated from the dry food; but the effect follows, because we mix and convey them both together, using (as Erasistratus phraseth it) the liquid as a vehicle for the dry.

Nicias having done, Protogenes the grammarian subjoined, that Homer was the first that observed the stomach was the vessel of the food, and the windpipe (which the ancients called [Greek omitted] of the breath, and upon the same account they called those who had loud voices [Greek omitted]). And when he describes how Achilles killed Hector, he says,

He pierced his weasand, where death enters soon;
and adds,
But not his windpipe, so that he could speak,
("Iliad," xxii. 325-329.)

taking the windpipe for the proper passage of the speech and breath....

Upon this, all being silent, Florus began thus: What, shall we tamely suffer Plato to be run down? By no means, said I, for if we desert him, Homer must be in the same condition, for he is so far from denying the windpipe to be the passage for our drink, that the dry food, in his opinion, goes the same way. For these are his words:–

> From his gullet [Greek omitted] flowed
> The clotted wine and undigested flesh.
> ("Odyssey," ix. 373.)

Unless perchance you will say that the Cyclops, as he had but one eye, so had but one passage for his food and voice; or would have [Greek omitted] to signify weasand, not windpipe, as both all the ancients and moderns use it. I produce this because it is really his meaning, not because I want other testimonies, for Plato hath store of learned and sufficient men to join with him. For not to mention Eupolis, who in his play called the "Flatterers" says,

> Protagoras bids us drink a lusty bowl,
> That when the Dog appears our lungs may still be moist;

or elegant Eratosthenes, who says,

> And having drenched his lungs with purest wine;

even Euripides, somewhere expressly saying,

> The wine passed through the hollows of the lungs,

shows that he saw better and clearer than Erasistratus. For he saw that the lungs have cavities and pores, through which the liquids pass. For the breath in expiration hath no need of pores, but that the liquids and those things which pass with them might go through, it is made like a strainer and full of pores. Besides, sir, as to the example of gruel which you proposed, the lungs can discharge themselves of the thicker parts together with the thin, as well as the stomach. For our stomach is not, as some fancy, smooth and slippery, but full of asperities, in which it is probable that the thin and small particles are lodged, and so not taken quite down. But neither this nor the other can we positively affirm; for the curious contrivance of Nature in her operation is too hard to be explained; nor can we be particularly exact upon those instruments (I mean the spirit and the heat) which she makes use of in her works. But besides those we have mentioned to confirm Plato's opinion, let us produce Philistion of Locri, very ancient and very famous physician, and Hippocrates too, with his disciple Dioxippus; for they thought of no other passage but that which Plato mentions. Dio says, that when we feed, the moist parts are about that separated from the dry, and the first are carried down the windpipe, the other down the weasand; and that the windpipe receives no parts of the food, but the stomach, together with the dry parts, receives some portion of the liquids. And this is probable, for the epiglottis lies over the windpipe, as a fence and strainer, that the drink may get in by little and little, lest descending in a large full stream, it stop the breath and endanger the life. And therefore birds have no epiglottis, because they do not sup or lap when they drink, but take up a little in their beak, and let it run gently down their windpipe.

These testimonies I think are enough; and reason confirms Plato's opinion by arguments drawn first from sense. For when the windpipe is wounded, no drink will go down; but as if the pipe were broken it runs out, though the weasand be whole and unhurt. And all know that in the inflammation of the lungs the patient is troubled with extreme thirst; the heat or dryness or some other cause, together with the inflammation, making the appetite intense. But a stronger evidence than all these follows. Those creatures that have very small lungs, or none at all, neither want nor desire drink, because to some parts there belongs a natural appetite to drink, and those that want those parts have no need to drink, nor any appetite to be supplied by it. But more, the bladder would seem unnecessary; for, if the weasand receives both meat and drink and conveys it to the belly, the superfluous parts of the liquids would not want a proper passage, one common one would suffice as a canal for both that were conveyed to the same vessel by the same passage. But now the bladder is distinct from the guts, because the drink goes from the lungs, and the meat from the stomach; they being separated as we take them down. And this is the reason that in our water nothing can be found that either in smell or color resembles dry food. But if the drink were mixed with the dry meat in the belly, it must be impregnant with its qualities, and not come forth so simple and untinged. Besides, a stone is never found in the stomach, though it is likely that the moisture should be coagulated there as well as in the bladder, if all the liquor were conveyed through the weasand then into the belly. But it is probable at the weasand robs the windpipe of a sufficient quantity of liquor as it is going down, and useth it to soften and concoct the meat. And therefore its excrement is never purely liquid; and the lungs, disposing of the moisture, as of the breath, to all of the parts that want it, deposit the superfluous portion in the bladder. And I am sure that this is a much more probable opinion than the other. But which is the truth cannot perhaps be discovered, and therefore it is not fit so peremptorily to find fault with the most acute and most famed philosopher, especially when the matter is so obscure, and the Platonists can produce such considerable reasons for their position.

QUESTION II. WHAT HUMORED MAN IS HE THAT PLATO CALLS [Greek omitted]? AND WHY DO THOSE SEEDS THAT FALL ON THE OXEN'S HORNS BECOME [Greek omitted]?

PLUTARCH, PATROCLES, EUTHYDEMUS, FLORUS.

We had always some difficulty started about [Greek omitted] and [Greek omitted], not what humor those words signified (for it is certain that some, thinking that those seeds which fall on the oxen's horns bear fruit which is very hard, did by a metaphor call a stiff untractable fellow by these names), but what was the cause that seeds falling on the oxen's horns should bear hard fruit. I had often desired my friends to search no farther, most of all fearing the passage of Theophrastus, in which he has collected many things whose causes we cannot discover. Such are the hen's using a straw to purify herself with after she has laid, the seal's consuming her rennet when she is caught, the deer's burying his horns, and the goat's stopping the whole herd by holding a branch of sea-holly in his mouth; and among the rest he reckoned this is a thing of which we are certain, but whose cause it is very difficult to find. But once at supper at Delphi, some of my companions—as if we were not only better counsellors when our bellies are full (as one hath it), but wine would make us brisker in our inquiries and bolder in our resolutions desired me to speak somewhat to that problem.

I refused, though I had some excellent men on my side, namely, Euthydemus my fellow-priest, and Patrocles my relative, who brought several the like instances, which they had gathered both from husbandry and hunting; for instance, that those officers that are appointed to watch the coming of the hail avert the storm by offering a mole's blood or a woman's cloths; that a wild fig being bound to a garden fig-tree will keep the fruit from falling and promote their ripening; that deer when they are taken shed salt tears, and boars sweet. But if you have a mind to such questions, Euthydemus will presently desire you to give an account of smallage and cummin; one of the which, if trodden down as it springs, will grow the better, and the other men curse and blaspheme whilst they sow it.

This last Florus thought to be an idle foolery; but he said, that we should not forbear to search into the causes of the other things as if they were incomprehensible. I have found, said I, your design to draw me on to this discourse, that you yourself may afterward give us a solution of the other proposed difficulties.

In my opinion it is cold that causes this hardness in corn and pulse, by contracting and constipating their parts till the substance becomes close and extremely rigid; while heat is a dissolving and softening quality. And therefore those that cite this verse against Homer,

The season, not the field, bears fruit,

do not justly reprehend him. For fields that are warm by nature, the air being likewise temperate, bear more mellow fruit than others. And therefore those seeds that fall immediately on the earth out of the sower's hand, and are covered presently, and cherished by being covered, partake more of the moisture and heat that is in the earth. But those that strike against the oxen's horns do not enjoy what Hesiod names the best position, but seem to be scattered rather than sown; and therefore the cold either destroys them quite, or else, lighting upon them as they lie naked, condenseth their moisture, and makes them hard and woody. Thus stones that lie under ground and, plant-animals have softer parts than those that lie above; and therefore stone-cutters bury the stones they would work, as if they designed to have them prepared and softened by the heat; but those that lie above ground are by the cold made hard, rigid, and very hurtful to the tools. And if corn lies long upon the floor, the grains become much harder than that which is presently carried away. And sometimes too a cold wind blowing whilst they winnow spoils the corn, as it hath happened at Philippi in Macedonia; and the chaff secures the grains whilst on the floor. For is it any wonder that as husband-men affirm, one ridge will bear soft and fruitful, and the very next to it hard and unfruitful corn or–which is stranger–that in the same bean-cod some beans are of this sort, some of the other, as more or less wind and moisture falls upon this or that?

QUESTION III. WHY THE MIDDLE OF WINE, THE TOP OF OIL, AND THE BOTTOM OF HONEY IS BEST. ALEXION, PLUTARCH, AND OTHERS.

My father-in-law Alexion laughed at Hesiod, for advising us to drink freely when the barrel is newly broached or almost out, but moderately when it is about the middle, since there is the best wine. For who, said he, doth not know, that the middle of wine, the top of oil, and the bottom of honey is the best? Yet he bids us spare the middle, and stay till worse wine runs, when the barrel is almost out. This said, the company minded Hesiod no more, but began to inquire into the cause of this difference.

We were not at all puzzled about the honey, everybody almost knowing that that which is lightest is so because it is rare, and that the heaviest parts are dense and compact, and by reason of their weight settle below the others. So, if you turn the vessel, each in a little time will recover its proper place, the heavier subsiding, and the lighter rising above the rest. And as for the wine, probable solutions presently appeared; for its strength consisting in heat, it is reasonable that it should be contained chiefly in the middle, and there best preserved; for the lower parts the lees spoil, and the upper are impaired by the neighboring air. For that the air will impair wine no man doubts, and therefore we usually bury or cover our barrels, that as little air as can be might come near them. And besides (which is an evident sign) a barrel when full is not spoiled so soon as when it is half empty; because a great deal of air getting into the empty space troubles and disturbs the liquor, whereas the wine that is in the unemptied cask is preserved and defended by itself, not admitting much of the external air, which is apt to injure and corrupt it.

But the oil gave us the most difficulty. One thought that the bottom of the oil was affected, because it was foul and troubled with the lees; and that the top was not really better than the rest, but only seemed so, because it was farthest removed from those corrupting particles. Others thought the thickness of the liquor to be the reason, which thickness keeps it from mixing with other humids, unless blended together and shaken violently; and therefore it will not mix with air, but keeps it off by its smoothness and close contexture, so that it hath no power to corrupt it. But Aristotle seems to be against this opinion, who hath observed that oil grows sweeter by being kept in vessels not exactly filled, and afterwards ascribes this melioration to the air; for more air, and therefore more powerful to produce the effect, flows into a vessel not well filled.

Well then! said I, the same quality in the air may spoil wine, and better oil. For long keeping improves wine, but spoils oil. Now the air keeps oil from growing old; for that which is cooled continues fresh and new, but that which is kept close up, having no way to exhale its corrupting parts, presently decays, and grows old. Therefore it is probable that the air coming upon the superficies of the oil keepeth it fresh and new. And this is the reason that the top of wine is worst, and of oil best; because age betters the one, and spoils the other.

QUESTION IV. WHAT WAS, THE REASON OF THAT CUSTOM OF THE ANCIENT ROMANS TO REMOVE THE TABLE BEFORE ALL THE MEAT WAS EATEN, AND NOT TO PUT OUT THE LAMP? FLORUS, EUSTROPHUS, CAESERNIUS, LUCIUS.

Florus, who observed the ancient manners, would not let the table be removed quite empty, but always left some meat upon it; declaring likewise that his father and grandfather were not only curious in this matter, but would never suffer the lamp after supper to be put out,–a thing about which the ancient Romans were very careful,–while those of to-day put it out immediately after supper, that they may lose no oil. Eustrophus the Athenian being present said: What could they get by that, unless they knew the cunning trick of our Polycharmus, who, after long deliberation how to find out a way to prevent the servants' stealing of the oil, at last with a great deal of difficulty happened upon this: As soon as you have put out the lamp, fill it up, and the next morning look carefully whether it remains full. Then Florus with a smile replied: Well, since we are agreed about that, let us inquire for what reason the ancients were so careful about their tables and their lamps.

First, about the lamps. And his son-in-law Caesernius was of opinion that the ancients abominated all extinction of fire, because of the relation that it had to the sacred and eternal flame. Fire, like man, may be destroyed two ways, either when it is violently quenched, or when it naturally decays. The sacred fire was secured against both ways, being always watched and continually supplied; but the common fire they permitted to go out of itself, not forcing or violently extinguishing it, but not supplying it with nourishment, like a useless beast, that they might not feed it to no purpose.

Lucius, Florus's son, subjoined, that all the rest of the discourse was very good, but that they did not reverence and take care of this holy fire because they thought it better or more venerable than other fire; but, as amongst the Egyptians some worship the whole species of dogs, wolves, or crocodiles, yet keep but one wolf, dog, or crocodile (for all could not be kept), so the particular care which the ancients took of the sacred fire was only a sign of the respect they had for all fires. For nothing bears such a resemblance to an animal as fire. It is moved and nourished by itself, and by its brightness, like the soul, discovers and makes everything apparent; but in its quenching it principally shows some power that seems to proceed from our vital principle, for it makes a noise and resists, like an animal dying or violently slaughtered. And can you (looking upon me) offer any better reason?

I can find fault, replied I, with no part of the discourse, yet I would subjoin, that this custom is an instruction for kindness and good-will. For it is not lawful for any one that hath eaten sufficiently to destroy the remainder of the food; nor for him that hath supplied his necessities from the fountain to stop it up; nor for him that hath made use of any marks, either by sea or land, to ruin or deface them; but every one ought to leave those things that may be useful to those persons that afterwards may have need of them. Therefore it is not fit, out of a saving covetous humor, to put out a lamp as soon as we need it not; but we ought to preserve and let it burn for the use of those that perhaps want its light. Thus, it would be very generous to lend our ears and eyes, nay, if possible, our reason and understanding, to others, whilst we are idle or asleep. Besides, consider whether to stir up men to gratitude these minute observances were practised. The ancients did not act absurdly when they highly reverenced an oak. The Athenians called one fig-tree sacred, and forbade any one to cut down an olive. For such observances do not (as some fancy) make men prone to superstition, but persuade us to be communicative and grateful to one another, by being accustomed to pay this respect to these senseless and inanimate creatures. Upon the same reason Hesiod, methinks, adviseth well, who would not have any meat or broth set on the table out of those pots out of which there had been no portion offered, but ordered the first-fruits to be given to the fire, as a reward for the service it did in preparing it. And the Romans, dealing well with the lamps, did not take away the nourishment they had once given, but permitted them to live and shine by it.

When I had said thus, Eustrophus subjoined: This gives us some light into that query about the table; for they thought that they ought to leave some portion of the supper for the servants and waiters, for those are not so well pleased with a supper provided for them apart, as with the relics of their master's table. And upon this account, they say, the Persian king did not only send portions from his own table to his friends, captains, and gentlemen of his bed-chamber, but had always what was provided for his servants and his dogs served up to his own table; that as far as possible all those creatures whose service was useful might seem to be his guests and companions. For, by such feeding in common and participation, the wildest of beasts might be made tame and gentle.

Then I with a smile said: But, sir, that fish there, that according to the proverb is laid up, why do not we bring out into play together with Pythagoras's choenix, which he forbids any man to sit upon, thereby teaching us that we ought to leave something of what we have before us for another time, and on the present day be mindful of the morrow? We Boeotians use to have that saying frequently in our mouths, "Leave something for the Medes," ever since the Medes overran and spoiled Phocis and the marches of Boeotia; but still, and upon all occasions, we ought to have that ready, "Leave something for the guests that may come." And therefore I must needs find fault with that always empty and starving table of Achilles; for, when Ajax and Ulysses came ambassadors to him, he had nothing ready, but was forced out of hand to dress a fresh supper. And when he would entertain Priam, he again bestirs himself, kills a white ewe, joints and dresses it, and in that work spent a great part of the night. But Eumaeus (a wise scholar of a wise master) had no trouble upon him when Telemachus came home, but presently desired him to sit down, and feasted him, setting before him dishes of boiled meat,

The cleanly reliques of the last night's feast.

But if this seems trifling, and a small matter, I am sure it is no small matter to command and restrain appetite while there are dainties before you to satisfy and please it. For those that are used to abstain from what is present are not so eager for absent things as others are.

Lucius subjoining said, that he had heard his grandmother say, that the table was sacred, and nothing that is sacred ought to be empty. Beside [omitted]. Therefore as we desire that the earth should always have and bear something that is useful for us, so we think that we should not let the table be altogether empty and void of all provision.

QUESTION V. THAT WE OUGHT CAREFULLY TO PRESERVE OURSELVES FROM PLEASURES ARISING FROM BAD MUSIC AND HOW IT MAY BE DONE. CALLISTRATUS, LAMPRIAS.

At the Pythian games Callistratus, procurator of the Amphictyons, forbade a piper, his citizen and friend, who did not give in his name in due time, to appear in the solemnity, according to the law. But afterward very fine tune; but afterwards, having tickled and sounded the humor of the whole company, and found that most were inclined to pleasure and would suffer him to play what effeminate and lascivious tunes he pleased, throwing aside all modesty, he showed that music was more intoxicating than wine to those that wantonly and unskilfully use it. For they were not content to sit still and applaud and clap, but many at last leaped from their seats, danced lasciviously, and made such gentle steps as became such effeminate and mollifying tunes. But after they had done, and the company, as it were recovered of its madness, began to come to itself again, Lamprias would have spoken to and severely chid the young men; but as fearing he would be too harsh and give offence, Callistratus gave him a hint, and drew him on by this discourse:–

For my part, I absolve all lovers of shows and music from intemperance; yet I cannot altogether agree with Aristoxenus, who says that those pleasures alone deserve the approbation "fine." For we call viands and ointments fine; and we say we have finely dined, when we have been splendidly entertained. Nor, in my opinion, doth Aristotle free those complacencies we take in shows and songs upon good reason from the charge of excess, saying, that those belong peculiarly to man, and of other pleasures beasts have a share. For I am certain that a great many irrational creatures are delighted with music, as deer with pipes; and to mares, whilst they are horsing, they play a tune called [Greek omitted]. And Pindar says, that his songs make him move,

> As brisk as Dolphins, whom a charming tune
> Hath raised from th' bottom of the quiet flood.

And certain fish are taken by means of dancing; for as the dance goes on they lift up their heads above water, being much pleased and delighted with the sight, and twisting their backs this way and that way, in imitation of the dancers. Therefore I see nothing peculiar in those pleasures, that they should be accounted proper to the mind, and all others to belong to the body, so far as to end there. But music, rhythm, dancing, song, passing through the sense, fix a pleasure and titilation in the sportive part of the soul and therefore none of these pleasures is enjoyed in secret, nor wants darkness nor walls about it, according to the women's phrase; but circuses and theatres are built for them. And to frequent shows and music-meetings with company is both more delightful and more genteel; because we take a great many witnesses, not of a luxurious and intemperate, but of a pleasant and respectable, manner of passing away our time.

Upon this discourse of Callistratus, my father Lamprias, seeing the musicians grow bolder, said: That is not the reason, sir, and, in my opinion, the ancients were much out when they named Bacchus the son of Forgetfulness. They ought to have called him his father; for it seems he hath made you forget that of those faults which are committed about pleasures some proceed from a loose intemperate inclination, and others from heedlessness or ignorance. Where the ill effect is very plain, there intemperate inclination captivates reason, and forces men to sin; but where the just reward of intemperance is not directly and presently inflicted, there ignorance of the danger and heedlessness make men easily wrought oil and secure. Therefore those that are vicious, either in eating, drinking, or venery, which diseases, wasting of estates, and evil reports usually attend, we call intemperate. For instance, Theodectes, who having sore eyes, when his mistress came to see him, said,

> All hail, delightful light;

or Anaxarchus the Abderite,

> A wretch who knew what evils wait on sin,
> Yet love of pleasure drove him back again.

Once almost free, he sank again to vice,
That terror and disturber of the wise.

Now those that take all care possible to secure themselves from all those pleasures that assault them either at the smelling, touch, or taste, are often surprised by those that make their treacherous approaches either at the eye or ear. But such, though as much led away as the others, we do not in like manner call incontinent and intemperate, since they are ruined through ignorance and want of experience. For they imagine they are far from being slaves to pleasures, if they can stay all day in the theatre without meat or drink; as if a pot forsooth should be mighty proud that a man cannot take it up by the bottom or the belly and carry it away, though he can easily do it by the ears. And therefore Agesilaus said, it was all one whether a man were a CINOE-DUS before or behind. We ought principally to dread those softening delights that please and tickle through the eyes and ears, and not think that city not taken which hath all its other gates secured by bars, portcullises, and chains, if the enemies are already entered through one and have taken possession; or fancy ourselves invincible against the assaults of pleasure, because stews will not provoke us, when the music-meeting or theatre prevails. For we in one case as much as the other resign up our souls to the impetuousness of pleasures, which pouring in those potions of songs, cadences, and tunes, more powerful and bewitching than the best mixtures of the most skilful cook or perfumer, conquer and corrupt us; and in the meantime, by our own confession as it were, the fault is chiefly ours. Now, as Pindar saith, nothing that the earth and sea hath provided for our tables can be justly blamed; but neither our meat nor broth, nor this excellent wine which we drink, hath raised such a noisy tumultous pleasure as those songs and tunes did, which not only filled the house with clapping and shouting, but perhaps the whole town. Therefore we ought principally to secure ourselves against such delights, because they are more powerful than others; as not being terminated in the body, like those which allure the touch, taste, or smelling, but affecting the very intellectual and judging faculties. Besides, from most other delights, though reason doth not free us, yet other passions very commonly divert us. Sparing niggardliness will keep a glutton from dainty fish, and covetousness will confine a lecher from a costly whore. As in one of Menander's plays, where every one of the company was to be enticed by the bawd who brought out a surprising whore, but each of them, though all boon companions,

Sat sullenly, and fed upon his cates.

For to pay interest for money is a severe punishment that follows intemperance, and to open our purses is no easy matter. But these pleasures that are called genteel, and solicit the ears or eyes of those that are frantic after shows and music, may be had without any charge at all, in every place almost, and upon every occasion; they may be enjoyed at the prizes, in the theatre, or at entertainments, at others cost. And therefore those that have not their reason to assist and guide them may be easily spoiled.

Silence following upon this, What application, said I, shall reason make, or how shall it assist? For I do not think it will apply those earcovers of Xenocrates, or force us to rise from the table as soon as we hear a harp struck or a pipe blown. No indeed, replied Lamprias, but as soon as we meet with the foresaid intoxications, we ought to make our application to the Muses, and fly to the Helicon of the ancients. To him that loves a costly strumpet, we cannot bring a Panthea or Penelope for cure; but one that delights in mimics and buffoons, loose odes, or debauched songs, we can bring to Euripides, Pindar, and Menander, that he might wash (as Plato phraseth it) his salt hearing with fresh reason. As the exorcists command the possessed to read over and pronounce Ephesian letters, so we in those possessions, during the madness of music and the dance, when

> We toss our hands with noise, and madly shout,

remembering those venerable and sacred writings, and comparing with them those odes, poems, and vain empty compositions, shall not be altogether cheated by them, or permit ourselves to be carried away sidelong, as by a smooth and undisturbed stream.

QUESTION VI. CONCERNING THOSE GUESTS THAT ARE CALLED SHADOWS, AND WHETHER BEING INVITED BY SOME TO GO TO ANOTHER'S HOUSE, THEY OUGHT TO GO; AND WHEN, AND TO WHOM.

PLUTARCH, FLORUS, CAESERNIUS.

Homer makes Menelaus come uninvited to his brother Agamemnon's treat, when he feasted the commanders;

> For well he knew great cares his brother vexed.

("Iliad," ii. 409.)

He did not take notice of the plain and evident omission of his brother, or show his resentments by not coming, as some surly testy persons usually do upon such oversights of their best friends; yet they had rather be overlooked than particularly invited, that they may have some color for their pettish anger. But about the introduced guests (which we call shadows) who are not invited by the entertainer, but by some others of the guests, a question was started, from whom that custom began. Some thought from Socrates, who persuaded Aristodemus, who was not invited, to go along with him to Agatho's, where there happened a pretty jest. For Socrates by chance staying somewhat behind, Aristodemus went in first; and this seemed very appropriate, for, the sun shining on their backs, the shadow ought to go before the body. Afterwards it was thought necessary at all entertainments, especially of great men, when the inviter did not know their favorites and acquaintance, to desire the invited to bring his company, appointing such a set number, lest they should be put to the same shifts which he was put to who invited King Philip to his country-house. The king came with a numerous attendance, but the provision was not equal to the company. Therefore, seeing his entertainer much cast down, he sent some about to tell his friends privately, that they should keep one corner of their bellies for a large cake that was to come. And they, expecting this, fed sparingly on the meat that was set before them, so that the provision seemed sufficient for them all.

When I had talked thus waggishly to the company Florus had a mind to talk gravely concerning these shadows, and have it discussed whether it was fit for those that were so invited to go, or no. His son-in-law Caesernius was positively against it. We should, says he, following Hesiod's advice,

> Invite a friend to feast,
> ("Works and Days," 342.)

or at least we should have our acquaintance and familiars to participate of our entertainments, mirth, and discourse over a glass of wine; but now, as ferry-men permit their passengers to bring in what fardel they please, so we permit others to fill our entertainments with any persons, let them be good companions or not. And I should wonder that any man of breeding being so (that is, not at all) invited, should go; since, for the most part, he must be unacquainted with the entertainer, or if he was acquainted, was not thought worthy to be bidden. Nay, he should be more ashamed to go to such a one, if he considers that it will look like an upbraiding of his unkindness, and yet a rude intruding into his company against his will. Besides, to go before or after the guest that invites him must look unhandsomely, nor is it creditable to go and stand in need of witnesses to assure the guests that he doth not come as a principally invited person, but such a one's shadow. Besides, to attend others bathing or anointing, to observe his hour, whether he goes early or late, is servile and gnathonical (for there never was such an excellent fellow as Gnatho to feed at another man's table). Besides, if there is no more proper time and place to say,

Speak, tongue, if thou wilt utter jovial things,

than at a feast, and freedom and raillery is mixed with everything that is either done or said over a glass of wine, how should he behave himself, who is not a true principally invited guest, but as it were a bastard and supposititious intruder? For whether he is free or not, he lies open to the exception of the company. Besides, the very meanness and vileness of the name is no small evil to those who do not resent it but can quietly endure to be called and answer to the name of shadows. For, by enduring such base names, men are insensibly accustomed and drawn on to base actions. Therefore, when I make an invitation, for it is hard to break the custom of a place, I give my guests leave to bring shadows; but when I myself am invited as a shadow, I assure you I refuse to go.

A short silence followed this discourse; then Florus began thus: This last thing you mentioned, sir, is a greater difficulty than the other. For it is necessary when we invite our friends to give them liberty to choose their own shadows, as was before hinted; for to entertain them without their friends is not very obliging, nor is it very easy to know whom the person we invite would be most pleased with. Then said I to him: Consider therefore whether those that give their friends this license to invite do not at the same time give the invited license to accept the invitation and come to the entertainment. For it is not fit either to allow or to desire another to do that which is not decent to be done, or to urge and persuade to that which no one ought to be persuaded or to consent to do. When we entertain a great man or stranger, there we cannot invite or choose his company, but must receive those that come along with him. But when we feast a friend, it will be more acceptable if we ourselves invite all, as knowing his acquaintance and familiars; for it tickles him extremely to see that others take notice that he hath chiefly a respect for such and such, loves their company most, and is well pleased when they are honored and invited as well as he. Yet sometimes we must deal with our friend as petitioners do when they make addresses to a god; they offer vows to all that belong to the same altar and the same shrine, though they make no particular mention of their names. For no dainties, wine, or ointment can incline a man to merriment, as much as a pleasant agreeable companion. For as it is rude and ungenteel to inquire and ask what sort of meat, wine, or ointment the person whom we are to entertain loves best; so it is neither disobliging nor absurd to desire him who hath a great many acquaintance to bring those along with him whose company he likes most, and in whose conversation he can take the greatest pleasure. For it is not so irksome and tedious to sail in the same ship, to dwell in the same house, or be a judge upon the same bench, with a person whom we do not like, as to be at the same table with him; and the contrary is fully as pleasant. An entertainment is a communion of serious or merry discourse or actions; and therefore, to make a merry company, we should not pick up any person at a venture, but take only such as are known to one another and sociable. Cooks, it is true, mix sour and sweet juices, rough and oily, to make their sauces; but there never was an agreeable table or pleasant entertainment where the guests were not all of a piece, and all of the same humor. Now, as the Peripatetics say, the first mover in nature moves only and is not moved, and the last moved is moved only but does not move, and between these there is that which moves and is moved by others; so there is the same analogy between those three sorts of persons that make up a company,–there is the simple inviter, the simple invited and the invited that invites another. We have spoken already concerning the inviter, and it will not be improper, in my opinion, to deliver my sentiments about the other two. He that is invited and invites others, should, in my opinion, be sparing in the number that he brings. He should not, as if he were to forage in an enemy's country, carry all he can with him; or, like those who go to possess a new-found land, by the excessive number of his own friends, incommode or exclude the friends of the inviter, so that the inviter must be in the same case with those that set forth suppers to Hecate and the gods who turn away evil, of which neither they nor any of their family partake, except of the smoke and trouble. It is true they only speak in waggery that say,

> He that at Delphi offers sacrifice
> Must after meat for his own dinner buy.

But the same thing really happens to him who entertains ill-bred guests or acquaintances, who with a great many shadows, as it were harpies, tear and devour his provision. Besides, he should not take anybody that he may come upon along with him to another's entertainment, but chiefly the entertainer's acquaintance, as it were contending with him and preceding him in the invitation. But if that cannot be effected, let him carry such of his own friends as the entertainer would choose himself; to a civil modest man, some of complaisant humor; to a learned man, ingenuous persons; to a man that hath borne office, some of the same rank; and, in short, such whose acquaintance he hath formerly sought and would be now glad of. For it will be extremely pleasing and obliging to bring such into company together; but one who brings to a feast men who have no likeness at all with the feast-maker, but who are entire aliens and strangers to him,–as hard drinkers to a sober man,–gluttons and sumptuous persons to a temperate thrifty entertainer,–or to a young, merry, boon companion, grave old philosophers solemnly speaking in their beards,–will be very disobliging, and turn all the intended mirth into an unpleasant sourness. The entertained should be as obliging to the entertainer as the entertainer to the entertained; and then he will be most obliging, when not only he himself, but all those that come by his means, are pleasant and agreeable.

The last of the three which remains to be spoken of is he that is invited by one man to another's feast. Now he that disdains and is so much offended at the name of a shadow will appear to be afraid of a mere shadow. But in this matter there is need of a great deal of caution, for it is not creditable readily to go along with every one and to everybody. But first you must consider who it is that invites; for if he is not a very familiar friend, but a rich or great man, such who, as if upon a stage, wants a large or splendid retinue, or such who thinks that he puts a great obligation upon you and does you a great deal of honor by this invitation, you must presently deny. But if he is your friend and particular acquaintance, you must not yield upon the first motion: but if there seems a necessity for some conversation which cannot be put off till another time, or if he is lately come from a journey or designs to go on one, and out of mere good-will and affection seems desirous of your company, and doth not desire to carry a great many, or strangers, but only some few friends along with him; or, besides all this, if he designs to bring you thus invited acquainted with the principal inviter, who is very worthy of your acquaintance, then consent and go. For as to ill-humored persons, the more they seize and take hold of us like thorns, we should endeavor to free ourselves from them or leap over them the more. If he that invites is a civil and well-bred person, yet doth not design to carry you to one of the same temper, you must refuse, lest you should take poison in honey, that is, get the acquaintance of a bad man by an honest friend. It is absurd to go to one you do not know, and with whom you never had any familiarity, unless, as I said before, the person be an extraordinary man, and, by a civil waiting, upon him at another man's invitation, you design to begin an acquaintance with him. And those friends you should chiefly go to as shadows, who would come to you again in the same quality. To Philip the jester, indeed, he seemed more ridiculous that came to a feast of his own accord than he that was invited; but to well-bred and civil friends it is more obliging for men of the same temper to come at the nick of time with other friends, when uninvited and unexpected; at once pleasing both to those that invite and those that entertain. But chiefly you must avoid going to rulers, rich or great men, lest you incur the deserved censure of being impudent, saucy, rude, and unseasonably ambitious.

QUESTION VII. WHETHER FLUTE-GIRLS ARE TO BE ALLOWED AT A FEAST? DIOGENIANUS, A SOPHIST, PHILIP.

At Chaeronea, Diogenianus the Pertamenian being present, we had a long discourse once at an entertainment about music; and we had a great deal of trouble to hold out against a great bearded sophister of the Stoic sect, who quoted Plato as blaming a company that admitted flute-girls and were not able to entertain one another with discourse. And Philip the Prusian, of the same sect, said: Those guests of Agatho, whose discourse was more sweet than the sound of any pipe in the world, were no good authority in this case; for it was no wonder that in their company the flute-girl was not regarded; but it is strange that, in the midst of the entertainment, the extreme pleasantness of the discourse had not made them forget their meat and drink. Yet Xenophon thought it not indecent to bring in to Socrates, Antisthenes, and the like the jester Philip; as Homer doth an onion to make the wine relish. And Plato brought in Aristophanes's discourse of love, as a comedy, into his entertainment; and at the last, as it were drawing all the curtains, he shows a scene of the greatest variety imaginable,–Alcibiades drunk, frolicking, and crowned. Then follows that pleasant raillery between him and Socrates concerning Agatho, and the encomium of Socrates; and when such discourse was going on, good gods! Had it not been allowable, if Apollo himself had come in with his harp ready to desire the god to forbear till the argument was out? These men, having such a pleasant way of discoursing, used these arts and insinuating methods, and graced their entertainment's by such facetious raillery. But shall we, being mixed with tradesmen and merchants, and some (as it now and then happens) ignorants and rustics, banish out of our entertainments this ravishing delight, or fly the musicians, as if they were Sirens, as soon as we see them coming? Clitomachus the wrestler, rising and getting away when any one talked of love, was much wondered at; and should not a philosopher that banisheth music from a feast, and is afraid of a musician, and bids his link boy presently light his link and be gone, be laughed at, since he seems to abominate the most innocent pleasures, as beetles do ointment? For, if at any time, certainly over a glass of wine, music should be permitted, and then chiefly the harmonious god should have the direction of our souls; so that Euripides, though I like him very well in other things, shall never persuade me that music, as he would have it, should be applied to melancholy and grief. For there sober and serious reason, like a physician, should take care of the diseased men; but those pleasures should be mixed with Bacchus, and serve to increase our mirth and frolic. Therefore it was a pleasant saying of that Spartan at Athens, who, when some new tragedians were to contend for the prize, seeing the preparations of the masters of the dances, the hurry and busy diligence of the instructors, said, the city was certainly mad which sported with so much pains. He that designs to sport should sport, and not buy his case and pleasure with great expense, or the loss of that time which might be useful to other things; but whilst he is feasting and free from business, those should be enjoyed. And it is advisable to try amidst our mirth, whether any profit is to be gotten from our delights.

QUESTION VIII. WHAT SORT OF MUSIC IS FITTEST FOR AN ENTERTAINMENT? DIOGENIANUS, A SOPHIST, PHILIP.

When Philip had ended, I hindered the sophister from returning an answer to the discourse, and said: Let us rather inquire, Diogenianus, since there are a great many sorts of music, which is fittest for an entertainment. And let us beg this learned man's judgment in this case; for since he is not prejudiced or apt to be biased by any sort, there is no danger that he should prefer that which is pleasantest before that which is best. Diogenianus joining with me in this request, he presently began. All other sorts I banish to the theatre and playhouse, and can only allow that which hath been lately admitted into the entertainments at Rome, and with which everybody is not yet acquainted. You know, continued he, that some of Plato's dialogues are purely narrative, and some dramatic. The easiest of this latter sort they teach their children to speak by heart; making them to imitate the actions of those persons they represent, and to form their voice and affections to be agreeable to the words. This all the grave and well-bred men exceedingly admire; but soft and effeminate fellows, whose ears ignorance and ill-breeding hath corrupted, and who, as Aristoxenus phraseth it, are ready to vomit when they hear excellent harmony, reject it; and no wonder, when effeminacy prevails.

Philip, perceiving some of the company uneasy at this discourse, said: Pray spare us, sir, and be not so severe upon us; for we were the first that found fault with that custom when it first began to be countenanced in Rome, and reprehended those who thought Plato fit to entertain us whilst we were making merry, and who would hear his dialogues whilst they were eating cates and scattering perfumes. When Sappho's songs or Anaereon's verses are recited, I protest I think it decent to set aside my cup. But should I proceed, perhaps you would think me much in earnest, and designing to oppose you, and therefore, together with this cup which I present my friend, I leave it to him to wash your salt ear with fresh discourse.

Then Diogenianus, taking the cup, said: Methinks this is very sober discourse, which makes me believe that the wine doth not please you, since I see no effect of it; so that I fear I ought to be corrected. Indeed, many sorts of music are not to be rejected; first, tragedy, as having nothing familiar enough for an entertainment, and being a representation of actions attended with grief and extremity of passion. I reject the sort of dancing which is called Pyladean from Pylades, because it is full of pomp, very pathetical, and requires a great many persons; but if we would admit any of those sorts that deserve those encomiums which Socrates mentions in his discourse about dancing, I like that sort called Bathyllean, which requires not so high a motion, but hath something of the character of the Cordax, and resembles the motion of an Echo, a Pan, or a Satyr frolicking with love. Old comedy is not fit for men that are making merry, by reason of the excuses that appear in it; for that vehemency which they use in the parabasis is loud and indecent, and the liberty they take to scoff and abuse is very surfeiting, too open, and full of filthy words and lewd expressions. Besides, as at great men's tables every man hath a servant waiting at his elbow, so each of his guests would need a grammarian to sit by him, and explain who is Laespodias in Eupolis, Cinesias in Plato, and Lampo in Cratinus, and who is each person that is jeered in the play. Concerning new comedy there is no need of any long discourse. It is so fitted, so interwoven with entertainments, that it is easier to have a regular feast without wine, than without Menander. Its phrase is sweet and familiar, the Humor innocent and easy, so that there is nothing for men whilst sober to despise, or when merry to be troubled at. The sentiments are so natural and unstudied, that midst wine, as it were in fire, they soften and bend the rigidest temper to be pliable and easy. And the mixture of gravity and jests seems to be contrived for nothing so aptly as for the pleasure and profit of those that are frolicking and making merry. The love-scenes in Menander are convenient for those who have already drunk their cups, and who in a short time must retire home to their wives; for in all his plays there is no love of boys mentioned, and all rapes committed on virgins and decently in marriages at last. As for misses, if they are impudent and jilting, they are bobbed, the young gallants turning sober, and repenting of their lewd courses. But if they are kind and constant, either their true parents are discovered, or a time is determined for intrigue, which brings them at last to obliging modesty and civil kindness. These things to men busied about other matters may seem scarce worth taking notice of; but whilst they are making merry, it is no wonder that the pleasantness and smoothness of the parts should work a neat conformity and distinction in the hearers and make their manners like the pattern they have from those genteel characters.

Diogenianus, either designedly or for want of breath ended thus. And when the sophister attacked him again, and contended that some of Aristophanes's verses should be read, Philip speaking to me said: Diogenianus hath had his wish in praising his beloved Menander, and seems not to care for any of the rest. There are a great many sorts which we have not at all considered, concerning which I should be very glad to have your opinion; and the prize for the carvers we will set up tomorrow, when we are sober, if Diogenianus and this stranger think fit. Of representations, said I, some are allegorical, and some are farces; neither of these are fit for an entertainment; the first by reason of their length and cost, and the latter being so full of filthy discourse and lewd actions, that they are not fit to be seen by the foot-boys that wait on civil masters. Yet the rabble, even with their wives and young sons, sit quietly to be spectators of such representations as are apt to disturb the soul more than the greatest debauch in drink. The harp ever since Homer's time was well acquainted with feasts and entertainments, and therefore it is not fitting to dissolve such an ancient friendship and acquaintance; but we should only desire the harpers to forbear their sad notes and melancholy tunes, and play only those that are delighting, and fit for such as are making merry. The pipe, if we would, we cannot reject, for the libation in the beginning of the entertainment requires that as well as the garland. Then it insinuates and passeth through the ears, spreading even to the very soul a pleasant sound, which produceth serenity and calmness; so that, if the wine hath not quite dissolved or driven away all vexing solicitous anxiety this, by the softness and delightful agreeableness of its sound, smooths and calms the spirits, if so be that it keeps within due bounds, and doth not elevate too much, and, by its numerous surprising divisions, raise an ecstasy in the soul which wine hath weakened and made easy to be perverted. For as brutes do not understand a rational discourse, yet lie down or rise up at the sound of a shell or whistle, or of a chirp or clap; so the brutish part of the soul, which is either incapable of understanding or obeying reason, men conquer by songs and tunes, and by music reduce it to tolerable order. But to speak freely what I think, no pipe nor harp simply played upon, and without a song with it, can be very fit for an entertainment. For we should still accustom ourselves to take our chiefest pleasure from discourse, and spend our leisure time in profitable talk, and use tunes and airs as a sauce for the discourse, and not singly by themselves, to please the unreasonable delicacy of our palate. For as nobody is against pleasure that ariseth from sauce or wine going in with our necessary food, but Socrates flouts and refuseth to admit that superfluous and vain pleasure which we take in perfumes and odors at a feast; thus the sound of a pipe or harp, when singly applied to our ears, we utterly reject, but if it accompanies words, and together with an ode feasts and delights our reason, we gladly introduce it. And we believe the famed Marsyas was punished by Apollo for pretending, when he had nothing but his single pipe, and his muzzle to apply to his lips, to contend with the harp and song of the god. Let us only take care that, when we have such guests as are able to cheer one another with philosophy and good discourse we do not introduce anything that may rather prove an uneasy hindrance to the conversation than promote it. For not only those are fools, who, as Euripides says, having safety at home and in their own power, yet would hire some from abroad; but those too who, having pleasantness enough within, are eager after some external pastimes to comfort and delight them. That extraordinary piece of honor which the Persian king showed Antalcidas the Spartan seemed rude and uncivil, when he dipped a garland composed of crocus and roses in ointment, and sent it him to wear, by that dipping putting a slight upon and spoiling the natural sweetness and beauty of the flowers. He doth as bad, who having a Muse in his own breast, and all the pleasantness that would fit an entertainment, will have pipes and harps play, and by that external adventitious noise destroy all the sweetness that was proper and his own. But in short, all ear-delights are fittest then, when the company begins to be disturbed, to fall out, and quarrel, for then they may prevent raillery and reproach, and stop the dispute that is running on to sophistical and unpleasant wrangling, and bridle all babbling declamatory altercations, so that the company may be freed of noise and quietly composed.

QUESTION IX. THAT IT WAS THE CUSTOM OF THE GREEKS AS WELL AS PERSIANS TO DEBATE OF STATE AFFAIRS AT THEIR ENTERTAINMENTS. NICOSTRATUS, GLAUCIAS.

At Nicostratus's table we discoursed of those matters which the Athenians were to debate of in their next assembly. And one of the company saying, It is the Persian fashion, sir, to debate midst your cups;

And why, said Glaucias rejoining, not the Grecian fashion? For it was a Greek that said,

After your belly's full, your counsel's best.

And they were Greeks who with Agamemnon besieged Troy, to whom, whilst they were eating and drinking,

Old Nestor first began a grave debate;

("Iliad," vii. 324.)

and he himself advised the king before to call the commanders together for the same purpose:–

For the commanders, sir, a feast prepare,

And see who counsels best, and follow him.

(Ibid, ix. 70 and 74.)

Therefore Greece, having a great many excellent institutions, and zealously following the customs of the ancients, hath laid the foundations of her polities in wine. For the assemblies in Crete called Andria, those in Sparta called Phiditia, were secret consultations and aristocratical assemblies; such, I suppose, as the Prytaneum and Thesmothesium here at Athens. And not different from these is that nightmeeting, which Plato mentions, of the best and most polite men, to which the greatest, the most considerable and puzzling matters are assigned. And those

Who, when they do design to seek their rest,

To Mercury their just libations pour,

("Odyssey," vii. 138.)

do they not join reason and wine together, since, when they are about to retire, they make their vows to the wisest god, as if he was present and particularly president over their actions? But the ancients indeed call Bacchus the good counsellor, as if he had no need of Mercury; and for his sake they named the night [Greek omitted] as it were, GOOD ADVISER.

QUESTION X. WHETHER THEY DID WELL WHO DELIBERATED MIDST THEIR CUPS. GLAUCIAS, NICOSTRATUS.

Whilst Glaucias was discoursing thus, the former tumultuous talk seemed to be pretty well lulled; and that it might be quite forgotten, Nicostratus started another question, saying, he never valued the matter before, whilst he thought it a Persian custom, but since it was discovered to be the Greek fashion too, it wanted (he thought) some reason to excuse or defend its seeming absurdity. For our reason (much moisture, is hard to be moved, and unable to perform its operations. And all sorts of troubles and discontents, like insects to the sun, creeping forth, and being agitated by a glass of wine, make the mind irresolute and inconstant. Therefore as a bed is more convenient for a man whilst making merry than a chair, because it contains the whole body and keeps it from all disturbing motion, so it is best to have the soul perfectly at quiet; or, if that cannot be, we must give it, as to children that will be doing, not a sword or spear, but a rattle or a ball,–in this following the example of the god himself, who puts into the hands of those that are making merry a ferula, the lightest and softest of all weapons, that, when they are most apt to strike, they may hurt least. Over a glass of wine men should make only ridiculous slips, and not such as may prove tragical, lamentable, or of any considerable concern. Besides, in serious debates, it is chiefly to be considered, that persons of mean understanding and unacquainted with business should be guided by the wise and experienced; but wine destroys this order. Insomuch that Plato says, wine is called [Greek omitted] because it makes those that drink it [Greek omitted] think that they have wit; for none over a glass of wine thinks himself so noble, beauteous, or rich (though he fancies himself all these), as wise; and therefore wine is babbling, full of talk, and of a dictating humor; so that we are rather for being heard than hearing, for leading than being led. But a thousand such objections may be raised, for they are very obvious. But let us hear which of the company, either old or young, can allege anything for the contrary opinion.

Then said my brother cunningly: And do you imagine that any, upon a sudden, can produce any probable reasons? And Nicostratus replying, Yes, no doubt, there being so many learned men and good drinkers in company; he with a smile continued: Do you think, sir, you are fit to treat of these matters, when wine hath disabled you to discourse of politics and state affairs? Or is not this all the same as to think that a man in his liquor doth not see very well nor understand those that talk and discourse with him, yet hears the music and the pipers very well? For as it is likely that useful and profitable things draw and affect the sense more than fine and gaudy; so likewise they do the mind too. And I shall not wonder that the nice philosophical speculation should escape a man who hath drunk freely; but yet, I think, if he were called to political debates, his wisdom would become more strong and vigorous. Thus Philip at Chaeronea, being well heated, talked very foolishly, and was the sport of the whole company; but as soon as they began to discourse of a truce and peace, he composed his countenance, contracted his brows, and dismissing all vain, empty and dissolute thoughts, he gave an excellent, wise, and sober answer to the Athenians. To drink freely is different from being drunk, and those that drink till they grow foolish ought to retire to bed. But as for those that drink freely and are otherwise men of sense, why should we fear that they will fail in their understanding or lose their skill, when we see that musicians play as well at a feast as in a theatre? For when skill and art are found in the soul, they make the body correct and proper in its operations, and obedient to the motions of the spirit. Besides, wine inspirits some men, and raises a confidence and assurance in them, but not such as is haughty and odious, but pleasing and agreeable. Thus they say that Aeschylus composed his tragedies over a bottle, and that all his plays (though Gorgias thought that one of them, the "Seven against Thebes," was full of Mars) were Bacchus's. For wine (according to Plato), heating the soul together with the body, makes the body pliable, quick, and active, and opens the passages; while the fancies draw in discourse with boldness, and daring.

For some have a good natural invention, yet whilst they are sober are too diffident and too close, but midst their wine, like frankincense, exhale and open at the heat. Besides, wine expels all fear, which is the greatest hindrance to all consultations, and quencheth many other degenerate and lazy passions; it opens the rancor and malice, as it were, the two-leaved doors of the soul, and displays the whole disposition and qualities of any person in his discourse. Freedom of speech, and, through that, truth it principally produceth; which it once wanting, neither quickness of wit nor experience availeth anything; and many proposing that which comes next rather hit the matter, than if they warily and designedly conceal their present sentiments. Therefore there is no reason to fear that wine will stir up our affections; for it never stirs up the bad, unless in the worst men, whose judgment is never sober. But as Theophrastus used to call the barbers' shops wineless entertainments; so there is a kind of an uncouth wineless drunkenness always excited either by anger, malice, emulation, or clownishness in the souls of the unlearned. Now wine, blunting rather than sharpening many of these passions, doth not make them sots and foolish, but simple and ingenuous; not negligent of what is profitable, but desirous of what is good and honest. Now those that think craft to be cunning, and vanity or closeness to be wisdom, have reason to think those that over a glass of wine plainly and ingenuously deliver their opinions to be fools. But, on the contrary, the ancients called the god the Freer and Loosener, and thought him considerable in divination; not, as Euripides says, because he makes men raging mad, but because he looseth and frees the soul from all base distrustful fear, and puts them in a condition to speak truth freely to one another.

Book Eight

THOSE, MY SOSSIUS Senecio, who throw philosophy out of entertainments do worse than those who take away a light. For the candle being removed, the temperate and sober guests will not become worse than they were before, being more concerned to reverence than to see one another. But if dulness and disregard to good learning wait upon the wine, Minerva's golden lamp itself could not make the entertainment pleasing and agreeable. For a company to sit silent and only cram themselves is, in good truth, swinish and almost impossible. But he that permits men to talk, yet doth not allow set and profitable discourses, is much more ridiculous than he who thinks that his guests should eat and drink, yet gives them foul wine, unsavory and nastily prepared meat. For no meat nor drink which is not prepared as it ought to be is so hurtful and unpleasant as discourse which is carried round in company insignificantly and out of season. The philosophers, when they would give drunkenness a vile name, call it doting by wine. Now doting is to use vain and trifling discourse; and when such babbling is accompanied by wine, it usually ends in most disagreeable and rude contumely and reproach. It is a good custom therefore of our women, who in their feasts called Agrionia seek after Bacchus as if he were run away, but in a little time give over the search, and cry that he is fled to the Muses and lurks with them; and some time after, when supper is done, put riddles and hard questions to one another. For this mystery teaches us, that midst our entertainments we should use learned and philosophical discourse, and such as hath a Muse in it; and that such discourse being applied to drunkenness, everything that is brutish and outrageous in it is concealed, being pleasingly restrained by the Muses.

This book, being the eighth of my Symposiacs, begins with that discourse in which about a year ago, on Plato's birthday, I was concerned.

QUESTION I. CONCERNING THOSE DAYS IN WHICH SOME
FAMOUS MEN WERE BORN; AND ALSO CONCERNING THE
GENERATION OF THE GODS. DIOGENIANUS, PLUTARCH,
FLORUS, TYNDARES.

On the sixth day of May we celebrated Socrates's birthday, and on the
seventh Plato's; and that first prompted us to such discourse as was suitable to the meeting, which Diogenianus the Pergamenian began thus:
Ion, said he, was happy in his expression, when he said that Fortune,
though much unlike Wisdom, yet did many things very much like her;
and that she seemed to have some order and design, not only in placing
the nativities of these two philosophers so near together, but in setting the birthday of the most famous of the two first, who was also the
master of the other. I had a great deal to say to the company concerning some notable things that fell out on the same day, as concerning
the time of Euripides's birth and death; for he was born the same day
that the Greeks beat Xerxes by sea at Salamis, and died the same day
that Dionysius the elder, the Sicilian tyrant, was born,–Fortune (as Timaeus hath it) at the same time taking out of the world a representer,
and bringing into it a real actor, of tragedies. Besides, we remembered
that Alexander the king and Diogenes the Cynic died upon the same
day. And all agreed that Attalus the king died on his own birthday. And
some said, that Pompey the great was killed in Egypt on his birthday,
or, as others will have it, a day before. We remember Pindar also, who,
being born at the time of the Pythian games, made afterwards a great
many excellent hymns in honor of Apollo.

To this Florus subjoined: Now we are celebrating Plato's nativity, why
should we not mention Carneades, the most famous of the whole Academy, since both of them were born on Apollo's feast; Plato, whilst they
were celebrating the Thargelia at Athens, Carneades, whilst the Cyre-
nians kept their Carnea; and both these feasts are, upon the same day.
Nay, the god himself you (he continued), his priests and prophets, call
Hebdomagenes, as if he were born on the seventh day. And therefore
those who make Apollo Plato's father do not, in my opinion, dishonor the
god; since by Socrates's as by another Chiron's instructions he is become
a physician for the diseases of the mind. And together with this, he mentioned that vision and voice which forbade Aristo, Plato's father, to come
near or lie with his wife for ten months.

To this Tyndares the Spartan subjoined: It is very fit we should apply
that to Plato,

> He seemed not sprung from mortal man, but God.
> ("*Iliad*," *xxiv. 258.*)

But, for my part, I am afraid to beget, as well as to be begotten, is repugnant to the incorruptibility of the deity. For that implies a change and passion; as Alexander imagined, when he said that he knew himself to be mortal as often as he lay with a woman or slept. For sleep is a relaxation of the body, occasioned by the weakness of our nature; and all generation is a corruptive parting with some of our own substance. But yet I take heart again, when I hear Plato call the eternal and unbegotten deity the father and maker of the world and all other begotten things; not as if he parted with any seed, but as if by his power he implanted a generative principle in matter, which acts upon, forms, and fashions it. Winds passing through a hen will on occasions impregnate her; and it seems no incredible thing, that the deity, though not after the fashion of a man, but by some other certain communication, fills a mortal creature with some divine conception. Nor is this my sense; but the Egyptians who say Apis was conceived by the influence of the moon, and make no question but that an immortal god may have communication with a mortal woman. But on the contrary, they think that no mortal can beget anything on a goddess, because they believe the goddesses are made of thin air, and subtle heat and moisture.

QUESTION II. WHAT IS PLATO'S MEANING, WHEN HE SAYS THAT GOD ALWAYS PLAYS THE GEOMETER? DIOGENIANUS, TYNDARES, FLORUS, AUTOBULUS.

Silence following this discourse, Diogenianus began again and said: Since our discourse is about the gods, shall we, especially on his own birthday, admit Plato to the conference, and inquire upon what account he says (supposing it to be his sentence) that God always plays the geometer? I said that this sentence was not plainly set down in any of his books; yet there are good arguments that it is his, and it is very much like his expression. Tyndares presently subjoining said: Perhaps, Diogenianus, you imagine that this sentence intimates some curious and difficult speculation, and not that which he hath so often mentioned, when he praiseth geometry as a science that takes off men from sensible objects, and makes them apply themselves to the intelligible and eternal Nature, the contemplation of which is the end of philosophy, as the view of the initiatory mysteries into holy rites. For the nail of pain and pleasure, that fastens the soul to the body, seems to do us the greatest mischief, by making sensible things more powerful over us than intelligible, and by forcing the understanding to determine the rather according to passion than reason. For this faculty, being accustomed by the vehemency of pain or pleasure to be intent on the mutable and uncertain body, as if it really and truly were, grows blind as to that which really is, and loses that instrument and light of the soul, which is worth a thousand bodies, and by which alone the deity can be discovered. Now in all sciences, as in plain and smooth mirrors, some marks and images of the truth of intelligible objects appear, but in geometry chiefly; which, according to Philo, is the chief and principal of all, and doth bring back and turn the understanding, as it were, purged and gently loosened from sense. And therefore Plato himself dislikes Eudoxus, Archytas, and Menaechmus for endeavoring to bring down the doubling the cube to mechanical operations; for by this means all that was good in geometry would be lost and corrupted, it falling back again to sensible things, and not rising upward and considering immaterial and immortal images, in which God being versed is always God.

After Tyndares, Florus, a companion of his, and who always jocosely pretended to be his admirer, said thus: Sir, we are obliged to you for making your discourse not proper to yourself, but common to us all; for you have made it possible to disprove it by demonstrating that geometry is not necessary to the gods, but to us. Now the deity doth not stand in need of science, as an instrument to withdraw his intellect from things created and to turn it to the real things; for these are all in him, with him, and about him. But pray consider whether Plato, though you do not apprehend it, doth not intimate something that is proper and peculiar to you, mixing Lycurgus with Socrates, as much as Dicaearchus thought he did Pythagoras. For Lycurgus, I suppose you know, banished out of Sparta all arithmetical proportion, as being democratical and favoring the crowd; but introduced the geometrical, as agreeable to an oligarchy and kingly government that rules by law; for the former gives an equal share to every one according to number, but the other gives according to the proportion of the deserts. It doth not huddle all things together, but in it there is a fair discretion of good and bad, every one having what is fit for him, not by lot or weight, but according as he is virtuous or vicious. The same proportion, my dear Tyndares, God introduceth, which is called [Greek omitted] and [Greek omitted], and which teacheth us to account that which is just equal, and not that which is equal just. For that equality which many affect, being often the greatest injustice, God, as much as possible, takes away; and useth that proportion which respects every man's deserts, geometrically defining it according to law and reason.

This exposition we applauded; and Tyndares, saying he envied him, desired Autobulus to engage Florus and confute his discourse. That he refused to do, but produced another opinion of his own. Geometry, said he, considers nothing else but the accidents and properties of the extremities of bodies; neither did God make the world any other way than by terminating matter, which was infinite before. Not that matter was actually without limits as to either magnitude or multitude; but the ancients used to call that infinite which by reason of its confusion and disorder is undetermined and unconfined. Now the terms of everything that is formed or figured are the form and figure of that thing, and without which the thing would be formless and unfigured. Now numbers and proportions being applied to matter, it is circumscribed and as it were bound up by lines, and through lines by surfaces and solids; and so were settled the first types and differences of bodies, as foundations from which to create the four elements, fire, air, water, and earth. For it was impossible that, out of an unsteady and confused matter, the equality of the sides, the likeness of the angles, and the exact proportion of octahedrons, icosahedrons, pyramids, and cubes should be deduced, unless by some power that terminated and shaped every particle of matter. Therefore, terms being fixed to that which was undetermined or infinite before, the whole became and still continues agreeable in all parts, and excellently terminated and mixed; the matter indeed always affecting an indeterminate state, and flying all geometrical confinement, but proportion terminating and circumscribing it, and dividing it into several differences and forms, out of which all things that arise are generated and subsist.

When he had said this, he desired me to contribute something to the discourse; and I applauded their conceits as their own devices, and very probable. But lest you despise yourselves (I continued) and altogether look for some external explication, attend to an exposition upon this sentence, which your masters very much approve. Amongst the most geometrical theorems, or rather problems, this is one: Two figures being given, to describe a third, which shall be equal to one and similar to the other. And it is reported that Pythagoras, upon the discovery of this problem, offered a sacrifice to the gods; for this is a much more exquisite theorem than that which lays down, that the square of the hypothenuse in a right-angled triangle is equal to the squares of the two sides. Right, said Diogenianus, but what is this to the present question? You will easily understand, I replied, if you call to mind how Timaeus divides that which gave the world its beginning into three parts. One of which is justly called God, the other matter, and the third form. That which is called matter is the most confused subject, the form the most beautiful pattern, and God the best of causes. Now this cause, as far as possible, would leave nothing infinite and indeterminate, but adorn

Nature with number, measure, and proportion making one thing of all the subjects together, equal to the matter, and similar to the form. Therefore proposing to himself this problem, he made and still makes a third, and always preserves it equal to the matter, and like the form; and that is the world. And this world, being in constant changes and alterations because of the natural necessity of body, is helped and preserved by the father and maker of all things, who by proportion terminates the substance according to the pattern.

QUESTION III. WHY NOISES ARE BETTER HEARD IN THE NIGHT THAN THE DAY. AMMONIUS, BOETHUS, PLUTARCH, THRASYLLUS, ARISTODEMUS.

When we supped with Ammonius at Athens, who was then the third time captain of the city-bands, there was a great noise about the house, some without doors calling, Captain! Captain! After he had sent his officers to quiet the tumult, and had dispersed the crowd, we began to inquire what was the reason that those that are within doors hear those that are without, but those that are without cannot hear those that are within as well. And Ammonius said, that Aristotle had given a reason for that already; for the sound of those within, being carried without into a large tract of air, grows weaker presently and is lost; but that which comes in from without is not subject to the like casualty, but is kept close, and is therefore more easy to be heard. But that seemed a more difficult question, Why sounds seem greater in the night than in the day, and yet altogether as clear. For my own part (continued he) I think Providence hath very wisely contrived that our hearing should be quickest when our sight can do us very little or no service; for the air of the "blind and solitary Night," as Empedocles calls it, being dark, supplies in the ears that defect of sense which it makes in the eyes. But since of natural effects we should endeavor to find the causes, and to discover what are the material and mechanical principles of things is the proper task of a natural philosopher, who shall first give us a rational account hereof?

Boethus began, and said: When I was a novice in letters, I then made use of geometrical postulates, and assumed as undoubted truths some undemonstrated suppositions; and now I shall make use of some propositions which Epicurus hath demonstrated already. Bodies move in a vacuum, and there are a great many spaces interspersed among the atoms of the air. Now when the air being rarefied is more extended, so as to fill the vacant space, there are only a few vacuities scattered and interspersed among the particles of matter; but when the atoms of air are condensed and laid close together, they leave a vast empty space, convenient and sufficient for other bodies to pass through. Now the coldness of the night makes such a constipation. Heat opens and separates parts of condensed bodies, and therefore bodies that boil, grow soft, or melt, require a greater space than before; but, on the contrary, the parts of the body that are condensed or freeze are contracted closer to one another, and leave those vessels and places from which they retired partly empty. Now the sound, meeting and striking against a great many bodies in its way, is either altogether lost or scattered, and very much and very frequently hindered in its passage; but when it hath a plain and smooth way through an empty space, and comes to the ear uninterrupted, the passage is so sudden, that it preserves its articulate distinctness, as well as the words it carries. You may observe that empty vessels, when knocked, answer presently, send out a noise to a great distance, and oftentimes the sound whirled round in the hollow breaks out with a considerable force; whilst a vessel that is filled either with a liquid or a solid body will not answer to a stroke, because the sound hath no room or passage to come through. And among solid bodies themselves, gold and stone, because they want pores, can hardly be made to sound; and when a noise is made by a stroke upon them, it is very flat, and presently lost. But brass is sounding, it being a porous, rare, and light metal, not consisting of parts tightly compacted, but being mixed with a yielding and uncompacted substance, which gives free passage to other motions, and kindly receiving the sound sends it forward; till some touching the instrument do, as it were, seize on it in the way, and stop the hollow; for then, by reason of the hindering force, it stops and goes no further. And this, in my opinion, is the reason why the night is more sonorous, and the day less; since in the day, the heat rarefying the air makes the empty spaces between the particles to be very little. But, pray, let none argue against the suppositions I assumed.

And I (Ammonius bidding me oppose him) said: Sir, your suppositions which demand a vacuum to be granted I shall admit; but you err in supposing that a vacuum is conducive either to the preservation or conveyance of sound. For that which cannot be touched, acted upon, or struck is peculiarly favorable to silence. But sound is a stroke of a sounding body; and a sounding body is that which has homogeneousness and uniformity, and is easy to be moved, light, smooth, and, by reason of its tenseness and continuity, it is obedient to the stroke; and such is the air. Water, earth, and fire are of themselves soundless; but each of them makes a noise when air falls upon or gets into it. And brass hath no vacuum; but being mixed with a smooth and gentle air it answers to a stroke, and is sounding. If the eye may be judge, iron must be reckoned to have a great many vacuities, and to be porous like a honey-comb, yet it is the dullest, and sounds worse than any other metal.

Therefore there is no need to trouble the night to contract and condense its air, that in other parts we may leave vacuities and wide spaces; as if the air would hinder and corrupt the substance of the sounds, whose very substance, form, and power itself is. Besides, if your reason held, misty and extreme cold nights would be more sonorous than those which are temperate and clear, because then the atoms in our atmosphere are constipated, and the spaces which they left remain empty; and, what is more obvious, a cold day should be more sonorous than a warm summer's night; neither of which is true. Therefore, laying aside that explication, I produce Anaxagoras, who teacheth that the sun makes a tremulous motion in the air, as is evident from those little motes which are seen tossed up and down and flying in the sunbeams. These (says he), being in the day-time whisked about by the heat, and making a humming noise, lessen or drown other sounds; but at night their motion, and consequently their noise, ceaseth.

When I had thus said, Ammonius began: Perhaps it will look like a ridiculous attempt in us, to endeavor to confute Democritus and correct Anaxagoras. Yet we must not allow that humming noise to Anaxagoras's little motes, for it is neither probable nor necessary. But their tremulous and whirling motion in the sunbeams is oftentimes sufficient to disturb and break a sound. For the air (as hath been already said), being itself the body and substance of sound, if it be quiet and undisturbed, makes a straight, easy, and continuous way to the particles or the motions which make the sound. Thus sounds are best heard in calm still weather; and the contrary is seen in stormy weather, as Simonides hath it:–

> *No tearing tempests rattled through the skies,*
> *Which hinder sweet discourse from mortal ears.*

For often the disturbed air hinders the articulateness of a discourse from coming to the ears, though it may convey something of the loudness and length of it. Now the night, simply considered in itself, hath nothing that may disturb the air; though the day hath,–namely the sun, according to the opinion of Anaxagoras.

To this Thrasyllus, Ammonius's son, subjoining said: What is the matter, for God's sake, that we endeavor to solve this difficulty by the unintelligible fancied motion of the air, and neglect the tossing and divulsion thereof, which are evident? For Jupiter, the great ruler above, doth not covertly and silently move the little particles of air; but as soon as he appears, he stirs up and moves everything.

He sends forth lucky signs,
And stirs up nations to their proper work,

And they obey; and (as Democritus saith) with fresh thoughts for each new day, as if newly born again, they fall to their worldly concerns with noisy and effectual contrivances. And upon this account, Ibycus oppositely calls the dawning [Greek omitted] (from [Greek omitted], TO HEAR), because then men first begin to hear and speak. Now at night, all things being at rest, the air being quiet and undisturbed must therefore probably transmit the voice better, and convey it whole and unbroken to our ears.

Aristodemus the Cyprian, being then in the company, said: But consider, sir, whether battles or the marches of great armies by night do not confute your reason; for the noise they make seems as loud as otherwise, though then the air is broken and very much disturbed. But the reason is partly in ourselves; for our voice at night is usually vehement, we either commanding others to do something or asking short questions with heat and concern. For that, at the same time when Nature requires rest, we should stir to do or speak anything, there must be some great and urgent necessity for it; and thence our voices become more vehement and loud.

QUESTION IV. WHY, WHEN IN THE SACRED GAMES ONE SORT OF GARLAND WAS GIVEN IN ONE, AND ANOTHER IN ANOTHER, THE PALM WAS COMMON TO ALL. AND WHY THEY CALL THE GREAT DATES [Greek omitted].

SOSPIS, HERODES, PROTOGENES, PRAXITELES, CAPHISUS.

The Isthmian games being celebrated, when Sospis was the second time director of the solemnity, we avoided other entertainments,–he treating a great many strangers and often all his fellow-citizens,–but once, when he entertained his nearest and most learned friends at his own house, I was one of the company. After the first course, one coming to Herodes the rhetorician brought a palm and a wreathed crown, which one of his acquaintance, who had won the prize for an encomiastic exercise, sent him. This Herodes received very kindly, and sent it back again, but added that he could not tell the reason why, since each of the games gave a particular garland, yet all of them bestowed the palm. For those do not satisfy me (said he) who say that the equality of the leaves is the reason, which growing out one against another seem to resemble some striving for the prize, and that victory is called [Greek omitted] from [Greek omitted], not to yield. For a great many other trees, almost by measure and weight dividing the nourishment to their leaves growing opposite to one another, show a decent order and wonderful equality. They seem to speak more probably who say the ancients were pleased with the beauty and figure of the tree. Thus Homer compares Nausicaa to a palm-branch. For you all know very well, that some threw roses at the victors, and others pomegranates and apples, to honor and reward them. But now the palm hath nothing evidently more taking than many other things, since here in Greece it bears no fruit that is good to eat, it not ripening and growing mature enough. But if, as in Syria and Egypt, it bore a fruit that is the most pleasant to the eyes of anything in the world, and the sweetest to the taste, then I must confess nothing could compare with it. And the Persian monarch (as the story goes), being extremely taken with Nicolaus the Peripatetic philosopher, who was a very sweet-humored man, tall and slender, and of a ruddy complexion, called the greatest and fairest dates Nicolai.

This discourse of Herodes seemed to give occasion for a query about Nicolaus, which would be as pleasant as the former. Therefore, said Sospis, let every one carefully give his sentiments of the matter before us. I begin, and think that, as far as possible, the honor of the victor should remain fresh and immortal. Now a palm-tree is the longest lived of any, as this line of Orpheus testifies:–

They lived like branches of a leafy palm.

And this almost alone has the privilege (though it is said to belong to many besides) of having always fresh and the same leaves. For neither the laurel nor the olive nor the myrtle, nor any other of those trees named evergreen, is always to be seen with the very same leaves; but as the old fall, new ones grow. So cities continue the same, where new parts succeed those that decay. But the palm, never shedding a leaf, is continually adorned with the same green. And this power of the tree, I believe, men think agreeable to, and fit to represent, the strength of victory.

When Sospis had done, Protogenes the grammarian, calling Praxiteles the commentator by his name, said. What then, shall we suffer those rhetoricians to be thought to have hit the mark when they bring arguments only from probabilities and conjectures? And can we produce nothing from history to club to this discourse? Lately, I remember, reading in the Attic annals, I found that Theseus first instituted games in Delos, and tore off a branch from the sacred palm-tree, which was called spadix (from [Greek omitted] TO TEAR).

And Praxiteles said: This is not certain; but perhaps some will demand of Theseus himself, upon what account when he instituted the game, he broke off a branch of palm rather than of laurel or of olive. But consider whether this be not a prize proper to the Pythian games, as appropriate to Amphictyon. For there they first, in honor of the god, crowned the victors with laurel and palm, as consecrating to the god, not the laurel or olive, but the palm. So Nicias did, who defrayed the charges of the solemnity in the name of the Athenians at Delos the Athenians themselves at Delphi; and before these, Cypselus the Corinthian. For this god is a lover of games, and delights in contending for the prize at harping, singing, and throwing the bar, and, as some say, at cuffing; and assists men when contending, as Homer witnesseth, by making Achilles speak thus,

> Let two come forth in cuffing stout, and try
> To which Apollo gives the victory.
> ("Iliad," xxiii. 659.)

And amongst the archers, he that made his address to Apollo made the best shot, and he that forgot to pray to him missed the mark. And besides, it is not likely that the Athenians would rashly, and upon no grounds, dedicate their place of exercise to Apollo. But they thought that the god which bestows health gives likewise a vigorous constitution, and strength for the encounter. And since some of the encounters are light and easy, others laborious and difficult, the Delphians offered sacrifices to Apollo the cuffer; the Cretans and Spartans to Apollo the racer; and the dedication of spoils taken in the wars and trophies to Apollo Pythias show that he is of great power to give victory in war.

Whilst he was speaking, Caphisus, Theon's son, interrupted him, and said: This discourse smells neither of history nor comment, but is taken out of the common topics of the Peripatetics, and endeavors to persuade; besides, you should, like the tragedians, raise your machine, and fright all that contradict you with the god. But the god, as indeed it is requisite he should be, is equally benevolent to all. Now let us, following Sospis (for he fairly leads the way), keep close to our subject, the palm-tree, which affords us sufficient scope for our discourse. The Babylonians celebrate this tree, as being useful to them three hundred and sixty several ways. But to us Greeks it is of very little use, but its lack of fruit makes it appropriate for contenders in the games. For being the fairest, greatest, and best proportioned of all sorts of trees, it bears no fruit amongst us; but by reason of its strong nature it exhausts all its nourishment (like an athlete) upon its body, and so has very little, and that very bad, left for seed. Besides all this, it hath something peculiar, which cannot be attributed to any other tree. The branch of a palm, if you put a weight upon it, doth not yield and bend downwards, but turns the contrary way as if it resisted the pressing force. The like is to be observed in these exercises. For those who, through weakness or cowardice, yield to them, their adversaries oppress; but those who stoutly endure the encounter have not only their bodies, but their minds too, strengthened and increased.

QUESTION V. WHY THOSE THAT SAIL UPON THE NILE TAKE UP THE WATER THEY ARE TO USE BEFORE DAY.

One demanded a reason why the sailors take up the water for their occasions out of the river Nile by night, and not by day. Some thought they feared the sun, which heating the liquid would make it more liable to putrefaction. For everything that is warmed becomes more easy to be changed, having already suffered when its natural quality was remitted. And cold constipating the parts seems to preserve everything in its natural state, and water especially. For that the cold of water is naturally constringent is evident from snow, which keeps flesh from corrupting a long time. And heat, as it destroys the proper quality of other things, so of honey, for it being boiled is itself corrupted, though when raw it preserves other bodies from corruption. And that this is the cause, I have a very considerable evidence from standing pools; for in winter they are as wholesome as other water, but in summer they grow bad and noxious. Therefore the night seeming in some measure to resemble the winter, and the day the summer, they think the water that is taken up at night is less subject to be vitiated and changed.

To these seemingly probable reasons another was added, which confirmed the ingenuity of the sailors by a very strong proof. For some said that they took up their water by night because then it was clear and undisturbed; but at day-time, when a great many fetched water together, and many boats were sailing and many beasts swimming upon the Nile, it grew thick and muddy, and in that condition it was more subject to corruption. For mixed bodies are more easily corrupted than simple and unmixed; for from mixture proceeds disagreement of the parts, from that disagreement a change, and corruption is nothing else but a certain change; and therefore painters call the mixing of their colors [Greek omitted], corrupting; and Homer expresseth dyeing by [Greek omitted] (TO STAIN OR CONTAMINATE). Commonly we call anything that is simple and unmixed incorruptible and immortal. Now earth being mixed with water soonest corrupts its proper qualities, and makes it unfit for drinking; and therefore standing water stinks soonest, being continually filled with particles of earth, whilst running waters preserve themselves by either leaving behind or throwing off the earth that falls into them. And Hesiod justly commends

The water of a pure and constant spring.

For that water is wholesome which is not corrupted, and that is not corrupted which is pure and unmixed. And this opinion is very much confirmed from the difference of earths; for those springs that run through a mountainous, rocky ground are stronger than those which are cut through plains or marshes, because they do not take off much earth. Now the Nile running through a soft country, like the blood mingled with the flesh, is filled with sweet juices that are strong and very nourishing; yet it is thick and muddy, and becomes more so if disturbed. For motion mixeth the earthly particles with the liquid, which, because they are heavier, fall to the bottom as soon as the water is still and undisturbed. Therefore the sailors take up the water they are to use at night, by that means likewise preventing the sun, which always exhales and consumes the subtler and lighter particles of the liquid.

QUESTION VI. CONCERNING THOSE WHO COME LATE TO AN ENTERTAINMENT; AND FROM WHENCE THESE WORDS, [Greek omitted] AND, [Greek omitted] ARE DERIVED.

PLUTARCH'S SONS, THEON'S SONS, THEON, PLUTARCH, SO-CLARUS.

My younger sons staying too long at the plays, and coming in too late to supper, Theon's sons waggishly and jocosely called them supper hinderers, night-suppers, and the like; and they in reply called their runners-to-supper. And one of the old men in the company said [Greek omitted] signified one that was too late for supper; because, when he found himself tardy, he mended his pace, and made more than common haste. And he told us a jest of Battus, Caesar's jester, who called those that came late supper-lovers, because out of their love to entertainments, though they had business, they would not desire to be excused.

And I said, that Polycharmus, a leading orator at Athens, in his apology for his way of living before the assembly, said: Besides a great many things which I could mention, fellow-citizens, when I was invited to supper, I never came the last man. For this is more democratical; and on the contrary, those that are forced to stay for others that come late are offended at them as uncivil and of an oligarchical temper.

But Soclarus, in defence of my sons, said: Alcaeus (as the story goes) did not call Pittacus a night-supper for supping late, but for delighting in base and scandalous company. Heretofore to eat early was accounted scandalous, and such a meal was called [Greek omitted], from [Greek omitted] INTEMPERANCE.

Then Theon interrupting him said: Not at all, if we must trust those who have delivered down to us the ancients way of living. For they say that those being used to work, and very temperate in a morning, ate a bit of bread dipped in wine, and nothing else, and that they called that meal [Greek omitted] from the [Greek omitted] (WINE). Their supper they called [Greek omitted], because returning from their business they took it [Greek omitted] (LATE). Upon this we began to inquire whence those two meals [Greek omitted] and [Greek omitted] took their names. In Homer [Greek omitted] and [Greek omitted] seem to be the same meal. For he says that Eumaeus provided [Greek omitted] by the break of day; and it is probable that [Greek omitted] was so called from [Greek omitted], because provided in the morning; and [Greek omitted] was so named from [Greek omitted], EASING FROM THEIR LABOR. For men used to take their [Greek omitted] after they had finished their business, or whilst they were about it. And this may be gathered from Homer, when he says,

> *Then when the woodman doth his supper dress.*
> *("Iliad," xi. 86.)*

But some perhaps will derive [Greek omitted] from [Greek omitted], EASIEST PROVIDED, because that meal is usually made upon what is ready and at hand; and [Greek omitted] from [Greek omitted], LABORED, because of the pains used in dressing it.

My brother Lamprias, being of a scoffing, jeering nature, said: Since we are in a trifling humor, I can show that the Latin names of these meals are a thousand times more proper than the Greek; [Greek omitted] SUPPER, they call coena ([Greek omitted]) from community; because they took their [Greek omitted] by themselves, but their coena with their friends. [Greek omitted] DINNER, they call prandium, from the time of the dry; for [Greek omitted] signifies NOON-TIDE, and to rest after dinner is expressed by [Greek omitted]; or else by prandium they denote a bit taken in the morning, [Greek omitted], BEFORE THEY HAVE NEED OF ANY. And not to mention stragula, from [Greek Omitted], vinum from [Greek omitted], oleum from [Greek omitted], mel from [Greek omitted], gustare from [Greek omitted], propinare from [Greek omitted], and a great many more words which they have plainly borrowed from the Greeks,–who can deny but that they have taken their comessatio, BANQUETING, from our [Greek omitted] and miscere, TO MINGLE, from the Greeks too? Thus in Homer,

She in a bowl herself mixt ([Greek omitted]) generous wine.
("Odyssey," x. 356.)

They call a table mensam, from [Greek omitted], PLACING IT IN
THE MIDDLE; bread, panem, from satisfying [Greek omitted], HUN-
GER; a garland, coronam, from [Greek omitted], THE HEAD;–and
Homer somewhat likens [Greek omitted], a HEAD-PIECE, to a garland;–caedere, TO BEAT, from [Greek omitted]; and dentes, TEETH,
from [Greek omitted]; lips they call labra, from [Greek omitted], TAK-
ING OUR VICTUALS WITH THEM. Therefore we must either listen
to such fooleries as these without laughing, or not give them so ready
entrance by means of words....

QUESTION VII. CONCERNING PYTHAGORAS'S SYMBOLS, IN
WHICH HE FORBIDS US TO RECEIVE A SWALLOW INTO OUR
HOUSE, AND BIDS US AS SOON AS WE ARE RISEN TO RUFFLE
THE BEDCLOTHES.

SYLLA, LUCIUS, PLUTARCH, PHILINUS.

Sylla the Carthaginian, upon my return to Rome after a long absence, gave me a welcoming supper, as the Romans call it, and invited
some few other friends, and among the rest, one Lucius an Etrurian, the
scholar of Moderatus the Pythagorean. He seeing my friend Philinus
ate no flesh, began (as the opportunity was fair) to talk of Pythagoras;
and affirmed that he was a Tuscan, not because his father, as others
have said, was one, but because he himself was born, bred, and taught
in Tuscany. To confirm this, he brought considerable arguments from
such symbols as these:–As soon as you are risen, ruffle the bedclothes;
leave not the print of the pot in the ashes; receive not a swallow into
your house; never step over a besom; nor keep in your house creatures
that have hooked claws. For these precepts of the Pythagoreans the
Tuscans only, as he said, carefully observe.

Lucius, having thus said, that precept about the swallow seemed
to be most unaccountable, it being a harmless and kind animal; and
therefore it seemed strange that that should be forbid the house, as
well as the hooked-clawed animals, which are ravenous, wild, and
bloody. Nor did Lucius himself approve that only interpretation of
the ancients, who say, this symbol aims directly at backbiters and tale-
bearing whisperers. For the swallow whispers not at all; it chatters indeed, and is noisy, but not more than a pie, a partridge, or a hen. What
then, said Sylla, is it upon the old fabulous account of killing her son,
that they deny the swallow entertainment, by that means showing

their dislike to those passions which (as the story goes) made Tereus and Procne and Philomel both act and suffer such wicked and abominable things? And even to this day they call the birds Daulides. And Gorgias the sophister, when a swallow muted upon him, looked upon her and said, Philomel, this was not well done. Or perhaps this is all without foundation; for the nightingale, though concerned in the same tragedy, we willingly receive.

Perhaps, sir, said I, what you have alleged may be some reason; but pray consider whether first they do not hate the swallow upon the same account that they abhor hook-clawed animals. For the swallow feeds on flesh; and grasshoppers, which are sacred and musical, they chiefly devour and prey upon. And, as Aristotle observes, they fly near the surface of the earth to pick up the little animals. Besides, that alone of all house-animals makes no return for her entertainment. The stork, though she is neither covered, fed, nor defended by us, yet pays for the place where she builds, going about and killing the efts, snakes, and other venomous creatures. But the swallow, though she receives all those several kindnesses from us, yet, as soon as her young are fledged, flies away faithless and ungrateful; and (which is the worst of all) of all house-animals, the fly and the swallow only never grow tame, suffer a man to touch them, keep company with or learn of him. And the fly is so shy because often hurt and driven away; but the swallow naturally hates man, suspects, and dares not trust any that would tame her. And therefore,–if we must not look on the outside of these things, but opening them view the representations of some things in others,–Pythagoras, setting the swallow for an example of a wandering, unthankful man, adviseth us not to take those who come to us for their own need and upon occasion into our familiarity, and let them partake of the most sacred things, our house and fire.

This discourse of mine gave the company encouragement to proceed, so they attempted other symbols, and gave moral interpretations of them. For Philinus said, that the precept of blotting out the print of the pot instructed us not to leave any plain mark of anger, but, as soon as ever the passion hath done boiling, to lay aside all thoughts of malice and revenge. That symbol which adviseth us to ruffle the bedclothes seemed to some to have no secret meaning, but to be in itself very evident; for it is not decent that the mark and (as it were) stamped image should remain to be seen by others, in the place where a man hath lain with his wife. But Sylla thought the symbol was rather intended to prevent men's sleeping in the day-time, all the conveniences for sleeping being taken away in the morning as soon as we are up. For night is the time for sleep, and in the day we should rise and follow our affairs, and not suffer so much as the print of our body in the bed, since a man asleep is of no more use than one dead. And this interpretation seems to be confirmed by that other precept, in which the Pythagoreans advise their followers not to take off any man's burthen from him, but to lay on more, as not countenancing sloth and laziness in any.

QUESTION VIII. WHY THE PYTHAGOREANS COMMAND FISH NOT TO BE EATEN, MORE STRICTLY THAN OTHER ANIMALS. EMPEDOCLES, SYLLA, LUCIUS, TYNDARES, NESTOR.

Our former discourse Lucius neither reprehended nor approved, but, sitting silent and musing, gave us the hearing. Then Empedocles addressing his discourse to Sylla, said: If our friend Lucius is displeased with the discourse, it is time for us to leave off; but if these are some of their mysteries which ought to be concealed, yet I think this may be lawfully divulged, that they more cautiously abstain from fish than from other animals. For this is said of the ancient Pythagoreans; and even now I have met with Alexicrates's scholars, who will eat and kill and even sacrifice some of the other animals, but will never taste fish. Tyndares the Spartan said, they spared fish because they had so great a regard for silence, and they called fish [Greek omitted], because they had their voice SHUT UP ([Greek omitted]); and my namesake Empedocles advised one who had been expelled from the school of Pythagoras to shut up his mind like a fish, and they thought silence to be divine, since the gods without any voice reveal their meaning to the wise by their works.

Then Lucius gravely and composedly saying, that perhaps the true reason was obscure and not to be divulged, yet they had liberty to venture upon probable conjectures, Theon the grammarian began thus: To demonstrate that Pythagoras was a Tuscan is a great and no easy task. But it is confessed that he conversed a long time with the wise men of Egypt, and imitated a great many of the rites and institutions of the priests, for instance, that about beans. For Herodotus delivers, that the Egyptians neither set nor eat beans, nay, cannot endure to see them; and we all know, that even now the priests eat no fish; and the stricter sort eat no salt, and refuse all meat that is seasoned with it. Various reasons are offered for this; but the only true reason is hatred to the sea, as being a disagreeable, or rather naturally a destructive element to man. For they do not imagine that the gods, as the Stoics did that the stars, were nourished by it. But, on the contrary, they think that the father and preserver of their country, whom they call the deflux of Osiris, is lost in it; and when they bewail him as born on the left hand, and destroyed in the right-hand parts, they intimate to us the ending and corruption of their Nile by the sea, and therefore they do not believe that its water is wholesome, or that any creature produced or nourished in it can be clean or wholesome food for man, since it breathes not the common air, and feeds not on the same food with him. And the air that nourisheth and preserves all other things is destructive to them, as if their production and life were unnecessary and against Nature; nor should we wonder that they think animals bred in the sea to be disagreeable to their bodies, and not fit to mix with their blood and spirits, since when they meet a pilot they will not speak to him, because he gets his living by the sea.

Sylla commended this discourse, and added concerning the Pythagoreans, that they then chiefly tasted flesh when they sacrificed to the gods. Now no fish is ever offered in sacrifice. I, after they had done, said that many, both philosophers and unlearned, considering with how many good things it furnisheth and makes our life more comfortable, take the sea's part against the Egyptians. But that the Pythagoreans should abstain from fish because they are not of the same kind, is ridiculous and absurd; nay, to butcher and feed on other animals, because they bear a nearer relation to us, would be a most inhuman and Cyclopean return. And they say that Pythagoras bought a draught of fishes, and presently commanded the fishers to let them all out of the net; and this shows that, he did not hate or not mind fishes, as things of another kind and destructive to man, but that they were his dearly beloved creatures, since he paid a ransom for their freedom.

Therefore the tenderness and humanity of those philosophers suggest a quite contrary reason, and I am apt to believe that they spare fishes to instruct men, or to accustom themselves to acts of justice; for other creatures generally give men cause to afflict them, but fishes neither do nor are capable of doing us any harm. And it is easy to show, both from the writings and religion of the ancients, that they thought it a great sin not only to eat but to kill an animal that did them no harm. But afterwards, being necessitated by the spreading multitude of men, and commanded (as they say) by the Delphic oracle to prevent the total decay of corn and fruit, they began to sacrifice, yet they were so disturbed and concerned at the action, that they called it [Greek omitted] and [Greek omitted] (TO DO), as if they did some strange thing in killing an animal; and they are very careful not to kill the beast before the wine has been cast upon his head and he nods in token of consent. So very cautious are they of injustice. And not to mention other considerations, were no chickens (for instance) or hares killed, in a short time they would so increase that there could be no living. And now it would be a very hard matter to put down the eating of flesh, which necessity first introduced, since pleasure and luxury hath espoused it. But the water-animals neither consuming any part of our air or water, or devouring the fruit, but as it were encompassed by another world, and having their own proper bounds, which it is death for them to pass, they afford our belly no pretence at all for their destruction; and therefore to catch or be greedy after fish is plain deliciousness and luxury, which upon no just reason unsettle the sea and dive into the deep. For we cannot call the mullet corn-destroying, the trout grape-eating, nor the barbel or seapike seed-gathering, as we do some land-animals, signifying their hurtfulness by these epithets. Nay, those little mischiefs which we complain of in these house-creatures, a weasel or fly, none can justly lay upon the greatest fish. Therefore the Pythagoreans, confining themselves not only by the law which forbids them to injure men, but also by Nature, which commands them to do violence to nothing, fed on fish very little, or rather not at all. But suppose there were no injustice in this case, yet to delight in fish would argue daintiness and luxury; because they are such costly and unnecessary diet. Therefore Homer doth not only make the Greeks whilst encamped near the Hellespont, eat no fish, but he mentions not any sea-provision that the dissolute Phaeacians or luxurious wooers had, though both islanders. And Ulysses's mates, though they sailed over so much sea, as long as they had any provision left, never let down a hook or net.

But when the victuals of their ship was spent,
("Odyssey," xii. 329-332.)
a little before they fell upon the oxen of the Sun, they caught fish, not to please their wanton appetite, but to satisfy their hunger,–
With crooked hooks, for cruel hunger gnawed.
The same necessity therefore forced them to catch fish and devour the oxen of the Sun. Therefore not only among the Egyptian and Syrians but Greeks too, to abstain from fish was a piece of sanctity, they avoiding (as I think), a superfluous curiosity in diet, as well as being just.

To this Nestor subjoining said: But sir, of my citizens as of the Megarians in the proverb, you make no account; although you have heard me often say that our priests of Neptune (whom we call Hieromnemons) never eat fish. For Neptune himself is called the Breeder. And the race of Hellen sacrificed to Neptune as the first father, imagining, as likewise the Syrians did, that man rose from a liquid substance. And therefore they worship a fish as of the same production and breeding with themselves, in this matter being more happy in their philosophy than Anaximander; for he says that fish and men were not produced in the same substances, but that men were first produced in fishes, and, when they were grown up and able to help themselves, were thrown out, and so lived upon the land. Therefore, as the fire devours its parents, that is, the matter out of which it was first kindled, so Anaximander, asserting that fish were our common parents, condemneth our feeding on them.

QUESTION IX. WHETHER THERE CAN BE NEW DISEASES, AND HOW CAUSED. PHILO, DIOGENIANUS, PLUTARCH.

Philo the physician stoutly affirmed that the elephantiasis was a disease but lately known; since none of the ancient physicians speak one word of it, though they oftentimes enlarge upon little, frivolous and obscure trifles. And I, to confirm it, cited Athenodorus the philosopher, who in his first book of Epidemical Diseases says, that not only that disease, but also the hydrophobia or water-dread (occasioned by the biting of a mad dog), were first discovered in the time of Asclepiades. At this the whole company were amazed, thinking it very strange that such diseases should begin then, and yet as strange that they should not be taken notice of in so long a time; yet most of them leaned to this last opinion, as being most agreeable to man, not in the least daring to imagine that Nature affected novelties, or would in the body of man, as in a city, create new disturbances and tumults.

And Diogenianus added, that even the passions and diseases of the mind go on in the same old road that formerly they did; and yet the viciousness of our inclination is exceedingly prone to variety, and our mind is mistress of itself, and can, if it please, easily change and alter. Yet all her inordinate motions have some sort of order, and the soul hath bounds to her passions, as the sea to her overflowings. And there is no sort of vice now among us which was not practised by the ancients. There are a thousand differences of appetites and various motions of fear; the schemes of grief and pleasure are innumerable.

> Yet are not they of late or now produced,
> And none can tell from whence they first arose.
> (Sophocles, "Antigone," 456.)

How then should the body be subject to new diseases, since it hath not, like the soul, the principle of its own alteration in itself, but by common causes is joined to Nature, and receives a temperature whose infinite variety of alterations is confined to certain bounds, like a ship moving and tossing in a circle about its anchor. Now there can be no disease without some cause, it being against the laws of Nature that anything should be without a cause. Now it will be very hard to find a new cause, unless we fancy some strange air, water, or food never tasted by the ancients, should out of other worlds or intermundane spaces descend to us. For we contract diseases from those very things which preserve our life; since there are no peculiar seeds of diseases, but the disagreement of their juices to our bodies, or our excess in using them, disturbs Nature. These disturbances have still the very same differences, though now and then called by new names. For names depend on custom, but the passions on Nature; and these being constant and those variable, this error has arisen. As, in the parts of a speech and the syntax of the words, some new sort of barbarism or solecism can suddenly arise; so the temperature of the body hath certain deviations and corruptions into which it may fall, those things which are against and hurtful to Nature being in some sort existent in Nature herself. The mythographers are in this particular very ingenious, for they say that monstrous uncouth animals were produced in the time of the Giants war, the moon being out of its course, and not rising where it used to do. And those who think Nature produces new diseases like monsters, and yet give neither likely nor unlikely reasons of the change, err, as I imagine, my dear Philo, in taking a less or a greater degree of the same disease to be a different disease. The intension or increase of a thing makes it more or greater, but does not make the subject of another kind. Thus the elephantiasis, being an intense scabbiness, is not a new kind; nor is the water-dread distinguished from other melancholic and stomachical affections but only by the degree. And I wonder we did not observe that Homer was acquainted with this disease, for it is evident that he calls a dog rabid from the very same rage with which when men are possessed they are said to be mad.

Against this discourse of Diogenianus Philo himself made some objections, and desired me to be the old physicians' patron; who must be branded with inadvertency and ignorance, unless it appears that those diseases began since their time. First then Diogenianus, methinks, very precariously desires us to think that the intenseness or remissness of degrees is not a real difference, and does not alter the kind. For, were this true, then we should hold that downright vinegar is not different from pricked wine, nor a bitter from a rough taste, darnel from wheat, nor garden-mint from wild mint. For it is evident that these differences are only the several degrees of the same qualities, in some being more intense, in some more remiss. So we should not venture to affirm that flame is different from a white spirit, sunshine from flame, hoarfrost from dew, or hail from rain; but that the former have only more intense qualities than the latter. Besides, we should say that blindness is of the same kind with short-sightedness, violent vomiting (or cholera) with weakness of the stomach, and that they differ only in degree. Though what they say is nothing to the purpose; for if they allow the increase in intensity and strength, but assert that this came but now of late,–the novelty showing itself in the quantity rather than the quality,–the same difficulties which they urged against the other opinion oppress them. Sophocles says very well concerning those things which are not believed to be now, because they were not heretofore,–

Once at the first all things their being had.

And it is probable that not all diseases, as in a race, the barrier being let down, started together; but that one rising after another, at some certain time, had its beginning and showed itself. It is rational but afterwards overeating, luxury, and surfeiting, encouraged by ease and plenty, raised bad and superfluous juices, and those brought various new diseases, and their perpetual complications and mixtures still create more new. Whatever is natural is determined and in order; for Nature is order, or the work of order. Disorder, like Pindar's sand, cannot be comprised by number, and that which is beside Nature is straight called indeterminate and infinite. Thus truth is simple, and but one; but falsities innumerable. The exactness of motions and harmony are definite, but the errors either in playing upon the harp, singing, or dancing, who can comprehend? Indeed Phrynichus the tragedian says of himself,

As many figures dancing doth propose
As waves roll on the sea when tempests toss.

And Chrysippus says that the various complications of ten single axioms amount to 1,000,000. But Hipparchus hath confuted that account, showing that the affirmative contains 101,049 complicated propositions, and the negative 310,952. And Xenocrates says, the number of syllables which the letters will make is 100,200,000. How then is it strange that the body, having so many different powers in itself, and getting new qualities every day from its meat and drink, and using those motions and alterations which are not always in the same time nor in the same order, should upon the various complications of all these be affected with new diseases? Such was the plague at Athens described by Thucydides, who conjectures that it was new because that birds and beasts of prey would not touch the dead carcasses. Those that fell sick about the Red Sea, if we believe Agatharcides, besides other strange and unheard diseases, had little serpents in their legs and arms, which did eat their way out, but when touched shrunk in again, and raised intolerable inflammations in the muscles; and yet this kind of plague, as likewise many others, never afflicted any beside, either before or since. One, after a long stoppage of urine, voided a knotty barley straw. And we know that Ephebus, with whom we lodged at Athens, threw out, together with a great deal of seed, a little hairy, many-footed, nimble animal. And Aristotle tells us, that Timon's nurse in Cilicia every year for two months lay in a cave, without any vital operation besides breathing. And in the Menonian books it is delivered as a symptom of a diseased liver carefully to observe and hunt after mice and rats, which we see now nowhere practised.

Therefore let us not wonder if something happens which never was before, or if something doth not appear among us with which the ancients were acquainted; for the cause of those accidents is the nature of our body, whose temperature is subject to be changed. Therefore, if Diogenianus will not introduce a new kind of water or air, we, having no need of it, are very well content. Yet we know some of Democritus's scholars affirm that, other worlds being dissolved, some strange effluvia fall into ours, and are the principle of new plagues and uncommon diseases. But let us not now take notice of the corruption of some parts of this world by earthquake, droughts, and floods, by which both the vapors and fountains rising out of the earth must be necessarily corrupted. Yet we must not pass by that change which must be wrought in the body by our meat, drink, and other exercises in our course of life. For many things which the ancients did not feed on are now accounted dainties; for instance, mead and swine's belly. Heretofore too, as I have heard, they hated the brain of animals so much, that they detested the very name of it; as when Homer says, "I esteem him at a brain's worth." And even now we know some old men, not bearing to taste cucumber, melon, orange, or pepper. Now by these meats and drinks it is probable that the juices of our bodies are much altered, and their temperature changed, new qualities arising from this new sort of diet. And the change of order in our feeding having a great influence on the alteration of our bodies, the cold courses, as they were called formerly, consisting of oysters, polyps, salads, and the like, being (in Plato's phrase) transferred "from tail to mouth," now make the first course, whereas they were formerly the last. Besides, the glass which we usually take before supper is very considerable in this case; for the ancients never drank so much as water before they ate, but now we drink freely before we sit down, and fall to our meat with a full and heated body, using sharp sauces and pickles to provoke appetite, and then we fall greedily on the other meat. But nothing conduceth more to alterations and new diseases in the body than our different baths; for here the flesh, like iron in the fire, grows soft and loose, and is presently constipated and hardened by the cold. For, in my opinion, if any of the last age had looked into our baths, he might have justly said,

There burning Phlegethon meets Acheron.

For they used such mild gentle baths, that Alexander the Great being feverish slept in one. And the Gauls' wives carry their pots of pulse to eat with their children whilst they are in the bath. But our baths now inflame, vellicate, and distress; and the air which we draw is a mixture of air and water, disturbs the whole body, tosses and displaces every atom, till we quench the fiery particles and allay their heat. Therefore, Diogenianus, you see that this account requires no new strange causes, no intermundane spaces; but the single alteration of our diet is enough to raise new diseases and abolish old.

QUESTION X. WHY WE GIVE LEAST CREDIT TO DREAMS IN AUTUMN. FLORUS, PLUTARCH, PLUTARCH'S SONS, FAVORINUS.

Florus reading Aristotle's physical problems, which were brought to him to Thermopylae, was himself (as philosophical wits used to be) filled with a great many doubts, and communicated them to others; thereby confirming Aristotle's saying, that much learning raises many doubts. Other topics made our walks every day very pleasant, but the common saying concerning dreams,–that those in autumn are the vainest,–I know not how, whilst Favorinus was engaged in other matters, was started after supper. Your friends and my sons thought Aristotle had given sufficient satisfaction in this point, and that no other cause was to be sought after or allowed but that which he mentions, the fruit. For the fruit, being new and flatulent, raises many disturbing vapors in the body; for it is not likely that only wine ferments, or new oil only makes a noise in the lamp, the heat agitating its vapor; but new corn and all sorts of fruit are plump and distended, till the unconcocted flatulent vapor is broke away. And that some sorts of food disturb dreams they said, was evident from beans and the polypus's head, from which those who would divine by their dreams are commanded to abstain.

But Favorinus himself, though in all other things he admires Aristotle exceedingly and thinks the Peripatetic philosophy to be most probable, yet in this case resolved to scour up an old musty opinion of Democritus. He first laid down that known principle of his, that images pass through the pores into the inmost parts of the body, and being carried upward cause dreams; and that these images fly from everything, vessels, garments, plants, but especially from animals, because of their heat and the motion of their spirits; and that these images not only carry the outward shape and likeness of the bodies (as Epicurus thinks, following Democritus so far and no farther), but the very designs, motions, and passions of the soul; and with those entering into the bodies, as if they were living things, discover to those that receive them the thoughts and inclinations of the persons from whom they come, if so be that they preserve their frame and order entire. And that is especially preserved when the air is calm and clear, their passage then being quick and undisturbed. Now the autumnal air, when trees shed their leaves, being very uneven and disturbed, ruffles and disorders the images, and, hindering them in their passage, makes them weak and ineffectual; when, on the contrary, if they rise from warm and vigorous subjects, and are presently applied, the notices which they give and the impressions they make are clear and evident.

Then with a smile looking upon Autobulus, he continued: But, sir, I perceive you design to have an airy skirmish with these images, and try the excellence of this old opinion, as you would a picture, by your nail. And Autobulus replied: Pray, sir, do not endeavor to cheat us any longer; for we know very well that you, designing to make Aristotle's opinion appear the better, have used this of Democritus only as its shade. Therefore I shall pass by that, and impugn Aristotle's opinion, which unjustly lays the blame on the new fruit. For both the summer and the early autumn witness in its favor, when, as Antimachus says, the fruit is most fresh and juicy; for then, though we eat the new fruit, yet our dreams are not so vain as at other times. And the months when the leaves fall, being next to winter, so concoct the corn and remaining fruit, that they grow shrivelled and less, and lose all their brisk agitating spirit. As for new wine, those that drink it soonest forbear till February, which is after winter; and the day on which we begin we call the day of the Good Genius, and the Athenians the day of cask-opening. For whilst wine is working, we see that even common, laborers will not venture on it. Therefore no more accusing the gifts of the gods, let us seek after another cause of vain dreams, to which the name of the season will direct us. For it is called LEAF-SHEDDING, because the leaves then fall off by reason of their dryness and coldness; except the leaves of hot and oily trees, as of the olive, the laurel, or the palm; or of the moist, as of the myrtle and the ivy. But the temperature of these preserves them, though not others; because in others the vicious humor that holds the leaves is constipated by the cold, or being weak and little is dried up. Now moisture and heat are necessary for the growth and preservation of plants, but especially of animals; and on the contrary, coldness and dryness are very noxious to both. And therefore Homer elegantly calls men moist and juicy: to rejoice he calls to be warmed; and anything that is grievous and frightful he calls cold and icy. Besides, the words [Greek omitted] and [Greek omitted] are applied to the dead, those names intimating their extreme dryness. But more, our blood, the principal thing in our whole body, is moist and hot. And old age hath neither of those two qualities. Now the autumn seems to be as it were the old age of the decaying year; for the moisture doth not yet fall, and the heat decays. And its inclining the body to diseases is an evident sign of its cold and dryness. Now it is necessary that the souls should be indisposed with the bodies and that, the subtile spirit being condensed, the divining faculty of the soul, like a glass that is breathed upon, should be sullied; and therefore it cannot represent anything plain, distinct, and clear, as long as it remains thick, dark, and condensed.

Book Nine

THIS NINTH BOOK, Sossius Senecio, contains the discourses we held at Athens at the Muses feast, for this number nine is agreeable to the number of the Muses. Nor must you wonder when you find more than ten questions (which number I have observed in my other books) in it; for we ought to give the Muses all that belongs to them, and be as careful of robbing them as of a temple, since we owe them much more and much better things than these.

QUESTION I. CONCERNING VERSES SEASONABLY AND UNSEASONABLY APPLIED. AMMONIUS, PLUTARCH, ERATO, CERTAIN SCHOOLMASTERS, AND FRIENDS OF AMMONIUS.

Ammonius, captain of the militia at Athens, would show Diogenianus the proficiency of those youths that learned grammar, geometry, rhetoric, and music; and invited the chief masters of the town to supper. There were a great many scholars at the feast, and almost all his acquaintance. Achilles invited only the single combatants to his feast, intending (as the story goes) that, if in the heat of the encounter they had conceived any anger or ill-will against one another, they might then lay it aside, being made partakers of one common entertainment. But the contrary happened to Ammonius, for the contentions of the masters increased and grew more sharp midst their cups and merriment; and all was disorder and confused babbling.

Therefore Ammonius commanded Erato to sing to his harp, and he sang some part of Hesiod's Works beginning thus,

> Contention to one sort is not confined;
> ("Works and Days," 11.)

and I commended him for choosing so apposite a song. Then he began to discourse about the seasonable use of verse, that it was not only pleasant but profitable. And straight every one's mouth was full of that poet who began Ptolemy's epithalamium (when he married his sister, a wicked and abominable match) thus,

> *Jove Juno called his sister and his wife;*
> *("Iliad," xviii. 356.)*

and another, who refused to sing after supper to Demetrius the king, but after he sent him his young son Philip to be educated sang thus,

> *Breed thou the boy as doth become*
> *Both Hercules's race and us;*

and Anaxarchus who, being pelted with apples by Alexander at supper, rose up and said,

> *Some god shall wounded be by mortal hand.*
> *(Euripides, "Orestes," 271.)*

But that Corinthian captive boy excelled all, who, when the city was destroyed, and Mummius, taking a survey of all the free-born children that understood letters, commanded each to write a verse, wrote thus:–

> *Thrice, four times blest, the happy Greeks that fell.*
> *("Odyssey," v. 306.)*

For they say that Mummius was affected with it, wept and gave all the free-born children that were allied to the boy their liberty. And some mentioned the wife of Theodorus the tragedian, who refused his embraces a little before he contended for the prize; but, when he was conqueror and came in unto her, clasped him and said,

> *Now, Agamemnon's son, you freely may*
> *(Sophocles "Electra," 2.)*

After this a great many sayings were mentioned as unseasonably spoken, it being fit that we should know such and avoid them;–as that to Pompey the Great, to whom, upon his return from a dangerous war, the schoolmaster brought his little daughter, and, to show him what a proficient she was, called for a book, and bade her begin at this line,

> *Returned from war; but hadst thou there been slain,*
> *My wish had been complete;*
> *("Iliad," iii. 428.)*

and that to Cassius Longinus, to whom a flying report of his son's dying abroad being brought, and he no ways appearing either to know the certain truth or to clear the doubt, an old senator came and said: Longinus, will you not despise the flying uncertain rumor, as if you did not know nor had read this line,

> *For no report is wholly false?*
> *(Hesiod, "Works and Days," 763.)*

And he that at Rhodes, to a grammarian demanding a line upon which he might show his skill in the theatre, proposed this,

Fly from the island, worst of all mankind,
("Odyssey," x. 72.)

either slyly put a trick upon him, or unwittingly blundered. And this discourse quieted the tumult.

QUESTIONS II. AND III. WHAT IS THE REASON THAT ALPHA IS PLACED FIRST IN THE ALPHABET, AND WHAT IS THE PROPORTION BETWEEN THE NUMBER OF VOWELS AND SEMI-VOWELS?

AMMONIUS, HERMEAS, PROTOGENES, PLUTARCH, ZOPYRION.

It being the custom of the Muses' feast to draw lots, and those that were matched to propose curious questions to one another, Ammonius, fearing that two of the same profession might be matched together, ordered, without drawing lots, a geometrician to propose questions to a grammarian, and a master of music to a rhetorician.

First, therefore, Hermeas the geometrician demanded of Protogenes the grammarian a reason why Alpha was the first letter of the alphabet. And he returned the common answer of the schools, that it was fit the vowels should be set before the mutes and semi-vowels. And of the vowels, some being long, some short, some both long and short, it is just that the latter should be most esteemed. And of these that are long and short, that is to be set first which is usually placed before the other two, but never after either; and that is Alpha. For that put after either Iota or Upsilon will not be pronounced, will not make one syllable with them, but as it were resenting the affront and angry at the position, seeks the first as its proper place. But if you place Alpha before either of those, they are obedient, and quietly join in one syllable, as in these words, [Greek omitted] and a thousand others. In these three respects therefore, as the conquerors in all the five exercises, it claims the precedence,–that of most other letters by being a vowel, that of other vowels by being dichronous, and lastly, that of these double-timed vowels themselves because it is its nature to go before and never after them.

Protogenes making a pause, Ammonius, speaking to me, said: What! have you, being a Boeotian, nothing to say for Cadmus, who (as the story goes) placed Alpha the first in order, because a cow is called Alpha by the Phoenicians, and they account it not the second or third (as Hesiod doth) but the first of their necessary things?

Nothing at all, I replied, for it is just that, to the best of my power,
I should rather assist my own than Bacchus's grandfather. For Lamprias my grandfather said, that the first articulate sound that is made
is Alpha; for the air in the mouth is formed and fashioned by the motion of the lips; now as soon as those are opened, that sound breaks
forth, being very plain and simple, not requiring or depending upon
the motion of the tongue, but gently breathed forth whilst that lies
still. And therefore that is the first sound that children make. Thus
[Greek omitted], TO HEAR, [Greek omitted], TO SING, [Greek
omitted], TO PIPE, [Greek omitted], TO HOLLOW, begin with the
letter Alpha; and I think that [Greek omitted], TO LIFT UP, and
[Greek omitted], TO OPEN, were fitly taken from that opening and
lifting up of the lips when his voice is uttered. Thus all the names of
the mutes besides one have an Alpha, as it were a light to assist their
blindness; for Pi alone wants it, and Phi and Chi are only Pi and
Kappa with an aspirate.

Hermeas saying that he approved both reasons, why then (continued
I) do not you explain the proportion, if there be any, of the number of
the letters; for, in my opinion, there is; and I think so, because the number of mutes and semi-vowels, compared between themselves or with
the vowels, doth not seem casual and undesigned, but to be according
to the first proportion which you call arithmetical. For their number
being nine, eight, and seven, the middle exceeds the last as much as it
wants of the first. And the first number being compared with the last,
hath the same proportion that the Muses have to Apollo; for nine is
appropriated to them, and seven to him. And these two numbers tied
together double the middle; and not without reason, since the semi-
vowels partake the power of both.

And Hermeas replied: It is said that Mercury was the first god that
discovered letters in Egypt; and therefore the Egyptians make the figure
of an Ibis, a bird dedicated to Mercury, for the first letter. But it is not
fit, in my opinion, to place an animal that makes no noise at the head of
the letters. Amongst all the numbers the fourth is peculiarly dedicated
to Mercury, because, as some say, the god was born on the fourth day of
the month. And the first letters called Phoenician from Cadmus are four
times four, or sixteen; and of those that were afterward added, Palamedes
found four, and Simonides four more. Now amongst numbers, three is
the first perfect, as consisting of a first, a middle, and a last; and after
that six, as being equal the sum of its own divisors (1+2+3). Of these, six
multiplied by four makes twenty-four; and also the first perfect number,
three, multiplied by the first cube, eight, make the same.

Whilst he was discoursing thus, Zopyrion the grammarian sneered and muttered between his teeth; and, as soon as he had done, cried out that he most egregiously trifled; for it was mere chance, and not design, that gave such a number and order to the letters, as it was mere chance that the first and last verses of Homer's Iliads have just as many syllables as the first and last of his Odysseys.

QUESTION IV. WHICH OF VENUS'S HANDS DIOMEDES WOUNDED. HERMEAS, ZOPYRION, MAXIMUS.

Hermeas would have replied to Zopyrion, but we desired him to hold; and Maximus the rhetorician proposed to him this far-fetched question out of Homer, Which of Venus's hands Diomedes wounded. And Zopyrion presently asking him again, of which leg was Philip lame?–Maximus replied, It is a different case, for Demosthenes hath left us no foundation upon which we may build our conjecture. But if you confess your ignorance in this matter, others will show how the poet sufficiently intimates to an understanding man which hand it was. Zopyrion being at a stand, we all, since he made no reply, desired Maximus to tell us.

And he began: The verses running thus

> Then Diomedes raised his mighty spear,
> And leaping towards her just did graze her hand;
> ("Iliad," v. 335. It is evident from what follows that
> Plutarch interprets [Greek omitted] in this passage HAVING
> LEAPED TO ONE SIDE. (G.))

it is evident that, if he designed to wound her left hand, there had been no need of leaping, since her left hand was opposite to his right. Besides, it is probable that he would endeavor to wound the strongest hand, and that with which she drew away Aeneas; and which being wounded, it was likely she would let him go. But more, after she returned to Heaven, Minerva jeeringly said,

> No doubt fair Venus won a Grecian dame,
> To follow her beloved Trojan youths,
> And as she gently stroked her with her hand,
> Her golden buckler scratched this petty wound.
> ("Iliad", v. 422.)

And I suppose, you sir, when you stroke any of your scholars, you use your right hand, and not your left; and it is likely that Venus, the most skilful of all the goddesses, soothed the heroines after the same manner.

QUESTION V. WHY PLATO SAYS THAT AJAX'S SOUL CAME TO
DRAW HER LOT IN THE TWENTIETH PLACE IN HELL. HYLAS,
SOSPIS, AMMONIUS, LAMPRIAS.

These discourses made all the other company merry; but Sospis the
rhetorician, seeing Hylas the grammarian sit silent and discomposed (for
he had not been very happy in his exercises), cried out,

But Ajax's soul stood far apart;

and raising his voice repeated the rest to him,

But sit, draw near, and patiently attend,
Hear what I say, and tame, your violent rage.

To this Hylas, unable to contain, returned a scurvy answer saying
that Ajax's soul, taking her lot in the twentieth place in hell, changed
her nature, according to Plato, for a lion's; but, for his part, he could not
but often think upon the saying of the old comedian,

'Tis better far to be an ass than see
Unworthwhile men in greater honor shine

At this Sospis, laughing heartily, said: But in the meantime, before
we have the pack-saddles on, if you have any regard for Plato, tell us
why he makes Ajax's soul, after the lots drawn, to have the twentieth
choice. Hylas, with great indignation, refused, thinking that this was a
jeering reflection on his former miscarriage. And therefore my brother began thus: What, was not Ajax counted the second for beauty,
strength, and courage, and the next to Achilles in the Grecian army?
And twenty is the second ten, and ten is the chiefest of numbers, as
Achilles of the Greeks. We laughing at this, Ammonius said: Well,
Lamprias, let this suffice for a joke upon Hylas; but since you have
voluntarily taken upon you to give an account of this matter, leave off
jesting, and seriously proceed.

This startled Lamprias a little, but, after a short pause, he continued
thus: Plato often tells merry stories under borrowed names, but when
he puts any fable into a discourse concerning the soul, he hath some
considerable meaning in it. The intelligent nature of the heavens he calls
a flying chariot, intimating the harmonious whirl of the world. And
here he introduceth one Er, the son of Harmonius, a Pamphylian, to tell
what he had seen in hell; intimating that our souls are begotten according to harmony, and are agreeably united to our bodies, and that, when
they are separated, they are from all parts carried together into the air,
and from thence return to second generations. And what hinders but
that [Greek omitted] twentieth should intimate that this was not a true
story, but only probable and fictitious [Greek omitted], and that the
lot fell casually [Greek omitted]. For Plato always toucheth upon three

causes, he being the first and chiefest philosopher that knew how fate accords with fortune, and how our free-will is mixed and complicated with both. And now he hath admirably discovered what influence each hath upon our affairs. The choice of our life he hath left to our free-will, for virtue and vice are free. But that those who have made a good choice should live religiously, and those who have made an ill choice should lead a contrary life, he leaves to the necessity of fate. But the chances of lots thrown at a venture introduce fortune into the several conditions of life in which we are brought up, and which pre-occupates and perverts our own choice. Now consider whether it is not irrational to inquire after a cause of those things that are done by chance. For if the lot seems to be disposed of by design, it ceaseth to be chance and fortune, and becomes fate and providence.

Whilst Lamprias was speaking, Marcus the grammarian seemed to be counting to himself, and when he had done, he began thus: Amongst the souls which Homer mentions in his [Greek omitted], Elpenor's is not to be reckoned as mixed with those in hell, but, his body being not buried, as wandering about the banks of the river Styx. Nor is it fit that we should reckon Tiresias's soul amongst the rest,–

> On whom alone, when deep in hell beneath,
> Wisdom Proserpina conferred,

to discourse and converse with the living even before he drank the sacrifice's blood. Therefore, Lamprias, if you subtract these two, you will find that Ajax was the twentieth that Ulysses saw, and Plato merrily alludes to that place in Homer's [Greek omitted].

QUESTION VI. WHAT IS SIGNIFIED BY THE FABLE ABOUT THE DEFEAT OF NEPTUNE? AND ALSO, WHY DO THE ATHENIANS OMIT THE SECOND DAY OF THE MONTH BOEDROMION? ME-NEPHYLUS, HYLAS, LAMPRIAS.

While all were making a disturbance, Menephylus, a Peripatetic philosopher, addressing Hylas: You see, he said, how this investigation is no foolery nor insolence. But leave now, my dear fellow, that obstinate Ajax, whose name is ill-omened, as Sophocles says, and side with Poseidon, whom you yourself are wont to tell has often been overcome, once by Athene here, in Delphi by Apollo, in Argos by Here, in Aegina by Zeus, in Naxos by Bacchus, yet in his misfortunes has always been mild and amiable. Here at least he shares a temple in common with Athene, in which there is an altar dedicated to Lethe. And Hylas, as if he had become better tempered: One thing has escaped you, Menephylus, that we have given up the second day of

September, not on account of the moon, but because on that day the gods seemed to have contended for the country. By all means, said Lamprias, by as much as Poseidon was more civilized than Thrasybulus, since not like him a winner but a loser....

(The rest of this book to Question XIII is lost; with the exception of the titles that follow, and the fragment of Question XII.)

QUESTION VII. WHY THE ACCORDS IN MUSIC ARE SEPARATED INTO THREE. QUESTION VIII. WHEREIN THE INTERVALS MELODIOUS DIFFER FROM THOSE THAT ARE HARMONIC. QUESTION IX. WHAT IS THE CAUSE OF ACCORD? AND ALSO, WHY, WHEN TWO ACCORDANT STRINGS ARE TOUCHED TOGETHER, IS THE MELODY ASCRIBED TO THE BASE? QUESTION X. WHY, WHEN THE ECLIPTIC PERIODS OF THE SUN AND THE MOON ARE EQUAL IN NUMBER, THE MOON APPEARS OFTENER ECLIPSED THAN THE SUN. QUESTION XI. THAT WE CONTINUE NOT ALWAYS THE SAME, IN REGARD OF THE DEFLUX OF OUR SUBSTANCE. QUESTION XII. IS IT MORE PROBABLE THAT THE NUMBER OF THE STARS IS EVEN OR ODD?

Men must be cheated by oaths. And Glaucias said: I have heard this saying used against Polycrates the tyrant; probably too it was said against others: but why do you ask these questions? Because, by Zeus, said Sospis, I see the children playing odd and even with jackstones and the Academics with words. For such tempers as these differ in no way from those who ask whether they hold clutched in their hands odd or even. Then Protogenes stood up and called me by name: What is the matter with us that we allow these rhetoricians to be so conceited, and to laugh down others while they are asked nothing, and contribute nothing in the way of argument,–unless they swear that they have no part in the wine as admirers and disciples of Demosthenes, a man who in his whole life never drank wine. That is not the cause of this, said I; but we have never asked them anything. But unless you have something more useful, I think I can put before them from Homer's poetry a case of antinomy in rhetorical theses.

QUESTION XIII. A MOOT-POINT OUT OF THE THIRD BOOK OF HOMER'S ILIADS. PLUTARCH, PROTOGENES, GLAUCIAS, SOSPIS.

What question will you put them, said Protogenes? I will tell you, continued I, and let them carefully attend. Paris makes his challenge in these express words:–

Let me and valiant Menelaus fight
For Helen, and for all the goods she brought;
And he that shall o'ercome, let him enjoy
The goods and woman; let them be his own.

And Hector afterwards publicly proclaiming this challenge in these plain words:–

He bids the Trojans and the valiant Greeks
To fix their arms upon the fruitful ground;
Let Menelaus and stout Paris fight
For all the goods; and he that beats have all.

Menelaus accepted the challenge, and the conditions were sworn to, Agamemnon dictating thus:–

If Paris valiant Menelaus kills,
Let him have Helen, and the goods possess;
If youthful Menelaus Paris kills,
The woman and the goods shall all be his.
(See "Iliad," iii. 68, 88, 255, and 281.)

Now since Menelaus only overcame but did not kill Paris, each party hath somewhat to say for itself, and against the other. The one may demand restitution, because Paris was overcome; the other deny it, because he was not killed. Now how to determine this case and clear the seeming repugnancies doth not belong to philosophers or grammarians, but to rhetoricians, that are well skilled both in grammar and philosophy.

Then Sospis said: The challenger's word decides; for the challenger proposed the conditions, and when they were accepted, the opposite party had no power to make additions. Now the condition proposed in this challenge was not killing, but overcoming; and there was reason that it should be so, for Helen ought to be the wife of the bravest. Now the bravest is he that overcomes; for it often happens that an excellent soldier might be killed by a coward, as is evident in what happened afterward, when Achilles was shot by Paris. For I do not believe that you will affirm, that Achilles was not so brave a man as Paris because he was killed by him, and that it should be called the victory, and not rather the unjust good fortune, of him that shot him. But Hector was overcome before he was killed by Achilles, because he would not stand, but trembled and fled at his approach. For he that refuseth the combat or flies cannot palliate his defeat, and plainly grants that his adversary is the better man. And therefore Iris tells Helen beforehand,

In single combat they shall fight for you,
And you shall be the glorious victor's wife.
(2 Ibid. iii. 137.)

And Jupiter afterwards adjudges the victory to Menelaus in these words:

The conquest leans to Menelaus's side.

(3 *Ibid.* iv. 13.)

For it would be ridiculous to call Menelaus a conqueror when he shot Podes, a man at a great distance, before he thought of or could provide against his danger, and yet not allow him the reward of conquest over him whom he made fly and sneak into the embraces of his wife, and whom he spoiled of his arms whilst he was yet alive, and who had himself offered the challenge, by the articles of which Menelaus now appeared to be the conqueror.

Glaucias subjoined: in all laws, decrees, contracts, and promises, those latest made are always accounted more valid than the former. Now the later contract was Agamemnon's, the condition of which was killing, and not only overcoming. Besides the former was mere words, the latter confirmed by oath; and, by the consent of all, those were cursed that broke them; so that this latter was properly the contract, and the other a bare challenge. And this Priam at his going away, after he had sworn to the conditions, confirms by these words:–

But Jove and other gods alone do know,
Which is designed to see the shades below;
("*Iliad,*" iii. 308.)

for he understood that to be the condition of the contract. And therefore a little after Hector says,

But Jove hath undetermined left our oaths,
(*Ibid.* vii. 69.)

for the combat had not its designed and indisputable determination, since neither of them fell. Therefore this question doth not seem to me to contain any contrariety of law, since the former contract is comprised and overruled by the latter; for he that kills certainly overcomes, but he that overcomes doth not always kill. But, in short, Agamemnon did not annul, but only explain the challenge proposed by Hector. He did not change anything, but only added the most principal part, placing victory in killing; for that is a complete conquest, but all others may be evaded or disputed, as this of Menelaus, who neither wounded nor pursued his adversary. Now as, where there are laws really contrary, the judges take that side which is plain and indisputable, and mind not that which is obscure; so in this case, let us admit that contract to be most valid which contained killing, as a known and undeniable evidence of victory. But (which is the greatest argument) he that seems to have had the victory, not being quiet, but running up and down the army, and searching all about,

To find neat Paris in the busy throng,
(Ibid. iii. 450.)

sufficiently testifies that he himself did not imagine that the conquest was perfect and complete. For when Paris had escaped he did not forget his own words:–

And which of us black fate and death design,
Let him be lost; the others cease from war.
(Iliad, iii. 101,)

Therefore it was necessary for him to seek after Paris, that he might kill him and complete the combat; but since he neither killed nor took him, he had no right to the prize. For he did not conquer him, if we may guess by what he said when he expostulated with Jove and bewailed his unsuccessful attempt:–

Jove, Heaven holds no more spiteful god than thou.
Now would I punish Paris for his crimes;
But oh! my sword is broke, my mighty spear,
Stretched out in vain, flies idly from my hand!
(Ibid. iii, 365.)

For in these words he confessed that it was to no purpose to pierce the shield or take the head-piece of his adversary, unless he likewise wounded or killed him.

QUESTION XIV. SOME OBSERVATIONS ABOUT THE NUMBER OF THE MUSES, NOT COMMONLY KNOWN. HERODES, AMMONIUS, LAMPRIAS, TRYPHON, DIONYSIUS, MENEPHYLUS, PLUTARCH.

This discourse ended, we poured out our offerings to the Muses, and together with a hymn in honor of Apollo, the patron of the Muses, we sung with Erato, who played upon the harp, the generation of the Muses out of Hesiod. After the song was done, Herod the rhetorician said: Pray, sirs, hearken. Those that will not admit Calliope to be ours say that she keeps company with kings, not such, I suppose, as are busied in resolving syllogisms or disputing, but such who do those things that belong to rhetoricians and statesmen. But of the rest of the Muses, Clio abets encomiums, for praises are called [Greek omitted]; and Polymnia history, for her name signifies the remembrance of many things; and it is said that all the Muses were somewhere called Remembrances. And for my part, I think Euterpe hath some relation to us too, if (as Chrysippus says) her lot be agreeableness in discourse and pleasantness in conversation. For it belongs to an orator to converse, as well as plead or give advice; since it is his part to gain the favor of his auditors, and to defend or excuse his client. To praise or dispraise is the commonest theme; and if we manage this artfully, it will turn to considerable account; if unskilfully, we are lost. For that saying,

Gods! how he is honored and beloved by all,
("Odyssey," x. 38.)

chiefly, in my opinion, belongs to those men who have a pleasing and persuasive faculty in discourse.

Then said Ammonius to Herod: We have no reason to be angry with you for grasping all the Muses, since the goods that friends have are common, and Jove hath begotten a great many Muses, that every man may be plentifully supplied; for we do not all need skill in hunting, military arts, navigation, or any mechanical trades; but learning and instruction is necessary for every one that

Consumes the fruits of the spacious earth.
(From Simonides.)

And therefore Jove made but one Minerva, one Diana, one Vulcan, but many Muses. But why there should be nine, and no more nor less, pray acquaint us; for you, so great a lover of, and so well acquainted with, the Muses, must certainly have considered this matter. What difficulty is there in that? replied Herod. The number nine is in everybody's mouth, as being the first square of the first odd number; and as doubly odd, since it may be divided into three equal odd numbers. Ammonius with a smile subjoined: Boldly said; and pray add, that this number is composed of the two first cubes, one and eight, and according to another composition of two triangles, three and six, each of which is itself perfect. But why should this belong to the Muses more than any other of the gods? For we have nine Muses, but not nine Cereses, nine Minervas or Dianas. For I do not believe that you take it for a good argument, that the Muses must be so many, because their mother's name (Mnemosyne) consists of just so many letters. Herod smiling, and everybody being silent, Ammonius desired our opinions.

My brother said, that the ancients celebrated but three Muses, and that to bring proofs for this assertion would be pedantic and uncivil in such a company. The reason of this number was (not as some say) the three different sorts of music, the diatonic, the chromatic, and harmonic, nor those stops that make the intervals nete, mese, and hypate, though the Delphians gave the Muses this name erroneously, in my opinion, appropriating it to one science, or rather to a part of one single science, the harmoniac part of music. But, as I think, the ancients, reducing all arts and sciences which are executed and performed by reason or discourse to three heads, philosophy, rhetoric, and mathematics, accounted them the gifts of three gods, and named them the Muses. Afterwards, about Hesiod's time, the sciences being better and more thoroughly looked into, and men subdividing them found that each science contained three different parts. In mathematics are comprehended music, arithmetic, and geometry; in philosophy are logic, ethics, and physics. In rhetoric, they say the first part was demonstrative or encomiastic, the second deliberative, the third judicial. None of all which they believed to be without a god or a Muse or some superior power for its patron, and did not, it is probable, make the Muses equal in number to these divisions, but found them to be so. Now, as you may divide nine into three threes, and each three into as many units; so there is but one rectitude of reason, which is employed about the highest truth, and which belongs to the whole in common, while each of the three kinds of science is assigned three Muses, and each of these has her distinct faculty assigned to her, which she disposes and orders. And I do not think the poets and astrologers will find fault with us for passing over their professions in silence, since they know, as well as we, that astrology is comprehended in geometry, and poetry in music.

As soon as he had said this, Trypho the physician subjoined: How hath our art offended you, that you have shut the Museum against us? And Dionysius of Melite added: Sir, you have a great many that will side with you in the accusation; for we farmers think Thalia to be ours, assigning her the care of springing and budding seeds and plants. But I interposing said: Your accusation is not just; for you have bountiful Ceres, and Bacchus who (as Pindar phraseth it) increaseth the trees, the chaste beauty of the fruits; and we know that Aesculapius is the patron of the Physicians, and they make their address to Apollo as Paean, but never as the Muses' leader. All men (as Homer says) stand in need of the gods, but all stand not in need of all. But I wonder Lamprias did not mind what the Delphians say in this matter; for they affirm that the Muses amongst them were not named so either from the strings or sounds in music; but the universe being divided into three parts, the first portion was of the fixed stars, the second of the planets, the third of those things that are under the concave of the moon; and all these are ordered according to harmonical proportions, and of each portion a Muse takes care; Hypate of the first, Nete of the last, and Mese in the middle, combining as much as possible, and turning about mortal things with the gods and earthly with heavenly. And Plato intimates the same thing under the names of the Fates, calling one Atropos, the other Lachesis, and the other Clotho. For he hath committed the revolutions of the eight spheres to so many Sirens, and not Muses.

Then Menephylus the Peripatetic subjoined: The Delphians' opinion hath indeed somewhat of probability in it; but Plato is absurd in committing the eternal and divine revolutions not to the Muses but to the Sirens, Daemons that neither love nor are benevolent to mankind, wholly passing by the Muses, or calling them by the names of the Fates, the daughters of Necessity. For Necessity is averse to the Muses; but Persuasion being more agreeable and better acquainted with them, in my opinion, than the grace of Empedocles,

Intolerable Necessity abhors.

No doubt, said Ammonius, as it is in us a violent and involuntary cause; but in the gods Necessity is not intolerable, uncontrollable, or violent, unless it be to the wicked; as the law in a commonwealth to the best man is its best gift, not to be violated or transgressed, not because they have no power, but because they have no will, to change it. And Homer's Sirens give us no just reason to be afraid; for he in that fable rightly intimates the power of their music not to be hurtful to man, but delightfully charming, and detaining the souls which pass from hence thither and wander after death; working in them a love for heavenly and divine things, and a forgetfulness of everything on earth; and they extremely pleased follow and attend them. And from thence some imperfect sound, and as it were echo of that music, coming to us by the means of reason and good precepts, rouseth our souls, and restores the notice of those things to our minds, the greatest part of which lie encumbered with and entangled in disturbances of the flesh and distracting passions. But the generous soul hears and remembers, and her affection for those pleasures riseth up to the most ardent passion, whilst she eagerly desires but is not able to free herself from the body.

It is true, I do not approve what he says; but Plato seems to me, as he hath strangely and unaccountably called the axes spindles and distaffs, and the stars whirls, so to have named the Muses Sirens, as delivering divine things to the ghosts below, as Ulysses in Sophocles says of the Sirens,

I next to Phorcus's daughters came,
Who fix the sullen laws below.

Eight of the Muses take care of the spheres, and one of all about the earth. The eight who govern the motions of the spheres maintain the agreement of the planets with the fixed stars and one another. But that one who looks after the place betwixt the earth and moon and takes care of mortal things, by means of discourse and song introduceth persuasion, aiding our natural consent to community and agreement, and giveth men as much harmony, grace, and order as is possible for them to take; introducing this persuasion to appease and quiet our disturbances, and as it were to recall our wandering desires out of the wrong way, and to set us in the right path. But, as Pindar says,

> *Whom Jove abhors, he starts to hear*
> *The Muses sounding in his ear.*
> *(Pindar, "Pythian," i. 25.)*

To this discourse Ammonius, as he used to do, subjoined that verse of Xenophanes,

> *This fine discourse seems near allied to truth,*

and desired every one to deliver his opinion. And I after a short silence, said: As Plato thinks by the name, as it were by tracks, to discover the powers of the gods, so let us place in heaven and over heavenly things one of the Muses, Urania. And it is likely that those require no distracting variety of cares to govern them, since they have the same single nature for the cause of all their motions. But where are a great many irregularities and disorders, there we must place the eight Muses, that we may have one to correct each particular irregularity and miscarriage. There are two parts in a man's life, the serious and the merry; and each must be regulated and methodized. The serious role, which instructs us in the knowledge and contemplation of the gods, Calliope, Clio, and Thalia appear chiefly to look after and direct. The other Muses govern our weak part, which changes presently into wantonness and folly; they do not neglect our brutish and violent passions and let them run their own course, but by appropriate dancing, music, song, and orderly motion mixed with reason, bring them down to a moderate temper and condition. For my part, since Plato admits two principles of every action, viz, the natural desire after pleasure, and acquired opinion which covets and wishes for the best, and calls one reason and the other passion, and since each of these is manifold, I think that each requires a considerable and, to speak the truth, a divine direction. For instance, one faculty of our reason is said to be political or imperial, over which Hesiod says Calliope presides; Clio's province is the noble and aspiring; and Polymnia's that faculty of the soul which inclines to attain and keep knowledge (and therefore the Sicyonians call one of their three Muses Polymathia); to Euterpe everybody allows the searches into nature and physical speculations, there being no greater, no sincerer pleasure belonging to any other sort of speculation in the world. The natural desire to meat and drink Thalia reduceth from brutish and uncivil to be sociable and friendly; and therefore we say [Greek omitted] of those that are friendly, merry, and sociable over their cups, and not of those that are quarrelsome and mad. Erato, together with Persuasion, that brings along with it reason and opportunity, presides over marriages; she takes away and extinguisheth all the violent fury of pleasure, and makes it tend to friendship, mutual confidence, and endearment, and not to effeminacy, lust, or discontent. The delight which the eye or ear receives is a sort of pleasure, either appropriate to reason or to passion, or common to them both. This the two other Muses, Terpsichore and Melpomene, so moderate, that the one may only tickle and not charm, the other only please and not bewitch.

QUESTION XV. THAT THERE ARE THREE PARTS IN DANCING: [Greek omitted], MOTION, [Greek omitted], GESTURE, AND [Greek omitted], REPRESENTATION. WHAT EACH OF THOSE IS AND WHAT IS COMMON TO BOTH POETRY AND DANCING.

AMMONIUS AND THRASYBULUS.

After this, a match of dancing was proposed, and a cake was the prize. The judges were Meniscus the dancing-master, and my brother Lamprias; for he danced the Pyrrhic very well, and in the Palaestra none could match him for the graceful motion of his hands and arms in dancing. Now a great many dancing with more heat than art, some desired two of the company who seemed to be best skilled and took most care to observe their steps, to dance in the kind called [Greek omitted]. Upon this Thrasybulus, the son of Ammonius, demanded what [Greek omitted] signified, and gave Ammonius occasion to run over most of the parts of dancing.

He said they were three,–[Greek omitted], [Greek omitted] and [Greek omitted]. For dancing is made up of motion and manner [Greek omitted] as a song of sounds and stops; stops are the ends of motion. Now the motions they call [Greek omitted], and the gestures and likeness to which the motions tend, and in which they end, they call [Greek omitted]: as, for instance, when by their own motions they represent the figure of Apollo, Pan, or any of the raging Bacchae. The third is [Greek omitted]; which is not an imitation, but a plain downright indication of the things represented. For as the poets, when they would speak of Achilles, Ulysses, the earth, or heaven, use their proper names, and such as the vulgar usually understand. But for the more lively representation, they use such words as by their very sound express some eminent quality in the thing, or metaphors; as when they say that streams do "babble and flash"; that arrows fly "desirous the flesh to wound"; or when they describe an equal battle by saying "the fight had equal heads." They have likewise a great many significative compositions in their verses. Thus Euripides of Perseus,

> *He that Medusa slew, and flies in air;*

and Pindar of a horse,

> *When by the smooth Alpheus's banks*
> *He ran the race, and never felt the spur;*

and Homer of a race,

> *The chariots, overlaid with tin and brass,*
> *By fiery horses drawn ran swiftly on.*
> *(Euripedes, Frag. 975; Pindar, "Olympian," i. 31;*
> *"Iliad," xxiii. 503.)*

So in dancing, the [Greek omitted] represents the shape and figure, the [Greek omitted] shows some action, passion, or power; but by the [Greek omitted] are properly and significatively shown the things themselves, for instance, the heaven, earth, or the company. Which, being done in a certain order and method, resembles the proper names used in poetry, decently clothed and attended with suitable epithets. As in these lines,

> *Themis the venerable and admired,*
> *And Venus beauteous with her bending brows,*
> *Fair Dione, and June crowned with gold.*
> *(Hesiod, "Theogony," 16.)*

And in these,

> *From Hellen kings renowned for giving laws,*
> *Great Dorus and the mighty Xuthus sprang,*
> *And Aeolus, whose chief delight was horse.*

For if poets did not take this liberty, how mean, how grovelling and flat, would be their verse! As suppose they wrote thus,

> *From this sprung Hercules, from the other Iphitus.*
> *Her father, husband, and her son were kings,*
> *Her brother and forefathers were the same;*
> *And she in Greece Olympias was called.*

The same faults may be committed in that sort of dancing called [Greek omitted] unless the representation be lively and graceful, decent and unaffected. And, in short, we may aptly transfer what Simonides said of painting to dancing, and call dancing mute poetry, and poetry speaking dancing; for poesy doth not properly belong to painting, nor painting to poesy, neither do they any way make use of one another. But poesy and dancing share much in common especially in that type of song called Hyporchema, in which is the most lively representation imaginable, dancing doing it by gesture, and poesy by words. So that poesy may bear some resemblance to the colors in painting, while dancing is like the lines which mark out the features. And therefore he who was the most famous writer of Hyporchemes, who here even surpassed himself, sufficiently proveth that these two arts stand in need of one another he shows what tendency poetry hath to dancing; whilst the sound excites the hands and feet, or rather as it were by some cords distends and raiseth every member of the whole body; so that, whilst such songs are recited or sung, they cannot be quiet. But nowadays no sort of exercise hath such bad depraved music applied to it as dancing; and so it suffers that which Ibyeus as to his own concerns was fearful of, as appears by these lines,

> *I fear lest, losing fame amongst the gods,*
> *I shall receive respect from men alone.*

For having associated to itself a mean paltry sort of music, and falling from that divine sort of poetry with which it was formerly acquainted, it rules now and domineers amongst foolish and inconsiderate spectators, like a tyrant, it hath subjected nearly all music, but hath lost all its honor with excellent and wise men.

These, my Sossius Senecio, were almost the last discourses which we had at Ammonius's house during the festival of the Muses.

Common Conceptions against the Stoics

LAMPRIAS, DIADUMENUS

LAMPRIAS. You, O Diadumenus, seem not much to care, if any one thinks that you philosophize against the common notions; since you confess that you contemn also the senses, from whence the most part of these notions in a manner proceed, having for their seat and foundation the belief of such things as appear to us. But I beseech you, with what speed you can, either by reasons, incantations, or some other manner of discourse, to cure me, who come to you full, as I seem to myself, of great and strange perturbations; so much have I been shaken, and into such a perplexity of mind have I been brought, by certain Stoics, in other things indeed very good men and my familiar friends, but most bitterly and hostility bent against the Academy. These, for some few words modestly spoken by me, have (for I will tell you no lie) rudely and unkindly reprehended me; angrily censuring and branding the ancient philosophers as Sophists and corrupters of philosophy, and subverters of regular doctrines; and saying things yet more absurd than these, they fell at last upon the conceptions, into which (they contend) the Academics had brought a certain confusion and disturbance. At length one of them said, that he thought it was not by fortune, but by the providence of the gods, that Chrysippus came into the world after Arcesilaus and before Carneades; of which the one was the author of the contumelies and injuries done to custom, and the other flourished most of all the Academics. Chrysippus then, coming between them, by his writings against Arcesilaus, stopped also the way against the eloquence of Carneades, leaving indeed many things to the senses, as provisions against a siege, but wholly taking away the trouble about anticipations and conceptions, directing every one of them and putting it in its proper place; so that they who will again embroil and disquiet matters should gain nothing, but be convinced of being malicious and deceitful Sophists. I, having been this morning set on fire by these discourses, want some cooling remedies to extinguish and take away this doubting, as an inflammation, out of my mind.

DIADUMENUS. You perhaps have suffered the same things with some of the vulgar. But if you believe the poets, who say that the ancient city Sipylus was overthrown by the providence of the gods when they punished Tantalus, believe also the companions of the Stoa saying that Nature, not by chance but by divine providence, brought forth Chrysippus, when she had a mind to turn things upside down and alter the course of life; for which purpose never any man was fitter than he. But as Cato said of Caesar, that never any but he came to the management of public affairs sober and considerately resolved on the ruin of the state; so does this man seem to me with the greatest diligence and eloquence to overturn and demolish custom, as those who magnify the man testify, when they dispute against him concerning the sophism called Pseudomenos (or the Liar). For to say, my best friend, that a conclusion drawn from contrary positions is not manifestly false, and again to say that some arguments having true premises and true inductions may yet moreover have the contrary to their conclusions true, what conception of demonstration or what assumption of confidence does it not overthrow? They say, that the polypus in the winter gnaws his own claws; but the logic of Chrysippus, taking away and cutting off its own chiefest parts and principles,–what other notion has it left unsuspected of falsehood? For the superstructures cannot be steady and sure, if the foundations remain not firm but are shaken with so many doubts and troubles. But as those who have dust or dirt upon their bodies, if they touch or rub the filth that is upon them, seem rather to increase than remove it; so some men blame the Academics, and think them guilty of the faults with which they show themselves to be burdened. For who do more subvert the common conceptions than the Stoic school? But if you please, let us leave accusing them, and defend ourselves from the things with which they charge us.

LAMPRIAS. Methinks, Diadumenus, I am this day become a various and unconstant man. For erewhile I came dejected and trembling, as one that wanted an apology; and now I am changed to an accuser, and desire to enjoy the pleasure of revenge, in seeing them all convicted of philosophizing against the common conceptions and presumptions, on which they think chiefly their doctrine is founded, whence they say that it alone agrees with Nature.

DIADUMENUS. Shall we then first attack those common and celebrated doctrines of theirs which themselves, gently admitting their absurdity, style paradoxes; as that only wise men are kings, that they only are rich and fair, they only citizens and judges? Or shall we send all this to the brokers, as old decayed frippery, and make our inquiry into such things as are most practical and with the greatest earnestness delivered by them?

LAMPRIAS. I indeed like this best. For who is there that is not already full of the arguments brought against those paradoxes?

DIADUMENUS. First, then, consider this, whether, according to the common conceptions, they can be said to agree with Nature, who think all natural things indifferent, and esteem neither health, strength of body, beauty, nor strength as desirable, commodious, profitable, or any way contributory to the completing of natural perfection; nor consider that their contraries, as maims, pains, disgraces, and diseases, are hurtful or to be shunned? To the latter of these they themselves say that Nature gives us an abhorrence, and an inclination to the former. Which very thing is not a little repugnant to common understanding, that Nature should incline us to such things as are neither good nor available, and avert us from such as are neither ill nor hurtful, and which is more, that she should render this inclination and this aversion so violent, that they who either possess not the one or fall into the other detest their life with good reason, and withdraw themselves out of it.

I think also that this is said by them against common sense, that Nature herself is indifferent, and yet that it is good to agree with Nature. For it is not our duty either to follow the law or be persuaded by argument, unless the law and argument be good and honest. And this indeed is the least of their errors. But if, as Chrysippus has written in his First Book concerning Exhortation, a happy life consists only in living according to virtue, other things (as he says) being nothing to us, nor cooperating any ways towards it, Nature is not only indifferent, but foolish also and stupid, in inclining us to such things as belong nothing to us; and we also are fools in thinking felicity to be an agreeing with Nature, which draws us after such things as contribute nothing to happiness. For what can be more agreeable to common sense, than that, as desirable things are requisite to live commodiously, so natural things are necessary that we may live according to Nature? Now these men say not so; but having settled the living according to Nature for their end, do nevertheless hold those things which are according to Nature to be indifferent.

Nor is this less repugnant to common sense, that an intelligent and prudent man should not be equally affected to equal good things, but should put no value on some, and be ready to undergo and suffer anything for others, though the things themselves are neither greater nor less one than another. For they say, It is the same thing to abstain from the enjoyment of an old woman that is about to die as to take part in the greatest actions with moderation... since in both cases we do what duty requires. And yet for this, as a great and glorious thing, they should be ready to die; when as to boast of the other would be shameful and ridiculous. And even Chrysippus himself in his commentary concerning Jupiter, and in the Third Book of the Gods, says, that it were a poor, absurd, and impertinent thing to glory in such acts, as proceeding from virtue, as bearing valiantly the stinging of a wasp, or abstaining chastely from an old woman that lies a dying. Do not they then philosophize against the common conception, who profess nothing to be more commendable than those things which yet themselves are ashamed to praise? For how can that be desirable or to be approved, which is worthy neither of praise nor admiration, but the praisers and admirers of which they esteem absurd and ridiculous?

And yet this will (I suppose) appear to you more against common sense, that a wise man should take no care whether he enjoys or not enjoys the greatest good things, but should carry himself after the same manner in these things, as in those that are indifferent both in their management and administration. For all of us, "whoever we are that eat the fruit of the broad earth," judge that desirable, good, and profitable, which being present we use, and absent we want and desire. But that which no man thinks worth his concern, either for his profit or delight, is indifferent. For we by no other means distinguish a laborious man from a trifler, who is for the most part also employed in action, but that the one busies himself in useless matters and indifferently, and the other in things commodious and profitable. But these men act quite contrary; for with them, a wise and prudent man, being conversant in many comprehensions and memories of comprehension, esteems few of them to belong to him; and not caring for the rest, he thinks he has neither more or less by remembering that he lately had the comprehension of Dion sneezing or Theon playing at ball. And yet every comprehension in a wise man, and every memory having assurance and firmness, is a great, yea, a very great good. When therefore his health fails, when some organ of his senses is disordered, or when his wealth is lost, is a wise man so careless as to think that none of these things concern him? Or does he, "when sick, give fees to the physicians: for the gaining of riches sail to Leucon, governor in the Bosphorus, or travel to Idanthyrsus, king of the Scythians," as Chrysippus says? And being deprived of some of his senses, does he not become weary even of life? How then do they not acknowledge that they philosophize against the common notions, employing so much care and diligence on things indifferent, and not minding whether they have or have not great good things?

But this is also yet against the common conceptions, that he who is a man should not rejoice when coming from the greatest evils to the greatest goods. Now their wise men suffer this. Being changed from extreme viciousness to the highest virtue, and at the same time escaping a most miserable life and attaining to a most happy one, he shows no sign of joy, nor does this so great change lift him up or yet move him, being delivered from all infelicity and vice, and coming to a certain sure and firm perfection of virtue. This also is repugnant to common sense, to hold that the being immutable in one's judgments and resolutions is the greatest of goods, and yet that he who has attained to the height wants not this, nor cares for it when he has it, nay, many times will not so much as stretch forth a finger for this security and constancy, which nevertheless themselves esteem the sovereign and perfect good. Nor do the Stoics say only these things, but they add also this to them,—that the continuance of time increases not any good thing; but if a man shall be wise but a minute of an hour, he will not be any way inferior in happiness to him who has all his time practised virtue and led his life happily in it. Yet, whilst they thus boldly affirm these things, they on the contrary also say, that a short-lived virtue is nothing worth; "For what advantage would the attainment of wisdom be to him who is immediately to be swallowed up by the waves or tumbled down headlong from a precipice? What would it have benefited Lichas, if being thrown by Hercules, as from a sling into the sea, he had been on a sudden changed from vice to virtue?" These therefore are the positions of men who not only philosophize against the common conceptions but also confound their own, if the having been but a little while endued with virtue is no way short of the highest felicity, and at the same time nothing worth. Nor is this the strangest thing you will find in their doctrine; but their being of opinion that virtue and happiness, when present, are frequently not perceived by him who enjoys them, nor does he discern that, having but a little before been most miserable and foolish, he is of a sudden become wise and happy. For it is not only childish to say that he who is possessed of wisdom is ignorant of this thing alone, that he is wise, and knows not that he is delivered from folly; but, to speak in general, they make goodness to have very little weight or strength, if it does not give so much as a feeling of it when it is present. For according even to them, it is not by nature imperceptible; nay, even Chrysippus in his books of the End expressly says that good is sensible, and demonstrates it also, as he maintains. It remains, then, that by its weakness and littleness it flies the sense, when being present it is unknown and concealed from the possessors. It were moreover absurd to imagine that the sight, perceiving those things which are but a little whitish or inclining to white, should not discern such as are white in perfection; or that the touch, feeling those things which are but warm or moderately hot, should be insensible of those that are hot in the highest degree. And yet more absurd it is, that a man who perceives what is commonly according to Nature–as are health and good constitution of body–should yet be ignorant of virtue when it is present, which themselves hold to be most of all and in the highest degree according to Nature. For how can it but be against sense, to conceive the difference between health and sickness, and yet so little to comprehend that between wisdom and folly as to think the one to be present when it is gone, and possessing the other to be ignorant that one has it? Now because there is from the highest progress a change made to felicity and virtue, one of these two things must of necessity follow; either that this progress is not vice and infelicity, or that virtue is not far distant from vice, nor happiness from misery, but that the difference between good and evil is very small and not to be perceived by sense; for otherwise they who have the one for the other could not be ignorant of it.

Since, then, they will not depart from any of these contrarieties, but confess and hold them all,–that those who are proceeding towards virtue are fools and vicious, that those who are become good and wise perceive not this change in themselves, and that there is a great difference between folly and wisdom,–they must assuredly seem to you wonderfully to preserve an agreement in their doctrines, and yet more so in their conduct, when affirming all men who are not wise to be equally wicked, unjust, faithless, and fools, they on the other side abhor and detest some of them,–nay, sometimes to such a degree that they refuse even to speak to them when they meet them,–while others of them they trust with their money, choose to offices, and take for husbands to their daughters. Now if they say these things in jest, let them smooth their brows; but if in earnest and as philosophers, it is against the common notions to reprove and blame all men alike in words, and yet to deal with some of them as moderate persons and with others as very wicked; and exceedingly to admire Chrysippus, to deride

Alexinus, and yet to think neither of them more or less mad than the other. "'Tis so," say they; "but as he who is not above a cubit under the superficies of the sea is no less drowned than he who is five hundred fathom deep, so they that are coming towards virtue are no less in vice their those that are farther off. And as blind men are still blind, though they shall perhaps a little after recover their sight; so these that have proceeded towards virtue, till such time as they have attained to it, continue foolish and wicked." But that they who are in the way towards virtue resemble not the blind, but such as see less clearly, nor are like to those who are drowned, but–those which swim, and that near the harbor–they themselves testify by their actions. For they would not use counsellors and generals and lawgivers as blind leaders, nor would they imitate the works and actions and words and lives of some, if they saw them all equally drowned in folly and wickedness. But leaving this, wonder at the men in this behalf, that they are not taught by their own examples to give up the doctrine that these men are wise being ignorant of it themselves, and neither knowing nor being sensible that they are recovered from being drowned and see the light, and that being gotten above vice, they fetch breath again.

This also is against common sense, that it should be convenient for a man who has all good things, and wants nothing requisite to felicity and happiness, to make away himself; and much more this, that for him who neither has nor ever shall have any good thing, but who is and ever shall be accompanied with all adversities, difficulties, and mishaps, it should not be fitting to quit this life unless some of the indifferent things befall him. These laws are enacted in the Stoa; and by these they incite many wise men to kill themselves, as if they would be thereby more happy; and they prevent many foolish men, as if it were proper for them to live on in misery. Although the wise man is fortunate, blessed, every way happy, secure, and free from danger; but the vicious and foolish man is "full, as I may say, of evils, so that there is not room to put them in"; and yet they think that continuing in life is fit for the latter, and departing out of it for the former. And not without cause, says Chrysippus, for we are not to measure life by good things or evil, but by those that are according to Nature. In this manner do they maintain custom, and philosophize according to the common conceptions. What do you say?–that he who enters upon a deliberation of life and death has no right to consider

What good or ill in his own house there is;
or to weigh, as in a balance, what things have the greatest sign of serving to felicity or infelicity; but must argue whether he should live or die from

those things which are neither profitable nor prejudicial, and follow such principles and sentences as command the choosing of a life full of all things to be avoided, and the shunning of one which wants nothing of all those things that are desirable? For though it is an absurd thing, friend Lamprias, to shun a life in which there is no evil, it is yet more absurd, if any one should leave what is good because he is not possessed of what is indifferent, as these men do who leave present felicity and virtue for want of riches and health which they have not.

Saturnian Jove from Glaucus took his wits,

when he went about to change his suit of golden armor for a brazen one, and to give what was worth a hundred oxen for that which was worth but nine. And yet the brazen armor was no less useful for fight than the golden; whereas beauty and health of body, as the Stoics say, contribute not the least advantage so far as happiness is concerned. And yet they seek health in exchange for wisdom. For they say, it would well enough have become Heraclitus and Pherecydes to have parted with their virtue and wisdom, if the one of them could have thereby been freed from his lousy disease, and the other from his dropsy; and if Circe had used two sorts of magical drinks, one to make wise men fools, and the other to make fools wise, Ulysses would rather have drunk that of folly, than have changed his shape for the form of a beast, though having with it wisdom, and consequently also happiness. And, they say, wisdom itself dictates to them these things, exhorting them thus: Let me go, and value not my being lost, if I must be carried about in the shape of an ass. But this, some will say, is an ass-like wisdom which teacheth thus; granting that to be wise and enjoy felicity is good, and to wear the shape of an ass is indifferent. They say, there is a nation of the Ethiopians where a dog reigns, is called king, and has all regal honors and services done to him; but men execute the offices of magistrates and governors of cities. Do not the Stoics act in the very same manner? They give the name and appearance of good to virtue, saying that it alone is desirable, profitable, and available; but in the meantime they act these things, they philosophize, they live and die, as at the command of things indifferent. And yet none of the Ethiopians kill that dog; but he sits in state, and is revered by all. But these men destroy and corrupt their virtue, that they may obtain health and riches.

But the corollary which Chrysippus himself has given for a conclusion to his doctrines seems to free us from the trouble of saying anything more about it. For there being, says he, in Nature some things good, some things bad, and some things between them both, which we call indifferent; there is no man but would rather have the good than the indifferent, and the indifferent than the bad. And of this we call the gods to witness, begging of them by our prayers principally the possession of good things, and if that may not be, deliverance from evil; not desiring that which is neither good nor bad instead of good, but willing to have it instead of evil. But this man, changing Nature and inverting its order, removes the middle out of its own place into the last, and brings back the last into the middle,–not unlike to those tyrants who give the first place to the wicked,–and he gives us a law, first to seek the good, and secondly the evil, and lastly to judge that worst which is neither good nor evil; as if any one should place infernal things next to celestial, thrusting the earth and earthly things into Tartarus,

> Where very far from hence, deep under ground,
> Lies a vast gulf.
> (Iliad, viii. 14.)

Having therefore said in his Third Book concerning Nature, that it is more expedient for a fool to live than not, though he should never attain to wisdom, he adds these words: "For such are the good things of men, that even evil things do in a manner precede other things that are in the middle place; not that these things themselves really precede, but reason, which makes us choose rather to live, though we were to be fools." Therefore also, though we were to be unjust, wicked, hated of the gods, and unhappy; for none of these things are absent from those that live foolishly. Is it then convenient rather to live miserably than not to live miserably, and better to be hurt than not hurt, to be unjust than not unjust, to break the laws than not to break them? That is, is it convenient to do things that are not convenient, and a duty to live even against duty? Yes indeed, for it is worse to want sense and reason than to be a fool. What then ails them, that they will not confess that to be evil which is worse than evil? Why do they say that folly alone is to be avoided, if it is not less but rather more convenient to shun that disposition which is not capable of folly?

But who can complain of this, that shall remember what he has written in his Second Book of Nature, declaring that vice was not unprofitably made for the universe? But it is meet I should set down his doctrine in his own words, that you may understand in what place those rank vice, and what discourses they hold of it, who accuse Xenocrates and Speusippus for not reckoning health indifferent and riches useless. "Vice," saith he, "has its limit in reference to other accidents. For it is also in some sort according to the reason of Nature, and (as I may so say) is not wholly useless in respect of the universe; for other wise there would not be any good." Is there then no good among the gods, because there is no evil? And when Jupiter, having resolved all matter into himself, shall be alone, other differences being taken away, will there then be no good, because there will be no evil? But is there melody in a choir though none in it sings faultily, and health in the body though no member is sick; and yet cannot virtue have its existence without vice? But as the poison of a serpent or the gall of an hyena is to be mixed with some medicines, was it also of necessity that there must have been some conjunction of the wickedness of Meletus with the justice of Socrates, and the dissolute conduct of Cleon with the probity of Pericles? And could not Jupiter have found a means to bring into the world Hercules and Lycurgus, if he had not also made for us Sardanapalus and Phalaris? It is now time for them to say that the consumption was made for the sound constitution of men's bodies, and the gout for the swiftness of their feet; and that Achilles would not have had a good head of hair if Thersites had not been bald. For what difference is there between such triflers and ravers, and those who say that intemperance was not brought forth unprofitably for continence, nor injustice for justice, so that we must pray to the gods, there may be always wickedness,

> *Lies, fawning speeches, and deceitful manners,*
> *(Hesiod, "Works and Days," 78.)*

if, when these are taken away, virtue will also vanish and be lost?

Or do you desire to understand the greatest sweetness of his eloquence and persuasion? "For," says he, "as comedies have in them sometimes ridiculous epigrams, which, though bad in themselves, give nevertheless a certain grace to the whole poem; so, though you may blame vice in itself, yet is it not useless to other things." First, then, to say that vice was made by the providence of God, as a wanton epigram by the will of the poet, transcends in absurdity all imagination. For this being granted, how will the gods be rather givers of good than evil? How will wickedness be displeasing to them, and hated by them? And what shall we have to oppose against these ill-sounding sentences of the poets.–

> *A cause to men God sends,*
> *When to chastise some house his wrath intends;*
> *(From the "Niobe" of Aeschylus, Frag. 151.)*

and again,

> *What God those seeds of strife 'twixt them did sow?*
> *(Iliad, i. 8.)*

Moreover, a lewd epigram adorns the comedy and contributes to its end, which is to delight the spectators and make them laugh. But Jupiter, who is surnamed fatherly, supreme, just, and (as Pindar has it) the most perfect artist, framing the world, not as a great interlude, full of variety and great learning, but as a common city of Gods and men, living together in concord and happiness with justice and virtue,–what need had he, for the attaining to this excellent end, of thieves, murderers, parricides, and tyrants? For vice entered not as a morris-dance, pleasing and delightful to the Divinity; nor was it brought in amongst the affairs of men, to cause mirth and laughter by its raillery and facetiousness, since there is not to be seen in it so much as a dream of that celebrated agreement with Nature. Besides, that foolish epigram is a very small part of the poem, and takes up but a very little place in the comedy; neither do such things abound in it, nor do they corrupt any of those things which seem to have been well done, or spoil their grace. But all human affairs are replete with vice, and the whole life, from the very prologue and beginning to the end, being disordered, depraved, and disturbed, and having no part of it pure or irreprehensible (as these men say), is the most filthy and most unpleasant of all farces.

Wherefore I would willingly ask, in what vice is profitable to the universe. Not surely in respect of heavenly things, and such as are divine by nature. For it would be ridiculous to say, that if there had not arisen, or were not amongst men, malice and covetousness and lying, or that if we did not rob, plunder, slander, and murder one another, the sun would not run his appointed course, the world enjoy its seasons and periods of time, or the earth, which is seated in the midst of the universe, afford the principles of the wind and rain. It remains, then, that the existence of vice must be profitable for us and our affairs; and that perhaps these men mean. Are we more healthy for being vicious, or do we more abound with necessaries? Or does vice contribute anything to our beauty and strength? They say, no. But where on earth is virtue to be met with? Is it then only a base name, and a visionary opinion of night-walking Sophists, and not an actual thing lying conspicuous to all, like vice, so that we cannot partake of anything as profitable,... but least, O ye gods! of virtue, for which we were created? Is it not then absurd, that the utensils of the husbandman, mariner, and charioteer should be serviceable and aiding towards his intended end, whilst that which was by God made for virtue destroys and corrupts virtue? But perhaps it is time now to leave this point, and pass to another.

LAMPRIAS. Not for my sake, my dear friend, I beseech you; for I desire to understand, in what manner these men bring in evil things before the good, and vice before virtue.

DIADUMENUS. It is indeed, sir, a thing worth knowing. They babble indeed much; but in conclusion they say that prudence, being the knowledge of good and evil, would be wholly taken away if there were no evil. For as, if there are truths, it is impossible but there must be some lies also near to them; so it stands with reason, that if there are good things, there must also be evil things.

LAMPRIAS. One of these things is not said amiss; and I think also that the other is not unapprehended by me. For I see a difference here: that which is not true must immediately be false; but that is not of necessity evil which is not good; because that between true and false there is no medium, but between good and evil there is the indifferent. Nor is it of necessity that the one must subsist with the other. For Nature may have good without having any need of evil, but only having that which is neither good nor evil. But if there is anything to be said by you to the former reason, let us hear it.

DIADUMENUS. Many things indeed are said; but at present we shall make use only of what is most necessary. In the first place, it is a folly to imagine that good and evil have their existence for the sake of prudence. For good and evil being already extant, prudence came afterwards; as the art of physic was invented, there being already things wholesome and unwholesome. For good and evil are not therefore extant that there may be prudence; but the faculty by which we judge good and evil that are already in being is named prudence. As sight is a sense distinguishing white from black; which colors were not therefore made that we might have sight, but we rather wanted sight to discern these things. Secondly, when the world shall be set on fire (as the Stoics hold), there will then no evil be left, but all will then be prudent and wise. There is therefore prudence, though there is no evil; nor is it of necessity for evil to exist that prudence may have a being. But supposing that prudence must always be a knowledge of good and evil, what inconvenience would it be if, evil being taken away, prudence should no longer subsist; but instead of this we should have another virtue, not being the knowledge of good and evil, but of good only? So, if black should be wholly lost from among the colors, and any one should therefore contend that sight is also lost, for that there is no more the sense of discerning black and white, what should hinder us from answering him: It is no prejudice to us, if we have not what you call sight, but in lieu of that have another sense and faculty, by which we apprehend colors that are white and not white. For I indeed think that neither our taste would be lost, if bitter things were wanting, nor our feeling, if pain were taken away, nor prudence, if evil had no being; but that these senses would remain, to apprehend things sweet and grateful and those that are not so, and prudence to be the science of things good and not good. But let those who think otherwise take the name to themselves, leaving us the thing.

Besides all this, what should hinder but there may be an understanding of evil, and an existence of good? As the gods, I believe, enjoy health, but understand the fever and pleurisy. Since even we, who, as they say, have abundance of evils but no good, are not yet destitute of the knowledge what prudence, what goodness, and what happiness is. And this also would be remarkable, that if virtue were absent, there should be those who could teach us what it is and give us a comprehension of it, when if vice were not extant, it should be impossible to have any understanding of it. For see what these men persuade us who philosophize against the conceptions,–that by folly indeed we comprehend prudence, but prudence without folly cannot so much as comprehend folly itself.

And if Nature had absolutely stood in need of the generation of evil, yet might one or two examples of vice have been sufficient; or if you will, it might have been requisite that ten, a thousand, or ten thousand vicious men should be brought forth, and not that the multitude of vices should be so great as "to exceed in number the sands of the sea, the dust of the earth, and the feathers of all the various kinds of birds in the world," and yet that there should not be so much all this while as a dream of virtue. Those who in Sparta had the charge of the public halls or eating places called Phiditia were wont to bring forth two or three Helots drunken and full of wine, that the young men, seeing what drunkenness was, might learn to keep sobriety. But in human life there are many such examples of vice. For there is not any one sober to virtue; but we all stagger up and down, acting shamefully and living miserably. Thus does reason inebriate us, and with so much trouble and madness does it fill us, that we fall in nothing short of those dogs of whom Aesop says, that seeing certain skins swimming in the water, they endeavored to gulp down the sea, but burst before they could get at them. For reason also, by which we hope to gain reputation and attain to virtue, does, ere we can reach to it, corrupt and destroy us, being before filled with abundance of heady and bitter vice;–if indeed, as these men say, they who are got even to the uppermost step have no ease, cessation, or breathing from folly and infelicity.

But let us see what manner of thing he shows vice to be who says that it was not brought forth unprofitably, and of what use and what a thing he makes it to be to those who have it, writing in his book of right conduct, that a wicked man wants nothing, has need of nothing, nothing is useful to him, nothing proper, nothing fit for him. How then is vice useful, with which neither health nor abundance of riches nor advancement in virtue is profitable? Who then does not want these things, of which some are "preferable" and "acceptable" and therefore highly useful, and others are "according to Nature," as themselves term them? But (they affirm) no one has need of them, unless he become wise. So the vicious man does not even stand in want of being made wise. Nor are men hungry and thirsty before they become wise. When thirsty, therefore, they have no need of water, nor when hungry, of bread.

> Be like to courteous guests, and him
> Who asks only fire and shelter:

does this man now not need entertainment? Nor had he need of a cloak, who said,

> Give Hipponax a cloak, for I'm stiff with cold.

But will you speak a paradox indeed, both extravagant and singular? Say then that a wise man has need of nothing, that he wants nothing, he is fortunate, he is free from want, he is self-sufficient, blessed, perfect. Now what madness is this, that he to whom nothing is wanting has need of the goods he has, but that the vicious indeed wants many things, and stands in need of nothing. For thus indeed says Chrysippus, that the vicious wants but stands not in need; removing the common notions, like chessmen, backwards and forwards. For all men think that having need precedes wanting, esteeming him who stands in need of things that are not at hand or easy to be got, to want them. For no man wants horns or wings, because no one has need of them. But we say that those want arms and money and clothes who are destitute of them, when they have occasion for them. But these men are so desirous of seeming always to say something against the common notions, that for the love of novelty they often depart from their own opinions, as they do here.

Recall yourself to the consideration of what has been said a little above. This is one of their assertions against the common conception, that no vicious man receives any utility. And yet many being instructed profit, many being slaves are made free; many being besieged are delivered, being lame are led by the hand, and being sick are cured. "But possessing all these things, they are never the better, neither do receive benefits, nor have they any benefactors, nor do they slight them." Vicious men then are not ungrateful, no more than are wise men. Ingratitude therefore has no being; because the good receiving a benefit fail not to acknowledge it, and the bad are not capable of receiving any. Behold, now, what they say to this,—that benefit is ranked among mean or middle things, and that to give and receive utility belongs only to the wise, but the bad also receive a benefit. Then they who partake of the benefit partake not also of its use; and whither a benefit extends, there is nothing useful or commodious. Now what else is there that makes a kind office a benefit, but that the bestower of it is, in some respect, useful to the needy receiver?

LAMPRIAS. But let these things pass. What, I beseech you, is this so highly venerated utility, which preserving as some great and excellent thing for the wise, they permit not so much as the name of it to the vicious?

DIADUMENUS. If (say they) one wise man does but any way prudently stretch out his finger, all the wise men all the world over receive utility by it. This is the work of their amity; in this do the virtues of the wise man terminate by their common utilities. Aristotle then and Xenocrates doted, saving that men receive utility from the gods, from their parents, from their masters, being ignorant of that wonderful utility which wise men receive from one another, being moved according to virtue, though they neither are together nor yet know it. Yet all men esteem, that laying up, keeping, and bestowing are then useful and profitable, when some benefit or profit is recovered by it. The thriving man buys keys, and diligently keeps his stores,

> With 's hand unlocking wealth's sweet treasury.
> *(From the "Bellerophontes" of Euripides, Frag. 287, vs. 8.)*

But to store up and to keep with diligence and labor such things as are for no use is not seemly or honorable, but ridiculous. If Ulysses indeed had tied up with the knot which Circe taught him, not the gifts he had received from Alcinous,–tripods, caldrons, cloths, and gold,–but heaping up trash, stones, and such like trumpery, should have thought his employment about such things, and the possession and keeping of them, a happy and blessed work, would any one have imitated this foolish providence and empty care? Yet this is the beauty, gravity, and happiness of the Stoical consent, being nothing else but a gathering together and keeping of useless and indifferent things. For such are things according to Nature, and more exterior things; if indeed they compare the greatest riches to fringes and golden chamberpots, and sometimes also, as it happens, to oil-cruets. Then, as those who seem proudly to have affronted and railed at some gods or demigods presently changing their note, fall prostrate and sit humbly on the ground, praising and magnifying the Divinity; so these men, having met with punishment of this arrogancy and vanity, again exercise themselves in these indifferent things and such as pertain nothing to them, crying out with a loud voice that there is only one thing good, specious, and honorable, the storing up of these things and the communication of them, and that it is not meet for those to live who have them not, but to despatch out of the way and famish themselves, bidding a long farewell to virtue.

They esteem indeed Theognis to have been a man altogether of a base and abject spirit, for saying, as one overfearful in regard to poverty, which is an indifferent thing:–

> *From poverty to fly, into the deep*
> *Throw thyself, Cyrnus, or from rocks so steep.*

Yet they themselves exhort the same thing in prose, and affirm that a man, to free himself from some great disease or exceedingly acute pain, if he have not at hand sword or hemlock, ought to leap into the sea or throw himself headlong from a precipice; neither of which is hurtful, or evil, or incommodious, or makes them who fall into it miserable.

With what, then, says he, shall I begin? And what shall I take for the principle of duty and matter of virtue, leaving Nature and that which is according to Nature?

With what, O good sir, do Aristotle and Theophrastus begin? What beginnings do Xenocrates and Polemo take? Does not also Zeno follow these, who hold Nature and that which is according to Nature to be the elements of happiness? But they indeed persisted in these things, as desirable, good, and profitable; and joining to them virtue, which employs them and uses every one of them according to its property, thought to complete and consummate a perfect life and one every way absolute, producing that concord which is truly suitable and consonant to Nature. For these men did not run into confusion, like those who leap up from the ground and presently fall down again upon it, terming the same things acceptable and not desirable, proper and not good, unprofitable and yet useful, nothing to us and yet the principles of duties. But their life was such as their speech, and they exhibited actions suitable and consonant to their sayings. But they who are of the Stoic sect–not unlike to that woman in Archilochus, who deceitfully carried in one hand water, in the other fire–by some doctrines draw Nature to them, and by others drive her from them. Or rather, by their deeds and actions they embrace those things which are according to Nature, as good and desirable, but in words and speeches they reject and contemn them, as indifferent and of no use to virtue for the acquiring felicity.

Now, forasmuch as all men esteem the sovereign good to be joyous, desirable, happy, of the greatest dignity, self-sufficient, and wanting nothing; compare their good, and see how it agrees with this common conception. Does the stretching out a finger prudently produce this joy? Is a prudent torture a thing desirable? Is he happy, who with reason breaks his neck? Is that of the greatest dignity, which reason often chooses to let go for that which is not good? Is that perfect and self-sufficient, by enjoying which, if they possess not too indifferent things, they neither can nor will endure to live? There is also another tenet of the Stoics, by which custom is still more injured, taking and plucking from her genuine notions, which are as her legitimate children, and supposing other bastardly, wild, and illegitimate ones in their room, and necessitating her to nourish and cherish the one instead of the other; and that too in those principles which concern things good and bad, desirable and avoidable, proper and strange, the energy of which ought to be more clearly distinguished than that of hot and cold, black and white. For the imaginations of these things are brought in by the senses from without; but those have their original bred from the good things which we have within us. But these men entering with their logic upon the topic of felicity, as on the sophism called Pseudomenos, or that named Kyrieuon, have removed no ambiguities, but brought in very many.

Indeed, of two good things, of which the one is the end and the other belongs to the end, none is ignorant that the end is the greater and perfecter good. Chrysippus also acknowledges this difference, as is manifest from his Third Book of Good Things. For he dissents from those who make science the end, and sets it down.... In his Treatise of Justice, however, he does not think that justice can be preserved, if any one makes pleasure to be the end; but allows it may, if pleasure is not said to be the end, but simply a good. Nor do I think that you need now to hear me repeat his words, since his Third Book of Justice is everywhere to be had. When, therefore, O my friend, they elsewhere say that no one good is greater or less than another, and that what is not the end is equal to the end, they contradict not only the common conceptions, but even their own words. Again, if of two evils, the one when it is present renders us worse, and the other hurts us but renders us not worse, it is against reason not to say that the evil which by its presence renders us worse is greater than that which hurts us but renders us not worse. Now Chrysippus indeed confesses, that there are some fears and sorrows and errors which hurt us, but render us not worse. Read his First Book of Justice against Plato; for in respect of other things, it is worth the while to note the babbling of the man in that place, expounding indifferently all matters and doctrines, as well proper to his own sect as foreign to it.

It is likewise against common sense when he says that there may be two ends or scopes proposed of life, and that all the things we do are not to be referred to one; and yet this is more against common sense, to say that there is an end, and yet that every action is to be referred to another. Nevertheless they must of necessity endure one of these. For if those things which are first according to Nature are not eligible for themselves, but the choice and taking of them agreeably to reason is, and if every one therefore does all his actions for the acquiring the first things according to Nature, then all things which are done must have their reference to this, that the principal things according to Nature may be obtained. But they think that they who aim and aspire to get these things do not have the things themselves as the end, but that to which they must make reference, namely, the choice and not the things. For the end indeed is to choose and receive these things prudently. But the things themselves and the enjoying of them are not the end, but the material ground, having its value only from the choice. For it is my opinion that they both use and write this very expression, to show the difference.

LAMPRIAS. You have exactly related both what they say and in what manner they deliver it.

DIADUMENUS. But observe how it fares with them, as with those that endeavor to leap over their own shadow; for they do not leave behind, but always carry along with them in their speech some absurdity most remote from common sense. For as, if any one should say that he who shoots does all he can, not that he may hit the mark, but that he may do all he can, such a one would rightly be esteemed to speak enigmatically and prodigiously; so these doting dreamers, who contend that the obtaining of natural things is not the end of aiming after natural things, but the taking and choosing them is, and that the desire and endeavor after health is not in every one terminated in the enjoyment of health, but on the contrary, the enjoyment of health is referred to the desire and endeavor after it, and that certain walkings and contentions of speech and suffering incisions and taking of medicines, so they are done by reason, are the end of health, and not health of them, they, I say, trifle like to those who say, Let us sup, that we may offer sacrifice, that we may bathe. But this rather changes order and custom, and all things which these men say carry with them the total subversion and confusion of affairs. Thus, we do not desire to take a walk in fit time that we may digest our meat; but we digest our meat that we may take a walk in fit time. Has Nature also made health for the sake of hellebore, instead of producing hellebore for the sake of health? For what is wanting to bring them to the highest degree of speaking paradoxes, but the saying of such things? What difference is there between him who says that health was made for the sake of medicines and not medicines for the sake of health, and him who makes the choice of medicines and their composition and use more desirable than health itself?–or rather who esteems health not at all desirable, but placing the end in the negotiation about these things, prefers desire to enjoyment, and not enjoyment to desire? For to desire, forsooth (they affirm), is joined the proceeding wisely and discreetly. It is true indeed, we will say, if respect be had to the end, that is, the enjoyment and possession of the things it pursues; but otherwise, it is wholly void of reason, if it does all things for the obtaining of that the enjoyment of which is neither honorable nor happy.

Now, since we are fallen upon this discourse, anything may rather be said to agree with common sense, than that those who have neither received nor have any conception of good do nevertheless desire and pursue it. For you see how Chrysippus drives Ariston into this difficulty, that he should understand an indifference in things inclining neither to good nor to bad, before either good or bad is itself understood; for so indifference will appear to have subsisted even before itself, if the understanding of it cannot be perceived unless good be first understood, while the good is nothing else than this very indifference. Understand now and consider this indifference which the Stoa refutes and calls consent, whence and in what manner it gives us the knowledge of good. For if without good the indifference to that which is not good cannot be understood, much less does the knowing of good things give any intelligence of itself to those who had not before some notion of the good. But as there can be no knowledge of the art of things wholesome and unwholesome in those who have not first some knowledge of the things themselves; so they cannot conceive any notion of the science of good and evil who have not some fore-knowledge of good and evil.

LAMPRIAS. What then is good? DIADUMENUS. Nothing but prudence. LAMPRIAS. And what is prudence? DIADUMENUS. Nothing but the science of good.

LAMPRIAS. There is much then of "Jupiter's Corinth" (that is, much begging the question) admitted into their reasoning. For I would have you let alone the saying about the turning of the pestle, lest you should seem to mock them; although an accident like to that has insinuated itself into their discourse. For it seems that, to the understanding of good, one has need to understand prudence, and to seek for prudence in the understanding of good, being forced always to pursue the one by the other, and thus failing of both; since to the understanding of each we have need of that which cannot be known without the other be first understood.

DIADUMENUS. But there is yet another way, by which you may perceive not only the perversion but the eversion of their discourse, and the reduction of it entirely to nothing. They hold the essence of good to be the reasonable election of things according to Nature. Now the election is not reasonable which is not directed to some end, as has been said before. What, then, is this end? Nothing else, say they, but to reason rightly in the election of things according to Nature. First, then, the conception of good is lost and gone. For to reason rightly in election is an operation proceeding from an habit of right reasoning, and therefore being constrained to get this from the end; and the end not without this, we fail of understanding either of them. Besides, which is more, this reasonable election ought strictly to be a choice of things good and useful, and cooperating to the end; for how can it be reasonable to choose things which are neither convenient nor honorable nor at all eligible? For be it, as they say, a reasonable election of things having a fitness for the causing felicity; see then to what a beautiful and solemn conclusion their discourse brings them. For the end is (it seems), according to them, to reason rightly in the choice of things which are useful in causing us to reason rightly.

LAMPRIAS. When I hear these words, my friend, what is laid down seems to me strangely extravagant; and I farther want to know how this happens.

DIADUMENUS. You must then be more attentive; for it is not for every one to understand this riddle. Hear therefore and answer. Is not the end, according to them, to reason rightly in the election of things according to Nature?

LAMPRIAS. So they say.

DIADUMENUS. And are these things according to Nature chosen as good, or as having some fitness or preferences... either for this end or for something else?

LAMPRIAS. I think not for anything else but for this end.

DIADUMENUS. Now, then, having discovered the matter, see what befalls them. They affirm that the end is to reason rightly in the selection of things which are of value in causing us to reason rightly, for they say that we neither have nor understand any other principle either of good or of felicity but this precious rectitude of reasoning in the election of things that are of worth. But there are some who think that this is spoken against Antipater, and not against the whole sect; for that he, being pressed by Carneades, fell into these fooleries.

But as for those things that are against the common conceptions taught in the Stoa concerning love, they are all of them concerned in

the absurdity. They say youths are deformed who are vicious and foolish, and that the wise are fair; and yet that none of these beautiful ones
is either beloved or worthy of being beloved. Nor yet is this the worst;
but they add, that those who love the deformed ones cease to do so
when they are become fair. Now whoever knew such a love as is kindled
and has its being at the sight of the body's deformity joined with that of
the soul, and is quenched and decays at the accession of beauty joined
with prudence, justice, and temperance? These men are not unlike to
those gnats which love to settle on the dregs of wine, or on vinegar, but
shun and fly away from potable and pleasant wine. As for that which
they call and term an appearance of beauty, saying that it is the induce-
ment of love,–first, it has no probability, for in those who are very foul
and highly wicked there cannot be an appearance of beauty, if indeed
(as is said) the wickedness of the disposition fills the face with deformity. And secondly, it is absolutely against all common experience for
the deformed to be worthy of love because he one day will be fair and
expects to have beauty, but that when he has got it and is become fair
and good, he is to be beloved of none.

LAMPRIAS. Love, they say, is a certain hunting after a young person who is as yet indeed undeveloped, but naturally well disposed
towards virtue.

DIADUMENUS. And what do we now else, O my best friend, but
demonstrate that their sect perverts and destroys all our common conceptions with improbable things and unusual expressions? For none
would hinder the solicitude of these wise men towards young persons, if
it were free from all passionate affection, from being named hunting or
love of instruction; but they ought to call love what all men and women
understand and call by this name, like that which Penelope's suitors in
Homer seem to acknowledge,

> *Who all desired to lie with her;*
> *("Odyssey," i. 366)*

or as Jupiter in another place says to Juno,

> *For neither goddess yet nor mortal dame*
> *E'er kindled in my heart so great a flame.*
> *("Iliad." xiv. 315.)*

Thus casting moral philosophy into these matters, in which all is

> *A mazy whirl, with nothing sound, and all perplexed,*
> *(Euripides, "Andromache," 448.)*

they contemn and deride it, as if boasting themselves to be the only
men who observe nature and custom as it ought to be, and who at
the same time adapted reason to each man by means of aversions,

desires, appetites, pursuits, and impulses. But custom has received no good from their logic, but, like the ear diseased by vain sounds, is filled with difficulty and obscurity,–of which, if you think good, we will elsewhere begin a new discourse. But now we will run through the chief and principal heads of their natural philosophy, which no less confounds the common conceptions than that other concerning ends. ============== First, this is altogether absurd and against sense, to say that is which is not, and things which are not are. But above all that is most absurd which they say of the universe. For, putting round about the circumference of the world an infinite vacuum, they say that the universe is neither a body nor bodiless. It follows then from this that the universe has no being, since with them body only has a being. Since therefore it is the part of that which has a being both to do and suffer, and the universe has no being, it follows that the universe will neither do nor suffer. Neither will it be in a place; for that which takes up place is a body, and the universe is not a body, therefore the universe exists nowhere. And since that only rests which continues in one and the same place, the universe rests not, because it takes not up place. Neither yet is it moved, for what is moved must have a place and space in which to move. Moreover, what is moved either moves itself, or suffers motion from another. Now, that which is moved by itself has some bents and inclinations proceeding from its gravity or levity; and gravity and levity are either certain habits or faculties or differences of bodies. But the universe is not a body. It follows then of necessity, that the universe is neither, heavy nor light, and consequently, that it has not in itself any principle of motion. Nor yet will the universe be moved by any other; for there is nothing else besides the universe. Thus are they necessitated to say as they do, that the universe neither rests nor is moved. Lastly since according to their opinion it must not be said that the universe is a body, and yet the heaven, the earth, animals, plants, men, and stones are bodies, it follows that that which is no body will have bodies for its parts, and things which have existence will be parts of that which has no existence, and that which is not heavy will have parts that are heavy, and what is not light will have parts that are light;–than which there cannot be any dreams imagined more repugnant to the common conceptions.

Moreover, there is nothing so evident or so agreeing to common sense as this, that what is not animate is inanimate, and what is not inanimate is animate. And yet they overthrow also this evidence, confessing the universe to be neither animate nor inanimate. Besides this, none thinks the universe, of which there is no part wanting to be imperfect; but they deny the universe to be perfect, saying that what is perfect may be defined, but the universe because of its infiniteness cannot be defined. Therefore, according to them, there is something which is neither perfect nor imperfect. Moreover, the universe is neither a part, since there is nothing greater than it; nor the whole, for the whole (they say) is predicated only of that which is digested into order; but the universe is, through its infiniteness, undetermined and unordered. Moreover, there is no other thing which can be the cause of the universe, there being nothing besides the universe; nor is the universe the cause of other things or even of itself; for its nature suffers it not to act, and a cause is understood by its acting. Suppose, now, one should ask all men what they imagine NOTHING to be, and what notion they have of it. Would they not answer, that it neither is a cause nor has a cause, that it is neither the whole nor a part that it is neither perfect nor imperfect, that it is neither animate nor inanimate, that it neither is moved nor rests nor subsists, that it is neither corporeal nor incorporeal; and that this and no other thing is meant by NOTHING? Since, then, they alone predicate that of the universe which all others do of NOTHING, it seems plain that they make the universe and NOTHING to be the same. Time must then be said to be nothing; the same also must be said of predicate, axiom, junction, conjunction, which terms they use more than any of the other philosophers, yet they say that they have no existence. But farther, to say that what is true has no being or subsistence but is comprehended, and that that is comprehensible and credible which no way partakes of the essence of being,–does not this exceed all absurdity?

But lest these things should seem to have too much of logical difficulty, let us proceed to such as pertain more to natural philosophy. Since, then, as themselves say,

> Jove is of all beginning, midst, and end,
> (See "Orphic Fragments," vi. 10 (Herm.).)

they ought chiefly to have applied themselves to remedy, redress, and reduce to the best order the conceptions concerning the gods, if there were in them anything confused or erroneous; or if not, to have left every one in those sentiments which they had from the laws and custom concerning the Divinity:–

> For neither now nor yesterday But always these things lived,   No one knows from whence they came.
> (Sophocles, "Antigone," 456.)

But these men, having begun (as it were) "from Vesta" to disturb the opinions settled and received in every country concerning the gods, have not (to speak sincerely) left anything entire and uncorrupted. For what man is there or ever was, except these, who does not believe the Divinity to be immortal and eternal? Or what in the common anticipations is more unanimously chanted forth concerning the gods than such things as these:–

> There the blest gods eternally enjoy
> Their sweet delights;
> ("Odyssey," vi. 46.)

and again,

> Both gods immortal, and earth-dwelling men;
> ("Iliad," v. 442.)

and again,

> Exempt from sickness and old age are they,
> And free from toil, and have escaped the stream
> Of roaring Acheron?
> (From Pindar.)

One may perhaps light upon some nations so barbarous and savage as not to think there is a God; but there was never found any man who, believing a God, did not at the same time believe him immortal and eternal. Certainly, those who were called Atheists, like Theodorus, Diagoras, and Hippo, durst not say that the Divinity is corruptible, but they did not believe that there is anything incorruptible; not indeed admitting the subsistence of an incorruptibility, but keeping the notion of a God. But Chrysippus and Cleanthes, having filled (as one may say) heaven, earth, air, and sea with gods, have not yet made any one of all these gods immortal or eternal, except Jupiter alone, in whom they consume all the rest; so that it is no more suitable for him to consume others than to be consumed himself. For it is alike an infirmity to perish by being resolved into another, and to be saved by being nourished by the resolution of others into himself. Now these are not like other of their absurdities, gathered by argument from their suppositions or drawn by consequence from their doctrines; but they themselves proclaim it aloud in their writings concerning the gods, Providence, Fate, and Nature, expressly saying that all the other gods were born, and shall die by the fire, melting away, in their opinion, as if they were of wax or tin. It is indeed as much against common sense that God should be mortal as the man should be immortal; nay, indeed, I do not see what the difference between God and man will be, if God also is a reasonable and corruptible animal. For if they oppose us with this subtle distinction, that man is mortal, and God not mortal but corruptible, see what they get by it. For they will say either that God is at the same time both immortal and corruptible, or else that he neither is mortal nor immortal; the absurdity of which even those cannot exceed who set themselves industriously to devise positions repugnant to common sense. I speak of others; for these men have left no one of the absurdest things unspoken or unattempted.

To these things Cleanthes, contending for the conflagration of the world, says, that the sun will make the moon and all the other stars like to himself, and will change them into himself. Indeed, if the stars, being gods, should contribute anything to the sun towards their own destruction by adding to its conflagration, it would be very ridiculous for us to make prayers to them for our salvation, and to think them the saviours of men, whose nature it is to accelerate their own corruption and dissolution.

And yet these men leave nothing unsaid against Epicurus, crying out, Fie, fie upon him, as confounding their presumption concerning God by taking away Providence; for God (they say) is presumed and understood to be not only immortal and happy, but also a lover of men and careful of them and beneficial to them, and herein they say true. Now if they who abolish Providence take away the preconception concerning God, what do they who say that the gods indeed have care of us, but deny them to be helpful to us, and make them not bestowers of good things but of indifferent ones, giving, to wit, not virtue, but wealth, health, children, and such like things, none of which is helpful, profitable, desirable, or available? Or shall we not rather think, that Epicurus does not take away the conceptions concerning the gods; but that these Stoics scoff at the gods and deride them, saying one is a god of fruits, another of marriage, another a physician, and another a diviner, while yet health, issue, and plenty of fruits are not good things, but indifferent things and unprofitable to those who have them?

The third point of the conception concerning the gods is, that the gods do in nothing so much differ from men as in happiness and virtue. But according to Chrysippus, they have not so much as this difference. For he says that Jupiter does not exceed Dion in virtue, but that Jupiter and Dion, being both wise, are equally aided by one another, when one comes into the motion of the other. For this and none else is the good which the gods do to men, and likewise men to the gods when they are wise. For they say, that a man who falls not short in virtue comes not behind them in felicity, and that he who, tormented with diseases and being maimed in the body, makes himself away, is equally happy with Jupiter the Saviour, provided he be but wise. But this man neither is nor ever was upon the earth; but there are infinite millions of men unhappy to the highest degree in the state and government of Jupiter, which is most excellently administered. Now what can be more against sense than that, when Jupiter governs exceedingly well, we should be exceedingly miserable? But if (which it is unlawful even to say) he would desire no longer to be a saviour, nor a deliverer, nor a protector, but the contrary to all these glorious appellations, there can no goodness be added to the things that are, either as to their multitude or magnitude, since, as these men say, all men live to the height miserably and wickedly, neither vice receiving addition, nor unhappiness increase.

Nor is this the worst; but they are angry with Menander for saying upon the stage,

The chief beginning of men's miseries
Are things exceeding good;

for that this is against sense. And yet they make God, who is good, the beginning of evils. "For matter," they contend, "produced not any evil of itself; for it is without quality, and whatever differences it has, it has received them all from that which moves and forms it." But that which moves and forms it is the reason dwelling in it, since matter is not made to move and form itself. So that of necessity evil, if it come by nothing, must have been produced from that which has no being; but if by some moving principle, from God. But if they think that Jupiter has not the command of his parts nor uses every one of them according to his reason, they speak against common sense, and imagine an animal, many of whose parts are not subservient to his will but use their own operations and actions, to which the whole gives no incitation nor begins their motion. For there is nothing which has life so ill compacted as that, against its will, its feet shall go, its tongue speak, its horns push, or its teeth bite. The most of which things God must of necessity suffer, if the wicked, being parts of him, do against his will lie, cheat, rob, and murder one another. But if, as Chrysippus says, the very least part cannot possibly behave itself otherwise than according to Jupiter's pleasure, and if every living thing is so framed by Nature as to rest and move according as he inclines it and as he turns, stays, and disposes it,

This saying is more impious than the first.
(See Nauck's "Tragic Fragments," p. 704 (No. 345).)

For it were more tolerable to say that many parts of Jupiter are, through his weakness and want of power, hurried on to do many absurd things against his nature and will, than that there is not any intemperance or wickedness of which Jupiter is not the cause. Moreover, since they affirm the world to be a city and the stars citizens, if this be so, there must be also tribes-men and magistrates, the sun must be some consul, and the evening star a praetor or mayor of a city. Now I know not whether any one that shall go about to disprove such things will not show himself more ridiculous than those who assert and affirm them.

Is it not therefore against sense to say that the seed is more and greater than that which is produced of it? For we see that Nature in all animals and plants, even those that are wild, has taken small, slender, and scarce visible things for principles of generation to the greatest. For it does not only from a grain of wheat produce an ear-bearing stalk, or a vine from the stone of a grape; but from a small berry or acorn which has escaped being eaten by the bird, kindling and setting generation on fire (as it were) from a little spark, it sends forth the stock of a bush, or the tall body of an oak, palm, or pine tree. Whence also they say that seed is in Greek called [Greek omitted], as it were, the [Greek omitted] or the WINDING UP of a great mass in a little compass; and that Nature has the name of [Greek omitted], as if it were the INFLATION [Greek omitted] and diffusion of reason and numbers opened and loosened by it. But now, in opposition to this, they hold that fire is the seed of the world, which shall after the conflagration change into seed the world, which will then have a copious nature from a smaller body and bulk, and possess an infinite space of vacuum filled by its increase; and the world being made, the form again recedes and settles, the matter being after the generation gathered and contracted into itself.

You may hear them and read many of their writings, in which they jangle with the Academics, and cry out against them as confounding all things with their paradox of indistinguishable identity, and as vehemently contending that there is but one quality in two substances. And yet there is no man who understands not this, and would not on the contrary think it wonderful and extremely strange if there should not in all time be found one kind of dove exactly and in all respects like to another dove, a bee to a bee, a grain of wheat to a grain of wheat, or (as the proverb has it) one fig to another. But these things are plainly against common sense which the Stoics say and feign,—that there are in one substance two individual qualities, and that the same substance, which has particularly one quality, when another quality is added, receives and equally conserves them both. For if there may be two, there may be also three, four, and five, and even more than you can name, in one and the same substance; I say not in its different parts, but all equally in the whole, though even infinite in number. For Chrysippus says, that Jupiter and the world are like to man, as is also Providence to the soul; when therefore the conflagration shall be, Jupiter, who alone of all the gods is incorruptible, will retire into

Providence, and they being together, will both perpetually remain in the one substance of the ether.

But leaving now the gods, and beseeching them to give these Stoics common sense and a common understanding, let us look into their doctrines concerning the elements. It is against the common conceptions that one body should be the place of another, or that a body should penetrate through a body, neither of them containing any vacuity, but the full passing into the full, and in which there is no vacuity–but is full and has no place by reason of its continuity–receiving the mixture. But these men, not thrusting one thing into one, nor yet two or three or ten together, but jumbling all the parts of the world, being cut piecemeal, into any one thing which they shall first light on, and saying that the very least which is perceived by sense will contain the greatest that shall come unto it, boldly frame a new doctrine, proving themselves here, as in many other things, to be holding for their suppositions things repugnant to common sense. And presently upon this they are forced to admit into their discourse many monstrous and strange positions, mixing whole bodies with whole; of which this also is one, that three are four. For this others put as an example of those things which cannot be conceived even in thought. But to the Stoics it is a matter of truth, that when one cup of wine is mixed with two of water, if it is not to disappear and if the mixture is to be equalized, it must be spread through the whole and be confounded therewith, so as to make that which was one two by the equalization of the mixture. For the one remains, but is extended as much as two, and thus is equal to the double of itself. Now if it happens in the mixture with two to take the measure of two in the diffusion, this is together the measure both of three and four,–of three because one is mixed with two, and of four because, being mixed with two, it has an equal quantity with those with which it is mixed. Now this fine subtilty is a consequence of their putting bodies into a body, and so likewise is the unintelligibleness of the manner how one is contained in the other. For it is of necessity that, of bodies passing one into another by mixture, the one should not contain and the other be contained, nor the one receive and the other be received within; for this would not be a mixture, but a contiguity and touching of the superficies, the one entering in, and the other enclosing it without, and the rest of the parts remaining unmixed and pure, and so it would be merely many different things. But there being a necessity, according to their axiom of mixture, that the things which are mixed should be mingled one within the other, and that the same things should together be contained by being within, and by receiving contain the other, and that neither of them could possibly exist again as it was before, it comes to pass that both the subjects of the mixture mutually penetrate each other, and that there is not any part of either remaining separate, but that they are necessarily all filled with each other.

Here now that famed leg of Arcesilaus comes in, with much laughter insulting over their absurdities; for if these mixtures are through the whole, what should hinder but that, a leg being cut off and putrefied and cast into the sea and diffused, not only Antigonus's fleet (as Arcesilaus said) might sail through it, but also Xerxes's twelve hundred ships, together with the Grecians' three hundred galleys, might fight in it? For the progress will not henceforth fail, nor the lesser cease to be in the greater; or else the mixture will be at an end, and the extremity of it, touching where it shall end, will not pass through the whole, but will give over being mingled. But if the mixture is through the whole, the leg will not indeed of itself give the Greeks room for the sea-fight, for to this there is need of putrefaction and change; but if one glass or but one drop of wine shall fall from hence into the Aegean or Cretan Sea, it will pass into the Ocean or main Atlantic Sea, not lightly touching its superficies, but being spread quite through it in depth, breadth, and length. And this Chrysippus admits, saying immediately in his First Book of Natural Questions, that there is nothing to hinder one drop of wine from being mixed with the whole sea. And that we may not wonder at this, he says that this one drop will by mixtion extend through the whole world; than which I know not anything that can appear more absurd.

And this also is against sense, that there is not in the nature of bodies anything either supreme or first or last, in which the magnitude of the body may terminate; but that there is always some phenomenon beyond the body, still going on which carries the subject to infinity and undeterminateness. For one body cannot be imagined greater or less than another, if both of them may by their parts proceed IN INFINITUM; but the nature of inequality is taken away. For of things that are esteemed unequal, the one falls short in its last parts, and the other goes on and exceeds. Now if there is no inequality, it follows that there is no unevenness nor roughness of bodies; for unevenness is the inequality of the same superficies with itself, and roughness is an unevenness joined with hardness; neither of which is left us by those who terminate no body in its last part, but extend them all by the multitude of their parts unto an infinity. And yet is it not evident that a man consists of more parts than a finger, and the world of more than a man? This indeed all men know and understand, unless they become Stoics; but if they are once Stoics, they on the contrary say and think that a man has no more parts than a finger, nor the world than a man. For division reduces bodies to an infinity; and of infinites neither is more or less or exceeds in multitude, or the parts of the remainder will cease to be divided and to afford a multitude of themselves.

LAMPRIAS. How then do they extricate themselves out of these difficulties?

DIADUMENUS. Surely with very great cunning and courage. For Chrysippus says: "If we are asked, if we have any parts, and how many, and of what and how many parts they consist, we are to use a distinction, making it a position that the whole body is compacted of the head, trunk, and legs, as if that were all which is inquired and doubted of. But if they extend their interrogation to the last parts, no such thing is to be undertaken, but we are to say that they consist not of any certain parts, nor yet of so many, nor of infinite, nor of finite." And I seem to myself to have used his very words, that you may perceive how he maintains the common notions, forbidding us to think of what or how many parts every body is compacted, and whether of infinite or finite. For if there were any medium between finite and infinite, as the indifferent is between good and evil, he should, by telling us what that is, have solved the difficulty. But if—as that which is not equal is presently understood to be unequal, and that which is not mortal to be immortal—we also understand that which is not finite to be immediately infinite, to say that a body consists of parts neither finite nor infinite is, in my opinion, the same thing as to affirm that an argument is compacted of positions neither true nor false....

To this he with a certain youthful rashness adds, that in a pyramid consisting of triangles, the sides inclining to the juncture are unequal, and yet do not exceed one another in that they are greater. Thus does he keep the common notions. For if there is anything greater and not exceeding, there will be also something less and not deficient, and so also something unequal which neither exceeds nor is deficient; that is, there will be an unequal thing equal, a greater not greater, and a less not less. See it yet farther, in what manner he answered Democritus, inquiring philosophically and to the point, if a cone is divided by a plane parallel with its base, what is to be thought of the superficies of its segments, whether they are equal or unequal; for if they are unequal, they will render the cone uneven, receiving many steplike incisions and roughnesses; but if they are equal, the sections will be equal, and the cone will seem to have the same qualities as the cylinder, to wit, to be composed not of unequal but of equal circles; which is most absurd. Here, that he may convince Democritus of ignorance, he says, that the superficies are neither equal or unequal, but that the bodies are unequal, because the superficies are neither equal nor unequal. Indeed to assert this for a law, that bodies are unequal while the superficies are not unequal, is the part of a man who takes to himself a wonderful liberty of writing whatever comes into his head. For reason and manifest evidence, on the contrary, give us to understand, that the superficies of unequal bodies are unequal, and that the bigger the body is, the greater also is the superficies, unless the excess, by which it is the greater, is void of a superficies. For if the superficies of the greater bodies do not exceed those of the less, but sooner fail, a part of that body which has an end will be without an end and infinite. For if he says that he is compelled to this. For those rabbeted incisions, which he suspects in a cone, are made by the inequality of the body, and not of the superficies. It is ridiculous therefore not to reckon the superficies, and to leave the inequality in the bodies themselves. But to persist still in this matter, what is more repugnant to sense than the imagining of such things? For if we admit that one superficies is neither equal nor unequal to another, we may say also of magnitude and of number, that one is neither equal nor unequal to another; and this, not having anything that we can call or think to be a neuter or medium between equal and unequal. Besides, if there are superficies neither equal nor unequal, what hinders but there may be also circles neither equal nor unequal? For indeed these superficies of conic sections are circles. And if circles, why may not also their diameters be neither equal nor unequal? And if so, why not also angles, triangles, parallelograms, parallelopipeds, and bodies? For if the longitudes are neither equal nor unequal to one another, so will the weight, percussion, and bodies be neither equal nor unequal. How then dare these men inveigh against those who introduce vacuums, and suppose that there are indivisible atoms, and who say that motion and rest are not incompatible with each other, when they themselves affirm such axioms as these to be false: If any things are not equal to one another, they are unequal to one another; and the same things are not equal and unequal to one another? But when he says that there is something greater and yet not exceeding, it were worth the while to ask, whether these things quadrate with one another. For if they quadrate, how is either the greater? And if they do not quadrate, how can it be but the one must exceed and the other fall short? For if neither of these are true, the other both will and will not quadrate with the greater. For those who keep not the common conceptions must of necessity fall into such perplexities.

It is moreover against sense to say that nothing touches another; nor is this less absurd, that bodies touch one another, but touch by nothing. For they are necessitated to admit these things, who allow not the least parts of a body, but assume something before that which appears to touch, and never ceases to proceed still farther. What, therefore, these men principally object to the patrons of those indivisible bodies called atoms is this, that there is neither a touching of the whole by the whole, nor of the parts by the parts; for that the one makes not a touching but a mixture, and that the other is not possible, these individuals having no parts. How then do not they themselves fall into the same inconvenience, leaving no first or last part, whilst they say, that whole bodies mutually touch one another by a term or extremity and not by a part? But this term is not a body; therefore one body shall touch one another by that which is incorporeal, and again shall not touch, that which is incorporeal coming between them. And if it shall touch, the body shall both do and suffer something by that which is incorporeal. For it is the nature of bodies mutually to do and suffer, and to touch. But if the body has a touching by that which is incorporeal, it will have also a contact, and a mixture, and a coalition. Again, in these contacts and mixtures the extremities of the bodies must either remain, or not remain but be corrupted. Now both of these are against sense. For neither do they themselves admit corruptions and generations of incorporeal things; nor can there be a mixture and coalition of bodies retaining their own extremities. For the extremity determines and constitutes the nature of the body; and mixtions, unless the mutual laying of parts by parts are thereby understood, wholly confound all those that are mixed. And, as these men say, we must admit the corruption of extremities in mixtures, and their generation again in the separation of them. But this none can easily understand. Now by what bodies mutually touch each other, by the same they press, thrust, and crush each other. Now that this should be done or take place in things that are incorporeal, is impossible and not so much as to be imagined. But yet this they would constrain us to conceive. For if a sphere touch a plane by a point, it is manifest that it may be also drawn over the plane upon a point; and if the superficies of it is painted with vermilion, it will imprint a red line on the plane; and if it is fiery hot, it will burn the plane. Now for an incorporeal thing to color, or a body to be burned by that which is incorporeal, is against sense. But if we should imagine an earthen or glassy sphere to fall from on high upon a plane of stone, it were against reason to think it would not be broken, being struck against that which is hard and solid; but it would be more absurd that it should be broken, falling upon an extremity or point that is incorporeal. So that the presumptions concerning things incorporeal and corporeal are wholly disturbed, or rather taken away, by their joining to them many impossibilities.

It is also against common sense, that there should be a time future and past, but no time present; and that EREWHILE and LATELY subsist, but NOW is nothing at all. Yet this often befalls the Stoics, who admit not the least time between, nor will allow the present to be indivisible; but whatsoever any one thinks to take and understand as present, one part of that they say to be future, and the other part past; so that there is no part remaining or left of the present time: but of that which is said to be present, one part is distributed to the future, the other to the past. Therefore one of these two things follows: either that, holding there was a time and there will be a time, we must deny there is a time; or we must hold that there is a time present, part of which has already been and part will be, and say that of that which now is, one part is future and the other past; and that of NOW, one part is before and the other behind; and that now is that which is neither yet now nor any longer NOW; for that which is past is no longer now, and that which is to come is not yet NOW. And dividing thus the present, they must needs say of the year and of the day, that part of it was of the year or day past, and part will be of the year or day to come; and that of what is together, there is a part before and a part after. For no less are they perplexed, confounding together these terms, NOT YET and ALREADY and NO LONGER and NOW and NOT NOW. But all other men suppose, esteem, and think EREWHILE and AWHILE HENCE to be different parts of time from NOW, which is followed by the one and preceded by the other. But Archedemus, saying that now is the beginning and juncture of that which is past and that which is near at hand, has (as it seems) without perceiving it thereby destroyeth all time. For if NOW is no time, but only a term or extremity of time, and if every part of time is such as now, all time seems to have no parts, but to be wholly dissolved into terms, joints, and beginnings. But Chrysippus, desiring to show more artifice in his division, in his book of Vacuity and some others, says, that the past and future time are not, but have subsisted (or will subsist), and that the present only is; but in his third, fourth, and fifth books concerning Parts, he asserts, that of the present time one part is past, the other to come. Thus it comes to pass, that he divides subsisting time into non-subsisting parts of a subsisting total, or rather leaves nothing at all of time subsisting, if the present has no part but what is either future or past.

These men's conception therefore of time is not unlike the grasping of water, which, the harder it is held, all the more slides and runs away. As to actions and motions, all evidence is utterly confounded. For if NOW is divided into past and future, it is of necessity that what is now moved partly has been moved and partly shall be moved, that the end and beginning of motion have been taken away, that nothing of any work has been done first, nor shall anything be last, the actions being distributed with time. For as they say that of present time, part is past and part to come; so of that which is doing, it will be said that part is done and part shall be done. When therefore had TO DINE, TO WRITE, TO WALK, a beginning, and when shall they have an end, if every one who is dining has dined and shall dine, and every one who is walking has walked and shall walk? But this is, as it is said, of all absurdities the most absurd, that if he who now lives has already lived and shall live, then to live neither had beginning nor shall have end; but every one of us, as it seems, was born without commencing to live, and shall die without ceasing to live. For if there is no last part, but he who lives has something of the present still remaining for the future, to say "Socrates shall live" will never be false so long as it shall be true to say "Socrates lives"; and so long also will it be false to say "Socrates is dead." So that, if "Socrates shall live" is true in infinite parts of time, it will in no part of time be true to say "Socrates is dead." And verily what end will there be of a work, and where will you terminate an action, if, as often as it is true to say "This is doing," it is likewise true to say "This shall be doing"? For he will lie who shall say, there will be an end of Plato's writing and disputing; since Plato will never give over writing and disputing, if it is never false to say of him who disputes that he shall dispute, and of him who writes that he shall write. Moreover, there will be no part of that which now is, but either has been or is to be, and is either past or future; but of what has been and is to be, of past and future, there is no sense; wherefore there is absolutely no sense of anything. For we neither see what is past and future, nor do we hear or have any other sense of what has been or is to be. Nothing, then, even what is present, is to be perceived by sense, if of the present, part is always future and part past,–if part has been and part is to be.

Now they indeed say, that Epicurus does intolerable things and violates the conceptions, in moving all bodies with equal celerity, and admitting none of them to be swifter than another. And yet it is much more intolerable and farther remote from sense, that nothing can be overtaken by another:–

> *Not though Adrastus's swift-footed steed*
> *Should chase the tortoise slow,*

as the proverb has it. Now this must of necessity fall out, if things move according to PRIUS and POSTERIUS, and the intervals through which they pass are (as these men's tenet is) divisible IN INFINITUM; for if the tortoise is but a furlong before the horse, they who divide this furlong in infinitum, and move them both according to PRIUS and POSTERIUS, will never bring the swiftest to the slowest; the slower always adding some interval divisible into infinite spaces. Now to affirm that, water being poured from a bowl or cup, it will never be all poured out, is it not both against common sense, and a consequence of what these men say? For no man can understand the motion according to PRIUS of things infinitely divisible to be consummated; but leaving always somewhat divisible, it will make all the effusion, all the running and flux of a liquid, motion of a solid, and fall of an heavy thing imperfect.

I pass by many absurdities of theirs, touching only such as are against sense. The dispute concerning increase is indeed ancient; for the question, as Chrysippus says, was put by Epicharmus. Now, whereas those of the Academy think that the doubt is not very easy and ready all of a sudden to be cleared, these men have mightily exclaimed against them, and accused them of taking away the fixed ideas, and yet themselves are so far from preserving the common notions, that they pervert even sense itself. For the discourse is simple, and these men grant the suppositions,–that all particular substances flow and are carried, some of them emitting forth somewhat from themselves, and others receiving things coming from elsewhere; and that the things to which there is made an accession or from which there is a decession by numbers and multitudes, do not remain the same, but become others by the said accessions, the substance receiving a change; and that these changes are not rightly called by custom increasings or diminutions, but it is fitter they should be styled generations and corruptions, because they drive by force from one state to another, whereas to increase and be diminished are passions of a body that is subject and permanent. These things being thus in a manner said and delivered, what would these defenders of evidence and canonical masters of common conceptions have? Every one of us (they say) is double, twin-like, and composed of a double nature; not as the poets feigned of the Molionidae, that they in some parts grow together and in some parts are separated,–but every one of us has two bodies, having the same color, the same figure, the same weight and place.... These things were never before seen by any man; but these men alone have discerned this composition, doubleness, and ambiguity, how every one of us is two subjects, the one substance, the other quality; and the one is in perpetual flux and motion, neither increasing nor being diminished nor remaining altogether; the other remains and increases and is diminished, and suffers all things contrary to the former, with which it is so concorporated, conjoined, and confounded, that it exhibits not any difference to be perceived by sense. Indeed, Lynceus is said to have penetrated stones and oaks with his sight; and a certain man sitting on a watch-tower in Sicily beheld the ships of the Carthaginians setting forth from their harbor, which was a day and a night's sail from thence. Callicrates and Myrmecides are said to have made chariots that might be covered with the wings of a fly, and to have engraved verses of Homer on a sesame seed. But none ever discerned or discovered this diversity in us; nor have we perceived ourselves to be double, in one part always flowing, and in the other remaining the same from our birth even to our death. But I make the discourse more simple, since they make four subjects in every one, or rather every one of us to be four. But two are sufficient to show their absurdity. For if, when we hear Pentheus in the tragedy affirm that he sees two suns and two cities of Thebes, (Euripides, "Bacchae," 918.) we say that he does not see, but that his sight is dazzled, he being transported and troubled in his head; why do we not bid those farewell, who assert not one city alone, but all men and animals, and all trees, vessels, instruments, and clothes, to be double and composed of two, as men who constrain us to dote rather than to understand? But this feigning other natures of subjects must perhaps be pardoned them; for there appears no other invention by which they can maintain and uphold the augmentations of which they are so fond.

But by what cause moved, or for the adorning of what other suppositions, they frame in a manner innumerable differences and forms of bodies in the soul, there is none can say, unless it be that they remove, or rather wholly abdicate and destroy, the common and usual notions, to introduce other foreign and strange ones. For it is very absurd that, making all virtues and vices–and with them all arts, memories, fancies, passions, impulses, and assents–to be bodies, they should affirm that they neither lie nor subsist in any subject, leaving them for a place one only hole, like a prick in the heart, where they crowd the principal part of the soul, enclosed with so many bodies, that a very great number of them lie hid even from those who think they can spare and distinguish them one from another. Nay that they should not only make them bodies, but also intelligent beings, and even a swarm of such creatures, not friendly or mild, but a multitude rebellious and having a hostile mind, and should so make of each one of us a park or menagerie or Trojan horse, or whatever else we may

call their inventions,–this is the very height of contempt and contradiction to evidence and custom. But they say, that not only the virtues
and vices, not only the passions, as anger, envy, grief, and malicious-
ness, not only comprehensions, fancies, and ignorances, not only arts,
as shoemaking and working in brass, are animals; but besides these,
also they make even the operations bodies and animals, saying that
walking is an animal, as also dancing, supposing, saluting, and railing. The consequence of this is that laughing and weeping are also
animals; and if so, then also are coughing, sneezing, groaning, spit-
ting, blowing the nose, and other such like things sufficiently known.
Neither have they any cause to take it ill that they are by reason, proceeding leisurely, reduced to this, if they shall call to mind how Chrysippus, in his First Book of Natural Questions, argues thus: "Is not
night a body? And are not then the evening, dawning, and midnight
bodies? Or is not a day a body? Is not then the first day of the month
a body? And the tenth, the fifteenth, and the thirtieth, are they not
bodies? Is not a month a body? Summer, autumn, and the year, are
they not bodies?"

These things they maintain against the common conceptions; but
those which follow they hold also against their own, engendering that
which is most hot by refrigeration, and that which is most subtile by condensation. For the soul, to wit, is a substance most hot and most subtile.
But this they make by the refrigeration and condensation of the body,
changing, as it were, by induration the spirit, which of vegetative is made
animal. Moreover, they say that the sun became animated, his moisture
changing into intellectual fire. Behold how the sun is imagined to be engendered by refrigeration! Xenophanes indeed, when one told him that
he had seen eels living in hot water, answered, We will boil them then
in cold. But if these men engender heat by refrigeration and lightness
by condensation, it follows, they must also generate cold things by heat,
thick things by dissolution, and heavy things by rarefaction, that so they
may keep some proportion in their absurdity.

And do they not also determine the substance and generation of conception itself, even against the common conceptions? For conception
is a certain imagination, and imagination an impression in the soul.
Now the nature of the soul is an exhalation, in which it is difficult for an
impression to be made because of its tenuity, and for which it is impossible to keep an impression it may have received. For its nutriment and
generation, consisting of moist things, have continual accession and
consumption. And the mixture of respiration with the air always makes
some new exhalation which is altered and changed by the flux of the

air coming from abroad and again going out. For one may more easily imagine that a stream of running water can retain figures, impressions, and images, than that a spirit can be carried in vapors and humors, and continually mingled with another idle and strange breath from without. But these men so far forget themselves, that, having defined the conceptions to be certain stored-up intelligences, and memoirs to be constant and habitual impressions, and having wholly fixed the sciences, as having stability and firmness, they presently place under them a basis and seat of a slippery substance, easy to be dissipated and in perpetual flux and motion.

Now the common conception of an element and principle, naturally imprinted in almost all men, is this, that it is simple, unmixed, and uncompounded. For that is not an element or principle which is mixed; but those things are so of which it is mixed. But these men, making God, who is the principle of all things, to be an intellectual body and a mind seated in matter, pronounce him to be neither simple nor uncompounded, but to be composed of and by another; matter being of itself indeed without reason and void of quality, and yet having simplicity and the property of a principle. If, then, God is not incorporeal and immaterial, he participates of matter as a principle. For if matter and reason are one and the same thing, they have not rightly defined matter to be reasonless; but if they are different things, then is God constituted of them both, and is not a simple but compound thing, having to the intellectual taken the corporeal from matter.

Moreover, calling these four bodies, earth, water, air, and fire, the first elements, they do (I know not how) make some of them simple and pure, and others compound and mixed. For they maintain that earth and water hold together neither themselves nor other things, but preserve their unity by the participation of air and force of fire; but that air and fire do both fortify themselves by their own strength, or being mixed with the other two, give them force, permanence, and subsistence. How, then, is either earth or water an element, if neither of them is either simple, or first or self-sufficient, but if each one wants somewhat from without to contain and keep it in its being? For they have not left so much as a thought of their substance; but this discourse concerning the earth has much confusion and uncertainty, when they say that it subsists of itself; for if the earth is of itself, how has it need of the air to fix and contain it? But neither the earth nor water can any more be said to be of itself; but the air, drawing together and thickening the matter, has made the earth, and again dissolving and mollifying it, has produced the water. Neither of these then is an element, since something else has contributed being and generation to them both.

Moreover, they say that subsistence and matter are subject to qualities, and do so in a manner define them; and again, they make the qualities to be also bodies. But these things have much perplexity. For if qualities have a peculiar substance, for which they both are and are called bodies, they need no other substance; for they have one of their own. But if they have under them in common only that which the Stoic school calls essence and matter, it is manifest they do but participate of the body; for they are not bodies. But the subject and recipient must of necessity differ from those things which it receives and to which it is subject. But these men see by halves; for they say indeed that matter is void of quality, but they will not call qualities immaterial. Now how can they make a body without quality, who understand no quality without a body? For the reason which joins a body to all quality suffers not the understanding to comprehend any body without some quality. Either, therefore, he who oppugns incorporeal quality seems also to oppugn unqualified matter; or separating the one from the other, he mutually parts them both. As for the reason which some pretend, that matter is called unqualified not because it is void of all quality, but because it has all qualities, it is most of all against sense. For no man calls that unqualified which is capable of every quality, nor that impassible which is by nature always apt to suffer all things, nor that immovable which is moved every way. And this doubt is not solved, that, however matter is always understood with quality, yet it is understood to be another thing and differing from quality.

Contradictions of the Stoics

I FIRST LAY THIS down for an axiom, that there ought to be seen in men's lives an agreement with their doctrines. For it is not so necessary that the pleader (as Aeschines has it) and the law speak one and the same thing, as that the life of a philosopher be consonant to his speech. For the speech of a philosopher is a law of his own and voluntarily imposed on himself, unless they esteem philosophy to be a game, or an acuteness in disputing invented for the gaining of applause, and not–what it really is–a thing deserving our greatest study.

Since, then, there are in their discourses many things written by Zeno himself, many by Cleanthes, and most of all by Chrysippus, concerning policy, governing, and being governed, concerning judging and pleading, and yet there is not to be found in any of their lives either leading of armies, making of laws, going to parliament, pleading before the judges, fighting for their country, travelling on embassies, or making of public gifts, but they have all, feeding (if I may so say) on rest as on the lotus, led their whole lives, and those not short but very long ones, in foreign countries, amongst disputations, books, and walkings; it is manifest that they have lived rather according to the writings and sayings of others than their own professions, having spent all their days in that repose which Epicurus and Hieronymus so much commend.

Chrysippus indeed himself, in his Fourth Book of Lives, thinks there is no difference between a scholastic life and a voluptuous one. I will set down here his very words: "They who are of opinion that a scholastic life is from the very beginning most suitable to philosophers seem to me to be in an error, thinking that men ought to follow this for the sake of some recreation or some other thing like to it, and in that manner to spin out the whole course of their life; that is, if it may be explained, to live at ease. For this opinion of theirs is not to be concealed, many of them delivering it clearly, and not a few more obscurely." Who therefore did more grow old in this scholastic life than Chrysippus, Cleanthes, Diogenes, Zeno, and Antipater, who left their countries not out of any discontent but that they might quietly enjoy their delight, studying, and disputing at their leisure. To verify which, Aristocreon, the disciple and intimate friend of Chrysippus, having erected his statue of brass upon a pillar, engraved on it these verses:–

This brazen statue Aristocreon
To's friend Chrysippus newly here has put,
Whose sharp-edged wit, like sword of champion,
Did Academic knots in sunder cut.

Such a one then was Chrysippus, an old man, a philosopher, one who praised the regal and civil life, and thought there was no difference between a scholastic and voluptuous one.

But those others of them who intermeddle in state affairs act yet more contradictorily to their own doctrines. For they govern, judge, consult, make laws, punish, and honor, as if those were indeed cities in the government of which they concern themselves, those truly counsellors and judges who are at any time allotted to such offices, those generals who are chosen by suffrages, and those laws which were made by Clisthenes, Lycurgus, and Solon, whom they affirm to have been vicious men and fools. Thus even over the management of state affairs are they at variance with themselves.

Indeed Antipater, in his writings concerning the difference between Cleanthes and Chrysippus, has related that Zeno and Cleanthes would not be made citizens of Athens, lest they might seem to injure their own countries. I shall not much insist upon it, that, if they did well, Chrysippus acted amiss in suffering himself to be enrolled as a member of that city. But this is very contradictory and absurd, that, removing their persons and their lives so far off amongst strangers, they reserved their names for their countries; which is the same thing as if a man, leaving his wife, and cohabiting and bedding with another, and getting children on her, should yet refuse to contract marriage with the second, lest he might seem to wrong the former.

Again, Chrysippus, writing in his treatise of Rhetoric, that a wise man will so plead and so act in the management of a commonwealth, as if riches, glory, and health were really good, confesses that his speeches are inextricable and impolitic, and his doctrines unsuitable for the uses and actions of human life.

It is moreover a doctrine of Zeno's, that temples are not to be built to the gods; for that a temple is neither a thing of much value nor holy; since no work of carpenters and handicrafts-men can be of much value.

And yet they who praise these things as well and wisely said are initiated in the sacred mysteries, go up to the Citadel (where Minerva's temple stands), adore the shrines, and adorn with garlands the sacraries, being the works of carpenters and mechanical persons. Again, they think that the Epicureans, who sacrifice to the gods and yet deny them to meddle with the government of the world, do thereby refute themselves; whereas they themselves are more contrary to themselves, sacrificing on altars and in temples, which they affirm ought not to stand nor to have been built.

Moreover, Zeno admits (as Plato does) several virtues having various distinctions—to wit, prudence, fortitude, temperance, and justice—as being indeed inseparable, but yet divers and different from one another. But again, defining every one of them, he says that fortitude is prudence in executing, justice prudence in distributing, as being one and the same virtue, but seeming to differ in its relation to different affairs when it comes to action. Nor does Zeno alone seem to contradict himself in these matters; but Chrysippus also, who blames Ariston for saying that the other virtues are different habits of one and the same virtue, and yet defends Zeno, who in this manner defines every one of the virtues. And Cleanthes, having in his Commentaries concerning Nature said, that vigor is the striking of fire, which, if it is sufficient in the soul to perform the duties presented to it, is called force and strength; subjoins these very words: "Now this force and strength, when it is in things apparent and to be persisted in, is continence; when in things to be endured, it is fortitude; when about worthiness, it is justice; and when about choosing or refusing, it is temperance." Against him, who said,

> Give not thy judgment till both sides are heard,
> (In the "Pseudo-Phocylidea," vs. 87 (Bergk).)

Zeno on the contrary made use of such an argument as this: "If he who spake first has plainly proved his cause, the second is not to be heard, for the question is at an end; and if he has not proved it, it is the same case as if being cited he did not appear, or appearing did nothing but wrangle; so that, whether he has proved or not proved his cause, the second is not to be heard." And yet he who made this dilemma has written against Plato's Commonweal, dissolved sophisms, and exhorted his scholars to learn logic, as enabling them to do the same. Now Plato has either proved or not proved those things which he writ in his Commonweal; but in neither case was it necessary to write against him, but wholly superfluous and vain. The same may be said concerning sophisms.

Chrysippus is of opinion, that young students should first learn logic, secondly, ethics, and after these, physics, and likewise in this to meddle last of all with the disputes concerning the gods. Now these things having been often said by him, it will suffice to set down what is found in his Fourth Book of Lives, being thus word for word: "First, then, it seems to me, according as it has been rightly said by the ancients, that there are three kinds of philosophical speculations, logical, ethical, and physical, and that of these, the logical ought to be placed first, the ethical second, and the physical third, and that of the physical, the discourse concerning the gods ought to be the last; wherefore also the traditions concerning this have been styled [Greek omitted], or the ENDINGS." But that very discourse concerning the gods, which he says ought to be placed the last, he usually places first and sets before every moral question. For he is seen not to say anything concerning the ends, or concerning justice, or concerning good and evil, or concerning marriage and the education of children, or concerning the law and the commonwealth; but, as those who propose decrees to states set before them the words To Good Fortune, so he also premises something of Jupiter, Fate, Providence, and of the world's being one and finite and maintained by one power. None of which any one can be persuaded to believe, who has not penetrated deeply into the discourses of natural philosophy. Hear what he says of this in his Third Book of the Gods: "For there is not to be found any other beginning or any other generation of Justice, but what is from Jupiter and common Nature. From thence must every such thing have its beginning, if we will say anything concerning good and evil." And again, in his Natural Positions he says: "For one cannot otherwise or more properly come to the discourse of good and evil, to the virtues, or to felicity, than from common Nature and the administration of the world." And going farther on, he adds: "For to these we must annex the discourse concerning good and evil, there being no other better beginning or relation thereof, and the speculation of Nature being learned for nothing else, but to understand the difference between good and evil." According to Chrysippus, therefore, the natural science is both before and after the moral; or rather, it is an inversion of order altogether absurd, if this must be put after those things none of which can be comprehended without this; and his contradicting himself is manifest, when he asserts the discourse of Nature to be the beginning of that concerning good and evil, and yet commands it to be delivered, not before, but after it.

Now, if any one shall say that Chrysippus in his book concerning the Use of Speech has written, that he who applies himself to logic first needs not absolutely to abstain from the rest, but should take as much of them as shall fall in his way, he will indeed say the truth, but will withal confirm the fault. For he oppugns himself, one while commanding that the science concerning God should be taken last and for a conclusion, as being therefore also called [Greek omitted], and again, another while saying that this is to be learned together with the very first. For order is at an end, if all things must be used at all times. But this is more, that having made the science concerning the gods the beginning of that concerning good and evil, he bids not those who apply themselves to the ethics to begin with that; but learning these, to take of that also as it shall come in their way, and then to go from these to that, without which, he says, there is no beginning or entrance upon these.

As for disputing on both sides, he says, that he does not universally reject it, but exhorts us to use it with caution, as is done in pleadings, not with the aim really to disprove, but to dissolve their probability. "For to those," says he, "who endeavor a suspension of assent concerning all things, it is convenient to do this, and it co-operates to what they desire; but as for those who would work and constitute in us a certain science according to which we shall professedly live, they ought, on the contrary, to state the first principles, and to direct their novices who are entered from the beginning to the end; and where there is occasion to make mention of contrary discourses, to dissolve their probability, as is done in pleadings." For this he hath said in express words. Now that it is absurd for philosophers to think that they ought to set down the contrary opinion, not with all its reasons, but like pleaders, disabling it, as if they contended not for truth but victory, we have elsewhere spoken against him. But that he himself has, not in one or two places in his disputations, but frequently, confirmed the discourses which are contrary to his own opinions, and that stoutly, and with so much earnestness and contention that it was not for every one to understand what he liked,–the Stoics themselves affirm, who admire the man's acuteness, and think that Carneades said nothing of his own, but that catching hold of those arguments which Chrysippus alleged for the contrary opinion, he assaulted with them his positions, and often cried out,

> Wretch, thy own strength will thee undo,
>
> ("*Iliad*", vi. 407.)

as if Chrysippus had given great advantages against himself to those who would disturb and calumniate his doctrines.

But of those things which he has written against Custom they are so proud and boastful, that they fear not to affirm, that all the sayings of all the Academics together, if they were collected into one body, are not comparable to what Chrysippus has writ in disparagement of the senses. Which is an evident sign of the ignorance or self-love of the speakers; but this indeed is true, that being afterwards desirous to defend custom and the senses, he was inferior to himself, and the latter treatise was much weaker than the former. So that he contradicts himself; for having always directed the proposing of an adversary's opinions not with approbation, but with a demonstration of their falsity, he has showed himself more acute in opposing than defending his own doctrines; and having admonished others to take heed of contrary arguments, as withdrawing comprehension, he has been more sedulous in framing such proofs as take away comprehension, than such as confirm it. And yet he plainly shows that he himself feared this, writing thus in his Fourth Book of Lives: "Repugnant arguments and probabilities on the contrary side are not rashly to be proposed, but with caution, lest the hearers distracted by them should let go their conceptions, not being able sufficiently to apprehend the solutions, but so weakly that their comprehensions may easily be shaken. For even those who have, according to custom, preconceived both sensible phenomena and other things depending on the senses quickly forego them, being distracted by Megarian interrogatories and by others more numerous and forcible." I would willingly therefore ask the Stoics, whether they think these Megarian interrogatories to be more forcible than those which Chrysippus has written in six books against custom; or rather this should be asked of Chrysippus himself. For observe what he has written about the Megarian reason, in his book concerning the Use of Speech, thus: "Some such things fell out in the discourse of Stilpo and Menedemus; for, whereas they were renowned for wisdom, their disputing has turned to their reproach, their arguments being part clumsy, and the rest plainly sophistical." And yet, good sir, you fear lest those arguments which you deride and term the disgrace of their proposers, as having a manifest faultiness, should divert some from comprehension. And did not you yourself, writing so many books against custom, in which you have added whatever you could invent, ambitiously striving to exceed Arcesilaus, expect that you should perplex some of your readers? For neither does he use slender arguments against custom; but as if he were pleading, he with some passion in himself stirs up the affections of others, telling his opponent that he talks foolishly and labors in vain. And that he may leave no room to deny his speaking of contradictions, he has in his Natural Positions written thus: "It may be lawful for those who comprehend a thing to argue on the contrary side, applying to it that kind of defence which the subject itself affords; and sometimes, when they comprehend neither, to discourse what is alleged for either." And having said in his book concerning the Use of Speech, that we ought no more to use the force of reason than of arms for such things as are not fitting, he subjoins this: "For they are to be employed for the finding out of truths and for the alliance of them, and not for the contrary, though many men do it." By "many" perhaps he means those who withhold their assent. But these teachers, understanding neither, dispute on both sides, believing that, if anything is comprehensible, thus only or chiefly does truth afford a comprehension of itself. But you, who accuse them, and do yourself write contrary to those things which you understood concerning custom, and exhort others under your authority to do the same, confess that you wantonly use the faculty of disputing, out of vain ambition, even on useless and hurtful things.

They say, that a good deed is the command, and sin the prohibition of the law; and therefore that the law forbids the wicked many things, but commands them nothing, because they cannot do a good deed. But who is ignorant that he who cannot do a good deed cannot also sin? Therefore they make the law to contradict itself, commanding men those things which they cannot perform, and forbidding them those things from which they cannot abstain. For a man who cannot be temperate cannot but act intemperately; and he who cannot be wise cannot but act foolishly. And they themselves affirm, that those who forbid say one thing, forbid another and command another. For he who says "Thou shalt not steal" at the same time that he says these words, "Thou shalt not steal, forbids also to steal and directs not to steal. The law therefor bids the wicked nothing, unless it also commands them something. And they say, that the physician bids his disciple to cut and cauterize, omitting to add these words, 'seasonably and moderately'; and the musician commands his scholar to play on the harp and sing, omitting 'tunably' and 'keeping time.'" Wherefore also they punish those who do these things unskilfully and faultily; for that they were commanded to do them well, and they have done them ill. If therefore a wise man commands his servant to say or do something, and punishes him for doing it unseasonably or not as he ought, is it not manifest that he commanded him to do a good action and not an indifferent one? But if wise men command wicked ones indifferent things, what hinders but the commands of the law may be also such? Moreover, the impulse (called [Greek omitted]) is, according to him, the reason of a man commanding him to do something, as he has written in his book of the law. Is not therefore also the aversion (called [Greek omitted]) a prohibiting reason, and a disinclination, a disinclination agreeable to reason? Caution therefore is also reason prohibiting a w cautious is proper only to the wise, and not to the wicked. If, then, the reason of a wise man is one thing and the law another, wise men have caution contrary to the law; but if the law is nothing else but the reason of a wise man, the law is found to forbid wise men the doing of those things of which they are cautious.

Chrysippus says, that nothing is profitable to the wicked, that the wicked have neither use nor need of anything. Having said this in his First Book of Good Deeds, he says again, that both commodiousness and grace pertain to mean or indifferent things, none of which according to them, is profitable. In the same place he affirms, that there is nothing proper, nothing convenient for a vicious man, in these words: "On the same principle we declare that there is nothing foreign or strange to the good man, and nothing proper or rightfully belonging to the bad man, since the one is good and the other bad." Why, then, does he break our heads, writing particularly in every one of his books, as well natural as moral, that as soon as we are born we are appropriated to ourselves, our parts, and our offspring? And why in his First Book of Justice does he say that the very brutes, proportionably to the necessity of their young, are appropriated to them, except fishes, whose young are nourished by themselves? For neither have they sense who have nothing sensible, nor they appropriation who have nothing proper; for appropriation seems to be the sense and perception of what is proper.

And this opinion is consequent to their principal ones. It is moreover manifest that Chrysippus, though he has also written many things to the contrary, lays this for a position, that there is not any vice greater or any sin more grievous than another, nor any virtue more excellent or any good deed better than another; so that he says in his Third Book of Nature: "As it well beseems Jupiter to glory in himself and his life, to magnify himself, and (if we may so say) to bear up his head, have an high conceit of himself, and speak big, for that he leads a life worthy of lofty speech; so the same things do not misbeseem all good men, since they are in nothing exceeded by Jupiter." And yet himself, in his Third Book of Justice, says, that they who make pleasure the end destroy justice, but they who say it is only a good do not destroy it. These are his very words: "For perhaps, if we leave this to pleasure, that it is a good but not the end, and that honesty is one of those things which are eligible for themselves, we may preserve justice, making the honest and the just a greater good than pleasure." But if that only is good which is honest, he who affirms pleasure to be a good is in an error, but he errs less than he who makes it also the end; for the one destroys justice, the other preserves it; and by the one human society is overthrown, but the other leaves a place to goodness and humanity. Now I let pass his saying farther in his book concerning Jupiter, that the virtues increase and go on, lest I may seem to catch at words; though Chrysippus is indeed in this kind very sharp upon Plato and others. But when he forbids the praising of everything that is done according to virtue, he shows that there is some difference between good deeds. Now he says thus in his book concerning Jupiter: "For since each virtue has its own proper effects, there are some of these that are to be praised more highly than others; for he would show himself to be very frigid, that should undertake to praise and extol any man for holding out the finger stoutly, for abstaining continently from an old woman ready to drop into the grave, and patiently hearing it said that three are not exactly four." What he says in his Third Book of the Gods is not unlike to this: "For I moreover think that the praises of such things as to abstain from an old woman who has one foot in the grave, and to endure the sting of a fly, though proceeding from virtue, would be very impertinent." What other reprehender of his doctrines does this man then expect? For if he who praises such things is frigid, he who asserts every one of them to be a great–nay, a very great good deed–is much more frigid. For if to endure a fly is equal to being valiant, and to abstain from an old woman now at the edge of the grave is equal to being temperate, there is, I think, no difference whether a virtuous man is prized for these or for those. Moreover, in his Second Book of Friendship, teaching that friendships are not for every fault to be dissolved, he has these very expressions: "For it is meet that some faults should be wholly passed by, others lightly reprehended, others more severely, and others deemed worthy a total dissolution of friendship." And which is more, he says in the same book, that we will converse with some more and some less, so that some shall be more and some less friends; and this diversity extending very far, some are worthy of such an amity, others of a greater; and these will deserve to be so far trusted, those not so far, and the like. For what else has he done in these places, but shown the great diversity there is between these things? Moreover, in his book concerning Honesty, to demonstrate that only to be good which is honest, he uses these words: "What is good is eligible; what is eligible is acceptable; what is acceptable is laudable; and what is laudable is honest." And again: "What is good is joyous; what is joyous is venerable; what is venerable is honest." But these speeches are repugnant to himself; for either all good is commendable, and then the abstaining chastely from an old woman is also commendable; or all good is neither venerable nor joyous, and his reasoning falls to the ground. For how can it possibly be frigid in others to praise any for such things, and not ridiculous for him to rejoice and glory in them?

Such indeed he frequently is; but in his disputations against others he takes not the least care of speaking things contrary and dissonant to himself. For in his books of Exhorting, reprehending Plato, who said, that to him who has neither learned nor knows how to live it is profitable not to live, he speaks in this manner: "For this speech is both repugnant to itself, and not at all conclusive. For first insinuating that it is best for us not to live, and in a sort counselling us to die, he will excite us rather to anything else than to be philosophers; for neither can he who does not live philosophize, nor he who shall live long wickedly and ignorantly become wise." And going on, he says that it is convenient for the wicked also to continue in life. And afterwards thus, word for word: "First, as virtue, barely taken, has nothing towards our living, so neither has vice anything to oblige us to depart." Nor is it necessary to turn over other books, that we may show Chrysippus's contradictoriness to himself; but in these same, he sometimes with commendation brings forth this saying of Antisthenes, that either understanding or a halter is to be provided, as also that of Tyrtaeus,

Come nigh the bounds of virtue or of death.

Now what else will this show, but that to wicked men and fools not to live is more profitable than to live? And sometimes correcting Theognis, he says, that the poet should not have written,

From poverty to fly;–

but rather thus,

From wickedness to fly, into the deep
Throw thyself, Cyrnus, or from rocks so steep.
(See "Theognis," vs. 175.)

What therefore else does he seem to do, but to set down himself those things and doctrines which, when others write them, he expunges; condemning, indeed, Plato for showing that not to live is better than to live viciously and ignorantly; and yet advising Theognis to let a man break his neck or throw himself into the sea, that he may avoid vice? For having praised Antisthenes for directing fools to an halter, he again blames him, saying that vice has nothing that should oblige us to depart out of life.

Moreover, in his books against the same Plato, concerning Justice, he immediately at the very beginning leaps into a discourse touching the gods, and says, that Cephalus did not rightly avert men from injustice by the fear of the gods, and that his teaching is easily refuted, and that it affords to the contrary many arguments and probabilities impugning the discourse concerning divine punishments, as nothing differing from the tales of Acco and Alphito (or Raw-Head and Bloody-Bones), with which women are wont to frighten little children from their unlucky pranks. Having thus traduced Plato, he in other places again praises him, and often alleges this saying of Euripides:–

Howe'er you may deride it, there's a Jove,
With other gods, who sees men's ills above.

And likewise, in his First Book of Justice citing these verses of Hesiod,

Then Jove from heaven punishments did send,
And plague and famine brought them to their end,
("Works and Days," 242.)

he says, the gods do these things, that the wicked being punished, others admonished by these examples may less dare to attempt the doing of such things.

Again, in his book of Justice, subjoining, that it is possible for those who make pleasure a good but not the end to preserve also justice, he said in express terms: "For perhaps if we leave this to pleasure, that it is a good but not the end, and that honesty is one of those things which are eligible for themselves, we may preserve justice, making the honest and the just a greater good than pleasure." So much he says in this place concerning pleasure. But in his book against Plato, accus temperance, and all the other virtues will be taken away, if we make pleasure, health, or anything else which is not honest, to be a good. What therefore is to be said for Plato, we have elsewhere written against him. But here his contradicting himself is manifest, when he says in one place, that if a man supposes that with honesty pleasure also is a good, justice is preserved, and in another, accuses those who make anything besides honesty to be a good of taking away all the virtues. But that he may not leave any means of making an apology for his contradictions, writing against Aristotle concerning justice, he affirms him not to have spoken rightly when he said, that pleasure being made the end, justice is taken away, and together with justice, every one also of the other virtues. For justice (he says) will indeed be taken away; but there is nothing to hinder the other virtues from remaining and being, though not eligible for themselves, yet good and virtues. Then he reckons up every one of them by name. But it will be better to set down his own words. "For pleasure," says he, "appearing according to this discourse to be made the end, yet all this seems not to me to be contained in it. Wherefore we must say, that neither any of the virtues is eligible nor any of the vices to be avoided for itself, but that all these things are to be referred to the proposed scope. Yet nothing, according to their opinion, will hinder but that fortitude, prudence, continence, and patience may be good, and their contraries to be avoided." Has there ever then been any man more peevish in his disputes than he, who has blamed two of the principal philosophers, the one for taking away all virtue, by not making that only to be good which is honest, and the other for not thinking all the virtues except justice to be preserved, though pleasure is made the end? For it is a wonderful licentiousness that, discoursing of the same matters, he should when accusing Plato take away again those very things which himself sets down when reprehending Aristotle. Moreover, in his demonstrations concerning justice, he says expressly, that every good deed is both a lawful action and a just operation; but that everything which is done according to continence, patience, prudence, or fortitude is a good deed, and therefore also a just operation. Why, then, does he not also leave justice to them to whom he leaves prudence, fortitude, and continence; since whatever they do well according to the said virtue, they do also justly?

Moreover, Plato having said, that injustice, as being the corruption and sedition of the soul, loses not its power even in those who have it within them, but sets the wicked man against himself, and molests and disturbs him; Chrysippus, blaming this, affirms that it is absurdly said, "A man injures himself"; for that injustice is to another, and not to one's self. But forgetting this, he again says, in his demonstrations concerning justice, that the unjust man is injured by himself and injures himself when he injures another, becoming to himself the cause of transgressing, and undeservedly hurting himself. In his books indeed against Plato, contending that we cannot talk of injustice against one's self, but as concerns another, he has these words: "For men cannot be unjust by themselves; injustice requires several on different sides, speaking contrary one unto another and the injustice must be taken in different ways. But no such thing extends to one alone, except inasmuch as he is affected towards his neighbor." But in his demonstrations he has such discourses as these, concerning the unjust man's being injurious also to himself: "The law forbids the being any way the author of transgression, and to act unjustly will be transgression. He therefore who is to himself the author of acting unjustly transgresses against himself. Now he that transgresses against any one also injures him; therefore he who is injurious to any one whomsoever is injurious also to himself." Again: "Sin is a hurt, and every one who sins sins against himself; every one therefore who sins hurts himself undeservedly, and if so, is also unjust to himself." And farther thus: "He who is hurt by another hurts himself, and that undeservedly. Now that is to be unjust. Every one therefore that is injured, by whomsoever it is, is unjust also to himself."

He says, that the doctrine concerning good and evil which himself introduces and approves is most agreeable to life, and does most of all reach the inbred prenotions; for this he has affirmed in his Third Book of Exhortations. But in his First Book he says, that this doctrine takes a man off from all other things, as being nothing to us, nor co-operating anything towards felicity. See, now, how consonant he is to himself, when he asserts a doctrine which takes us off from life, health, indolence, and integrity of the senses, and says that those things we beg of the gods are nothing to us, though most agreeable to life and to the common presumptions. But that there may be no denial of his speaking contradictions, in his Third Book of Justice he has said thus: "Wherefore also, from the excellence of their greatness and beauty, we seem to speak things like to fictions, and not according to man or human nature." Is it then possible that any one can more plainly confess his speaking things contrary to himself than this man does, who affirms those things which (he says) for their excellency seem to be fictions and to be spoken above man and human nature, to be agreeable to life, and most of all to reach the inbred prenotions?

In every one of his natural and ethical books, he asserts vice to be the very essence of unhappiness; writing and contending that to live viciously is the same thing as to live unhappily. But in his Third Book of Nature, having said that it is profitable for a fool to live rather than to die, though he is never to become wise, he subjoins: "For such is the nature of good things among mortals, that evil things are in some sort chosen before indifferent ones." I let pass therefore, that having elsewhere said that nothing is profitable to fools, he here says that to live foolishly is profitable to them. Now those things being by them called indifferent which are neither bad nor good, when he says that bad things precede them, he says nothing else but that evil things precede those that are not evil, and that to be unhappy is more profitable than not to be unhappy; and if so, he esteems not to be unhappy to be more unprofitable–and if more unprofitable, more hurtful–than to be unhappy. Desiring therefore to mitigate this absurdity, he adds concerning evils: "But it is not these evils that have precedence, but reason; with which it is more convenient to live, though we shall be fools." First therefore he says that vice and things participating of vice are evil, and that nothing else is so. Now vice is something reasonable, or rather depraved reason. For those therefore who are fools to live with reason, is nothing else but to live with vice.

Thence to live being fools is to live being unhappy. In what then is this to be preferred to indifferent things? For he surely will not say that with regard to happiness unhappiness is to be preferred. But neither, say they, does Chrysippus altogether think that the remaining in life is to be reckoned amongst good things, or the going out of it amongst bad; but both of them amongst indifferent ones, according to Nature. Wherefore also it sometimes becomes meet for the happy to make themselves away, and again for the unhappy to continue in life. Now what greater repugnance can there be than this in the choice and avoiding of things, if it is convenient for those who are in the highest degree happy to forsake those good things that are present, for the want of some one indifferent thing? And yet they esteem none of the indifferent things either desirable or to be avoided; but only good desirable, and only evil to be avoided. So that it comes to pass, according to them, that the reasoning about actions regards neither things desirable nor things refusable; but that aiming at other things, which they neither shun nor choose, they make life and death to depend on these.

Chrysippus confesses that good things are totally different from bad; and it must of necessity be so, if these make them with whom they are present miserable to the very utmost point, and those render their possessors in the highest degree happy. Now he says, that good and evil things are sensible, writing thus in his First Book of the End: "That good and evil things are perceptible by sense, we are by these reasons forced to say; for not only the passions, with their species, as sorrow, fear, and such others, are sensible; but we may also have a sense of theft, adultery, and the like, and generally, of folly, cowardice, and other vices not a few; and again, not only of joy, beneficence, and many other dependences on good deeds, but also of prudence, fortitude, and the other virtues." Let us pass by the other absurdities of these things; but that they are repugnant to those things which are delivered by him concerning "the wise man that knows nothing of his being so," who does not confess? For good, when present, being sensible and having a great difference from evil, is it not most absurd, that he who is of bad become good should be ignorant of it, and not perceive virtue when present, but think that vice is still within him? For either none who has all virtues can be ignorant and doubt of his having them; or the difference of virtue from vice, of happiness from misery, and of a most honest life from a most shameful one, is little and altogether difficult to be discerned, if he who has taken the one in exchange for the other does not perceive it.

He has written one volume of lives divided into four books; in the fourth of these he says, that a wise man meddles with no business but his own, and is employed about his own affairs. His words are these: "For I am of opinion, that a prudent man shuns affairs, meddles little, and at the same time minds his own occasions; civil persons being both minders of their own affairs and meddlers with little else." He has said almost the same in his book of Things eligible for Themselves, in these very words: "For indeed a quiet life seems to have in it a certain security and freedom from danger, though there are not very many who can comprehend it." It is manifest that he does not much dissent from Epicurus, who takes away Providence that he may leave God in repose. But the same Chrysippus in his First Book of Lives says, that a wise man willingly takes upon him a kingdom, making his profit by it; and if he cannot reign himself, will dwell with a king, and go to the wars with a king like Hydanthyrsus the Scythian or Leucon the Pontic. But I will here also set down his very discourse, that we may see whether, as from the treble and the base strings there arises a symphony in music, so the life of a man who chooses quietness and meddling with little accords with him who, upon any necessity, rides along with the Scythians and manages the affairs of the tyrants in the Bosphorus: "For that a wise man will both go to the wars and live with potentates, we will again consider this hereafter; some indeed upon the like arguments not so much as suspecting this, and we for semblable reasons admitting it." And a little after: "Not only with those who have proceeded well, and are become proficients in discipline and good manners, as with Leucon and Hydanthyrsus."

Some there are who blame Callisthenes for sailing to Alexander in hopes to obtain the rebuilding of Olynthus, as Aristotle had procured that of Stagira; and commend Ephorus, Xenocrates, and Menedemus, who rejected Alexander's solicitation. But Chrysippus thrusts his wise man headforwards for the sake of gain, as far as Panticapaeum and the desert of the Scythians. And that he does this for the sake of profit and gain, he has showed before, supposing three ways of gaining most suitable for a wise man,–the first by a kingdom, the second by his friends, and the third, besides these, by teaching philosophy. And yet he frequently even tires us with his praises of this saying:–

What need have men of more than these two things?

And in his books of Nature he says, that a wise man, if he has lost the greatest wealth imaginable, seems to have lost but a single groat. But having there thus elevated and puffed him up, he again here throws him down to mercenariness and sophistry; nay, to asking money and even to receiving it beforehand, sometimes at the very entrance of his scholar, and otherwhiles after some time past. The last, he says indeed, is the more polite, but to receive beforehand the more sure; delay allowing of injuries. Now he says thus: "All who are well advised do not require their salary in the same manner, but differently; a multitude of them, as opportunity offers, not promising to make their scholars good men, and that within a year, but to do this, as far as in them lies, within a time agreed on." And again going on, he says: "But he will know his opportunity, whether he ought to receive his recompense presently at the very entrance (as many have done), or to give them time, this manner being more liable to injuries, but withal, seeming the more courteous." And how is the wise man a contemner of wealth, who upon a contract delivers virtue for money, and if he has not delivered it, yet requires his reward, as having done what is in him? Or how is he above being endamaged, when he is so cautious lest he be wronged of his recompense? For no man is wronged who is not endamaged. Therefore, though he has elsewhere asserted that a wise man cannot be injured, he here says, that this manner of dealing is liable to injury.

In his book of a Commonweal he says, that his citizens will neither act nor prepare anything for the sake of pleasure, and praises Euripides for having uttered this sentence:–

> What need have men of more than these two things,
> The fruits of Ceres, and thirst-quenching springs?

And yet a little after this, going on, he commends Diogenes, who forced his nature to pass from himself in public, and said to those that were present: I wish I could in the same manner drive hunger also out of my belly. What reason then is there to praise in the same books him who rejects all pleasure, and withal, him who for the sake of pleasure does such things, and proceeds to such a degree of filthiness? Moreover, having in his book of Nature written, that Nature has produced many creatures for the sake of beauty, delighting in pulchritude and pleasing herself with variety, and having added a most absurd expression, that the peacock was made for the sake of his tail and for the beauty of it; he has, in his treatise of a Commonweal, sharply reprehended those who bred peacocks and nightingales, as if he were making laws contrary to the lawgiver of the world, and deriding Nature for pleasing herself in the beauty of animals to which a wise man would not give a place in his city. For how can it but be absurd to blame those who nourish these creatures, if he commends Providence which created them? In his Fifth Book of Nature, having said, that bugs profitably awaken us out of our sleep, that mice make us cautious not to lay up everything negligently, and that it is probable that Nature, rejoicing in variety, takes delight in the production of fair creatures, he adds these words: "The evidence of this is chiefly shown in the peacock's tail; for here she manifests that this animal was made for the sake of his tail, and not the contrary; so, the male being made, the female follows." In his book of a Commonweal, having said that we are ready to paint even dunghills, a little after he adds, that some beautify their cornfields with vines climbing up trees, and myrtles set in rows, and keep peacocks, doves, and partridges, that they may hear them cry and coo, and nightingales. Now I would gladly ask him, what he thinks of bees and honey? For it was of consequence, that he who said bugs were created profitably should also say that bees were created unprofitably. But if he allows these a place in his city, why does he drive away his citizens from things that are pleasing and delight the ear? To be brief,– as he would be very absurd who should blame the guests for eating sweetmeats and other delicacies and drinking of wine, and at the same time commend him who invited them and prepared such things for them; so he that praises Providence, which has afforded fishes, birds, honey, and wine, and at the same time finds fault with those who reject not these things, nor content themselves with

The fruits of Ceres and thirst-quenching springs,

which are present and sufficient to nourish us, seems to make no scruple of speaking things contradictory to himself.

Moreover, having said in his book of Exhortations, that the having carnal commerce with our mothers, daughters, or sisters, the eating forbidden food, and the going from a woman's bed or a dead carcass to the temple, have been without reason blamed, he affirms, that we ought for these things to have a regard to the brute beasts, and from what is done by them conclude that none of these is absurd or contrary to Nature; for that the comparisons of other animals are fitly made for this purpose, to show that neither their coupling, bringing-forth, nor dying in the temples pollutes the Divinity. Yet he again in his Fifth Book of Nature says, that Hesiod rightly forbids urinating into rivers and fountains, and that we should rather abstain from doing this against any altar, or statue of the gods; and that it is not to be admitted for an argument, that dogs, asses, and young children do it, who have no discretion or consideration of such things. It is therefore absurd to say in one place, that the savage example of irrational animals is fit to be considered, and in another, that it is unreasonable to allege it.

To give a solution to the inclinations, when a man seems to be necessitated by exterior causes, some philosophers place in the principal faculty of the soul a certain adventitious motion, which is chiefly manifested in things differing in no way from one another. For when, with two things altogether alike and of equal importance, there is a necessity to choose the one, there being no cause inclining to either, for that neither of them differs from the other, this adventitious power of the soul, seizing on its inclination, determines the doubt. Chrysippus, discoursing against these men, as offering violence to Nature by imagining an effect without a cause, in many places alleges the die and the balance, and several other things, which cannot fall or incline either one way or the other without some cause or difference, either wholly within them or coming to them from without; for that what is causeless (he says) is wholly insubsistent, as also what is fortuitous; and in those motions devised by some and called adventitious, there occur certain obscure causes, which, being concealed from us, move our inclinations to one side or other. These are some of those things which are most evidently known to have been frequently said by him; but what he has said contrary to this, not lying so exposed to every one's sight, I will set down in his own words. For in his book of Judging, having supposed two running for a wager to have exactly finished their race together, he examines what is fit for the judge in this case to do. "Whether," says he, "may the judge give the palm to which of them he will, since they both happen to be so familiar to him, that he would in some sort appear to bestow on them somewhat of his own? Or rather, since the palm is common to both, may it be, as if lots had been cast, given to either, according to the inclination he chances to have? I say the inclination he chances to have, as when two groats, every way else alike, being presented to us, we incline to one of them and take it." And in his Sixth Book of Duties, having said that there are some things not worthy of much study or attention, he thinks we ought, as if we had cast lots, to commit the choice of those things to the casual inclination of the mind: "As if," says he, "of those who try the same two drams in a certain time, some should approve this and others that, and there being no more cause for the taking of one than the other, we should leave off making any farther investigation and take that which chances to come first; thus casting the lot (as it were) according to some uncertain principle, and being in danger of choosing the worse of them." For in these passages, the casting of lots and the casual inclining of the mind, which is without any cause, introduce the choice of indifferent things.

In his Third Book of Dialectics, having said that Plato, Aristotle, and those who came after them, even to Polemon and Straton, but especially Socrates, diligently studied dialectics, and having cried out that one would even choose to err with such and so great men as these, he brings in these words: "For if they had spoken of these things cursorily, one might perhaps have cavilled at this place; but having treated of dialectic skill as one of the greatest and most necessary faculties, it is not probable they should have been so much mistaken, having been such in all the parts of philosophy as we esteem them." Why, then (might some one say to him), do you never cease to oppose and argue against such and so great men, as if you thought them to err in the principal and greatest matters? For it is not probable that they writ seriously of dialectics, and only transitorily and in sport of the beginning, end, gods, and justice, in which you affirm their discourse to be blind and contradictory to itself, and to have a thousand other faults.

In one place he says, that the vice called [Greek omitted], or the rejoicing at other men's harms, has no being; since no good man ever rejoiced at another's evils. But in his Second Book of Good, having declared envy to be a sorrow at other men's good,–to wit, in such as desire the depression of their neighbors that themselves may excel, he joins to it this rejoicing at other men's harms, saying thus: "To this is contiguous the rejoicing at other men's harms, in such as for like causes desire to have their neighbors low; but in those that are turned according to other natural motions, is engendered mercy." For he manifestly admits the joy at other men's harms to be subsistent, as well as envy and mercy; though in other places he affirms it to have no subsistence; as he does also the hatred of wickedness, and the desire of dishonest gain.

Having in many places said, that those who have a long time been happy are nothing more so, but equally and in like manner with those who have but a moment been partakers of felicity, he has again in many other places affirmed, that it is not fit to stretch out so much as a finger for the obtaining momentary prudence, which flies away like a flash of lightning. It will be sufficient to set down what is to this purpose written by him in his Sixth Book of Moral Questions. For having said, that neither does every good thing equally cause joy, nor every good deed the like glorying, he subjoins these words: "For if a man should have wisdom only for a moment of time or the final minute of life, he ought not so much as to stretch out his finger for such a shortlived prudence." And yet men are neither more happy for being longer so, nor is eternal felicity more eligible than that which lasts but a moment. If he had indeed held prudence to be a good, producing felicity, as Epicurus thought, one should have blamed only the absurdity and the paradoxicalness of this opinion; but since prudence of itself is not another thing differing from felicity, but felicity itself, how is it not a contradiction to say, that momentary happiness is equally desirable with eternal, and yet that momentary happiness is nothing worth?

Chrysippus also says, that the virtues follow one another, and that not only he who has one has all, but also that he who acts according to any one of them acts according to them all; and he affirms, that there is not any man perfect who is not possessed of all the virtues, nor any action perfect to the doing of which all the virtues do not concur. But yet in his Sixth Book of Moral Questions he says, that a good man does not always act valiantly, nor a vicious man always fearfully; for certain objects being presented to the fancies, the one must persist in his judgments, and the other depart from them; and he says that it is not probable a wicked man should be always indulging his lust. If then to act valiantly is the same thing as to use fortitude; and to act timorously as to yield to fear, they cannot but speak contradictions who say, that he who is possessed of either virtue or vice acts at she same time according to all the virtues or all the vices, and yet that a valiant man does not always act valiantly nor a vicious man timorously.

He defines Rhetoric to be an art concerning the ornament and the ordering of a discourse that is pronounced. And farther in his First Book he has written thus: "And I am of opinion not only that a regard ought to be had to a liberal and simple adorning of words, but also that care is to be taken for proper delivery, as regards the right elevation of the voice and the compositions of the countenance and hands." Yet he, who is in this place so curious and exact, again in the same book, speaking of the collision of the vowels, says: "We ought not only to let these things pass, minding somewhat that is better, but also to neglect certain obscurities and defects, nay, solecisms also, of which others, and those not a few, would be ashamed." Certainly, in one place to allow those who would speak eloquently so carefully to dispose their speech as even to observe a decorum in the very composition of their mouth and hands, and in another place to forbid the taking care of defects and inelegancies, and the being ashamed even of committing solecisms, is the property of a man who little cares what he says, but rashly utters whatever comes first into his mouth.

Moreover, in his Natural Positions having warned us not to trouble ourselves but to be at quiet about such things as require experience and scientific investigation, he says: "Let us not think after the same manner with Plato, that liquid nourishment is conveyed to the lungs, and dry to the stomach; nor let us embrace other errors like to these." Now it is my opinion, that to reprehend others, and then not to keep one's self from falling into those things which one has reprehended, is the greatest of contradictions and shamefullest of errors. But he says, that the connections made by ten axioms amount to above a million in number, having neither searched diligently into it by himself nor attained to the truth by men experienced in it. Yet Plato had to testify for him the most renowned of the physicians, Hippocrates, Philistion, and Dioxippus the disciple of Hippocrates; and of the poets, Euripides, Aleaeus, Eupolis, and Eratosthenes, who all say that the drink passes through the lungs. But all the arithmeticians refute Chrysippus, amongst whom also is Hipparchus, demonstrating that the error of his computation is very great; since the affirmative makes of the ten axioms one hundred and three thousand forty and nine connections, and the negative three hundred and ten thousand nine hundred fifty and two.

Some of the ancients have said, that the same befell Zeno which befalls him who has sour wine which he can sell neither for vinegar nor wine; for his "things preferable," as he called them, cannot be disposed of, either as good or as indifferent. But Chrysippus has made the matter yet far more intricate; for he sometimes says, that they are mad who make no account of riches, health, freedom from pain, and integrity of the body, nor take any care to attain them; and having cited that sentence of Hesiod,

> Work hard, O God-born Perses,
> ("Works and Days," 299.)

he cries out, that it would be a madness to advise the contrary and say,

> Work not, O God-born Perses.

And in his book of Lives he affirms, that a wise man will for the sake of gain live with kings, and teach for money, receiving from some of his scholars his reward beforehand, and making contract with others of them; and in his Seventh Book of Duties he says, that he will not scruple to turn his heels thrice over his head, if for so doing he may have a talent. In his First Book of Good Things, he yields and grants to those that desire it to call these preferable things good and their contraries evil, in these very words: "Any one who likes, according to these permutations, may call one thing good and another evil, if he has a regard to the things themselves, not wandering elsewhere, not failing in the understanding of the thing signified, and in the rest accommodating himself to custom in the denomination." Having thus in this place set his things preferable so near to good, and mixed them therewith, he again says, that none of these things belongs at all to us, but that reason withdraws and averts us from all such things; for he has written thus in his First Book of Exhortations. And in his Third Book of Nature he says, that some esteem those happy who reign and are rich, which is all one as if those should be reputed happy who make water in golden chamber-pots and wear golden fringes; but to a good man the losing of his whole estate is but as the losing of one groat, and the being sick no more than if he had stumbled. Wherefore he has not filled virtue only, but Providence also, with these contradictions. For virtue would seem to the utmost degree sordid and foolish, if it should busy itself about such matters, and enjoin a wise man for their sake to sail to Bosphorus or tumble with his heels over his head. And Jupiter would be very ridiculous to be styled Ctesius, Epicarpius, and Charitodotes, because forsooth he gives the wicked golden chamber-pots and golden fringes, and the good such things as are hardly worth a groat, when through Jupiter's providence they become rich. And yet much more ridiculous is Apollo, if he sits to give oracles concerning golden fringes and chamber-pots and the recovering of a stumble.

But they make this repugnancy yet more evident by their demonstration. For they say, that what may be used both well and ill, the same is neither good nor bad; but fools make an ill use of riches, health, and strength of body; therefore none of these is good. If therefore God gives not virtue to men,–but honesty is eligible of itself,–and yet bestows on them riches and health without virtue, he confers them on those who can use them not well but ill, that is hurtfully, shamefully, and perniciously. Now, if the gods can bestow virtue and do not, they are not good; but if they cannot make men good, neither can they help them, for outside of virtue nothing is good and advantageous. Now to judge those who are otherwise made good according to virtue and strength... is nothing to the purpose, for good men also judge the gods according to virtue and strength; so that they do no more aid men than they are aided by them.

Now Chrysippus neither professes himself nor any one of his disciples and teachers to be virtuous. What then do they think of others, but those things which they say,–that they are all mad fools, impious, transgressors of laws, and in the most degree of misery and unhappiness? And yet they say that our affairs, though we act thus miserably, are governed by the providence of the gods. Now if the gods, changing their minds, should desire to hurt, afflict, overthrow, and quite crush us, they could not put us in a worse condition than we already are; as Chrysippus demonstrates that life can admit only one degree either of misery or of unhappiness; so that if it had a voice, it would pronounce these words of Hercules:

> I am so full of miseries, there is
> No place to stow them in.
> (Euripides, "Hercules Furens," 1245.)

Now who can imagine any assertions more repugnant to one another than chat of Chrysippus concerning the gods and that concerning men; when he says, that the gods do in the best manner possible provide for men, and yet men are in the worst condition imaginable?

Some of the Pythagoreans blame him for having in his book of Justice written concerning cocks, that they are usefully procreated, because they awaken us from our sleep, hunt out scorpions, and animate us to battle, breeding in us a certain emulation to show courage; and yet that we must eat them, lest the number of chickens should be greater than were expedient. But he so derides those who blame him for this, that he has written thus concerning Jupiter the Saviour and Creator, the father of justice, equity, and peace, in his Third Book of the Gods: "As cities overcharged with too great a number of citizens send forth colonies into other places and make war upon some, so does God give the beginnings of corruption." And he brings in Euripides for a witness, with others who say that the Trojan war was caused by the gods, to exhaust the multitude of men.

But letting pass their other absurdities (for our design is not to inquire what they have said amiss, but only what they have said dissonantly to themselves), consider how he always attributes to the gods specious and kind appellations, but at the same time cruel, barbarous, and Galatian deeds. For those so great slaughters and earnages, as were the productions of the Trojan war and again of the Persian and Peloponnesian, were no way like to colonies unless these men know of some cities built in hell and under the earth. But Chrysippus makes God like to Deiotarus, the Galatian king, who having many sons, and being desirous to leave his kingdom and house to one of them, killed all the rest; as he that cuts and prunes away all the other branches from the vine, that one which he leaves remaining may grow strong and great. And yet the vine-dresser does this, the sprigs being slender and weak; and we, to favor a bitch, take from her many of her new-born puppies, whilst they are yet blind. But Jupiter, having not only suffered and seen men to grow up, but having also both created and increased them, plagues them afterwards, devising occasions of their destruction and corruption; whereas he should rather not have given them any causes and beginnings of generation.

However, this is but a small matter; but that which follows is greater. For there is no war amongst men without vice. But sometimes the love of pleasure, sometimes the love of money, and sometimes the love of glory and rule is the cause of it. If therefore God is the author of wars, he must be also of sins, provoking and perverting men. And yet himself says in his treatise of Judgment and his Second Book of the Gods, that it is no way rational to say that the Divinity is in any respect the cause of dishonesty. For as the law can in no way be the cause of transgression, so neither can the gods of being impious; therefore neither is it rational that they should be the causes of anything that is filthy. What therefore can be more filthy to men than the mutual killing of one another?–to which Chrysippus says that God gives beginnings. But some one perhaps will say, that he elsewhere praises Euripides for saying,

If gods do aught dishonest, they're no gods;
and again,
'Tis a most easy thing t' accuse the gods;
(From the "Bellerophontes" of Euripides, Frag. 294;
and the "Archelaus," Frag. 256.)

as if we were now doing anything else than setting down such words and sentences of his as are repugnant to one another. Yet that very thing which is now praised may be objected, not once or twice or thrice, but even ten thousand times, against Chrysippus:–

'Tis a most easy thing t' accuse the gods.

For first having in his book of Nature compared the eternity of motion to a drink made of divers species confusedly mixed together, turning and jumbling the things that are made, some this way, others that way, he goes on thus: "Now the administration of the universe proceeding in this manner, it is of necessity we should be in the condition we are, whether contrary to our own nature we are sick or maimed, or whether we are grammarians or musicians." And again a little after, "According to this reason we shall say the like of our virtue and vice, and generally of arts or the ignorance of arts, as I have said." And a little after, taking away all ambiguity, he says: "For no particular thing, not even the least, can be otherwise than according to common Nature and its reason." But that common Nature and the common reason of Nature are with him Fate and Providence and Jupiter, is not unknown even to the antipodes. For these things are everywhere inculcated in the Stoic system; and Chrysippus affirms that Homer said very well,

Jove's purposes were ripening,
("Iliad," i. 5.)

having respect to Fate and the Nature of the universe, according to which everything is governed. How then do these agree, both that God is no way the cause of any dishonest thing, and again, that not even the least thing imaginable can be otherwise done than according to common Nature and its reason? For amongst all things that are done, there must of necessity be also evil things attributed to the gods. And though Epicurus indeed turns himself every way, and studies artifices, devising how to deliver and set loose our voluntary free will from this eternal motion, that he may not leave vice irreprehensible; yet Chrysippus gives vice a most absolute liberty, as being done not only of necessity or according to Fate, but also according to the reason of God and best Nature. And these things are yet farther seen in what he says afterwards, being thus word for word: "For common Nature extending to all things, it will be of necessity that everything, howsoever done in the whole or in any one soever of its parts, must be done according to this common Nature and its reason, proceeding on regularly without any impediment. For there is nothing without that can hinder the administration, nor is there any of the parts that can be moved or habituated otherwise than according to common Nature." What, then, are these habits and motions of the parts? It is manifest, that the habits are vices and diseases, covetousness, luxury, ambition, cowardice, injustice; and that the motions are adulteries, thefts, treasons, murders, parricides. Of these Chrysippus thinks, that no one, either little or great, is contrary to the reason of Jupiter, or to his law, justice, and providence; so neither is the transgressing of the law done against the law, nor the acting unjustly against justice, nor the committing of sin against Providence.

And yet he says, that God punishes vice, and does many things for the chastising of the wicked. And in his Second Book of the Gods he says, that many adversities sometimes befall the good, not as they do the wicked, for punishment, but according to another dispensation, as it is in cities. And again in these words: "First we are to understand of evils in like manner as has been said before: then that these things are distributed according to the reason of Jupiter, whether for punishment, or according to some other dispensation, having in some sort respect to the universe." This therefore is indeed severe, that wickedness is both done and punished according to the reason of Jupiter. But he aggravates this contradiction in his Second Book of Nature, writing thus: "Vice in reference to grievous accidents, has a certain reason of its own. For it is also in some sort according to the reason of Nature, and, as I may so say, is not wholly useless in respect of the universe. For otherwise also there would not be any good." Thus does he reprehend those that dispute indifferently on both sides, who, out of a desire to say something wholly singular and more exquisite concerning everything, affirms, that men do not unprofitably cut purses, calumniate, and play madmen, and that it is not unprofitable there should be unprofitable, hurtful, and unhappy persons. What manner of god then is Jupiter,–I mean Chrysippus's Jupiter,–who punishes an act done neither willingly nor unprofitably? For vice is indeed, according to Chrysippus's discourse, wholly reprehensible; but Jupiter is to be blamed, whether he has made vice which is an unprofitable thing, or, having made it not unprofitable, punishes it.

Again, in his First Book of Justice, having spoken of the gods as resisting the injustices of some, he says: "But wholly to take away vice is neither possible nor expedient." Whether it were not better that law-breaking, injustice, and folly should be taken away, is not the design of this present discourse to inquire. But he himself, as much as in him lies, by his philosophy taking away vice, which it is not expedient to take away, does something repugnant both to reason and God. Besides this, saying that God resists some injustices, he again makes plain the impiety of sins.

Having often written that there is nothing reprehensible, nothing to be complained of in the world, all things being finished according to a most excellent nature, he again elsewhere leaves certain negligences to be reprehended, and those not concerning small or base matters. For having in his Third Book of Substance related that some such things befall honest and good men, he says: "May it not be that some things are not regarded, as in great families some bran–yea, and some grains of corn also–are scattered, the generality being nevertheless well ordered; or maybe there are evil Genii set over those things in which there are real and faulty negligence?" And he also affirms that there is much necessity intermixed. I let pass, how inconsiderate it is to compare such accidents befalling honest and good men, as were the condemnation of Socrates, the burning of Pythagoras, whilst he was yet living, by the Cyloneans, the putting to death–and that with torture–of Zeno by the tyrant Demylus, and of Antiphon by Dionysius, with the letting of bran fall. But that there should be evil Genii placed by Providence over such charges,–how can it but be a reproach to God, as it would be to a king, to commit the administration of his provinces to evil and rash governors and captains, and suffer the best of his subjects to be despised and ill-treated by them? And furthermore, if there is much necessity mixed amongst affairs, then God has not power over them all, nor are they all administered according to his reason.

He contends much against Epicurus and those that take away providence from the conceptions we have of the gods, whom we esteem beneficial and gracious to men. And these things being frequently said by them, there is no necessity of setting down the words. Yet all do not conceive the gods to be good and favorable to us. For see what the Jews and Syrians think of the gods; consider also with how much superstition the poets are filled. But there is not any one, in a manner to speak of, that imagines God to be corruptible or to have been born. And to omit all others, Antipater the Tarsian, in his book of the gods writes thus, word for word: "At the opening of our discourse we will briefly repeat the opinion we have concerning God. We understand therefore God to be an animal, blessed and incorruptible, and beneficial to men." And then expounding every one of these terms he says: "And indeed all men esteem the gods to be incorruptible." Chrysippus therefore is, according to Antipater, not one of "all men"; for he thinks none of the gods, except Fire, to be incorruptible, but that they all equally were born and will die. These things are, in a manner, everywhere said by him. But I will set down his words out of his Third Book of the Gods: "It is otherwise with the gods. For some of them are born and corruptible, but others not born. And to demonstrate these things from the beginning will be more fit for a treatise of Nature. For the Sun, the Moon, and other gods who are of a like nature, were begotten; but Jupiter is eternal." And again going on: "But the like will be said concerning dying and being born, both concerning the other gods and Jupiter. For they indeed are corruptible, but his past incorruptible." With these I compare a few of the things said by Antipater: "Whosoever they are that take away from the gods beneficence, they affect in some part our conception of them; and according to the same reason they also do this, who think they participate of generation and corruption." If, then, he who esteems the gods corruptible is equally absurd with him who thinks them not to be provident and gracious to men, Chrysippus is no less in an error than Epicurus. For one of them deprives the gods of beneficence, the other of incorruptibility. ============ And moreover, Chrysippus, in his Third Book of the Gods treating of the other gods being nourished, says thus: "The other gods indeed use nourishment, being equally sustained by it; but Jupiter and the World are maintained after another manner from those who are consumed and were engendered by fire." Here indeed he declares, that all the other gods are nourished except the World and Jupiter; but in his First Book of Providence he says: "Jupiter increases till he has consumed all things into himself. For since death is the separation of the soul from the body, and the soul of the World is not indeed separated, but increases continually till it has consumed all matter into itself, it is not to be said that the World dies." Who can therefore appear to speak things more contradictory to himself than he who says that the same god is now nourished and again not nourished? Nor is there any need of gathering this by argument: for himself has plainly written in the same place: "But the World alone is said to be self-sufficient, because it alone has in itself all things it stands in need of, and is nourished and augmented of itself, the other parts being mutually changed into one another." He is then repugnant to himself, not only by declaring in one place that all the gods are nourished except the World and Jupiter, and saying in another, that the World also is nourished; but much more, when he affirms that the World increases by nourishing itself. Now the contrary had been much more probable, to wit, that the World alone does not increase, having its own destruction for its food; but that addition and increase are incident to the other gods, who are nourished from without, and the World is rather consumed into them, if so it is that the World feeds on itself, and they always receive something and are nourished from that.

Secondly, the conception of the gods contains in it felicity, blessedness, and self-perfection. Wherefore also Euripides is commanded for saying:–

> For God, if truly God, does nothing want,
> So all these speeches are the poets' cant.
> ("Hercules Furens," 1345.)

But Chrysippus in the places I have alleged says, that the World only is self-sufficient, because this alone has in itself all things it needs. What then follows from this, that the World alone is self-sufficient? That neither the Sun, Moon, nor any other of the gods is self-sufficient, and not being self-sufficient, they cannot be happy or blessed.

He says, that the infant in the womb is nourished by Nature, like a plant; but when it is brought forth, being cooled and hardened by the air, it changes its spirit and becomes an animal; whence the soul is not unfitly named Psyche because of this refrigeration [Greek omitted]. But again he esteems the soul the more subtile and fine spirit of Nature, therein contradicting himself; for how can a subtile thing be made of a gross one, and be rarefied by refrigeration and condensation? And what is more, how does he, declaring an animal to be made by refrigeration, think the sun to be animated, which is of fire and made of an exhalation changed into fire? For he says in his Third Book of Nature: "Now the change of fire is such, that it is turned by the air into water; and the earth subsiding from this, the air exhales; the air being subtilized, the ether is produced round about it; and the stars are, with the sun, kindled from the sea." Now what is more contrary to kindling than refrigeration, or to rarefaction than condensation? For the one makes water and earth of fire and air, and the other changes that which is moist and earthy into fire and air. But yet in one place he makes kindling, in another cooling, to be the beginning of animation. And he moreover says, that when the inflammation is throughout, it lives and is an animal, but being again extinct and thickened, it is turned into water and earth and corporeity. Now in his First Book of Providence he says: "For the world, indeed, being wholly set on fire, is presently also the soul and guide of itself; but when it is changed into moisture, and has altered the soul remaining within it by some method into a body and soul, so as to consist of these two it exists then after another manner." Here, forsooth, he plainly says, that the inanimate parts of the world are by inflammation turned into an animated thing, and that again by extinction the soul is relaxed and moistened, being changed into corporeity. He seems therefore very absurd, one while by refrigeration making animals of senseless things, and again, by the same changing the greatest part of the world's soul into senseless and inanimate things.

But besides this, his discourse concerning the generation of the soul has a demonstration contrary to his own opinion; or he says, that the soul is generated when the infant is already brought forth, the spirit being changed by refrigeration, as by hardening. Now for the soul's being engendered, and that after the birth, he chiefly uses this demonstration, that the children are for the most part in manners and inclinations like to their parents. Now the repugnancy of these things is evident. For it is not possible that the soul, which is not generated till after the birth, should have its inclination before the birth; or it will fall out that the soul is like before it is generated; that is, it will be in likeness, and yet not be, because it is not yet generated. But if any one says that, the likeness being bred in the tempers of the bodies, the souls are changed when they are generated, he destroys the argument of the soul's being generated. For thus it may come to pass, that the soul, though not generated, may at its entrance into the body be changed by the mixture of likeness.

He says sometimes, that the air is light and mounts upwards, and sometimes, that it is neither heavy nor light. For in his Second Book of Motion he says, that the fire, being without gravity, ascends upwards, and the air like to that; the water approaching more to the earth, and the air to the fire. But in his Physical Arts he inclines to the other opinion, that the air of itself has neither gravity nor levity.

He says that the air is by nature dark, and uses this as an argument of its being also the first cold; for that its darkness is opposite to the brightness, and its coldness to the heat of fire. Moving this in his First Book of Natural Questions, he again in his treatise of Habits says, that habits are nothing else but airs; for bodies are contained by these, and the cause that every one of the bodies contained in any habit is such as it is, is the containing air, which they call in iron hardness, in stone solidness, in silver whiteness. These words have in them much absurdity and contradiction. For if the air remains such as it is of its own nature, how comes black, in that which is not white, to be made whiteness; and soft, in that which is not hard, to be made hardness; and rare, in that which is not thick, to be made thickness? But if, being mixed with these, it is altered and made like to them, how is it a habit or power or cause of these things by which it is subdued? For such a change, by which it loses its own qualities, is the property of a patient, not of an agent, and not of a thing containing, but of a thing languishing. Yet they everywhere affirm, that matter, being of its own nature idle and motionless, is subjected to qualities, and that the qualities are spirits, which, being also aerial tensions, give a form and figure to every part of matter to which they adhere. These things they cannot rationally say, supposing the air to be such as they affirm it. For if it is a habit and tension, it will assimilate every body to itself, so that it shall be black and soft. But if by the mixture with these things it receives forms contrary to those it has, it will be in some sort the matter, and not the cause or power of matter.

It is often said by Chrysippus, that there is without the world an infinite vacuum, and that this infinity has neither beginning, middle, nor end. And by this the Stoics chiefly refute that spontaneous motion of the atoms downward, which is taught by Epicurus; there not being in infinity any difference according to which one thing is thought to be above, another below. But in his Fourth Book of Things Possible, having supposed a certain middle place and middle region, he says that the world is situated there. The words are these: "Wherefore, if it is to be said of the world that it is corruptible, this seems to want proof; yet nevertheless it rather appears to me to be so. However, its occupation of the place wherein it stands cooperates very much towards its immunity from corruption, because it is in the midst; since if it were conceived to be anywhere else, corruption would absolutely happen to it." And again, a little after: "For so also in a manner has essence happened eternally to possess the middle place, being immediately from the beginning such as it is; so that both by another manner and through this chance it admits not any corruption, and is therefore eternal." These words have one apparent and visible contradiction, to wit, his admitting a certain middle place and middle region infinity. They have also a second, more obscure indeed, but withal more absurd than this. For thinking that the world would not have remained incorruptible if its situation had happened to have been in any other part of the vacuum, he manifestly appears to have feared lest, the parts of essence moving towards the middle, there should be a dissolution and corruption of the world. Now this he would not have feared, had he not thought that bodies do by nature tend from every place towards the middle, not of essence, but of the region containing essence; of which also he has frequently spoken, as of a thing impossible and contrary to Nature; for that (as he says) there is not in the vacuum any difference by which bodies are drawn rather this way than that way, but the construction of the world is the cause of motion, bodies inclining and being carried from every side to the centre and middle of it. It is sufficient to this purpose, to set down the text out of his Second Book of Motion; for having discoursed, that the world indeed is a perfect body, but that the parts of the world are not perfect, because they have in some sort respect to the whole and are not of themselves; and going forward concerning its motion, as having been framed by Nature to be moved by all its parts towards compaction and cohesion, and not towards dissolution and breaking, he says thus: "But the universe thus tending and being moved to the same point, and the arts having the same motion from the nature of the body, it is probable that all bodies have this first motion according to Nature towards the centre of the world,–the world being thus moved as concerns itself, and the parts being moved as being its parts." What, then, ailed you, good sir (might some one say to him), that you have so far forgotten those words, as to affirm that the world, if it had not casually possessed the middle place, would have been dissoluble and corruptible? For if it is by nature so framed as always to incline towards the middle, and its parts from every side tend to the same, into what place soever of the vacuum it should have been transposed,–thus containing and (as it were) embracing itself,–it would have remained incorruptible and without danger of breaking. For things that are broken and dissipated suffer this by the separation and dissolution of their parts, every one of them hasting to its own place from that which it had contrary to Nature. But you, being of opinion that, if the world should have been seated in any other place of the vacuum, it would have been wholly liable to corruption, and affirming the same, and therefore asserting a middle in that which naturally can have no middle,–to wit, in that which is infinite,–have indeed dismissed these tensions, coherences, and inclinations, as having nothing available to its preservation, and attributed all the cause of its permanency to the possession of place. And, as if you were ambitious to confute yourself, to the things you have said before you join this also: "In whatsoever manner every one of the parts moves, being coherent to the rest, it is agreeable to reason that in the same also the whole should move by itself; yea, though we should, for argument's sake, imagine and suppose it to be in some vacuity of this world; for as, being kept in on every side, it would move towards the middle, so it would continue in the same motion, though by way of disputation we should admit that there were on a sudden a vacuum round about it." No part then whatsoever, though encompassed by a vacuum, loses its inclination moving it towards the middle of the world; but the world itself, if chance had not prepared it a place in the middle, would have lost its containing vigor, the parts of its essence being carried some one way, some another.

And these things indeed contain great contradictions to natural reason; but this is also repugnant to the doctrine concerning God and Providence, that assigning to them the least causes, he takes from them the most principal and greatest. For what is more principal than the permanency of the world, or that its essence, united in its parts, is contained in itself? But this, as Chrysippus says, fell out casually. For if the possession of place is the cause of incorruptibility, and this was the production of chance, it is manifest that the preservation of the universe is a work of chance, and not of Fate and Providence.

Now, as for his doctrine of possibles, how can it but be repugnant to his doctrine of Fate? For if that is not possible which either is true or shall be true, as Diodorus has it, but everything which is capable of being, though it never shall be, is possible, there will be many things possible which will never be according to invincible, inviolable, and all-conquering Fate. And thus either Fate will lose its power; or if that, as Chrysippus thinks, has existence, that which is susceptible of being will often fall out to be impossible. And everything indeed which is true will be necessary, being comprehended by the principal of all necessities; and everything that is false will be impossible, having the greatest cause to oppose its ever being true. For how is it possible that he should be susceptible of dying on the land, who is destined to die at sea? And how is it possible for him who is at Megara to come to Athens, if he is prohibited by Fate?

But moreover, the things that are boldly asserted by him concerning fantasies or imaginations are very opposite to Fate. For desiring to show that fantasy is not of itself a perfect cause of consent, he says, that the Sages will prejudice us by imprinting false imaginations in our minds, if fantasies do of themselves absolutely cause consent; for wise men often make use of falsity against the wicked, representing a probable imagination,–which is yet not the cause of consent, for then it would be also a cause of false apprehension and error. Any one therefore, transferring these things from the wise man to Fate, may say, that consents are not caused by Fate; for if they were, false consents and opinions and deceptions would also be by Fate. Thus the reason which exempts the wise man from doing hurt also demonstrates at the same time that Fate is not the cause of all things. For if men neither opine nor are prejudiced by Fate, it is manifest also that they neither act rightly nor are wise nor remain firm in their sentiments nor have utility by Fate, but that there is an end of Fate's being the cause of all things. Now if any one shall say that Chrysippus makes not Fate the absolute cause of all things, but only a PROCATARCLICAL (or antecedent) one, he will again show that he is contradictory to himself, since he excessively praises Homer for saying of Jupiter,

> Receive whatever good or ill
> He sends to each of you;

as also Euripides for these words,

> O Jove, how can I say that wretched we,
> Poor mortals, aught do understand? On thee
> We all depend, and nothing can transact,
> But as thy sacred wisdom shall enact.
> (Euripides, "Suppliants," 734.)

And himself writes many things agreeable to these. In fine, he says that nothing, be it never so little, either rests or is moved otherwise than according to the reason of Jupiter, which is the same thing with Fate. Moreover, the antecedent cause is weaker than the absolute one, and attains not to its effect when it is subdued by others that rise up against it. But he himself declaring Fate to be an invincible, unimpeachable, and inflexible cause, calls it Atropos, (That is, Unchangeable.) Adrasteia, (That is, Unavoidable.) Necessity, and Pepromene (as putting a limit to all things). Whether then shall we say, that neither consents nor virtues nor vices nor doing well nor doing ill is in our power? Or shall we affirm, that Fate is deficient, that terminating destiny is unable to determine, and that the motions and habits of Jupiter cannot be effective? For the one of these two consequences will follow from Fate's being an absolute, the other from its being only an antecedent cause. For if it is an absolute cause, it takes away our free will and leaves nothing in our control; and if it is only antecedent, it loses its being unimpeachable and effectual. For not once or ten times, but everywhere, especially in his Physics, he has written, that there are many obstacles and impediments to particular natures and motions, but none to that of the universe. And how can the motion of the universe, extending as it does to particular ones, be undisturbed and unimpeached, if these are stopped and hindered? For neither can the nature of man be free from impediment, if that of the foot or hand is not so; nor can the motion of a ship but be hindered, if there are any obstacles about the sails or the operation of the oars.

Besides all this, if the fantasies are not according to Fate, neither are they causes of consents; but if, because it imprints fantasies leading to consent, the consents are said to be according to Fate, how is it not contrary to itself, imprinting in the greatest matters different imaginations and such as draw the understanding contrary ways? For (they say) those who adhere to one of them, and withhold not their consent, do amiss: if they yield to obscure things, they stumble; if to false, they are deceived; if to such as are not commonly comprehended, they opine. And yet one of these three is of necessity,—either that every fantasy is not the work of Fate, or that every receipt and consent of fantasy is faultless, or that Fate itself is not irreprehensible. For I do not know how it can be blameless, proposing to us such fantasies that not the resisting or going against them, but the following and yielding to them, is blamable. Moreover, both Chrysippus and Antipater, in their disputes against the Academics, take not a little pains to prove that we neither act nor are incited without consent, saying, that they build on fictions and false suppositions who think that, a proper fantasy being presented, we are presently incited, without having either yielded or consented. Again, Chrysippus says, that God imprints in us false imaginations, as does also the wise man; not that they would have us consent or yield to them, but only that we should act and be incited with regard to that which appears; but we, being evil, do through infirmity consent to such fantasies. Now, the perplexity and discrepancy of these discourses among themselves are not very difficult to be discerned. For he that would not have men consent but only act according to the fantasies which he offers unto them—whether he be God or a wise man—knows that the fantasies are sufficient for acting, and that consents are superfluous. For if, knowing that the imagination gives us not an instinct to work without consent, he ministers to us false and probable fantasies, he is the voluntary cause of our falling and erring by assenting to incomprehensible things.

The Eating of Flesh

TRACT I. YOU ASK of me then for what reason it was that Pythagoras abstained from eating of flesh. I for my part do much wonder in what humor, with what soul or reason, the first man with his mouth touched slaughter, and reached to his lips the flesh of a dead animal, and having set before people courses of ghastly corpses and ghosts, could give those parts the names of meat and victuals, that but a little before lowed, cried, moved, and saw; how his sight could endure the blood of slaughtered, flayed, and mangled bodies; how his smell could bear their scent; and how the very nastiness happened not to offend the taste, while it chewed the sores of others, and participated of the saps and juices of deadly wounds.

> Crept the raw hides, and with a bellowing sound
> Roared the dead limbs; the burning entrails groaned.
> ("Odyssey," xii. 395.)

This indeed is but a fiction and fancy; but the fare itself is truly monstrous and prodigious,—that a man should have a stomach to creatures while they yet bellow, and that he should be giving directions which of things yet alive and speaking is fittest to make food of, and ordering the several kinds of the seasoning and dressing them and serving them up to tables. You ought rather, in my opinion, to have inquired who first began this practice, than who of late times left it off.

And truly, as for those people who first ventured upon eating of flesh, it is very probable that the whole reason of their so doing was scarcity and want of other food; for it is not likely that their living together in lawless and extravagant lusts, or their growing wanton and capricious through the excessive variety of provisions then among them, brought them to such unsociable pleasures as these, against Nature. Yea, had they at this instant but their sense and voice restored to them, I am persuaded they would express themselves to this purpose:

"Oh! happy you, and highly favored of the gods, who now live! Into what an age of the world are you fallen, who share and enjoy among you a plentiful portion of good things! What abundance of things spring up for your use! What fruitful vineyards you enjoy! What wealth you gather from the fields! What delicacies from trees and plants, which you may gather! You may glut and fill yourselves without being polluted. As for us, we fell upon the most dismal and affrighting part of time, in which we were exposed by our production to manifold and inextricable wants and necessities. As yet the thickened air concealed the heaven from our view, and the stars were as yet confused with a disorderly huddle of fire and moisture and violent fluxions of winds. As yet the sun was not fixed to a regular and certain course, so as to separate morning and evening, nor did the seasons return in order crowned with wreaths from the fruitful harvest. The land was also spoiled by the inundations of disorderly rivers; and a great part of it was deformed with marshes, and utterly wild by reason of deep quagmires, unfertile forests, and woods. There was then no production of tame fruits, nor any instruments of art or invention of wit. And hunger gave no time, nor did seed-time then stay for the yearly season. What wonder is it if we made use of the flesh of beasts contrary to Nature, when mud was eaten and the bark of wood, and when it was thought a happy thing to find either a sprouting grass or a root of any plant! But when they had by chance tasted of or eaten an acorn, they danced for very joy about some oak or esculus, calling it by the names of life-giver, mother, and nourisher. And this was the only festival that those times were acquainted with; upon all other occasions, all things were full of anguish and dismal sadness. But whence is it that a certain ravenousness and frenzy drives you in these happy days to pollute yourselves with blood, since you have such an abundance of things necessary for your subsistence? Why do you belie the earth as unable to maintain you? Why do you profane the lawgiver Ceres, and shame the mild and gentle Bacchus, as not furnishing you with sufficiency? Are you not ashamed to mix tame fruits with blood and slaughter? You are indeed wont to call serpents, leopards, and lions savage creatures; but yet yourselves are defiled with blood, and come nothing behind them in cruelty. What they kill is their ordinary nourishment, but what you kill is your better fare."

For we eat not lions and wolves by way of revenge; but we let those go, and catch the harmless and tame sort, and such as have neither stings nor teeth to bite with, and slay them; which, so may Jove help us, Nature seems to us to have produced for their beauty and comeliness only. [Just as if one seeing the river Nilus overflowing its banks, and thereby filling the whole country with genial and fertile moisture, should not at all admire that secret power in it that produces plants and plenteousness of most sweet and useful fruits, but beholding somewhere a crocodile swimming in it, or an asp crawling along, or mice (savage and filthy creatures), should presently affirm these to be the occasion of all that is amiss, or of any want or defect that may happen. Or as if indeed one contemplating this land or ground, how full it is of tame fruits, and how heavy with ears of corn, should afterwards espy somewhere in these same cornfields an ear of darnel or a wild vetch, and thereupon neglect to reap and gather in the corn, and fall a complaining of these. Such another thing it would be, if one–listening to the harangue of some advocate at some bar or pleading, swelling and enlarging and hastening towards the relief of some impending danger, or else, by Jupiter, in the impeaching and charging of certain audacious villanies or indictments, flowing and rolling along, and that not in a simple and poor strain, but with many sorts of passions all at once, or rather indeed with all sorts, in one and the same manner, into the many and various and differing minds of either hearers or judges that he is either to turn and change, or else, by Jupiter, to soften, appease, and quiet–should overlook all this business, and never consider or reckon upon the labor or struggle he had undergone, but pick up certain loose expressions, which the rapid motion of the discourse had carried along with it, as by the current of its course, and so had slipped and escaped the rest of the oration, and, hereupon undervalue the orator.]

But we are nothing put out of countenance, either by the beauteous gayety of the colors, or by the charmingness of the musical voices, or by the rare sagacity of the intellects, or by the cleanliness and neatness of diet, or by the rare discretion and prudence of these poor unfortunate animals; but for the sake of some little mouthful of flesh, we deprive a soul of the sun and light, and of that proportion of life and time it had been born into the world to enjoy. And then we fancy that the voices it utters and screams forth to us are nothing else but certain inarticulate sounds and noises, and not the several deprecations, entreaties, and pleadings of each of them, as it were saying thus to us: "I deprecate not thy necessity (if such there be), but thy wantonness. Kill me for thy feeding, but do not take me off for thy better feeding." O horrible cruelty! It is truly an affecting sight to see the very table of rich people laid before them, who keep them cooks and caterers to furnish them with dead corpses for their daily fare; but it is yet more affecting to see it taken away, for the mammocks remaining are more than that which was eaten. These therefore were slain to no purpose. Others there are, who are so offended by what is set before them that they will not suffer it to be cut or sliced; thus abstaining from them when dead, while they would not spare them when alive.

Well, then, we understand that that sort of men are used to say, that in eating of flesh they follow the conduct and direction of Nature. But that it is not natural to mankind to feed on flesh, we first of all demonstrate from the very shape and figure of the body. For a human body no ways resembles those that were born for ravenousness; it hath no hawk's bill, no sharp talon, no roughness of teeth, no such strength of stomach or heat of digestion, as can be sufficient to convert or alter such heavy and fleshy fare. But even from hence, that is, from the smoothness of the tongue, and the slowness of the stomach to digest, Nature seems to disclaim all pretence to fleshy victuals. But if you will contend that yourself was born to an inclination to such food as you have now a mind to eat, do you then yourself kill what you would eat. But do it yourself, without the help of a chopping-knife, mallet, or axe,–as wolves, bears, and lions do, who kill and eat at once. Rend an ox with thy teeth, worry a hog with thy mouth, tear a lamb or a hare in pieces, and fall on and eat it alive as they do. But if thou hadst rather stay until what thou greatest is become dead, and if thou art loath to force a soul out of its body, why then dost thou against Nature eat an animate thing? Nay, there is nobody that is willing to eat even a lifeless and a dead thing as it is; but they boil it, and roast it, and alter it by fire and medicines, as it were, changing and quenching the slaughtered gore with thousands of sweet sauces, that the palate being thereby deceived may admit of such uncouth fare. It was indeed a witty expression of a Lacedaemonian, who, having purchased a small fish in a certain inn, delivered it to his landlord to be dressed; and as he demanded cheese, and vinegar, and oil to make sauce, he replied, if I had had those, I would not have bought the fish. But we are grown so wanton in our bloody luxury, that we have bestowed upon flesh the name of meat [Greek omitted], and then require another seasoning [Greek omitted], to this same flesh, mixing oil, wine, honey, pickle, and vinegar, with Syrian and Arabian spices, as though we really meant to embalm it after its disease. Indeed when things are dissolved and made thus tender and soft, and are as it were turned into a sort of a carrionly corruption, it must needs be a great difficulty for concoction to master them, and when it hath mastered them, they must needs cause grievous oppressions and qualmy indigestions.

Diogenes ventured once to eat a raw pourcontrel, that he might disuse himself from meat dressed by fire; and as several priests and other people stood round him, he wrapped his head in his cassock, and so putting the fish to his mouth, he thus said unto them: It is for your sake, sirs, that I undergo this danger, and run this risk. A noble and gallant risk, by Jupiter! For far otherwise than as Pelopidas ventured his life for the liberty of the Thebans, and Harmodius and Aristogiton for that of the Athenians, did this philosopher encounter with a raw pourcontrel, to the end he might make human life more brutish. Moreover, these same flesh-eatings not only are preternatural to men's bodies, but also by clogging and cloying them, they render their very minds and intellects gross. For it is well known to most, that wine and much flesh-eating make the body indeed strong and lusty, but the mind weak and feeble. And that I may not offend the wrestlers, I will make use of examples out of my own country. The Athenians are wont to call us Boeotians gross, senseless, and stupid fellows, for no other reason but our over-much eating; by Pindar we are called hogs, for the same reason. Menander the comedian calls us "fellows with long jaws." It is observed also that, according to the saying of Heraclitus, "the wisest soul is like a dry light." Earthen jars, if you strike them, will sound; but if they be full, they perceive not the strokes that are given them. Copper vessels also that are thin communicate the sound round about them, unless some one stop and dull the ambient stroke with his fingers. Moreover, the eye, when seized with an over-great plenitude of humors, grows dim and feeble for its ordinary work. When we behold the sun through a humid air and a great quantity of gross and indigested vapors, we see it not clear and bright, but obscure and cloudy, and with glimmering beams. Just so in a muddy and clogged body, that is swagged down with heavy and unnatural nourishments; it must needs happen that the gayety and splendor of the mind be confused and dulled, and that it ramble and roll after little and scarce discernible objects, since it wants clearness and vigor for higher things.

But to pass by these considerations, is not accustoming one's self to mildness and a human temper of mind an admirable thing? For who would wrong or injure a man that is so sweetly and humanly disposed with respect to the ills of strangers that are not of his kind? I remember that three days ago, as I was discoursing, I made mention of a saying of Xenocrates, and how the Athenians gave judgment upon a certain person who had flayed a living ram. For my part I cannot think him a worse criminal that torments a poor creature while living, than a man that shall take away its life and murder it. But (as it seems) we are more sensible of what is done against custom than against Nature. There, however, I discussed these matters in a more popular style. But as for that grand and mysterious principle which (as Plato speaks) is incredible to base minds and to such as affect only mortal things, I as little care to move it in this discourse as a pilot doth a ship in a storm, or a comedian his machine while the scenes are moving; but perhaps it would not be amiss, by way of introduction and preface, to repeat certain verses of Empedocles.... For in these, by way of allegory, he hints at men's souls, as that they are tied to mortal bodies, to be punished for murders, eating of flesh and of one another, although this doctrine seems much, ancienter than his time. For the fables that are storied and related about the discerption of Bacchus, and the attempts of the Titans upon him, and of their tasting of his slain body, and of their several punishments and fulminations afterwards, are but a representation of the regeneration. For what in us is unreasonable, disorderly, and boisterous, being not divine but demoniac, the ancients termed Titans, that is, TORMENTED and PUNISHED (from [Greek omitted])....

TRACT II. Reason persuades us now to return with fresh cogitations and dispositions to what we left cold yesterday of our discourse about flesh-eating. It is indeed a hard and a difficult task to undertake (as Cato once said) to dispute with men's bellies, that have no ears; since most have already drunk that draught of custom, which is like that of Ciree,

> Of groans and frauds and sorcery replete.

> *("Odyssey," x. 234.)*

And it is no easy task to pull out the hook of flesh-eating from the jaws of such as have gorged themselves with luxury and are (as it were) nailed down with it. It would indeed be a good action, if as the Egyptians draw out the stomach of a dead body, and cut it open and expose it to the sun, as the only cause of all its evil actions, so we could, by cutting out our gluttony and blood-shedding, purify and cleanse the remainder of our lives. For the stomach itself is not guilty of bloodshed, but is involuntarily polluted by our intemperance. But if this may not be, and we are ashamed by reason of custom to live unblamably, let us at least sin with discretion. Let us eat flesh; but let it be for hunger and not for wantonness. Let us kill an animal; but let us do it with sorrow and pity, and not abusing and tormenting it, as many nowadays are used to do, while some run red-hot spits through the bodies of swine, that by the tincture of the quenched iron the blood may be to that degree mortified, that it may sweeten and soften the flesh in its circulation; others jump and stamp upon the udders of sows that are ready to pig, that so they may crush into one mass (O Piacular Jupiter!) in the very pangs of delivery, blood, milk, and the corruption of the mashed and mangled young ones, and so eat the most inflamed part of the animal; others sew up the eyes of cranes and swans, and so shut them up in darkness to be fattened, and then souse up their flesh with certain monstrous mixtures and pickles.

By all which it is most manifest, that it is not for nourishment, or want, or any necessity, but for mere gluttony, wantonness, and expensiveness, that they make a pleasure of villany. Just as it happens in persons who cannot satiate their passion upon women, and having made trial of everything else and falling into vagaries, at last attempt things not to be mentioned; even so inordinateness in feeding, when it hath once passed the bounds of nature and necessity, studies at last to diversify the lusts of its intemperate appetite by cruelty and villany. For the senses, when they once quit their natural measures, sympathize with each other in their distempers, and are enticed by each other to the same consent and intemperance. Thus a distempered ear first debauched music, the soft and effeminate notes of which provoke immodest touches and lascivious tickling. These things first taught the eye not to delight in Pyrrhic dances, gesticulations of hands, or elegant pantomimes, nor in statues and fine paintings; but to reckon the slaughtering and death of mankind and wounds and duels the most sumptuous of shows and spectacles. Thus unlawful tables are accompanied with intemperate copulations, with unmusicianlike balls, and theatres become monstrous through shameful songs and rehearsals; and barbarous and brutish shows are again accompanied with an unrelenting temper and savage cruelty towards mankind. Hence it was that the divine Lycurgus in his Three Books of Laws gave orders that the doors and ridges of men's houses should be made with a saw and an axe, and that no other instrument should so much as be brought to any house. Not that he did hereby intend to declare war against augers and planes and other instruments of finer work; but because he very well knew that with such tools as these you will never bring into your house a gilded couch, and that you will never attempt to bring into a slender cottage either silver tables, purple carpets, or costly stones; but that a plain supper and a homely dinner must accompany such a house, couch table, and cup. The beginning of a vicious diet is presently followed by all sorts of luxury and expensiveness,

Ev'n as a mare is by her thirsty colt.

And what meal is not expensive? One for which no animal is put to death. Shall we reckon a soul to be a small expense? I will not say perhaps of a mother, or a father, or of some friend, or child, as Empedocles did; but one participating of feeling, of seeing, of hearing, of imagination, and of intellection; which each animal hath received from Nature for the acquiring of what is agreeable to it, and the avoiding what is disagreeable. Do but consider this with yourself now, which sort of philosophers render us most tame and civil, they who bid people to feed on their children, friends, fathers, and wives, when they are dead; or Pythagoras and Empedocles, that accustom men to be just towards even the other members of the creation. You laugh at a man that will not eat a sheep: but we (they will say again)–when we see you cutting off the parts of your dead father or mother, and sending it to your absent friends, and calling upon and inviting your present friends to eat the rest freely and heartily–shall we not smile? Nay, peradventure we offend at this instant time while we touch these books, without having first cleansed our hands, eyes, feet, and ears; if it be not (by Jupiter) a sufficient purgation of them to have discoursed of these matters in potable and fresh language (as Plato speaketh), thereby washing off the brackishness of hearing. Now if a man should set these books and discourses in opposition to each other, he will find that the philosophy of the one sort suits with the Seythians, Sogdians, and Melanchlaenians, of whom Herodotus's relation is scarce believed; but the sentiments of Pythagoras and Empedocles were the laws and customs of the ancients Grecians.

Who, then, were the first authors of this opinion, that we owe no justice to dumb animals?

Who first beat out accursed steel,
And made the lab'ring ox a knife to feel.

In the very same manner oppressors and tyrants begin first to shed blood. For example, the first man that the Athenians ever put to death was one of the basest of all knaves, who had the reputation of deserving it; after him they put to death a second and a third. After this, being now accustomed to blood, they patiently saw Niceratus the son of Nicias, and their own general Theramenes, and Polemarchus the philosopher suffer death. Even so, in the beginning, some wild and mischievous beast was killed and eaten, and then some little bird or fish was entrapped. And the desire of slaughter, being first experimented and exercised in these, at last passed even to the laboring ox, and the sheep that clothes us, and to the poor cock that keeps the house; until by little and little, unsatiableness, being strengthened by use, men came to the slaughter of men, to bloodshed and wars. Now even if one cannot demonstrate and make out, that souls in their regenerations make a promiscuous use of all bodies, and that that which is now rational will at another time be irrational, and that again tame which is now wild,–for that Nature changes and transmutes everything,

With different fleshy coats new clothing all,–

this thing should be sufficient to change and show men, that it is a savage and intemperate habit, that it brings sickness and heaviness upon the body, and that it inclines the mind the more brutishly to bloodshed and destruction, when we have once accustomed ourselves neither to entertain a guest nor keep a wedding nor to treat our friends without blood and slaughter.

And if what is argued about the return of souls into bodies is not of force enough to beget faith, yet methinks the very uncertainty of the thing should fill us with apprehension and fear. Suppose, for instance, one should in some night-engagement run on with his drawn sword upon one that had fallen down and covered his body with his arms, and should in the meantime hear one say, that he was not very sure, but that he fancied and believed, that the party lying there was his own son, brother, father, or tent-companion; which were more advisable, think you,–to hearken to a false suggestion, and so to let go an enemy under the notion of a friend, or to slight an authority not sufficient to beget faith, and to slay a friend instead of a foe? This you will all say would be insupportable. Do but consider the famous Merope in the tragedy, who taking up a hatchet, and lifting it at her son's head, whom she took for her son's murderer, speaks thus as she was ready to give the fatal blow,

Villain, this holy blow shall cleave thy head;
(Euripides, "Cresphontes," Frag. 457.)

what a bustle she raises in the whole theatre while she raises herself to give the blow, and what a fear they are all in, lest she should prevent the old man that comes to stop her hand, and should wound the youth. Now if another old man should stand by her and say, "Strike, it is thy enemy," and this, "Hold, it is thy son"; which, think you, would be the greater injustice, to omit the punishing of an enemy for the sake of one's child, or to suffer one's self to be so carried away with anger at an enemy as to slay one's child? Since then neither hatred nor wrath nor any revenge nor fear for ourselves carries us to the slaughter of a beast, but the poor sacrifice stands with an inclined neck, only to satisfy thy lust and pleasure, and then one philosopher stands by and tells thee, "Cut him down, it is but an unreasonable animal," and another cries, "Hold, what if there should be the soul of some kinsman or god enclosed in him?"–good gods! is there the like danger if I refuse to eat flesh, as if I for want of faith murder my child or some other friend?

The Stoics' way of reasoning upon this subject of flesh-eating is no way equal nor consonant with themselves. Who is this that hath so many mouths for his belly and the kitchen? Whence comes it to pass, that they so very much womanize and reproach pleasure, as a thing that they will not allow to be either good or preferable, or so much as agreeable, and yet all on a sudden become so zealous advocates for pleasures? It were indeed but a reasonable consequence of their doctrine, that, since they banish perfumes and cakes from their banquets, they should be much more averse to blood and to flesh. But now, just as if they would reduce their philosophy to their account-books, they lessen the expenses of their suppers in certain unnecessary and needless matters, but the untamed and murderous part of their expense they nothing boggle at. "Well! What then?" say they. "We have nothing to do with brute beasts." Nor have you any with perfumes, nor with foreign sauces, may some one answer; therefore leave these out of your banquets, if you are driving out everything that is both useless and needless.

Let us therefore in the next place consider, whether we owe any justice to the brute beasts. Neither shall we handle this point artificially, or like subtle sophisters, but by casting our eye into our own breasts, and conversing with ourselves as men, we will weigh and examine the whole matter....

Concerning Fate

("THIS LITTLE TREATISE is so pitiously torne, maimed, and dismembred thorowout, that a man may sooner divine and guess thereat (as I have done) than translate it."–HOLLAND.)

I will endeavor, my dearest Piso, to send you my opinion concerning Fate, written with all the clearness and compendiousness I am capable of; since you, who are not ignorant how cautious I am of writing, have thought fit to make it the subject of your request.

You are first, then, to know that this word Fate is spoken and understood two manner of ways; the one as it is an energy, the other as it is a substance. First, therefore, as it is an action, Plato (See Plato, "Phaedrus," p. 248 C; "Timaeus," p.41 E; "Republic," x. p.617 D.) has under a type described it, saying thus in his dialogue entitled Phaedrus: "And this is a sanction of Adrastea (or an inevitable ordinance), that whatever soul being an attendant on God," &c. And in his treatise called Timaeus: "The laws which God in the nature of the universe has established for immortal souls." And in his book of a Commonweal he entitles Fate "the speech of the virgin Lachesis, who is the daughter of Necessity." By which sentences he not tragically but theologically shows us what his sentiments are in this matter. Now if any one, paraphrasing the fore-cited passages, would have them expressed in more familiar terms, the description in Phaedrus may be thus explained: That Fate is a divine sentence, intransgressible since its cause cannot be divested or hindered. And according to what he has said in his Timaeus, it is a law ensuing on the nature of the universe, according to which all things that are done are transacted. For this does Lachesis effect, who is indeed the daughter of Necessity,–as we have both already related, and shall yet better understand by that which will be said in the progress of our discourse. Thus you see what Fate is, when it is taken for an action.

But as it is a substance, it seems to be the universal soul of the world, and admits of a threefold distribution; the first destiny being that which errs not; the second, that which is thought to err; and the third that which, being under the heaven, is conversant about the earth. Of these, the highest is called Clotho, the next Atropos, and the lowest, Lachesis; who, receiving the celestial influences and efficacies of her sisters, transmits and fastens them to the terrestrial things which are under her government. Thus have we declared briefly what is to be said of Fate, taken as a substance; what it is, what are its parts, after what manner it is, how it is ordained, and how it stands, both in respect to itself and to us. But as to the particularities of these things, there is another fable in his Commonweal, by which they are in some measure covertly insinuated, and we ourselves have, in the best manner we can, endeavored to explain them to you.

But we now once again turn our discourse to Fate, as it is an energy. For concerning this it is that there are so many natural, moral, and logical questions. Having therefore already in some sort sufficiently defined what it is, we are now in the next place to say something of its quality, although it may to many seem absurd. I say then that Fate, though comprehending as it were in a circle the infinity of all those things which are and have been from infinite times and shall be to infinite ages, is not in itself infinite, but determinate and finite; for neither law, reason, nor any other divine thing can be infinite. And this you will the better understand, if you consider the total revolution and the total time in which the revolutions of the eight circles (that is, of the eight spheres of the fixed stars, sun, moon, and five planets), having (as Timaeus (Plato, "Timaeus," p.39 D.) says) finished their course, return to one and the same point, being measured by the circle of the Same, which goes always after one manner. For in this order, which is finite and determinate, shall all things (which, as well in heaven as in earth, consist by necessity from above) be reduced to the same situation, and restored again to their first beginning. Wherefore the habitude of heaven alone, being thus ordained in all things, as well in regard of itself as of the earth and all terrestrial matters, shall again (after long revolutions) one day return; and those things that in order follow after, and being linked together in a continuity are maintained in their course, shall follow, every one of them by necessity bringing what is its own. But for the better clearing of this matter, let us understand that whatever is in us or about us is not wrought by the course of the heavens and heavenly influences, as being entirely the efficient cause both of my writing what I now write, and of your doing also what you at present do, and in the same manner as you do it. Hereafter, then, when the same cause shall return, we shall do the same things we now do and in the same manner, and shall again become the same men; and so it will be with all others. And that which follows after shall also happen by the following cause; and in brief, all things that shall happen in the whole and in every one of these universal revolutions shall again become the same. By this it appears (as we have said before) that Fate, being in some sort infinite, is nevertheless determinate and finite; and it may be also in some sort seen and comprehended, as we have farther said, that it is as it were a circle. For as a motion of a circle is a circle, and the time that measures it is also a circle; so the order of things which are done and happen in a circle may be justly esteemed and called a circle.

This, therefore, though there should be nothing else, almost shows us what sort of thing Fate is; but not particularly or in every respect. What kind of thing then is it in its own form? It is, as far as one can compare it, like to the civil or politic law. For first it orders the most part of things at least, if not all, conditionally; and then it comprises (as far as is possible for it) all things that belong to the public in general; and the better to make you understand both the one and the other, we must specify them by an example. The civil law speaks and ordains in general of a valiant man, and also of a deserter and a coward; and in the same manner of others. Now this is not to make the law speak of this or that man in particular, but principally to propose such things as are universal or general, and consequently such as fall under them. For we may very well say, that it is legal to reward this from his colors; because the law has virtually–though not in express terms and particularly yet in such general ones as they are comprehended under,–so determined of them. As the law (if I may so speak) of physicians and masters of corporal exercises potentially comprehends particular and special things within the general; so the law of Nature, determining first and principally general matters, secondarily and subordinately determines such as are particular. Thus, general things being decreed by Fate, particular and individual things may also in some sort be said to be so, because they are so by consequence with the general. But perhaps some one of those who more accurately examine and more subtly search into these things may say, on the contrary, that particular and individual things precede the composition of general things, and that the general exist only for the particular, since that for which another thing is always goes before that which is for it. Nevertheless, this is not the proper place to treat of this difficulty, but it is to be remitted to another. However, that Fate comprehends not all things clearly and expressly, but only such as are universal and general, let it pass for resolved on at present, as well for what we have already said a little before, as for what we shall say hereafter. For that which is finite and determinate, agreeing properly with divine Providence, is seen more in universal and general things than in particular; such therefore is the divine law, and also the civil; but infinity consists in particulars and individuals.

After this we are to declare what this term "conditionally" means; for it is to be thought that Fate is also some such thing. That, then, is said to be conditionally, which is supposed to exist not of itself or absolutely, but as really dependent upon and joined to another; which signifies a suit and consequence. "And this is the sanction of Adrastea (or an inevitable ordinance), that whatever soul, being an attendant on God, shall see anything of truth, shall till another revolution be exempt from punishment; and if it is ever able to do the same, it shall never suffer any damage." This is said both conditionally and also universally. Now that Fate is some such thing is clearly manifest, as well from its substance as from its name. For it is called [Greek omitted] as being [Greek omitted], that is, dependent and linked; and it is a sanction or law, because things are therein ordained and disposed consequentially, as is usual in civil government.

We ought in the next place to consider and treat of mutual relation and affection; that is, what reference and respect Fate has to divine Providence, what to Fortune, what also to "that which is in our power," what to contingent and other such like things; and furthermore we are to determine, how far and in what it is true or false that all things happen and are done by and according to Fate. For if the meaning is, that all things are comprehended and contained in Fate, it must be granted that this proposition is true; and if any would farther have it so understood, that all things which are done amongst men, on earth, and in heaven are placed in Fate, let this also pass as granted for the present. But if (as the expression seems rather to imply) the "being done according to Fate" signifies not all things, but only that which is a direct consequent of Fate, then it must not be said that all things happen and are done by and according to Fate, though all things are so according to Fate as to be comprised in it. For all things that the law comprehends and of which it speaks are not legal or according to law; for it comprehends treason, it treats of the cowardly running away from one's colors in time of battle, of adultery, and many other such like things, of which it cannot be said that any one of them is lawful. Neither indeed can I affirm of the performing a valorous act in war, the killing of a tyrant, or the doing any other virtuous deed, that it is legal; because that only is proper to be called legal, which is commanded by the law. Now if the law commands these things, how can they avoid being rebels against the law and transgressors of it, who neither perform valiant feats of arms, kill tyrants, nor do any other such remarkable acts of virtue? And if they are transgressors of the law, why is it not just they should be punished? But if this is not reasonable, it must then be also confessed that these things are not legal or according to law; but that legal and according to law is only that which is particularly prescribed and expressly commanded by the law, in any action whatsoever. In like manner, those things only are fatal and according to Fate, which are the consequences of causes preceding in the divine disposition. So that Fate indeed comprehends all things which are done; yet many of those things that are comprehended in it, and almost all that precede, should not (to speak properly) be pronounced to be fatal or according to Fate.

These things being so, we are next in order to show, how "that which is in our power" (or free will), Fortune, possible, contingent, and other like things which are placed among the antecedent causes, can consist with Fate, and Fate with them; for Fate, as it seems, comprehends all things, and yet all these things will not happen by necessity, but every one of them according to the principle of its nature. Now the nature of the possible is to presubsist, as the genus, and to go before the contingent; and the contingent, as the matter and subject, is to be in the sphere of free will; and our free will ought as a master to make use of the contingent; and Fortune comes in by the side of free will, through the property of the contingent of inclining to either part. Now you will more easily apprehend what has been said, if you shall consider that everything which is generated, and the generation itself, is not done without a generative faculty or power, and the power is not without a substance. As for example, neither the generation of man, nor that which is generated, is without a power; but this power is about man, and man himself is the substance. Now the power or faculty is between the substance, which is the powerful, and the generation and the thing generated, which are both possibles. There being then these three things, the power, the powerful, and the possible; before the power can exist, the powerful must of necessity be presupposed as its subject, and the power must also necessarily subsist before the possible. By this deduction then may in some measure be understood what is meant by possible; which may be grossly defined as "that which power is able to produce;" or yet more exactly, if to this same there be added, "provided there be nothing from without to hinder or obstruct it." Now of possible things there are some which can never be hindered, as are those in heaven, to wit, the rising and setting of the stars, and the like to these; but others may indeed be hindered, as are the most part of human things, and many also of those which are done in the air. The first, as being done by necessity, are called necessary; the others, which may fall one way or other, are called contingent; and they may both thus be described. The necessary possible is that whose contrary is impossible; and the contingent possible is that whose contrary is also possible. For that the sun should set is a thing both necessary and possible, forasmuch as it is contrary to this that the sun should not set, which is impossible; but that, when the sun is set, there should be rain or not rain, both the one and the other is possible and contingent. And then again of things contingent, some happen oftener, others rarely and not so often, others fall out equally or indifferently, as well the one way as the other, even as it happens. Now it is manifest that those are contrary to one another,–to wit, those which fall out oftener and those which happen but seldom,–and they both for the most part are dependent on Nature; but that which happens equally, as much one way as another, depends on ourselves. For that under the Dog it should be either hot or cold, the one oftener, the other seldomer, are both things subject to Nature; but to walk and not to walk, and all such things of which both the one and the other are submitted to the free will of man, are said to be in us and our election; but rather more generally to be in us. For there are two sorts of this "being in our power"; the one of which proceeds from some sudden passion and motion of the mind, as from anger or pleasure; the other from the discourse and judgment of reason, which may properly be said to be in our election. And some reason there is to hold that this possible and contingent is the same thing with that which is said to be in our power and according to our free will, although named differently. For in respect to the future, it is called possible and contingent; and in respect of the present, it is named "in our power" and "in our free choice." These things may thus be defined: The contingent is that which is itself–as well as its contrary–possible; and "that which is in our power" is one part of the contingent, to wit, that which now takes place according to our choice. Thus have we in a manner declared, that the possible in the order of Nature precedes the contingent, and that the contingent exists before free will; as also what each of them is, whence they are so named, and what are the qualities adjoined or appertaining to them.

It now remains, that we treat of Fortune and casual adventure, and whatever else is to be considered with them. It is therefore certain that Fortune is a cause. Now of causes, some are causes by themselves, and others by accident. Thus for example, the proper cause by itself of an house or a ship is the art of the mason, the carpenter, or the shipwright; but accidental causes are music, geometry, and whatever else may happen to be joined with the art of building houses or ships, in respect either of the body, the soul, or any exterior thing. Whence it appears, that the cause by itself must needs be determinate and one; but the causes by accident are never one and the same, but infinite and undetermined. For many–nay, infinite–accidents, wholly different one from the other, may be in one and the same subject. Now the cause by accident, when it is found in a thing which not only is done for some end but has in it free will and election, is then called Fortune; as is the finding a treasure while one is digging a hole to plant a tree, or the doing or suffering some extraordinary thing whilst one is flying, following, or otherwise walking, or only turning about, provided it be not for the sake of that which happens, but for some other intention. Hence it is, that some of the ancients have declared Fortune to be a cause unknown that cannot be foreseen by the human reason. But according to the Platonics, who have approached yet nearer to the true reason of it, it is thus defined: Fortune is a cause by accident, in those things which are done for some end, and which are of our election. And afterwards they add, that it is unforeseen and unknown to the human reason; although that which is rare and strange appears also by the same means to be in this kind of cause by accident. But what this is, if it is not sufficiently evidenced by the oppositions and disputations made against it, will at least most clearly be seen by what is written in Plato's Phaedo, where you will find these words:–

PHAED. Have you not heard how and in what manner the judgment passed? ECH. Yes indeed; for there came one and told us of it. At which we wondered very much that, the judgment having been given long before, it seems that he died a great while after. And what, Phaedo, might be the cause of it? PHAED. It was a fortune which happened to him, Echecrates. For it chanced that, the day before the judgment, the prow of the galley which the Athenians send every year to the isle of Delos was crowned. (Plato, "Phaedo," p.58 A.)

In which discourse it is to be observed, that the expression HAPPENED TO HIM is not simply to be understood by WAS DONE or CAME TO PASS, but it much rather regards what befell him through the concurrence of many causes together, one being done in connection with another. For the priest crowned the ship and adorned it with garlands for another end and intention, and not for the sake of Socrates; and the judges also had for some other cause condemned him. But the event was con-

trary to experience, and of such a nature that it might seem to have been effected by the foresight of some human creature, or rather of the superior powers. And so much may suffice to show with what Fortune must of necessity subsist, and that there must subsist first such things as are in our free will: what it effects is, like itself called Fortune. ===============
But chance or casual adventure is of a larger extent than Fortune; which it comprehends, and also several other things which may of their own nature happen sometimes one way, sometimes another. And this, as it appears by the derivation of the word, which is in Greek [Greek omitted] CHANCE, is that which happens of itself, when that which is ordinary happens not, but another thing in its place; such as cold in the dog-days seems to be; for it is sometimes then cold.... Once for all, as "that which is in our power" is a part of the contingent, so Fortune is a part of chance or casual adventure; and both the two events are conjoined and dependent on the one and the other, to wit, chance on contingent, and Fortune on "that which is in our choice,"–and yet not on all, but on what is in our election, as we have already said. Wherefore chance is common to things inanimate, as well as to those which are animated; whereas Fortune is proper to man only, who has his actions voluntary. And an argument of this is, that to be fortunate and to be happy are thought to be one and the same thing. Now happiness is a certain well-doing, and well-doing is proper only to man, and to him perfect.

These, then, are the things which are comprised in Fate, to wit, contingent, possible, election, "that which is in our power," Fortune, chance, and their adjuncts, as are the things signified by the words perhaps and peradventure; all which indeed are contained in Fate. Yet none Of them is fatal. It now remains, that we discourse of divine Providence, and show how it comprehends even Fate itself.

The supreme therefore and first Providence is the understanding or (if you had rather) the will of the first and sovereign God, doing good to everything that is in the world, by which all divine things have universally and throughout been most excellently and most wisely ordained and disposed. The second Providence is that of the second gods, who go through the heaven, by which temporal and mortal things are orderly and regularly generated, and which pertains to the continuation and preservation of every kind. The third may probably be called the Providence and procuration of the Daemons, which, being placed on the earth, are the guardians and overseers of human actions. This threefold Providence therefore being seen, of which the first and supreme is chiefly and principally so named, we shall not be afraid to say, although we may in this seem to contradict the sentiments of some philosophers, that all things are done by Fate and by Providence, but not also by Nature. But some are done according to Providence, these according to one, those according to another,–and some according to Fate; and Fate is altogether according to Providence, while Providence is in no wise according to Fate. But let this discourse be understood of the first and supreme Providence. Now that which is done according to another, whatever it is, is always posterior to that according to which it is done; as that which is according to the law is after the law, and that which is according to Nature is after Nature, so that which is according to Fate is after Fate, and must consequently be more new and modern. Wherefore supreme Providence is the most ancient of all things, except him whose will or understanding it is, to wit, the sovereign author, maker, and father of all things. "Let us therefore," says Timaeus, "discourse for what cause the Creator made and framed this machine of the universe. He was good, and in him that is good there can never be imprinted or engendered any envy against anything. Being therefore wholly free from this, he desired that all things should, as far as it is possible, resemble himself. He, therefore, who admits this to have been chiefly the principal original of the generation and creation of the world, as it has been delivered to us by wise men, receives that which is most right. For God, who desired that all things should be good, and nothing, as far as possibly might be, evil, taking thus all that was visible,–restless as it was, and moving rashly and confusedly,–reduced it from disorder to order, esteeming the one to be altogether better than the other. For it neither was nor is convenient for him who is in all perfection good, to make anything that should not be very excellent and beautiful." (Plato, "Timaeus," p.29 D.) This, therefore, and all that follows, even to his disputation concerning human souls, is to be understood of the first Providence, which in the beginning constituted all things. Afterwards he speaks thus: "Having framed the universe, he ordained souls equal in number to the stars, and distributed to each of them one; and having set them, as it were, in a chariot, showed the nature of the universe, and appointed them the laws of Fate." (Ibid. p.41 D.) Who, then, will not believe, that by these words he expressly and manifestly declares Fate to be, as it were, a foundation and political constitution of laws, fitted for the souls of men? Of which he afterwards renders the cause.

As for the second Providence, he thus in a manner explains it, saying: "Having prescribed them all these laws, to the end that, if there should afterwards happen any fault, he might be exempt from being the cause of any of their evil, he dispersed some of them upon the earth, some into the moon, and some into the other instruments of time. And after this dispersion, he gave in charge to the young gods the making of human bodies, and the making up and adding whatever was wanting and deficient in human souls; and after they had perfected whatever is adherent and consequent to this, they should rule and govern, in the best manner they possibly could, this mortal creature, so far as it might not be the cause of its own evils." (Ibid. p.42 D.) For by these words, "that he might be exempt from being the cause of any of their evil," he most clearly signifies the cause of Fate; and the order and office of the young gods manifests the second Providence; and it seems also in some sort to have touched a little upon the third, if he therefore established laws and ordinances that he might be exempt from being the cause of any of their evil. For God, who is free from all evil, has no need of laws or Fate; but every one of these petty gods, drawn on by the providence of him who has engendered them, performs what belongs to his office. Now that this is true and agreeable to the opinion of Plato, these words of the lawgiver, spoken by him in his Book of Laws, seems to me to give sufficient testimony: "If there were any man so sufficient by Nature, being by divine Fortune happily engendered and born, that he could comprehend this, he would have no need of laws to command him. For there is not any law or ordinance more worthy and powerful than knowledge; nor is it suitable that Mind, provided it be truly and really free by Nature, should be a subject or slave to any one, but it ought to command all." (Plato, "Laws," ix. p.875 C.)

I therefore do for mine own part thus understand and interpret this sentence of Plato. There being a threefold Providence, the first, as having engendered Fate, does in some sort comprehend it; the second, having been engendered with Fate, is with it totally comprehended and embraced by the first; the third, as having been engendered after Fate, is comprehended by it in the same manner as are free choice and Fortune, as we have already said. "For they whom the assistance of a Daemon's power does help in their intercourse" says Socrates, declaring to Theages what is the almost settled ordinance of Adrastea "are those whom you also mean; for they advance quickly." (Plato, "Theages", p.129 E.) In which words, what he says of a Daemon's aiding some is to be ascribed to the third Providence, and the growing and coming forward with speed to Fate. In brief, it is not obscure or doubtful but that this also is a kind of Fate. And perhaps it may be found much more probable that the second Providence is also comprehended under Fate, and indeed all things that are done; since Fate, as a substance, has been rightly divided by us into three parts, and the simile of the chain comprehends the revolutions of the heavens in the number and rank of those things which happen conditionally. But concerning these things I will not much contend, to wit, whether they should be called conditional, or rather conjoined with Fate, the precedent cause and commander of Fate being also fatal.

Our opinion, then, to speak briefly, is such. But the contrary sentiment not only places all things in Fate, but affirms them all to be done by Fate. It agrees indeed in all things to the other (the Stoic) doctrine; and that which accords to another thing, 'tis clear, is the same with it. In this discourse therefore we have first spoken of the contingent; secondly, of "that which is in our power"; thirdly, of Fortune and chance, and whatever depends on them; fourthly, of praise, blame, and whatever depends on them; the fifth and last of all may be said to be prayers to the gods, with their services and ceremonies.

For the rest, as to those which are called idle and cropping arguments, and that which is named the argument against destiny, they are indeed but vain subtleties and captious sophisms, according to this discourse. But according to the contrary opinion, the first and principal conclusion seems to be, that there is nothing done without a cause, but that all things depend upon antecedent causes; the second, that the world is governed by Nature, and that it conspires, consents, and is compatible with itself; the third seems rather to be testimonies,–of which the first is divination, approved by all sorts of people, as being truly in God; the second is the equanimity and patience of wise men, who take mildly and bear patiently whatever befalls, as happening by divine ordinance and as it ought; the third is the speech so common and usual in every one's mouth, to wit, that every proposition is true or false. Thus have we contracted this discourse into a small number of short articles, that we might in few words comprehend the whole matter of Fate; into which a scrutiny ought to be made, and the reasons of both opinions to be weighed with a most exact balance. But we shall come to discuss particulars later.

Against Colotes, the Disciple and Favorite of Epicurus

COLOTES, WHOM EPICURUS was wont diminutively and by way of familiarity or fondness to call Colotaras and Colotarion, composed, O Saturninus, and published a little book which he entitled, "That according to the opinions of the other philosophers one cannot so much as live." This was dedicated to King Ptolemy. Now I suppose that it will not be unpleasant for you to read, when set down in writing, what came into my mind to speak against this Colotes, since I know you to be a lover of all elegant and honest treatises, and particularly of such as regard the science of antiquity, and to esteem the bearing in memory and having (as much as possible may be) in hand the discourses of the ancient sages to be the most royal of all studies and exercises.

Not long since, therefore, as this book was being read, Aristodemus of Aegium, a familiar friend of ours (whom you well know to be one of the Academy, and not a mere thyrsus-bearer, but one of the most frantic celebrators of Plato's name), did, I know not how, keep himself contrary to his custom very still all the while, and patiently gave ear to it even to the end. But the reading was scarce well over when he said: Well, then, whom shall we cause to rise up and fight against this man, in defence of the philosophers? For I am not of Nestor's opinion, who, when the most valiant of those nine warriors that presented themselves to enter into combat was to be chosen, committed the election to the fortune of a lot.

Yet, answered I, you see he so disposed himself in reference to the lot, that the choice might pass according to the arbitrament of the wisest man;

> And th' lot drawn from the helmet, as they wished,
> On Ajax fell.

But yet since you command me to make the election,
> *How can I think a better choice to make*
> *Than the divine Ulysses?*
> *("Iliad," vii. 182; x. 243.)*

Consider therefore, and be well advised, in what manner you will chastise this man.

But you know, replied Aristodemus, that Plato, when highly offended with his boy that waited on him, would not himself beat him, but requested Speusippus to do it for him, saying that he himself was angry. As much therefore may I say to you; Take this fellow to you, and treat him as you please; for I am in a fit of choler.

When therefore all the rest of the company desired me to undertake this office; I must then, said I, speak, since it is your pleasure. But I am afraid that I also shall seem more vehemently transported than is fitting against this book, in the defending and maintaining Socrates against the rudeness, scurrility, and insolence of this man; who, because Socrates affirmed himself to know nothing certainly, instead of bread (as one would say) present him hay, as if he were a beast, and asks him why he puts meat into his mouth and not into his ear. And yet perhaps some would make but a laughing matter of this, considering the mildness and gentleness of Socrates; "but for the whole host of the Greeks," that is, of the other philosophers, amongst which are Democritus, Plato, Stilpo, Empedocles, Parmenides, and Melissus, who have been basely traduced and reviled by him, it were not only a shame to be silent, but even a sacrilege in the least point to forbear or recede from freedom of speech in their behalf, who have advanced philosophy to that honor and reputation it has gotten.

And our parents indeed have, with the assistance of the gods, given us our life; but to live well comes to us from reason, which we have learned from the philosophers, which favors law and justice, and restrains our concupiscence. Now to live well is to live sociably, friendly, temperately, and justly; of all which conditions they leave us not one, who cry out that man's sovereign good lies in his belly, and that they would not purchase all the virtues together at the expense of a cracked farthing, if pleasure were totally and on every side removed from them. And in their discourses concerning the soul and the gods, they hold that the soul perishes when it is separated from the body, and that the gods concern not themselves in our affairs. Thus the Epicureans reproach the other philosophers, that by their wisdom they bereave man of his life; whilst the others on the contrary accuse them of teaching men to live degenerately and like beasts.

Now these things are scattered here and there in the writings of Epicurus, and dispersed through all his philosophy. But this Colotes, by having extracted from them certain pieces and fragments of discourses, destitute of any arguments whatever to render them credible and intelligible, has composed his book, being like a shop or cabinet of monsters and prodigies; as you better know than any one else, because you have always in your hands the works of the ancients. But he seems to me, like the Lydian, to open not only one gate against himself, but to involve Epicurus also in many and those the greatest doubts and difficulties. For he begins with Democritus, who receives of him an excellent and worthy reward for his instruction; it being certain that Epicurus for a long time called himself a Democritean, which as well others affirm, as Leonteus, a principal disciple of Epicurus, who in a letter which he writ to Lycophron says, that Epicurus honored Democritus, because he first attained, though a little at a distance, the right and sound understanding of the truth, and that in general all the treatise concerning natural things was called Democritean, because Democritus was the first who happened upon the principles and met with the primitive foundations of Nature. And Metrodorus says openly of philosophy, If Democritus had not gone before and taught the way, Epicurus had never attained to wisdom. Now if it be true, as Colotes holds, that to live according to the opinions of Democritus is not to live, Epicurus was then a fool in following Democritus, who led him to a doctrine which taught him not to live.

Now the first thing he lays to his charge is, that, by supposing everything to be no more individual than another, he wholly confounds human life. But Democritus was so far from having been of this opinion, that he opposed Protagoras the philosopher who asserted it, and writ many excellent arguments concluding against him, which this fine fellow Colotes never saw nor read, nor yet so much as dreamed of; but deceived himself by misunderstanding a passage which is in his works, where he determines that [Greek omitted] is no more than [Greek omitted], naming in that place the body by [Greek omitted], and the void by [Greek omitted], and meaning that the void has its own proper nature and subsistence, as well as the body.

But he who is of opinion that nothing has more of one nature than another makes use of a sentence of Epicurus, in which he says that all the apprehensions and imaginations given us by the senses are true. For if of two saying, the one, that the wine is sour, and the other, that it is sweet, neither of them shall be deceived by his sensation, how shall the wine be more sour than sweet? And we may often see that some men using one and the same bath find it to be hot, and others find it to be cold; because those order cold water to be put into it, as these do hot. It is said that, a certain lady going to visit Berenice, wife to King Deiotarus, as soon as ever they approached each other, they both immediately turned their backs, the one, as it seemed, not being able to bear the smell of perfume, nor the other of butter. If, then, the sense of one is no truer than the sense of another, it is also probable, that water is no more cold than hot, nor sweet ointment or butter better or worse scented one than the other. For if any one shall say that it seems the one to one, and the other to another, he will, before he is aware, affirm that they are both the one and the other.

And as for these symmetries and proportions of the pores, or little passages in the organs of the senses, about which they talk so much, and those different mixtures of seeds, which, they say, being dispersed through all savors, odors, and colors, move the senses of different persons to perceive different qualities, do they not manifestly drive them to this, that things are no more of one nature than another? For to pacify those who think the sense is deceived and lies because they see contrary events and passions in such as use the same objects, and to solve this objection, they teach,–that when almost everything was confused and mixed up together, since it has been arranged by Nature that one thing shall fit another thing, it was not the contact or the apprehension of the same quality nor were all parts affected in the same way by what was influencing them. But those only coalesced with anything to which they had a characteristic, symmetrical in a corresponding proportion; so that they are in error so obstinately to insist that a thing is either good or bad, white or not white, thinking to establish their own senses by destroying those of others; whereas they ought neither to combat the senses,–because they all touch some quality, each one drawing from this confused mixture, as from a living and large fountain, what is suitable and convenient,–nor to pronounce of the whole, by touching only the parts, nor to think that all ought to be affected after one and the same manner by the same thing, seeing that one is affected by one quality and faculty of it, and another by another. Let us investigate who those men are which bring in this opinion that things are not more of one quality than another, if they are not those who affirm that every sensible object is a mixture, compounded of all sorts of qualities, like a mixture of new wine fermenting, and who confess that all their rules are lost and their faculty of judging quite gone, if they admit any sensible object that is pure and simple, and do not make each one thing to be many?

See now to this purpose, what discourse and debate Epicurus makes Polyaenus to have with him in his Banquet concerning the heat of wine. For when he asked, "Do you, Epicurus, say, that wine does not heat?" some one answered, "It is not universally to be affirmed that wine heats." And a little after: "For wine seems not to be universally a heater; but such a quantity may be said to heat such a person." And again subjoining the cause, to wit, the compressions and disseminations of the atoms, and having alleged their commixtures and conjunctions with others when the wine comes to be mingled in the body, he adds this conclusion: "It is not universally to be said that wine is endued with a faculty of heating; but that such a quantity may heat such a nature and one so disposed, while such a quantity to such a nature is cooling. For in such a mass there are such natures and complexions of which cold might be composed, and which, united with others in proper measure, would yield a refrigerative virtue. Wherefore some are deceived, who say that wine is universally a heater; and others, who say that it is universally a cooler." He then who says that most men are deceived and err, in holding that which is hot to be heating and that which is cold to be cooling, is himself in an error, unless he should allow that his assertion ends in the doctrine that one thing is not more of one nature than another. He farther adds afterwards that oftentimes wine entering into a body brings with it thither neither a calefying nor refrigerating virtue, but, the mass of the body being agitated and disturbed, and a transposition made of the parts, the heat-effecting atoms being assembled together do by their multitude cause a heat and inflammation in the body, and sometimes on the contrary disassembling themselves cause a refrigeration.

But it is moreover wholly evident, that we may employ this argument to all those things which are called and esteemed bitter, sweet, purging, dormitive, and luminous, not any one of them having an entire and perfect quality to produce such effects, nor to act rather than to be acted on when they are in the bodies, but being there susceptible, of various temperatures and differences. For Epicurus himself, in his Second Book against Theophrastus, affirming that colors are not connatural to bodies, but are engendered there according to certain situations and positions with respect to the sight of man, says: "For this reason a body is no more colored than destitute of color." And a little above he writes thus, word for word: "But apart from this, I know not how a man may say that those bodies which are in the dark have color; although very often, an air equally dark being spread about them, some distinguish diversities of colors, others perceive them not through the weakness of their sight. And moreover, going into a dark house or room, we at our first entrance see no color, but after we have stayed there awhile, we do. Wherefore we are to say that every body is not more colored than not colored. Now, if color is relative and has its being in regard to something else, so also then is white, and so likewise blue; and if colors are so, so also are sweet and bitter. So that it may truly be affirmed of every quality, that it cannot more properly be said to exist than not to exist. For to those who are in a certain manner disposed, they will be; but to those who are not so disposed, they will not be." Colotes therefore has bedashed and bespattered himself and his master with that dirt, in which he says those lie who maintain that things are not more of one quality than another.

But is it in this alone, that this excellent man shows himself–

To others a physician, whilst himself
Is full of ulcers?
(Euripides, Frag. 1071.)

No indeed; but yet much farther in his second reprehension, without any way minding it, he drives Epicurus and Democritus out of this life. For he affirms that the statement of Democritus–that the atoms are to the senses color by a certain human law or ordinance, that they are by the same law sweetness, and by the same law concretion–is at war with our senses, and that he who uses this reason and persists in this opinion cannot himself imagine whether he is living or dead. I know not how to contradict this discourse; but this I can boldly affirm, that this is as inseparable from the sentences and doctrines of Epicurus as they say figure and weight are from atoms. For what is it that Democritus says? "There are substances, in number infinite, called atoms (because they cannot be divided), without difference, without quality, and passibility, which move, being dispersed here and there, in the infinite voidness; and that when they approach one another, or meet and are conjoined, of such masses thus heaped together, one appears water, another fire, another a plant, another a man; and that all things are thus properly atoms (as he called them), and nothing else; for there is no generation from what does not exist; and of those things which are nothing can be generated, because these atoms are so firm, that they can neither change, alter, nor suffer; wherefore there cannot be made color of those things which are without color, nor nature or soul of those things which are without quality and impassible." Democritus then is to be blamed, not for confessing those things that happen upon his principles, but for supposing principles upon which such things happen. For he should not have supposed immutable principles; or having supposed them, he should have seen that the generation of all quality is taken away; but having seen the absurdity, to deny it is most impudent. But Epicurus says, that he supposes the same principles with Democritus, but that he says not that color, sweet, white, and other qualities, are by law and ordinance. If therefore NOT TO SAY is the same as NOT TO CONFESS, he does merely what he is wont to do. For it is as when, taking away divine Providence, he nevertheless says that he leaves piety and devotion towards the gods; and when, choosing friendship for the sake of pleasure, that he suffers most grievous pains for his friends; and supposing the universe to be infinite, that he nevertheless takes not away high and low.... Indeed having taken the cup, one may drink what he pleases, and return the rest. But in reasoning one ought chiefly to remember this wise apothegm, that where the principles are not necessary, the ends and consequences are necessary. It was not then necessary for him to suppose or (to say better) to steal from Democritus, that atoms are the principles of the universe; but having supposed this doctrine, and having pleased and glorified himself in the first probable and specious appearances of it, he must afterwards also swallow that which is troublesome in it, or must show how bodies which have not any quality can bring all sorts of qualities to others only by their meetings and joining together. As–to take that which comes next neither had heat when they came, nor are become hot after their being joined together? For the one presupposes that they had some quality, and the other that they were fit to receive it. And you affirm, that neither the one nor the other must be said to be congruous to atoms, because they are incorruptible.

How then? Do not Plato, Aristotle, and Xenocrates produce gold from that which is not gold, and stone from that which is not stone, and many other things from the four simple first bodies? Yes indeed; but with those bodies immediately concur also the principles for the generation of everything, bringing with them great contributions, that is, the first qualities which are in them; then, when they come to assemble and join in one the dry with the moist, the cold with the hot, and the solid with the soft,–that is, active bodies with such as are fit to suffer and receive every alteration and change,–then is generation wrought by passing from one temperature to another. Whereas the atom, being alone, is alone, is deprived and destitute of all quality and generative faculty, and when it comes to meet with the others, it can make only a noise and sound because of its hardness and firmness, but nothing more. For they always strike and are stricken, not being able by this means to compose or make an animal, a soul, or a nature, nay, not so much as a mass or heap of themselves; for that as they beat upon one another, so they fly back again asunder.

But Colotes, as if he were speaking to some ignorant and unlettered king, again attacks Empedocles for expressing the same thought:–

I've one thing more to say. 'Mongst mortals there
No Nature is; nor that grim thing men fear
So much, called death. There only happens first
A mixture, and mixt things asunder burst
Again, when them disunion does befall.
And this is that which men do Nature call.

For my part, I do not see how this is repugnant and contrary to life or living, especially amongst those who hold that there is no generation of that which is not, nor corruption of that which is, but that the assembling and union of the things which are is called generation, and their dissolution and disunion named corruption and death. For that he took Nature for generation, and that this is his meaning, he has himself declared, when he opposed Nature to death. And if they neither live nor can live who place generation in union and death in disunion, what else do these Epicureans? Yet Empedocles, gluing, (as it were) and conjoining the elements together by heats, softnesses, and humidifies, gives them in some sort a mixtion and unitive composition; but these men who hunt and drive together the atoms, which they affirm to be immutable and impassible, compose nothing proceeding from them, but indeed make many and continual percussions of them.

For the interlacement, hindering the dissolution, more and more augments the collision and concussion; so that there is neither mixtion nor adhesion and conglutination, but only a discord and combat, which according to them is called generation. And if the atoms do now recoil for a moment by reason of the shock they have given, and then return again after the blow is past, they are above double the time absent from one another, without either touching or approaching, so as nothing can be made of them, not even so much as a body without a soul. But as for sense, soul, understanding, and prudence, there is not any man who can in the least conceive or imagine how it is possible they should be made in a voidness, and atoms which neither when separate and apart have any quality, nor any passion or alteration when they are assembled and joined together, especially seeing this their meeting together is not an incorporation or congress, making a mixture or coalition, but rather percussions and repercussions. So that, according to the doctrine of these people, life is taken away, and the existence of an animal denied, since they posit principles void, impassible, godless, and soulless, and such as cannot allow or receive any mixture or commingling whatever.

How then is it, that they admit and allow Nature, soul, and living creature? Even in the same manner as they do an oath, prayer, and sacrifice, and the adoration of the gods. Thus they adore by word and mouth, only naming and feigning that which by their principles they totally take away and abolish. If now they call that which is born Nature, and that which is engendered generation,–as those who are accustomed to call wood wood-work and the voices that accord and sound together symphony,– whence came it into his mind to object these words against Empedocles? "Why," says he, "do we tire ourselves in taking such care of ourselves, in desiring and longing after certain things, and shunning and avoiding others? For we neither are ourselves, nor do we live by making use of others." But be of good cheer, my dear little Colotes, may one perhaps say to him: there is none who hinders you from taking care of yourself by teaching that the nature of Colotes is nothing else but Colotes himself, or who forbids you to make use of things (now things with you are pleasures) by showing that there is no nature of tarts and marchpanes, of sweet odors, or of venereal delights, but that there are tarts, marchpanes, perfumes, and women. For neither does the grammarian who says that the "strength of Hercules" is Hercules himself deny the being of Hercules; nor do those who say that symphonies and roofings are but absolute derivations affirm that there are neither sounds nor timbers; since also there are some who, taking away the soul and intelligence, do not yet seem to take away either living or being intelligent.

And when Epicurus says that the nature of things is to be found in bodies and their place, do we so comprehend him as if he meant that Nature were something else than the things which are, or as if he insinuated that it is merely the things which are, and nothing else?–as, to wit, he is wont to call voidness itself the nature of voidness, and the universe, by Jupiter, the nature of the universe. And if any one should thus question him; What sayst thou, Epicurus, that this is voidness, and that the nature of voidness? No, by Jupiter, would he answer; but this transference of names is in use by law and custom. I grant it is. Now what has Empedocles done else, but taught that Nature is nothing else save that which is born, and death no other thing but that which dies? But as the poets very often, forming as it were an image, say thus in figurative language,

> Strife, tumult, noise, placed by some angry god,
> Mischief, and malice there had their abode;
> ("Iliad," xvii. 525.)

so do some authors attribute generation and corruption to things that are contracted together and dissolved. But so far has he been from stirring and taking away that which is, or contradicting that which evidently appears, that he casts not so much as one single word out of the accustomed use; but taking away all figurative fraud that might hurt or endamage things, he again restored the ordinary and useful signification to words in these verses:–

> When from mixed elements we sometimes see
> A man produced, sometimes a beast, a tree,
> Or bird, this birth and geniture we name;
> But death, when this so well compacted frame
> And juncture is dissolved.

And yet I myself say that Colotes, though he alleged these verses, did not understand that Empedocles took not away men, beasts, trees, or birds, which he affirmed to be composed of the elements mixed together; and that, by teaching how much they are deceived who call this composition Nature and life, and this dissolution unhappy destruction and miserable death, he did not abrogate the using of the customary expressions in this respect.

And it seems to me, indeed, that Empedocles did not aim in this place at the disturbing the common manner of expression, but that he really, as it has been said, had a controversy about generation from things that have no being, which some call Nature. Which he manifestly shows by these verses:–

> Fools, and of little thought, we well may deem
> Those, who so silly are as to esteem
> That what ne'er was may now engendered be,
> And that what is may perish utterly.

For these are the words of one who cries loud enough to those which have ears, that he takes not away generation, but procreation from nothing; nor corruption, but total destruction that is, reduction to nothing. For to him who would not so savagely and foolishly but more gently calumniate, the following verses might give a colorable occasion of charging Empedocles with the contrary, when he says:–

> No prudent man can e'er into his mind
> Admit that, whilst men living here on earth
> (Which only life they call) both fortunes find,
> They being have, but that before the birth
> They nothing were, nor shall be when once dead.

For these are not the expressions of a man who denies those that are born to be, but rather of him who holds those to be that are not yet born or that are already dead. And Colotes also does not altogether accuse him of this, but says that according to his opinion we shall never be sick, never wounded. But how is it possible, that he who affirms men to have being both before their life and after their death, and during their life to find both fortunes (or to be accompanied both by good and evil), should not leave them the power to suffer? Who then are they, O Colotes, that are endued with this privilege never to be wounded, never to be sick? Even you yourselves, who are composed of atoms and voidness, neither of which, you say, has any sense. Now there is no great hurt in this; but the worst is, you have nothing left that can cause you pleasure, seeing an atom is not capable to receive those things which are to effect it, and voidness cannot be affected by them.

But because Colotes would, immediately after Democritus, seem to inter and bury Parmenides, and I have passed over and a little postponed his defence, to bring in between them that of Empedocles, as seeming to be more coherent and consequent to the first reprehensions, let us now return to Parmenides. Him, then, does Colotes accuse of having broached and set abroad certain shameful and villanous sophistries; and yet by these his sophisms he has neither rendered friendship less honorable, nor voluptuousness or the desire of pleasures more audacious and unbridled. He has not taken from honesty its attractive property or its being venerable or recommendable of itself, nor has he disturbed the opinions we ought to have of the gods. And I do not see how, by saying that the All (or the universe) is one, he hinders or obstructs our living. For when Epicurus himself says that the All is infinite, that it is neither engendered nor perishable, that it can neither increase nor be diminished, he speaks of the universe as of one only thing. And having in the beginning of his treatise concerning this matter said, that the nature of those things which have being consists of bodies and of vacuum, he makes a division (as it were) of one thing into two parts, one of which has in reality no subsistence, being, as you yourselves term it, impalpable, void, and incorporeal; so that by this means, even with you also, all comes to be one; unless you desire, in speaking of voidness, to use words void of sense, and to combat the ancients, as if you were fighting against a shadow.

But these atomical bodies, you will say, are, according to the opinion of Epicurus, infinite in number, and everything which appears to us is composed of them. See now, therefore, what principles of generation you suppose, infinity and voidness; one of which, to wit, voidness, is inactive, impassible, and incorporeal; the other, to wit, infinity, is disorderly, unreasonable, and unintelligible, dissolving and confounding itself, because it cannot for its multitude be contained, circumscribed, or limited. But Parmenides has neither taken away fire, nor water, nor precipices, nor yet cities (as Colotes says) which are inhabited as well in Europe as in Asia; since he has both constructed an order of the world, and mixing the elements, to wit, light and dark, does of them and by them arrange and finish all things that appear in the world. For he has written very largely of the earth, heaven, sun, moon, and stars, and has spoken of the generation of man; and being, as he was, an ancient author in physiology, and one who in writing sought to save his own and not to destroy another's doctrine, he has overlooked none of the essential things in Nature. Moreover, Plato, and before him Socrates himself, understood that in Nature there is one part subject to opinion, and another subject to intelligence. As for that which is subject to opinion, it is always unconstant, wandering, and carried away with several passions and changes, liable to diminution and increase, and to be variously disposed to various men, and not always appearing after one manner even to the same individual. But as to the intelligible part, it is quite of another kind,

Constant, entire, and still engenerable,

as himself says, always like to itself, and perdurable in its being.

Here Colotes, sycophant-like, catching at his expressions and drawing the discourse from things to words, flatly affirms that Parmenides in one word destroys the existence of all things by supposing ENS (or that which is) to be one. But, on the contrary, he takes away neither the one nor the other part of Nature; but rendering to each of them what belongs to it and is convenient for it, he places the intelligible in the idea of one and of "that which is," calling it ENS because it is eternal and incorruptible, and one because it is always like itself and admits no diversity. And as for that part which is sensible, he places it in the rank of uncertain, disorderly, and always moving. Of which two parts, we may see the distinct judgment:–

One certain truth and sincere knowledge is,

as regarding that which is intelligible, and always alike and of the same sort;

The other does on men's opinions rest,
Which breed no true belief within our breast,

because it is conversant in things which receive all sorts of changes, passions, and inequalities. Now how he could have left sense and opinion, if he had not also left any sensible and opinable object, it is impossible for any man to say. But because to that which truly IS it appertains to continue in its being, and because sensible things sometimes are, sometimes are not, continually passing from one being to another and perpetually changing their state, he thought they required some other name than that of ENTIA, or things which always are. This speech therefore concerning ENS (or that which is), that it should be but one, is not to take away the plurality of sensible things, but to show how they differ from that which is intelligible. Which difference Plato in his discussion of Ideas more fully declaring, has thereby afforded Colotes an opportunity of cavilling.

Therefore it seems not unfitting to me to take next into our consideration, as it were all in a train, what he has also said against him. But first let us contemplate a little the diligence–together with the manifold and profound knowledge–of this our philosopher, who says, that Aristotle, Xenocrates, Theophrastus, and all the Peripateties have followed these doctrines of Plato. For in what corner of the uninhabitable world have you, O Colotes, written your book, that, composing all these accusations against such personages, you never have lighted upon their works, nor have taken into your hands the books of Aristotle concerning Heaven and the Soul, nor those of Theophrastus against the Naturalists, nor the Zoroaster of Heraclides, nor his books of Hell, nor that of Natural Doubts and Difficulties, nor the book of Dicaearchus concerning the Soul; in all which books they are in the highest degree contradictory and repugnant to Plato about the principal and greatest points of natural philosophy? Nay, Strato himself, the very head and prince of the other Peripatetics, agrees not in many things with Aristotle, and holds opinions altogether contrary to Plato, concerning motion, the understanding, the soul, and generation. In fine, he says that the world is not an animal, and that what is according to Nature follows what is according to Fortune; for that Chance gave the beginning, and so every one of the natural effects was afterwards finished.

Now as to the ideas,–for which he quarrels with Plato,–Aristotle, by moving this matter at every turn, and alleging all manner of doubts concerning them, in his Ethics, in his Physics, and in his Exoterical Dialogues seems to some rather obstinately than philosophically to have disputed against these doctrines, as having proposed to himself the debasing and undervaluing of Plato's philosophy; so far he was from following it. What an impudent rashness then is this, that having neither seen nor understood what these persons have written and what were their opinions, he should go and devise such things as they never imagined; and persuading himself that he reprehends and refutes others, he should produce a proof, written with his own hand, arguing and convincing himself of ignorance, licentiousness, and shameful impudence, in saying that those who contradict Plato agree with him, and that those who oppose him follow him.

Plato, says he, writes that horses are in vain by us considered horses, and men men. And in which of Plato's commentaries has he found this hidden? For as to us, we read in all his books, that horses are horses, that men are men, and that fire is by him esteemed fire, because he holds that every one of these things is sensible and subject to opinion. But this Colotes, as if he were not a hair's breadth distance from wisdom, takes it to be one and the same thing to say, "Man is not" and "Man is a NON ENS."

Now to Plato there seems to be a wonderful great difference between not being at all and being a NON ENS; because the first imports an annihilation and abolishment of all substance, and the other shows the diversity there is between that which is participated and that which participates. Which diversity those who came after distinguished only into the difference of genus and species, and certain common and proper qualities or accidents, as they are called, but ascended no higher, falling into more logical doubts and difficulties. Now there is the same proportion between that which is participated and that which participates, as there is between the cause and the matter, the original and the image, the faculty and the result. Wherein that which is by itself and always the same principally differs from that which is by another and never remains in one and the same manner; because the one never was nor ever shall be non-existent, and is therefore totally and essentially an ENS; but to the other that very being, which it has not of itself but happens to take by participation from another, does not remain firm and constant, but it goes out of it by its imbecility,–the matter always gliding and sliding about the form, and receiving several functions and changes in the image of the substance, so that it is continually moving and shaking. As therefore he who says that the image of Plato is not Plato takes not away the sense and substance of the image, but shows the difference of that which is of itself from that which is only in regard to some other, so neither do they take away the nature, use, or sense of men, who affirm that every one of us, by participating in a certain common substratum, that is, in the idea, is become the image of that which afforded the likeness for our generation. For neither does he who says that a red-hot iron is not fire, or that the moon is not the sun, but, as Parmenides has it,

> *A torch which round the earth by night*
> *Does bear about a borrowed light,*

take away therefore the use of iron, or the nature of the moon. But if he should deny it to be a body, or affirm that it is not illuminated, he would then contradict the senses, as one who admitted neither body, animal, generation, nor sense. But he who by his opinion imagines that these things subsist only by participation, and reflects how far remote and distant they are from that which always is and which communicates to them their being, does not reject the sensible, but affirms that the intelligible is; nor does he take away and abolish the results which are wrought and appear in us; but he shows to those who follow him that there are other things, firmer and more stable than these in respect of their essence, because they are neither engendered, nor perish, nor suffer anything; and he teaches them, more purely touching the difference, to express it by names, calling these [Greek omitted] or [Greek omitted] (THINGS THAT HAVE BEING), and those [Greek omitted] or FIENTIA (THINGS ENGENDERED). And the same also usually befalls the moderns; for they deprive many–and those great things–of the appellation of ENS or BEING; such as are voidness, time, place, and simply the entire genus of things spoken, in which are comprised all things true. For these things, they say, are not ENTIA but SOME THINGS; and they perpetually treat of them in their lives and in their philosophy, as of things having subsistence and existence.

But I would willingly ask this our fault-finder, whether themselves do not in their affairs perceive this difference, by which some things are permanent and immutable in their substances,–as they say of their atoms, that they are at all times and continually after one and the same manner, because of their impassibility and hardness,–but that all compound things are fluxible, changeable, generated, and perishing; forasmuch as infinite images are always departing and going from them, and infinite others as it is probable, repair to them from the ambient air, filling up what was diminished from the mass, which is much diversified and transvasated, as it were, by this change, since those atoms which are in the very bottom of the said mass can never cease stirring and reciprocally beating upon one another; as they themselves affirm. There is then in things such a diversity of substance. But Epicurus is in this wiser and more learned than Plato, that he calls them all equally ENTIA,–to wit, the impalable voidness, the solid and resisting body, the principles, and the things composed of them,–and thinks that the eternal participates of the common substance with that which is generated, the immortal with the corruptible, and the natures that are impassible, perdurable, unchangeable, and that can never fall from their being, with those which have their essence in suffering and changing, and can never continue in one and the same state. But though Plato had with all the justness imaginable deserved to be condemned for having offended in this, yet should he have been sentenced by these gentlemen, who use Greek more elegantly and discourse more correctly than he, only as having confounded the terms, and not as having taken away the things and driven life from us, because he named them FIENTIA (or things engendered), and not ENTIA (things that have being), as these men do.

But because we have passed over Socrates, who should have come next after Parmenides, we must now turn back our discourse to him. Him therefore has Colotes begun at the very first to remove, as the common proverb has it, from the sacred line; and having mentioned how Chaerephon brought from Delphi an oracle, well known to us all, concerning Socrates, he says thus: "Now as to this narration of Chaerephon's, because it is odious and entirely sophistical, we will overpass it." Plato, then, that we may say nothing of others, is also odious, who has committed it to writing; and the Lacedaemonians are yet more odious, who keep the oracle of Lycurgus amongst their most ancient and most authentic inscriptions. The oracle also of Themistocles, by which he persuaded the Athenians to quit their town, and in a naval fight defeated the barbarous Xerxes, was a sophistical fiction. Odious also were all the ancient legislators and founders of Greece who established the most part of their temples, sacrifices, and solemn festivals by the answer of the Pythian Oracle. But if the oracle brought from Delphi concerning Socrates, a man ravished with a divine zeal to virtue, by which he is styled and declared wise, is odious, fictitious, and sophistical, by what name shall we call your cries, noises, and shouts, your applauses, adorations and canonizations, with which you extol and celebrate him who incites and exhorts you to frequent and continual pleasures? For thus has he written in his epistle to Anaxarchus: "I for my part incite and call you to continual pleasures, and not to vain and empty virtues, which have nothing but turbulent hopes of uncertain fruits." And yet Metrodorus, writing to Timarchus, says: "Let us do some extraordinarily excellent thing, not suffering ourselves to be plunged in reciprocal affections, but retiring from this low and terrestrial life, and elevating ourselves to the truly holy and divinely revealed ceremonies and mysteries of Epicurus." And even Colotes himself, hearing one day Epicurus discoursing of natural things, fell suddenly at his feet and embraced his knees, as Epicurus himself, glorying in it, thus writes: "For as if you had adored what we were then saying, you were suddenly taken with a desire, proceeding not from any natural cause, to come to us, prostrate yourself on the ground, embrace our knees, and use all those gestures to us which are ordinarily practised by those who adore and pray to the gods. So that you made us also," says he, "reciprocally sanctify and adore you." Those, by Jupiter, well deserve to be pardoned, who say, they would willingly give any money for a picture in which should be presented to the life this fine story of one lying prostrate at the knees and embracing the legs of another, who mutually again adores him and makes his devout prayers to him. Nevertheless this devout service, how well soever it was ordered and composed by Colotes, received not the condign fruit he expected; for he was not declared wise; but it was only said to him: Go they ways, and walk immortal; and understand that we also are in like manner immortal.

These men, knowing well in their consciences that they have used such foolish speeches, have had such motions, and such passions, dare nevertheless call others odious. And Colotes, having shown us these fine first-fruits and wise positions touching the natural senses,–that we eat meat, and not hay or forage; and that when rivers are deep and great, we pass them in boats, but when shallow and easily fordable, on foot,–cries out, "You use vain and arrogant speeches, O Socrates; you say one thing to those who come to discourse with you, and practise another." Now I would fain know what these vain and arrogant speeches of Socrates were, since he ordinarily said that he knew nothing, that he was always learning, and that he went inquiring and searching after the truth. But if, O Colotes, you had happened on such expressions of Socrates as are those which Epicurus writ to Idomeneus, "Send me then the first-fruits for the entertainment of our sacred body, for ourself and for our children: for so it comes upon me to speak;" what more arrogant and insolent words could you have used? And yet that Socrates spake otherwise than he lived, you have wonderful proofs in his gests at Delium, at Potidaea, in his behavior during the time of the Thirty Tyrants, towards Archelaus, towards the people of Athens, in his poverty, and in his death. For are not these things beseeming and answerable to the doctrine of Socrates? They would indeed, good sir, have been indubitable testimonies to show that he acted otherwise than he taught, if, having proposed pleasure for the end of life, he had led such a life as this.

Thus much for the calumnies he has uttered against Socrates. Colotes besides perceives not that he is himself found guilty of the same offences in regard to theory and practice which he objects against Socrates. For this is one of the sentences and propositions of Epicurus, that none but the wise man ought irrevocably and unchangeably to be persuaded of anything. Since then Colotes, even after those adorations he performed to Epicurus, became not one of the sages, let him first make these questions and interrogatories his own: How is it that being hungry he eats meat and not hay, and that he puts a robe about his body and not about a pillar, since he is not indubitably persuaded either that a robe is a robe or that meat is meat? But if he not only does these things, but also passes not over rivers, when they are great and high, on foot, and flies from wolves and serpents, not being irrevocably persuaded that any of these things is such as it seems, but yet doing everything according to what appears to him; so likewise the opinion of Socrates concerning the senses was no obstacle to him, but that he might in like manner make use of things as they appeared to him. For it is not likely that bread appeared bread and hay hay to Colotes, because he had read those holy rules of Epicurus which came down from heaven, while Socrates on account of his vanity imagined that hay was bread and bread hay. For these wise men use better opinions and reasons than we; but to have sense, and to receive an impression from objects as they appear, is common as well to the ignorant as to the wise, as proceeding from causes where there needs not the discourse of reason. And the proposition which affirms that the natural senses are not perfect, nor certain enough to cause an entire belief, hinders not that everything may appear to us; but leaving us to make use of our senses in our actions according to that which appears, it permits us not so to give credit to them as if they were exactly true and without error. For it is sufficient that in what is necessary and commodious for use there is nothing better. But as for the science and knowledge which the soul of a philosopher desires to have concerning everything, the senses have it not.

But as to this, Colotes will farther give us occasion to speak of it hereafter, for he brings this objection against several others. Furthermore, whereas he profusely derides and despises Socrates for asking what man is, and in a youthful bravery (as he terms it) affirming that he was ignorant of it, it is manifest that he himself, who scoffs at it, never so much as thought of this matter; but Heraclitus on the contrary, as having done some great and worthy thing, said, I have been seeking myself. And of the sentences that were written in Apollo's temple at Delphi, the most excellent and most divine seems to have been this, Know thyself. And this it was which gave Socrates an occasion and beginning of doubting and inquiring into it, as Aristotle says in his Platonics. And yet this appears to Colotes ridiculous and fit to be scoffed at. And I wonder that he derides not also his master himself, who does as much whenever he writes concerning the substance of the soul and the creation of man. For if that which is compounded of both, as they themselves hold,–of the body, to wit, and the soul,–is man, he who searches into the nature of the soul consequently also searches into the nature of man, beginning from his chiefest principle. Now that the soul is very difficult to be comprehended by reason, and altogether incomprehensible by the exterior senses, let us not learn from Socrates, who is a vainglorious and sophistical disputer, but let us take it from these wise men, who, having forged and framed the substance of the soul of somewhat hot, spiritual, and aerial, as far as to the faculties of the flesh, by which she gives heat, softness and strength to the body, proceed not to that which is the principal, but give over faint and tired by the way. For that by which she judges, remembers, loves, hates,–in a word, that which is prudent and rational, is,–say they, made afterwards of I know not what nameless quality. Now we well know, that this nameless thing is a confession of their shameful ignorance, whilst they pretend they cannot name what they are not able to understand or comprehend. But let this, as they say, be pardoned them. For it seems not to be a light and easy matter, which every one can at the first attempt find out and attain to, but has retired itself to the bottom of some very remote place, and there lies obscurely concealed. So that there is not, amongst so many words and terms as are in use, any one that can explain or show it. Socrates therefore was not a fool or blockhead for seeking and searching what himself was; but they are rather to be thought shallow coxcombs, who inquire after any other thing before this, the knowledge of which is so necessary and so hard to find. For how could he expect to gain the knowledge of other things, who has not been able to comprehend the principal element even of himself?

But granting a little to Colotes, that there is nothing so vain, useless, and odious as the seeking into one's self, let us ask him, what confession of human life is in this, and how it is that a man cannot continue to live, when he comes once thus to reason and discourse in himself: "Go to now, what am I? Am I a composition, made up of soul and body; or rather a soul, serving itself and making use of the body, as an horseman using his horse is not a subject composed of horse and man? Or is every one of us the principal part of the soul, by which we understand, infer, and act; and are all the other parts, both of soul and body, only organs and utensils of this power? Or, to conclude, is there no proper substance of the soul at all apart, but is only the temperature and complexion of the body so disposed, that it has force and power to understand and live?" But Socrates does not by these questions overthrow human life, since all natural philosophers treat of the same matter. But those perhaps are the monstrous questions and inquiries that turn everything upside down, which are in Phaedrus, (Plato, "Phaedrus," p. 230 A.) where he says, that every one ought to examine and consider himself, whether he is a savage beast, more cautelous, outrageous, and furious than ever was the monster Typhon; or on the contrary, an animal more mild and gentle, partaking by Nature of a certain divine portion, and such as is free from pride. Now by these discourses and reasonings he overturns not the life of man, but drives from it presumption and arrogance, and those haughty and extravagant opinions and conceits he has of himself. For this is that monster Typhon, which your teacher and master has made to be so great in you by his warring against the gods and divine men.

Having done with Socrates and Plato, he next attacks Stilpo. Now as for those his true doctrines and good discourses, by which he managed and governed himself, his country, his friends, and such kings and princes as loved him and esteemed him, he has not written a word; nor yet what prudence and magnanimity was in his heart, accompanied with meekness, moderation, and modesty. But having made mention of one of those little sentences he was wont in mirth and raillery to object against the sophisters, he does, without alleging any reason against it or solving the subtlety of the objection, stir up a terrible tragedy against Stilpo, saying that the life of man is subverted by him, inasmuch as he affirms that one thing cannot be predicated of another. "For how," says he, "shall we live, if we cannot style a man good, nor a man a captain, but must separately name a man a man, good good, and a captain a captain; nor can say ten thousand horsemen, or a fortified town, but only call horsemen horsemen, and ten thousand ten thousand, and so of the rest?" Now what man ever was there that lived the worse for this? Or who is there that, hearing this discourse, does not immediately perceive and understand it to be the speech of a man who rallies gallantly, and proposes to others this logical question for the exercise of their wits? It is not, O Colotes, a great and dangerous scandal not to call any man good, or not to say ten thousand horsemen; but not to call God God, and not to believe him to be God,–as you and the rest do, who will not confess that there is a Jupiter presiding over generation, or a Ceres giving laws, or a Neptune nourishing the plants,–it is this separation of names that is pernicious, and fills our life with audaciousness and an atheistical contempt of the gods. When you pluck from the gods the names and appellations that are tied to them, you abolish also the sacrifices, mysteries, processions, and feasts. For to whom shall we offer the sacrifices preceding the tilling of the ground? To whom those for the obtaining of preservation? How shall we celebrate the Phosphoria or torch-festivals, the Bacchanals, and the ceremonies that go before marriage, if we admit neither Bacchantes, gods of light, gods who protect the sown field, nor preservers of the state? For this it is that touches the principal and greatest points, being an error in things,–not in words, in the structure of propositions, or use of terms.

Now if these are the things that disturb and subvert human life, who are there that more offend in speech than you? For you take utterly away the whole category of namable things, which constitute the substance of language; and leave only words and their accidental objects, while you take away in the meantime the things particularly signfied by them, by which are wrought disciplines, doctrines, preconceptions, intelligences, inclination, and assent, which you hold to be nothing at all.

But as for Stilpo, thus his reasoning proceeds. "If of a man we predicate good, and of an horse running, the predicate or thing predicated is not the same with the subject or that of which it is predicated, but the essential definition of man is one, and of good another. And again, to be a horse differs from to be running. For being asked the definition of the one and of the other, we do not give the same for them both; and therefore those err who predicate the one of the other. For if good is the same with man, and to run the same with a horse, how is good affirmed also of food and medicine, and again (by Jupiter) to run of a lion and a dog? But if the predicate is different, then we do not rightly say that a man is good, and a horse runs." Now if Stilpo is in this exorbitant and grossly mistaken, not admitting any copulation of such things as are in the subject, or affirmed of the subject, with the subject itself; but holding that every one of them, if it is not absolutely one and the same thing with that to which it happens or of which it is spoken, ought not to be spoken or affirmed of it,–no, not even as an accident; it is nevertheless manifest, that he was only offended with some words, and opposed the usual and accustomed manner of speaking, and not that he overthrew man's life, and turned his affairs upside down.

Colotes, then, having got rid of the old philosophers, turns to those of his own time, but without naming any of them; though he would have done better either to have reproved by name these moderns, as he did the ancients, or else to have named neither of them. But he who has so often employed his pen against Socrates, Plato, and Parmenides, evidently demonstrates that it is through cowardice he dares not attack the living, and not for any modesty or reverence, of which he showed not the least sign to those who were far more excellent than these. But his meaning is, as I suspect, to assault the Cyrenaics first, and afterwards the Academics, who are followers of Arcesilaus. For it was these who doubted of all things; but those, placing the passions and imaginations in themselves, were of opinion that the belief proceeding from them is not sufficient for the assuring and affirming of things but, as if it were in the siege of a town, abandoning what is without, they have shut themselves up in the passions, using only it seems, and not asserting it is, of things without. And therefore they cannot, as Colotes says of them, live or have the use of things. And then speaking comically of them, he adds: "These deny that there is a man, a horse, a wall; but say that they themselves (as it were) become walls, horses, men," or "take on the images of walls, horses, or men." In which he first maliciously abuses the terms, as caluminators are usually wont to do. For though these things follow from the sayings of the Cyrenaics, yet he ought to have declared the fact as they themselves teach it. For they affirm that things then become sweet, bitter, lightsome, or dark, when each thing has in itself the natural unobstructed operation of one of these impressions. But if honey is said to be sweet, an olive-branch bitter, hail cold, wine hot, and the nocturnal air dark, there are many beasts, things, and men that testify the contrary. For some have an aversion for honey, others feed on the branches of the olive-tree; some are scorched by hail, others cooled with wine; and there are some whose sight is dim in the sun but who see well by night. Wherefore opinion, containing itself within these sensations, remains safe and free from error; but when it goes forth and attempts to be curious in judging and pronouncing concerning exterior things, it often deceives itself, and opposes others, who from the same objects receive contrary sensations and different imaginations.

And Colotes seems properly to resemble those young children who are but beginning to learn their letters. For, being accustomed to learn them where they see them in their own horn-books and primers, when they see them written anywhere else, they doubt and are troubled; so those very discourses, which he praises and approves in the writings of Epicurus, he neither understands nor knows again, when they are spoken by others. For those who say that the sense is truly informed and moulded when there is presented one image round and another broken, but nevertheless permit us not to pronounce that the tower is round and the oar broken, confirm their own sensations and imaginations, but they will not acknowledge and confess that the things without are so affected. But as the Cyrenaics must say that they are imprinted with the figure of a horse or of a wall, but refuse to speak of the horse or the wall; so also it is necessary to say that the sight is imprinted with a figure round or with three unequal sides, and not that the tower is in that manner triangular or round. For the image by which the sight is affected is broken; but the oar whence that image proceeds is not broken. Since, then, there is a difference between the sensation and the external subject, the belief must either remain in the sensation, or else–if it maintains the being in addition to the appearing–be reproved and convinced of untruth. And whereas they cry out and are offended in behalf of the sense, because the Cyrenaics say not that the thing without is hot, but that the effect made on the sense is such; is it not the same with what is said touching the taste, when they say that the thing without is not sweet, but that some function and motion about the sense is such? And for him who says that he has received the apprehension of an human form, but perceives not whether it is a man, whence has he taken occasion so to say? Is it not from those who affirm that they receive an apprehension of a bowed figure and form, but that the sight pronounces not that the thing which was seen is bowed or round, but that a certain image of it is such? Yes, by Jupiter, will some one say; but I, going near the tower or touching the oar, will pronounce and affirm that the one is straight and the other has many angles and faces; but he, when he comes near it, will confess that it seems and appears so to him, and no more. Yes, certainly, good sir, and more than this, when he sees and observes the consequence, that every imagination is equally worthy of belief for itself, and none for another; but that they are all in like condition. But this your opinion is quite lost, that all the imaginations are true and none false or to be disbelieved, if you think that these ought to pronounce positively of that which is without, but those you credit no farther than that they are so affected. For if they are in equal condition as to their being believed, when they are near or when they are far off, it is just that either upon all of them, or else not upon these, should follow the judgment pronouncing that a thing is. But if there is a difference in the being affected between those that are near and those that are far off, it is then false that one sense and imagination is not more express and evident than another. Therefore those they call attestations and counterattestations are nothing to the sense, but are concerned only with opinion. So, if they would have us following these to pronounce concerning exterior things, making being a judgment of opinion, and what appears an affection of sense, they transfer the judicature from which is totally true to that which often fails.

But how full of trouble and contradictions in respect of one another these things are, what need is there to say at present? But the reputation of Arcesilaus, who was the best beloved and most esteemed of all the philosophers in his time, seems to have been no small eyesore to Epicurus; who says of him that delivering nothing peculiar to himself or of his own invention, he imprinted in illiterate men the opinion and esteem of his being very knowing and learned. Now Arcesilaus was so far from desiring any glory by being a bringer-in of new opinions, and from arrogating to himself those of the ancients, that the sophisters of that time blamed him for attributing to Socrates, Plato, Parmenides, and Heraclitus the doctrines concerning the retention of assent, and the incomprehensibility of things; having no need so to do, but only that he might strengthen them and render them recommendable by ascribing them such illustrious personages. For this, therefore, thanks to Colotes, and to every one who declares that the academic doctrine was from a higher times derived to Arcesilaus. Now as for retention of assent and the doubting of all things, not even those who have much labored in the manner, and strained themselves to compose great books and large treatises concerning it, were ever able to stir it; but bringing at last out of the Stoa itself the cessation from all actions, as the Gorgon to frighten away the objections that came against them, they were at last quite tired and gave over. For they could not, what attempts and stirs soever they made, obtain so much from the instinct by which the appetite is moved to act, as to suffer itself to be called an assent, or to acknowledge sense for the origin and principle of its propension, but it appeared of its own accord to present itself to act, as having no need to be joined with anything else. For against such adversaries the combat and dispute is lawful and just. And

> Such words as you have spoke, the like you may
> Expect to hear.
> ("Iliad," xx. 250.)

For to speak to Colotes of instinct and consent is, I suppose, all one as to play on the harp before an ass. But to those who can give ear and conceive, it is said that there are in the soul three sorts of motions,–the imaginative, the appetitive, and the consenting. As to the imaginative or the apprehension, it cannot be taken away, though one would. For one cannot, when things approach, avoid being informed and (as it were) moulded by them, and receiving an impression from them. The appetite, being stirred up by the imaginative, effectually moves man to that which is proper and agreeable to his nature, just as when there is made a propension and inclination in the principal and reasonable part. Now those who withhold their assent and doubt of all things take not away this, but make use of the appetition or instinct naturally conducting every man to that which seems convenient for him. What, then, is the only thing that they shun? That in which is bred falsehood and deceit,–that is, opining, and haste in giving consent,–which is a yielding through weakness to that which appears, and has not any true utility. For action stands in need of two things, to wit, the apprehension or imagination of what is agreeable to Nature, and the instinct or appetition driving to that which is so imagined; of which, neither the one nor the other is repugnant to the retention of assent. For reason withdraws us from opinion, and not from appetition or imagination. When, therefore, that which is delectable seems to us to be proper for us, there is no need of opinion to move and carry us to it, but appetition immediately exerts itself, which is nothing else but the motion and inclination of the soul.

It is their own axiom, that a man must only have sense and be flesh and blood and pleasure will appear to be good. Wherefore also it will seem good to him who withholds his assent. For he also participates of sense, and is made of flesh and blood, and as soon as he has conceived an imagination of good, desires it and does all things that it may not escape from him; but as much as possibly he can, he will keep himself with that which is agreeable to his nature, being drawn by natural and not by geometrical constraints. For these goodly, gentle, and tickling motions of the flesh are, without any teacher, attractive enough of themselves–even as these men forget not to say–to draw even him who will not in the least acknowledge and confess that he is softened and rendered pliable by them. "But how comes it to pass," perhaps you will say, "that he who is thus doubtful and withholds his assent hastens not away to the mountain, instead of going to the bath? Or that, rising up to go forth into the market-place, he runs not his head against the wall, but takes his way directly to the door?" Do you ask this, who hold all the senses to be infallible, and the apprehensions of the imagination certain and true? It is because the bath appears to him not a mountain, but a bath; and the door seems not a wall, but a door; and the same is to be said of every other thing. For the doctrine of retention does not pervert the sense, nor by absurd passions and motions work in it an alteration disturbing the imaginative faculty; but it only takes away opinions, and for the rest, makes use of other things according to their nature.

But it is impossible, you will say, not to consent to things that are evident; for to deny such things as are believed is more absurd than neither to deny nor affirm. Who then are they that call in question things believed, and contend against things that are evident? They who overthrow and take away divination, who say that there is not any government of Divine Providence, who deny the sun and the moon–to whom all men offer sacrifices and whom they honor and adore–to be animated. And do not you take away that which is apparent to all the world, that the young are contained in the nature of their parents? Do you not, contrary to the sense of all men, affirm that there is no medium between pleasure and pain, saying that not to be in pain is to be in the fruition of pleasure, that not to do is to suffer, and that not to rejoice is to be grieved?

But to let pass all the rest, what is more evident and more generally believed by all men, than that those who are seized with melancholy distempers, and whose brain is troubled and whose wits are distracted, do, when the fit is on them and their understanding altered and transported, imagine that they see and hear things which they neither see nor hear? Whence they frequently cry out:–

Women in black arrayed bear in their hands,
To burn mine eyes, torches and fiery brands.

And again:–

See, in her arms she holds my mother dear.
(Euripides, "Iphigenia in Tauris," 289.)

These, and many other illusions more strange and tragical than these,–resembling those mormos and bugbears which they themselves laugh at and deride, as they are described by Empedocles to be, "with sinuous feet and undeveloped hands, bodied like ox and faced like man,"–with certain other prodigious and unnatural phantoms, these men have gathered together out of dreams and the alienations of distracted minds, and affirm that none of them is a deception of the sight, a falsity, or inconsistence; but that all these imaginations are true, being bodies and figures that come from the ambient air. What thing then is there so impossible in Nature as to be doubted of, if it is possible to believe such reveries as these? For these men, supposing that such things as never any mask-maker, potter, designer of wonderful images, or skilful and all-daring painter durst join together, to deceive or make sport for the beholders, are seriously and in good earnest existent,–nay, which is more, affirming that, if they are not really so, all firmness of belief, all certainty of judgment and truth, is forever gone,–do by these their suppositions and affirmations cast all things into obscurity, and bring fears into our judgments, and suspicions into our actions,–if the things which we apprehend, do, are familiarly acquainted with, and have at hand are grounded on the same imagination and belief with these furious, absurd, and extravagant fancies. For the equality which they suppose to be in all apprehensions rather derogates from the credit of such as are usual and rational, than adds any belief to those that are unusual and repugnant to reason. Wherefore we know many philosophers who would rather and more willingly grant that no imagination is true than that all are so, and that would rather simply disbelieve all the men they never had conversed with, all the things they had not experimented, and all the speeches they had not heard with their own ears, than persuade themselves that any one of these imaginations, conceived by these frantic, fanatical, and dreaming persons, is true. Since then there are some imaginations which may, and others which may not be rejected, it is lawful for us to retain our assent concerning them, though there were no other cause but this discordance, which is sufficient to work in us a suspicion of things, as having nothing certain and assured, but being altogether full of obscurity and perturbation. For in the disputes about the infinity of worlds and the nature of atoms and individuums and their inclinations, although they trouble and disturb very many, there is yet this comfort, that none of all these things that are in question is near us, but rather every one of them is far remote from sense. But as to this diffidence, perplexity, and ignorance concerning sensible things and imaginations, found even in our eyes, our ears, and our hands, what opinion does it not shock? What consent does it not turn upside down? For if men neither drunk, intoxicated, nor otherwise disturbed in their senses, but sober, sound in mind, and professedly writing of the truth and of the canons and rules by which to judge it, do in the most evident passions and motions of the senses set down either that which has no existence for true, or that which is existent for false, it is not strange that a man should be silent about all things, but rather that he assent to anything; nor is it incredible that he should have no judgment about things which appear, but rather that he should have contrary judgments. For it is less to be wondered, that a man should neither affirm the one nor the other but keep himself in a mean between two opposite things, than that he should set down things repugnant and contrary to one another. For he that neither affirms nor denies, but keeps himself quiet, is less repugnant to him who affirms an opinion than he who denies it, and to him who denies an opinion than he who affirms it. Now if it is possible to withhold one's assent concerning these things, it is not impossible also concerning others, at least according to your opinion, who say that one sense does not exceed another, nor one imagination another.

The doctrine then of retaining the assent is not, as Colotes thinks, a fable or an invention of rash and light-headed young men who please themselves in babbling and prating; but a certain habit and disposition of men who desire to keep themselves from falling into error, not leaving the judgment at a venture to such suspected and inconstant senses, nor suffering themselves to be deceived by those who hold that in doubtful matters things which do not appear to the senses are credible and ought to be believed, when they see so great obscurity and uncertainty in things which do appear. But the infinity you assert is a fable, and so indeed are the images you dream of: and he breeds in young men rashness and self-conceitedness who writ of Pythocles, not yet eighteen years of age, that there was not in all Greece a better or more excellent nature, that he admirably well expressed his convictions, and that he was in other respects behaved like a women,–praying that all these extraordinary endowments of the young man might not work him hatred and envy. But these are sophists and arrogant, who write so impudently and proudly against great and excellent personages. I confess indeed, that Plato, Aristotle, Theophrastus and Democritus contradicted those who went before them; but never durst any man besides Colotes set forth with such an insolent title as this against all at once.

Whence it comes to pass that, like to such as have offended some Divinity, confessing his fault, he says thus towards the end of His book: "Those who have established laws and ordinances and instituted monarchies and other governments in towns and cities, have placed human life in great repose and security and delivered it from many troubles; and if any one should go about to take this away, we should lead the life of savage beasts, and should be every one ready to eat up one another as we meet." For these are the very words of Colotes, though neither justly nor truly spoken. For if any one, taking away the laws, should leave us nevertheless the doctrines of Parmenides, Socrates, Plato, and Heraclitus, we should be far from mutually devouring one another and leading the life of beasts. For we should fear dishonest things, and should for honesty alone venerate justice, the gods our superiors, and magistrates, believing that we have spirits and daemons who are the guardians and superintendents of human life, esteeming all the gold that is upon and within the earth not to be equivalent to virtue; and doing that willingly by reason, as Xenocrates says, which we now do by force and through fear of the law. When then will our life become savage, uncivilized, and bestial? When, the laws being taken away, there shall be left doctrines inciting men to pleasure; when the world shall bethought not to be ruled and governed by Divine Providence; when those men shall be esteemed wise who spit at honesty if it is not joined with pleasure; and when such discourses and sentences as these shall be scoffed at and derided:–

For Justice has an eye which all things sees;
and again:–
God near us stands, and views whate'er we do;
and once more: "God, as antiquity has delivered to holding the beginning, middle, and end of the universe, makes a direct line, walking according to Nature. After him follows Justice, a punisher of those who have been deficient in their duties by transgressing the divine law."

For they who contemn these things as if they were fables, and think that the sovereign good of man consists about the belly, and in those other passages by which pleasure is admitted, are such as stand in need of the law, and fear, and stripes, and some king, prince, or magistrate, having in his hand the sword of justice; to the end that they may not devour their neighbors through their gluttony, rendered confident by their atheistical impiety. For this is the life of brutes, because brute beasts know nothing better nor more honest than pleasure, understand not the justice of the gods, nor revere the beauty of virtue; but if Nature has bestowed on them any point of courage, subtlety, or activity, they make use of it for the satisfaction of their fleshly pleasure and the accomplishment of their lusts. And the sapient Metrodorus believes that this should be so, for he says: "All the fine, subtle, and ingenious inventions of the soul have been found out for the pleasure and delight of the flesh, or for the hopes of attaining to it and enjoying it, and every act which tends not to this end is vain and unprofitable." The laws being by such discourses and philosophical reasons as these taken away, there wants nothing to a beast-like life but lions' paws, wolves' teeth, oxen's paunches, and camels' necks; and these passions and doctrines do the beasts themselves, for want of speech and letters, express by their bellowings, neighings, and brayings, all their voice being for their belly and the pleasure of their flesh, which they embrace and rejoice in either present or future; unless it be perhaps some animal which naturally takes delight in chattering and garrulity.

No sufficient praise therefore or equivalent to their deserts can be given those who, for the restraining of such bestial passions, have set down laws, established policy and government of state, instituted magistrates and ordained good and wholesome laws. But who are they that utterly confound and abolish this? Are they not those who withdraw themselves and their followers from all part in the government? Are they not those who say that the garland of tranquillity and a reposed life are far more valuable than all the kingdoms and principalities in the world? Are they not those who declare that reigning and being a king is a mistaking the path and straying from the right way of felicity? And they write in express terms: "We are to treat how a man may best keep and preserve the end of Nature, and how he may from the very beginning avoid entering of his own free will and voluntarily upon offices of magistracy, and government over the people." And yet again, these other words are theirs: "There is no need at all that a man should tire out his mind and body to preserve the Greeks, and to obtain from them a crown of wisdom; but to eat and drink well, O Timocrates, without prejudicing, but rather pleasing the flesh." And yet in the constitution of laws and policy, which Colotes so much praises, the first and most important article is the belief and per-suasion of the gods. Wherefore also Lycurgus heretofore consecrated the Lacedaemonians, Numa the Romans, the ancient Ion the Athenians, and Deucalion universally all the Greeks, through prayers, oaths, oracles, and omens, making them devout and affectionate to the gods by means of hopes and fears at once. And if you will take the pains to travel through the world, you may find towns and cities without walls, without letters, without kings, without houses, without wealth, without money, without theatres and places of exercise; but there was never seen nor shall be seen by man any city without temples and gods, or without making use of prayers, oaths, auguries, and sacrifices for the obtaining of blessings and benefits, and the averting of curses and calamities. Nay, I am of opinion, that a city might sooner be built without any ground to fix it on, than a commonweal be constituted altogether void of any religion and opinion of the gods,–or being constituted, be preserved. But this, which is the foundation and ground of all laws, do these men, not going circularly about, nor secretly and by enigmatical speeches, but attacking it with the first of their most principal opinions directly subvert and overthrow; and then afterwards, as if they were haunted by the Furies, they come and confess that they have grievously offended in thus taking away the laws, and confounding the ordinances of justice and policy, that they may not be capable of pardon. For to err in opinion, though it be not the part of wise men, is at least human; but to impute to others the errors and of-fences they commit themselves, how can any one declare what it is, if he forbears to give it the name it deserves?

For if, in writing against Antidorus or Bion the sophister, he had made mention of laws, policy, order, and justice, might not either of them have said to him, as Electra did to her mad brother Orestes:–

> Lie still at ease, poor wretch; keep in thy bed,
> *(Euripides, "Orestes," 258.)*

and there cherish thy bit of body, leaving those to expostulate and find fault with me who have themselves lived the life of a citizen and house-holder? Now such are all those whom Colotes has reviled and railed at in his book. Amongst whom, Democritus in his writings advises and exhorts to the learning of the science of politics, as being the greatest of all, and to the accustoming one's self to bear fatigues, by which men attain to great wealth and honor. And as for Parmenides, he beautified and adorned his native country with most excellent laws which he there established, so that even to this day the officers every year, when they enter first on the exercise of their charges, are obliged to swear that they will observe the laws and ordinances of Parmenides. Empedocles brought to justice some of the principal of his city, and caused them to be condemned for their insolent behavior and embezzling of the public treasure, and also delivered his country from sterility and the plague–to which calamities it was before subject–by immuring and stopping up the holes of certain mountains, whence there issued an hot south wind, which overspread all the plain country and blasted it. And Socrates, after he was condemned, when his friends offered him, if he pleased, an opportunity of making his escape, absolutely refused to make use of it, that he might maintain the authority of the laws, choosing rather to die unjustly than to save himself by disobeying the laws of his country. Melissus, being captain general of his country, vanquished the Athenians in a battle at sea. Plato left in his writings excellent discourses concerning the laws, government, and policy of a commonweal; and yet he imprinted much better in the hearts and minds of his disciples and familiars, which caused Sicily to be freed by Dion, and Thrace to be set at liberty by Pytho and Heraclides, who slew Cotys. Chabrias also and Phocion, those two great generals of the Athenians, came out of the Academy.

As for Epicurus, he indeed sent certain persons into Asia to chide Timocrates, and caused him to be removed out of the king's palace, because he had offended his brother Metrodorus; and this is written in their own books. But Plato sent of his disciples and friends, Aristonymus to the Arcadians, to set in order their commonweal, Phormio to the Eleans, and Menedemus to the Pyrrhaeans. Eudoxus gave laws to the Cnidians, and Aristotle to the Stagirites, who were both of them the intimates of Plato. And Alexander the Great demanded of Xenocrates rules and precepts for reigning well. And he who was sent to the same Alexander by the Grecians dwelling in Asia, and who most of all inflamed and stimulated him to embrace and undertake the war against the barbarian king of Persia, was Delius the Ephesian, one of Plato's familiars. Zeno, the disciple of Parmenides, having attempted to kill the tyrant Demylus, and failing in his design, maintained the doctrine of Parmenides, like pure and fine gold tried in the fire, that there is nothing which a magnanimous man ought to dread but dishonor, and that there are none but children and women, or effeminate and women-hearted men, who fear pain. For, having with his own teeth bitten off his tongue, he spit it in the tyrant's face.

But out of the school of Epicurus, and from among those who follow his doctrine, I will not ask what tyrant-killer has proceeded, nor yet what man valiant and victorious in feats of arms, what lawgiver, what prince, what counsellor, or what governor of the people; neither will I demand, who of them has been tormented or has died for supporting right and justice. But which of all these sages has for the benefit and service of his country undertaken so much as one voyage at sea, gone of an embassy, or expended a sum of money? What record is there extant of one civil action in matter of government, performed by any of you? And yet, because Metrodorus went down one day from the city as far as the haven of Piraeus, taking a journey of forty stadia to assist Mithres a Syrian, one of the king of Persia's court who had been arrested and taken prisoner, he writ of it to every one and in all his letters, Epicurus also highly magnifying and extolling this wonderful voyage. What value then, think you, would they have put upon it, if they had done such an act as Aristotle did, who procured the restoration and rebuilding of Stagira, the town of his nativity, after it had been destroyed by King Philip? Or as Theophrastus, who twice delivered his city, when possessed and held by tyrants? Would not the river Nile sooner have given over to bear the paper-reed, than they have been weary of writing their brave exploits?

And it is not the greatest dishonor, that, of so many sects of philosophers as have existed, they alone should enjoy the benefits that are in cities, without having ever contributed to them anything of their own; but far more serious is it that, while there are not even any tragical or comical poets who do not always endeavor to do or say some good thing or other in defence of the laws and policy these men, if peradventure they write, write of policy, that we may not concern ourselves in the government of the commonweal,–of rhetoric, that we may not perform an act of eloquence,–and of royalty, that we may shun the living and conversing with kings. Nor do they ever name any of those great personages who have intermeddled in civil affairs, but only to scoff at them and abolish their glory. Thus they say that Epaminondas had something of good, but that infinitesimal, or [Greek omitted], for that is the very word they use. They moreover call him iron-hearted, and ask what ailed him that he went marching his army through all Peloponnesus, and why he did not rather keep himself quiet at home with a garland on his head, employed only in cherishing and making much of his body. But methinks I ought not in this place to omit what Metrodorus writ in his book of Philosophy, when, utterly abjuring all meddling in the management of the state, he said thus: "Some, through an excess of vanity and arrogance, have so deep a comprehension into the business of it, that in discussing the precepts of good life and virtue, they allow themselves to be carried away with the very same desires as were Lycurgus and Solon." What is this? Was it then vanity and abundance of vanity, to set free the city of Athens, to render Sparta well-policied and governed by wholesome laws, that young men might do nothing licentiously, nor get children upon common courtesans and whores, and that riches, delights, intemperance, and dissolution might no longer bear sway and have command in cities, but law and justice? For these were the desires of Solon. To this Metrodorus, by way of scorn and contumely, adds this conclusion: "It is then very well beseeming a native born gentleman to laugh heartily, as at other men, so especially at these Solons and Lycurguses." But such a one, O Metrodorus, is not a gentleman, but a servile and dissolute person, and deserves to be scourged, not with that whip which is for free-born persons, but with that scourge made with ankle-bones, with which those eunuch sacrificers called Galli were wont to be chastised, when they failed of performing their duty in the ceremonies and sacrifices of the Goddess Cybele, the great Mother of the Gods.

But that they made war not against the lawgivers but against the laws themselves, one may hear and understand from Epicurus. For in his questions, he asks himself, whether a wise man, being assured that it will not be known, will do anything that the laws forbid. To which he answers: "That is not so easy to settle simply,"–that is "I will do it indeed, but I am not willing to confess it." And again, I suppose writing to Idomeneus, he exorts him not to make his life a slave to the laws or to the options of men, unless it be to avoid the trouble they prepare, by the scourge and chastisement, so near at hand. If those who abolish laws, governments, and polices of men subvert and destroy human life, and if Metrodorus and Epicurus do this, by dehorting and withdrawing their friends from concerning themselves in public affairs, by hating those who intermeddle in them, by reviling the first most wise lawgivers, and by advising contempt of the laws provided there is no fear and danger of the whip punishment. I do not see that Colotes has brought so many false accusations against the other philosophers as he has alleged and advanced true ones against the writings and doctrines of Epicurus.

Platonic Questions

QUESTION I. WHY DID GOD COMMAND SOCRATES TO ACT THE MIDWIFE'S PART TO OTHERS, BUT CHARGED HIMSELF NOT TO GENERATE; AS HE AFFIRMS IN THEAETETUS? (See Plato, "Theaetetus," p. 149 B.)

For he would never have used the name of God in such a merry, jesting manner, though Plato in that book makes Socrates several times to talk with great boasting and arrogance, as he does now. "There are many, dear friend, so affected towards me, that they are ready even to snap at me, when I offer to cure them of the least madness. For they will not be persuaded that I do it out of goodwill, because they are ignorant that no god bears ill-will to man, and that therefore I wish ill to no man; but I cannot allow myself either to stand in a lie or to stifle the truth." (Ibid. p. 151 C.) Whether therefore did he style his own nature, which was of a very strong and pregnant wit, by the name of God,–as Menander says, "For our mind is God," and as Heraclitus, "Man's genius is a Deity"? Or did some divine cause or some daemon or other impart this way of philosophizing to Socrates, whereby constantly interrogating others, he cleared them of pride, error, and ignorance, and of being troublesome both to themselves and to others? For about that time there happened to be in Greece several sophists; to these some young men paid great sums of money, for which they purchased a strong opinion of learning and wisdom, and of being stout disputants; but this sort of disputation spent much time in trifling squabblings, which were of no credit or profit. Now Socrates, using an argumentative discourse by way of a purgative remedy procured belief and authority to what he said, because in refuting others he himself affirmed nothing; and he the sooner gained upon people, because he seemed rather to be inquisitive after the truth as well as they, than to maintain his own opinion.

Now, however useful a thing judgment is, it is mightily infected By the begetting of a man's own fancies. For the lover is blinded with the thing loved; and nothing of a man's own is so beloved as is the opinion and discourse he has begotten. And the distribution of children said to be the justest, in respect of discourses is the unjustest; for there a man must take his own, but here a man must choose the best, though it be another man's. Therefore he that has children of his own, is a worse judge of other men's; it being true, as the sophister said well, "The Eleans would be the most proper judges of the Olympic games, were no Eleans gamesters." So he that would judge of disputations cannot be just, if he either seeks the bays for himself, or is himself antagonist to either of the antagonists. For as the Grecian captains, when they were to settle by their suffrages who had behaved himself the best, every man of them voted for himself; so there is not a philosopher of them all but would do the like, besides those that acknowledge, like Socrates, that they can say nothing that is their own; and these only are the pure uncorrupt judges of the truth. For as the air in the ears, unless it be still and void of noise in itself, without any sound or humming, does not exactly take sounds so the philosophical judgment in disputations, if it be disturbed and obstreperous within, is hardly comprehensive of what is said without. For our familiar and inbred opinion will not allow that which disagrees with itself, as the number of sects and parties shows, of which philosophy–if she deals with them in the best manner–must maintain one to be right, and all the others to be contrary to the truth in their positions.

Furthermore, if men can comprehend and know nothing, God did justly interdict Socrates the procreation of false and unstable discourses, which are like wind-eggs, and did him convince others who were of any other opinion. And reasoning, which rids us of the greatest of evils, error and vanity of mind, is none of the least benefit to us; "For God has not granted this to the Esculapians." (Theognis, vs. 432,) Nor did Socrates give physic to the body; indeed he purged the mind of secret corruption. But if there be any knowledge of the truth, and if the truth be one, he has as much that learns it of him that invented it, as the inventor himself. Now he the most easily attains the truth, that is persuaded he has it not; and he chooses best, just as he that has no children of his own adopts the best. Mark this well, that poetry, mathematics, oratory, and sophistry, which are the things the Deity forbade Socrates to generate, are of no value; and that of the sole wisdom about what is divine and intelligible (which Socrates called amiable and eligible for itself), there is neither generation nor invention by man, but reminiscence. Wherefore Socrates taught nothing, but suggesting principles of doubt, as birth-pains, to young men, he excited and at the same time confirmed the innate notions. This he called his Art of Midwifery, which did not (as others professed) extrinsically confer intelligence upon his auditors; but demonstrated it to be innate, yet imperfect and confused, and in want of a nurse to feed and fortify it.

QUESTION II. WHY DOES HE CALL THE SUPREME GOD FATHER AND MAKER OF ALL THINGS? (Plato, "Timaeus," p. 28 C.)

Is it because he is (as Homer calls him) of created gods and men the Father, and of brutes and things that have no soul the maker? If Chrysippus may be believed, he is not properly styled the father of the afterbirth who supplied the seed, although it arose from the seed. Or has Plato figuratively called the maker of the world the father of it? In his Convivium he calls Phaedrus the father of the amatorious discourse which he had commenced; and so in his Phaedrus ("Phaedrus," p. 261 A.) he calls him "father of noble children," when he had been the occasion of many pre-eminent discourses about philosophical questions. Or is there any difference between a father and a maker? Or between procreation and making? For as what is procreated is also made, but not the contrary recreated did also make, for the procreation of an animal is the making of it. Now the work of a maker–as of a builder, a weaver, a musical-instrument maker, or a statuary–is altogether apart and separate from its author; but the principle and power of the procreator is implanted in the progeny, and contains his nature, the progeny being a piece pulled off the procreator. Since therefore the world is neither like a piece of potter's work nor joiner's work, but there is a great share of life and divinity in it, which God from himself communicated to and mixed with matter, God may properly be called Father of the world–since it has life in it–and also the maker of it.

And since these things come very near to Plato's opinion, consider, I pray, whether there may not be some probability in them. Whereas the world consists of two parts, body and soul, God indeed made not the body; but matter being at hand, he formed and fitted it, binding up and confirming what was infinite within proper limits and figures. But the soul, partaking of mind, reason, and harmony, was not only the work of God, but part of him not only made by him, but begot by him.

QUESTION III. In the Republic, ("Republic," vi. pp. 509 D-511 E.) he assumes the universe, as one line to be cut into two unequal parts; again he cuts each of these parts in two after the same manner, and supposes the two sections first made to form the two genera of things sensible and things intelligible. The first stands for the genus of intelligibles, comprehending in the first subdivision the primitive forms, in the second the mathematics. Of sensibles, the first subdivision comprehends solid bodies, the second comprehends the images and representations of them. Moreover, to every one of these four he has assigned its proper criterion;–to the first reason; to the mathematics, the understanding; to sensibles, belief; to images and likenesses, conjecture.

BUT WHAT DOES HE MEAN BY DIVIDING THE UNIVERSE INTO UNEQUAL PARTS? AND WHICH OF THE SECTIONS, THE INTELLIGIBLE OR THE SENSIBLE, IS THE GREATER? FOR IN THIS HE HAS NOT EXPLAINED HIMSELF.

At first glance it will appear that the sensible is the greater portion. For the essence of intelligibles being indivisible, and in the same respect ever the same, is contracted into a little, and pure; but an essence divisible and running through bodies constitutes the sensible part. Now what is immaterial is limited; but body in respect of matter is infinite and unlimited, and it becomes sensible only when it is limited by partaking of the intelligible. Besides, as every sensible has many images, shadows, and representations, and from one and the same original several copies may be taken both by nature and art; so the latter must surpass the former in number, according to Plato, who makes things of the intellect to be patterns or ideas of things sensible, as if the last were images and reflections. Further, Plato derives the knowledge of ideas by abstraction and cutting away of body, leading us by mathematical discipline from arithmetic to geometry, thence to astronomy, and placing harmony above them all. For things become geometrical by the accession of magnitude to quantity; solid, by the accession of profundity to magnitude; astronomical, by the accession of motion to solidity; harmonical, by the accession of sound to motion. Take then sound from moving bodies, motion from solids, profundity from superficies, magnitude from quantity, we then reach pure intelligible ideas, which have no difference among themselves as regards the one single intelligible essence. For unity makes no number unless joined by the infinite binary; then it makes a number. And thence we proceed to points, thence to lines, from them to superficies, and solids, and bodies, and to the qualities of the bodies so and so affected. Now the reason is the only criterion of intelligibles; and the understanding is the reason in the mathematics, where intelligibles appear as if in mirrors. But as to the knowledge of bodies, because of their multitude, Nature has given us five powers or distinctions of senses; nor are all bodies discerned by them, many escaping sense by reason of their smallness. And though every one of us consists of a body and soul, yet the hegemonic and intellectual faculty is small, being hid in the huge mass of flesh. And the case is the same in the universe, as to sensible and intelligible. For intelligibles are the principles of bodily things, but everything is greater than the principle whence it came.

Yet, on the contrary, some will say that, by comparing sensibles with intelligibles, we match things mortal with divine, in some measure; for God is in intelligibles. Besides, the thing contained is ever less than the containing, and the nature of the universe contains the sensible in the intelligible. For God, having placed the soul in the middle, hath extended it through all, and hath covered it all round with bodies. The soul is invisible, and cannot be perceived by any of the senses, as Plato says in his Book of Laws; therefore every man must die, but the world shall never die. For mortality and dissolution surround every one of our vital faculties. The case is quite otherwise in the world; for the corporeal part, contained in the middle by the more noble and unalterable principle, is ever preserved. And a body is said to be without parts and indivisible for its minuteness; but what is incorporeal and intelligible is so, as being simple and sincere, and void of all firmness and difference. Besides, it were folly to think to judge of incorporeal things by corporeal. The present, or now, is said to be without parts and indivisible, since it is everywhere and no part of the world is void of it. But all affections and actions, and all corruptions and generations in the world, are contained by this same now. But the mind is judge only of what is intelligible, as the sight is of light, by reason of its simplicity and similitude. But bodies, having several differences and diversities, are comprehended, some by one judicatory function, others by another, as by several organs. Yet they do not well who despise the discriminative faculty in us; for being great, it comprehends all sensibles, and attains to things divine. The chief thing he himself teaches in his Banquet, where he shows us how we should use amatorious matters, turning our minds from sensible goods to things discernible only by the mind, that we ought not to be enslaved by the beauty of any body, study, or learning, but laying aside such weakness, should turn to the vast ocean of beauty. (See Plato's "Symposium," p. 210 D.)

QUESTION IV. WHAT IS THE REASON THAT, THOUGH PLA-
TO ALWAYS SAYS THAT THE SOUL IS ANCIENTER THAN THE
BODY, AND THAT IT IS THE CAUSE AND PRINCIPLE OF ITS
RISE, YET HE LIKEWISE SAYS, THAT NEITHER COULD THE
SOUL EXIST WITHOUT THE BODY, NOR THE REASON WITH-
OUT THE SOUL, BUT THE SOUL IN THE BODY AND THE REA-
SON IN THE SOUL? FOR 80 THE BODY WILL SEEM TO BE AND
NOT TO BE, BECAUSE IT BOTH EXISTS WITH THE SOUL, AND
IS BEGOT BY THE SOUL.

Perhaps what we have often said is true; viz., that the soul without
reason and the body without form did mutually ever coexist, and neither
of them had generation or beginning. But after the soul did partake of
reason and harmony, and being through consent made wise, it wrought
a change in matter, and being stronger than the other's motions, it drew
and converted these motions to itself. So the body of the world drew its
original from the soul, and became conformable and like to it. For the
soul did not make the nature of the body out of itself, or out of nothing; but it wrought an orderly and pliable body out of one disorderly and
formless. Just as if a man should say that the virtue of the seed is with the
body, and yet that the body of the fig-tree or olive-tree was made of the
seed, he would not be much out; for the body, its innate motion and mutation proceeding from the seed, grew up and became what it is. So, when
formless and indefinite matter was once formed by the inbeing soul, it
received such a form and disposition.

QUESTION V. WHY, SINCE BODIES AND FIGURES ARE CON-
TAINED PARTLY BY RECTILINEARS AND PARTLY BY CIRCLES,
DOES HE MAKE ISOSCELES TRIANGLES AND TRIANGLES
OF UNEQUAL SIDES THE PRINCIPLES OF RECTILINEARS; OF
WHICH THE ISOSCELES TRIANGLE CONSTITUTES THE CUBE,
THE ELEMENT OF THE EARTH; AND A SCALENE TRIANGLE
FORMS THE PYRAMID, THE OCTAHEDRON THE SEED OF
FIRE, AIR AND WATER RESPECTIVELY, AND THE ICOSAHE-
DRON;–WHILE HE PASSES OVER CIRCULARS, THOUGH HE
DOES MENTION THE GLOBE, WHERE HE SAYS THAT EACH
OF THE AFORE-RECKONED FIGURES DIVIDES A ROUND
BODY THAT CIRCUMSCRIBES IT INTO EQUAL PARTS. (See "Ti-
maeus," pp. 53-56.)

Is their opinion true who think that he ascribed a dodecahedron to
the globe, when he says that God made use of it in delineating the universe? For upon account of the multitude of its bases and the obtuseness

of its angles, avoiding all rectitude, it is flexible, and by circumtension, like globes made of twelve skins, it becomes circular and comprehensive. For it has twenty solid angles, each of which is contained by three obtuse planes, and each of these contains one and the fifth part of a right angle. Now it is made up of twelve equilateral and equangular quinquangles (or pentagons), each of which consists of thirty of the first scalene triangles. Therefore it seems to resemble both the Zodiac and the year, it being divided into the same number of parts as these.

Or is a right line in Nature prior to circumference; or is circumference but an accident of rectilinear? For a right line is said to bend; and a circle is described by a centre and distance, which is the place of a right line from which a circumference is measured, this being everywhere equally distant from the middle. And a cone and a cylinder are made by rectilinears; a cone by keeping one side of a triangle fixed and carrying another round with the base,–a cylinder, by doing the like with a parallelogram. Further, that is nearest to principle which is less; but a right is the least of all lines, as it is simple; whereas in a circumference one part is convex without, another concave within. Besides, numbers are before figures, as unity is before a point, which is unity in position. But indeed unity is triangular; for every triangular number (Triangular numbers are those of which equilateral triangles can be formed in this way:

Such are: 3, 6, 10, 15, 21, 28, 36, 45, etc.; that is, numbers formed by adding the digits in regular order. (G.)) taken eight times, by adding unity, becomes quadrate; and this happens to unity. Therefore a triangle is before a circle, whence a right line is before a circumference. Besides, no element is divided into things compounded of itself; indeed there is a dissolution of all other things into the elements. Now a triangle is divided into no circumference, but two diameters cut a circle into four triangles; therefore a rectilinear figure is before a circular, and has more of the nature of an element. And Plato himself shows that a rectilinear is in the first place, and a circular is only consequential and accidental. For when he says the earth consists of cubes, each of which is contained with rectilinear superficies, he says the earth is spherical and round. Therefore there was no need of making a peculiar element for round things, since rectilinears, fitted after a certain manner among themselves, do make up this figure.

Besides, a right line, whether great or little, preserves the same rectitude; but as to the circumference of a circle, the less it is, the crookeder it is; the larger, the straighter. Therefore if a convex surface stands on a plane, it sometimes touches the under plane in a point, sometimes in a line. So that a man may imagine that a circumference is made up of little right lines.

But observe whether this be not true, that no circle or sphere in this world is exactly drawn; but since by the tension and circumtension of the straight lines, or by the minuteness of the parts, the difference is hidden, the figure seems circular and round. Therefore no corruptible body moves circularly, but altogether in a right line. To be truly spherical is not in a sensible body, but is the element of the soul and mind, to which he has given circular motion, as being agreeable to their nature.

QUESTION VI. HOW COMES IT TO PASS THAT IN PHAEDRUS IT IS SAID, THAT THE NATURE OF A WING, BY WHICH ANYTHING THAT IS HEAVY IS CARRIED UPWARDS, PARTICIPATES MOST OF THE BODY OF GOD? (See "Phaedrus," p. 246 D.)

Is it because the discourse is of love, and love is of beauty inherent in a body? Now beauty, by similitude to things divine, moves and reminds the soul. Or it may be (without too much curiosity) he may be understood in plain meaning, to wit, that the several faculties of the soul being employed about bodies, the power of reasoning and understanding partakes most about divine and heavenly things; which he did not improperly call a wing, it raising the soul from mean and mortal things to things above.

QUESTION VII. IN WHAT SENSE DOES PLATO SAY, THAT THE ANTIPERISTASIS (OR REACTION) OF MOTION–BY REASON THERE IS NO VACUUM–IS THE CAUSE OF THE PHENOMENA IN PHYSICIANS' CUPPING-GLASSES, IN SWALLOWING, IN CASTING WEIGHTS, IN THE RUNNING OF WATER, IN THUNDER, IN THE ATTRACTION OF THE LOADSTONE, AND IN THE HARMONY OF SOUNDS? (See "Timaeus," pp. 79-81.)

For it seems unreasonable to ascribe the reason of such different effects to the selfsame cause.

How respiration is made by the reaction of the air, he has sufficiently shown. But the others, he says, seem to be effected miraculously, but really the bodies force each other aside and change places with one another; while he has left for us to discover how each is particularly done.

As to cupping-glasses, the case is thus: the air next to the flesh being comprehended and inflamed by the heat, and being made more rare than the pores of the brass, does not go into a vacuum (for there is no such thing), but into the air that is without the cupping-glass, and has an impulse upon it. This air drives that before it; and each, as it gives way, strives to succeed into the place which was vacuated by the cession of the first. And so the air approaching the flesh comprehended by the cupping-glass, and attracting it, draws the humors into the cupping-glass.

Swallowing takes place in the same way. For the cavities about the mouth and stomach are full of air; when therefore the meat is squeezed down by the tongue and tonsils, the elided air follows what gives way, and also forces down the meat.

Weights also thrown cleave the air and dissipate it, as they fall with force; the air recoiling back, according to its proper tendency to rush in and fill the vacuum, follows the impulse, and accelerates the motion.

The fall also of thunderbolts is like to darting anything. For by the blow in the cloud, the fiery matter exploded breaks into the air; and it being broken gives way, and again being contracted above, by main force it presses the thunderbolt downwards contrary to Nature.

And neither amber nor the loadstone draws anything to it which is near, nor does anything spontaneously approach them. But this stone emits strong exhalations, by which the surrounding air being impelled forceth that which is before it; and this being drawn round in the circle, and returning into the vacuated place, forcibly draws the iron in the same movement. In amber there is a flammeous and spirituous nature, and this by rubbing on the surface is emitted by recluse passages, and does the same that the loadstone does. It also draws the lightest and driest of adjacent bodies, by reason of their tenuity and weakness; for it is not so strong nor so endued with weight and strength as to force much air and to act with violence and to have power over great bodies, as the magnet has. But what is the reason the air never draws a stone, nor wood, but iron only, to the loadstone? This is a common question both by those who think the coition of these bodies is made by the attraction of the loadstone, and by such as think it done by the incitement of the iron. Iron is neither so rare as wood, nor altogether so solid as gold or a stone; but has certain pores and asperities, which as far as inequality is concerned are proportionable to the air; and the air being received in certain positions, and having (as it were) certain stays to hang to, does not slip off; but when it is carried up to the stone and is forced against it, it draws the iron by force along with it to the stone. Such then may be the reason of this.

But the manner of the waters running over the earth is not so evident. But it is observable that the waters of lakes and ponds stand immovable, because the air about them stagnates immovable and admits of no vacuity. For the water on the surface of lakes and seas is troubled and fluctuates as the air is moved, it following the motion of the air, and moving as it is moved. For the force from below causes the hollowness of the wave, and from above the swelling thereof; until the air ambient and containing the water is still. Therefore the flux of such waters as follow the motion of the receding air, and are impelled by that which presses behind, is continued without end. And this is the reason that the stream increases with the waters, and is slow where the water is weak, the air not giving way, and therefore enduring less reaction. So the water of fountains must needs go upwards, the extrinsic air succeeding into the vacuity and throwing the water out. In a close house, that keeps in the air and wind, the floor sprinkled with water causes an air or wind, because, as the sprinkled water falls, the air gives way. For it is so provided by Nature that air and water force one another and give way to one another; because there is no vacuity in which one can be fixed without experiencing the change and alteration in the other.

Concerning symphony, he shows how sounds harmonize. A quick sound is acute, a slow is grave. Therefore acute sounds move the senses the quicker; and these dying and grave sounds supervening, what arises from the contemperation of one with the other causes pleasure to the ear, which we call harmony. And by what has been said, it may easily be understood that air is the instrument of these things. For sound is the stroke upon the sense of the hearer, caused by the air; and the air strikes as it is struck by the thing moving,–if violent, acutely,–if languid, softly. The violent stroke comes quick to the ear; then the circumambient air receiving a slower, it affects and carries the sense along with it.

QUESTION VIII. WHAT MEANS TIMAEUS (See "Timaeus," p. 42 D.) WHEN HE SAYS THAT SOULS ARE DISPERSED INTO THE EARTH, THE MOON, AND INTO OTHER INSTRUMENTS OF TIME?

Does the earth move like the sun, moon, and five planets, which for their motions he calls organs or instruments of time? Or is the earth fixed to the axis of the universe; yet not so built as to remain immovable, but to turn and wheel about, as Aristarchus and Seleucus have shown since; Aristarchus only supposing it, Seleucus positively asserting it? Theophrastus writes how that Plato, when he grew old, repented him that he had placed the earth in the middle of the universe, which was not its place.

Or is this contradictory to Plato's opinion elsewhere, and in the Greek instead of [Greek omitted] should it be written [Greek omitted], taking the dative case instead of the genitive, so that the stars will not be said to be instruments, but the bodies of animals? So Aristotle has defined the soul to be "the actualization of a natural organic body, having the power of life." The sense then must be this, that souls are dispersed into meet organical bodies in time. But this is far besides his opinion. For it is not once, but several times, that he calls the stars instruments of time; as when he says, the sun was made, as well as other planets, for the distinction and conservation of the numbers of time.

It is therefore most proper to understand the earth to be here an instrument of time; not that the earth is moved, as the stars are; but that, they being carried about it, it standing still makes sunset and sunrising, by which the first measures of time, nights and days, are circumscribed. Wherefore he called it the infallible guard and artificer of night and day. For the gnomons of dials are instruments and measures of time, not in being moved with the shadows, but in standing still; they being like the earth in closing out the light of the sun when it is down,–as Empedocles says that the earth makes night by intercepting light. This therefore may be Plato's meaning.

And so much the rather might we consider whether the sun is not absurdly and without probability said to be made for the distinction of time, with the moon and the rest of the planets. For as in other respects the dignity of the sun is great; so by Plato in his Republic (Plato, "Republic." vi. pp. 508, 509.) the sun is called the king and lord of the whole sensible nature, as the Chief Good is of the intelligible. For it is said to be the offspring of Good, it supplying both generation and appearance to things visible; as it is from Good that things intelligible both are and are understood. But that this God, having such a nature and so great power, should be only an instrument of time, and a sure measure of the difference that happens among the eight orbs, as they are slow or swift in motion, seems neither decent nor highly rational. It must therefore be said to such as are startled at these things, that it is their ignorance to think that time is the measure of motion in respect of sooner or later, as Aristotle calls it; or quantity in motion, as Speusippus; or an interval of motion and nothing else, as some of the Stoics define it, by an accident, not comprehending its essence and power, which Pindar has not ineptly expressed in these words: Time, who surpasses all in the seats of the blest. Pythagoras also, when he was asked what time was, answered, it was the soul of the universe. For time is no affection or accident of motion, but the cause, power, and principle of that symmetry and order that confines all created beings, by which the animated nature of the universe is moved. Or rather, this order and symmetry itself–so far as it is motion–is called time. For this,

> *Walking by still and silent ways,*
> *Mortal things with justice leads.*
> *(Euripides, "Troades," 887.)*

According to the ancients, the principle of the soul is a number moving itself. Therefore Plato says that time and heaven were coexistent, but that motion was before heaven had being. But time was not. For then there neither was order, nor measure, nor determination; but indefinite motion, as it were, the formless and rude matter of time.... But when matter was informed with figures, and motion with circuitions, from that came the world, from this time. Both are representations of God; the world, of his essence; time, of his eternity in the sphere of motion, as the world is God in creation. Therefore they say heaven and motion, being bred together, will perish together, if ever they do perish. For nothing is generated without time, nor is anything intelligible without eternity; if this is to endure forever, and that never to die when once bred. Time, therefore, having a necessary connection and affinity with heaven, cannot be called simple motion, but (as it were) motion in order having terms and periods; whereof since the sun is prefect and overseer, to determine, moderate, produce, and observe changes and seasons, which (according to Heraclitus) produce all things, he is coadjutor to the governing and chief God, not in trivial things, but in the greatest and most momentous affairs.

QUESTION IX. Since Plato in his Commonwealth, discoursing of the faculties of the soul, has very well compared the symphony of reason and of the irascible and the concupiscent faculties to the harmony of the middle, lowest, and highest chord, (See "Republic," iv. p. 443.) some men may properly inquire:–

DID PLATO PLACE THE RATIONAL OR THE IRASCIBLE FACULTY IN THE MIDDLE? FOR HE IS NOT CLEAR IN THE POINT.

Indeed, according to the natural system of the parts, the place of the irascible faculty must be in the middle, and of the rational in the highest, which the Greeks call hypate. For they of old called the chief and supreme [Greek omitted]. So Xenocrates calls Jove, in respect of immutable things, [Greek omitted] (or HIGHEST), in respect of sublunary things [Greek omitted] (or LOWEST). And long before him, Homer calls the chief God [Greek omitted], HIGHEST OF RULERS. And Nature has of due given the highest place to what is most excellent, having placed reason as a steersman in the head, and the appetitive faculty at a distance, last of all and lowest. And the lowest place they call [Greek omitted], as the names of the dead, [Greek omitted] and [Greek omitted], do show. And some say, that the south wind, inasmuch as it blows from a low and obscure place, is called [Greek omitted]. Now since the appetitive faculty stands in the same opposition to reason in which the lowest stands to the highest and the last to the first, it is not possible for the reason to be uppermost and first, and yet for any other part to be the one called [Greek omitted] (or HIGHEST). For they that ascribe the power of the middle to it, as the ruling power, are ignorant how they deprive it of a higher power, namely, of the highest, which is compatible neither to the irascible nor to the concupiscent faculty; since it is the nature of them both to be governed by and obsequious to reason, and the nature of neither of them to govern and lead it. And the most natural place of the irascible faculty seems to be in the middle of the other two. For it is the nature of reason to govern, and of the irascible faculty both to govern and be governed, since it is obsequious to reason, and commands the appetitive faculty when this is disobedient to reason. And as in letters the semi-vowels are middling between mutes and vowels, having something more than those and less than these; so in the soul of man, the irascible faculty is not purely passive, but hath often an imagination of good mixed with the irrational appetite of revenge. Plato himself, after he had compared the soul to a pair of horses and a charioteer, likened (as every one knows) the rational faculty to the charioteer, and the concupiscent to one of the horses, which was resty and unmanageable altogether, bristly about the ears, deaf and disobedient both to whip and spur; and the irascible he makes for the most part very obsequious to the bridle of reason, and assistant to it. As therefore in a chariot, the middling one in virtue and power is not the charioteer, but that one of the horses which is worse than his guider and yet better than his fellow; so in the soul, Plato gives the middle place not to the principal part, but to that faculty which has less of reason than the principal part and more than the third. This order also keeps the analogy of the symphonies, i.e. the proportion of the irascible to the rational (which is placed as hypate) making the diatessaron (or fourth), that of the irascible to the concupiscent (or nete) making the diapente (or fifth), and that of the rational to the concupiscent (as hypate to nete) making an octave or diapason. But should you place the rational in the middle, you would make the irascible farther from the concupiscent; though some of the philosophers have taken the irascible and the concupiscent faculty for the selfsame, by reason of their likeness.

But it may be ridiculous to describe the first, middle, and last by their place; since we see hypate highest in the harp, lowest in the pipe; and wheresoever you place the mese in the harp, provided it is tunable, it sounds more acute than hypate, and more grave than nete. Nor does the eye possess the same place in all animals; but whereever it is placed, it is natural for it to see. So a pedagogue, though he goes not foremost but follows behind, is said to lead ([Greek omitted]), as the general of the Trojan army,

>   Now in the front, now in the rear was seen,
>   And kept command;
>   ("Iliad," xi. 64.)

but wherever he was, he was first and chief in power. So the faculties of the soul are not to be ranged by mere force in order of place or name, but according to their power and analogy. For that in the body of man reason is in the highest place, is accidental. But it holds the chief and highest power, as mese to hypate, in respect of the concupiscent; as mese to nete, in respect of the irascible; insomuch as it depresses and heightens,–and in fine makes a harmony,–by abating what is too much and by not suffering them to flatten and grow dull. For what is moderate and symmetrous is defined by mediocrity. Still more is it the end of the rational faculty to bring the passions to moderation, which is called sacred, as making a harmony of the extremes with reason, and through reason with each other. For in chariots the best of the team is not in the middle; nor is the skill of driving to be placed as an extreme, but it is a mean between the inequality of the swiftness and the slowness of the horses. So the force of reason takes up the passions irrationally moved, and reducing them to measure, constitutes a mean betwixt too much and too little.

QUESTION X. WHY SAID PLATO, THAT SPEECH WAS COMPOSED OF NOUNS AND VERBS? (Plato's "Sophist," p. 262 A.)

For he seems to make no other parts of speech but them. But Homer in a playful humor has comprehended them all in one verse:–

[Greek omitted] ("Iliad", i. 185.)

For in it there is pronoun, participle, noun, preposition, article, conjunction, adverb, and verb, the particle–[Greek omitted] being put instead of the preposition [Greek omitted]; for [Greek omitted], TO THE TENT, is said in the same sense as [Greek omitted], TO ATHENS. What then shall we say for Plato?

Is it that at first the ancients called that [Greek omitted], or speech, which once was called protasis and now is called axiom or proposition,–which as soon as a man speaks, he speaks either true or false? This consists of a noun and verb, which logicians call the subject and predicate. For when we hear this said, "Socrates philosphizeth" or "Socrates is changed," requiring nothing more, we say the one is true, the other false. For very likely in the beginning men wanted speech and articulate voice, to enable them to express clearly at once the passions and the patients, the actions and the agents. Now, since actions and affections are adequately expressed by verbs, and they that act and are affected by nouns, as he says, these seem to signify. And one may say, the rest signify not. For instance, the groans and shrieks of stage players, and even their smiles and silence, make their discourse more emphatic. But they have no absolute power to signify anything, as a noun and verb have, but only an ascititious power to vary speech; just as they vary letters who mark spirits and quantities upon letters, these being the accidents and differences of letters. This the ancients have made manifest, whom sixteen letters sufficed to speak and write anything.

Besides, we must not fail to observe, that Plato says that speech is composed OF these, not BY these; nor must we find fault with Plato for omitting conjunctions, prepositions, and the rest, any more than we should criticise a man who should say such a medicine is composed of wax and galbanum, because fire and utensils are omitted, without which it cannot be produced. For speech is not composed of these; yet by their means, and not without them, speech must be composed. As, if a man says BEATS or IS BEATEN, and adds Socrates and Pythagoras to the same, he gives us something to conceive and understand. But if a man pronounce INDEED or FOR or ABOUT and no more, none can conceive any notion of a body or matter; and unless such words as these be uttered with verbs and nouns, they are but empty noise and chattering. For neither alone nor joined one with another do they signify anything. And join and confound together conjunctions, articles, and prepositions, supposing you would make something of them; yet you will be taken to babble, and not to speak sense. But when there is a verb in construction with a noun, the result is speech and sense. Therefore some do with justice make only these two parts of speech; and perhaps Homer is willing to declare himself of this mind, when he says so often,

[Greek omitted]

For by [Greek omitted] he usually means a verb, as in these verses.

[Greek omitted],

and,

[Greek omitted] ("Odyssey," xxiii. 183; viii. 408.)

For neither conjunction, article, nor preposition could be said to be [Greek omitted] (TERRIBLE) or [Greek omitted] (SOUL GRIEVING), but only a verb signifying a base action or a foolish passion of the mind. Therefore, when we would praise or dispraise poets or writers, we are wont to say, such a man uses Attic nouns and good verbs, or else common nouns and verbs; but none can say that Thucydides or Euripides used Attic or common articles.

What then? May some say, do the rest of the parts conduce nothing to speech? I answer, They conduce, as salt does to victuals; or water to barley cakes. And Euenus calls fire the best sauce. Though sometimes there is neither occasion for fire to boil, nor for salt to season our food, which we have always occasion for. Nor has speech always occasion for articles. I think I may say this of the Latin tongue, which is now the universal language; for it has taken away all prepositions, saving a few, nor does it use any articles, but its nouns are (as it were) without skirts and borders. Nor is it any wonder, since Homer, who in fineness of epic surpasses all men, has put articles only to a few nouns, like handles to cans, or crests to helmets. Therefore these verses are remarkable wherein the articles are suppressed.–

[Greek omitted] ("Iliad," xiv. 459.)

and,

[Greek omitted] (Ibid. xx. 147.)

and some few besides. But in a thousand others, the omission of the articles hinders neither perspicuity nor elegance of phrase.

Now neither an animal nor an instrument nor arms nor anything else is more fine, efficacious, or pleasanter, for the loss of a part. Yet speech, by taking away conjunctions, often becomes more persuasive, as here:–

> *One rear'd a dagger at a captive's breast;*
> *One held a living foe, that freshly bled*
> *With new-made wounds, another dragg'd a dead.*
> *(Ibid. xviii. 536.)*

And this of Demosthenes:–

"A bully in an assault may do much which his victim cannot even report to another person,–by his attitude, his look, his voice,–when he insults, when he attacks as an enemy, when he smites with his fist, when he strikes a blow on the face. These rouse a man; these make a man beside himself who is unused to such foul abuse."

And again:–

"Not so with Midias; but from the very day, he talks, he abuses, he shouts. Is there an election of magistrates? Midias the Anagyrrasian is nominated. He is the advocate of Plutarchus; he knows state secrets; the city cannot contain him." ("Demosthenes against Midias," p. 537,25, and p. 578, 29.)

Therefore the figure asyndeton, whereby conjunctions are omitted, is highly commended by writers of rhetoric. But such as keep overstrict to the law, and (according to custom) omit not a conjunction, rhetoricians blame for using a dull, flat, tedious style, without any variety in it. And inasmuch as logicians mightily want conjunctions for the joining together their axioms, as much as charioteers want yokes, and Ulysses wanted withs to tie Cyclop's sheep; this shows they are not parts of speech, but a conjunctive instrument thereof, as the word conjunction imports. Nor do conjunctions join all, but only such as are not spoken simply; unless you will make a cord part of the burthen, glue a part of a book, or distribution of money part of the government. For Demades says, that money which is given to the people out of the exchequer for public shows is the glue of a democracy. Now what conjunction does so of several propositions make one, by fitting and joining them together, as marble joins iron that is incited with it in the fire? Yet the marble neither is nor is said to be part of the iron; although in this case the substances compose the mixture and are melted together, so as to make a common substance from several and to be mutually affected. But there be some who think that conjunctions do not make anything one, but that this kind of speech is merely an enumeration, as when magistrates or days are reckoned in order.

Moreover, as to the other parts of speech, a pronoun is manifestly a sort of noun; not only because it has cases, but because some pronouns, when they are used of objects already defined, by their mere utterance give the most distinct designation of them. Nor do I know whether he that says SOCRATES or he that says THIS ONE does more by name declare the person.

The thing we call a participle, being a mixture of a verb and noun is nothing of itself, as are not the common names of male and female qualities (i.e, adjectives), but in construction it is put with others, in regard of tenses belonging to verbs, in regard of cases to nouns. Logicians call them [Greek omitted], (i.e., REFLECTED),–as [Greek omitted], comes from [Greek omitted], and from [Greek omitted],–having the force both of nouns and appellatives.

And prepositions are like to the crests of a helmet, or footstools and pedestals, which (one may rather say) do belong to words than are words themselves. See whether they rather be not pieces and scraps of words, as they that are in haste write but dashes and points for letters. For it is plain that [Greek omitted] and [Greek omitted] are abbreviations of the whole words [Greek omitted] and [Greek omitted]. As undoubtedly for haste and brevity's sake, instead of [Greek omitted] and [Greek omitted] men first said [Greek omitted] and [Greek omitted].

Therefore every one of these is of some use in speech; but nothing is a part or element of speech (as has been said) except a noun and a verb, which make the first juncture allowing of truth or falsehood, which some call a proposition or protasis, others an axiom, and which Plato called speech.

The Life and Poetry of Homer

(HOMERIC QUOTATIONS ARE almost all taken from Lord Derby's "Iliad" and Butcher and Long's "Odyssey." The first is indicated by the letter I, the second by O.)

Homer, who was in time first among most poets and by his power first of all poets, we justly read first, thereby gaining the greatest advantages for our language, for our intellect, and for practical knowledge. Let us speak of his poetry, first having shortly recalled his origin.

Homer, Pindar says, was a Chian and of Smyrnae; Simonides says a Chian; Antimachus and Nicander, a Colophonion; but the philosopher Aristotle says he was of Iete; the historian Ephorus says he was from Kyme. Some do not hesitate to say he was from Salamis in Cyprus; some, an Argive. Aristarchus and Dionysius the Thracian say that he was an Athenian. By some he is spoken of as the son of Maeon and Kritheus; by others, (a son) of the river-god Meles.

Just as there is a difficulty about his origin, so there is about the time in which he flourished. Aristarchus says he lived about the period of the Ionian emigration; this happened sixty years after the return of the Heraclidae. But the affair of the Heraclidae took place eighty years after the destruction of Troy. Crates reports that he lived before the return of the Heraclidae, so he was not altogether eighty years distant from the Trojan War. But by very many it is believed that he was born one hundred years after the Trojan War, not much before the foundation of the Olympic games, from which the time according to the Olympics is reckoned.

There are two poems of his, the "Iliad" and the "Odyssey," both, of which are arranged according to the number of letters in the alphabet, not by the poet himself, but by Aristarchus, the grammarian. Of these, the "Iliad" records the deeds of the Greeks and Barbarians in Ilium on account of the rape of Helen, and particularly the valor displayed in the war by Achilles. In the "Odyssey" are described the return of Ulysses home after the Trojan War, and his experiences in his wanderings, and how he took vengeance on those who plotted against his house. From this it is evident that Homer sets before us, through the "Iliad," bodily courage; in the "Odyssey," nobility of soul.

But the poet is not to be blamed because in his poetry he sets forth not only the virtues but the evils of the soul, its sadness and its joys, its fears and desires; for being a poet, it is necessary for him to imitate not only good but evil characters. For without these the deeds would not get the admiration of the hearer, who must pick out the better characters. And he has made the gods associating with men not only for the sake of interest and entertainment, but that he might declare by this that the gods care for and do not neglect men.

To sum up, an extraordinary and mythical narration of events is employed in order to stir his readers with wonder and to make his hearers strongly impressed. Whence he seems to have said some things contrary to what is likely. For the persuasive always follows where the remarkable and elevated are previously conjoined. Therefore he not only elevates actions, and turns them from their customary course, but words as well. That he always handles novel things and things out of the common sphere, and leads on his hearers, is evident to every one. And indeed in these fabulous narratives, if one reads not unattentively but carefully each element of what is said, Homer appears to have been at home in the whole sphere and art of logic, and to have supplied many incentives, and as it were seeds of all kinds of thought and action to his posterity, not to poets alone, but to the authors of historical and scientific works. Let us first look at his varied form of speech, and afterward at his sound knowledge on matters of fact. All poetry grips the hearer by definite order of coordinated expressions, by rhythm and metre, since the smooth and flowing, by becoming at the same time grave and sweet, forces the attention by its action on the senses. Whence it comes to pass also that it delights not only by the striking and attractive parts, but easily persuades by the parts tending to virtue.

The poems of Homer have the most perfect metre, the hexameter, which is also called heroic. It is called hexameter because each line has six feet: one of these is of two long syllables, called spondee; the other, of three syllables, one long and two short, which is called dactyl. Both are isochronic. These in interchangeable order fill out the hexameter verse. It is called heroic because in it the deeds of the heroes are recounted.

He makes use of a sound diction, combining the characteristics of every Greek dialect, from which it is plain that he travelled over the whole of Greece and among every people in it. He uses the ellipse of the Dorians, due to their practice of shortening their speech, saying for [Greek omitted], as (O. i. 392): "Immediately a beautiful horse ([Greek omitted]) was his," and for [Greek omitted] he uses [Greek omitted], as (O. xix. 543): "Because ([Greek omitted]) an eagle killed my geese"; and for [Greek omitted], "back," [Greek omitted], changing the o into a, the [Greek letter omitted] and the [Greek letter omitted] into its related letter. And [Greek omitted] he changes to [Greek omitted](I. xiv. 249): "For before at another time ([Greek omitted]) your precepts made me modest," and similar cases. Likewise, dropping the middle syllable, he says for [Greek omitted], "of like hair," and [Greek omitted], "of the same years," [Greek omitted]; and for [Greek omitted], that is, "of the same father," [Greek omitted]; for [Greek omitted]; "to tremble," [Greek omitted] for [Greek omitted], "I honour," [Greek omitted]. It is a characteristic of the Dorians also to transpose letters, as when they say for [Greek omitted], [Greek omitted].

In composite words he makes use of the syncope of the Aeolians, saying [Greek omitted] instead of [Greek omitted], "they went to sleep," and [Greek omitted], for [Greek omitted], "to subject."

Then when the third person of the imperfect among other Greek peoples ends in the diphthong [Greek letter], the Eolians end in [Greek letter], as when they say for [Greek omitted], "he was loving," [Greek omitted], and for [Greek omitted], "he was thinking," [Greek omitted]. This custom Homer followed, saying (I. xi. 105): "He bound ([Greek omitted]) in tender twigs," instead of [Greek omitted], and (O. v. 478): "Which neither any humid power of the wind penetrates" [Greek omitted]. Besides this they change [Greek letter] into [Greek letter], as they say [Greek omitted] for [Greek omitted], "odor," and [Greek Omitted] for [Greek omitted], "we knew."

Besides, they use pleonasm in some expressions, as when they put for [Greek omitted], "calm," [Greek omitted], [Greek omitted] for [Greek omitted], "but," [Greek omitted] got [Greek omitted], "having cried." And when to the second person of verbs they add [Greek omitted], for [Greek omitted] "thou speakest," [Greek omitted], and for [Greek omitted], "thou hast spoken," [Greek omitted]. Some attribute the doubling of the consonant to the Dorians, some to the Aeolians. Such as we find in I. v. 83: "Black death laid hold on [Greek omitted] him," [Greek omitted]; for [Greek omitted] as I. iii. 321: "Each did these deeds."

He preserves the peculiarity of the Ionians for the preterite tenses of verbs the aphaeresis, as where he says [Greek omitted] for [Greek omitted]. So in past tenses they are want to begin with the same letter as in present tenses and to leave off the [Greek letter] in the word [Greek omitted], "priest" and [Greek omitted], "hawk." Besides, they add [Greek letter] to the third persons of the subjunctive mood, as when they say for [Greek omitted] "may have come," [Greek omitted], and for [Greek omitted], "may have taken," [Greek omitted]. This participle they add to the dative, [Greek omitted], "to the gates," "to the woods." Besides, they say [Greek omitted] for "name", and [Greek omitted] for [Greek omitted], "disease" and [Greek omitted] for [Greek omitted], "empty," and [Greek omitted] for [Greek omitted], "black." And then they change long [Greek letter] into [Greek letter], as [Greek omitted] for [Greek omitted], "Juno," and for [Greek omitted], Minerva. And sometimes they change [Greek letter] into [Greek letter], saying for [Greek omitted], "having forgotten." Moreover, they write in full by diaeresis words which are circumflexed, for [Greek omitted], "intelligent," [Greek omitted]. In the same way they lengthen genitive singulars in [Greek omitted], as [Greek omitted], and genitive feminines in [Greek omitted], as [Greek omitted], "of gates," [Greek omitted], "of nymphs," and finally regular plurals of nouns in the neuter gender ending in [Greek letter] as [Greek omitted], [Greek omitted], "breasts," "darts," and their genitives likewise. They say in their way [Greek omitted] for [Greek omitted].

But he most largely used the Attic dialect for it was combined with others. For just as in Attic they say [Greek omitted] for [Greek omitted], "people," so he did, as [Greek omitted] and [Greek omitted], "debt." It is a custom with them sometimes to use contractions and to put one syllable for two, as for [Greek omitted], "word," [Greek omitted], and for [Greek omitted], "clothes," [Greek omitted]. Related to these is that Homeric expression, "the Trojans in crowds bent over" [Greek omitted], and another case, "fields bearing the lotos" [Greek omitted], instead of [Greek omitted]. Besides they take [Greek letter] from that type of optative, saying for [Greek omitted], "it might seem good to thee," [Greek omitted], for [Greek omitted], "mightiest thou be honored," [Greek omitted]. There is also an Atticism [Greek omitted] for [Greek omitted] in his verse (I. iii. 102):–

But you others discerned most quickly.

Likewise this, too, is Attic, "the more were worse [Greek omitted], the few better [Greek omitted], than their fathers;" we say [Greek omitted] or [Greek omitted]. And they do not prolong these by di-aeresis, [Greek omitted], as "oxen [Greek omitted] falling down," and, "fishes [Greek omitted] and birds." And that, too, is said in the Attic fashion (O. xii. 331):–

> Nor flowing do they break ([Greek omitted] for
> [Greek omitted]) by their violence.

In the same way as [Greek omitted], [Greek omitted].

And the taking away short vowels is Attic: [Greek omitted], "he is washed," [Greek omitted], "I think," [Greek omitted]; in the same way for [Greek omitted], "he is loosed," he says [Greek omitted]. The Attics say [Greek omitted], adding an unnecessary [Greek letter], whence also comes [Greek omitted], "he was pouring out wine." They contract the iota in words of this sort, as for [Greek omitted], "shores," [Greek omitted], "shores," and for [Greek omitted], [Greek omitted]. So also (I. xi. 782):–

> You two [Greek omitted] wished it very much.

Finally in datives ending in pure iota with a penultimate of alpha the same is done, as [Greek omitted], "horn," [Greek omitted], "old age," [Greek omitted], "ray." And this, too, is Attic, where it is said [Greek omitted], "let them be," and [Greek omitted], "let them follow," for [Greek omitted] and [Greek omitted]. The use of the dual which Homer repeatedly employs is of the same type. Also with feminine substantives he joins masculine articles, participles, and adjectives, as [Greek omitted]. This is a practice with Plato, as when he uses [Greek omitted] "pillaging," and [Greek omitted], "the wise just woman." So, too, Homer (I. viii. 455), speaking of Here and Athene, says:–

> In vain smitten [Greek omitted] with a thunderbolt on
> our chariots,–

and (I. iv. 22):–

> Athene was indeed unwilling [Greek omitted],–

and (I. ii. 742):–

> Famous [Greek omitted] Hippodamea.

Moreover the dialects have many peculiarities of construction. When the poet says (I. iv. 100):–

> But seek with your javelins of divine Menelaos,–

instead of the accusative, he presents an Attic usage. But when he says (I. ii. 186):–

> He took for him the sceptre and he took the cup for
> fair-cheeked Themis–

instead of "from him" and "from Themis," he is employing a Dorian usage.

Accordingly it appears how he makes his diction varied by throwing together words of all the Greek dialects, and sometimes he makes use of foreign words as are the aforesaid, sometimes archaic words, as when he says [Greek omitted], "falchion," and [Greek omitted], "sword," sometimes common and ordinary words, as when he says [Greek omitted], "sword and shield"; one might wonder how well common words in his poetry preserve dignity of speech.

But an artificially wrought style cultivates variation from the customary, by which it becomes clever, more dignified, and altogether more attractive. The turn of expression is called a Trope, and change of construction is called a Schema. The forms of these are described in technical treatises. Let us examine if any of these is omitted by Homer or whether anything else was discovered by his successors which he himself did not use first.

Among Tropes, Onomatopoeia is very common. For he knew the early origin of words. The first who gave names to things called many of them from what had taken place, and therefore introduced inarticulate sounds into writing. As when they said [Greek omitted], "to blow," [Greek omitted], "to cut," [Greek omitted], "to woo," [Greek omitted], "to thunder," and others like these. Whence he himself created certain words not previously existing, copying the things they signified, as [Greek omitted], "sound," and other things also indicating sounds, [Greek omitted], and others of the same kind. None could be found more significant. And again where some words pertaining to certain things he attributes to others, as when he says (I. xxi. 337):–

Bearing an evil fire,–

which signifies its power in burning, and "fever" he uses for "fire." Like these is the expression (I. xix. 25):–

Brass striking wounds,–

he writes to express wounds inflicted by brass. And to sum up he uses much novelty of speech, with great freedom, changing some from their customary use, giving distinction to others for the sake of infusing in his language beauty and grandeur.

He has also much fertility in epithets; these being fitted to their objects properly and naturally have the force of proper names, as when he gives to the several gods each some proper designation, so he calls Zeus the "all-wise and high thundering," and the Sun, Hyperion, "advancing aloft," and Apollo, Phoebus, that is, shining. But after the Onomatopoeia let us examine other Tropes.

Catechresis, which changes a word from a customary significa-tion to another not recognized. This is to be found in the poet when he says golden chain [Greek omitted], but [Greek omitted] properly means a rope, and when he says a goat helmet [Greek omitted]; now a helmet is [Greek omitted] in Homer, because it used to be made of dog's skin, not of goat's skin.

Metaphor, so-called because it transfers a thing from its proper signifi-cance to another with an analogous likeness to both, occurs in many and varied forms in verse, as is the line (O. ix. 481):–

He comes, having broken off the crown of a great mountain,–
and (O. x. 195):
An island which the sea laves and crowns.

For the relation a crown has to him whom it encircles, the same the sea has to an island. By making use of related but not usual words he makes his speech not only more beautiful but more picturesque.

There are in Homer various kinds of metaphors; some applied from animate things to animate, as, "the driver of the caerulean ship spoke" instead of the sailor, and "he went to Agamemnon the son of Atreus, the shepherd of the people" instead of king. Some are applied from ani-mate to inanimate, as (I. ii. 824):–

Under the extreme foot of Ida,–
that is, the rising ground. Also (I. ix. 141):–
The breast of the field,–
that is, the fertility. Others, on the contrary, from inanimate to ani-mate, as (I. xxiv. 205):–

The iron breast.

From inanimate to animate, as (O. v. 490):–
Preserving the seed of fire,–
instead of the generating origin. Then he has metaphors of verbs as well as substantives (I. xvii. 265):–

As the shores bellow with the smiting salt and gale,–
instead of "resound."

Another Trope which is called Metalepsis, signifying a different thing by a synonym (O. xv. 299):–

I beached the ship in the sharp islands,–
for he wishes to signify islands properly called jagged. Both words in Greek are synonyms. For in Greek sharp not only signifies swiftness of motion, but also in a figure that which rises into a slender shape. Such is the quotation (O. ix. 327):–

accompanied him and sharpened my pace.

Another Trope is named Synecdoche, called from this reason; that from what is properly meant, another of the like kind is understood. This Trope has also many varieties. For either we perceive the part from the whole, as (I. xii. 137):–

They advanced straight to the walls the burning bulls,–

for he wishes to indicate by the appellation "bulls" the leather out of which shields are wont to be made. Or from a part the whole (O. i. 343):–

I long for such a head,–

for from the head he signifies the man. And when for beautiful he says "endowed with beautiful cheeks," and for well armed he says "well greaved." Or from one the many, as when he speaks of Odysseus (O. i. 2):–

When he wasted the sacred citadel of Troy.

Not he by himself took Troy, but along with the rest of the Greeks. From the many one, as (I. iii. 397), "happy breasts," i.e. breast. From the species the genus, as (I. xii. 380):–

Casting on the hard marble,–

for marble is a species of rock. From the genus the species (O. ii. 159).–

To know the birds and to say many fitting things.

He wishes to say not all birds, but only the birds of auspices. From the instruments the action, as (I. ii. 827):–

Pandorus to whom he gave the bow of Apollo.

By the bow he indicates the skill in using it. And (O. xii. 172):–

Sitting they made the water white,–

and (O. iii. 486):–

Now others moved the whole day the thong of their sandal.

This comes from an accidental feature; in the first case "they were rowing," in the next "they were running," is to be implied. Besides there is the consequent to the precedent, as (O. xi. 245):–

She loosed the virgin zone.

It follows that she defiled it. From the consequent the precedent, as when instead of saying "to kill" he says "to disarm," that is, to spoil.

There is another Trope called Metonymy, i.e. when an expression applied properly to one thing indicates another related to it, such as (I. ii. 426):–

But the young men proceed to grind Demeter,–

for he means the crop of grain named from its inventor, Demeter. And when he says (O. xix. 28):–

They held the transfixed entrails over Hephaestus.

By the name Hephaestus he signifies fire. Like what has previously been mentioned is this (I. i. 223).–

Whoever shall touch my choenix,–

for what is contained in the choenix is intended.

There is besides another Trope, Autonomasia, when an epithet or co-title is used for a proper name, as in this example (I. viii. 39):–

The son of Peleus again attacked the son of Atreus
with petulant words.

By this he indicates Achilles and Agamemnon respectively. And again (I. xxii. 183):–

Be of good cheer, Tritonia, dear daughter,–

and in other places (I. xx. 39):–

Shorn Phoebus.

In the one case he means Athene and in the other Apollo.

There is, too, Antiphrasis, or an expression signifying the opposite from what it appears to do (I. i. 330):–

Seeing these Achilles did not rejoice.

He wishes to say the contrary, that seeing them he was disgusted.

There is also Emphasis, which through reflection adds vigor to what is said (O. xi. 523):–

But descending into the home which Epeus constructed.

In the word "descending" he reveals the great size of the house. Of the same kind is the line (I. xvi. 333):–

The whole sand was hot with blood,–

for in this he furnishes a more intense description, as if the sand was so bathed with blood that it was hot. These kind of Tropes were invented by Homer first of all.

Let us look at the changes of construction which are called figures to see if Homer also first invented these. Figure is a method of expression divergent from ordinary custom for the sake of ornament or utility, altered by a kind of fiction. For beauty is added to narrative by variety and change of expression, and these make the style more impressive. They are also useful because they exalt and intensify innate qualities and powers.

Among the figures Pleonasm is sometimes used for the sake of the metre; as in (I. xix. 247):–

Odysseus adding all ten talents of gold,–

for the word "all" is added without contributing to the sense. It is done for the sake of ornament, cf. (I. xviii. 12).–

Certainly the strenuous son of Menoetius is quite dead,–

for the word "quite" is pleonastic after the Attic fashion.

Sometimes by several forms of speech he unfolds his meaning. This is called Periphrasis. As when he says "Sons of the Achaeans" for Achaeans, and the "Herculean might" for Hercules.

Things are said figuratively by Mutation when the ordinary order is inverted. But he puts in an expression in the midst which is called Hyperbaton, as in this (I. xvii. 542):—

Just as a lion feeds on an eaten bull,—

instead of saying the lion eats up the bull. And so he passes the limits of the sentence (I. ii. 333):—

He said, and loudly cheered the Greeks–and loud
From all the hollow ships came back the cheers–
In admiration of Ulysses' speech.

The order is the Argives applauded with a great shout the speech of divine Odysseus.

Of the same kind is the figure called Parembole, or interposition, when something outside having nothing to do with the subject is introduced. If it is removed, the construction is not affected (I. i. 234):—

By this I say and with an oath confirm
By this my royal staff, which never more
Shall put forth leaf nor spray, since first it left
Upon the mountain side its parent stem
Nor blossom more; since all around the axe
Hath lopped both leaf and bark–...

and the rest as much as he has said about the sceptre, then joining what follows with the beginning (I. i. 340):—

The time shall come when all the sons of Greece
  Shall mourn Achilles' loss.

He uses also Palillogia–that is the repetition of some part of a sentence, or several parts are repeated. This figure is called Reduplication, such as (I. xx. 371):—

Encounter him well! Though his hands were hands of fire,
Of fire, his hands, his strength as burnished steel.

Sometimes certain insertions are made and they are repeated, as in (O. i. 22):—

Howbeit Poseidon had now departed for the distant Ethiopians,
the Ethiopians that are sundered in twain, the uttermost
of men.

This is a figure revealing the feeling of the speaker and at the same time affecting the hearer.

Of the same kind is Relation; when at the commencement of several members of a sentence the same part is repeated. An example of this from the poet is (I. ii. 671):–

Nireus three well-trimmed ships from Syme brought.
Nireus to Charops whom Aglaia bore.
Nireus the goodliest man of all the Greeks.

This figure is likewise adapted to excite the emotions and give sweetness to the expression.

He has also Regression. This is when one puts forward two names of objects. When the sense is not yet complete, the poet returns to both of the names, completing what is lacking in the sense, as (I. v. 518).–

Followed the thronging bands of Troy, by Mars and fierce
Bellona led: she by the hand wild uproar held; while Mars
a giant spear brandished aloft.

The characteristic of this figure is variety and perspicuity.

He has also the figure called Homoioteleuton in which the parts of the sentence have endings similar in sound and have the same syllables at the end (O. xv. 74):–

Men should love a guest while he is with them, and send
him on his way when he would depart,–

and in the following (O. vi. 42):–

And she departed to Olympus, where they say is the seat of the gods that standeth fast forever. Not by the wind is it shaken nor ever wet with rain nor doth the snow come nigh thereto, but most clear air is spread about it cloudless and the white light floats over it.

When periods or their members end in nouns which are of the same declension this is properly called Homoioptolon, as the following (I. ii. 87):–

[Greek omitted]

As swarms of bees, that pour in ceaseless stream
From out the crevice of some hollow rock.

The above and others like them add grace and attractiveness to the narrative.

As a proof of his care in composition we often see he employs two figures in the same verses, as Epanaphora and Homoioteleuton (I. ii. 382):–

Each sharpen well his spear, his shield prepare
Each to his fiery steeds their forage give.

Belonging to these is the figure called Parison, which is formed out of two or more numbers having an equal number of words (I. vii. 93):–

Shamed to refuse, but fearful to accept.–

and again (I. xvi. 282):–
Had cast away difference, had resumed friendship,–
That this figure gives much ornament of style is very clear.

The like grace comes from Paranomasia, when besides the name in question another similar one is added at a slight interval (I. vi. 130):–
Not long did Dryas' son, Lycurgus brave,–
and in another (I. ii. 758):–
Swift-footed Protheus led.

But the above examples are arranged either by Pleonasm or by some such like artifice. But there is another due to absence of a word. Of thes omitted the sense is plain from what has gone before, as in the following (I. ix. 328):–
Twelve cities have I taken with my ships,
Eleven more by land on Trojan soil,–
where the words "have I taken" are wanting in last line, but are supplied from the preceding one. This is said to be by Ellipse (I. xii. 243):–
One bird best to defend the fatherland,–
where the word "is" is lacking. And (I. xx. 293):–
Alas I the grief to me of great-hearted Aeneas,–
when the words "is present," "comes," or something of the kind, are understood.

There are many kinds of Ellipses in Homer; the effect of the figure is quickness.

Of this sort is Asyndeton when the conjunctions uniting sentences are removed. This is done not only for the sake of celerity, but also of the sake of emotional emphasis. Such as is the following (O. x. 251):–
We went on our way, noble Odysseus, up through the coppice
even as thou didst command; we found within the forest glades
the fair halls builded of polished stone of Circe.
In these the conjunction is dropped since the speaker seeks the quickest method of expressing his message. There is among the figures what is called the Incongruous or the Variation. It is used when the ordinary arrangement is made different. And the variety is due either to impressing grace and elegance to the words; the ordinary movements not seeming to be followed, but the alteration has an arrangement of its own.

It often takes place when the genders of nouns are changed as [Greek omitted] instead of [Greek omitted] and [Greek omitted]. It was not unusual for the ancients, and especially among the people of Attica, to use masculine for feminine as superior and more vigorous. Nor did they do this without rhyme and reason, but when they made use of a word, as an epithet apart from the body which was spoken of. For the words concerned with the body are "great, beautiful," those not connected with it, "glorious, fortunate." Besides, they are ambiguous on account of their composition. For in general all compound things are common to either gender. And wherever a verb or participle is used with a masculine and feminine noun, the masculine prevails (I. vi. 567):–

The virgins and the youths minding childish things,–

where the participle is masculine.

Certain things, owing to the peculiarity of the dialect or the custom of that time, are said differently, [Greek omitted] feminine instead of [Greek omitted] (O. i. 53):–

And himself upholds the tall pillars which keep earth
and sky asunder.

Often as the narrative proceeds he changes the genders, as in (O, xv. 125):–

I give to you the gift, my dear son.

Son is a neuter substantive to which the adjective agrees; the poet refers it to the person. Of the same kind is that which is said by Dione to Venus (I. v. 382):–

Have patience, dearest child; though much enforced.

Analogous to it is that (O. xi. 90):–

Anon came the soul of Theban Teiresias, with a golden sceptre
in his hand,–

for he made the participle [Greek omitted] agree not with the gender of soul [Greek omitted], but the gender of the body, that is, Teiresias. For often he looks not to the word but to the sense, as in this passage (I. xvi. 280):–

In all their spirit stirred, and the phalanxes moved hoping
for the idle son of Peleus from the ships,–

for the participle [Greek omitted] does not agree with the word "phalanxes," but with the men composing them.

In another way he changes genders, as when he says (O. xii. 75):–

And a dark cloud encompasses it; this never streams away,–

since [Greek omitted] and [Greek omitted], "cloud," are synonyms, using first [Greek omitted] he afterward makes his adjectives agree with [Greek omitted] understood. Like this are these verses (I. ii. 459):–

As various tribes of winged fowl or geese
Or cranes or long necked swans
Besides Coysters stream, now here, now there,
Disporting, ply their wings.

For having first set down generically the kinds of birds, which are neuter, then after speaking of the species in the masculine he comes back again to the neuter–settling down with a noise giving the proper agreement to the general word of the species.

The poet often changes the number as well as the gender (I. xv. 305):–

The crowd approach the ships of the Achaeans.

First comes a singular then a plural verb, plainly looking to the sense, for although the word "crowd" is called singular, yet it embraces many individuals.

Like it in the opposite way is when the plural precedes the singular follows (I. xvi. 264):–

They having a martial heart each one rushes on.

The word [Greek omitted] is singular, being applied to a multitude has the same effect as all ([Greek omitted]). The same kind of figure is the following (O. iii. 4):–

And they reached Pylas, the stablished castle of Neleus, and
the people were doing sacrifice on the seashore.

The people of Pylas are meant.

He has changes of cases, the nominative and the vocative being interchanged in the following verse (I. ii. 107):–

To Agamemnon last Thyestis left it,–

and (I. i. 411):–

Cloud-compelling Zeus,–

and (o. xvii. 415):–

Friend [Greek omitted] give me for thou dost not seem to me
to be the worst of the Greeks.

The genitive and dative are changed in the next example (I. iii. 16):–

Godlike Paris fights in front for the Trojans,–

instead of "in front of." And the contrary in the next (O. v. 68):–

There about the hollow cave trailed a gadding vine.

Where in the original the Greek word "cave" is in the genitive case, not as it should be, dative. And the cause of the mutation is that the nominative accusative and vocative seem to have a certain relation to one another. On which account nouns of the neuter gender and many masculine and feminine ones have these three cases alike. Likewise the genitive has a certain affinity with the dative. This is found in the dual number of all words. Hence the cases are changed contrary to what is usual. Sometimes it is possible to discover the reason for the change, as in the expression (I. v. 222):–

Understanding of the field,–

and (I. ii. 785):–

They crossed the field,–

just as if he had used the preposition "through."

A fine example of change of case is found in the beginning of both his poems:–

Sing, O Muse, the vengeance, etc., whence to Greece unnumbered ills arose.

Tell me, Muse, of that man, of many a shift and many the woes he suffered.

Sometimes after the genitive he brings in the nominative, as in this (I. i. 272):–

Of others who are now mortal.

He arranges many things in figures in various ways, as the following passage (I. ii. 350):–

For well I ween, that on the day when first
We Grecians hitherward our course address'd
To Troy the messengers of blood and death
Th' o'erruling son of Saturn, on our right
His lightning flashing, with auspicious sign
Assur'd us of his favor.

And the following is not unlike it (I. vi. 510):–

His bright arms flashing like the gorgeous sun
Hasten'd with boastful mien and rapid step.

And these things, according to the ancient fashion, he exalts not unreasonably. If any one changes the participles into verbs, he will discover the sequence, for the word "lightning" has the same value as "when it was lightning," and "relying" "since he relied." Like these cases are the following (O. xii. 73):–

There are two crags, one reaches the broad sky,

and (I. vii. 306):–

They parted: Ajax to the Grecian camp
And Hector to the ranks of Troy returned.

And others of the same kind. For it is reasonable when one is about to speak of two individuals to put first what is common to the two, keeping the nominative in both cases. It is plain that this common use displays much grace. Sometimes employing a common case he signifies only one, as in the following (I. iii. 211):–

Both sat down, Ulysses was the higher in honor.

The form of words he often changes, sometimes putting the comparative instead of the absolute (I. i. 32):–

That you may return a more sane being.

Sometimes the superlative for the positive, as (I. xi. 832);–
    Most just of Centaurs.
Such is the change in nouns. But in verbs there is a change in moods, as when the infinitive is used for the imperative, as (I. v. 124):–
    Go fearless onward, Diomed, to meet the Trojan darts,–
where the imperative "meet" might be expected.
Or the indicative in place of the optative, as (I. ii. 488):–
    The crowd I shall not relate nor name,–
where one would expect "I could not relate nor name." And, on the contrary, the optative for the indicative, as (I. v. 388):–
    Mars would then be lost,–for "was lost."
There is a variation of tenses when the present is used for the future (I. l. 29)–
    Her I release not till her youth be fled,–
instead of "shall flee." Or for the imperfect (O. vi. 86):–
    Where truly were the unfailing cisterns, and bright water
    wells up free from beneath,–
instead of "welled up." And the future for the present (O. i. 24):–
    Abiding some, where Hyperion will sink; and some, where
    he rises.
Or in place of the past (O. v. 300):–
    I fear that indeed the goddess may spake all things truly.
And the voices are often changed. Instead of the active, the passive and middle are often used, as (I. i. 194):–
    A great sword is drawn from its sheath,–
instead of "he drew." And (I. xiii. 4):–
    His keen glance turning to view,–instead of "seeing."
And, on the other hand, the active instead of the passive:–
    I shall give a tripod with a golden handle,–instead of
    "shall be given."
It can be seen how he changes numbers, putting the plural for the singular as often happens in common speech when one speaks of himself as if of several, as in the following (O. i. 10):–
    Of these things, goddess daughter of Zeus, from whatsoever
    source thou wilt declare even to us,–
instead of "to me."
We find with him a change of persons of one sort, as (I. v. 877):–
    The other gods, who in Olympus dwell,
    Are to thee obedient and we are submissive.
For since there are many gods, among whom is the person speaking, both classes are well indicated by saying, "they are obedient" and "we

are submissive." In another way leaving the person who is spoken of, he changes from one to another. This is called specifically Apostrophe, and affects us by its emotional character and stimulates the hearer, as in the following stanza (I. xv. 346):–

While loudly Hector to the Trojans called
To assail the ships and leave the bloody spoils
Whom I elsewhere and from the ships aloof
Shall find,–

changing from the narrative to direct discourse. In the narration itself he often uses Apostrophe (I. xx. 2.):

Round thee eager for the fray stood the sons of Greece.

But he makes use of direct narrative and change of persons, as in the following passage (I. ii. 337):–

Like children, Grecian warriors, ye debate
Like babes to whom unknown are feats of arms.
Atrides thou, as is thy wont, maintain
Unchang'd thy counsel; for the stubborn fight
Array the Greeks.

There is another kind of this Apostrophe (I. ii. 344):–

Thou wouldst not know to whom Tydides may join himself,–

instead of "no one can know."

And again (O. ix. 210):–

And a marvellous sweet smell went up from the mixing bowl:
then truly it was no pleasure to refrain.

58. He uses participles in the place of verbs, as in these words (I. viii. 306):–

Weighed down in a garden by this fruit,–

instead of "it is weighed," and (O. xiii. 113):–

Thither they as having knowledge of that place drive
their ships,–

instead of "before they knew."

And articles he often changes, setting demonstrative instead of relatives (I. xvi. 150):–

Whom Podarge, swift of foot, to Zephyr bore,–and the contrary
(I. xvii. 460):–
And breastplate: for his own his faithful friend hath lost.

So he was wont to change prepositions (I. i. 424):–

Yesterday he went through the banquet,–instead of "to the
banquet."

And (I. i. 10):–

And he stirred up an evil plague through the army.

Likewise he joins with a preposition a noun improperly, as in the verse (I. x. 101):–

Lest perchance they wish to decide the contest in the night,–

where the preposition is followed by, the accusative, not the genitive. And as to other prepositions, some he changes, some he omits (I. ii. 696):–

Of whom he lies lamenting,–instead of "concerning whom."

And (O. xxiii. 91):–

Expecting whether he would bespeak him,–instead of
"speak to him."

And other prepositions he in the same fashion changes or leaves out. And adverbs he changes, using indifferently motion towards, rest in, and motion from a place (I. xx. 151):–

His grandchildren were setting down from elsewhere,–instead of
"elsewhere" (I. vii. 219):–
And Ajax came from near,–instead of "near."

Finally he has changes of conjunctions, as (O. i. 433):–

He never lay with her and he shunned the wrath of his lady,–
instead of "for he shunned," etc. And these are the figures of
speech which not only all poets but the writers of prose have
employed.

But significance is given by him in many ways. One of which is Proanaphonesis, which is used when any one in the midst of a narration uses an order proper to other things, as in the following line (O. xxi, 98):–

He was to be the first that should taste the arrow,–

and Epiphonesis (I. xvii. 32):–

After the event may e'en a fool be wise.

The use of Prosopopoiia is frequent and varied with him. For he introduces many different people speaking together, to whom he attributes various characteristics. Sometimes he re-creates characters no longer living, as when he says (I. vii. 125):–

What grief would fill the aged Pellus's soul.

There is, too, Diatyposis, which is the working out of things coming into being or actually existent or that have come to pass, brought in to make what is said clearer, as in the following (I. ix. 593):–

The slaughtered men, the city burnt with fire,
The helpless children and deep-bosomed dames.

Or, to produce pity (I. xxii. 60):–

Look, too, on me with pity: me on whom
E'en on the threshold of mine age, hath Jove

> *A bitter burthen cast, condemned to see*
> *My sons struck down, my daughters dragged away*
> *In servile bonds: our chamber's sanctity*
> *Invaded; and our babes by hostile hands*
> *Dashed to the ground.*

There is also to be found in him Irony, i.e. an expression revealing the opposite of what is said with a certain ethical artifice; as in the speech of Achilles (I. ix. 391):–

> *Let him choose among the Greeks a fitter King.*

For he hints that he would not find one of more royal temper. And this is the same Trope used when one speaks about himself in extenuation and gives a judgment contrary to one's own. There is another form when any one pretends to praise another and really censures him. As the verse in Homer, put in the mouth of Telemachus (O. xvii. 397):–

> *Antinous–verily thou hast good care of me, as it were a*
> *father for his son.*

For he says to an enemy that he cares as a father for his son, and, again, when any one by way of jest extolls his neighbor, as the suitors (O. ii. 325):–

> *In my truth Telemachus planneth our destruction. He will*
> *bring a rescue either from sandy Pylos, or it may be from*
> *Sparta, so terribly is he set on slaying us.*

Sarcasm is a species of Irony used when any one jibes at another with a pretence of smiling. As Achilles, in the following passage (I. ix. 335):–

> *He meted out*
> *Their several portions, and they hold them still.*
> *From me, from me alone of all the Greeks,*
> *He bore away and keeps my cherished wife.*
> *Well! let him keep her, solace of his bed.*

Like this in kind is Allegory, which exhibits one thing by another, as in the following (O. xxii. 195):–

> *Now in good truth Melanthiusi shalt thou watch all night,*
> *lying on, a soft bed as beseems thee.*

For being in chains and hanging, he says he can rest on a soft bed.

Often, too, he makes use of Hyperbole, which, by exaggerating the truth, indicates emphasis, as (I. x. 437):–

> *These surpass in brilliancy the snow, in speed the eagle.*

Homer used Tropes and figures of this sort and handed them down to posterity, and justly obtains glory beyond all others.

Since there are also Characters of speech called Forms, of which one is Copiousness, the other Gracefulness, and the third Restraint, let us see if Homer has all these separate classes, on which poets and orators have worked after him. There are examples of these–copiousness in Thucydides, gracefulness in Lysias, restraint in Demosthenes. That is copious which by combination of words and sentences has great emphasis. An example of this is (O. v. 291):–

> With that he gathered the clouds and troubled the waters of
> the deep, rasping his trident in his hands: and he roused all
> storms of all manner of winds and shrouded in clouds the land
> and sea: and down sped night from heaven.

The graceful is delicate by the character of the matter. It is drawn out by the way it is expressed (I. vi. 466).–

> Thus he spake, great Hector stretch'd his arms
> To take the child: but back the infant shrank,
> Crying, and sought his nurse's sheltering breast,
> Scar'd by the brazen helm and horse-hair plume.

The restrained is between the two, the copious and the graceful, as (O. xxii. 291):–

> Then Odysseus, rich in counsel, stripped him of his rags and
> leaped on the great threshold with his bow and quiver full of
> arrows, and poured forth all the swift shafts there before his
> feet, and spake among the wooers.

But the florid style of speech, which has beauty and capacity for creating delight and pleasure, like a flower, is frequent in our poet; his poetry is full of such examples. The kinds of phrasing have much novelty in Homer, as we shall go on to show, by giving a few examples from which the rest may be gathered.

Every type of style practised among men is either historical, theoretic, or political. Let us examine whether the beginnings of these are to be found in him. Historical style contains a narration of facts. The elements of such a narration are character, cause, place, time, instrument, action, feeling, manner. There is no historical narration without some of these. So it is with our poet, who relates many things in their development and happening. Sometimes in single passages can be found relations of this kind.

Of character, as the following (I. v. 9):–

> There was one Dores 'mid the Trojan host,
> The priest of Vulcan, rich, of blameless life;
> Two gallant sons he had, Idaeus named
> And Phegeus, skilled in all the points of war.

He describes features, also, as in the case of Thersites (I. ii. 217):–

With squinting eyes, and one distorted foot,
His shoulders round, and buried in his breast
His narrow head, with scanty growth of hair.

And many other things, in which he often pictures the type or appearance or character, or action or fortune of a person, as in this verse (I. xx. 215):–

Dardanus first, cloud-compelling
Zeus begot,–and the rest.

There is in his poetry description of locality; where he speaks about the island near that of the Cyclops, in which he describes the look of the place, its size, its quality, and the things in it, and what is near it. Also, when he describes the things adjacent to the island of Calypso (O. v. 63):–

And round about the cave there was a wood-blossoming alder
and poplar, and sweet-smelling cypress.

And what follows. And innumerable other things of the same kind. Time narratives are found as follows (I. ii. 134):–

Already now nine weary years have passed.

And (I. ii. 303):–

Not long ago, when ships of Greece were met at Aulis charged
with evil freight for Troy.

Then there are the causes, in which he shows why something is coming to pass or has come to pass. Such are the things said at the beginning of the "Iliad" (I. i. 8):–

Say then, what god the fatal strife provoked
Jove's and Latona's son; he filled with wrath
Against the King, with deadly pestilence
The Camp afflicted–and the people died
For Chryses' sake, his priest, whom Atreus' son
With scorn dismissed,

–and the rest. In this passage he says the cause of the difference between Achilles and Agamemnon was the plague; but the plague was caused by Apollo, and his wrath was due to the insult put upon his priest.

Description of the instrument he gives, as when he tells of the shield made by Vulcan for Achilles. And there is a briefer one on the spear of Hector (I. viii. 493):–

In his hand
His massive spear he held twelve cubits long,
Whose glittering point flash'd bright with hoop of gold
Encircled round.

Narrations of fact are of several kinds, some like the following (I. vii. 60):–

> *When in the midst they met, together rush'd*
> *Bucklers and lances, and the furious might*
> *Of mail-clad warriors; bossy shield on shield*
> *Clattered in conflict; loud the clamor rose.*

The emotional narrative is where the incident is connected with some personal cause or energy, as when he speaks about things arising from anger or fear or sorrow, or when people are wounded, killed, or any other such thing happens to them. As a specimen of cause, take the following (I. i. 103):–

> *His dark soul filled with fury, and his eyes*
> *Flashed like flames of fire.*

Of an action (I. xvii. 51):–

> *Those locks, that with the Graces hair might vie,*
> *Those tresses bright, with gold and silver bound,*
> *Were dabbled all with blood.*

A Trope is constructive of action, or experience, or form, according as one acts in a special way or is acted upon. He follows the whole scene in this sort of narrative. An example of it would be as follows (O. xxii. 15):–

> *But Odysseus aimed and smote him with the arrow in his throat,*
> *and the point passed clean out through his delicate neck and*
> *he fell back, and the cup dropped from his hand as he was*
> *smitten, and at once through his nostrils there came up a*
> *thick jet of slain man's blood.*

There is also in Homer narration which has for the most part copious expression, a method of working in full, fitting the subject. Sometimes, however, it is concise, as in the following (I. xviii. 20):–

> *Patroclus lies in death,*
> *And o'er his body now the war is waged,*
> *His naked body, for his arms are now*
> *The prize of Hector of the glancing helmet.*

This type is often useful, for the quickness of the words make the reader and speaker more intent, and he immediately takes in the subject.

Sometimes he tells his story lightly; sometimes by an image or likeness or simile. An image, as when he says (O. xix. 53):–

> *Now forth from her chamber came the wise Penelope like*
> *Artemis or golden Aphrodite.*

A likeness as (I. iii. 196):–

> *He like a goat crossed the serried lines first.*

A simile, when he makes a comparison of closely related things that has a connection with subject narrated. There are in Homer various kinds of similes. Constantly and in many ways he compares the behavior and nature of animals to the arts and habits of men.

Sometimes he takes a similitude from very small things, not considering the size of the body, but the nature of each; whence he likens boldness to a fly (I. xvii. 570):–

And she breathed in his breast the courage of the fly.

And he compares assiduity to the same creature (I. ii. 469):–

As the many generations of numberless flies.

The packing together and orderly moving crowd to bees (I. ii. 87):–

As are the crowds of countless bees.

So he shows anger and irritation (I. xvi. 259):–

Like skilful wasps.

And he adds in the same place "when boys are wont to tease," in order that he might heighten their passionate temper by being stirred up by children. Of a continuous sound, he says (I. iii. 151):–

Abundant as the cricket.

For it is a most chattering creature and incessant in it.

But those that produce with no order all kinds of sounds, he likens to (I. iii. 3):–

Just as the clamor of geese strikes to heaven.

But the multitudes resting in order, he likens to birds settling down (I. ii. 493):–

Sitting down with clamor.

Sharpness of sight and act he sometimes likens to the falcon (I. xv. 238):–

Like to a falcon, swooping on a dove, swiftest of birds.

But sometimes to an eagle (I. xvii. 676):–

Like to an eagle, famed of sharpest sight
Of all that fly beneath the vault of Heav'n
Whom, soaring in the clouds, the crouching dove
Eludes not.

He declares its sharpness by its seeing from afar off; its swiftness, by its seizing a very active animal. A man, overcome by the sight of an enemy he compares to one who sees a snake, for he does not hesitate to take examples from reptiles (I. iii. 33):–

As when some traveller spies, could in his path upon the
mountain side, a deadly snake.

From the other animals he takes examples; of timidity from the hare and also from the stag (I. iv. 243):–

Why stand ye thus like timid fawns?
From dogs sometimes he takes daring (I. x. 360):–
  And as the hounds, well practis'd in the chase.
Sometimes love for their offspring (I. x. 14):–
  As a dog loves and defends its pups.
But sometimes their readiness in watching (I. x. 183):–
  As round a sheepfold keep their anxious watch
  The dogs.
A capture done with passion and boldness he is wont to compare to
wolves (I. xvi. 352):–
  As rav'ning wolves that lambs or kids assail.
Bravery and constancy he shows by wild boars, panthers, and lions,
dividing to each one what belongs to its nature. From boars, the on-
slaught they have, in fighting, making it irresistible (I. iv. 253):–
  Idomeneus of courage stubborn as the forest boar.
From panthers, inexhaustible daring (I. xxi. 577):–
  As when a panther by the spear transfixed does not remit
  her rage.
From lions, hesitation, finally bravery, as (I. xx. 171):–
  And with his tail he lashes both his flanks and limbs.
Again the rush of a valiant man he likens to a horse which has had a
full meal (I. vi. 506):–
  As some proud steed, at well-fill'd manger fed.
And, on the contrary, one slow to move; but in endurance not easily
overcome, he shows in this way (I. xi. 558):–
  As near a field of corn, a stubborn ass o'powers his
  boyish guides.
The kingly temper and dignity he expresses in the following (I. ii.
480):–
  As 'mid the thronging heifers in a herd
  Stands, proudly eminent, the lordly bull.
He does not omit similes taken from marine creatures, the persever-
ance of a polypus and the difficulty of removing it from a rock (O. v.
432):–
  As when the cuttlefish is dragged forth from his chamber.
The leadership and prominence of the dolphin over the rest (I. xxi.
22):–
  As fishes flying from a dolphin.
Oftentimes things made by men he compares to others similarly
made, as in this (I. xi. 67):–
  The rival bands of reapers mow the swathe.

Showing the resistance and bravery of men. But one lamenting ignobly, he blames in a clear comparison (I. xvi. 7):–

Why weeps Patroclus like an infant girl?

He dared to compare human actions to the elements of nature, as in the following passage (I. ii. 394):–

From th' applauding ranks of Greece
Rose a loud sound, as when the ocean wave,
Driv'n by the south wind on some lofty beach,
Dashes against a prominent crag expos'd
To blasts from every storm that wars around.

In these it is plain he used Hyperbola and Amplification, for he was not satisfied with comparing the clamor to the sound of the wind, but to the waves beating on a craggy shore, where the high sea makes the noise greater. Nor is the tempest an ordinary one, but it comes from the south, which especially stirs up the billows, and it is driven against a projecting crag stretching out into the sea, and surrounded by it, and it has the sea over it constantly, and from every side the winds blow and fall upon it. Such things as these are worked out by him in his descriptions. From a few examples we can become acquainted with many.

Let us see if the other forms of narrative are to be found in our author and how he took cognizance of them and clearly prepared them. We will give a few examples and so facilitate acquaintance with the rest.

There is the theoretic style, which embraces what is called speculative matter, which is a knowledge of the truth conceived in art. By these it is possible to know the nature of reality, both divine and human things, and to discriminate virtues and vices in morals and to learn how to attain truth by logical skill. These things are the province of those who are occupied in philosophy, which is divided into natural, ethical, and dialectical. If we find out Homer supplying the beginnings and the seeds of all these, is he not, beyond all others, worthy of admiration? Because he shows matters of intelligence by dark sayings and mythical expressions, it ought not to be considered strange. The reason is to be found in poetic art and ancient custom. So those who desired to learn, being led by a certain intellectual pleasure, might the easier seek and find the truth, and that the unlearned might not despise what they are not able to understand. For what is indicated indirectly is stimulating, while what is said clearly is valued more moderately.

Let us begin with the beginning and creation of the whole universe, which Thales the Milesian refers to the substance water, and let us see whether Homer first discovered this when he said (I. xiv. 246):–

Even to the stream of old Oceanus Prime origin of all.

After him Xenophanes of Colophon, laying down that the first elements were water and land, seems to have taken this conception from the Homeric poems (I. vii. 99):–

To dust and water turn all ye who here inglorious sit.

For he indicates their dissolution into the original elements of the universe. But the most likely opinion makes four elements,–fire, air, water, earth. These Homer shows he knows, as in many places he makes mention of them.

He knew, too, the order of their arrangement. We shall see that the land is the lowest of them all, for as the world is spherical, the sky, which contains all things, can reasonably be said to have the highest position. The earth being in the midst everywhere is below what surrounds it. This the poet declares chiefly in the lines where he says if Zeus let a chain down from Olympus, he could turn over the land and sea so that everything would be in the air (I. viii. 23):–

But if I choose to make my pow'r be known,
The earth itself and ocean I could raise,
And binding round Olympus' ridge the cord
Leave them suspended so in middle air.

Although the air is around the earth, he says the ether is higher in the following lines (I. xiv. 287):–

And going up on a lofty pine, which then grew on the summit
of Ida and through the air reached into the ether.

But higher than the ether is heaven (I. xvii. 424):–

And thus they fought: the iron clangor pierc'd
The airless ether and brazen vault of Heaven.

And, besides, in the following (I. i. 497):–

The vapor ascended to the great heaven and to Olympus.

The top part of the air is finer and more distant from the earth and its exhalations. Therefore it is said Olympus is called "wholly shining." Where the poet says Hera is the wife of Zeus, although she is his sister, he seems to speak in an allegory, since Hera stands for the air, which is a humid substance. Therefore he says (I. xxi. 6):–

Hera spread before their path clouds of thick darkness.

By Zeus is signified the ether, that is the fiery and heated substance (I. xv. 192):–

Broad Heav'n amid the sky and clouds, to Jove.

They seem brother and sister on account of a certain likeness and relationship, because both are light and mobile; they dwell together and are intimate, because from their intercourse all things are generated. Therefore they meet in Ida, and the land produces for them plants and flowers.

The same explanation have those words in which Zeus says he will, hang Hera and fasten two weights to her feet, namely, the land and the sea. He works out especially the principles of the elements in what Poseidon says to him (I. xv. 187):–

> *We were brethren, all of Rhaea born*
> *To Saturn: Jove and I and Pluto third,*
> *Who o'er the nether regions holds his sway,*

and (I. xv. 189):–

> *Threefold was our partition: each obtain'd*
> *His meed of honor due.*

And in the division of the whole, Zeus obtained the element fire, Poseidon water, and Hades that of air. Him he also calls "aerial darkness," because the air has no proper light, but is lightened by the sun, moon, and other planets.

The fourth part was left common to all, for the primal essence of the three elements is always in motion. The earth alone remains unmoved, to which he added also Olympus; it may have been because it is a mountain, being a part of the earth. If it belongs to heaven, as being the most brilliant and purest part of it, this may be the fifth essence in the elements, as certain distinguished philosophers think. So he, with reason, has conjectured it was common, the lowest part belonging to the earth by its weight, and the top parts to Olympus by their lightness. The natures between the two are borne upward to the one and downward to the other.

Since the nature of the elements is a combination of contraries, of dryness and moisture, hot and cold, and since by their relation and combination all things are constructed and undergo partial changes,– the whole not admitting of dissolution,–Empedocles says all things exist in this manner: "Sometimes in love all things meeting together in one. Sometimes, again, each being carried away by animosity of hate." The concord and unity of the elements he calls love, their opposition, hate.

Before his time Homer foreshadowed love and hate in what he says in his poetry (I. xiv. 200):–

> *I go to visit old Oceanus*
> *The sire of gods, and Tethys,*
> *I go to visit them and reconcile a lengthen'd feud.*

A similar meaning has the myth about, Aphrodite and Ares, the one having the same force as Empedocles's love, the other his hate. When they sometimes come together, and again separate, the sun reveals them, Hephaestus binds them, and Poseidon releases them. Whence it is evident that the warm and dry essence, and the contrary of these, the cold and wet, sometimes combine all things and again dissolve them.

Related to these is what is said by other poets that by the intercourse of Ares and Aphrodite arises Harmony; a combination of contraries grave and acute analogously accommodating themselves to one another. By which arrangement things which are endowed with a contrary nature are all mutually opposed. The poet seems to have signified this enigmatically in the conflict of the gods, in which he makes some help the Greeks and some the Trojans, showing allegorically the character of each. And he set over against Poseidon Phoebus, the cold and wet against the hot and dry: Athene to Ares, the rational to the irrational, that is, the good to the bad. Hera to Artemis, that is, the air to the moon, because the one is stable and the other unstable. Hermes to Latona, because speech investigates and remembers, but oblivion is contrary to these. Hephaestus to the River God, for the same reason that the sun is opposed to the sea. The spectator of the fight was the primary god, and he is made taking joy in it.

From the afore-mentioned matter Homer seems to show this: that the world is one and finite. For if it had been infinite, it would never have been divided in a number having a limit. By the name "all" he signifies the collective whole. For in many other cases he uses the plural for the singular. He signifies the same thing more clearly in saying (I. xiv. 200):–

The ends of the earth,–and again where he says (I. vii. 478):–
Nor should I care
Though thou wert thrust beneath the lowest deep
Of earth and ocean,–and in
On the very top of many-peaked Olympus where there is a top,
there, too, is a limit.

His opinions about the sun are plain. That it has an orbicular energy sometimes appearing over the earth, sometimes going under it, this he makes evident by saying (O. x. 190):–

My friends, lo we know not where is the place of darkness or
of dawning, nor where the sun that gives light to men goes
beneath the earth, nor where he rises.

And that he is always preceding over us and on this account is called Hyperion by our poet; that he makes the sun rising from the water which surrounds the earth the ocean, that the sun descends into it, is clearly expressed. First, as to the rising (O. iii. l):–

Now the sun arose and left the lovely mere speeding to the
brazen heaven, to give light to the immortals and to mortal
men on the earth.

Its setting (I. vii. 486):–

The sun, now sunk beneath the ocean wave,
Drew o'er the teeming earth the veil of night.

And he declares its form (O. xix. 234):–

He was brilliant as the sun,

and its size (I. xi. 735):–

We as sunlight overspread the earth.

and more in the following (O. iv. 400):–

So often as the sun in his course has reached the
mid-heaven,–and its power (O. ii. log):–
Of Helios, who overseeth all and ordereth all things.

Finally that it has a soul, and in its movement is guided by choice in
certain menaces it makes (O. xii. 383):–

I will go down to Hades and shine among the dead.

And on this thus Zeus exhorts him:–

Helios, see that thou shine on amidst the deathless gods amid
mortal men upon the earth, the grain giver.

From which it is plain that the sun is not a fire, but some more potent
being, as Aristotle conjectured. Assuredly, fire is borne aloft, is without
a soul, is easily quenchable and corruptible; but the sun is orbicular and
animate, eternal and imperishable.

And as to the other planets scattered through the heavens, that
Homer is not ignorant is evident in his poems (I. xviii. 480):–

Pleiads and Hyads and Orions might.

The Bear which always encircles the North Pole is visible to us.
By reason of its height it never touches the horizon, because in an
equal time, the smallest circle in which the Bear is, and the largest in
which Orion is, revolves in the periphery of the world. And Bootes,
slowly sinking because it makes a frequent setting, has that kind of
position, that is carried along in a straight line. It sinks with the four
signs of Zodiac, there being six zodiacal signs divided in the whole
night. That he has not gone through all observations of the stars, as
Aratus or some of the others, need be surprising to no one. For this
was not his purpose.

He is not ignorant of the causes of disturbances to the elements as
earthquakes and eclipses, since the whole earth shares in itself air, fire,
and water, by which it is surrounded. Reasonably, in its depths are
found vapors full of spirit, which they say being borne outward move

the air; when they are restrained, they swell up and break violently forth. That the spirit is held within the earth they consider is caused by the sea, which sometimes obstructs the channels going outward, and sometimes by withdrawing, overturns parts of the earth. This Homer knew, laying the cause of earthquakes on Poseidon, calling him Earth Container and Earth Shaker.

Now, then, when these volatile movements are kept within the earth, the winds cease to blow, then arises the darkness and obscurity of the sun. Let us see whether he was aware also of this. He made Poseidon moving the earth after Achilles issued forth to fight. For he had previously mentioned on the day before what the state of the air was. In the incident of Sarpedon (I. xvi. 567):-

> *Zeus extended opaque shadows over the fight,-*

and again in the case of Patroclus (I. xvii. 366):-

> *Now might ye deem the glorious sun himself nor moon was safe,*
> *for darkest clouds of night overspread the warriors.*

And a little while afterward Ajax prays (I. xvii. 645):-

> *O Father Jove, from o'er the sons of Greece,*
> *Remove this cloudy darkness; clear the sky*
> *That we may see our fate.*

But after the earthquake, the vapor issuing forth, there are violent winds, whence Hera says (I. xxi. 334):-

> *While from the sea I call the strong blast*
> *Of Zephyr and brisk Notus who shall drive*
> *The raging flames ahead.*

On the following day Iris calls the winds to the pyre of Patroclus (I. xxiii. 212):-

> *They with rushing sound rose and before them drove the*
> *hurrying clouds.*

So the eclipse of the sun takes place in a natural manner, when the moon on its passage by it goes under it perpendicularly and is darkened. This he seems to have known. For he said before that Odysseus was about to come (O. xiv. 162):-

> *As the old moon wanes, and the new is born;-*

that is, when the month ends and begins, the sun being conjoined with the moon at the time of his coming. The seer says to the suitors (O. xiv. 353):-

> *Ah, wretched men, what woe is this ye suffer, shrouded in*
> *night are your heads and your faces and knees, and kindled is*
> *the voice of wailing and the path is full of phantoms and full*
> *is the court, the shadows of men hasting hellwards beneath the*

gloom, and the sun is perished out of heaven, and an evil mist
has overspread the world.

He closely observed the nature of the winds, how they arise from
the moist element. For the water transformed goes into air. The wind
is air in motion. This he shows in very many places, and where he says
(O. v. 478):–

The force of the wet winds blew,–

he arranged the order of their series (O. v. 295):–

*The East wind and the South wind clashed and the stormy West
and the North that is born in the bright air, welling onwards
a great wave.*

Of these one comes from the rising, one from the midday quarter,
one from the setting, one from the north.

And Subsolanus, being humid, changes into the South, which is warm.
And the South, rarefying, is changed into the East; but the East, becoming
further rarefied, is purified into the North wind, therefore (O. v. 385):–

She roused the swift North and brake the waves before him.

Their contention he explains naturally (O. v. 331):–

*Now the South would toss it to the North to carry, and now
again the East would yield it to the West.*

He knew besides that the North Pole is suspended over the earth,
and how it weighs on the men who dwell in that climate. But the
South Pole, on the contrary, is profound; as when he says of the North
Pole (O. v. 296):–

*And the North that is born in the bright air rolling on a
great wave on the Southwest wind.*

(O. iii. 295):–

*Where the Southwest wind drives a great wave against the
left headland."*

For by saying "rolling" he notes the force of the wave rushing on
from above, but the wind "driving" signifies a force applied to what is
higher, coming from what is lower.

That the generation of rains comes from the evaporation of the humid, he demonstrates, saying (I. xi. 54):–

Who sent from Heav'n a show'r of blood-stained rain,–

and (I. xvi. 459):–

But to the ground some drops of blood let fall,–

for he had previously said (I. vii. 329):–

*Whose blood, beside Scamander's flowing stream,
Fierce Mars has shed, while to the viewless shade
Their spirits are gone,–*

where it is evident that humors of this sort exhaled from the waters about the earth, mixed with blood, are borne upward. The same argument is found in the following (I. xvi. 385):–

As in the autumnal season when the earth with weight of rain is saturate,–for then the sun on account of the dryness of the ground draws out humors from below and brings from above terrestrial disturbances. The humid exhalations produce rains, the dry ones, winds. When the wind is in impact with a cloud and by its force rends the cloud, it generates thunder and lightning. If the lightning falls, it sends a thunderbolt. Knowing this our poet speaks as follows (I. xvii. 595):–

His lightnings flash, his rolling thunders roar.

And in another place (O. xii. 415):–

In that same hour Zeus thundered and cast his bolt upon
the ship.

Justly thinking men consider that gods exist, and first of all Homer. For he is always recalling the gods (I. i. 406):–

The blessed gods living a happy life.

For being immortal they have an easy existence and an inexhaustible abundance of life. And they do not need food of which the bodies of mortal men have need (I. v. 341):–

They eat no bread, they drink no ruddy wine,
And bloodless and deathless they become.

But poetry requires gods who are active; that he may bring the notion of them to the intelligence of his readers he gives bodies to the gods. But there is no other form of bodies than man's capable of understanding and reason. Therefore he gives the likeness of each one of the gods the greatest beauty and adornment. He has shown also that images and statues of the gods must be fashioned accurately after the pattern of a man to furnish the suggestion to those less intelligent, that the gods exist.

But the leader and head of all these, the chief god the best philosophers think, is without a body, and is rather comprehensible by the intelligence. Homer seems to assume this; by him Zeus is called (I. iv. 68):–

The Sire of gods and men. O father ours, son of Kronos, chief
of the greater beings.

And Zeus himself says (I. viii. 27):–

As much as I am better than gods and men.

And Athene says of him (I. viii. 32):–

Well do we know thy power invincible.

If it is necessary to ask how he knew that God was an object of the intelligence, it was not directly shown, as he was using poetic form combined with myth. Yet we can gather it from the things he says (I. i. 498):–

The all-seeing son of Saturn there she found sitting apart.
And where he himself says (I. xx. 22):–
*Yet he will upon Olympus' lofty ridge remain and view serene
the combat."*

That solitude and the not mingling with the other gods, but being gladly by himself and using leisure for one directing and ordering all things, these constitute the character of an "intelligible" God. He knew besides that God is mind and understands all things, and governs all. For censuring Poseidon, he says (I. xiii. 354):–
*Equal the rank of both, their birth the same,
But Jupiter in wisdom as in years the first.*

And this expression frequently is used "when he again thought over other things." This shows that he was ever in thought.

But to the mind of God pertain Providence and Fate, concerning which the philosophers have spoken much. The stimulus to this came from Homer,–why should any one insist on the providence of the gods? Since in all his poetry not only do they speak to one another on behalf of men, but descending on the earth they associate with men. A few things we shall look at for the sake of illustrations; among these is Zeus speaking to his brother (I. xx. 20):–
*The purpose, Neptune, well thou know'st thyself
For which I called thee; true, they needs must die,
But still they claim my care.*

And in other places (I. xxii. 168):–
*A woful sight mine eyes behold: a man
I love in plight around the walls! my heart
For Hector grieves.*

He refers to the royal dignity of the gods and their loving care of men, saying (O. i. 65):–
*How should I forget divine Odysseus, who in understanding is
beyond mortals, and beyond all men hath done sacrifice to the
deathless gods who keep the wide heaven?*

How he makes the gods mingling with and working with men themselves it is possible to learn completely in many passages for just as he represents Athene once helping Achilles and always aiding Odysseus, so he represents Hermes helping Priam, and again Odysseus, for he says (O. xvii. 485):–
*Yea even the gods, in the likeness of strangers from far
countries, put on all manner of shapes, and wander through
cities to watch the violence and the righteousness of men.*

It is the characteristic of divine providence to wish men to live justly. This the poet indicates very clearly (O. xiv. 83):–

> *Verily it is not forward deeds the gods love, but they*
> *reverence justice and the righteous acts of men.*

And (O. xvi. 386):–

> *When Jove*
> *Pours down his fiercest storms in wrath to men,*
> *Who in their courts unrighteous judgments pass.*

Then just as he introduces the gods caring for men, so he represents men as mindful of them in every crisis. As the leader, succeeding in an action, says (I. viii. 526):–

> *Hopeful to Jove I pray, and all the gods*
> *To chase from hence these fate-inflicted hounds.*

And in danger (I. xvii. 646):–

> *Father Jove, from o'er the sons of Greece,*
> *Remove this cloudy darkness.*

And again when one has slayed another (I. xxii. 379):–

> *Since heaven has granted us this man to slay.*

And dying (I. xxii. 358):–

> *But see I bring not down upon thy head the wrath of heaven.*

From what other place than here did originate that doctrine of the Stoics? I mean this, that the world is one and in it both gods and men minister, sharing in justice by their nature. For when he says (I. xx. 4):–

> *Then Jove to Themis gave command to call*
> *The gods to council from the lofty height*
> *Of many ridg'd Olympus.*
> *Why, Lord of lightning, hast thou summoned here*
> *The gods of council, dost thou aught desire*
> *Touching the Greeks and Trojans?*

What does this mean except that the world is conducted by civilized laws and the gods consult under the presidency of the father of gods and men?

His opinion on fate he shows clearly in his poems (I. vi. 488):–

> *Dearest, wring not thus my heart,*
> *For till my day of destiny is come*
> *No man may take my life, and when it comes*
> *Nor brave, nor coward can escape that day.*

But among the other things in which he confirms the power of fate, he thinks as the most-approved philosophers have thought after him,–Plato, Aristotle, and Theophrastus,–that not all things happen by fate, but some things are in the power of men, the choice of whom is free. The same man in a way acts as he desires and falls into what he does not desire. And this point of view he has clearly expounded in many places, as in the beginning of each of his poems: in the "Iliad" saying the wrath of Achilles was the cause of the destruction of the Greeks and that the will of Zeus was fulfilled; in the "Odyssey" that the comrades of Odysseus went to their destruction by their own folly. For they had offended by touching the sacred oxen of the Sun, although they could have abstained from doing so. Yet it was foreordained (O. xi. 110):–

> But if thou hurtest them, I signify ruin for thy ships, and
> for thy men, and even though thou shalt thyself escape.
> If thou doest them no hurt and art careful to return, so may
> ye yet reach Ithaca, albeit in evil case.

So not to violate them depended on themselves, but that those who had done the evil should perish follows from fate.

It is possible to avoid what happens accidentally by foresight as he shows in the following (O. v. 436):–

> Then of a truth would luckless Odysseus have perished beyond
> what was ordained had not gray-eyed Athene given him some
> counsel. He rushed in and with both his hands clutched the
> rock whereto he clung till the great wave went by.

Then on the other hand running a great danger as he was, he had perished by fortune; yet by prudence he was saved.

Just as about divine things there are many divine reasonings in the philosophers taking their origin from Homer, so also with human affairs it is the same. First we will take up the subject of the soul. The most noble of the doctrines of Pythagoras and Plato is that the soul is immortal. To it in his argument Plato affixed wings. Who first determined this? Homer says this among other things (I. xvi. 856):–

But the soul flying on its members came to Hades,–i.e. into a formless and invisible place, whether you think it in the air or under the earth. But in the "Iliad" he makes the soul of Patroclus stand by the side of Achilles (I. xxiii. 65):–

> The soul of wretched Patroclus came.

He makes a small speech for him in which he says this (I. xxiii. 72):–

> The spirits and spectres of departed men
> Drove me from them, nor allow to
> Cross the abhorred river.

In the "Odyssey" through the whole account of the descent to Hades what else does he show but that souls survive after death, and when they drink blood can speak. For he knows that blood is the food and drink of the spirit, but spirit is the same thing as soul or the vehicle of the soul.

123. Most clearly he reveals that he considers man is nothing else but soul, where he says (O. xi. 90):–

There came up the soul of the Theban
Tiresias having a golden sceptre.

Purposely he changes the word for soul to the masculine, to show that it was Tiresias. And afterward (O. xi. 601):–

And after him I described the mighty Heracles, his phantom
I say; but as for himself he hath joy at the banquet among the
deathless gods.

For here again he showed that the semblance thrown off from the body appeared, but no longer connected with its matter. The purest part of the soul had gone away; this was Heracles himself.

124. Whence that seems to philosophers a probable theory that the body is in a way the prison house of the soul. And this Homer first revealed; that which belongs to the living he calls [Greek omitted] (from "binding") as in this line (I. i. 115):–

Not the body nor the nature.

O. iv. 196:–

A body came to the woman.

O. xvi. 251:–

By my form, my virtue, my body.

But that which has put off the soul he calls nothing else but body as in these lines (I. vii. 79):–

To bring home my body again.

And (O. xxiv. 187):–

The bodies lie uncared for in the hall of Odysseus.

O. xi. 53:–

And we left the body in the house of Circe.

For the same thing, while a man lives, was the bond of the soul; when he dies it is left, as it were, his monument.

To this is related also another doctrine of Pythagoras, namely, that the souls of the dead pass into other forms of bodies. This did not escape Homer's notice, for he made Hector talking with horses, and Antilochus and Achilles himself not only talking with them but listening to them, and a dog recognizing Odysseus before men, even before his intimates. What other thing is he establishing but a community of speech and a relation of soul between men and beasts? Besides, there are those who ate up the oxen of the Sun and after this fell into destruction. Does he not show that not only oxen but all other living creatures, as sharers of the same common nature, are beloved by the gods?

The change of the comrades of Odysseus into swine and that type of animal signifies this, that the souls of undeserving men are changed into the likeness of brute beasts; they fall into the circular periphery of the whole, which he calls Circe; whereas she is justly represented as the child of the Sun, dwelling in the island of Aeaea, for this word [Greek omitted] is so called because men lament and wail by reason of death. But the prudent man Odysseus did not suffer the change, because from Hermes, i.e. reason, he had received immortality. He went down into Hades, as it were, dissolving and separating the soul from the body, and became a spectator of souls both good and bad.

The Stoics define the soul as a cognate spirit, sensible to exhalations. It has its origin from the humid portions of the body. In this they follow Homer, who says (I. ix. 609).–

While the breath abides in the breast.

And again (I. xxiii. 100):–

Vanish'd like smoke, the spirit beneath the earth.

Here he makes the vital spirit, being humid, a breath; when it is extinguished he likens it to smoke. And the word "spirit" itself he uses for soul (I. xv. 262):–

His words fresh vigor in the chief infus'd.

And (I. iv. 524):–

Breathing away his spirit.

And (I. xxii. 475):–

But when her breath and spirit returned again.

That is, she collected her distracted spirit (I. v. 697):–

But soon revived, as on his forehead blew,
While yet he gasped for breath, the cooling breeze.

While his spirit was failing him in a faint, the outside breeze having a natural affinity to it brought him back to life. This argument is strengthened because for the external spirit he uses the word "soul," saying (I. xxiii. 440):–

He turned aside with lightest breath.

He wishes to say: "Having got back his breath."

Plato and Aristotle considered the soul incorporeal, but always associating with the body and needing it as a vehicle. On this account, then, it drew along the spiritual matter with it, oftentimes as an image, which had the shape of the body impressed upon it. So therefore Homer is never in his poetry found calling the soul body, but to what is deprived of soul he always gives the name, as we have mentioned in what has gone before.

The soul has, according to the views of the philosophers, a rational part, seated in the head, and an irrational part of which one element, the passionate, dwells in the heart and another, the appetitive, in the intestines. Did not Homer see this distinction when he made in the case of Achilles, the rational struggling with the passionate, deliberating in the same moment whether he should drive off the one who had filled him with grief or should stay his anger (I. i. 193):–

> *Up to this time he revolved these things in his mind*
> *and heart,*

that is, the intelligent part and what is opposed to it? The emotional anger is represented by him as overcome by prudence. For the appearance of Athene signifies this. And in these places he makes reason admonish the emotions, as a ruler giving orders to a subject (O. xx. 18):–

> *Endure my heart; yea, a baser thing thou once didst bear.*

And often the passionate element gives way to reason (I. xx. 22):–

> *Pallas indeed sat silent and though inly wroth with Jove,*
> *yet answered not a word.*

Likewise injury (I. xviii. 112):–

> *Though still my heart be sore,*
> *Yet will I school my angry spirit down.*

Sometimes he shows the passionate element getting the better of reason. This he does not praise, but openly blames; as when Nestor speaks upbraiding the insult offered by Agamemnon to Achilles (I. ix. 108):–

> *Not by my advice*
> *I fain would have dissuaded thee; but thou,*
> *Swayed by the promptings of a lofty soul,*
> *Didst to our bravest wrong dishonoring him*
> *Whom ev'n the Immortals honor'd.*

Achilles speaks like things to Ajax (I. ix. 645):–

> *All thou hast said hath semblance just and fair,*
> *But swells my heart with fury at the thought of him,*
> *Of Agamemnon, who, amid the Greeks*
> *Assembled, held me forth to scorn.*

So, too, reason is paralysed by fear, where Hector deliberates whether he will abide the conflict with Achilles (I. xxii. 129):–

> *Better to dare the fight and know at once*
> *To whom Olympian Jove the triumph wills,*

Then he withdraws when he gets near Achilles (I. xxii. 136):–

> *Nor dared he there await th' attack, but left*
> *The gates behind, and terror-stricken fled.*

It is also plain that he places the emotions about the heart. Anger as
(O. xx. 13):–

> *The heart within barked for him.*

Grief (I. xiv. 128):–

> *How long, my son, wilt thou thy soul consume with grief*
> *an mourning?*

Then fear (I. x. 95):–

> *And leaps my troubled heart as tho' it would burst*
> *My bosom's bounds; my limbs beneath me shake.*

In the same way just as fear, so he declares daring to be about the
heart (I. xvi. 11):–

> *And fix'd in every breast*
> *The fierce resolve to wage unwearied war.*

From these passages the Stoics took the opinion that the leading
element is about the heart. That the appetitive element is placed in
the intestines in many places he declares; in these verses, for example
(O. xviii. 54):–

> *But my belly's call is urgent on me, that evil worker,–*

and (O. xvii. 286):–

> *But now may conceal a ravening belly, a thing accursed.*

And the causes which belong to the passionate element of the soul
he says happen by nature. For wrath created by grief he shows is a
kind of effervescence of the blood and the spirit in it as in the following (I. i. 103):–

> *His dark soul filled with fury, and his eyes flashing like*
> *flames of fire.*

For he seemed to call spirit [Greek omitted], i.e. wrath, and this
in the case of those who are angry he thinks is extended and inflamed. Again the spirit, if there is fear, is perturbed and made
cold, generates tremors and terrors and pallors in the body. Pallor,
by the heat coursing into the interior ruddiness leaves the surface.
Tremor, because being, confined within the spirit it shakes the body.
Terror, because when the moisture is congealed the hairs are contracted and stand on end. All of these Homer clearly indicates when
he says (I. xv. 4):–

> *Pallid from fear.*

And (I. vii. 479):–

> *Pallid fear lay hold on him.*

(I. x. 95):–

> *My valiant members tremble.*

And (I. xxiv. 358):–

The old man heard, his mind confus'd with dread,
So grievously he fear'd that every hair
Upon his bended head did stand on end.

According to these passages for "feared" he says "frozen" and "fear" he calls "freezing." On the other hand, for "daring" and "courage" he uses [Greek omitted], "heat." Evil effects, he distinguishes in these ways.

Again when Aristotle considers indignation a mercy among the generous emotions (for when good men are stirred because their neighbors seem to succeed beyond their worth, it is called indignation. When they, beyond their desert, have misfortunes, it is called pity.) These two Homer considers to belong, to the good, for he reckons them as belonging to Zeus. Other passages he has as well as the following (I. xi. 542):–

But Jove, high-throned, the soul of Ajax filled with fear.

And in other places he pities him being chased about the wall.

What opinion the poet had about virtue and vice he shows in many places. For since one part of the soul is intelligent and rational, and the other devoid of reason and open to emotions, and on this account man has a middle position between God and brute, he thinks the highest, virtue, is divine, and the other extremity, evil, is brutelike. Just as later on Aristotle thought, he adopts these principles in his companions. For he always considers good men to be like gods, and as he says (I. ii. 167):–

By a counsel not, unworthy of Zeus.

Among the evil ones he names cowards (I. xiii. 102):–

Like to timid stags,–

and to sheep without a shepherd and to hares in flight. About those borne headlong and heedlessly to anger (I. xvii. 20):–

Nor pard, nor lion, nor the forest boar,
Fiercest of beasts, and provident of his strength
In their own esteem
With Panthous' sons for courage nor may vie.

The laments of those grieving to no purpose he compares to the sounds of birds (O. xvi. 218):–

Where Younglings the country folk have taken from the nest
ere yet they are fledged.

The Stoics who place virtue in apathy follow the passages in which he takes up every feeling, saying about grief (I. xix. 218):–

Behoves us bury out of sight our dead,
Steeling our heart and weeping but a day.

And (I. xvi. 7):–

Why weep over Patroclus as a girl?

About anger (I. xviii. 107):–

May strife perish from gods and men.

About fear (I. v. 252):–

Do not speak of fear, if thou thinkest to persuade me.

And (O. xv. 494):–

Struck and smitten seeing fate and death, he fell heroicly
from the sword. So those challenged to single combat obey
fearlessly, and several arise to take the place of one.
And the wounded man has none the less abiding courage.

(I. xi. 388):–

And now because thy shaft has grazed my foot, thou mak'st
thy empty boast.

And every valiant person is likened to a lion, boar, to a torrent and whirlwind.

Now the Peripatetics think that freedom from emotion is unattainable by men. They bring in a certain mean; by taking away excess of feeling, they define virtue by moderation. And Homer brings in the best men neither feeble nor altogether fearless nor devoid of pain, but yet differing from the worst in not being overcome extravagantly by their feelings. For he says (I. xiii. 279):–

The cowards color changes, nor his soul
Within his heart its even balance keeps
But changing still, from foot to foot he shifts,
And in his bosom loudly beats his heart
Expecting death; and chatter all his teeth.
The brave man's color changes not with fear,
He knows the ambush ent'ring.

For it is evident that by taking away excessive fear from the good man he leaves the mean between the two. The same must be thought about the like emotions, pain and anger. To this effect is that verse of his (I. vii. 215):–

The Trojans' limbs beneath them shrank with fear,   E'en Hector's heart beat quicker in his breast,   The others, even at the sight, trembled.

But he, in the midst of dangers being brave, was only troubled. So he makes Dolon and Lycaon feeling fear; Ajax and Menelaus, turning gradually and going away step by step, as lions driven from their quarry. In the same way he shows the differences of those who grieve and also of those who rejoice. As Odysseus, relating the way he deceived the Cyclops, says (O. ix. 413):–

My heart within me laughed.

The suitors seeing the beggar laying on the ground (O. xviii. 100):–

> But the proud wooers threw up their hands, and cried outright
> for laughter.

But in more trivial matters the difference of moderation appears. Odysseus though loving his wife, and seeing her lamenting on his account, contains himself (O. xix. 211):–

> His eyes kept steadfast between his eyelids as it were
> horn or iron.

But the suitors who were in love with her when they saw her (O. xviii. 212):–

> And straightways the knees of the wooers were loosened, and
> their hearts were enchanted with love, and each one uttered
> a prayer that he might be her bedfellow.

Such is the poet's treatment of the powers and passions of the soul.

Although there are various things said by the philosophers about the chief end of virtue and happiness, it is agreed by all that virtue of the soul is the greatest of goods. But the Stoics consider that virtue by itself is sufficient for happiness, taking the cue from the Homeric poems in which he has made the wisest and most prudent man on account of virtue despising trouble and disregarding pleasure. As to the first point in this way (O. iv. 242):–

> Now all of them I could not tell or number, so many as were
> the adventures of the patient Odysseus. He bruised himself
> with unseemly stripes and cast a sorry covering over his
> shoulders, and in the fashion of a servant he went into the
> wide-wayed city of the foemen.

And as to the second, i.e. (O. ix. 29):–

> Vainly Calypso, the fair goddess, would fain have kept me
> with her in her hollow caves longing to have me for her lord.
> Circe of Aia would have stayed me in her halls, longing to
> have me for her lord. But never did they prevail upon my
> heart within my breast.

Especially does he expound his opinion of virtue in the passages in which he makes Achilles not only brave but most beautiful in form, and swiftest of foot, and most illustrious in birth and distinguished in race and aided by the chiefest of the gods; and Odysseus understanding and firm in soul–in other respects not enjoying an equal fortune. His stature and aspect not conspicuous, his parentage not altogether noteworthy, his country obscure, hated by a god who was all but first. None of these things prevented him from being famous, from gaining the chief good of the soul.

But the Peripatetic School think the goods of the soul have the pre-eminence, such as prudence, fortitude, temperance, justice. Afterward are those of the body, such as health, strength, beauty, swiftness; and there are besides external goods such as reputation, nobility, wealth. For they think any one worthy of praise and admiration if he, fortified by the protective virtues of the soul, holds out against evils in the midst of sufferings, disease, want, unforeseen accidents, but that this situation is not a desirable nor a happy one. For not only the possession of virtue do they think good, but its use and its activity. And these distinctions Homer directly showed, for he always makes the gods (O. viii. 325):–

The givers of good things,–

these things also men pray the gods to furnish them, as being plainly neither useless to them nor indifferent, but advantageous to happiness.

What the goods are men aim at, and through which they are called happy, he declares in many places. But all of them together were centred in Hermes (I. xxiv. 376):–

Blessed are thy parents in a son so grac'd,
In face and presence, and of mind so wise.

He bears witness to his beauty of body, his intelligence, and his lineage. Separately he takes them up (I. vi. 156):–

On whom the gods bestowed
The gifts of beauty and of manly grace,
And Zeus poured out lordly wealth,–

for this, too, is a gift of God (O. vi. 188):–

For Zeus himself gives prosperity to mortals.

Sometimes he esteems honor a good (I. viii. 540):–

Would that I might be adored as Athene and Apollo.

Sometimes good fortune in children (O. iii. 196):–

So good a thing it is that a son of the dead should be left.

Sometimes, too, the benefit of one's family (O. xiii. 39):–

Pour ye the drink offering, and send me safe on my way, and
as for you, fare ye well. For now I have all my heart's
desire,–an escort and loving gifts. May the gods of heaven
give me good fortune with them and may I find my noble wife
in my home, and my friends unharmed while ye, for your part,
abide here, and make glad your gentle wives and children, and
may the gods vouchsafe all manner of good and may no evil
come, nigh the people.

That in a comparison of goods valor is better than wealth, he shows in the following (I. ii. 872):–

> *With childish folly to the war he came,*
> *Laden with stress of gold; yet naught availed*
> *His gold to save him from the doom of death.*

And (O. iv. 93):–

> *I have no joy of my lordship among these my possessions.*

And that intelligence is better than beauty of form (O. viii. 169):–

> *For one man is feebler than another in presence, yet the*
> *gods crown his words with beauty.*

It is evident that bodily excellence and external things he considers as good, and that without these virtue alone is not sufficient for happiness he declares in the following way. He created two men who attained to the height of virtue, Nestor and Odysseus, different indeed from one another, but like one another in prudence and valor and power of eloquence. He has made them not at all equal in fortune, but on the side of Nestor he has placed the gods (O. iv. 208):–

> *Right easily is known that man's seed for whom Cronion*
> *weaves the skein of luck at bridal and at birth, even as now*
> *hath he granted prosperity to Nestor forever, for all his*
> *days, that he himself should grow into smooth old age in his*
> *halls, and his sons moreover should be wise and the best*
> *of spearsmen.*

But Odysseus, though shrewd and clever and prudent, he often calls unfortunate. For Nestor goes back home quickly and safely, but Odysseus wanders about for a long time and endures constantly innumerable sufferings and dangers. So it is a desirable and blessed thing if fortune is at hand helping and not opposing virtue.

How the possession of virtue is of no use unless it accomplishes something, is evident from the passages where Patroclus complains to Achilles and says (I. xvi. 31):–

> *Whoe'er may hope in future days by thee*
> *To profit, if thou now forbear to save*
> *The Greeks from shame and loss.*

So he speaks to him because he makes his virtue useless by inactivity. Achilles himself deplores his inactivity (I. xviii. 104:):–

> *But idly here I sit cumb'ring the ground,*
> *I, who amid the Greeks no equal own*
> *In fight,–*

for he laments because though possessing virtue he does not make use of it; but being indignant with the Greeks (I. i. 490):–

> *No more he sought*
> *The learned council, nor the battlefield;*

But wore his soul away, and only pined
For the fierce joy and tumult of the fight.

And so Phoenix admonished him (I, ix. 433):–

To teach thee how to frame
Befitting speech, and mighty deeds achieve.

After his death he is indignant at that inertia, saying (O. xi. 489):–

Rather would I live upon the soil as the hireling of another
with a lordless man who had no great livelihood, than bear
sway among the dead that are no more.

And he adds the cause (O. xi. 498):–

For I am no longer his champion under the sun, so mighty a
man as once I was, when in wide Troy I slew the best of the
host, succoring the Argives.

That saying of the Stoics, that good men are friends of the gods, is taken from Homer, who says about Amphiaerus (O. xv. 245):–

Whom Zeus, lord of the ages, and Apollo loved with all
manner of love.

And of Odysseus (O. iii. 52):–

And Athene rejoiced in the wisdom and judgment of the man.

There is, too, an opinion of the same philosophic school that virtue is teachable, and has for its beginning good birth. For Homer says (O. iv. 206):–

And from such a sire thou too art sprung, wherefore thou dost
even speak wisely.

And by training it is brought to perfection. For virtue is the knowledge of living rightly, i.e. of doing the things which it is necessary for those who live well to do. These principles can also be found in Homer, for he says (I. ix. 440):–

Inexperienced yet in war, that sorrow brings alike on all
And sage debate in which attends renown.

And in other places (I. vi. 446):–

Nor did my heart compel me, since I had learnt to be good,

And Phoenix says of Achilles (I. ix. 442):–

Me then he sent, to teach thee how to frame
Befitting speech, and mighty deeds achieve.

For since life is made up of acts and speech, therefore he says he was the young man's teacher in these things. From what has been said it is plain that he declares the whole of virtue to be teachable. So, then, Homer is the first philosopher in ethics and in philosophy.

Now to the same science belongs arithmetic and music, which Pythagoras especially honored. Let us see whether these are mentioned by our poet. Very often. A few examples from very many will suffice. For Pythagoras thought number had the greatest power and reduced everything to numbers–both the motions of the stars and the creation of living beings. And he established two supreme principles,–one finite unity, the other infinite duality. The one the principle of good, the other of evil. For the nature of unity being innate in what surrounds the whole creation gives order to it, to souls virtue, to bodies health, to cities and dwellings peace and harmony, for every good thing is conversant with concord. The nature of duality is just the contrary,–to the air disturbance, to souls evil, to bodies disease, to cities and dwellings factions and hostilities. For every evil comes from discord and disagreement. So he demonstrates of all the successive numbers that the even are imperfect and barren; but the odd are full and complete, because joined to the even they preserve their own character. Nor in this way alone is the odd number superior, but also added to itself it generates an even number. For it is creative, it keeps its original force and does not allow of division, since PER SE the mind is superior. But the even added to itself neither produces the odd nor is indivisible. And Homer seems to place the nature of the one in the sphere of the good, and the nature of the dual in the opposite many times. Often he declares a good man to be [Greek omitted] "kind" and the adjective from it is "benignity"; as follows (I. ii. 204):–

It is not good for many to reign, let there be but one ruler.
And (O. iii. 127):–
We never spake diversely either in the assembly or in the
council, but always were of one mind.
He always makes use of the uneven number as the better. For making the whole world to have five parts, three of these being the mean, he divides it (I. xv. 189):–
Threefold was our portion each obtained,
His need of honor due.
Therefore, too, Aristotle thought there were five elements, since the uneven and perfect number had everywhere the predominance. And to the heavenly gods he gives the uneven shares. For Nestor nine times to Poseidon sacrificed nine bulls; and Tiresias bids Odysseus sacrifice (O. xi. 131):–
A ram and a bull and a boar, the mate of swine.
But Achilles immolated for Patroclus, all in even numbers, four horses and (I. xxiii. 175):–
Twelve noble sons he slew, the sons of Troy,–

and of nine dogs he casts two on the pyre, in order to leave for himself seven. And in many places he uses the ternary, quinary, and septenary number, especially the number nine (I. vii. 161):-

The old man spoke reproachfully; at his words
Uprose nine warriors.

And (O. xi. 311):-

At nine seasons old they were of breadth nine cubits, and
nine fathoms in height.

(I. i. 53):–

Nine days the heavenly Archer on the troops hurl'd his
dread shafts.

And (I. vi 174):–

Nine days he feasted him, nine oxen slew.

Why pray, is the number nine the most perfect? Because it is the square of the first odd number, and unevenly odd since it is divided into three triads, of which again each is divided into three units.

But not only the virtue of numbers but a natural way of counting he showed, as in the catalogue of ships he made (I. ii. 509):-

With these came fifty ships; and in each
Were sixscore youths, Boeotia's noblest flow'r.

And again (I. xvi. 170):–

They were fifty men.

Whence it is possible to compute that as all the ships were near 1200, and each had 100 men, the whole number is 12 myriads–120,000.

Again speaking. of the Trojans (I. viii. 563):-

A thousand fires burnt brightly; and round each
Sat fifty warriors in the ruddy glare.

He enables one to compute that without counting allies they were 50,000 men.

Now music being closest to the soul, since it is a harmony produced by different elements, by melodies, and by rhythms, intensifies what is relaxed and relaxes the intense. The Pythagoreans have clearly proved this, and before them Homer. For he gives praise to music, in the case of the Sirens, to which he adds the following (O. xii. 188)

And had joy thereof and gone on his way the wiser.

In another place he introduces in banquets the lyre, as among the suitors (O. xvii. 271):-

And the voice of the lyre is heard there which the gods made
to be mate of the feast.

And at the house of Alcinous the player on the lyre (O. vii. 266):-

Was composing a beautiful song.

And at marriages (I. xviii. 495):–

The pipes and lyres were sounding.

And in the works of the vintage (I. xvii. 569):–

A boy amid them, from a clear-ton'd pipe
Drew lovely music; well his liquid voice
The strings accompanied.

Besides in war (I. x. 13):–

Of pipes and flutes he heard the sound.

Also he uses music to express grief (I. xxiv. 721):–

Poured forth the music of the mournful dirge,

by the sweetness of melodies softening the bitterness of the soul.

It is clear that melody is twofold,–one of the voice, the other of instruments, partly wind, partly string. Of sound some are bass, some treble. These differences Homer knew, since he represents women and boys with treble voices, by reason of the tenuity of their breath; men, he makes with bass voices. As in the following (I. xviii. 70):–

She with bitter cry
Clasped in her hands his head, and
Sorrowing spoke.

And again (I. ix. 16):–

So with deep groans he thus addressed the Greeks.

But old men like the locusts (I. iii. 151) he compares to shrill-voiced creatures. Instruments whose strings are thin and vibrate quickly, easily cut the air, and give an acute sound. Those with thick ones, through the slow movement, have a deep sound. Homer calls the pipe acute–acute because being thin it gives an acute sound. Homer has this information about music.

Since we are speaking here about Pythagoras, to whom taciturnity and not expressing those things which it is wrong to speak were especially pleasing, let us see whether Homer had also this opinion. For about those drunken with wine he says (O. xiv. 466):–

And makes him speak out a word which were better unsaid.

And Odysseus upbraids Thersites (I. ii. 246):–

Thou babbling fool Therites, prompt of speech,
Restrain thy tongue.

And Ajax speaks, blaming Idomeneus (I. xxiii. 478):–

But thou art ever hasty in thy speech.
And ill becomes thee this precipitance

And while the armies are entering the fight (I. iii. 2-8):–

With noise and clarmor, as a flight of birds,

> *The men of Troy advanced,*
> *On th'other side the Greeks in silence mov'd.*

Clamor is barbaric, silence is Greek. Therefore he has represented the most prudent man as restrained, in speech. And Odysseus exhorts his son (O. xvi. 300):–

> *If in very truth thou art my son and of our blood, then let*
> *no man hear that Odysseus is come home; neither let Laertes*
> *know it nor the swineherd nor any of the household nor*
> *Penelope herself.*

And again he exhorts him (O. xix. 42):–

> *Hold thy peace and keep all this in thine heart and ask*
> *not thereof.*

So the opinions of famous philosophers have their origin in Homer.

If it is necessary to mention those who elected for themselves certain individual views, we could find them taking their source in Homer. Democritus in constructing his "idola," or representative forms, takes the thought from the following passage (I. v. 449):–

> *Meanwhile Apollo of the silver bow*
> *A phantom form prepar'd, the counterpart*
> *Of great Aeneas and alike in arms.*

Others deviated into error in ways he would not approve of, but he represented them as fitting to the special time. For when Odysseus was detained with Alcinous, who lived in pleasure and luxury, he speaks to him in a complimentary way (O. ix. 5):–

> *Nay, as for me I say that there is no more gracious or perfect*
> *delight than when a whole people make merry, and the men sit*
> *orderly at feasts in the halls and listen to the singer, and*
> *the tables by them laden with food and flesh, and a winebearer*
> *drawing the wine serves it into the cups. The fashion seems*
> *to me the fairest thing in the world.*

Led by these words, Epicurus took up the opinion that pleasure was the SUMMUM BONUM. And Odysseus himself is at one time covered with a precious and thin woven garment, sometimes represented in rags with a wallet. Now he is resting with Calypso, now insulted by Iros and Melantheus. Aristippus taking the model of this life not only struggled valiantly with poverty and toil, but also intemperately made use of pleasure.

But it is possible to take these as specimens of Homer's wisdom, because he first enunciated the many excellent sayings of the Wise Men, as "follow God" (I. i. 218):–

> *Who hears the gods, of them his prayers are heard,*

And "nothing too much" (O. xv. 70):–
> *I think it shame even in another heart, who loves overmuch*
> *or hates overmuch; measure is in all things best.*

And the expression (O. viii. 351):–
> *A pledge is near to evil,*
> *Evil are evil folks' pledges to hold.*

And that saying of Pythagoras to one who asked who is a friend said "an ALTER EGO."

Homer's parallel saying is (O. xviii. 82):–
> *The equal to my head.*

Belonging to the same species of Apothegm is what is called the Gnome, a universal expression about life stated briefly. All poets and philosophers and orators have used it and have attempted to explain things gnomically. Homer was the first to introduce in his poetry many excellent Gnomes stating a principle he wishes to lay down; as when he says (I. i. 80):–
> *And terrible to men of low estate the anger of a king.*

And again what must needs be done or not done (I. ii 24):–
> *To sleep all night but ill becomes a chief.*

Of Homer's many good sayings and admonitions not a few afterward have been paraphrased. Some examples of these should find a place here; as the following passage of Homer (I. xv. 104):–
> *Fools are we all, who madly strive with Jove,*
> *Or hope, by access to his throne, to sway*
> *By word or deed his course! From all apart,*
> *He all our counsels heeds not, but derides!*
> *And boasts o'er all the immortal gods to reign.*
> *Prepare, then, each his several woes to bear.*

Like this is a saying of Pythagoras:–
> *Whatever pains mortals have from the gods, whatever fate*
> *thou hast, bear it nor murmur.*

And also these words of Euripides:–
> *Nor is it fitting to be indignant at events, no good comes*
> *of it; but when things go wrong, if one bears them right,*
> *they do go well.*

Again Homer says (I. xxiv. 128):–
> *How long, my son, wilt thou thy soul consume with grief*
> *and mourning?*

So Pythagoras:–
> *Spare thy life, do not wear out thy soul.*

Then Homer says (O. xviii. 136):–

> For the spirit of men upon the earth is even as their day,
> that comes upon them from the father of gods and men.

Archilochus, who imitates other things of Homer, has paraphrased this too, saying:–

> Such for mortal men, O Glaucus, son of Leptineus, is their
> mind, as Zeus directs for a day.

And in other words, Homer says (I. xiii. 730):–

> To one the gods have granted warlike might,
> While in another's breast all-seeing Jove
> Hath plac'd the spirit of wisdom and mind
> Discerning for the common good of all.
> By him are states preserved! and he himself
> Best knows the value of the precious gift.

Euripides has followed this original:–

> Cities are well ordered by the instructions of one man.
> So, too, a house. One again is mighty in war. For one wise
> judgment conquers many hands, but ignorance with a crowd
> brings the most evil.

Where he makes Idomeneus exhorting his comrade, he says (I. xii. 322):–

> O friend, if we survivors of this war
> Could live from age and death forever free,
> Thou shouldst not see me foremost in the fight,
> Nor would I urge thee to the glorious field;
> But since in man ten thousand forms of death
> Attend, which none may 'scape, then on that we
> May glory in others' gain, or they on us!

Aeschylus saying after him:–

> Nor receiving many wounds in his heart does any one die,
> unless the goal of life is run. Nor does any one sitting by
> the hearth flee any better the decreed fate.

In prose, Demosthenes speaks as follows (O. xviii. 9):–

> For all mortals, death is the end of life even if one keeps
> himself shut up in a cell; it is necessary ever for good men
> to attempt noble things and bravely to bear whatever God
> may give.

Again take Homer (I. iii. 65):–

> The gifts of Heav'n are not to be despis'd.

Sophocles paraphrases this, saying:–

> This is God's gift; whatever the gods may give, one must never
> avoid anything, my son.

In Homer there are the words (I. i. 249):–
> *From whose persuasive lips. Sweeter than*
> *Honey flowed the stream of speech.*

Theocritus said (I. vii. 82):–
> *Therefore the Muse poured in his mouth*
>   *Sweet nectar.*

How, also, Aratus paraphrased this (I. xviii. 489):–
> *Sole star that never bathes in th' ocean wave,–*

saying:–
> *The Bears protected from cerulean ocean.*

(I. xv. 628):–
> *They win their soul from death,*

is paraphrased:–
> *He escaped Hades by a small peg.*

Let this be enough on this subject.

But civil discourse belongs to the rhetorical art, with which it seems Homer was first to be familiar. If Rhetoric is the power of persuasive speaking, who more than Homer depended on this power? He excels all in eloquence; also in the grasp of his subject he reveals an equal literary power.

And the first part of this art is Arrangement, which he exhibits in all his poetry, and especially at the beginning of his narratives. For he did not make the beginning of the "Iliad" at a distant period, but at the time when affairs were developing with energy and had come to a head. The more inactive periods, which came into past time, he goes over in other places succinctly. The same he did in the "Odyssey," beginning from the close of the times of Odysseus's wanderings, in which it was clearly time to bring in Telemachus and to show the haughty conduct of the suitors. Whatever happened to Odysseus in his wanderings before this he introduces into Odysseus's narrative. These things he prefers to show as more probable and more effective, when said by the one who experienced them.

As therefore all orators make use of introductory remarks to get the benevolent attention of their audience, so our poet makes use of exordiums fitted to move and reach the hearer. In the "Iliad" he first declares that he is about to say how many evils happened to the Achaeans through the wrath of Achilles and the high-handed conduct of Agamemnon; and in the "Odyssey" how many labors and dangers Odysseus encountered and surmounted all of them by the judgment and perseverance of his soul. And in each one of the exordiums he invokes the Muse that she may make the value of what is said greater and more divine.

While the characters introduced by him are made to say many things either to their relatives or friends or enemies or the people, yet to each he assigns a fitting type of speech, as in the beginning he makes Chryseis in his words to the Greeks use a most appropriate exordium. First he desires for them that they may be superior to their enemies and may return home, in order that he might gain their kindly feeling. Then he demands his daughter. But Achilles being angered by the threat of Agamemnon combines a speech for the Greeks and for himself, in order to make them more friendly disposed. For, he says, all had proceeded to the war, not on account Of some private enmity, but to please Agamemnon himself and his brother, and he went on to say he had done many things himself and had received a present not from Agamemnon and Menelaus, but from the whole body of the Greeks. Agamemnon replying to him has no difficulty in winning the crowd. For when Achilles says he means to sail back home, on account of the insult he has received, he does not say "go" but "flee," changing what is said abruptly into an attack on Achilles reputation. And his words are:–

I do not exhort you to remain; there are here who value me.

And this was agreeable to his hearers.

And afterward he introduces Nestor, whom he had previously called sweet in speech and a shrewd orator (I. i. 249):–

Whose voice flowed from his tongue sweeter than honey.

There could be no greater praise for an orator. He starts off with an exordium by which he tries to change the minds of the contesting chiefs, bidding them consider by opposing one another they give occasion of joy to their enemies. He goes on to admonish both and to exhort them to give heed to him as their elder. And by telling one to be prudent, he says what gratifies the other. He advises Agamemnon not to take away what has been given to a man who has labored much; Achilles, not to strive with the king who is his superior. And he gives suitable praise to both: to the one as ruling over more people; to the other, as having more prowess. In this way he seeks to moderate them.

Again, in what follows, when Agamemnon saw the dream bearing good hopes to him from Zeus, and exhorting him to arm the Greeks, did he not use rhetorical art speaking to the multitude, saying the contrary of what he wishes, to try their feeling and to see if they will be disgusted by being compelled to do battle for him. But he speaks to please them. Another of the men able to influence them bids them stay in their tents, as if the king really wished this. For to those he speaks to he indicates that he desires the contrary. Odysseus taking up these words, and making use of a convenient freedom, persuades the leaders by his mild language; the common people he compels by threats to heed their superiors. Stopping the mutiny and agitation of the crowd, he persuades all by his shrewd words, moderately blaming them for not carrying out what they promised, and at the same time excusing them on the ground that they have been idle for some time and have been deprived of what is dearest to them. He persuades them to remain by the hope of the seer's prophecy.

Likewise Nestor, using arguments unchanged indeed but tending to the same end, and also using greater freedom to those who have been spoilt by inaction, brings over the crowd. He places the blame of their negligence on a few unworthy people and advises the rest. He threatens the disobedient and immediately takes counsel with the king as to how the forces are to be drawn up.

Again, when in the deeds of war the Greeks have partly succeeded and partly failed and been reduced to terror, Diomed, since he has the audacity of youth and freedom of speech by reason of his success, before he had shown his valor, took the king's reproof in silence, but afterward he turns on Agamemnon as if he had counselled flight through cowardice. For he says (I. ix. 32):–

> Atrides I thy folly must confront,
> As is my right in council! thou, O King,
> Be not offended.

In his speech he tries to advise him and at the same time deprecate his anger. He then recites the things just performed by him, without envy, saying (I. ix. 36):–

> How justly so
> Is known to all the Greeks both young and old.

Afterward he exhorts the Greeks, giving them indirect praise (I. ix. 40):–

> How canst thou hope the sons of Greece shall prove
> Such heartless cowards as thy words suppose?

And he shames Agamemnon, excusing him if he wishes to depart, saying the others will be sufficient, or if all flee, he will remain alone with his comrade and fight (I. ix. 48):–

> Yet I and Sthenelaus, we two, will fight.

Nestor commends the excellence of his judgment and his actions. As to the aim of the council he considers that, as the eldest, he has the right to offer advice. And he continues endeavoring to arrange for sending ambassadors to Achilles.

And in the embassy itself he makes the speakers employ different devices of arguments. For Odysseus, at the opening of his speech, did not say immediately that Agamemnon repented the taking away of Briseis, and would give the girl back, and that he was giving some gifts immediately and promised the rest later. For it was not useful, while his feelings were excited, to remember these things. But first he wished to provoke Achilles to sympathize with the misfortunes of the Greeks. Then he suggests that later on he will want to remedy these disasters and will not be able to. After this he recalls to him the advice of Peleus; removing any resentment toward himself, he attributes it to the character of his father as being more able to move him. And when he seemed mollified, then he mentioned the gifts of Agamemnon and again goes back to entreaties on behalf of the Greeks, saying that if Agamemnon is justly blamed, at least it was a good thing to save those who had never injured him.

It was necessary to have a peroration of this kind containing nothing to irritate the hearer. He specifically recalls the purpose of the speech. The final exhortation has something to stir him against the enemy, for they are represented as despising him. "For now you can take Hector if he stands opposed to you! Since he says none of the Greeks is his equal." But Phoenix, fearing that he has used less entreaties than were befitting, sheds tears. And first he agrees with his impulse, saying he will not leave him if he sails away. This was pleasant for him to hear. And he tells Achilles how Peleus intrusted Phoenix to bring Achilles up, taking him as a child, and how he was thought worthy to be his teacher in words and deeds. In passing he relates Achilles' youthful errors, showing how this period of life is inconsiderate. And proceeding he omits no exhortation, using briefly all rhetorical forms, saying that it is a good thing to be reconciled with a suppliant, a man who has sent gifts, and has despatched the best and most honored ambassadors; that he himself was worthy to be heard, being his tutor and teacher; that if he let the present occasion go, he would repent. He makes use of the example of Meleager who, when called upon to help his fatherland, did not heed until by the necessity of the calamities that overtook the city he turned to defend, it. But Ajax used neither entreaty nor pity, but freedom of speech. He determined to remove Achilles' haughtiness partly by blaming him seasonably, partly by exhorting him genially not to be completely embittered. For it befitted his excellency in virtue. Replying to each of these Achilles shows nobility and simplicity. The others he refutes cleverly and generously by bringing out worthy causes of his anger; to Ajax he excuses himself.

And to Odysseus he says that he will sail away on the following day; then being stirred by the entreaties of Phoenix, he says he will take counsel about leaving. Moved by the free speech of Ajax, he confesses all that he intends to do: that he will not go forth to fight until Hector gets as far as his tents and the ships, after killing many of the Greeks. Then he says, "I think I shall stop Hector no matter how earnestly he fights." And this argument he offers in rebuttal to Odysseus about resisting the onslaught of Hector.

In the words of Phoenix he shows that there is such a thing as the art of Rhetoric. For he says to Achilles that he had taken him over (I. ix. 440):–

> *Inexperienced yet in war that sorrow brings alike on all*
> *And sage debate, on which attends renown*
> *Me then he sent, to teach thee how to frame*
> *Befitting speech and mighty deeds achieve.*

These words show that the power of speech especially makes men renowned.

It is besides possible to find in many other parts of his poems passages pertaining to the art of Rhetoric. For he shows the method of accusation and purgation elsewhere and in the place where Hector taxes his brother, accusing him of cowardice and dissoluteness. Because he had this character, he had injured those who were far different from him; so he had become the cause of evil to his family. And Alexander softens his brothers' temper by confessing he was rightly blamed; he wipes off the charge of cowardice by promising to meet Menelaus in combat. And that Homer was a skilful speaker, no one in his right mind would deny, for it is all clear from reading his poems.

He did not overlook to give certain types to his speakers. He introduces Nestor as agreeable and attractive to his hearers; Menelaus, fond of brevity, attractive, and sticking to his subject; Odysseus, abundant subtilty of speech. These things Antenor testifies about the two heroes; he had heard them when they came to Ilium as ambassadors. And these characteristics of speech Homer himself introduces, displaying them in all his poetry.

He was acquainted with Antithesis in eloquence. This in every subject introduces the contrary, and proves and disproves the same thing by clever handling of the art of logic. For he says (I. xx. 248):–

> *For glibly runs the tongue, and can at will*
> *Give utt'rance to discourse in every vein;*
> *Wide is the range of language, and such words*
> *As one may speak, another may return.*

He knew how to say the same things at length, and to repeat them briefly, which is called Recapitulation, and is used by orators whenever it is necessary to recall briefly the numerous things which have been said. For what Odysseus related in four books in the Phaeacians, these he goes over again shortly in the passage beginning (O. xxiii. 310):–

> *He began by setting forth how he overcame the Cicones, etc.*

But civil discourse embraces also knowledge of laws. No one can really say whether the word "law" was used in his time. Some say that he certainly knew it, for he said (O. xvii. 487):–

> *To watch the violence and righteousness of men.*

Aristachus says the word "righteousness" ([Greek omitted]) comes from the words "to distribute well." Hence law ([Greek omitted]) seems to be called, because it distributes ([Greek omitted]) equal parts to all or to each according to his worth. But that he knew the force of law was conserved, if not in writing at least in the opinion of men, he shows in many ways. For he makes Achilles talking about the sceptre say (I. i. 237):–

> *And now 'tis borne,*
> *Emblem of justice, by the sons of Greece,*
> *Who guard the sacred ministry of law*
> *Before the face of Jove.*

For usages and customs, the laws of which Zeus is reported as the lawgiver, with whom Minos the king of the Cretans had converse men say; which converse is, as Plato bears witness, the learning of the laws. Clearly in his poems he reveals that it is necessary to follow the laws and not to do wrong (O. xviii. 141):–

> *Wherefore let no man forever be lawless any more, but keep*
> *quietly the gifts of the gods, whatsoever they may give.*

Homer first of all divided into different parts civil polity. For in the shield which was made in imitation of the whole world by Hephaestus (that is, spiritual power) he imagined two cities to be contained: one enjoying peace and happiness; the other at war, and exposing the advantages of each he shows that the one life is civil and the other military. Neither did he pass over even the agricultural. But he showed this, too, making it clear and beautiful in his language.

In every city it is sanctioned by the law that there is to be a meeting of a council to consider before the popular assembly is called together. This is evident from the words of Homer (I. ii. 53):–

> *But first of all the Elders*
> *A secret conclave Agamemnon called.*

Agamemnon collects the Elders, and examines with them how to arm the people for the fight.

And that it is necessary for the leader before all things to care for the salvation of the whole, he teaches in his characters by the advice he gives (I. ii. 24):–

> To sleep all night but ill becomes a chief.

And how it is necessary for subjects to obey their leader, and how the commander should bear himself toward each class; Odysseus shows this, persuading the superior class by soft words, but using toward the crowd bitter words of rebuke.

To rise up for one's superiors is sanctioned in all laws. This the gods themselves do in the case of Zeus (I. i. 535):–

> At his entrance all
> Rose from their seats at once; not one presumed
> To wait his coming.

There is a rule among most that the eldest shall speak. Diomed by necessity of the war having dared to speak first, requests to be pardoned (I. xiv. 111):–

> Nor take offence that I,
> The youngest of all, presume to speak.

And it is an universal rule that voluntary offences are punished and involuntary ones are excused. This, too, the poet shows, in what the minstrel says (O. xxii. 350):–

> And Telemachus will testify of this, thine own dear son, that
> not by mine own will or desire did I resort to thy house to
> sing to the wooers after their feasts; but being so many and
> stronger than I, they led me by constraint.

There are three forms of polity intended to attain justice and good laws,–Royalty, Aristocracy, and Democracy. To these are opposed three which end in injustice and lawlessness,–Tyranny, Oligarchy, and Mob Rule. Homer does not seem ignorant of these. Through-out his whole poem he names kingly rule and praises it; for example (I. ii. 196):–

> For fierce his anger, and the Lord of counsel, Jove,
> From whom proceeds all honor, loves him well.

And what sort of a man a king must be, he plainly reveals (O. ii. 236):–

> Be kind and gentle with all his heart.

And (O. iv. 690):–

> One that wrought no iniquity toward any man, nor spake aught
> unrighteous in the township, as is the wont of divine kings.

And severally where he enumerates five kings of the Boeotians, and among the Phaeacians (O. viii. 390):–

> *Behold there are twelve glorious princes who rule among this*
> *people and bear sway, and I myself am the thirteenth.*

The image of democracy he shows clearly on the shield, in which he makes two cities. The one he says is ruled democratically, since they have no leader, yet all by their own will conduct themselves according to the laws; then, too, he introduces a trial proceeding. And he exhibits a democracy when he says (O. xvi. 425):–

> *In fear of the people, for they were exceedingly wroth against*
> *him, because he had followed with Topheon sea-robbers and*
> *harried the Thesprotians, who were at peace with us.*

A man ruling with violence and contrary to the laws he does not call a tyrant, for the name is of more recent date. But his nature he exhibits in his deeds (O. vxiii. 85):–

> *And send thee to the mainland to Echetus the king, the maimer*
> *of all mankind, who will cut off thy nose and ears with the*
> *pitiless steel.*

And he shows Aegisthus tyrannical, who killed Agamemnon and lorded over Mycenae. And when he was killed he says he would have had no sepulchre if Menelaus had been there. For this was the custom with tyrants (O. iii. 258):–

> *Then even in his death would they not have heaped the piled*
> *earth over him, but dogs and fowls of the air would have*
> *devoured him as he lay on the plain far from the town:*
> *so dread was the deed he contrived.*

Oligarchy he seems to show in the ambition of the suitors, about whom he says (O. i. 247):–

> *As many as lord it in rocky Ithaca.*

He describes the mob rule in the Trojan government in which all are accomplices of Alexander and all are involved in misfortunes. Priam accuses his sons of being the cause (I. xxiv. 253):–

> *Haste, worthless sons, my scandal and my shame!*

And also another Trojan, Antimachus (I. xi. 124):–

> *'Twas he who chief*
> *Seduc'd by Paris' gold and splendid gifts*
> *Advis'd the restitution to refuse*
> *Of Helen to her lord.*

It is esteemed just among men to distribute to each according to his worth. This principle concerns especially reverencing the gods, and honoring parents and relations. Piety toward the gods he teaches in many passages, introducing the heroes sacrificing, praying, offering gifts to the gods, and celebrating them in hymns, and as a reward for their piety they receive from the gods.

Honor to parents he shows especially, in the character of Telemachus, and in his praise of Orestes (O. i. 298):--

> *Or hast thou not heard what renown the goodly Orestes got*
> *among all men in that he slew the slayer of his father?*

For parents to be cared for in their old age by their children is just by nature and a debt of retribution; this he showed in one passage where he says (I. xvii. 302):-

> *Not destin'd he his parents to repay their early care.*

The good will and good faith of brothers to one another he shows in Agamemnon and Menelaus, of friends in Achilles and Patroclus, prudence and wifely love in Penelope, the longing of a man for his wife in Odysseus.

How we should act toward our country he showed especially in these words (I. xii. 243):-

> *The best of omens is our country's cause.*

And how citizens should share a common friendship (I. ix. 63):-

> *Outcast from kindred, law, and hearth is he*
> *Whose soul delights in fierce, internal strife.*

That truthfulness is honorable and the contrary to be avoided (I. ix. 312):-

> *Him as the gates of hell my soul abhors*
> *Where outward speech his secret thought belies.*

And (O. xviii. 168):-

> *Who speak friendly with their lips, but imagine evil in the*
> *latter end.*

Households are chiefly well ordered when the wife does not make a fuss over the undeclared plans of her husband nor without his counsel undertakes to do any thing. Both he shows in the person of Hera; the former he attributes to Zeus as speaker (I. i. 545):-

> *Expect not Juno, all my mind to know.*

And the latter Hera herself speaks (I. xiv. 310):-

> *Lest it displease thee, if, to thee unknown,*
> *I sought the Ocean's deeply flowing stream,*

There is a custom among all people for those who go to a war or who are in danger to send some message to their families. Our poet was familiar with this custom. For Andromache, bewailing Hector, says (I. xxiv. 743):-

> *For not to me was giv'n to clasp the hand extended from thy*
> *dying bed,*

> *Nor words of wisdom catch, which night and day,*
> *With tears, I might have treasur'd in my heart.*

Penelope recalls the commands of Odysseus when he set forth (O. xviii. 265):–

> *Wherefore I know not if the gods will suffer me to return, or*
> *whether I shall be cut off there in Troy; so do thou have a*
> *care for all these things. Be mindful of my father and my*
> *mother in the halls, even as thou art or yet more than now,*
> *while I am far away. But when thou see'st thy son a bearded*
> *man, marry whom thou wilt and leave thine own house.*

He knew also the custom of having stewards (O. ii. 226):–

> *He it was to whom Odysseus, as he departed in the fleet, had*
> *given the charge over all his house that it should obey the*
> *old man, and that he should keep all things safe.*

Grief at the death in one's household he thinks should not be unmeasured; for this is unworthy, nor does he allow it altogether to be repressed; for apathy is impossible for mankind, whence he says the following (I. xxiv. 48):–

> *He mourns and weeps, but time his grief allays,*
> *For fate to man a patient mind hath given.*

Other places he says (I. xix. 228):–

> *Behooves us bury out of sight our dead*
> *Steeling our hearts and weeping but a day.*

He also knew the customs used now at funerals, in other passages and in the following (I. xvi. 456):–

> *There shall his brethren and his friends perform*
> *His fun'ral rites, and mound and column raise*
> *The fitting tribute to the mighty dead*

And as Andromache says (before) the naked and prostrate body of Hector (I. xxii. 509):–

> *But now on thee, beside the beaked ships*
> *Far from thy parents, when the rav'ning dogs*
> *Have had their fill, the wriggling worms shall feed*
> *In thee all naked; while within thy house*
> *Lies store of raiment, rich and rare, the work*
> *Of women's hands: these I will burn with fire*
> *Not for thy need–thou ne'er shalt wear them more*
> *But for thine honor in the sight of Troy.*

So, too, Penelope prepares the shroud (O. ii. 99):–

> *Even this shroud for the hero Laertes.*

But these are examples of moderation. But exceeding these are the living creatures and men Achilles burns on the pyre of Patroclus. He tells us of them, but does not do so in words of praise. Therefore he exclaims (I. xxi. 19):–

> *On savage deeds intent.*

And he first of all mentions monuments to the slain (I. vii. 336):–

> *And on the plains erect*
> *Around the pyre one common pyre for all.*

And he gave the first example of funeral games. These are common to times of peace and war.

Experience in warlike affairs, which some authorities call Tactics, his poetry being varied by infantry, siege, and naval engagements, and also by individual contests, covers many types of strategy. Some of these are worth mentioning. In drawing up armies it is necessary always to put the cavalry in front, and after it the infantry. This he indicates in the following verses (I. ii. 297):–

> *In the front rank, with chariot and with horse,*
> *He plac'd the car-borne warriors; in the rear,*
> *Num'rous and brave, a cloud of infantry!*

And as to placing leaders among the soldiers as they are arranged in files (I. ix. 86):–

> *Seven were the leaders; and with each went forth,*
> *A hundred gallant youths, with lances armed.*

Some of the leaders fight in the front rank; some in the rear exhort the rest to fight (I. iv. 252):–

> *And come where round their chief*
> *Idomeneus, the warlike bards of Crete*
> *Were coming for the fight; Idomeneus*
> *Of courage stubborn as the forest boar*
> *The foremost ranks array'd; Meriones*
> *The rearmost squadrons had in charge.*

It is necessary for those who are valiant to camp in the extreme limits, making as it were a wall for the rest; but for the king is pitched his tent in the safest place, that is, in the midst. He shows this by making the most valorous men, Achilles and Ajax, encamp in the most exposed spaces of the fleet, but Agamemnon and the rest in the middle.

The custom of surrounding the camp with earth-works, and digging around it a deep and wide ditch and planting it in a circle with stakes so that no one can jump over it by reason of its breadth, nor go down into it because of its depth, is found in the warlike operations of Homer (I. xii. 52):–

> *In vain we seek to drive*
> *Our horses o'er the ditch: it is hard to cross,*
> *'Tis crowned with pointed stakes, and then behind*
> *Is built the Grecian wall; these to descend,*
> *And from our cars in narrow space to fight,*
> *Were certain ruin.*

And in battle those who follow the example of Homer's heroes die bravely (I. xxii. 304):–

> *Yet not without a struggle let me die,*
> *Nor all inglorious; but let some great act,*
> *Which future days may hear of, mark my fall.*

And another time (O. xv. 494):–

> *And if there be among you who this day shall meet his doom by*
> *sword or arrow slain, e'en let him die! a glorious death is*
> *his who for his country falls.*

To those who distinguish themselves he distributes gifts (I. ix. 334):–

> *To other chiefs and kings he meted out their several portions.*

And he threatens deserters (I. xv. 348):–

> *Whom I elsewhere, and from the ships aloof*
> *Shall find, my hand shall down him on the spot.*

Why is it necessary to speak of the heroes in battle? How differently and variously he makes them give and receive wounds. One he thinks worthy of mention, because he thinks those wounded in front are the more honorable because they prove steadfastness and a desire to abide the shock. Those who are struck in the back or neck were less honorable, since these blows they received in flight. Both of these are mentioned in Homer (I. xii. 288):–

> *Not in the neck behind, nor in thy back*
> *Should fall the blow, but in thy breast in front,*
> *Thy courage none might call in doubt*
> *Shouldst thou from spear or sword receive a wound.*

And again (I. xxii. 213):–

> *Not in my back will I receive thy spear,*
> *But through my heart.*

In putting enemies to flight he gives useful advice, not to be busied with the spoil, nor give time for flight, but to press on and pursue (I. vi. 68):–

> *Loiter not now behind, to throw yourselves   Upon the prey, and bear*
> *it to the ships;   Let all your aim be now to kill, then   Ye may at leisure*
> *spoil your slaughtered foe.*

There are in his poetry successful deeds achieved by every age, by which every one, no matter who he may be, can be encouraged: the man in the flower of his strength by Achilles, Ajax, and Diomed; by younger ones Antilochus and Meriones; the mature by Idomeneus and Odysseus; the old men by Nestor; and every king by all of these named and by Agamemnon. Such are in Homer the examples of the discourse and action of civilized life.

Let us see now whether Homer had any familiarity with medicine. That he held the art in high regard is clear from the following (I. xi. 514):–

Worth many a life is his, the skilful leech.

Medical science appears to be the science of disease and health. That it is a science any one can learn from this (O. iv. 23):–

There each one is a leech skilled beyond all men.

That it deals with disease and health (O. iv. 230):–

Many that are healing in the cup, and many baneful,–

he indicates with these things.

Medicine has, too, a theoretical side which reaches the knowledge of particulars by universal reasoning and by inductive method. The parts of this are the study of symptoms and the knowledge of the courses of disease. The active part treating of action and effect; the parts of it diatetic, surgical, medicinal. How did Homer appraise each of these? That he knew the theoretical side is evident from this (O. iv. 227):–

Medicines of such virtue and so helpful had the daughters
of Zeus.

He calls them "of such virtue" because they were prepared by theoretic art.

But the study of symptoms he goes over in the case of Achilles. For he was a disciple of Charon. He first observed, then, the causes of the pestilence which was attacking the Greeks. For he knew that the causes of common diseases were from Apollo, who seems to be the same as the Sun. For he notices the seasons of the year. If these are intemperate, they become the causes of disease. For, in general, the safety and destruction of men are to be ascribed to Apollo, of women to Artemis, i.e. to the Sun and Moon, making them the casters of arrows by reason of the rays they throw out. So dividing the male and female he makes the male of the warmer temperament. On this account, at any rate, he says Telemachus is of this type, "by the guidance of Apollo"; but the daughters of Tyndarus grew up, he says, under the protection of Artemis. Moreover, to these gods he attributes death in many places, and among others in the following (I. xxiv. 605):–

The youths, Apollo with his silver bow;
The maids, the Archer Queen Diana slew.

Where he relates the rising of the Dog Star, the same is a sign and cause of fever and disease (I. xxii. 30):–

> *The highest he but sign to mortal man*
> *Of evil augury and fiery heat.*

He gives the causes of disease where he speaks about the gods (I. v. 341):–

> *They eat no bread, they drink no ruddy wine,*
> *Thence are they bloodless and exempt from death.*

For food, whether dry or humid, is generative of blood. And this nourishes the body; if it is excessive or corrupt, it becomes the cause of disease.

The practical part of medicine he carefully distinguishes. In this is the dietetic. First, he knew the periods and cures of diseases, as when he says (O. xi. 171):–

> *What doom overcame thee of death that lays men at their*
> *length? Was it a slow disease, or did Artemis the archer slay*
> *them with the visitation of her gentle shafts?*

It is evident that he thinks a light diet is healthful. For he pictures his heroes making use of cooked food and so removes extravagant attention about things to eat. And since the stomach needs constant repletion, when cooked food, which has the closest relation to the body, is digested in the heart and veins, and the surfeit is cast forth, he says words like the following (O. vii. 215):–

> *But as for me suffer me to sup afflicted as I am; for naught*
> *is there more shameless than a ravening belly, which biddeth a*
> *man perforce be mindful of him.*

And again (O. vii. 219):–

> *Yet ever more he biddeth me eat and drink, and maketh utterly*
> *to forget all my sufferings and commandeth me to take my fill.*

He knew, too, the difference in the use of wine: that immoderate drinking is harmful but moderate profitable; as follows (O. xxi. 294):–

> *Honey sweet wine, that is the bane of others too, even of all*
> *who take great draughts and drink out of measure.*

The other so (I. vi. 261):–

> *But great the strength,*
> *Which gen'rous wine imparts to men who toil*
> *And that gives additional force.*

and (I. xix. 167):–

> *But he who first with food and wine refreshed*
> *All day maintains the combat with the foe.*

His spirit retains unbroken, and his limbs
Unwearied till both armies quit the field.

And he thinks the agreeable taste contributes to good fellowship
(O. vii. 182):–

So spake he, and Pontonous mixed the gladdening wine.

The strong and heady kind Odysseus gives to the Cyclops, the sharp
kind for a medicine, for such is the Promneon brand, which he gives to
wounded Machaon.

That he advises the use of gymnastics is evident in many places, for he
makes his characters always at work, some in appropriate occupations,
some for the sake of exercise. Although the Phaeacians are externally
given to softness, and the suitors are dissolute, he introduces them doing
gymnastic feats. And moderate exercise he thinks is the cause of health.
For a tired body sleep is a remedy. For he says "sleep came upon Odysseus" after he had been tired out by the sea (O. v. 493):–

That so it might soon release him from his weary travail,
overshadowing his eyelids.

Nature requires a tired body to take rest. And where there is too little
heat, as it is not able to penetrate everywhere, it remains at the lowest
level. Why does the body rest? Because the tension of the soul is remitted
and the members are dissolved and this he clearly says (O. iv. 794):–

And she sank back in sleep, and all her joints were loosened.

As in other things, immoderation is not advantageous; so he declares
the same with regard to sleep, at one time saying (O, xiv. 394):–

Weariness and much sleep.

And another (O. xx. 52):–

To wake and watch all night, this, too, is vexation of spirit.

He knew, too, that clearness of air contributes to health, where he
says (O. iv. 563):–

But the deathless gods will convey thee to the Elysian plain
and the World's end, where is Rhadamanthus of the fair hair,
where life is easiest for men. No snow is there, nor yet
great storm, nor any rain; but always ocean sendeth forth the
breeze of the shrill west to blow cool on men.

He knew remedies for sufferings; for cold revives those who are
fainting, as in the case of Sarpedon (I. v. 697):–

He swooned, and giddy mists o'erspread his eyes,
But soon revived as on his forehead blew
While yet he gasped for breath the cooling breeze.

Heat is a remedy for cold, as in the case of storm-tossed Odysseus,
who bends down in the thicket, where there is a protection against winds

and rains, and he covers himself with the wood about him. And other places he mentions baths and anointing, as in the case of Diomed and Odysseus returning from their night expedition. The special usefulness of baths he shows especially in the following (O. x. 362):–

> *She bathed me with water from out a great caldron, pouring it*
> *over head and shoulders, where she had mixed it to a pleasant*
> *warmth till from my limbs she took away consuming weariness.*

It is plain that the nerves have their origin in the head and shoulders. So probably from this he makes the healing of fatigue to be taken. This takes place by the wetting and warming; for labors are parching.

We have now to consider how he treated the function of surgery. Machaon heals Menelaus by first removing the javelin; then he examines the wound and presses out the blood, and scatters over it dry medicaments. And it is evident that this is done by him in a technical fashion. Eurypalus, who is wounded in the thigh, first treats it with a sharp knife, then he washes it with clear water; afterward to diminish the pain, he employs an herb. For there are many in existence that heal wounds. He knew this, too, that bitter things are suitable; for to dry up wounds requires exsiccation. After Patroclus has applied the healing art, he did not go away immediately, but (I. xv. 393):–

> *Remaining, with his converse soothed the chief.*

For a sufferer needs sympathy. Machaon wounded not with a great or fatal wound on the shoulder, he makes using intentionally a somewhat careless diet. Perhaps here he shows his art. For he who takes care of himself at ordinary times is able to heal himself.

This is noted, too, in Homer, that he knows the distinction of drugs. Some are to be used as plasters, others as powders, as when he says (I. iv. 218):–

> *And applied with skilful hand the herbs of healing power.*

But some are to be drunk, as where Helen mixes a medicine in a bowl (O. iv. 221):–

> *A drug to lull all pain and anger, and bring forgetfulness of*
> *every sorrow.*

He knows, too, that some poisonous drugs are to be applied as ointments (O. i. 261):–

> *To seek a deadly drug, that he might have wherewithal to*
> *smear his bronze-shod arrows.*

Others are to be drunk, as in these words (O. ii. 330):–

> *To fetch a poisonous drug that he may cast it into the bowl*
> *and make an end of all of us.*

So much for medicines in the Homeric poems.

Divination is useful to man like medicine. A part of this the Stoics call artificial, as the inspection of entrails and birds' oracles, lots, and signs. All of these they call in general artificial. But what is not artificial, and is not acquired by learning, are trances and ecstasy, Homer knew, too, of these phenomena. But he also knew of seers, priests, interpreters of dreams, and augurs. A certain wise man in Ithaca he tells of (O. ii 159):–

> He excelled his peers in knowledge of birds and in uttering
> words of fate.

And Odysseus, praying, says (O. xx. 100):–

> Let some one I pray of the folk that are waking show me a
> word of good omen within and without; let soon other sign be
> revealed to me from Zeus.

Snoring with him is a good sign. A divinely inspired seer is with the suitors, telling the future by divine inspiration. Once, too, Helenus says (I. vii. 53):–

> He was the recipient of a divine voice.
> By revelation from th' eternal gods.

He gives cause of believing that Socrates had actually communications from the voice of the daemon.

What natural or scientific art is left untouched? Tragedy took its start from Homer, and afterward was raised to supremacy in words and things. He shows that there is every form of tragedy; great and extraordinary deeds, appearances of the gods, speech full of wisdom, revealing all sorts of natures. In a word, his poems are all dramas, serious and sublime in expression, also in feeling and in subject. But they contain no exhibition of unholy deeds, lawless marriages, or the murder of parents and children, or the other marvels of more recent tragedy. But when he mentions a thing of this kind, he seems to conceal rather than to condemn the crime. As he does in the case of of Clytemnestra. For he says (O. iii. 266):–

> That she was endowed with an excellent mind as she had with
> her a teacher appointed by Agamemnon, to give her the
> best advice.

Aegisthus got this tutor out of the way and persuaded her to sin. He allows that Orestes justly avenged his father's death by killing Aegisthus; but he passes over in silence the murder of his mother. Many of the like examples are to be seen in the poet, as a writer of majestic, but not inhuman, tragedy.

None the less, however, Comedy took from him its origin; for he contains, although he relates the gravest and most serious things, episodes which move to laughter, as in the "Iliad" Hephaestus is introduced limping and pouring out wine for the gods (I. i. 599):–

Rose laughter irrepressible, at sight
Of Vulcan hobbling round the spacious hall.

Thersites is most contemptible in body and most evil in disposition, from his raising a disturbance, and his slanderous speech and boastfulness. Odysseus attacks him on this account and gives occasion to all to laugh (I. ii. 270):–

The Greeks, despite their anger, laugh'd aloud.

In the "Odyssey" among the pleasure-loving Phaeacians their bard sings the adultery of Ares and Aphrodite. He tells how they fell into the snares of Hepheastus, and were taken in the act, and caused all the gods to laugh, and how they joked frequently with one another. And among the dissolute suitors Irus the beggar is brought in, contesting for a prize with the most noble Odysseus, and how he appeared ridiculous in the action. Altogether it is the character of human nature, not only to be intense, but to take "a moral holiday" so that the men may be equal to the troubles of life. Such relaxation for the mind is to be found in our poet. Those who in later days introduced Comedy to produce laughter made use of bare and naked language, but they cannot claim to have invented anything better. Of erotic feelings and expression, Homer makes but a moderate use; as Zeus says (I. iii. 442):–

For never did thy beauty so inflame my sense.

And what follows, and about Helen (I. iii. 156):–

And 'tis no marvel, one to other said,
The valiant Trojans and the well-greaved Greeks
For beauty such as this should long endure
The toils of war.

And other things of the same kind. Other poets have represented men taken by this passion uncontrollably and immoderately. This is sufficient for this subject.

Epigrams are a pleasing variety of speech; they are found on statues and on monuments indicating succinctly to whom they are dedicated. And this, too, is a mark of Homer where he says (I. vii. 89):–

Lo! there a warrior's tomb of days gone by,
A mighty chief whom glorious Hector slew.

And again (I. vi. 460):–

Lo! this was Hector's wife, who, when they fought
On plains of Troy, was Ilion's bravest chief.

But if any one should say that Homer was a master of painting, he would make no mistake. For some of the wise men said that poetry was speaking painting, and painting silent poetry. Who before or who more than Homer, by the imagination of his thoughts or by the harmony of his verse, showed and exalted gods, men, places, and different kinds of deeds? For he showed by abundance of language all sorts of creatures and the most notable things–lions, swine, leopards. Describing their forms and characters and comparing them to human deeds, he showed the properties of each. He dared to liken the forms of gods to those of men. Hephaestus prepared Achilles' shield; he sculptured in gold, land, sky, sea, the greatness of the Sun and the beauty of the Moon and the host of the stars crowning all. He placed on it cities in different states and fortunes, and animals moving and speaking. Who has more skill than the artificer of such an art?

Let us see in another example out of many how poems resemble more those things that are seen than those that are heard. As for example, in the passage where he tells of the wound of Odysseus, he introduces what Eurychleias did (O. xix. 468):–

> Now the old woman took the scarred limb and passed her hand down it, and knew it by the touch and let the foot drop suddenly, so that the knees fell into the bath, and the vessel broke, being turned over on the other side, and that water was spilled on the ground. Then grief and joy came on her in one moment, and her eyes filled with tears, and the voice of her utterance was stayed, and touching the chin of Odysseus, she spake to him saying, "Yea, verily, thou art Odysseus, my dear child, and I knew thee not before till I had handled all the body of my lord." Therewithal she looked toward Penelope, as minded to make a sign and the rest.

For here more things are shown than can be in a picture and those can be weighed by the eyes. They are not to be taken in by the eyes, but by the intelligence alone: such as the letting go of the foot through emotion, the sound of the tears, the spilt water and the grief, and at the same time the joy of the old women, her words to Odysseus, and what she is about to say as she looks toward Penelope. Many other things are graphically revealed in the poet which come out when he is read.

It is time to close a work which we have woven, like a crown from a beflowered and variegated field, and which we offer to Muses. And we, we shall not lay it to the heart if any one censures us, because the Homeric poems contain the basis of evil things, if we ascribe to him various political, ethical, and scientific discussions. Since good things are by themselves simple, straightforward, and unprepared;

but what is mixed with evil has many different modes and all kinds of combinations, from which the substance of the matter is derived. If evil is added to the others, the knowledge and choice of the good is made easier. And on the whole a subject of this sort gives occasion to the poet for originating discourse of all kinds, some belonging to himself, some proper to the characters he introduces. From this circumstance be gives much profit to his readers. Why should we not ascribe to Homer every excellence? Those things that he did not work up, they who came after him have noticed. And some make use of his verses for divination, like the oracles of God. Others setting forward other projects fit to them for our use what he has said by changing or transposing it.

The Banquet of the Seven Wise Men

THE SEVEN,–SOLON, DIAS, THALES, ANACHARSIS, CLEOBU-
LUS, PITTACUS, CHILO.

NILOXENUS, EUMETIS, ALEXIDEMUS PERIANDER, ARDALUS,
AESOP, CLEODEMUS, MNESIPHILUS, CHERSIAS, GORGIAS, DI-
OCLES. DIOCLES TO NICARCHUS

No wonder, my friend Nicarchus, to find old truths so disguised, and
the words and actions of men so grossly and misrepresented and lamely
delivered, seeing people are so disposed to give ear and credit to fictions
of yesterday's standing. For there were not merely seven present at that
feast, as you were informed; there were more than double the number. I
was there myself in person familiarly acquainted with Periander (my art
had gained me his acquaintance); and Thales boarded at my house, at
the request and upon the recommendation of Periander. Whoever then
gave you that account of our feast did it very inadequately; it is plain he
did it upon hearsay and that he was not there among us. Now, that we are
together and at leisure, and possibly we may not live to find an opportunity so convenient another time, I will (as you wish it) give you a faithful
account of the whole proceedings at that meeting.

Periander had prepared a dinner for us, not in the town, but in a din-
ing-hall which stands close to the temple of Venus, to whom there was
a sacrifice that day. For having neglected the duty ever since his mother died for love, he was resolved now to atone for the omission, being
warned so to do by the dreams of Melissa. In order thereunto, there was
provided a rich chariot for every one of the guests. It was summer-time,
and every part of the way quite to the seaside was hardly passable, by
reason of throngs of people and whole clouds of dust. As soon as Thales
espied the chariot waiting at the door, he smilingly discharged it, and we
walked through the fields to avoid the press and noise. There was in our
company a third person, Niloxenus a Naucratian, an eminent man, who

was very intimately acquainted with Solon and Thales in Egypt; he had a message to deliver to Bias, and a letter sealed, the contents whereof he knew not; only he guessed it contained a second question to be resolved by Bias, and in case Bias undertook not to answer it, he had in commission to impart it to the wisest men in Greece. What a fortune is this (quoth Niloxenus) to find you all together! This paper (showing it us) I am bringing to the banquet. Thales replied, after his wonted smiling way, If it contains any hard question, away with it to Priene. Bias will resolve it with the same readiness he did your former problem. What problem was that? quoth he. Why, saith Thales, a certain person sent him a beast for sacrifice with this command, that he should return him that part of his flesh which was best and worst; our philosopher very gravely and wisely pulled out the tongue of the beast, and sent it to the donor;–which single act procured him the name and reputation of a very wise man. It was not this act alone that advanced him in the estimation of the world, quoth Niloxenus; but he joyfully embraces what you so carefully shun, the acquaintance and friendship of kings and great men; and whereas he honors you for divers great accomplishments, he particularly admires you for this invention, that with little labor and no help of any mathematical instrument you took so truly the height of one of the pyramids; for fixing your staff erect at the point of the shadow which the pyramid cast, two triangles being thus made by the tangent rays of the sun, you demonstrated that what proportion one shadow had to the other, such the pyramid bore to the stick.

But, as I said, you are accused of being a hater of kings, and certain false friends of yours have presented Amasis with a paper of yours stuffed with sentences reproachful to majesty; as for instance, being at a certain time asked by Molpagoras the Ionian, what the most absurd thing was you had observed in your notice, you replied, An old king. Another time, in a dispute that happened in your company about the nature of beasts, you affirmed that of wild beasts, a king, of tame, a flatterer, was the worst. Such apothegms must needs be unacceptable to kings, who pretend there is vast difference between them and tyrants. This was Pittacus's reply to Myrsilus, and it was spoken in jest, quoth Thales; nor was it an old king I said I should marvel at, but an old pilot. In this mistake however, I am much of the youth's mind who, throwing a stone at a dog, hit his stepmother, adding, Not so bad. I therefore esteemed Solon a very wise and good man, when I understood he refused empire; and if Pittacus had not taken upon himself a monarchy, he had never exclaimed, O ye gods! how hard a matter it is to be good! And Periander, however he seems to be sick of his father's disease, is yet to be commended that he gives ear to wholesome discourses and converses only with wise and good men, rejecting the advice of Thrasybulus my countryman who would have persuaded him to chop off the heads of the leading men. For a prince that chooses rather to govern slaves than freemen is like a foolish farmer, who throws his wheat and barley in the streets, to fill his barns with swarms of locusts and whole cages of birds. For government has one good thing to make amends for its many evils, namely, honor and glory, provided one rules good men as being better than they and great men because greater than they. But he that having ascended the throne minds only his own interest and ease, is fitter to tend sheep or to drive horses or to feed cattle than to govern men.

But this stranger (continues he) has engaged us in a deal of impertinent chat, for we have omitted to speak or offer any discourse suitable to the occasion and end of our meeting; for doubtless it becomes the guest as well as the host, to make preparation beforehand. It is reported that the Sybarites used to invite their neighbors' wives a whole twelve-month before to their entertainments, that they might have convenient time to trim and adorn themselves; for my part, I am of opinion, that he who would feast as he should ought to allow himself more time for preparation than they, it being a more difficult matter to compose the mind into an agreeable temper than to fit one's clothes for the outward ornament of the body. For a prudent man comes not hither only to fill his belly, as if he were to fill a bottle, but to be sometimes grave and serious, sometimes pleasant, sometimes to listen to others, and sometimes to speak himself what may benefit or divert the company, if the meeting is intended for any good use or purpose. For if the victuals be not good, men may let them alone, or if the wine be bad, men may use water; but for a weak-brained, impertinent, unmannerly, shallow fellow-commoner there is no cure; he mars all the mirth and music, and spoils the best entertainment in the world. And it will be no easy business to lay aside a sullen temper; since we find divers men, angered in their debauches, have yet remembered the provocation to their dying day, the spite remaining like a surfeit arising from wrong done or an insult received in drinking. Wherefore Chilo did very well and wisely; for when he invited yesterday, he would not promise to come till he had a particular given him of all their names who were to meet him. For, quoth he, if my business calls me to sea or I am pressed to serve my prince in his wars, there is a necessity upon me to rest contented with whatever company I fall into, though never so unsuitable to my quality or disagreeable to my nature and humor; but voluntarily and needlessly to associate myself with any riffraff rabble would ill become any man pretending to but common discretion.

The Egyptian skeleton which they brought into their feasts and exposed to the view of their guests, with this advice, that they should not in their merriment forget they would shortly be themselves such as that was,–though it was a sight not so acceptable (as may be supposed),–had yet this conveniency and use, to incite the spectators not to luxury and drunkenness but to mutual love and friendship, persuading them not to protract a life in itself short and uncertain by a tedious course of wickedness.

In discourses of this kind we spent our time by the way, and were now come to the house. Here Thales would not be washed, for he had but a while before anointed himself; wherefore he took a round to view the horse-race and the wrestling-place, and the grove upon the water-side, which was neatly trimmed and beautified by Periander; this he did, not so much to satisfy his own curiosity (for he seldom or never admired anything he saw), but that he might not disoblige Periander or seem to overlook or despise the glory and magnificence of our host. Of the rest every one, after he had anointed and washed himself, the servants introduced into a particular room, purposely fitted and prepared for the men; they were guided thither through a porch, in which Anacharsis sat, and there was a certain young lady with him combing his hair. This lady stepping forward to welcome Thales, he kissed her most courteously, and smiling said: Madam, make our host fair and pleasant, so that, being (as he is) the mildest man in the world, he may not be fearful and terrible for us to look on. When I was curious to inquire who this lady was, he said, Do you not yet know the wise and famous Eumetis? for so her father calls her, though others call her after her father's name Cleobulina. Doubtless, saith Niloxenus, they call her by this name to commend her judgment and wit, and her reach into the more abstruse and recondite part of learning; for I have myself in Egypt seen and read some problems first started and discussed by her. Not so, saith Thales, for she plays with these as with cockal-bones, and deals boldly with all she meets; she is a person of an admirable understanding, of a shrewd capacious mind, of a very obliging conversation, and one that prevails upon her father to govern his subjects with the greatest mildness. How democratic she is appears, saith Niloxenus, plainly to any that observes her simple innocent garb. But pray, continues he, wherefore is it that she shows such affection to Anacharsis? Because, replied Thales, he is a temperate and learned man, who fully and freely makes known to her those mysterious ways of dieting and physicing the sick which are now in use among the Scythians; and I doubt not she now coaxes and courts the old gentleman at the rate you see, taking this opportunity to discourse with him and learn something of him.

As we were come near the dining-room, Alexidemus the Milesian, a bastard son of Thrasybulus the Tyrant, met us. He seemed to be disturbed, and in an angry tone muttered to himself some words which we could not distinctly hear; but espying Thales, and recovering himself out of his disorder, he complained how Periander had put an insufferable affront upon him. He would not permit me, saith he, to go to sea, though I earnestly importuned him, but he would press me to dine with him. And when I came as invited, he assigned me a seat unbecoming my person and character, Aeolians and islanders and others of inferior rank being placed above me; whence it is easy to infer how meanly he thinks of my father, and it is undeniable how this affront put upon me rebounds disgracefully in my parent's face. Say you so? quoth Thales, are you afraid lest the place lessen or diminish your honor and worth, as the Egyptians commonly hold the stars are magnified or lessened according to their higher or lower place and position? And are you more foolish than that Spartan who, when the prefect of the music had appointed him to sit in the lowest seat in the choir, replied, This is prudently done, for this is the ready way to bring this seat into repute and esteem? It is a frivolous consideration, where or below whom we sit; and it is a wiser part to adapt ourselves to the judgment and humor of our right and left hand man and the rest of the company, that we may approve ourselves worthy of their friendship, when they find we take no pet at our host, but are rather pleased to be placed near such good company. And whosoever is disturbed upon the account of his place seems to be more angry with his neighbor than with his host, but certainly is very troublesome and nauseous to both.

These are fine words, and no more, quoth Alexidemus, for I observe you, the wisest of men, as ambitious as other men; and having said thus, he passed by us doggedly and trooped off. Thales, seeing us admiring the insolence of the man, declared he was a fellow naturally of a blockish, stupid disposition; for when he was a boy, he took a parcel of rich perfume that was presented to Thrasybulus and poured it into a large bowl and mixing it with a quantity of wine, drank it off and was ever hated for it. As Thales was talking after this fashion, in comes a servant and tells us it was Periander's pleasure we would come in and inform him what we thought of a certain creature brought into his presence that instant, whether it were so born by chance or were a monster and omen;–himself seeming mightily affected and concerned, for he judged his sacrifice polluted by it. At the same time he walked before us into a certain house adjoining to his garden-wall, where we found a young beardless shepherd, tolerably handsome, who having opened a leathern bag produced and showed us a child born (as he averred) of a mare. His upper parts as far as his neck and his hands, was of human shape, and the rest of his body resembled a perfect horse; his cry was like that of a child newly born. As soon as Niloxenus saw it, he cried out. The gods deliver us; and away he fled as one sadly affrighted. But Thales eyed the shepherd a considerable while, and then smiling (for it was his way to jeer me perpetually about my art) says he, I doubt not, Diocles, but you have been all this time seeking for some expiatory sacrifice, and meaning to call to your aid those gods whose province and work it is to avert evils from men, as if some greet and grievous thing had happened. Why not? quoth I, for undoubtedly this prodigy portends sedition and war, and I fear the dire portents thereof may extend to myself, my wife, and my children, and prove all our ruin; since, before I have atoned for my former fault, the goddess gives us this second evidence and proof of her displeasure. Thales replied never a word, but laughing went out of the house. Periander, meeting him at the door, inquired what we thought of that creature; he dismissed me, and taking Periander by the hand, said, Whatsoever Diocles shall persuade you to do, do it at your best leisure; but I advise you either not to have such youthful men to keep your mares, or to give them leave to marry. When Periander heard him out, he seemed infinitely pleased, for he laughed outright, and hugging Thales in his arms he kissed him; then saith he, O Diocles, I am apt to think the worst is over, and what this prodigy portended is now at an end; for do you not apprehend what a loss we have sustained in the want of Alexidemus's good company at supper?

When we entered into the house, Thales raising his voice inquired where it was his worship refused to be placed; which being shown him, he sat himself in that very place, and prayed us to sit down by him, and said, I would gladly give any money to have an opportunity to sit and eat with Ardalus. This Ardalus was a Troezenian by birth, by profession a minstrel, and a priest of the Ardalian Muses, whose temple old Ardalus had founded and dedicated. Here Aesop, who was sent from Croesus to visit Periander, and withal to consult the oracle at Delphi, sitting by and beneath Solon upon a low stool, told the company this fable: A Lydian mule, viewing his own picture in a river, and admiring the bigness and beauty of his body, raises his crest; he waxes proud, resolving to imitate the horse in his gait and running; but presently, recollecting his extraction, how that his father was but an ass at best, he stops his career and cheeks his own haughtiness and bravery. Chilo replied, after his short concise way, You are slow and yet try to run, in imitation of your mule.

Amidst these discourses in comes Melissa and sits her down by Periander; Eumetis followed and came in as we were at supper; then Thales calls to me (I sat me down above Bias), Why do you not make Bias acquainted with the problems sent him from the King by Niloxenus this second time, that he may soberly and warily weigh them? Bias answered, I have been already scared with that news. I have known that Bacchus is otherwise a powerful deity, and for his wisdom is termed [Greek omitted] that is, THE INTERPRETER; therefore I shall undertake it when my belly is full of wine. Thus they jested and reparteed and played one upon another all the while they sat at table. Observing the unwonted frugality of Periander at this time, I considered with myself that the entertainment of wise and good men is a piece of good husbandry, and that so far from enhancing a man's expenses in truth it serves to save charge, the charge (to wit) of costly foreign unguents and junkets, and the waste of the richest wines, which Periander's state and greatness required him every day in his ordinary treats to expend. Such costly provisions were useless here, and Periander's wisdom appeared in his frugality. Moreover, his lady had laid aside her richer habit, and appeared in an ordinary, but a very becoming dress.

Supper now ended, and Melissa having distributed the garlands, we offered sacrifice; and when the minstrel had played us a tune or two, she withdrew. Then Ardalus inquired of Anacharsis, if there were women fiddlers at Scythia. He suddenly and smartly replied, There are no vines there. Ardalus asked a second question, whether the Scythians had any gods among them. Yes, quoth Anacharsis, and they understand what men say to them; nor are the Scythians of the Grecian opinion (however these last may be the better orators), that the gods are better pleased with the sounds of flutes and pipes than with the voice of men. My friend, saith Aesop, what would you say if you saw our present pipe-makers throw away the bones of fawns and hind-calves, to use those of asses, affirming they yield the sweeter and more melodious sound? Whereupon Cleobulina made one of her riddles about the Phrygian flute,... in regard to the sound, and wondered that an ass, a gross animal and so alien from music should yet supply bones so fit for harmony. Therefore it is doubtless, quoth Niloxenus, that the people of Busiris blame us Naucratians for using pipes made of asses' bones it being an insufferable crime in an of them to listen to the flute or cornet, the sound thereof being (as they esteem it) so like the braying of an ass; and you know an ass is hateful to the Egyptians on account of Typhon.

There happening here a short silence, Periander, observing Niloxenus willing but not daring to speak, said: I cannot but commend the
civility of those magistrates who give audience first to strangers and
afterwards to their own citizens; wherefore I judge it convenient that
we inhabitants and neighbors should proceed no farther at present in
our discourse, and that now attention be given to those royal propositions sent us from Egypt, which the worthy Niloxenus is commissioned
to deliver to Bias, who wishes that he and we may scan and examine
them together. And Bias said: For where or in what company would a
man more joyfully adventure to give his opinion than here in this? And
since it is his Majesty's pleasure that I should give my judgment first, in
obedience to his commands I will do so, and afterwards they shall come
to every one of you in order.

Then Niloxenus delivered the paper to Bias, who broke up the seal
and commanded it to be read in all their hearing. The contents were
these:

Amasis the king of Egypt, to Bias, the wisest of the Grecians, greet-
ing. There is a contest between my brother of Ethiopia and myself about
wisdom; and being baffled in divers other particulars, he now demands
of me a thing absurd and impracticable; for he requires me to drink up
the ocean dry. If I be able to read this his riddle, divers cities and towns
now in his possession are to be annexed to my kingdom; but if I cannot
resolve this hard sentence, and give him the right meaning thereof, he
requires of me my right to all the towns bordering upon Elephantina.
Consider with speed the premises, and let me receive your thoughts by
Niloxenus. Pray lose no time. If in anything I can be serviceable to your
city or friends, you may command me. Farewell.

Bias, having perused and for a little time meditated upon the letter,
and whispering Cleobulus in the ear (he sat by him), exclaimed: What
a narration is here, O Niloxenus! Will Amasis, who governs so many
men and is seized of so many flourishing territories, drink up the ocean
for the gain of a few paltry, beggarly villages? Niloxenus replied with a
smile: Consider, good sir, what is to be done, if he will obey. Why then,
said Bias, let Amasis require the Ethopian king to stop the stream which
from all parts flow and empty themselves in the ocean, until he have
drunk out the whole remainder; for I conceive he means the present
waters, not those which shall flow into it hereafter. Niloxenus was so
overjoyed at this answer, that he could not contain himself. He hugged
and kissed the author, and the whole company liked his opinion admirably well; and Chilo laughing desired Niloxenus to get aboard immediately before the sea was consumed, and tell his master he should mind

more how to render his government sweet and potable to his people, than how to swallow such a quantity of salt water. For Bias, he told him, understands these things very well, and knows how to oblige your lord with very useful instructions, which if he vouchsafe to attend, he shall no more need a golden basin to wash his feet, to gain respect from his subjects; all will love and honor him for his virtue, though he were ten thousand times more hateful to them than he is. It were well and worthily done, quoth Periander, if all of us did pay him our first-fruits in this kind by the poll (as Homer said). Such a course would bring him an accession of profit greater than the whole proceeds of the voyage, besides being of great use to ourselves.

To this point it is fit that Solon should first speak, quoth Chilo, not only because he is the eldest in the company and therefore sits uppermost at table, but because he governs and gives laws to the amplest and most complete and flourishing republic in the world, that of Athens. Here Niloxenus whispered me in the ear: O Diocles, saith he, how many reports fly about and are believed, and how some men delight in lies which they either feign of their own heads or most greedily swallow from the mouths of others. In Egypt I heard it reported how Chilo had renounced all friendship and correspondence with Solon, because he maintained the mutability of laws. A ridiculous fiction, quoth I, for then he and we must have renounced Lycurgus, who changed the laws and indeed the whole government of Sparta.

Solon, pausing awhile, gave his opinion in these words. I conceive that monarch, whether king or tyrant, were infinitely to be commanded, who would exchange his monarchy for a commonwealth. Bias subjoined, And who would be first and foremost in conforming to the laws of his country. Thales added, I reckon that prince happy, who, being old, dies in his bed a natural death. Fourthly, Anacharsis, If he alone be a wise man. Fifthly, Cleobulus said, If he trust none of his courtiers. Sixthly, Pittacus spake thus, If he could so treat his subjects that they feared not him but for him. Lastly, Chilo concluded thus, A magistrate ought to meditate no mortal thing but everything immortal.

When all had given in their judgments upon this point, we requested Periander to let us know his thoughts. Disorder and discontent appearing in his countenance, he said, These opinions are enough to scare any wise man from affecting, empire. These things, saith Aesop after his reproving way, ought rather to have been discussed privately among ourselves, lest we be accounted antimonarchical while we desire to be esteemed friends and loyal counsellors. Solon, gently touching him on the head and smiling, answered: Do you not perceive that any one would make a king more moderate and a tyrant more favorable, who should persuade him that it is better not to reign than to reign? Who would believe you before the oracle delivered unto you, quoth Aesop which pronounced that city happy that heard but one crier. Yes, quoth Solon, and Athens, now a commonwealth, hath but one crier and one magistrate, the law, though the government be democratical; but you, my friend, have been so accustomed to the croaking of ravens and the prating of jays, that you do not hear clearly your own voice. For you maintain it to be the happiness of a city to be under the command of one man, and yet account it the merit of a feast if liberty is allowed every man to speak his mind freely upon what subject he pleases. But you have not prohibited your servants' drunkenness at Athens, Aesop said, as you have forbidden them to love or to use dry ointments. Solon laughed at this; but Cleodorus the physician said: To use dry ointment is like talking when a man is soaked with wine; both are very pleasant. Therefore, saith Chilo, men ought the more carefully to avoid it. Aesop proceeds, Thales seemed to imply that he should soon grow old.

Periander said laughing: We suffer deservedly, for, before we have perfected any remarks upon the letter, we are fallen upon disputes foreign to the matter under consideration; and therefore I pray, Niloxenus, read out the remainder of your lord's letter, and slip not this opportunity to receive what satisfaction all that are present shall be able to give you. The command of the king of Ethiopia, says Niloxenus, is no more and no less than (to use Archilochus's phrase) a broken scytale; that is, the meaning is inscrutable and cannot be found out. But your master Amasis was more mild and polite in his queries; for he commanded him only to resolve him what was most ancient, most beautiful, greatest, wisest, most common, and withal, what was most profitable, most pernicious, most strong, and most easy. Did he resolve and answer every one of these questions? He did, quoth Niloxenus, and do you judge of his answers and the soundness thereof: and it is my Prince's purpose not to misrepresent his responses and condemn unjustly what he saith well, so, where he finds him under a mistake, not to suffer that to pass without correction. His answers to the foresaid questions I will read to you.–What is most ancient? Time. What is greatest? The World. What is wisest? Truth. What is most beautiful? The light. What is most common? Death. What is most profitable? God. What is most Pernicious? An evil genius. What is strongest? Fortune. What is most easy? That which is pleasant.

When Niloxenus had read out these answers, there was a short silence among them; by and by Thales desires Niloxenus to inform him if Amasis approved of these answers. Niloxenus said, he liked some and disliked others. There is not one of them right and sound, quoth Thales, but all are full of wretched folly and ignorance. As for instance, how can that be most ancient whereof part is past, part is now present, and part is yet to come; every man knows it is younger than ourselves and our actions. As to his answer that truth is the most wise thing, it is as incongruous as if he had affirmed the light to be an eye if he judged the light to be the most beautiful how could he omit the sun; as to his solutions concerning the gods and evil genuises, they are full of presumption and peril. What he saith of Fortune is void of sense, for her inconstancy and fickleness proceed from want of strength and power. Nor is death the most common thing; the living are still at liberty, it hath not arrested them. But lest we be blamed as having a faculty to find fault only, we will lay down our opinions of these things, and compare them with those of the Ethiopian; I offer my self first, if Niloxenus pleases, to deliver my opinion on every one singly and I will relate both questions and answers in that method and order in which they were sent to Ethiopia and read to us. What is most ancient Thales answered, God, for he had no beginning. What is greatest? Place; the World contains all other things, this surrounds and contains the world. What is most beautiful? The world; for whatever is framed artificially and methodically is a part of it. What is most wise? Time; for it has found out some things already, it will find out the rest in due time. What is most common Hope; for they that want other things are masters of this. What is most profitable? Virtue; for by a right managery of other things she makes them all beneficial and advantageous. What is most pernicious? Vice; for it depraves the best things we enjoy. What is most strong? Necessity; for this alone is insuperable. What is most easy? That which is most agreeable to nature; for pleasures themselves are sometimes tedious and nauseating.

All the consult approved of Thale's solutions. Cleodemus said: My friend Niloxenus, it becomes kings to propound and resolve such questions; but the insolence of that barbarian who would have Amasis drink the sea would have been better fitted by such a smart reprimand as Pittacus gave Alyattes, who sent an imperious letter to the Lesbians. He made him no other answer, but to bid him spend his time in eating his hot bread and onions.

Periander, here assumed the discourse, and said: It was the manner of the ancient Grecians heretofore, O Cleodemus, to propound doubts to one another; and it hath been told us, that the most famous and eminent poets used to meet at the grave of Amphidamas in Chalcis. This Amphidamas was a leading commander, one that had perpetual wars with the Eretrians, and at last lost his life in one of the battles fought for the possession of the Lelantine plain. Now, because the writings of those poets were set to verse and so made the argument more knotty and the decision more arduous, and the great names of the antagonists, Homer and Hesiod, whose excellence was so well known, made the umpires timorous and shy to determine; they therefore betook themselves to these sorts of questions, and Homer, says Lesches, propounded this riddle:–

> Tell me, O Muse, what never was
> And never yet shall be.

Hesiod answered readily and extempore in this wise:–

> When steeds with echoing hoof, to win
> The prize, shall run amain;
> And on the tomb of lofty Jove
> Their chariots break in twain.

For this reply he was infinitely commended and got the tripod. Pray tell me, quoth Cleodemus, what difference there is between these riddles and those of Eumetis, which she frames and invents to recreate herself with as much pleasure as other virgins make nets and girdles? They may be fit to offer and puzzle women withal; but for men to beat their brains to find out their mystery would be mighty ridiculous. Eumetis looked like one that had a great mind to reply; but her modesty would not permit her, for her face was filled with blushes. But Aesop in her vindication asked: Is it not much more ridiculous that all present cannot resolve the riddle she propounded to us before supper? This was as follows:–

> A man I saw, who by his fire
> Did set a piece of brass
> Fast to a man, so that it seemed
> To him it welded was.

Can you tell me, said he, how to construe this, and what the sense of it may be? No, said Cleodemus, it is no profit to know what it means. And yet, quoth Aesop, no man understands this thing better and practises it more judiciously and successfully than yourself. If you deny it, I have my witnesses ready; for there are your cupping-glasses. Cleodemus laughed outright; for of all the physicians in his time, none used cupping-glasses like him, he being a person that by his frequent and fortunate application thereof brought them first into request in the world.

Mnesiphilus the Athenian, a friend and favorite of Solon's, said: O Periander, our discourse, as our wine, ought to be distributed not according to our power or priority, but freely and equally, as in a popular state; for what hath been already discoursed concerning kingdoms and empires signifies little to us who live in a democracy. Wherefore I judge it convenient that every one of you, commencing with Solon, should freely and impartially declare his sense of a popular state. The motion pleased all the company; then saith Solon: My friend Mnesiphilus, you heard, together with the rest of this good company, my opinion concerning republics; but since you are willing to hear it again, I hold that city or state happy and most likely to remain free, in which those that are not personally injured are yet as forward to try and punish wrongdoers as that person who is wronged. Bias added, Where all fear the law as they fear a tyrant. Thirdly, Thales said, Where the citizens are neither too rich nor too poor. Fourthly, Anacharsis said, Where, though in all other respects they are equal, yet virtuous men are advanced and vicious persons degraded. Fifthly, Cleobulus said, Where the rulers fear reproof and shame more than the law. Sixthly, Pittacus said, Where evil men are kept from ruling, and good men from not ruling. Chilo, pausing a little while, determined that the best and most enduring state was where the subject minded the law most and the lawyers least. Periander concluded with his opinion, that all of them would best approve that democracy which came next and was likest to an aristocracy.

After they had ended this discourse, I begged they would condescend to direct me how to govern a house; for they were few who had cities and kingdoms to govern, compared with those who had houses and families to manage. Aesop laughed and said: I hope you except Anacharsis out of your number; for having no house he glories because he can be contented with a chariot only, as they say the sun is whirled about from one end of the heavens to the other in his chariot. Therefore, saith Anacharsis, he alone, or he principally, is most free among the gods, and ever at his own liberty and dispose. He governs all, and is governed and subject to none, but he rides and reigns; and you know not how magnificent and broad his chariot is; if you did, you would not thus floutingly depreciate our Scythian chariots. For you seem in my apprehension to call these coverings made of wood and mud houses, as if you should call the shell and not the living creature a snail. Therefore you laughed when Solon told you how, when he viewed Croesus's palace and found it richly and gloriously furnished, he yet could not yield he lived happily until he had tried the inward and invisible state of his mind; for a man's felicity consists not in the outward and visible favors and blessings of fortune, but in the inward and unseen perfections and riches of the mind. And you seem to have forgot your own fable of the fox, who, contending with the leopard as to which possessed more colors and spots, and having referred the matter in controversy to the arbitration of an umpire, desired him to consider not so much the outside as the inside; for, saith he, I have more various and different fetches and tricks in my mind than he has marks or spots in his body. You regard only the handiwork of carpenters and masons and stone-cutters, and call this a house; not what one hath within, his children, his wife, his friends and attendants, with whom if a man lived in an emmet's bed or a bird's nest, enjoying in common the ordinary comforts of life, this man may be affirmed to live a happy and a fortunate life.

This is the answer I purpose to return Aesop, quoth Anacharsis, and I tender it to Diocles as my share in this discourse; only let the rest give in their opinions, if they please. Solon thought that house most happy where the estate was got without injustice, kept without distrust, and spent without repentance. Bias said, That house is happy where the master does freely and voluntarily what the law would else compel him to do. Thales held that house most happy where the master had most leisure and respite from business. Cleobulus said, That in which the master is more beloved than feared. Pittacus said, most that is happy where superfluities are not required and necessaries are not wanting. Chilo added, that house is most happy where one rules as a monarch in his kingdom. And he proceeded, when a certain Lacedaemonian desired Lycurgus to establish a democracy in the city. Go you, friend, replied he, and try the experiment first in your own house.

When they had all given in their opinions upon this point, Eumetis and Melissa withdrew. Then Periander called for a large bowl full of wine, and drank to Chilo; and Chilo too drank to Bias. Ardalus then standing up called to Aesop, and said: Will you not hand the cup to your friends at this end of the table, when you behold those persons there swilling up all that good liquor, and imparting none to us here as if the cup were that of Bathycles. But this cup, quoth Aesop, is no public cup, it hath stood so long by Solon's trenchard. Then Pittacus called to Mnesiphilus: Why, saith he, does not Solon drink, but act in contradiction to his own verses?–

I love that ruby god, whose blessings flow
In tides, to recreate my thirsty maw;
Venus I court, the Muses I adore,
Who give us wine and pleasures evermore.

Anacharsis subjoined: He fears your severe law, my friend Pittacus, wherein you decreed the drunkard a double punishment. You seem, said Pittacus, a little to fear the penalty, who have adventured heretofore, and now again before my face, to break that law and to demand a crown for the reward of your debauch. Why not, quoth Anacharsis, when there is a reward promised to the hardest drinker? Why should I not demand my reward, having drunk down all my fellows?–or inform me of any other end men drive at in drinking much wine, but to be drunk. Pittacus laughed at this reply, and Aesop told them this fable: The wolf seeing a parcel of shepherds in their booth feeding upon a lamb, approaching near them,–What a bustle and noise and uproar would there have been, saith he, if I had but done what you do! Chilo said: Aesop hath very justly revenged himself upon us, who awhile ago stopped his mouth; now he observes how we prevented Mnesiphilus's discourse, when the question was put why Solon did not drink up his wine.

Mnesiphilus then spake to this effect: I know this to be the opinion of Solon, that in every art and faculty, divine and human, the work which is done is more desired than the instrument wherewith it is done, and the end than the means conducing to that end; as, for instance, a weaver thinks a cloak or coat more properly his work than the ordering of his shuttles or the divers motions of his beams. A smith minds the soldering of his irons and the sharpening of the axe more than those little things accessory to these main matters, as the kindling of the coals and preparing the stone-dust. Yet farther, a carpenter would justly blame us, if we should affirm it is not his work to build houses or ships but to bore holes or to make mortar; and the Muses would be implacably incensed with him that should say their business is only to make harps, pipes and such musical instruments, not the institution and correcting of manners and the government of those men's passions who are lovers of singing and masters of music. And agreeably copulation is not the work of Venus, nor is drunkenness that of Bacchus; but love and friendship, affection and familiarity, which are begot and improved by and the means of these. Solon terms these works divine, and he professes he loves and now prosecutes them in his declining years as vigorously as ever in his youthful days. That mutual love between man and wife is the work of Venus, the greatness of the pleasure affecting their bodies mixes and melts their very souls; divers others, having little or no acquaintance before, have yet contracted a firm and lasting friendship over a glass of wine, which like fire softened and melted their tempers, and disposed them for a happy union. But in such a company, and of such men as Periander hath invited, there is no need of can and chalice, but the Muses themselves throwing a subject of discourse among you, as it were a sober cup, wherein is contained much of delight and drollery and seriousness too, do hereby provoke, nourish, and increase friendship among you, allowing the cup to rest quietly upon the bowl, contrary to the rule which Hesiod (Hesiod, "Works and Days," 744.) gives for those who have more skill for carousing than for discoursing.

> *Though all the rest with stated rules we bound*
> *Unmix'd, unmeasured are thy goblets crown'd*
> *("Iliad" iv. 261.)*

for it was the old Greek way, as Homer here tells us, to drink one to another in course and order. So Ajax gave a share of his meat to his next neighbor.

When Mnesiphilus had discoursed after this manner, in comes Chersias the poet, whom Periander had lately pardoned and received into favor upon Chilo's mediation. Saith Cherias: Does not Jupiter distribute to the gods their proportion and share sparingly and severally, as Agamemnon did to his commanders when his guests pledged one another? If, O Chersias, quoth Cleodemus, as you narrate, certain pigeons bring him ambrosia every meal, winging with a world of hardship through the rocks called PLANCTAE (or WANDERING), can you blame him for his sparingness and frugality and dealing out to his guests by measure?

I am satisfied, quoth Chersias, and since we are fallen upon our old discourse of housekeeping, which of the company can remember what remains to be said thereof? There remains, if I mistake not, to show what that measure is which may content any man. Cleobulus answered: The law has prescribed a measure for wise men; but as touching foolish ones I will tell you a story I once heard my father relate to my brother. On a certain time the moon begged of her mother a coat that would fit her. How can that be done, quoth the mother, for sometime you are full, sometimes the one half of you seems lost and perished, sometimes only a pair of horns appear. So, my Chersias, to the desires of a foolish immoderate man no certain measure can be fitted; for according to the ebbing and flowing of his lust and appetite, and the frequent or seldom casualties that befall him, accordingly his necessities ebb and flow, not unlike Aesop's dog, who, being pinched and ready to starve with the cold winter, was a mind to build himself a house; but when summer came on, he lay all along upon the ground, and stretching himself in the sun thought himself monstrous big, and thought it unnecessary and besides no small labor to build him a house portionable to that bulk and bigness. And do you not observe, O Chersias, continues he, many poor men,–how one while they pinch their bellies, upon what short commons they live, how sparing and niggardly and miserable they are; and another while you may observe the same men as distrustful and covetous withal, as if the plenty of the city and county, the riches of king and kingdom were not sufficient to preserve them from want and beggary.

When Chersias had concluded this discourse, Cleodemus began thus: We see you that are wise men possessing these outward goods after an unequal manner. Good sweet sir, answered Cleobulus, the law weaver-like hath distributed to every man a fitting, decent, adequate portion, and in your profession your reason does what the law does here,–when you feed, or diet, or physic your patient, you give not the quantity he desires, but what you judge to be convenient for each in his circumstances. Arda-lus inquires: Epimenides, to abstain from all other victuals, and to con-tent himself with a little composition of his own, which the Greeks call [Greek omitted] (HUNGER-RELIEVING)? This he takes into his mouth and chews, and eats neither dinner nor supper. This instance obliged the whole company to be a little while silent, until Thales in a jesting way replied, that Epimenides did very wisely, for hereby he saved the trouble and charge of grinding and boiling his meat, as Pittacus did. I myself sojourning as Lesbos overheard my landlady, as she was very busy at her hand-mill, singing as she used to do her work, "Grind mill; grind mill; for even Pittacus the prince of great Mitylene, grinds" [Greek footnote ommitted]. Quoth Solon: Ardalus, I wonder you have not read the law of Epimenides's frugality in Hesiod's writings, who prescribes him and oth-ers this spare diet; for he was the person that gratified Epimenides with the seeds of this nutriment, when he directed him to inquire how great benefit a man might receive by mallows and asphodel (Hesiod, "Works and Days," 41.) Do you believe, said Periander, that Hesiod meant this literally; or rather that, being himself a great admirer of parsimony, he hereby intended to exhort men to use mean and spare diet, as most healthful and pleasant? For the chewing of mallows is very wholesome, and the stalk of asphodel is very luscious; but this "expeller of hunger and thirst" I take to be rather physic than natural food, consisting of honey and I know not what barbarian cheese, and of many and costly drugs fetched from foreign parts. If to make up this composition so many in-gredients were requisite, and so difficult to come by and so expensive, Hesiod might have kept his breath to cool his pottage, and never blessed the world with the discovery. And yet I admire how your landlord, when he went to perform the great purification for the Delians not long since, could overlook the monuments and patterns of the first aliment which the people brought into the temple,–and, among other cheap fruits such as grow of themselves, the mallows and the asphodel; the usefulness and innocency whereof Hesiod seemed in his work to magnify. Moreover, quoth Anacharsis, he affirms both plants to be great restoratives. You are in the right, quoth Cleodemus; for it is evident Hesiod was no ordinary physician, who could discourse so learnedly and judiciously of diet, of the nature of wines, and of the virtue of waters and baths, and of women, the proper times for procreation, and the site and position of infants in the womb; insomuch, that (as I take it) Aesop deserves much more the name of Hesiod's scholar and disciple than Epimenides, whose great and excellent wisdom the fable of the nightingale and hawk demonstrates. But I would gladly hear Solon's opinion in this matter; for having sojourned long at Athens and being familiarly acquainted with Epimenides, it is more than probable he might learn of him the grounds upon which he accustomed himself to so spare a diet.

To what purpose, said Solon, should I trouble him or myself to make inquiry in a matter so plain? For if it be a blessing next to the greatest to need little victuals, then it is the greatest felicity to need none at all. If I may have leave to deliver my opinion, quoth Cleodemus, I must profess myself of a different judgment, especially now we sit at table; for as soon as the meat is taken away, what belongs to those gods that are the patrons of friendship and hospitality has been removed. As upon the removal of the earth, quoth Thales, there must needs follow an universal confusion of all things, so in forbidding men meat, there must needs follow the dispersion and dissolution of the family, the sacred fire, the cups, the feasts and entertainment's, which are the principal and most innocent diversions of mankind; and so all the comforts of society are at end. For to men of business some recreation is necessary, and the preparation and use of victuals conduces much thereunto. Again, to be without victuals would tend to the destruction of husbandry, for want whereof the earth would soon be overgrown with weeds, and through the sloth of men overflowed with waters. And together with this, all arts would fail which are supported and encouraged hereby; nay, more, take away hospitality and the use of victuals and the worship and honor of the gods will sink and perish; the sun will have but small and the moon yet smaller reverence if thy afford men only light and heat. And who will build an altar or offer sacrifices to Jupiter Pluvius, or to Ceres the patroness of husbandmen, or to Neptune the preserver of plants and trees? Or how can Bacchus be any longer termed the donor of all good things, if men make no further use of the good things he gives? What shall men sacrifice? What first-fruits shall they offer? In short, the subversion and confusion of the greatest blessings attend this opinion. Promiscuously and indefatigable to pursue all sorts of pleasures I own to be brutish, and to avoid all with a suitable aversion equally blockish, let the mind then freely enjoy such pleasures as are agreeable to its nature and temper. But for the body, there is certainly no pleasure more harmless and commendable and fitting than that which springs from a plentiful table,–which is granted by all men, for, placing this in the middle, men converse with one another and share in the provision. As to the pleasures of the bed, men use these in the dark, reputing the use thereof shameful and beastly as well as the total disuse of the pleasures of the table.

Cleodemus having finished this long harangue, I began to this effect. You omit one thing, my friend, how they that decry food decry sleep too, and they that declaim against sleep declaim against dreams in the same breath, and so destroy the primitive and ancient way of divination. Add to this, that our whole life will be of one form and fashion, and our soul enclosed in a body to no purpose; many and those the principal parts thereof are naturally so formed and fashioned as to be organs of nutriment; so the tongue, the teeth, the stomach, and the liver, whereof none are idle, none framed for other use, so that whosoever hath no need of nutriment has no need of his body; that is, in other words, no man hath any need of himself, for every man hath a body of his own. This I have thought fit to offer in vindication of our bellies; if Solon or any other has anything to object to what I have said, I am willing to hear him.

Yea, doubtless, replies Solon, or we may be reputed more injudicious than the Egyptians. For when any person dies among them, they open him and show him so dissected to the sun; his guts they throw into the river, to the remaining parts they allow a decent burial, for they think the body now pure and clean; and to speak truly they are the foulest parts of the body, and like that lower hell crammed with dead carcasses and at the same time flowing with offensive rivers, such as flame with fire and are disturbed with tempests. No live creature feeds upon another living creature, but we first take away their lives, and in that action we do them great wrong. Now the very plants have life in them,–that is clear and manifest, for we perceive they grow and spread. But to abstain from eating flesh (as they say Orpheus of old did) is more a pretence than a real avoiding of an injury proceeding from the just use of meat. One way there is, and but one way, whereby a man may avoid offence, namely by being contented with his own, not coveting what belongs to his neighbor. But if a man's circumstances be such and so hard that he cannot subsist without wronging another man, the fault is God's, not his. The case being such with some persons, I would fain learn if it be not advisable to destroy, at the same time with injustice, these instruments of injustice, the belly, stomach, and liver, which have no sense of justice or appetite to honesty, and therefore may be fitly compared to your cook's implements, his knives and his caldrons, or to a baker's chimney and bins and kneading-tubs. Verily one may observe the souls of some men confined to their bodies, as to a house of correction, barely to do the drudgery and to serve the necessities thereof. It was our own case but even now. While we minded our meat and our bellies, we had neither eyes to see nor ears to hear; but now the table is taken away, we are free to discourse among ourselves and to enjoy one another; and now our bellies are full, we have nothing else to do or care for. And if this condition and state wherein we at present are would last our whole life, we having no wants to fear nor riches to covet (for a desire of superfluities attends a desire of necessaries), would not our lives be much more comfortable and life itself much more desirable?

Yea, but Cleodemus stiffly maintains the necessity of eating and drinking, else we shall need tables and cups, and shall not be able to offer sacrifice to Ceres and Proserpina. By a parity of reason there is a necessity there should be contentions and wars, that men may have bulwarks and citadels and fortifications by land, fleets and navies abroad at sea, and that having slain hundreds, we may offer Hecatombs after the Messenian manner. By this reason we shall find men grudging their own health, for (they will say) there will be no need of down or feather beds unless they are sick; and so those healing gods, and particularly Esculapius, will be vast sufferers, for they will infallibly lose so many fat and rich sacrifices yearly. Nay, the art of chirurgery will perish, and all those ingenious instruments that have been invented for the cure of man will lie by useless and insignificant. And what great difference is there between this and that? For meat is a medicine against hunger, and such as use a constant diet are said to cure themselves,–I mean such as use meat not for wantonness but of necessity. For it is plain, the prejudices we receive by feeding far surmount the pleasures. And the enjoyment of eating fills a very small place in our bodies and very little time. But why should I trouble you or myself with a catalogue of the many vexations which attend that man who is necessitated to provide for a family, and the many difficulties which distract him in his undertaking? For my part, I verily believe Homer had an eye to this very thing, when, to prove the immortality of the gods, he made use of this very argument, that they were such because they used no victuals;

> *For not the bread of man their life sustains,*
> *Nor wine's inflaming juice supplies their veins;*
> *("Iliad," v. 341.)*

intimating meat to be the cause of death as well as the means of sustaining and supporting life. From hence proceed divers fatal distempers caused much more by fulness than by fasting; and to digest what we have eaten proves frequently a harder matter than to provide and procure what we eat. And when we solicitously inquire beforehand what we should do or how we should employ ourselves if we had not such care and business to take up our time, this is as if Danaus's daughters should trouble their heads to know what they should do if they had no sieves to fill with water. We drudge and toil for necessaries, for want of better and nobler occupation. As slaves then who have gained their freedom do now and then those drudgeries and discharge those servile employments and offices for their own benefit which they undertook heretofore for their masters' advantage, so the mind of man, which at present is enslaved to the body and the service thereof, when once it becomes free from this slavery, will take care of itself, and spend its time in contemplation of truth without distraction or disturbance. Such were our discourses upon this head, O Nicarchus.

And before Solon had fully finished, in came Gorgias, Periander's brother, who was just returned from Taenarum, whither he had been sent by the advice of the oracle to sacrifice to Neptune and to conduct a deputation. Upon his entrance we welcomed him home; and Periander having among the rest saluted him, Gorgias sat by him upon a bed, and privately whispered something to his brother which we could not hear. Periander by his various gestures and motions discovered different affections; sometimes he seemed sad and melancholic, by and by disturbed and angry; frequently he looked as doubtful and distrustful men use to do; awhile after he lifts up his eyes, as is usual with men in a maze. At last recovering himself, saith he, I have a mind to impart to you the contents of this embassy; but I scarce dare do it, remembering Thales's aphorism, how things impossible or incredible are to be concealed and only things credible and probable are to be related. Bias answered, I crave leave to explain Thales's saying, We may distrust enemies, even though they speak things credible, and trust friends, even though they relate things incredible; and I suppose by enemies he meant vicious men and foolish, and by friends, wise and good men. Then, brother Gorgias, quoth Periander, I pray relate the whole story particularly.

Gorgias in obedience to his brother's command began his story thus:–

When we had fasted now for three days and offered sacrifice upon each of those days, we were all resolved to sit up the third night and spend it in pastime and dancing. The moon shone very bright upon the water, and the sea was exceeding calm and still; this we saw, for we sported ourselves upon the shore. Being thus taken up, all of a sudden we espied a wonderful spectacle off at sea, making with incredible expedition to the adjoining promontory. The violence of the motion made the sea foam again, and the noise was so loud, that the whole company forsook their sport and ran together toward the place, admiring what the matter should be. Before we could make a full discovery of the whole, the motion was so rapid, we perceived divers dolphins, some swimming in a ring or circle, others hastening amain to that part of the shore which was most shallow, and others following after and (as it were) bringing up the rear. In the middle there was a certain heap which we could perceive above the water; but we could not distinctly apprehend what it was, till drawing near the shore we saw all the dolphins flocking together, and having made near the land they safely surrendered their charge, and left out of danger a man breathing and shaking himself. They returned to the promontory, and there seemed to rejoice more than before for this their fortunate undertaking. Divers in the company were affrighted and ran away; myself and a few more took courage, and went on to see and satisfy ourselves what this unusual matter might be; there we found and instantly knew our old acquaintance Arion the musician, who told us his name. He wore that very garment he used when he strove for mastery. We brought him into our tent and found he had received no damage in his passage, save only a little lassitude by the violence of the motion. He told us the whole story of his adventure,–a story incredible to all but such as saw it with their eyes. He told us how, when he had determined to leave Italy, being hastened away by Periander's letters, he went aboard a Corinthian merchantman then in port and ready to sail; being off at sea with the winds favorable, he observed the seamen bent to ruin him, and the master of the vessel told him as much, and that they purposed to execute their design upon him that very night. In this distress, the poor man (as if inspired by his good Genius) girds about him his heretofore victorious, now his mourning cloak, with a brave resolution to compose and sing his own epitaph, as the swans when they apprehend the approaches of death are reported to do. Being thus habited, he told the seamen he was minded to commit the protection of himself and his fellow-passengers to the providence of the gods in a Pythian song; then standing upon the poop near the side of the vessel, and having invoked the help and assistance of all the sea gods, he strikes up briskly and sings to his harp. Before he had half finished his carol, the sun set, and he could discern Peloponnesus before him. The seamen thought it tedious to tarry for the night, wherefore they resolved to murder him immediately, to which purpose they unsheathed their swords. Seeing this, and observing the steersman covering his face, he leaped into the sea as far as he could; but before his body sunk he found himself supported by dolphins. At first he was surprised with care and trouble; but by and by, finding himself marching forward with much ease and security, and observing a whole shoal of dolphins flocking about him and joyfully contending which should appear most forward and serviceable in his preservation, and discerning the vessel at a considerable distance behind, he apprehended the nimbleness of his porters; then, and not till then, his fears forsook him, and he professed he was neither so fearful of death nor desirous of life as he was full of ambitious desire, that he might show to all men that he stood in the grace and favor of the gods, and that he might himself have a firm belief in them. In his passage, as he lifted up his eyes toward heaven, and beheld the stars glittering and twinkling and the moon full and glorious, and the sea calm all about her as she seemed to rise out of it, and yielding him (as it were) a beaten track; he declared, he thought God's justice had more eyes than one, and that with these innumerable eyes the gods beheld what was acted here below both by sea and land. With such contemplations he performed his voyage less anxiously, which much abated the tediousness thereof and was a comfort and refreshment to him in his solitude and danger. At last, arriving near the promontory which was both steep and high, and fearing danger in a straight course and direct line, they unanimously veered about, and making to shore with a little compass for security they delivered Arion to us in safety, so that he plainly perceived and with thanks acknowledged a Providence.

When Arion had finished this narrative of his escape, I asked him (quoth Gorgias) whither the ship was bound; he told me for Corinth, but it would not be there very suddenly, for when he leaped out of the ship and was carried (as he conceived) about five hundred furlongs, he perceived a calm, which must needs much retard their arrival who were aboard. Gorgias added that, having learned the names of the pilot and master and the colors of the ship, he immediately despatched out ships and soldier to examine all the ports, all this while keeping Arion concealed, lest the criminals should upon notice of His deliverance escape the pursuit of justice. This action happened very luckily; for as soon as he arrived at Corinth, news was brought him that the same ship was in port, and that his party had seized it and secured all the men, merchants and others. Whereupon Periander commanded Gorgias's discretion and zeal, desiring him to proceed and lose no time, but immediately to clap them in close prison, and to suffer none to come at them to give the least notice of Arion's miraculous escape.

Gentlemen, quoth Aesop, I remember you derided my dialogue of the daws and rooks; and now you can admire and believe as improbable a story of dolphins. You are mightily out, said I, for this is no novel story which we believe, but it is recorded in the annals of Ino and Athamas above a thousand years ago. These passages are supernatural, quoth Solon and much above our reason; what befell Hesiod is of a lower kind, and more proper for our discourse, and if you have not heard of it before, it is worth your hearing.

Hesiod once sojourned at the same house in Locris with a certain Milesian. In this his sojourning time it happened the gentleman's daughter was got with child by the Milesian which being discovered, the whole family concluded Hesiod, if not guilty, must be privy to the fact. His innocence was but a weak fence against their jealousy and aspersions; and therefore, rashly censuring him guilty, the brothers of the woman waylaid him in his return home, and slew him and his companion Troilus near the shrine of Nemean Jove in Locris. Their carcasses they threw into the sea; that of Troilus was carried into the river Daphnus, and rested upon a certain rock compassed with waters, just above the surface of the sea, which rock bears his name to this day. The body of Hesiod was no sooner fallen upon the surface of the water, but a company of dolphins received it, and conveyed it to Rhium and Molyeria. It happened the Locrians were assembled at Rhium that day to feast and make merry according to the custom which continues still among them. As soon as they perceived a carcass floating or rather swimming towards them, they hastened, not without admiration, to see what it was; and knowing the body to be Hesiod's, they instantly resolved to find out the murderers. It proved an easy discovery. After conviction they threw them headlong alive into the sea, and ordered their houses to be demolished to the very foundations. The body they buried in the grove of the temple of Jove, that no foreigner might find it out; the reason of this act was that the Orchomenians had searched far and near for it at the instigation of the oracle, who promised them the greatest felicity if they could get the bones of Hesiod and bury them in their city. Now if dolphins are so favorable to dead men, it is very probable they have a strong affection for the living, especially for such as delight in music, whether vocal or instrumental. And this we know undoubtedly, that these creatures delight infinitely in music; they love it, and if any man sings or plays, they will quietly come by the side of the ship, and listen till the music is ended.

When children bathe in the water and sport themselves, you shall have a parcel of them flock together and sport and swim by them; and they may do it the more securely, since it is a breach of the law of Nature to hurt them. You never heard of any man that fishes for them purposely or hurts them wilfully, unless falling into the nets they spoil the sport, and so, like bad children, are corrected for their misdemeanors. I very well remember the Lesbians told me how a maid of their town was preserved from drowning by them.

It was a very true story, quoth Pittacus, and there are divers still alive who will attest it, if need be. The builders or founders of Lesbos were commanded by the oracle to sail till they came to a haven called Mesogaeum, there they should sacrifice a bull to Neptune, and for the honor of Amphitrite and the sea-nymphs they should offer a virgin. The principal persons in this colony were seven in number; the eighth was one Echelaus by name, and appointed head of the rest by the oracle himself; and he was a bachelor. A daughter of one of these seven was to be sacrificed, but who it should be was to be decided by lot, and the lot fell upon Smintheus's sister. Her they dressed most richly, and so apparelled they conveyed her in abundance of state to the water-side, and having composed a prayer for her, they were now ready to throw her overboard. There was in the company a certain ingenuous young gentleman whose name was Enalus; he was desperately in love with this young lady, and his love prompted him to endeavor all he could for her preservation, or at least to perish in the attempt. In the very moment she was to be cast away, he clasps her in his arms and throws himself and her together into the sea. Shortly after there was a flying report they were both conveyed safe to land. A while after Enalus was seen at Lesbos, who gave out they were preserved by dolphins. I could tell you stories more incredible than these, such as would amuse some and please others; but it is impossible to command men's faith. The sea was so tempestuous and rough, the people were afraid to come too near the waters, when Enalus arrived. A number of polypuses followed him even to Neptune's temple, the biggest and strongest of which carried a great stone. This Enalus dedicated, and this stone is therefore called Enalus to this day. To be short and to speak all in a few words,–he that knows how to distinguish between the impossible and the unusual, to make a difference between the unlikely and the absurd, to be neither too credulous nor too distrustful,–he hath learned your lesson, Do not overdo. ([Greek omitted], NE QUID NIMIS.)

Anacharsis after all this discourse spake to this purpose: Since Thales has asserted the being of a soul in all the principal and most noble parts of the universe, it is no wonder that the most commendable acts are governed by an overruling Power; for, as the body is the organ of the soul, so the soul is an instrument in the hand of God. Now as the body has many motions of its own proceeding from itself, but the best and most from the soul, so the soul acts some things by its own power, but in most things it is subordinate to the will and power of God, whose glorious instrument it is. To me it seems highly unreasonable–and I should be but too apt to censure the wisdom of the gods, if I were convinced–that they use fire, and water, and wind, and clouds, and rain for the preservation and welfare of some and for the detriment and destruction of others, while at the same time they make no use of living creatures that are doubtless more serviceable to their ends than bows are to the Scythians or harps or pipes to the Greeks.

Chersias the poet broke off this discourse, and told the company of divers that were miraculously preserved to his certain knowledge, and more particularly of Cypselus, Periander's father, who being newly born, his adversary sent a party of bloody fellows to murder him. They found the child in his nurse's arms, and seeing him smile innocently upon them, they had not the heart to hurt him, and so departed; but presently recalling themselves and considering the peremptoriness of their orders, they returned and searched for him, but could not find him, for his mother had hid him very carefully in a chest. (Called [Greek omitted] in Greek, whence the child was named Cypelus.(G.)) When he came to years of discretion, and understood the greatness of his former danger and deliverance, he consecrated a temple at Delphi to Apollo, by whose care he conceived himself preserved from crying in that critical time, and by his cries from betraying his own life. Pittacus, addressing his discourse to Periander, said: It is well done of Chersias to make mention of that shrine, for this brings to my mind a question I several times purposed to ask you but still forgot, namely,–To what intent all those frogs were carved upon the palm-tree before the door, and how they affect either the deity or the dedicator? Periander remitted him to Chersias for answer, as a person better versed in these matters for he was present when Cypselus consecrated the shrine. But Chersias smiling would not satisfy them, until they resolved him the meaning of these aphorisms; "Do not overdo," "Know thyself," but particularly and principally this,–which had scared divers from wedlock and others from suretyship and others for speaking at all,–"promise, and you are ruined." What need we to explain to you these, when you yourself have so mightily magnified Aesop's comment upon each of them. Aesop replied:

When Chersias is disposed to jest with me upon these subjects, and to jest seriously, he is pleased to father such sayings and sentences upon Homer, who, bringing in Hector furiously flying upon others, yet at another time represents him as flying from Ajax son of Telamon, ("Iliad," xi. 542.)–an argument that Hector knew himself. And Homer made Ulysses use the saying "Do not overdo," when he besought his friend Diomedes not to commend him, too much nor yet to censure him too much. And for suretyship he exposes it as a matter unsafe, nay highly dangerous, declaring that to be bound for idle and wicked men is full of hazard. ("Iliad," x. 249; "Odyssey," viii. 351.) To confirm this, Chersias reported how Jupiter had thrown Ate headlong out of heaven, because she was by when he made the promise about the birth of Hercules whereby he was circumvented.

Here Solon broke in: I advise, that we now give ear to Homer,–

But now the night extends her awful shade:
The Goddess parts you: be the night obeyed.
("Iliad," vii. 282.)

If it please the company then, let us sacrifice to the Muses, to Neptune, and to Amphitrite, and so bid each adieu for this night.

This was the conclusion of that meeting, my dear Nicarchus.

How a Young Man Ought to hear Poems

Though it may be allowed to be a question fit for the determination of those concerning whom Cato said, Their palates are more sensitive than their minds, whether that saying of Philoxenus the poet be true or no, The most savory flesh is that which is no flesh, and fish that is no fish. Yet this to me, Marcus Sedatus, is out of question, that those precepts of philosophy which seem not to be delivered with a designed gravity, such as becomes philosophers, take most with persons that are very young, and meet with a more ready acceptance and compliance from them. Whence it is that they do not only read through Aesop's fables and the fictions of poets and the Abaris of Heraclides and Ariston's Lyco; but also such doctrines as relate to the souls of men, if something fabulous be mixed with them, with an excess of pleasure that borders on enthusiasm. Wherefore we are not only to govern their appetites in the delights of eating and drinking, but also (and much more) to inure them to a like temperance in reading and hearing, that, while they make use of enjoyment as a sauce, they may pursue that which is wholesome and profitable in those things which they read. For neither can a city be secure if but one gate be left open to receive the enemy, though all the rest be shut; nor a young man safe, though he be sufficiently fortified against the assaults of all other pleasures, whilst he is without any guard against those of the ear. Yea, the nearer the commerce is betwixt the delights of that sense and those of the mind and reason, by so much the more, when he lies open on that side, is he apt to be debauched and corrupted thereby. Seeing therefore we cannot (and perhaps would not if we could) debar young men of the size of my Soclarus and thy Cleander altogether from the reading of poets, yet let us keep the stricter guard upon them, as those who need a guide to direct them in their reading more than on their journeys. Upon which consideration, I find myself disposed to send thee at present in writing that discourse concerning Poetry which I had lately an occasion to deliver by word of mouth; that, when thou hast read it over thyself, thou mayst also make such use of it, if thou judgest it may be serviceable to that purpose, as those which are engaged to drink hard do of amulets (or preservatives against drunkenness),–that is, that thou mayst communicate it to Cleander, to prepossess him therewith; seeing he is naturally endowed with a brisk, piercing, and daring wit, and therefore more prone to be inveigled by that sort of study.

They say of the fish called polypus that

> His head in one respect is very good,
> But in another very naughty food;

because, though it be very luscious to eat, yet it is thought to disturb the fancy with frightful and confused dreams. And the like observation may be made concerning poetry, that it affords sweet and withal wholesome nourishment to the minds of young men, but yet it contains likewise no less matter of disturbance and emotion to them that want a right conduct in the study thereof. For of it also, as well as of Egypt, may it be said that (to those who will use it)

> Its over-fertile and luxuriant field
> Medicines and poisons intermixt doth yield;

for therein

> Love with soft passions and rich language drest
> Oft steals the heart out of th' ingenuous breast.
> ("Odyssey," iv. 230; "Iliad," xiv. 216.)

And indeed such only are endangered thereby, for the charms of that art ordinarily affect not those that are downright sots and naturally incapable of learning. Wherefore, when Simonides was asked why of all men he could not deceive the Thessalians, his answer was, Because they are not so well bred as to be capable of being cajoled by me. And Gorgias used to call tragical poems cheats, wherein he that did cheat was juster than he that did not cheat, and he that was cheated was wiser than he that was not cheated.

It deserves therefore our consideration, whether we shall put young men into Epicurus's boat,–wherein, having their ears stopped with wax, as those of the men of Ithaca were, they shall be obliged to sail by and not so much as touch at poetry,–or rather keep a guard on them, so as to oblige their judgments by principles of right reason to use it aright, and preserve them from being seduced to their hurt by that which affords them so much delight. For neither did Lycurgus, the valiant son of Dryas (as Homer calls him) ("Iliad," vi. 130.) act like a man of sound reason in the course which he took to reform his people that were much inclined to drunkenness, by travelling up and down to destroy all the vines in the country; whereas he should have ordered that every vine should have a well of water near it, that (as Plato saith) the drunken deity might be reduced to temperance by a sober one. For water mixed with wine takes away the hurtful spirits, while it leaves the useful ones in it. Neither should we cut down or destroy the Muses' vine, poetry; but where we perceive it luxuriates and grows wild through an ungoverned appetite of applause, there ought we to prune away or keep under the fabulous and theatrical branches thereof; and where we find any of the Graces linked to any of the Muses,–that is, where the lusciousness and tempting charms of language are not altogether barren and unprofitable,–there let us make use of philosophy to incorporate with it.

For as, where the mandrake grows near the vine and so communicates something of its force thereto, the wine that is made of its grapes makes the sleep of those that drink it more refreshing; so doth the tempering poetry with the principles of philosophy and allaying their roughness with its fictions render the study of them more easy and the relish of them more grateful to young learners. Wherefore those that would give their minds to philosophical studies are not obliged to avoid poetry altogether, but rather to introduce themselves to philosophy by poems, accustoming themselves to search for and embrace that which may profit in that which pleaseth them, and rejecting and discarding that wherein they find nothing of this nature. For this discrimination is the first step to learning; and when this is attained, then, according to what Sophocles saith,–

> *To have begun well what we do intend*
> *Gives hope and prospect of as good an end.*

Let us therefore in the first place possess those whom we initiate in the study of poetry with this notion (as one which they ought always to have at hand), that

> *'Tis frequently the poet's guise*
> *To intermingle truth with lies;–*

which they do sometimes with and sometimes against their wills. They do it with their wills, because they find strict truth too rigid to comply with that sweetness and gracefulness of expression, which most are taken with, so readily as fiction doth. For real truth, though it disgust never so much, must be told as it is, without alteration; but that which is feigned in a discourse can easily yield and shift its garb from the distasteful to that which is more pleasing. And indeed, neither the measures nor the tropes nor the grandeur of words nor the aptness of metaphors nor the harmony of the composition gives such a degree of elegance and gracefulness to a poem as a well-ordered and artificial fiction doth. But as in pictures the colors are more delightful to the eye than the lines because those give them a nearer resemblance to the persons they were made for, and render them the more apt to deceive the beholder; so in poems we are more apt to be smitten and fall in love with a probable fiction than with the greatest accuracy that can be observed in measures and phrases, where there is nothing fabulous or fictitious joined with it. Wherefore Socrates, being induced by some dreams to attempt something in poetry, and finding himself unapt, by reason that he had all his lifetime been the champion of severe truth, to hammer out of his own invention a likely fiction, made choice of Aesop's fables to turn into verse; as judging nothing to be true poetry that had in it nothing of falsehood. For though we have known some sacrifices performed without pipes and dances, yet we own no poetry which is utterly destitute of fable and fiction. Whence the verses of Empedocles and Parmenides, the Theriaca of Nicander, and the sentences of Theognis, are rather to be accounted speeches than poems, which, that they might not walk contemptibly on foot, have borrowed from poetry the chariot of verse, to convey them the more creditably through the world. Whensoever therefore anything is spoken in poems by any noted and eminently famous man, concerning gods or daemons or virtue, that is absurd or harsh, he that takes such sayings for truths is thereby misled in his apprehension and corrupted with an erroneous opinion. But he that constantly keeps in his mind and maintains as his principle that the witchcraft of poetry consists in fiction, he that can at all turns accost it in this language,–

> Riddle of art! like which no sphinx beguiles;
> Whose face on one side frowns while th' other smiles!
> Why cheat'st thou, with pretence to make us wise,
> And bid'st sage precepts in a fool's disguise?–

such a one, I say, will take no harm by it, nor admit from it any absurd thing into his belief. But when he meets in poetry with expressions of Neptune's rending the earth to pieces and dicovering infernal regions, ("See Iliad," xx. 57.) he will be able to check his fears of the reality of any such accident; and he will blame himself for his anger against Apollo for the chief commander of the Greeks,–

> Whom at a banquet, whiles he sings his praise
> And speaks him fair, yet treacherously he slays.
> ("From Aeschylus" The whole passage is quoted in Plato's

"Republic," end of book II. (G.).)

Yea, he will repress his tears for Achilles and Agamemnon, while they are resented as mourning after their death, and stretching forth their limber and feeble hands to express their desire to live again. And if at any time the charms of poetry transport him into any disquieting passions, he will quickly say to himself, as Homer very elegantly (considering the propension of that sex to listen after fables) says in his Necyia, or relation of the state of the dead,–

> *But from the dark dominions speed thy way,*
> *And climb the steep ascent to upper day;*
> *To thy chaste bride the wondrous story tell,*
> *The woes, the horrors, and the laws of hell.*
> *("Odyssey," xi. 223.)*

Such things as I have touched upon are those which the poets willingly feign. But more there are which they do not feign, but believing themselves as their own proper judgments, they put fictitious colors upon them to ingratiate them to us. As when Homer says of Jupiter,–

> *Jove lifts the golden balances, that show*
> *The faces of mortal men, and things below.*
> *Here each contending hero's lot he tries,*
> *And weighs with equal hand their destinies*
> *Low sinks the scale surcharged with Hector's fate;*
> *Heavy with death it sinks, and hell receives the weight.*
> *("Iliad," xxii. 210.)*

To this fable Aeschylus hath accommodated a whole tragedy which he calls Psychostasia, wherein he introduceth Thetis and Aurora standing by Jupiter's balances, and deprecating each of them the death of her son engaged in a duel. Now there is no man but sees that this fable is a creature of the poet's fancy, designed to delight or scare the reader. But this other passage,–

> *Great Jove is made the treasurer of wars;*
> *(Ibid. iv. 84.)*

and this other also,–

> *When a god means a noble house to raze,*
> *He frames one rather than he'll want a cause:*
> *(From the "Niobe" of Aeschylus, Frag. 151.)*

these passages, I say, express their judgment and belief who thereby discover and suggest to us the ignorant or mistaken apprehensions they had of the Deities. Moreover, almost every one knows nowadays, that the portentous fancies and contrivances of stories concerning the state of the dead are accommodated to popular apprehensions,–that the spectres and phantasms of burning rivers and horrid regions and terrible tortures expressed by frightful names are all mixed with fable and fiction, as poison with food; and that neither Homer nor Pindar nor Sophocles ever believed themselves when they wrote at this rate:–

> *There endless floods of shady darkness stream*
> *From the vast caves, where mother Night doth teem;*

and,

> *There ghosts o'er the vast ocean's waves did glide,*
> *By the Leucadian promontory's side;*
> *("Odyssey," xxiv. 11.)*

and,

> *There from th' unfathomed gulf th' infernal lake*
> *Through narrow straits recurring tides doth make.*

And yet, as many of them as deplore death as a lamentable thing, or the want of burial after death as a calamitous condition, are wont to break out into expressions of this nature:–

> *O pass not by, my friend; nor leave me here*
> *Without a grave, and on that grave a tear;*
> *("Odyssey," xi. 72.)*

and,

> *Then to the ghosts the mournful soul did fly,*
> *Sore grieved in midst of youth and strength to die;*
> *("Iliad," xvi. 856.)*

and again,

> *'Tis sweet to see the light. O spare me then,*
> *Till I arrive at th' usual age of men:*
> *Nor force my unfledged soul from hence, to know*
> *The doleful state of dismal shades below.*
> *(Euripides, "Iphigenia at Aulus," 1218.)*

These, I say, are the speeches of men persuaded of these things, as being possessed by erroneous opinions; and therefore they touch us the more nearly and torment us inwardly, because we ourselves are full of the same impotent passion from which they were uttered. To fortify us therefore against expressions of this nature, let this principle continually ring in our ears, that poetry is not at all solicitous to keep to the strict measure of truth. And indeed, as to what that truth in these matters is, even those men themselves who make it their only study to learn and search it out confess that they can hardly discover any certain footsteps to guide them in that inquiry. Let us therefore have these verses of Empedocles, in this case, at hand:–

> *No sight of man's so clear, no ear so quick,*

> *No mind so piercing, that's not here to seek;*

as also those of Xenophanes:–

> *The truth about the gods and ghosts, no man*
> *E'er was or shall be that determine can;*

and lastly, that passage concerning Socrates, in Plato, where he by the solemnity of an oath disclaims all knowledge of those things. For those who perceive that the searching into such matters makes the heads of philosophers themselves giddy cannot but be the less inclined to regard what poets say concerning them.

And we shall fix our young men more if, when we enter him in the poets, we first describe poetry to him and tell him that it is an imitating art and is in many respects like unto painting; not only acquainting him with that common saying, that poetry is vocal painting and painting silent poetry, but showing him, moreover, that when we see a lizard or an ape or the face of a Thersites in a picture, we are surprised with pleasure and wonder at it, not because of any beauty in the things, but for the likeness of the draught. For it is repugnant to the nature of that which is itself foul to be at the same time fair; and therefore it is the imitation–be the thing imitated beautiful or ugly–that, in case it do express it to the life, is commanded; and on the contrary, if the imitation make a foul thing to appear fair, it is dispraised because it observes not decency and likeness. Now some painters there are that paint uncomely actions; as Timotheus drew Medea killing her children; Theon, Orestes murdering his mother; and Parrhasius, Ulysses counterfeiting madness; yea, Chaerephanes expressed in picture the unchaste converse of women with men. Now in such cases a young man is to be familiarly acquainted with this notion, that, when men praise such pictures, they praise not the actions represented but only the painter's art which doth so lively express what was designed in them. Wherefore, in like manner, seeing poetry many times describes by imitation foul actions and unseemly passions and manners, the young student must not in such descriptions (although performed never so cleverly and commendably) believe all that is said as true or embrace it as good, but give its due commendation so far only as it suits the subject treated of. For as, when we hear the grunting of hogs and the shrieking of pulleys and the rustling of wind and the roaring of seas, we are, it may be, disturbed and displeased, and yet when we hear any one imitating these or the like noises handsomely (as Parmenio did that of an hog, and Theodorus that of a pulley), we are well pleased; and as we avoid (as an unpleasing spectacle) the sight of sick persons and of a man full of ulcers, and yet are delighted to be spectators of the Philoctetes of Aristophon and the Jocasta of Silanion, wherein such wasting and dying persons are well acted; so must the young scholar, when he reads in a poem of Thersites the buffoon or Sisyphus the whoremaster or Batrachus the bawd speaking or doing anything, so praise the artificial managery of the poet, adapting the expressions to the persons, as withal to look on the discourses and actions so expressed as odious and abominable. For the goodness of things themselves differs much from the goodness of the imitation of them; the goodness of the latter consisting only in propriety and aptness to represent the former. Whence to foul acts foul expressions are most suitable and proper. As the shoes of Demonides the cripple (which, when he had lost them, he wished might suit the feet of him that stole them) were but poor shoes, but yet fit for him; so we may say of such expressions as these:–

> If t'is necessary an unjust act to do,
> It is best to do it for a throne;
> (Euripides, "Phoenissae," 524.)
> Get the repute of Just,
> And in it do all things whence gain may come;
> A talent dowry! Could I
> Sleep, or live, if thee I should neglect?
> And should I not in hell tormented be,
> Could I be guilty of such sacrilege?
> (From Menander.)

These, it is true, are wicked as well as false speeches, but yet are decent enough in the mouth of an Eteocles, an Ixion, and a griping usurer. If therefore we mind our children that the poets write not such things as praising and approving them, but do really account them base and vicious and therefore accommodate such speeches to base and vicious persons, they will never be damnified by them from the esteem they have of the poets in whom they meet with them. But, on the contrary, the suspicions insinuated into them of the persons will render the words and actions ascribed to them suspected for evil, because proceeding from such evil men. And of this nature is Homer's representation of Paris, when he describes him running out of the battle into Helen's bed. For in that he attributes no such indecent act to any other, but only to that incontinent and adulterous person, he evidently declares that he intends that relation to import a disgrace and reproach to such intemperance.

In such passages therefore we are carefully to observe whether or not the poet himself do anywhere give any intimation that he dislikes the things he makes such persons say; which, in the prologue to his Thais Menander does, in these words:–

> Therefore, my Muse, describe me now a whore,

Fair, bold, and furnished with a nimble tongue;
One that ne'er scruples to do lovers wrong;
That always craves, and denied shuts her door;
That truly loves no man, yet, for her ends,
Affection true to every man pretends.

But Homer of all the poets does it best. For he doth beforehand, as it were, bespeak dislike of the evil things and approbation of the good things he utters. Of the latter take these instances:–

He readily did the occasion take,
And sweet and comfortable words he spake;
("Odyssey," vi. 148.)
By him he stood, and with soft speeches quelled
The wrath which in his heated bosom swelled.
("Iliad," ii. 180.)

And for the former, he so performs it as in a manner solemnly to forbid us to use or heed such speeches as those he mentions, as being foolish and wicked. For example, being to tell us how uncivilly Agamemnon treated the priest, he premises these words of his own,–

Not so Atrides: he with kingly pride
Repulsed the sacred sire, and thus replied;
(Ibid. i. 24.)

intimating the insolency and unbecomingness of his answer. And when he attributes this passionate speech to Achilles,–

O monster, mix'd of insolence and fear,
Thou dog in forehead, and in heart a deer!
(Ibid. i. 225.)

he accompanies it with this censure,–

Nor yet the rage his boiling breast forsook,
Which thus redoubling on Atrides broke;
(Ibid. i. 223.)

for it was unlikely that speaking in such anger he should observe any rules of decency.

And he passeth like censures on actions. As on Achilles's foul usage of Hector's carcass,–

Gloomy he said, and (horrible to view)
Before the bier the bleeding Hector threw.
("Iliad," xxiii. 24.)

And in like manner he doth very decently shut up relations of things said or done, by adding some sentence wherein he declares his judgment of them. As when he personates some of the gods saying, on the occasion of the adultery of Mars and Venus discovered by

Vulcan's artifice,–

> *See the swift god o'ertaken by the lame!*
> *Thus ill acts prosper not, but end in shame.*
> *("Odyssey," viii. 329.)*

And thus concerning Hector's insolent boasting he says,–

> *With such big words his mind proud Hector eased,*
> *But venerable Juno he displeased.*
> *("Iliad," viii. 198.)*

And when he speaks of Pandarus's shooting, he adds,–

> *He heard, and madly at the motion pleased,*
> *His polish'd bow with hasty rashness seized.*
> *(Ibid. iv. 104.)*

Now these verbal intimations of the minds and judgments of poets are not difficult to be understood by any one that will heedfully observe them. But besides these, they give us other hints from actions. As Euripides is reported, when some blamed him for bringing such an impious and flagitious villain as Ixion upon the stage, to have given this answer: But yet I brought him not off till I had fastened him to a torturing wheel. This same way of teaching by mute actions is to be found in Homer also, affording us useful contemplations upon those very fables which are usually most disliked in him. These some men offer force to, that they may reduce them to allegories (which the ancients called [Greek omitted]), and tell us that Venus committing adultery with Mars, discovered by the Sun, is to be understood thus: that when the star called Venus is in conjunction with that which hath the name of Mars, bastardly births are produced, and by the Sun's rising and discovering them they are not concealed. So will they have Juno's dressing herself so accurately to tempt Jupiter, and her making use of the girdle of Venus to inflame his love, to be nothing else but the purification of that part of the air which draweth nearest to the nature of fire. As if we were not told the meaning of those fables far better by the poet himself. For he teacheth us in that of Venus, if we heed it, that light music and wanton songs and discourses which suggest to men obscene fancies debauch their manners, and incline them to an unmanly way of living in luxury and wantonness, of continually haunting the company of women, and of being

> *Given to fashions, that their garb may please,*
> *Hot baths, and couches where they loll at case.*

And therefore also he brings in Ulysses directing the musician thus,–

> *Leave this, and sing the horse, out of whose womb*

> *The gallant knights that conquered Troy did come;*
> *("Odyssey," viii. 249 and 492.)*

evidently teaching us that poets and musicians ought to receive the arguments of their songs from sober and understanding men. And in the other fable of Juno he excellently shows that the conversation of women with men, and the favors they receive from them procured by sorcery, witchcraft, or other unlawful arts, are not only short, unstable, and soon cloying, but also in the issue easily turned to loathing and displeasure, when once the pleasure is over. For so Jupiter there threatens Juno, when he tells her,–

> *Hear this, remember, and our fury dread,*
> *Nor pull the unwilling vengeance on thy head;*
> *Lest arts and blandishments successless prove*
> *Thy soft deceits and well dissembled love.*
> *("Iliad," xv. 32.)*

For the fiction and representation of evil acts, when it withal acquaints us with the shame and damage befalling the doers, hurts not but rather profits him that reads them. For which end philosophers make use of examples for our instruction and correction out of historical collections; and poets do the very same thing, but with this difference, that they invent fabulous examples themselves. There was one Melanthius, who (whether in jest or earnest he said it, it matters not much) affirmed that the city of Athens owed its preservation to the dissensions and factions that were among the orators, giving withal this reason for his assertion, that thereby they were kept from inclining all of them to one side, so that by means of the differences among those statesmen there were always some that drew the saw the right way for the defeating of destructive counsels. And thus it is too in the contradictions among poets, which, by lessening the credit of what they say, render them the less powerful to do mischief; and therefore, when comparing one saying with another we discover their contrariety, we ought to adhere to the better side. As in these instances:–

> *The gods, my son, deceive poor men oft-times.* ANS. *'Tis easy, sir, on God to lay our crimes.*
>
> *'Tis comfort to thee to be rich, is't not!* ANS. *No, sir, 'tis bad to be a wealthy sot.*
>
> *Die rather than such toilsome pains to take.* ANS. *To call God's service toil's a foul mistake.*

Such contrarieties as these are easily solved, if (as I said) we teach youth to judge aright and to give the better saying preference. But if we chance to meet with any absurd passages without any others at their heels to confute them, we are then to overthrow them with such others as elsewhere are to be found in the same author. Nor must we be offended with the poet or grieved at him, but only at the speeches themselves, which he utters either according to the vulgar manner of speaking or, it may be, but in drollery. So, when thou readest in Homer of gods thrown out of heaven headlong one by another, or gods wounded by men and quarrelling and brawling with each other, thou mayest readily, if thou wilt, say to him,–

Sure thy invention here was sorely out,
Or thou hadst said far better things, no doubt;
("Iliad," viii. 358.)

yea, and thou dost so elsewhere, and according as thou thinkest, to wit, in these passages of thine:–

The gods, removed from all that men doth grieve,
A quiet and contented life do live.
Herein the immortal gods forever blest
Feel endless joys and undisturbed rest.
The gods, who have themselves no cause to grieve,
For wretched man a web of sorrow weave.
(Ibid. vi. 138; "Odyssey," vi. 46; "Iliad," xxiv, 526.)

For these argue sound and true opinions of the gods; but those other were only feigned to raise passions in men. Again, when Euripides speaks at this rate,–

The gods are better than we men by far,
And yet by them we oft deceived are,–

may do well to quote him elsewhere against himself where he says better,–

If gods do wrong, surely no gods there are.

So also, when Pindar, saith bitterly and keenly,

No law forbids us anything to do,
Whereby a mischief may befall a foe,

tell him: But, Pindar, thou thyself sayest elsewhere,

The pleasure which injurious acts attends
Always in bitter consequences ends.

And when Sophocles speaks thus,

Sweet is the gain, wherein to lie and cheat
Adds the repute of wit to what we get,

tell him: But we have heard thee say far otherwise,

When the account's cast up, the gain's but poor

Which by a lying tongue augments the store.
And as to what he saith of riches, to wit:–
   Wealth, where it minds to go, meets with no stay;
   For where it finds not, it can make a way;
   Many fair offers doth the poor let go,
   And lose his talent because his purse is low;
   The fair tongue makes, where wealth can purchase it,
   The foul face beautiful, the fool a wit:–
against this the reader may set in opposition divers other sayings of the same author. For example,
   From honor poverty doth not debar,
   Where poor men virtuous and deserving are.
   Whate'er fools think, a man is ne'er the worse
   If he be wise, though with an empty purse.
   The comfort which he gets who wealth enjoys,
   The vexing care by which 'tis kept destroys.
And Menander also somewhere magnifies a voluptuous life, and inflames the minds of vain persons with these amorous strains,
   The glorious sun no living thing doth see,
   But what's a slave to love as well as we.
But yet elsewhere, on the other side, he fastens on us and pulls us back to the love of virtue, and checks the rage of lust, when he says thus,
   The life that is dishonorably spent,
   Be it ne'er so pleasant, yields no true content.
For these lines are contrary to the former, as they are also better and more profitable; so that by comparing them considerately one cannot but either be inclined to the better side, or at least flag in the belief of the worse.

But now, supposing that any of the poets themselves afford no such correcting passages to solve what they have said amiss, it will then be advisable to confront them with the contrary sayings of other famous men, and therewith to sway the scales of our judgment to the better side. As, when Alexis tempts to debauchery in these verses,
   The wise man knows what of all things is best,
   Whilst choosing pleasure he slights all the rest.
   He thinks life's joys complete in these three sorts,
   To drink and eat, and follow wanton sports;
   And what besides seems to pretend to pleasure,
   If it betide him, counts it over measure,
we must remember that Socrates said the contrary, to wit: that they

are bad men who live that they may eat and drink, whereas good men eat and drink that they may live. And against the man that wrote in this manner,

> He that designs to encounter with a knave,
> An equal stock of knavery must have,

seeing he herein advises us to follow other vicious examples, that of Diogenes may well be returned, who being asked by what means a man might revenge himself upon his enemy, answered, By becoming himself a good and honest man. And the same Diogenes may be quoted also against Sophocles, who, writing of the sacred mysteries, caused great grief and despair to multitudes of men:–

> Most happy they whose eyes are blest to see
> The mysteries which here contained be,
> Before they die! For only they have joy.
> In th' other world; the rest all ills annoy.

This passage being read to Diogenes, What then! says he, shall the condition of Pataecion, the notorious robber, after death be better than that of Epaminondas, merely for his being initiated in these mysteries? In like manner, when one Timotheus on the theatre, singing of the Goddess Diana, called her furious, raging, possessed, mad, Cinesias suddenly interrupted him, May thy daughter, Timotheus, be such a goddess! And witty also was that of Bion to Theognis, who said,–

> One cannot say nor do, if poor he be;
> His tongue is bound to th' peace, as well as he.
> ("Theognis," vss. 177, 178.)

How comes it to pass then, said he, Theognis that thou thyself being so poor pratest and gratest our ears in this manner?

Nor are we to omit, in our reading those hints which, from some other words or phrases bordering on those that offend us, may help to rectify our apprehensions. But as physicians use cantharides, believing that, though their bodies be deadly poison, yet their feet and wings are medicinal and are antidotes to the poison itself, so must we deal with poems. If any noun or verb near at hand may assist to the correction of any such saying, and preserve us from putting a bad construction upon it, we should take hold of it and employ it to assist a more favorable interpretation. As some do in reference to those verses of Homer,–

> Sorrows and tears most commonly are seen
> To be the gods' rewards to wretched men:–
> The gods, who have no cause themselves to grieve,
> For wretched man a web of sorrow weave.

("Odyssey," iv. 197; "Iliad," xxiv. 526.)

For, they say, he says not of men simply, or of all men, that the gods weave for them the fatal web of a sorrowful life, but he affirms it only of foolish and imprudent men, whom, because their vices make them such, he therefore calls wretched and miserable.

Another way whereby those passages which are suspicious in poets maybe transferred to a better sense may be taken from the ordinary use of words, which a young man ought indeed to be more exercised in than in the use of strange and obscure terms. For it will be a point of philology which it will not be unprofitable to him to understand, that when he meets with [Greek omitted] in a poet, that word means an EVIL DEATH; for the Macedonians use the word [Greek omitted] to signify DEATH. So the Aeolians call victory gotten by patient endurance of hardships [Greek omitted] and the Dryopians call daemons [Greek omitted].

But of all things it is most necessary, and no less profitable if we design to receive profit and not hurt from the poets, that we understand how they make use of the names of gods, as also of the terms of Evil and Good; and what they mean by Soul and Fate; and whether these words be always taken by them in one and the same sense or rather in various senses, as also many other words are. For so the word [Greek omitted] sometimes signifies a MATERIAL HOUSE, as, Into the high-roofed house; and sometimes ESTATE, as, My house is devoured. So the word [Greek omitted] sometimes signifies life, and sometimes wealth. And [Greek omitted] is sometimes taken for being uneasy and disquieted in mind, as in

[Greek omitted] ("Iliad," v. 352.)

and elsewhere for boasting and rejoicing, as in

[Greek omitted] ("Odyssey," xviii. 333.)

In like manner [Greek omitted] signifies either to MOVE, as in Euripides when he saith,

[Greek omitted]–

or TO SIT, as in Sophocles when he writes thus,

[Greek omitted] (Sophocles, "Oedipus Tyranus," 2.)

It is elegant also when they fit to the present matter, as grammarians teach, the use of words which have another signification. As here:–

[Greek omitted]

For here [Greek omitted] signifies TO PRAISE (instead of [Greek omitted]), and TO PRAISE is used for TO REFUSE. So in conversation it is common with us to say, [Greek omitted], IT IS WELL (i.e., NO, I THANK YOU), and to bid anything FAREWELL [Greek omitted]; by which forms of speech we refuse a thing which we do not want, or receive it not, but still with a civil compliment. So also some say that Proserpina is called [Greek omitted] in the notion of [Greek omitted], TO BE DEP-RECATED, because death is by all men shunned.

And the like distinction of words we ought to observe also in things more weighty and serious. To begin with the gods, we should teach our youth that poets, when they use the names of gods, sometimes mean properly the Divine Beings so called, but otherwhiles understand by those names certain powers of which the gods are the donors and authors, they having first led us into the use of them by their own practice. As when Archilochus prays,

> *King Vulcan, hear thy suppliant, and grant*
> *That what thou'rt wont to give and I to want,*

it is plain that he means the god himself whom he invokes. But when elsewhere he bewails the drowning of his sister's husband, who had not obtained lawful burial, and says,

> *Had Vulcan his fair limbs to ashes turned,*
> *I for his loss had with less passion mourned,*

he gives the name of Vulcan to the fire and not to the Deity. Again, Euripides, when he says,

> *No; by the glorious stars I swear,*
> *And bloody Mars and Jupiter,*
> *(Euripides, "Phoenissae," 1006.)*

means the gods themselves who bare those names. But when Sophocles saith,

> *Blind Mars doth mortal men's affairs confound,*
> *As the swine's snout doth quite deface the ground,*

we are to understand the word Mars to denote not the god so called, but war. And by the same word we are to understand also weapons made of hardened brass, in those verses of Homer,

> *These, are the gallant men whose noble blood*
> *Keen Mars did shed near swift Scamander's flood.*
> *("Iliad," vii. 329.)*

Wherefore, in conformity to the instances given, we must conceive and bear in mind that by the names of Jupiter also sometimes they mean the god himself, sometimes Fortune, and oftentimes also Fate. For when they say,–

> *Great Jupiter, who from the lofty hill*
> *Of Ida govern'st all the world at will;*
> *("Iliad," iii. 276.)*
> *That wrath which hurled to Pluto's gloomy realm*

The souls of mighty chiefs:–
Such was the sovereign doom, and such the will of Jove;
(Ibid. i. 3 and 5.)
For who (but who himself too fondly loves)
Dares lay his wisdom in the scale with Jove's?–

they understand Jupiter himself. But when they ascribe the event of all things done to Jupiter as the cause, saying of him,–

Many brave souls to hell Achilles sent,
And Jove's design accomplished in th' event,–

they mean by Jove no more but Fate. For the poet doth not conceive that God contrives mischief against mankind, but he soundly declares the mere necessity of the things themselves, to wit, that prosperity and victory are destined by Fate to cities and armies and commanders who govern themselves with sobriety, but if they give way to passions and commit errors, thereby dividing and crumbling themselves into factions, as those of whom the poet speaks did, they do unhandsome actions, and thereby create great disturbances, such as are attended with sad consequences.

For to all unadvised acts, in fine,
The Fates unhappy issues do assign.
(From Euripides.)

But when Hesiod brings in Prometheus thus counselling his brother Epimetheus,

Brother, if Jove to thee a present make,
Take heed that from his hands thou nothing take,
(Hesiod, "Works and Days," 86.)

he useth the name of Jove to express Fortune; for he calls the good things which come by her (such as riches, and marriages, and empires, and indeed all external things the enjoyment whereof is profitable to only them who know how to use them well) the gifts of Jove. And therefore he adviseth Epimetheus (an ill man, and a fool withal) to stand in fear of and to guard himself from prosperity, as that which would be hurtful and destructive to him.

Again, where he saith,

Reproach thou not a man for being poor;
His poverty's God's gift, as is thy store,
(Hesiod "Works and Days," 717.)

he calls that which befalls men by Fortune God's gift, and intimates that it is an unworthy thing to reproach any man for that poverty which he falls into by Fortune, whereas poverty is then only a matter of disgrace and reproach when it is attendant on sloth and idleness, or wantonness and prodigality. For, before the name of Fortune was used, they knew there was a powerful cause, which moved irregularly and unlimitedly and with such a force that no human reason could avoid it; and this cause they called by the names of gods. So we are wont to call divers things and qualities and discourses, and even men themselves, divine. And thus may we rectify many such sayings concerning Jupiter as would otherwise seem very absurd. As these, for instance:–

> *Before Jove's door two fatal hogsheads, filled*
> *With human fortunes, good and bad luck yield.–*
> *Of violated oaths Jove took no care,*
> *But spitefully both parties crushed by war:–*
> *To Greeks and Trojans both this was the rise*
> *Of Mischief, suitable to Jove's device.*
> *("Iliad," xxiv. 527; vii. 69; "Odyssey," viii. 81.)*

These passages we are to interpret as spoken concerning Fortune or Fate, of the casuality of both which no account can be given by us, nor do their effects fall under our power. But where anything is said of Jupiter that is suitable, rational, and probable, there we are to conceive that the names of that god is used properly. As in these instances:–

> *Through others' ranks he conquering did range,*
> *But shunned with Ajax any blows t' exchange;*
> *But Jove's displeasure on him he had brought,*
> *Had he with one so much his better fought.*
> *("Iliad," xi. 540.)*
> *For though great matters are Jove's special care,*
> *Small things t' inferior daemons trusted are.*

And other words there are which the poets remove and translate from their proper sense by accommodation to various things, which deserve also our serious notice. Such a one, for instance, is [Greek omitted], VIRTUE. For because virtue does not only render men prudent, just, and good, both in their words and deeds, but also oftentimes purchaseth to them honor and power, therefore they call likewise these by that name. So we are wont to call both the olive-tree and the fruit [Greek omitted], and the oak-tree and its acorn [Greek omitted] communicating the name of the one to the other. Therefore, when our young man reads in the poets such passages as these,–

> *This law th' immortal gods to us have set,*
> *That none arrive at virtue but by sweat;*
> *(Hesiod, "Works and Days," 289.)*
> *The adverse troops then did the Grecians stout*
> *By their mere virtue profligate and rout;*

("Iliad," xi. 90.)
> *If now the Fates determined have our death,*
> *To virtue we'll consign our parting breath;–*

let him presently conceive that these things are spoken of that most excellent and divine habit in us which we understand to be no other than right reason, or the highest attainment of the reasonable nature, and most agreeable to the constitution thereof. And again, when he reads this,

> *Of virtue Jupiter to one gives more,*
> *And lessens, when he lifts, another's store;*

and this,

> *Virtue and honor upon wealth attend;*
> *(Ibid. xx. 242; Hesiod "Works and Days," 313.)*

let him not sit down in an astonishing admiration of rich men, as if they were enabled by their wealth to purchase virtue, nor let him imagine that it is in the power of Fortune to increase or lessen his own wisdom; but let him conceive that the poet by virtue meant either glory or power or prosperity or something of like import. For poets use the same ambiguity also in the word [Greek omitted], EVIL, which sometimes in them properly signifies a wicked and malicious disposition of mind, as in that of Hesiod,

> *Evil is soon acquired; for everywhere*
> *There's plenty on't and t'all men's dwellings near;*
> *(Hesiod, "Works and Days," 287.)*

and sometimes some evil accident or misfortune, as when Homer says,

> *Sore evils, when they haunt us in our prime,*
> *Hasten old age on us before our time.*
> *("Odyessy," xix. 360.)*

So also in the word [Greek omitted], he would be sorely deceived who should imagine that, wheresoever he meets with it in poets, it means (as it does in philosophy) a perfect habitual enjoyment of all good things or the leading a life every way agreeable to Nature, and that they do not withal by the abuse of such words call rich men happy or blessed, and power or glory felicity. For, though Homer rightly useth terms of that nature in this passage,–

> *Though of such great estates I am possest,*
> *Yet with true inward joy I am not blest;*
> *(Ibid. iv. 93.)*

and Menander in this,–

> *So great's th' estate I am endowed withal:*

> *All say I'm rich, but none me happy call;–*

yet Euripides discourseth more confusedly and perplexedly when he writes after this manner,–

> *I do not want a happy life that is tedious;*
> *And, man, why praisest thou*
> *Th' unjust beatitude of tyranny?*
> *(Euripides, "Medea," 598; "Phoenissae," 549.)*

except, as I said, we allow him the use of these words in a metaphorical and abusive meaning. But enough hath been spoken of these matters.

Nevertheless, this principle is not once only but often to be inculcated and pressed on young men, that poetry when it undertakes a fictitious argument by way of imitation, though it make use of such ornament and illustration as suit the actions and manners treated of, yet disclaims not all likelihood of truth, seeing the force of imitation, in order to the persuading of men, lies in probability. Wherefore such imitation as does not altogether shake hands with truth carries along with it certain signs of virtue and vice mixed together in the actions which it doth represent. And of this nature is Homer's poetry, which totally bids adieu to Stoicism, the principles whereof will not admit any vice to come near where virtue is, nor virtue to have anything to do where any vice lodgeth, but affirms that he that is not a wise man can do nothing well, and he that is so can do nothing amiss. Thus they determine in the schools. But in human actions and the affairs of common life the judgment of Euripides is verified, that

> *Virtue and vice ne'er separately exist,*
> *But in the same acts with each other twist.*
> *(From the "Aeolus" of Euripides.)*

Next, it is to be observed that poetry, waiving the truth of things, does most labor to beautify its fictions with variety and multiplicity of contrivance. For variety bestows upon fable all that is pathetical, unusual, and surprising, and thereby makes it more taking and graceful; whereas what is void of variety is unsuitable to the nature of fable, and so raiseth no passions at all. Upon which design of variety it is, that the poets never represent the same persons always victorious or prosperous or acting with the same constant tenor of virtue;–yea, even the gods themselves, when they engage in human actions, are not represented as free from passions and errors;–lest, for the want of some difficulties and cross passages, their poems should be destitute of that briskness which is requisite to move and astonish the minds of men.

These things therefore so standing, we should, when we enter a young man into the study of the poets, endeavor to free his mind from that degree of esteem of the good and great personages in them described as may incline him to think them to be mirrors of wisdom and justice, the chief of princes, and the exemplary measures of all virtue and goodness. For he will receive much prejudice, if he shall approve and admire all that comes from such persons as great, if he dislike nothing in them himself, nor will endure to hear others blame them, though for such words and actions as the following passages import:–

> *Oh! would to all the immortal powers above,*
> *Apollo, Pallas, and almighty Jove!*
> *That not one Trojan might be left alive,*
> *And not a Greek of all the race survive.*
> *Might only we the vast destruction shun,*
> *And only we destroy the accursed town!*
> *Her breast all gore, with lamentable cries,*
> *The bleeding innocent Cassandra dies,*
> *Murdered by Clytemnestra's faithless hand:*
> *Lie with thy father's whore, my mother said,*
> *That she th' old man may loathe; and I obeyed:*
> *Of all the gods, O father Jove, there's none*
> *Thus given to mischief but thyself alone.*
> *("Iliad," xvi. 97; "Odyssey," xi. 421; "Iliad," ix, 452;*
> *Ibid. iii, 365.)*

Our young man is to be taught not to commend such things as these, no, nor to show the nimbleness of his wit or subtlety in maintaining argument by finding out plausible colors and pretences to varnish over a bad matter. But we should teach him rather to judge that poetry is an imitation of the manners and lives of such men as are not perfectly pure and unblameable, but such as are tinctured with passions, misled by false opinions, and muffled with ignorance; though oftentimes they may, by the help of a good natural temper, change them for better qualities. For the young man's mind, being thus prepared and disposed, will receive no damage by such passages when he meets with them in poems, but will on the one side be elevated with rapture at those things which are well said or done, and on the other, will not entertain but dislike those which are of a contrary character. But he that admires and is transported with everything, as having his judgment enslaved by the esteem he hath for the names of heroes, will be unawares wheedled into many evil things, and be guilty of the same folly with those who imitate the crookedness of Plato or the stammering of Aristotle. Neither must he carry himself timorously herein, nor, like a superstitious person in a temple, tremblingly adore all he meets with; but use himself to such confidence as may enable him openly to pronounce, This was ill or incongruously said, and, That was bravely and gallantly spoken. For example, Achilles in Homer, being offended at the spinning out that war by delays, wherein he was desirous by feats of arms to purchase to himself glory, calls the soldiers together when there was an epidemical disease among them. But having himself some smattering skill in physic, and perceiving after the ninth day, which useth to be decretory in such cases, that the disease was no usual one nor proceeding from ordinary causes, when he stands up to speak, he waives applying himself to the soldiers, and addresseth himself as a councillor to the general, thus:–

> *Why leave we not the fatal Trojan shore,*
> *And measure back the seas we cross'd before?*
> *(For this and the four following quotations, see*
> *"Iliad," i. 59, 90, 220, 349; ix, 458.)*

And he spake well, and with due moderation and decorum. But when the soothsayer Chalcas had told him that he feared the wrath of the most potent among the Grecians, after an oath that while he lived no man should lay violent hands on him, he adds, but not with like wisdom and moderation,

> *Not e'en the chief by whom our hosts are led,*
> *The king of kings, shall touch that sacred head;*

in which speech he declares his low opinion or rather his contempt of his chief commander. And then, being farther provoked, he drew his weapon with a design to kill him, which attempt was neither good nor expedient. And therefore by and by he repented his rashness,–

> *He said, observant of the blue-eyed maid;*
> *Then in the sheath returned the shining blade;*

wherein again he did rightly and worthily, in that, though he could not altogether quell his passion, yet he restrained and reduced it under the command of reason, before it brake forth into such an irreparable act of mischief. Again, even Agamemnon himself talks in that assembly ridiculously, but carries himself more gravely and more like a prince in the matter of Chryseis. For whereas Achilles, when his Briseis was taken away from him,

> *In sullenness withdraws from all his friends,*
> *And in his tent his time lamenting spends;*

Agamemnon himself hands into the ship, delivers to her friends, and so sends from him, the woman concerning whom a little before he declared that he loved her better than his wife; and in that action did nothing unbecoming or savoring of fond affection. Also Phoenix, when his father bitterly cursed him for having to do with one that was his own harlot, says,

> *Him in my rage I purposed to have killed,*
> *But that my hand some god in kindness held;*
> *And minded me that, Greeks would taunting say,*
> *Lo, here's the man that did his father slay.*

It is true that Aristarchus was afraid to permit these verses to stand in the poet, and therefore censured them to be expunged. But they were inserted by Homer very aptly to the occasion of Phoenix's instructing Achilles what a pernicious thing anger is, and what foul acts men do by its instigation, while they are capable neither of making use of their own reason nor of hearing the counsel of others. To which end he also introduceth Meleager at first highly offended with his citizens, and afterwards pacified; justly therein reprehending disordered passions, and praising it as a good and profitable thing not to yield to them, but to resist and overcome them, and to repent when one hath been overcome by them.

Now in these instances the difference is manifest. But where a like clear judgment cannot be passed, there we are to settle the young man's mind thus, by way of distinction. If Nausicaa, having cast her eyes upon Ulysses, a stranger, and feeling the same passion for him as Calypso had before, did (as one that was ripe for a husband) out of wantonness talk with her maidens at this foolish rate,–

> *O Heaven! in my connubial hour decree*
> *This man my spouse, or such a spouse as he!*
> *("Odyssey," vi. 254.)*

she is blameworthy for her impudence and incontinence. But if, perceiving the man's breeding by his discourse, and admiring the prudence of his addresses, she rather wisheth to have such a one for a husband than a merchant or a dancing gallant of her fellow-citizens, she is to be commended. And when Ulysses is represented as pleased with Penelope's jocular conversation with her wooers, and at their presenting her with rich garments and other ornaments,

> *Because she cunningly the fools cajoled,*
> *And bartered light words for their heavy gold;*
> *("Odyssey," xvii, 282.)*

if that joy were occasioned by greediness and covetousness, he discovers himself to be a more sordid prostituter of his own life than Poliager is wont to be represented on the stage to have been, of whom it is said,–

> *Happy man he, whose wife, like Capricorn,*

Stores him with riches from a golden horn!

But if through foresight he thought thereby to get them the more within his power, as being lulled asleep in security for the future by the hopes she gave them at present, this rejoicing, joined with confidence in his wife, was rational. Again, when he is brought in numbering the goods which the Phaeacians had set on shore together with himself and departed; if indeed, being himself left in such a solitude, so ignorant where he was, and having no security there for his own person, he is yet solicitous for his goods, lest

The sly Phaeacians, when they stole to sea,
Had stolen some part of what they brought away;
(Ibid. xiii. 216.)

the covetousness of the man deserved in truth to be pitied, or rather abhorred. But if, as some say in his defence, being doubtful whether or no the place where he was landed were Ithaca, he made use of the just tale of his goods to infer thence the honesty of the Phaeacians,–because it was not likely they would expose him in a strange place and leave him there with his goods by him untouched, so as to get nothing by their dishonesty,–then he makes use of a very fit test for this purpose, and deserves commendation for his wisdom in that action. Some also there are who condemn that passage of the putting him on shore when he was asleep, if it really so happened, and they tell us that the people of Tuscany have still a traditional story among them concerning Ulysses, that he was naturally sleepy, and therefore a man whom many people could not freely converse with. But if his sleep was but shammed, and he made use of this pretence only of a natural infirmity, by counterfeiting a nap, to hide the strait he was in at the time in his thoughts, betwixt the shame of sending away the Phaeacians without giving them a friendly collation and hospitable gifts, and the fear he had of being discovered to his enemies by the treating such a company of men together, they then approve it.

Now, by showing young men these things, we shall preserve them from being carried away to any corruption in their manners, and dispose them to the election and imitation of those that are good, as being before instructed readily to disapprove those and commend these. But this ought with the most care to be done in the reading of tragedies wherein probable and subtle speeches are made use of in the most foul and wicked actions. For that is not always true which Sophocles saith, that

From evil acts good words can never come.

For even he himself is wont to apply pleasant reasonings and plausible arguments to those manners and actions which are wicked or unbecoming. And in another of his fellow-tragedians, we may see even Phaedra herself represented as justifying her unlawful affection for Hippolytus by accusing Theseus of ill-carriage towards her. And in his Troades, he allows Helen the same liberty of speech against Hecuba, whom she judgeth to be more worthy of punishment than herself for her adultery, because she was the mother of Paris that tempted her thereto. A young man therefore must not be accustomed to think anything of that nature handsomely or wittily spoken, nor to be pleased with such colorable inventions; but rather more to abhor such words as tend to the defence of wanton acts than the very acts themselves.

And lastly, it will be useful likewise to inquire into the cause why each thing is said. For so Cato, when he was a boy, though he was wont to be very observant of all his master's commands, yet withal used to ask the cause or reason why he so commanded. But poets are not to be obeyed as pedagogues and promulgators of laws are, except they have reason to back what they say. And that they will not want, when they speak well; and if they speak ill, what they say will appear vain and frivolous. But nowadays most young men very briskly demand the reason of such trivial speeches as these, and inquire in what sense they are spoken:–

> *It bodes ill, when vessels you set up,*
> *To put the ladle on the mixing-cup.*
> *Who from his chariot to another's leaps,*
> *Seldom his seat without a combat keeps.*
> *(Hesiod "Works and Days," 744; "Iliad," iv. 306.)*

But to those of greater moment they give credence without examination, as to those that follow:–

> *The boldest men are daunted oftentimes,*
> *When they're reproached with their parents' crimes:*
> *(Euripides, "Hippolytus," 424.)*
> *When any man is crushed by adverse fate,*
> *His spirit should be low as his estate.*

And yet such speeches relate to manners, and disquiet men's lives by begetting in them evil opinions and unworthy sentiments, except they have learned to return answer to each of them thus: "Wherefore is it necessary that a man who is crushed by adverse fate should have a dejected spirit? Yea, why rather should he not struggle against Fortune, and raise himself above the pressures of his low circumstances? Why, if I myself be a good and wise son of an evil and foolish father, does it not rather become me to bear myself confidently upon the account of my own virtue, than to be dejected and dispirited because of my father's defects?" For he that can encounter such speeches and oppose them after this manner, not yielding himself up to be overset with the blast of every saying, but approving that speech of Heraclitus, that

> Whate'er is said, though void of sense and wit,
>   The size of a fool's intellect doth fit,

will reject many such things as falsely and idly spoken.

These things therefore may be of use to preserve us from the hurt we might get by the study of poems.

Now, as on a vine the fruit oftentimes lies concealed and hidden under its large leaves and luxuriant branches, so in the poet's phrases and fictions that encompass them there are also many profitable and useful things concealed from the view of young men. This, however, ought not to be suffered; nor should we be led away from things themselves thus, but rather adhere to such of them as tend to the promoting of virtue and the well forming of our manners. It will not be altogether useless, therefore, to treat briefly in the next place of passages of that nature. Wherein I intend to touch only at some particulars, leaving all longer discussion, and the trimming up and furnishing them with a multitude of instances, to those who write more for display and ostentation.

First, therefore, let our young man be taught to understand good and bad manners and persons, and from thence apply his mind to the words and deeds which the poet decently assigns to either of them. For example, Achilles, though in some wrath, speaks to Agamemnon thus decently:–

> Nor, when we take a Trojan town, can I
>   With thee in spoils and splendid prizes vie;
>   (For this and the five following quotations,
>   see "Iliad," i. 163; ii. 226; i. 128; ii. 231;
>   iv. 402 and 404.)

whereas Thersites to the same person speaks reproachfully in this manner:–

> 'Tis thine whate'er the warrior's breast inflames,
>   The golden spoil, thine the lovely dames.
>   With all the wealth our wars and blood bestow,
>   Thy tents are crowded and thy chests o'erflow.

Again, Achilles thus:–

> Whene'er, by Jove's decree, our conquering powers
>   Shall humble to the dust Troy's lofty towers;

but Thersites thus:–

Whom I or some Greek else as captive bring.

Again, Diomedes, when Agamemnon taking a view of the army spoke reproachfully to him,

To his hard words forbore to make reply,
For the respect he bare to majesty;

whereas Sthenelus, a man of small note, replies on him thus:–

Sir, when you know the truth, what need to lie?
For with our fathers we for valor vie.

Now the observation of such difference will teach the young man the decency of a modest and moderate temper, and the unbecoming nauseousness of the contrary vices of boasting and cracking of a man's own worth. And it is worth while also to take notice of the demeanor of Agamemnon in the same place. For he passeth by Sthenelus unspoken to; but perceiving Ulysses to be offended, he neglects not him, but applies himself to answer him:–

Struck with his generous wrath, the king replies.
("Iliad," iv. 357. For the four following, see "Iliad," ix. 34
and 70; iv. 431; x. 325.)

For to have apologized to every one had been too servile and misbecoming the dignity of his person; whereas equally to have neglected every one had been an act of insolence and imprudence. And very handsome it is that Diomedes, though in the heat of the battle he answers the king only with silence, yet after the battle was over useth more liberty towards him, speaking thus:–

You called me coward, sir, before the Greeks.

It is expedient also to take notice of the different carriage of a wise man and of a soothsayer popularly courting the multitude. For Chalcas very unseasonably makes no scruple to traduce the king before the people, as having been the cause of the pestilence that was befallen them. But Nestor, intending to bring in a discourse concerning the reconciling Achilles to him, that he might not seem to charge Agamemnon before the multitude with the miscarriage his passion had occasioned, only adviseth him thus:–

But thou, O king, to council call the old....
Wise weighty counsels aid a state distressed,
And such a monarch as can choose the best;

which done, accordingly after supper he sends his ambassadors. Now this speech of Nestor tended to the rectifying of what he had before done amiss; but that of Chalcas, only to accuse and disparage him.

There is likewise consideration to be had of the different manners of nations, such as these. The Trojans enter into battle with loud outcries and great fierceness; but in the army of the Greeks,

> *Sedate and silent move the numerous bands;*
> *No sound, no whisper, but the chief's commands;*
> *Those only heard, with awe the rest obey.*

For when soldiers are about to engage an enemy, the awe they stand in of their officers is an argument both of courage and obedience. For which purpose Plato teacheth us that we ought to inure ourselves to fear, blame and disgrace more than labor and danger. And Cato was wont to say that he liked men that were apt to blush better than those that looked pale.

Moreover, there is a particular character to be noted of the men who undertake for any action. For Dolon thus promiseth:–

> *I'll pass through all their host in a disguise*
> *To their flag-ship, where she at anchor lies.*

But Diomedes promiseth nothing, but only tells them he shall fear the less if they send a companion with him; whereby is intimated, that discreet foresight is Grecian and civil, but rash confidence is barbarous and evil; and the former is therefore to be imitated, and the latter to be avoided.

It is a matter too of no unprofitable consideration, how the minds of the Trojans and of Hector too were affected when he and Ajax were about to engage in a single combat. For Aeschylus, when, upon one of the fighters at fisticuffs in the Isthmian games receiving a blow on the face, there was made a great outcry among the people, said: "What a thing is practice! See how the lookers-on only cry out, but the man that received the stroke is silent." But when the poet tells us, that the Greeks rejoiced when they saw Ajax in his glistering armor, but

> *The Trojans' knees for very fear did quake,*
> *And even Hector's heart began to ache;*
> *("Iliad," vii. 215. For the three following,*
> *see "Iliad," ii. 220; v. 26 and 231.)*

who is there that wonders not at this difference,–when the heart of him that was to run the risk of the combat only beats inwardly, as if he were to undertake a mere wrestling or running match, but the very bodies of the spectators tremble and shake, out of the kindness and fear which they had for their king?

In the same poet also we may observe the difference betwixt the humor of a coward and a valiant man. For Thersites

> *Against Achilles a great malice had,*

And wise Ulysses he did hate as bad;

but Ajax is always represented as friendly to Achilles; and particularly he speaks thus to Hector concerning him:–

Hector I approach my arm, and singly know
What strength thou hast, and what the Grecian foe.
Achilles shuns the fight; yet some there are
Not void of soul, and not unskill'd in war:

wherein he insinuates the high commendation of that valiant man. And in what follows, he speaks like handsome things of his fellow-soldiers in general, thus:–

Whole troops of heroes Greece has yet to boast,
And sends thee one, a sample of her host;

wherein he doth not boast himself to be the only or the best champion, but one of those, among many others, who were fit to undertake that combat.

What hath been said is sufficient upon the point of dissimilitudes; except we think fit to add this, that many of the Trojans came into the enemy's power alive, but none of the Grecians; and that many Trojans supplicated to their enemies,–as (for instance) Adrastus, the sons of Antimachus, Lycaon,–and even Hector himself entreats Achilles for a sepulture; but not one of these doth so, as judging it barbarous to supplicate to a foe in the field, and more Greek-like either to conquer or die.

But as, in the same plant, the bee feeds on the flower, the goat on the bud, the hog on the root, and other living creatures on the seed and the fruit; so in reading of poems, one man singleth out the historical part, another dwells upon the elegancy and fit disposal of words, as Aristophanes says of Euripides,–

His gallant language runs so smooth and round,
That I am ravisht with th' harmonious sound;
(See "Aristophanes," Frag. 397.)

but others, to whom this part of my discourse is directed, mind only such things as are useful to the bettering of manners. And such we are to put in mind that it is an absurd thing, that those who delight in fables should not let anything slip them of the vain and extravagant stories they find in poets, and that those who affect language should pass over nothing that is elegantly and floridly expressed; and that only the lovers of honor and virtue, who apply themselves to the study of poems not for delight but for instruction's sake, should slightly and negligently observe what is spoken in them relating to valor, temperance, or justice. Of this nature is the following:–

And stand we deedless, O eternal shame!

Till Hector's arm involve the ships in flame?
Haste, let us join, and combat side by side.
("Iliad," xi. 313. For the four following see
"Odyssey," iii. 52; "Iliad," xxiv. 560 and 584;
"Odyssey," xvi. 274.)

For to see a man of the greatest wisdom in danger of being totally cut off with all those that take part with him, and yet affected less with fear of death than of shame and dishonor, must needs excite in a young man a passionate affection for virtue. And this,

Joyed was the Goddess, for she much did prize
A man that was alike both just and wise,

teacheth us to infer that the Deity delights not in a rich or a proper or a strong man, but in one that is furnished with wisdom and justice. Again, when the same goddess (Minerva) saith that the reason why she did not desert or neglect Ulysses was that he was

Gentle, of ready wit, of prudent mind,

she therein tells us that, of all things pertaining to us, nothing is dear to the gods and godlike but our virtue, seeing like naturally delights in like.

And seeing, moreover, that it both seemeth and really is a great thing to be able to moderate a man's anger, but a greater by far to guard a man's self beforehand by prudence, that he fall not into it nor be surprised by it, therefore also such passages as tend that way are not slightly to be represented to the readers; for example, that Achilles himself–who was a man of no great forbearance, nor inclined to such meekness–yet admonishes Priam to be calm and not to provoke him, thus,

Move me no more (Achilles thus replies,
While kindling anger sparkled in his eyes),
Nor seek by tears my steady soul to bend:
To yield thy Hector I myself intend:
Cease; lest, neglectful of high Jove's command,
I show thee, king, thou tread'st on hostile land;

and that he himself first washeth and decently covereth the body of Hector and then puts it into a chariot, to prevent his father's seeing it so unworthily mangled as it was,–

Lest the unhappy sire,
Provoked to passion, once more rouse to ire
The stern Pelides; and nor sacred age,
Nor Jove's command, should check the rising rage.

For it is a piece of admirable prudence for a man so prone to anger, as being by nature hasty and furious, to understand himself so well as to set a guard upon his own inclinations, and by avoiding provocations to keep his passion at due distance by the use of reason, lest he should be unawares surprised by it. And after the same manner must the man that is apt to be drunken forearm himself against that vice; and he that is given to wantonness, against lust, as Agesilaus refused to receive a kiss from a beautiful person addressing to him, and Cyrus would not so much as endure to see Panthea. Whereas, on the contrary, those that are not virtuously bred are wont to gather fuel to inflame their passions, and voluntarily to abandon themselves to those temptations to which of themselves they are endangered. But Ulysses does not only restrain his own anger, but (perceiving by the discourse of his son Telemachus, that through indignation conceived against such evil men he was great-ly provoked) he blunts his passion too beforehand, and composeth him to calmness and patience, thus:–

> *There, if base scorn insult my reverend age,*
> *Bear it, my son! repress thy rising rage.*
> *If outraged, cease that outrage to repel;*
> *Bear it, my son! howe'er thy heart rebel.*

For as men are not wont to put bridles on their horses when they are running in full speed, but bring them bridled beforehand to the race; so do they use to preoccupy and predispose the minds of those per-sons with rational considerations to enable them to encounter passion, whom they perceive to be too mettlesome and unmanageable upon the sight of provoking objects.

Furthermore, the young man is not altogether to neglect names themselves when he meets with them; though he is not obliged to give much heed to such idle descants as those of Cleanthes, who, while he professeth himself an interpreter, plays the trifler, as in these passages of Homer: [Greek omitted], ("Iliad," iii. 320; xvi. 233.) For he will needs read the two of these words joined into one, and make them [Greek omitted] for that the air evaporated from the earth by exhala-tion [Greek omitted] is so called. Yea, and Chrysippus too, though he does not so trifle, yet is very jejune, while he hunts after improbable etymologies. As when he will need force the words [Greek omitted] to import Jupiter's excellent faculty in speaking and powerfulness to persuade thereby.

But such things as these are fitter to be left to the examination of grammarians and we are rather to insist upon such passages as are both profitable and persuasive. Such, for instance, as these;–

> *My early youth was bred to martial pains,*

My soul impels me to the embattled plains!
How skill'd he was in each obliging art;
The mildest manners, and the gentlest heart.
(Ibid. vi. 444; xvii. 671.)

For while the author tells us that fortitude may be taught, and that an obliging and graceful way of conversing with others is to be gotten by art and the use of reason, he exhorts us not to neglect the improvement of ourselves, but by observing our teachers' instructions to learn a becoming carriage, as knowing that clownishness and cowardice argue ill-breeding and ignorance. And very suitable to what hath been said is that which is said of Jupiter and Neptune:–

Gods of one source, of one ethereal race,
Alike divine, and heaven their native place;
But Jove the greater; first born of the skies,
And more than men or Gods supremely wise.
("Iliad," xiii. 354.)

For the poet therein pronounceth wisdom to be the most divine and royal quality of all; as placing therein the greatest excellency of Jupiter himself, and judging all virtues else to be necessarily consequent thereunto. We are also to accustom a young man attentively to hear such things as these:–

Urge him with truth to frame his fair replies:
And sure he will, for wisdom never lies:
The praise of wisdom, in thy youth obtain'd,
An act so rash, Antilochus, has stain'd:
Say, is it just, my friend, that Hector's ear
From such a warrior such a speech should hear?
I deemed thee once the wisest of thy kind,
But ill this insult suits a prudent mind.
("Odyssey," iii. 20; "Iliad," xxiii. 570; xvii. 170.)

These speeches teach us that it is beneath wise men to lie or to deal otherwise than fairly, even in games, or to blame other men without just cause. And when the poet attributes Pindarus's violation of the truce to his folly, he withal declares his judgment that a wise man will not be guilty of an unjust action. The like may we also infer concerning continence, taking our ground for it from these passages:–

For him Antaea burn'd with lawless flame,
And strove to tempt him from the paths of fame:
In vain she tempted the relentless youth,
Endued with wisdom, sacred fear, and truth:
At first, with worthy shame and decent pride,

The royal dame, his lawless suit denied!
For virtue's image yet possessed her mind:
("Iliad," vi. 160; "Odyssey," iii. 265.)

in which speeches the poet assigns wisdom to be the cause of continence. And when in exhortations made to encourage soldiers to fight, he speaks in this manner:–

What mean you, Lycians? Stand! O stand, for shame!
Yet each reflect who prizes fame or breath,
On endless infamy, on instant death;
For, lo! the fated time, the appointed shore;
Hark! the gates burst, the brazen barriers roar!
("Iliad," xvi. 422; xiii. 121.)

he seems to intimate that prudent men are valiant men; because they fear the shame of base actions, and can trample on pleasures and stand their ground in the greatest hazards. Whence Timotheus, in the play called Persae, takes occasion handsomely to exhort the Grecians thus:–

Brave soldiers of just shame in awe should stand;
For the blushing face oft helps the fighting hand.

And Aeschylus also makes it a point of wisdom not to be blown up with pride when a man is honored, nor to be moved or elevated with the acclamations of a multitude, writing thus of Amphiaraus:–

His shield no emblem bears; his generous soul
Wishes to be, not to appear, the best;
While the deep furrows of his noble mind
Harvests of wise and prudent counsel bear.
(See note in the same passage of
Aeschylus (Sept. 591), i. 210. (G).)

For it is the part of a wise man to value himself upon the consciousness of his own true worth and excellency.

Whereas, therefore, all inward perfections are reducible to wisdom, it appears that all sorts of virtue and learning are included in it

Again, boys may be instructed, by reading the poets as they ought, to draw even from those passages that are most suspected as wicked and absurd something that is useful and profitable; as the bee is taught by Nature to gather the sweetest and most pleasant honey from the harshest flowers and sharpest thorns. It does indeed at the first blush cast a shrewd suspicion on Agmemnon of taking a bribe, when Homer tells us that he discharged that rich man from the wars who presented him with his fleet mare Aethe:–

Whom rich Echepolus, more rich than brave,

To 'scape the wars, to Agamemnon gave
(Aethe her name), at home to end his days;
Base wealth preferring to eternal praise.
("Iliad," xxiii. 297.)

Yet, as saith Aristotle, it was well done of him to prefer a good beast before such a man. For, the truth is, a dog or ass is of more value than a timorous and cowardly man that wallows in wealth and luxury. Again, Thetis seems to do indecently, when she exhorts her son to follow his pleasures and minds him of companying with women. But even here, on the other side, the continency of Achilles is worthy to be considered; who, though he dearly loved Briseis,—newly returned to him too,—yet, when he knew his life to be near its end, does not hasten to the fruition of pleasures, nor, when he mourns for his friend Patroclus, does he (as most men are wont) shut himself up from all business and neglect his duty, but only bars himself from recreations for his sorrow's sake, while yet he gives himself up to action and military employments. And Archilochus is not praiseworthy either, who, in the midst of his mourning for his sister's husband drowned in the sea, contrives to dispel his grief by drinking and merriment. And yet he gives this plausible reason to justify that practice of his,

To drink and dance, rather than mourn, I choose;
Nor wrong I him, whom mourning can't reduce.

For, if he judged himself to do nothing amiss when he followed sports and banquets, sure, we shall not do worse, if in whatever circumstances we follow the study of philosophy, or manage public affairs, or go to the market or to the Academy, or follow our husbandry. Wherefore those corrections also are not to be rejected which Cleanthes and Antisthenes have made use of. For Antisthenes, seeing the Athenians all in a tumult in the theatre, and justly, upon the pronunciation of this verse,—

Except what men think wrong, there's nothing ill,
(From the "Aeolus" of Euripides, Frag. 19.)

presently subjoined this corrective,

What's wrong is so,—believe men what they will.

And Cleanthes, hearing this passage concerning wealth:—

Great is th' advantage that great wealth attends,
For oft with it we purchase health and friends,
(Euripides, "Electra," 428.)

presently altered it thus:

Great disadvantage oft attends on wealth;
We purchase whores with't and destroy our health.

And Zeno corrected that of Sophocles,

> *The man that in a tyrant's palace dwells*
> *His liberty for's entertainment sells,*

after this manner:–

> *No: if he came in free, he cannot lose*
> *His liberty, though in a tyrant's house;*

meaning by a free man one that is undaunted and magnanimous, and one of a spirit too great to stoop beneath itself. And why may not we also, by some such acclamations as those, call off young men to the better side, by using some things spoken by poets after the same manner? For example, it is said,

> *'Tis all that in this life one can require,*
> *To hit the mark he aims at in desire.*

To which we may reply thus:–

> *'Tis false; except one level his desire*
> *At what's expedient, and no more require.*

For it is an unhappy thing and not to be wished, for a man to obtain and be master of what he desires if it be inexpedient. Again this saying,

> *Thou, Agamemnon, must thyself prepare*
> *Of joy and grief by turns to take thy share,*
> *Thy father, Atreus, sure, ne'er thee begat,*
> *To be an unchanged favorite of Fate:*
> *(Euripides, "Iphigenia at Aulus," 29.)*

we may thus invert:–

> *Thy father, Atreus, never thee begat,*
> *To be an unchanged favorite of Fate:*
> *Therefore, if moderate thy fortunes are,*
> *Thou shouldst rejoice always, and grief forbear.*

Again it is said,

> *Alas! this ill comes from the powers divine*
> *That oft we see what's good, yet it decline.*
> *(From the "Chrysippus" of Euripides, Frag. 838.)*

Yea, rather, say we, it is a brutish and irrational and wretched fault of ours, that when we understand better things, we are carried away to the pursuit of those which are worse, through our intemperance and effeminacy. Again, one says,

> *For not the teacher's speech but practice moves.*
> *(From Menander.)*

Yea, rather, say we, both the speech and practice,–or the practice by the means of speech,–as the horse is managed with the bridle, and the ship with the helm. For virtue hath no instrument so suitable and agreeable to human nature to work on men withal, as that of rational discourse.

Again, we meet with this character of some person:–

    A. *Is he more inclined to male or female love?*

    B. *He bends both ways, where beauty moves.*

But it had been better said thus:–

    He's flexible to both, where virtue moves.

For it is no commendation of a man's dexterity to be tossed up and down as pleasure and beauty move him, but an argument rather of a weak and unstable disposition. Once more, this speech,

    Religion damps the courage of our minds,

    And ev'n wise men to cowardice inclines,

is by no means to be allowed; but rather the contrary,

    Religion truly fortifies men's minds,

    And a wise man to valiant acts inclines,

and gives not occasion of fear to any but weak and foolish persons and such as are ungrateful to the Deity, who are apt to look on that divine power and principle which is the cause of all good with suspicion and jealousy, as being hurtful unto them. And so much for that which I call correction of poets' sayings.

There is yet another way of improving poems, taught us well by Chrysippus; which is, by accommodation of any saying, to transfer that which is useful and serviceable in it to divers things of the same kind. For whereas Hesiod saith,

    If but a cow miscarry, the common fame

    Upon the next ill neighbor lays the blame;

    (Hesiod, "Work and Days," 348.)

the same may be applied to a man's dog or ass or any other beast of his which is liable to the like mischance. Again, Euripides saith,

    How can that man be called a slave, who slights

    Ev'n death itself, which servile spirits frights?

the like whereof may be said of hard labor or painful sickness. For as physicians, finding by experience the force of any medicine in the cure of some one disease, make use of it by accommodation, proportionably to every other disease of affinity thereto, so are we to deal with such speeches as are of a common import and apt to communicate their value to other things; we must not confine them to that one thing only to which they were at first adapted, but transfer them to all other of like nature, and accustom young men by many parallel instances to see the communicableness of them, and exercise the promptness of their wits in such applications so that when Menander says,

    Happy is he who wealth and wisdom hath,

they may be able to judge that the same is fitly applicable to glory and authority and eloquence also. And the reproof which Ulysses gives Achilles, when he found him sitting in Scyrus in the apartment of the young ladies,

> *Thou, who from noblest Greeks deriv'st thy race,*
> *Dost thou with spinning wool thy birth disgrace?*

may be as well given to the prodigal, to him that undertakes any dishonest way of living, yea, to the slothful and unlearned person, thus:–

> *Thou, who from noblest Greeks deriv'st thy race,*
> *Dost thou with fuddling thy great birth disgrace?*

or dost thou spend thy time in dicing, or quail-striking, (The word here used [Greek omitted] denotes a game among the Grecians, which Suidas describes to be the setting of quails in a round compass or ring and striking at the heads of them; and he that in the ring struck one had liberty to strike at the rest in order, but he that missed was obliged to set up quails for others; and this they did by turns.) or deal in adulterate wares or griping usury, not minding anything that is great and worthy thy noble extraction? So when they read,

> *For wealth, the God most served, I little care,*
> *Since the worst men his favors often wear,*
> *(From the "Aeolus," of Euripides, Frag. 20.)*

they may be able to infer, therefore, as little regard is to be had to glory and bodily beauty and princely robes and priestly garlands, all which also we see to be the enjoyments of very bad men. Again, when they read this passage,

> *A coward father propagates his vice,*
> *And gets a son heir to his cowardice,*

they may in truth apply the same to intemperance, to superstition, to envy, and all other diseases of men's minds. Again, whereas it is handsomely said of Homer,

> *Unhappy Paris, fairest to behold!*

and

> *Hector, of noble form.*
> *("Iliad," iii. 39; xvii. 142.)*

for herein he shows that a man who hath no greater excellency than that of beauty to commend him deserves to have it mentioned with contempt and ignominy,–such expressions we should make use of in like cases to repress the insolence of such as bear themselves high upon the account of such things as are of no real value, and to teach young men to look upon such compellations as "O thou richest of men," and "O thou that excellest in feasting, in multitudes of attendants, in herds of cattle, yea, and in eloquent speaking itself," to be (as they are indeed) expressions that import reproach and infamy. For, in truth, a man that designs to excel ought to endeavor it in those things that are in themselves most excellent, and to become chief in the chiefest, and great in the greatest things. Whereas glory that ariseth from things in themselves small and inconsiderable is inglorious and contemptible. To mind us whereof we shall never be at a loss for instances, if, in reading Homer especially, we observe how he applieth the expressions that import praise or disgrace; wherein we have clear proof that he makes small account of the good things either of the body or Fortune. And first of all, in meetings and salutations, men do not call others fair or rich or strong, but use such terms of commendation as these:–

> Son of Laertes, from great Jove deriving
> Thy pedigree, and skilled in wise contriving;
> Hector, thou son of Priam, whose advice
> With wisest Jove's men count of equal price;
> Achilles, son of Peleus, whom all story
> Shall mention as the Grecians greatest glory;
> Divine Patroclus, for thy worth thou art,
> Of all the friends I have, lodged next my heart.
> ("Iliad," ii. 173; vii. 47; xix. 216; xi. 608.)

And moreover, when they speak disgracefully of any person, they touch not at bodily defects, but direct all their reproaches to vicious actions; as for instance:–

> A dogged-looking, drunken beast thou art,
> And in thy bosom hast a deer's faint heart;
> Ajax at brawling valiant still,
> Whose tongue is used to speaking ill;
> A tongue so loose hung, and so vain withal,
> Idomeneus, becomes thee not at all;
> Ajax thy tongue doth oft offend;
> For of thy boasting there's no end.
> (Ibid. i. 225; xxiii. 483 and 474-479; xiii. 824.)

Lastly, when Ulysses reproacheth Thersites, he objecteth not to him his lameness nor his baldness nor his hunched back, but the vicious quality of indiscreet babbling. On the other side, when Juno means to express a dalliance or motherly fondness to her son Vulcan, she courts him with an epithet taken from his halting, thus,

> Rouse thee, my limping son!
> (Ibid, xxi. 331.)

In this instance, Homer does (as it were) deride those who are ashamed of their lameness or blindness, as not thinking anything a disgrace that is not in itself disgraceful, nor any person liable to a reproach for that which is not imputable to himself but to Fortune. These two great advantages may be made by those who frequently study poets;–the learning moderation, to keep them from unseasonable and foolish reproaching others with their misfortunes, when they themselves enjoy a constant current of prosperity; and magnanimity, that under variety of accidents they be not dejected nor disturbed, but meekly bear the being scoffed at, reproached, and drolled upon. Especially, let them have that saying of Philemon ready at hand in such cases:–

> *That spirit's well in tune, whose sweet repose*
> *No railer's tongue can ever discompose.*

And yet, if one that so rails do himself merit reprehension, thou mayst take occasion to retort upon him his own vices and inordinate passions; as when Adrastus in the tragedy is assaulted thus by Alcmaeon,

> *Thy sister's one that did her husband kill,*

he returns him this answer,

> *But thou thyself thy mother's blood did spill.*

For as they who scourge a man's garments do not touch the body, so those that turn other men's evil fortunes or mean births to matter of reproach do only with vanity and folly enough lash their external circumstances, but touch not their internal part, the soul, nor those things which truly need correction and reproof.

Moreover, as we have above taught you to abate and lessen the credit of evil and hurtful poems by setting in opposition to them the famous speeches and sentences of such worthy men as have managed public affairs, so will it be useful to us, where we find any things in them of civil and profitable import, to improve and strengthen them by testimonies and proofs taken from philosophers, withal giving these the credit of being the first inventors of them. For this is both just and profitable to be done, seeing by this means such sayings receive an additional strength and esteem, when it appears that what is spoken on the stage or sung to the harp or occurs in a scholar's lesson is agreeable to the doctrines of Pythagoras and Plato, and that the sentences of Chile and Bias tend to the same issue with those that are found in the authors which children read. Therefore must we industriously show them that these poetical sentences,

> *Not these, O daughter, are thy proper cares,*
> *Thee milder arts befit, and softer wars;*
> *Sweet smiles are thine, and kind endearing charms;*
> *To Mars and Pallas leave the deeds of arms;*

> *Jove's angry with thee, when thy unmanaged rage*
> *With those that overmatch thee doth engage;*
> *("Iliad," v. 248; xi. 543.)*

differ not in substance but bear plainly the same sense with that philosophical sentence, Know thyself, And these

> *Fools, who by wrong seek to augment their store,*
> *And know not how much half than all is more;*
> *Of counsel giv'n to mischievous intents,*
> *The man that gives it most of all repents;*
> *(Hesiod, "Works and Days," 40 and 266.)*

are of near kin to what we find in the determination of Plato, in his books entitled Gorgias and Concerning the Commonwealth, to wit, that it is worse to do than to suffer injury, and that a man more endamageth himself when he hurts another, than he would be damnified if he were the sufferer. And that of Aeschylus,

> *Cheer up, friend; sorrows, when they highest climb,*
> *What they exceed in measure want in time,*

we must inform them, is but the same famous sentence which is so much admired in Epicurus, that great griefs are but short, and those that are of long continuance are but small. The former clause whereof is that which Aeschylus here saith expressly, and the latter but the consequent of that. For if a great and intense sorrow do not last, then that which doth last is not great nor hard to be borne. And those words of Thespis,

> *Seest not how Jove,–because he cannot lie*
> *Nor vaunt nor laugh at impious drollery,*
> *And pleasure's charms are things to him unknown,–*
> *Among the gods wears the imperial crown?*

wherein differ they from what Plato says, that the divine nature is remote from both joy and grief? And that saying of Bacchylides,

> *Virtue alone doth lasting honor gain,*
> *But men of basest souls oft wealth attain;*

and those of Euripides much of the same import,

> *Hence temperance in my esteem excels,*
> *Because it constantly with good men dwells;*
> *However you may strive for honor*
> *And you may seem to have secured by wealth virtue,*
> *Good men will place you among the miserable;*

do they not evidently confirm to us what the philosophers say of riches and other external good things, that without virtue they are fruitless and unprofitable enjoyments?

Now thus to accommodate and reconcile poetry to the doctrines of philosophy strips it of its fabulous and personated parts, and makes those things which it delivers usefully to acquire also the reputation of gravity; and over and above, it inclines the soul of a young man to receive the impressions of philosophical precepts. For he will hereby be enabled to come to them not altogether destitute of some sort of relish of them, not as to things that he has heard nothing of before, nor with an head confusedly full of the false notions which he hath sucked in from the daily tattle of his mother and nurse,–yea, sometimes too of his father and pedant,–who have been wont to speak of rich men as the happy men and mention them always with honor, and to express themselves concerning death and pain with horror, and to look on virtue without riches and glory as a thing of nought and not to be desired. Whence it comes to pass, that when such youths first do hear things of a quite contrary nature from philosophers, they are surprised with a kind of amazement, trouble, and stupid astonishment, which makes them afraid to entertain or endure them, except they be dealt with as those who come out of very great darkness into the light of the bright sun, that is, be first accustomed for a while to behold those doctrines in fabulous authors, as in a kind of false light, which hath but a moderate brightness and is easy to be looked on and borne without disturbance to the weak sight. For having before heard or read from poets such things as these are,–

> *Mourn one's birth, as the entrance of all ills;*
> *But joy at death, as that which finishes misery;*
> *Of worldly things a mortal needs but two;*
> *A drink of water and the gift of Ceres:*
> *O tyranny, to barbarous nations dear!*
> *This in all human happiness is chief,*
> *To know as little as we can of grief;*

they are the less disturbed and offended when they hear from philosophers that no man ought to be overconcerned about death; that riches are limited to the necessities of nature; that the happiness of man's life doth not consist in the abundance of wealth or vastness of employments or height of authority and power, but in freedom from sorrow, in moderation of passions, and in such a temper of mind as measures all things by the use of Nature.

Wherefore, upon all these accounts, as well as for all the reasons before mentioned, youth stands in need of good government to manage it in the reading of poetry, that being free from all prejudicate opinions, and rather instructed beforehand in conformity thereunto, it may with more calmness, friendliness, and familiarity pass from thence to the study of philosophy.

Abstract of a Comparison between Aristophane and Menander

To SPEAK IN SUM and in general, he prefers Menander by far; and as to particulars, he adds what here ensues. Aristophanes, he saith, is importune, theatric, and sordid in his expression; but Menander not so at all. For the rude and vulgar person is taken with the things the former speaketh; but the well-bred man will be quite out of humor with them. I mean, his opposed terms, his words of one cadence, and his derivatives. For the one makes use of these with due observance and but seldom, and bestows care upon them; but the other frequently, unseasonably, and frigidly. "For he is much commended," said he, "for ducking the chamberlains, they being indeed not chamberlains [Greek omitted] but witches."[Greek omitted]. And again,–"This rascal breathes out nothing but roguery and sycophancy"; and "Smite him well in his belly with the entrails and the guts"; and, "By laughing I shall get to Laughington [Greek omitted]"; and, "Thou poor sharded ostracized pot, what shall I do with thee?" and, "To you women surely he is a mad plague, for he was brought up among these mad worts";–and, "Look here, how the moths have eaten away my crest"; and, "Bring me hither the gorgon-backed circle of my shield"; "Give me the round-backed circle of a cheese-cake";–and much more of the same kind. (See Aristophanes, "Knights," 437, 455; "Thesmophoriazusae," 455; Acharnians," 1109, 1124.) There is then in the structure of his words something tragic and something comic, something blustering and something low, an obscurity, a vulgarness, a turgidness, and a strutting, with a nauseous prattling and fooling. And as his style has so great varieties and dissonances in it, so neither doth he give to his persons what is fitting and proper to each,–as state (for instance) to a prince, force to an orator, innocence to a woman, meanness of language to a poor man, and sauciness to a tradesman,–but he deals out to every person, as it were by lot, such words as come next to his hand, and you would scarce discern whether he be a son a father, a peasant, a god, an old woman, or a hero that is talking.

But now Menander's phrase is so well turned and contempered with itself, and so everywhere conspiring, that, while it traverses many passions and humors and is accommodated to all sorts of persons, it still shows the same, and retains its semblance even in trite, familiar, and everyday expressions. And if his master do now and then require something of rant and noise, he doth but (like a skilful flutist) set open all the holes of his pipe, and their presently stop them again with good decorum and restore the tune to its natural state. And though there be a great number of excellent artists of all professions, yet never did any shoemaker make the same sort of shoe, or tireman the same sort of visor, or tailor the same sort of garment, to fit a man, a woman, a child, an old man, and a slave. But Menander hath so addressed his style, as to proportion it to every sex, condition, and age; and this, though he took the business in hand when he was very young, and died in the vigor of his composition and action, when, as Aristotle tells us, authors receive most and greatest improvement in their styles. If a man shall then compare the middle and last with the first of Menander's plays, he will by them easily conceive what others he would have added to them, had he had but longer life.

He adds further, that of dramatic exhibitors, some address themselves to the crowd and populace, and others again to a few; but it is a hard matter to say which of them all knew what was befitting in both the kinds. But Aristophanes is neither grateful to the vulgar, nor tolerable to the wise; but it fares with his poesy as it doth with a courtesan who, when she finds she is now stricken and past her prime, counterfeits a sober matron, and then the vulgar cannot endure her affectation, and the better sort abominate her lewdness and wicked nature. But Menander hath with his charms shown himself every way sufficient for satisfaction, being the sole lecture, argument, and dispute at theatres, schools, and at tables; hereby rendering his poesy the most universal ornament that was ever produced by Greece, and showing what and how extraordinary his ability in language was, while he passes every way with an irresistible persuasion, and gains every man's ear and understanding who has any knowledge of the Greek tongue. And for what other reason in truth should a man of parts and erudition be at the pains to frequent the theatre, but for the sake of Menander only? And when are the playhouses better filled with men of letters, than when his comic mask is exhibited?

And at private entertainments among friends, for whom doth the table more justly make room or Bacchus give place than for Menander? To philosophers also and hard students (as painters are wont, when they have tired out their eyes at their work, to divert them to certain florid and green colors) Menander is a repose from their auditors and intense thinkings, and entertains their minds with gay shady meadows refreshed with cool and gentle breezes.

He adds, moreover, that though this city breeds at this time very many and excellent representers of comedy, Menander's plays participate of a plenteous and divine salt, as though they were made of the very sea out of which Venus herself sprang. But that of Aristophanes is harsh and coarse, and hath in it an angry and biting sharpness. And for my part I cannot tell where his so much boasted ability lies, whether in his style or persons. The parts he acts I am sure are quite overacted and depraved. His knave (for instance) is not fine, but dirty; his peasant is not assured, but stupid; his droll is not jocose, but ridiculous; and his lover is not gay, but lewd. So that to me the man seems not to have written his poesy for any temperate person, but to have intended his smut and obscenity for the debauched and lewd, his invective and satire for the malicious and ill-humored.

The Malice of Herodotus

THE STYLE, O Alexander, of Herodotus, as being simple, free, and easily suiting itself to its subject, has deceived many; but more, a persuasion of his dispositions being equally sincere. For it is not only (as Plato says) an extreme injustice, to make a show of being just when one is not so; but it is also the highest malignity, to pretend to simplicity and mildness and be in the meantime really most malicious. Now since he principally exerts his malice against the Boeotians and Corinthians, though without sparing any other, I think myself obliged to defend our ancestors and the truth against this part of his writings, since those who would detect all his other lies and fictions would have need of many books. But, as Sophocles has it, the face of persuasion, is prevalent, especially when delivered in the good language, and such as has power to conceal both the other absurdities and the ill-nature of the writer. King Philip told the Greeks who revolted from him to Titus Quinctius that they had got a more polished, but a longer lasting yoke. So the malice of Herodotus is indeed more polite and delicate than that of Theopompus, yet it pinches closer, and makes a more severe impression,–not unlike to those winds which, blowing secretly through narrow chinks, are sharper than those that are more diffused. Now it seems to me very convenient to delineate, as it were, in the rough draught, those signs and marks that distinguish a malicious narration from a candid and unbiassed one, applying afterwards every point we shall examine to such as appertain to them.

First then, whoever in relating a story shall use the odious terms when gentler expressions might do as well, is it not to be esteemed impartial, but an enjoyer of his own fancy, in putting the worst construction on things; as if any one, instead of saying Nicias is too superstitious, should call him fanatic, or should accuse Cleon of presumption and madness rather than of inconsiderateness in speech.------Secondly, when a writer, catching hold of a fault which has no reference to his story, shall draw it into the relation of such affairs as need it not, extending his narrative with cicumlocutions, only that he may insert a man's misfortune, offence, or discommendable action, it is manifest that he delights in speaking evil. Therefore Thucydides would not clearly relate the faults of Cleon, which were very numerous; and as for Hyperbolus the orator, having touched at him in a word and called him an ill man, he let him go. Philistus also passed over all those outrages committed by Dionysius on the barbarians which had no connection with the Grecian affairs. For the excursions and digressions of history are principally allowed for fables and antiquities, and sometimes also for encomiums. But he who makes reproaches and detractions an addition to his discourse seems to incur the tragedian's curse on the "collector of men's calamities."

Now the opposite to this is known to every one, as the omitting to relate some good and laudable action, which, though it may seem not to be reprehensible, yet is then done maliciously when the omission happens in a place that is pertinent to the history. For to praise unwillingly is so far from being more civil than to dispraise willingly, that it is perhaps rather more uncivil.

The fourth sign of a partial disposition in writing of history I take to be this: When a matter is related in two or more several manners, and the historian shall embrace the worst. Sophisters indeed are permitted, for the obtaining either of profit or reputation, to undertake the defence of the worst cause; for they neither create any firm belief of the matter, nor yet do they deny that they are often pleased in maintaining paradoxes and making incredible things appear probable. But an historian is then just, when he asserts such things as he knows to be true, and of those that are uncertain reports rather the better than the worse. Nay, there are many writers who wholly omit the worse. Thus Ephorus writes of Themistocles, that he was acquainted with the treason of Pausanias and his negotiations with the King's lieutenants, but that he neither consented to it, nor hearkened to Pausanias's proffers of making him partaker of his hopes; and Thucydides left the whole matter out of his story, as judging it to be false.

Moreover, in things confessed to have been done, but for doing which the cause and intention is unknown, he who casts his conjectures on the worst side is partial and malicious. Thus do the comedians, who affirm the Peloponnesian war to have been kindled by Pericles for the love of Aspasia or the sake of Phidias, and not through any desire of honor, or ambition of pulling down the Peloponnesian pride and giving place in nothing to the Lacedaemonians. For those who suppose a bad cause for laudable works and commendable actions, endeavoring by calumnies to insinuate sinister suspicions of the actor when they cannot openly discommend the act,–as they that impute the killing of Alexander the tyrant by Theba not to any magnanimity or hatred of vice, but to a certain feminine jealousy and passion, and those that say Cato slew himself for fear Caesar should put him to a more shameful death,–such as these are manifestly in the highest degree envious and malicious.

An historical narration is also more or less guilty of malice, according as it relates the manner of the action; as if one should be said to have performed an exploit rather by money than bravery, as some affirm of Philip; or else easily and without any labor, as it is said of Alexander; or else not by prudence, but by Fortune, as the enemies of Timotheus painted cities falling into his nets as he lay sleeping. For they undoubtedly diminish the greatness and beauty of the actions, who deny the performer of them to have done them generously, industriously, virtuously, and by themselves.

Moreover, those who will directly speak ill of any one incur the reproach of moroseness, rashness, and madness, unless they keep within measure. But they who send forth calumnies obliquely, as if they were shooting arrows out of corners, and then stepping back think to conceal themselves by saying they do not believe what they most earnestly desire to have believed, whilst they disclaim all malice, condemn themselves also of farther disingenuity.

Next to these are they who with their reproaches intermix some praises, as did Aristoxenus, who, having termed Socrates unlearned, ignorant, and libidinous, added, Yet was he free from injustice. For, as they who flatter artificially and craftily sometimes mingle light reprehensions with their many and great praises, joining this liberty of speech as a sauce to their flattery; so malice, that it may gain belief to its accusations, adds also praise.

We might here also reckon up more notes; but these are sufficient to let us understand the nature and manners of Herodotus.

First therefore,–beginning, as the proverb is, with Vesta,–whereas all the Grecians affirm Io, daughter to Inachus, to have been worshipped with divine honor by the barbarians, and by her glory to have left her name to many seas and principal ports, and to have given a source and original to most noble and royal families; this famous author says of her, that she gave herself to certain Phoenician merchants, having been not unwillingly defloured by a mariner, and fearing lest she should be found by her friends to be with child (Herodotus, i. 5.) And he belies the Phoenicians as having delivered these things of her, and says that the Persian stories testify of her being carried away by the Phoenicians with other women. (Ibid. i. 1.) Presently after, he gives sentence on the bravest and greatest exploits of Greece, saying that the Trojan war was foolishly undertaken for an ill woman. For it is manifest, says he, that had they not been willing they had never been ravished. (Ibid. i. 4.) Let us then say, that the gods also acted foolishly, in inflicting their indignation on the Spartans for abusing the daughters of Scedasus the Leuctrian, and in punishing Ajax for the violation of Cassandra. For it is manifest, if we believe Herodotus, that if they had not been willing they had never been defiled. And yet he himself said that Aristomenes was taken alive by the Spartans; and the same afterwards happened to Philopoemen, general of the Achaeans; and the Carthaginians took Regulus, the consul of the Romans; than whom there are not easily to be found more valiant and warlike men. Nor is it to be wondered, since even leopards and tigers are taken alive by men. But Herodotus blames the poor women that have been abused by violence, and patronizes their ravishers.

Nay, he is so favorable to the barbarians, that, acquitting Busiris of those human sacrifices and that slaughter of his guests for which he is accused, and attributing by his testimony to the Egyptians much religion and justice, he endeavors to cast that abominable wickedness and those impious murders on the Grecians. For in his Second Book he says, that Menelaus, having received Helen from Proteus and having been honored by him with many presents, showed himself a most unjust and wicked man; for wanting a favorable wind to set sail, he found out an impious device, and having taken two of the inhabitants' boys, consulted their entrails; for which villany being hated and persecuted, he fled with his ships directly into Libya. (See Herodotus, ii. 45.) From what Egyptian this story proceeds, I know not. For, on the contrary, many honors are even at this day given by the Egyptians to Helen and Menelaus.

The same Herodotus, that he may still be like himself, says that the Persians learned the defiling of the male sex from the Greeks. (Ibid, i. 135.) And yet how could the Greeks have taught this impurity to the Persians, amongst whom, as is confessed by many, boys had been castrated before ever they arrived in the Grecian seas? He writes also, that the Greeks were instructed by the Egyptians in their pomps, solemn festivals, and worship of the twelve gods; that Melampus also learned of the Egyptians the name of Dionysus (or Bacchus) and taught it the other Greeks; that the mysteries likewise and rites of Ceres were brought out of Egypt by the daughters of Danaus; and that the Egyptians were wont to beat themselves and make great lamentation, but yet he himself refused to tell the names of their deities, but concealed them in silence. As to Hercules and Bacchus, whom the Egyptians named gods, and the Greeks very aged men, he nowhere has such scruples and hesitation; although he places also the Egyptian Hercules amongst the gods of the second rank, and Bacchus amongst those of the third, as having had some beginning of their being and not being eternal, and yet he pronounces those to be gods; but to the gods Bacchus and Hercules, as having been mortal and being now demi-gods, he thinks we ought to perform anniversary solemnities, but not to sacrifice to them as to gods. The same also he said of Pan, overthrowing the most venerable and purest sacrifices of the Greeks by the proud vanities and mythologies of the Egyptians. (For the passages referred to in this chapter, see Herodotus, ii. 48, 51, 145, 146, 171.)

Nor is this impious enough; but moreover, deriving the pedigree of Hercules from Perseus, he says that Perseus was an Assyrian, as the Persians affirm. "But the leaders," says he, "of the Dorians may appear to be descended in a right line from the Egyptians, reckoning their ancestors from before Danae and Acrisius." (Herodotus, vi. 53, 54.) Here he has wholly passed by Epaphus, Io, Iasus, and Argus, being ambitious not only to make the other Herculeses Egyptians and Phoenicians but to carry this also, whom himself declares to have been the third, out of Greece to the barbarians. But of the ancient learned writers, neither Homer, nor Hesiod, nor Archilochus, nor Pisander, nor Stesichorus, nor Alcman, nor Pindar, makes any mention of the Egyptian or the Phoenician Hercules, but all acknowledge this our own Boeotian and Argive Hercules.

Now of the seven sages, whom he calls Sophisters, he affirms Thales to have been a barbarian, descended of the Phoenicians. (Ibid, i. 170.) Speaking ill also of the gods under the person of Solon, he has these words: "Thou, O Croesus, askest me concerning human affairs, who know that every one of the deities envious and tumultuous." (Ibid, i. 32.) Thus attributing to Solon what himself thinks of the gods, he joins malice to blasphemy. Having made use also of Pittacus in some trivial matters, not worth the mentioning, he has passed over the greatest and gallantest action that was ever done by him. For when the Athenians and Mitylenaeans were at war about Sigaeum, Phrynon, the Athenian general, challenging whoever would come forth to a single combat, Pittacus advanced to meet him, and catching him in a net, slew that stout and giant-like man; for which when the Mitylaenans offered him great presents, darting his javelin as far as he could out of his hand, he desired only so much ground as he should reach with that throw; and the place is to this day called Pittacium. Now what does Herodotus, when he comes to this? Instead of Pittacus's valiant act, he tells us the fight of Alcaeus the poet, who throwing away his arms ran out of the battle; by thus not writing of honorable deeds and not passing over such as are dishonorable, he offers his testimony to those who say, that from one and the same malice proceed both envy and a rejoicing at other men's harms. (Herodotus v. 95.)

After this, he accuses of treason the Alcmaeonidae who showed themselves generous men, and delivered their country from tyranny. (Ibid. i. 61.) He says, that they received Pisistratus after his banishment and got him called home, on condition he should marry the daughter of Megacles; but the damsel saying to her mother, Do you see, mother, how I am known by Pisistratus contrary to nature? The Alcmaeonidae were so offended at this villany, that they expelled the tyrant.

Now that the Lacedaemonians might have no less share of his malice than the Athenians, behold how he bespatters Othryadas, the man most admired and honored by them. "He only," says Herodotus, "remaining alive of the three hundred, and ashamed to return to Sparta, his companions being lost, slew himself on the spot at Thyreae." (Ibid. i. 82.) For having before said the victory was doubtful on both sides, he here, by making Othryadas ashamed, witnesses that the Lacedaemonians were vanquished. For it was shameful for him to survive, if conquered; but glorious, if conqueror.

I pass by now, that having, represented Croesus as foolish, vainglorious, and ridiculous in all things, he makes him, when a prisoner, to have taught and instructed Cyrus, who seems to have excelled all other kings in prudence, virtue, and magnanimity. (Ibid. i. 155, 156, 207, 208.) Having testified of the same Croesus nothing else that was commendable but his honoring the gods with many and great oblations, he shows that very act of his to have been the most impious of all. For he says, that he and his brother Pantoleon contended for the kingdom while their father was yet alive; and that Croesus, having obtained the crown, caused a companion and familiar friend of Pantoleon's to be torn in pieces in a fulling-mill, and sent presents to the gods from his property. (Ibid. i. 92.) Of Deioces also, the Median, who by virtue and justice obtained the government, he says that he got it not by real but pretended justice. (Ibid. i. 96.)

But I let pass the barbarian examples, since he has offered us plenty enough in the Grecian affairs. He says, that the Athenians and many other Ionians were so ashamed of that name that they wholly refused to be called Ionians; and that those who esteemed themselves the noblest among them, and who had come forth from the very Prytaneum of Athens, begat children on barbarian wives whose parents, husbands, and former children they had slain; that the women had therefore made a law among themselves, confirmed it by oath, and delivered it to be kept by their daughters, never to eat with their husbands, nor to call any of them by his name; and that the present Milesians are descended from these women. Having afterwards added that those are true Ionians who celebrate the feast called Apaturia; they all, says he, keep it except the Ephesians and Colophonians. (Herodotus, i. 143-148.) In this manner does he deprive these two states of their nobility.

He says moreover, that the Cumaeans and Mitylenaeans agreed with Cyrus to deliver up to him for a price Pactyas, who had revolted from him. I know not indeed, says he, for how much; since it is not certain what it was. Bravo!–not to know what it was, and yet to cast such an infamy on a Grecian city, without an assured knowledge! He says farther, that the Chians took Pactyas, who was brought to them out of the temple of Minerva Poliuchus (or Guardianess of the city), and delivered him up, having received the city Atarneus for their recompense. And yet Charon the Lampsacenian, a more ancient writer, relating this matter concerning Pactyas, charges neither the Mitylenaeans nor the Chians with any such action. These are his very words: "Pactyas, hearing that the Persian army drew near, fled first to Mitylene, then to Chios, and there fell into the hands of Cyrus." (See Herodotus, i. 157. etc.)

Our author in his Third Book, relating the expedition of the Lacedaemonians against the tyrant Polycrates, affirms, that the Samians think and say that the Spartans, to recompense them for their former assistance against the Messenians, both brought back the Samians that were banished, and made war on the tyrant; but that the Lacedaemonians deny this, and say, they undertook this design not to help or deliver the Samians, but to punish them for having taken away a cup sent by them to Croesus, and besides, a breastplate sent them by Amasis. (Ibid. iii. 47, 48.) And yet we know that there was not at that time any city so desirous of honor, or such an enemy to tyrants, as Sparta. For what breastplate or cup was the cause of their driving the Cypselidae out of Corinth and Ambracia, Lygdamis out of Naxos, the children of Pisistratus out of Athens, Aeschines out of Sicyon, Symmachus out of Thasus, Aulis out of Phocis, and Aristogenes out of Miletus; and of their overturning the domineering powers of Thessaly, pulling down Aristomedes and Angelus by the help of King Leotychides?–which facts are elsewhere more largely described. Now, if Herodotus says true, they were in the highest degree guilty both of malice and folly, when, denying a most honorable and most just cause of their expedition, they confessed that in remembrance of a former injury, and too highly valuing an inconsiderable matter, they invaded a miserable and afflicted people.

Now perhaps he gave the Lacedaemonians this stroke, as directly falling under his pen; but the city of Corinth, which was wholly out of the course of his story, he has brought in–going out of his way (as they say) to fasten upon it–and has bespattered it with a most filthy crime and most shameful calumny. "The Corinthians," says he, "studiously helped this expedition of the Lacedaemonians to Samos, as having themselves also been formerly affronted by the Samians." The matter was this. Periander tyrant of Corinth sent three hundred boys, sons to the principal men of Corcyra, to King Alyattes, to be gelt. These, going ashore in the island of Samos, were by the Samians taught to sit as suppliants in the temple of Diana, where they preserved them, setting before them for their food sesame mingled with honey. This our author calls an affront put by the Samians on the Corinthians, who therefore instigated the Lacedaemonians against them, to wit, because the Samians had saved three hundred children of the Greeks from being unmanned. By attributing this villany to the Corinthians, he makes the city more wicked than the tyrant. He indeed was revenging himself on those of Corcyra who had slain his son; but what had the Corinthians suffered, that they should punish the Samians for putting an obstacle to so great a cruelty and wickedness?–and this, after three generations, reviving the memory of an old quarrel for the sake of that tyranny, which they found so grievous and intolerable that they are still endlessly abolishing all the monuments and marks of it, though long since extinct. Such then was the injury done by the Samians to the Corinthians. Now what a kind of punishment was it the Corinthians would have inflicted on them? Had they been indeed angry with the Samians, they should not have incited the Lacedaemonians, but rather diverted them from their war against Polycrates, that the Samians might not by the tyrant's overthrow recover liberty, and be freed from their slavery. But (what is most to be observed) why were the Corinthians so offended with the Samians, that desired indeed but were not able to save the Corcyraeans children, and yet were not displeased with the Cnidians, who both preserved them and restored them to their friends? Nor indeed have the Corcyraeans any great esteem for the Samians on this account; but of the Cnidians they preserve a grateful recollection, having granted them several honors and privileges, and made decrees in their favor. For these, sailing to Samos, drove away Periander's guards from the temple, and taking the children aboard their ships, carried them safe to Corcyra; as it is recorded by Antenor the Cretan, and by Dionysius the Chalcidian in his foundations. Now that the Spartans undertook not this war on any design of punishing the Samians, but to save them by delivering them from the tyrant, we have the testimony of the Samians themselves. For they affirm that there is in Samos a monument erected at the public charge, and honors there done to Archias a Spartan, who fell fighting valiantly in that quarrel; for which cause also his posterity still keep a familiar and friendly correspondence with the Samians, as Herodotus himself witnesses.

In his Fifth Book, he says, that Clisthenes, one of the best and noblest men in Athens, persuaded the priestess Pythia to be a false prophetess, and always to exhort the Lacedaemonians to free Athens from the tyrants; calumniating this most excellent and just action by the imputation of so great a wickedness and imposture, and taking from Apollo the credit of that true and good prophecy, beseeming even Themis herself, who is also said to have joined with him. He says farther, that Isagoras prostituted his wife to Cleomenes, who came to her. (Herodotus, v. 63, 70.) Then, as his manner is, to gain credit by mixing some praises with his reproaches, he says: Isagoras the son of Tisander was of a noble family, but I cannot tell the original of it; his kinsmen, however, sacrifice to the Carian Jupiter. (Herodotus, v. 66.) O this pleasant and cunning scoffer of a writer, who thus disgracefully sends Isagoras to the Carians, as it were to the ravens. As for Aristogiton, he puts him not forth at the back door, but thrusts him directly out of the gate into Phoenicia, saying that he had his original from the Gephyraeans, and that the Gephyraeans were not, as some think, Euboeans or Eretrians, but Phoenicians, as himself has heard by report. (Ibid, v. 58.) And since he cannot altogether take from the Lacedaemonians the glory of having delivered the Athenians from the tyrants, he endeavors to cloud and disgrace that most honorable act by as foul a passion. For he says, they presently repented of it, as not having done well, in that they had been persuaded by spurious and deceitful oracles to drive the tyrants, who were their allies and had promised to put Athens into their hands, out of their country, and had restored the city to an ungrateful people. He adds, that they were about to send for Hippias from Sigeum, and bring him back to Athens; but that they were opposed by the Corinthians, Sosicles telling them how much the city of Corinth had suffered under the tyranny of Cypselus and Periander. (Ibid, v. 90, 91.) And yet there was no outrage of Periander's more abominable and cruel than his sending the three hundred children to be emasculated, for the delivering and saying of whom from that contumely the Corinthians, he says, were angry and bore a grudge against the Samians, as having put an affront upon them. With so much repugnance and contradiction is that malice of his discourse filled, which on every occasion insinuates itself into his narrations.

After this, relating the action of Sardis, he, as much as in him lies, diminishes and discredits the matter; being so audacious as to call the ships which the Athenians sent to the assistance of the Ionians, who had revolted from the King the beginning of evils, because they endeavored to deliver so many and so great Grecian cities from the barbarians. (Ibid, v. 97.) As to the Eretrians, making mention of them only by the way, he passes over in silence a great, gallant, and memorable action of theirs. For when all Ionia was in a confusion and uproar, and the King's fleet drew nigh, they, going forth to meet him, overcame in a sea-fight the Cyprians in the Pamphylian Sea. Then turning back and leaving their ships at Ephesus, they invaded Sardis and besieged Artaphernes, who was fled into the castle, that so they might raise the siege of Miletus. And this indeed they effected, causing the enemies to break up their camp and remove thence in a wonderful fright, and then seeing themselves in danger to be oppressed by a multitude, retired. This not only others, but Lysanias of Mallus also in his history of Eretria relates, thinking it convenient, if for no other reason, yet after the taking and destruction of the city, to add this valiant and heroic act. But this writer of ours says, they were defeated, and pursued even to their ships by the barbarians; though Charon the Lampsacenian has no such thing, but writes thus, word for word: "The Athenians set forth with twenty galleys to the assistance of the Ionians, and going to Sardis, took all thereabouts, except the King's wall; which having done, they returned to Miletus."

In his Sixth Book, our author, discoursing of the Plataeans,–how they gave themselves to the Lacedaemonians, who exhorted them rather to have recourse to the Athenians, who were nearer to them and no bad defenders,–adds, not as a matter of suspicion or opinion, but as a thing certainly known by him, that the Lacedaemonians gave the Plataeans this advice, not so much for any goodwill, as through a desire to find work for the Athenians by engaging them with the Boeotians. (Herodotus, vi. 108.) If then Herodotus is not malicious, the Lacedaemonians must have been both fraudulent and spiteful; and the Athenians fools, in suffering themselves to be thus imposed on; and the Plataeans were brought into play, not for any good-will or respect, but as an occasion of war.

He is farther manifestly convinced of belying the Lacedaemonians, when he says that, whilst they expected the full moon, they failed of giving their assistance to the Athenians at Marathon. For they not only made a thousand other excursions and fights at the beginning of the month, without staying for the full moon; but wanted so little of being present at this very battle, which was fought the sixth day of the month Boedromion, that at their coming they found the dead still lying in the field. And yet he has written thus of the full moon: "It was impossible for them to do these things at that present, being unwilling to break the law; for it was the ninth of the month, and they said, they could not go forth on the ninth day, the orb of the moon being not yet full. And therefore they stayed for the full moon." (Herodotus, vi. 106.) But thou, O Herodotus, transferest the full moon from the middle to the beginning of the month, and at the same time confoundest the heavens, days, and all things; and yet thou dost claim to be the historian of Greece!

And professing to write more particularly and carefully of the affairs of Athens, thou dost not so much as say a word of that solemn procession which the Athenians even at this day send to Agrae, celebrating a feast of thanksgiving to Hecate for their victory. But this helps Herodotus to refel the crime with which he is charged, of having flattered the Athenians for a great sum of money he received of them. For if he had rehearsed these things to them, they would not have omitted or neglected to remark that Philippides, when on the ninth he summoned the Lacedaemonians to the fight, must have come from it himself, since (as Herodotus says) he went in two days from Athens to Sparta; unless the Athenians sent for their allies to the fight after their enemies were overcome. Indeed Diyllus the Athenian, none of the most contemptible as an historian, says, that he received from Athens a present of ten talents, Anytus proposing the decree. Moreover Herodotus, as many say, has in relating the fight at Marathon derogated from the credit of it, by the number he sets down of the slain. For it is said that the Athenians made a vow to sacrifice so many kids to Diana Agrotera, as they should kill barbarians; but that after the fight, the number of the dead appearing infinite, they appeased the goddess by making a decree to immolate five hundred to her every year.

But letting this pass, let us see what was done after the fight. "The barbarians," say he, "retiring back with the rest of their ships, and taking the Eretrian slaves out of the island, where they had left them, doubled the point of Sunium, desiring to prevent the Athenians before they could gain the city. The Athenians suspected this to have been done by a plot of the Alcmaeonidae, who by agreement showed a shield to the Persians when they were got into their ships. They therefore doubled the cape of Sunium." (Herodotus, vi. 115, 121-124.) Let us in this place take no notice of his calling the Eretrians slaves, who showed as much courage and gallantry in this war as any other of the Grecians, and suffered things unworthy their virtue. Nor let us insist much on the calumny with which he defames the Alcmaeonidae, some of whom were both the greatest families and noblest men of the city. But the greatness of the victory itself is overthrown, and the end of that so celebrated action comes to nothing, nor does it seem to have been a fight or any great exploit, but only a light skirmish with the barbarians, as the envious and ill-willers affirm, if they did not after the battle fly away, cutting their cables and giving themselves to the wind, to carry them as far as might be from the Attic coast, but having a shield lifted up to them as a signal of treason, made straight with their fleet for Athens, in hope to surprise it, and having at leisure doubled the point of Sunium, were discovered above the port Phalerum, so that the chief and most illustrious men, despairing to save the city would have betrayed it. For a little after, acquitting the Alcmaeonidae, he charges others with the treason. "For the shield indeed was shown, nor can it be denied," says he, as if he had seen it himself. But this could no way be, since the Athenians obtained a solid victory; and if it had been done, it could not have been seen by the barbarians, flying in a hurry amidst wounds and arrows into their ships, and leaving every one the place with all possible speed. But when he again pretends to excuse the Alcmaeonidae of those crimes which he first of all men objected against them, and speaks thus: "I cannot credit the report that the Alcmaeonidae by agreement would ever have lifted up a shield to the Persians, and have brought the Athenians under the power of the barbarians and Hippias"; it reminds me of a certain proverbial saving,–Stay and be caught, crab, and I'll let you go. For why art thou so eager to catch him, if thou wilt let him go when he is caught? Thus you first accuse, then apologize; and you write calumnies against illustrious men, which again you refute. And you discredit yourself; for you heard no one else but yourself say that the Alcmaeonidae lifted up a shield to the vanquished and flying barbarians. And in those very things which you allege for the Alcmaeonidae, you show yourself a sycophant. For if, as here you write, the Alcmaeonidae were more or no less enemies to tyrants than Callias, the son of Phaenippus and father of Hipponicus, where will you place their conspiracy, of which you write in your First Book, that assisting Pisistratus they brought him back from exile to the tyranny and did not drive him away till he was accused of unnaturally abusing his wife? Such then are the repugnances of these things; and by his intermixing the praises of Callias, the son of Phaenippus, amidst the crimes and suspicions of the Alcmaeonidae, and joining to him his son Hipponicus, who was (as Herodotus himself says) one of the richest men in Athens, he confesses that he brought in Callias not for any necessity of the story, but to ingratiate himself and gain favor with Hipponicus.

Now, whereas all know that the Argives denied not to enter into the common league of the Grecians, though they thought not fit to follow and be under the command of the Lacedaemonians, who were their mortal enemies, and that this was no otherways, our author subjoins a most malicious cause for it, writing thus: "When they saw they were comprised by the Greeks, knowing that the Lacedaemonians would not admit them into a share of the command, they requested it, that they might have a pretence to lie still." "And of this," he says, "the Argive ambassadors afterwards put Artaxerxes in mind, when they attended him at Susa, and the King said, he esteemed no city more his friend than Argos." Then adding, as his manner is, to cover the matter, he says: "Of these things I know nothing certainly; but this I know, that all men have faults, and that the worst things were not done by the Argives; but I must tell such things as are reported, though I am not bound to believe them all; and let this be understood of all my narrations. For it is farther said that the Argives, when they were not able to sustain the war against the Lacedaemonians, called the Persians into Greece, willing to suffer anything rather than the present trouble." (Herodotus, vii. 148-152.) Therefore, as himself reports the Ethiopian to have said of the ointment and purple, "Deceitful are the beauties, deceitful the garments of the Persians," (Herodotus, iii. 22.) may not any one say also of him, Deceitful are the phrases, deceitful the figures of Herodotus's speeches; as being perplexed, unsound, and full of ambiguities? For as painters set off and render more eminent the luminous part of their pictures by adding shadows, so he by his denials extends his calumnies, and by his dubious speeches makes his suspicions take deeper impression. If the Argives joined not with the other Greeks, but stood out through an emulation of the Lacedaemonians command and valor, it cannot be denied but that they acted in a manner not beseeming their nobility and descent from Hercules. For it had been more honorable for the Argives under the leadership of Siphnians and Cythnians to have defended the Grecian liberty, than contending with the Spartans for superiority to have avoided so many and such signal combats. And if it was they who brought the Persians into Greece, because their war against the Lacedaemonians succeeded ill, how came it to pass, that they did not at the coming of Xerxes openly join themselves to the Medes? Or if they would not fight under the King, why did they not, being left at home, make incursions into Laconia or again attempt Thyreae or by some other way disturb and infest the Lacedaemonians? For they might have greatly damaged the Grecians, by hindering the Spartans from going with so great an army to Plataea.

But in this place indeed he has highly magnified the Athenians and pronounced them the saviours of Greece, doing herein rightly and justly, if he had not intermixed many reproaches with their praises. But now, when he says (Ibid. vii. 139.) that (but for the Athenians) the Lacedaemonians would have been betrayed by the other Greeks, and then, being left alone and having performed great exploits, they would have died generously; or else, having before seen that the Greeks were favoring the Medes, they would have made terms with Xerxes; it is manifest, he speaks not these things to the commendation of the Athenians, but he praises the Athenians that he may speak ill of all the rest. For how can any one now be angry with him for so bitterly and intemperately upbraiding the Thebans and Phocians at every turn, when he charges even those who exposed themselves to all perils for Greece with a treason which was never acted, but which (as he thinks) might have been. Nay, of the Lacedaemonians themselves, he makes it doubtful whether they might have fallen in the battle or have yielded to the enemy, minimizing the proofs of their valor which were shown at Thermopylae;– and these indeed were small!

After this, when he declares the shipwreck that befell the King's fleet, and how, an infinite mass of wealth being cast away, Aminocles the Magnesian, son of Cresines, was greatly enriched by it, having gotten an immense quantity of gold and silver; he could not so much as let this pass without snarling at it. "For this man," say she, "who had till then been none of the most fortunate, by wrecks became exceeding rich; for the misfortune he had in killing his son much afflicted his mind." (Herodotus, vii. 190.) This indeed is manifest to every one, that he brought this golden treasure and this wealth cast up by the sea into his history, that he might make way for the inserting Aminocles's killing his son.

Now Aristophanes the Boeotian wrote, that Herodotus demanded money of the Thebans but received none and that going about to discourse and reason with the young men, he was prohibited by the magistrates through their clownishness and hatred of learning; of which there is no other argument. But Herodotus bears witness to Aristophanes, whilst he charges the Thebans with some things falsely, with others ignorantly, and with others as hating them and having a quarrel with them. For he affirms that the Thessalians at first upon necessity inclined to the Persians, (Ibid, vii. 172.) in which he says the truth; and prophesying of the other Grecians that they would betray the Lacedaemonians, he added, that they would not do it willingly, but upon necessity, one city being taken after another. But he does not allow the Thebans the same plea of necessity, although they sent to Tempe five hundred men under the command of Mnamias, and to Thermopylae as many as Leonidas desired, who also alone with the Thespians stood by him, the rest leaving him after he was surrounded. But when the barbarian, having possessed himself of the avenues, was got into their confines, and Demaratus the Spartan, favoring in right of hospitality Attaginus, the chief of the oligarchy, had so wrought that he became the King's friend and familiar, whilst the other Greeks were in their ships, and none came on by land; then at last being forsaken did they accept conditions of peace, to which they were compelled by great necessity. For they had neither the sea and ships at hand, as had the Athenians; nor did they dwell far off, as the Spartans, who inhabited the most remote parts of Greece; but were not above a day and half's journey from the Persian army, whom they had already with the Spartans and Thespians alone resisted at the entrance of the straits, and were defeated.

But this writer is so equitable, that having said, "The Lacedaemonians, being alone and deserted by their allies, would perhaps have made a composition with Xerxes," he yet blames the Thebans, who were forced to the same act by the same necessity. But when he could not wholly obliterate this most great and glorious act of the Thebans, yet went he about to deface it with a most vile imputation and suspicion, writing thus: "The confederates who had been sent returned back, obeying the commands of Leonidas; there remained only with the Lacedaemonians the Thespians and the Thebans: of these, the Thebans stayed against their wills, for Leonidas retained them as hostages; but the Thespians most willingly, as they said they would never depart from Leonidas and those that were with him." (Herodotus, vii. 222.) Does he not here manifestly discover himself to have a peculiar pique and hatred against the Thebans, by the impulse of which he not only falsely and unjustly calumniated the city, but did not so much as take care to render his contradiction probable, or to conceal, at least from a few men, his being conscious of having knowingly contradicted himself? For having before said that Leonidas, perceiving his confederates not to be in good heart nor prepared to undergo danger, wished them to depart, he a little after adds that the Thebans were against their wills detained by him; whereas, if he had believed them inclined to the Persians, he should have driven them away though they had been willing to tarry. For if he thought that those who were not brisk would be useless, to what purpose was it to mix among his soldiers those that were suspected? Nor was the king of the Spartans and general of all Greece so senseless as to think that four hundred armed Thebans could be detained as hostages by his three hundred, especially the enemy being both in his front and rear. For though at first he might have taken them along with him as hostages; it is certainly probable that at last, having no regard for him, they would have gone away from him, and that Leonidas would have more feared his being encompassed by them than by the enemy. Furthermore, would not Leonidas have been ridiculous, to have sent away the other Greeks, as if by staying they should soon after have died, and to have detained the Thebans, that being himself about to die, he might keep them for the Greeks? For if he had indeed carried them along with him for hostages, or rather for slaves, he should not have kept them with those that were at the point of perishing, but have delivered them to the Greeks that went away. There remained but one cause that might be alleged for Leonidas's unwillingness to let them go, to wit, that they might die with him; and this our historian himself has taken away, writing thus of Leonidas's ambition: "Leonidas, considering these things, and desirous that this glory might redound to the Spartans alone, sent away his confederates rather for this than because they differed in their opinions." (Herodotus, vii. 220.) For it had certainly been the height of folly to keep his enemies against their wills, to be partakers of that glory from which he drove away his confederates. But it is manifest from the effects, that Leonidas suspected not the Thebans of insincerity, but esteemed them to be his steadfast friends. For he marched with his army into Thebes, and at his request obtained that which was never granted to any other, to sleep within the temple of Hercules; and the next morning he related to the Thebans the vision that had appeared to him. For he imagined that he saw the most illustrious and greatest cities of Greece irregularly tossed and floating up and down on a very stormy and tempestuous sea; that Thebes, being carried above all the rest, was lifted up on high to heaven, and suddenly after disappeared. And this indeed had a resemblance of those things which long after befell that city.

Now Herodotus, in his narration of that fight, hath obscured also the bravest act of Leonidas, saying that they all fell in the straits near the hill. (Herodotus, vii. 225.) But the affair was otherwise managed. For when they perceived by night that they were encompassed by the barbarians, they marched straight to the enemies' camp, and got very near the King's pavilion, with a resolution to kill him and leave their lives about him. They came then to his tent, killing or putting to flight all they met; but when Xerxes was not found there, seeking him in that vast camp and wandering about, they were at last with much difficulty slain by the barbarians, who surrounded them on every side. What other acts and sayings of the Spartans Herodotus has omitted, we will write in the Life of Leonidas; yet that hinders not but we may here set down also some few. Before Leonidas went forth to that war, the Spartans exhibited to him funeral spectacles, at which the fathers and mothers of those that went along with him were spectators. Leonidas himself, when one said to him, You lead very few with you to the battle, answered, There are many to die there. When his wife, at his departure, asked him what commands he had for her; he, turning to her, said, I command you to marry a good man, and bring him good children. After he was enclosed by the enemy at Thermopylae, desiring to save two that were related to him, he gave one of them a letter and sent him away; but he rejected it, saying angrily, I followed you as a soldier, not as a postman. The other he commanded to go on a message to the magistrates of Sparta; but he, answering, that is a messenger's business, took his shield, and stood up in his rank. Who would not have blamed another that should have omitted these things? But he who has collected and recorded the fart of Amasis, the coming of the thief's asses, and the giving of bottles, and many such like things, cannot seem to have omitted these gallant acts and these remarkable sayings by negligence and oversight, but as bearing ill-will and being unjust to some.

He says that the Thebans, being at the first with the Greeks, fought compelled by necessity. (Ibid, vii. 233.) For belike not only Xerxes, but Leonidas also, had whipsters following his camp, by whom the Thebans were scourged and forced against their wills to fight. And what more ruthless libeller could there be than Herodotus, when he says that they fought upon necessity, who might have gone away and fled, and that they inclined to the Persians, whereas not one came in to help them. After this, he writes that, the rest making to the hill, the Thebans separated themselves from them, lifted up their hands to the barbarian, and coming near, cried with a most true voice, that they had favored the Persians, had given earth and water to the King, that now being forced by necessity they were come to Thermopylae, and that they were innocent of the King's wound. Having said these things, they obtained quarter; for they had the Thessalians for witnesses of all they said. Behold, how amidst the barbarians, exclamations, tumults of all sorts, flights and pursuits, their apology was heard, the witnesses examined; and the Thessalians, in the midst of those that were slain and trodden under foot, all being done in a very narrow passage, patronized the Thebans, to wit, because the Thebans had but a little before driven away them, who were possessed of all Greece as far as, Thespiae, having conquered them in a battle, and slain their leader Lattamyas! For thus at that time stood matters between the Boeotians and the Thessalians, without any friendship or good-will. But yet how did the Thebans escape, the Thessalians helping them with their testimonies? Some of them, says he, were slain by the barbarians; many of them were by command of Xerxes marked with the royal mark, beginning with their leader Leontiades. Now the captain of the Thebans at Thermopylae was not Leontiades, but Anaxander, as both Aristophanes, out of the Commentaries of the Magistrates, and Nicander the Colophonian have taught us. Nor did any man before Herodotus know that the Thebans were stigmatized by Xerxes; for otherwise this would have been an excellent plea for them against his calumny, and this city might well have gloried in these marks, that Xerxes had punished Leonidas and Leontiades as his greatest enemies, having outraged the body of the one when he was dead, and caused the other to be tormented whilst living. But as to a writer who makes the barbarian's cruelty against Leonidas when dead a sign that he hated him most of all men when living, (Herodotus, vii. 238.) and yet says that the Thebans, though favoring the Persians, were stigmatized by them at Thermopylae, and having been thus stigmatized, again cheerfully took their parts at Plataea, it seems to me that such a man–like that Hippoclides (See Herodotus, vi. 126-130.) who gesticulating with his limbs by standing on his head on a table–would dance away the truth and say, It makes no difference to Herodotus.

In the Eighth Book our author says, that the Greeks being frighted designed to fly from Artemisium into Greece, and that, being requested by the Euboeans to stay a little till they could dispose of their wives and families, they regarded them not, till such time as Themistocles, having taken money of them, divided it between Eurybiades and Adimantus, the captain of the Corinthians, and that then they stayed and had a sea-fight with the barbarians (Ibid. viii. 4.) Yet Pindar, who was not a citizen of any of the confederate cities, but of one that was suspected to take part with the Medians, having made mention of Artemisium, brake forth into this exclamation: "This is the place where the sons of the Athenians laid the glorious foundation of liberty." But Herodotus, by whom, as some will have it, Greece is honored, makes that victory a work of bribery and theft, saying that the Greeks, deceived by their captains, who had to that end taken money, fought against their wills. Nor does he here put an end to his malice. All men in a manner confess that, although the Greeks got the better at sea, they nevertheless abandoned Artemisium to the barbarians after they had received the news of the overthrow at Thermopylae. For it was to no purpose for them to stay there and keep the sea, the war being already within Thermopylae, and Xerxes having possessed himself of the avenues. But Herodotus makes the Greeks contriving to fly before they heard anything of Leonidas's death. For thus he says: "But they having been ill-treated, and especially the Athenians, half of whose ships were sorely shattered, consulted to take their flight into Greece." (Ibid. viii. 18.) But let him be permitted so to name (or rather reproach) this retreat of theirs before the fight; but having before called it a flight, he both now styles it a flight, and will again a little after term it a flight; so bitterly does he adhere to this word "flight." "Presently after this," says he, "there came to the barbarians in the pinnace a man of Hestiaea, who acquainted them with the flight of the Grecians from Artemisium. They, because the thing seemed incredible, kept the messenger in custody, and sent forth some light galleys to discover the truth." (Herodotus, viii. 23.) But what is this you say? That they fled as conquered, whom the enemies after the fight could not believe to have fled, as having got much the better? Is then this a fellow fit to be believed when he writes of any man or city, who in one word deprives Greece of the victory, throws down the trophy, and pronounces the inscriptions they had set up to Diana Proseoa (EASTWARD-FACING) to be nothing but pride and vain boasting? The tenor of the inscription was as follows:–

When Athens youth had in a naval fight
All Asia's forces on this sea o'verthrown,
And all the Persian army put to flight,
Than which a greater scare was ever known,
To show how much Diana they respected,
This trophy to her honor they erected.

Moreover, not having described any order of the Greeks, nor told us what place every city of theirs held during the sea-fight, he says that in this retreat, which he calls their flight, the Corinthians sailed first and the Athenians last. (Ibid. viii, 21.)

He indeed ought not to have too much insulted over the Greeks that took part with the Persians, who, being by others thought a Thurian, reckons himself among the Halicarnassians, who, being Dorians by descent, went with their wives and children to the war against the Greeks. But he is so far from giving first an account of the straits they were in who revolted to the Persians, that, having related how the Thessalians sent to the Phocians, who were their mortal enemies, and promised to preserve their country free from all damage if they might receive from them a reward of fifty talents, he writ thus of the Phocians: "For the Phocians were the only people in these quarters who inclined not to the Persians, and that, as far as I upon due consideration can find, for no other reason but because they hated the Thessalians; for if the Thessalians had been affected to the Grecian affairs, I suppose the Phocians would have joined themselves to the Persians." And yet, a little after he would say that thirteen cities of the Phocians were burned by the barbarians, their country laid waste, and the temple which was in Abae set on fire, and all of both sexes put to the sword, except those that by flight escaped to Parnassus. (Herodotus, viii. 30-33. Compare ix. 17.) Nevertheless, he puts those who suffered all extremities rather than lose their honesty in the same rank with those who most affectionately sided with the Persians. And when he could not blame the Phocians actions, writing at his desk invented false causes and got up suspicions against them, and bids us judge them not by what they did, but by what they would have done if the Thessalians had not taken the same side, as if they had been prevented from treason because they found the place already occupied by others! Now if any one, going about to excuse the revolt of the Thessalians to the Persians, should say that they would not have done it but for the hatred they bare the Phocians,–whom when they saw joined to the Greeks, they against their inclinations followed the party of the Persians,–would not such a one be thought most shamefully to flatter, and for the sake of others to pervert the truth, by reigning good causes for evil actions? Indeed, I think, he would. Why then would not he be thought openly to calumniate, who says that the Phocians chose the best, not for the love of virtue, but because they saw the Thessalians on the contrary side? For neither does he refer this device to other authors, as he is elsewhere wont to do, but says that himself found it out by conjecture. He should therefore have produced certain arguments, by which he was persuaded that they, who did things like the best, followed the same counsels with the worst. For what he alleges of their hatreds is ridiculous. For neither did the difference between the Aeginetans and the Athenians, nor that between the Chalcidians and the Eretrians, nor yet that between the Corinthians and the Megarians, hinder them from fighting together for Greece. Nor did the Macedonians, their most bitter enemies, turn the Thessalians from their friendship with the barbarians, by joining the Persian party themselves. For the common danger did so bury their private grudges, that banishing their other passions, they applied their minds either to honesty for the sake of virtue, or to profit through the impulse of necessity. And indeed, after that necessity which compelled them to obey the Persians was over, they returned again to the Greeks, as Lacrates the Spartan has openly testified of them. And Herodotus, as constrained to it, in his relation of the affairs at Plataea, confessed that the Phocians took part with the Greeks. (Herodotus, ix. 31.)

Neither ought it to seem strange to any, if he thus bitterly inveighs against the unfortunate; since he reckons amongst enemies and traitors those who were present at the engagement, and together with the other Greeks hazarded their safety. For the Naxians, says he, sent three ships to the assistance of the barbarians; but Democritus, one of their captains, persuaded the others to take the party of the Greeks. (Ibid. viii. 46.) So unable he is to praise without dispraising, that if he commends one man he must condemn a whole city or people. But in this there give testimony against him, of the more ancient writers Hellanicus, and of the later Ephorus, one of which says that the Naxians came with six ships to aid the Greeks, and the other with five. And Herodotus convinces himself of having feigned these things. For the writers of the Naxian annals say, that they had before beaten back Megabates, who came to their island with two hundred ships, and after that had put to flight the general Datis who had set their city on fire. Now if, as Herodotus has elsewhere said, the barbarians burned their city so that the men were glad to save themselves by flying into the mountains, had they not just cause rather to send aid to the destroyers of their country than to help the protectors of the common liberty? But that he framed this lie not so much to honor Democritus, as to cast infamy on the Naxians, is manifest from his omitting and wholly passing over in silence the valiant acts then performed by Democritus, of which Simonides gives us an account in this epigram:–

When as the Greeks at sea the Medes did meet,
And had near Salamis a naval fight,
Democritus as third led up the fleet,
Charging the enemy with all his might;
He took five of their ships, and did another,
Which they had taken from the Greeks, recover.

But why should any one be angry with him about the Naxians? If we have, as some say, antipodes inhabiting the other hemisphere, I believe that they also have heard of Themistocles and his counsel, which he gave to the Greeks, to fight a naval battle before Salamis, on which, the barbarian being overcome, he built in Melite a temple to Diana the Counsellor. This gentle writer, endeavoring, as much as in him lies, to deprive Themistocles of the glory of this, and transfer it to another, writes thus word for word: "Whilst things were thus, Mnesiphilus, an Athenian, asked Themistocles, as he was going aboard his ship, what had been resolved on in council. And being answered, that it was decreed the ships should be brought back to Isthmus, and a battle fought at sea before Peloponnesus; he said, If then they remove the navy from Salamis, you will no longer be fighting for one country for they will return every one to his own city. Wherefore, if there be any way left, go and endeavor to break this resolution; and, if it be possible, persuade Eurybiades to change his mind and stay here." Then adding that this advice pleased Themistocles, who, without making any reply, went straight to Eurybiades, he has these very expressions: "And sitting by him he related what he had heard from Mnesiphilus, feigning as if it came from himself, and adding other things." (Herodotus, viii. 57, 58.) You see how he accuses Themistocles of disingenuity in arrogating to himself the counsel of Mnesiphilus.

And deriding the Greeks still further, he says, that Themistocles, who was called another Ulysses for his wisdom, was so blind that he could not foresee what was fit to be done; but that Artemisia, who was of the same city with Herodotus, without being taught by any one, but by her own consideration, said thus to Xerxes: "The Greeks will not long be able to hold out against you, but you will put them to flight, and they will retire to their own cities; nor is it probable, if you march your army by land to Peloponnesus, that they will sit still, or take care to fight at sea for the Athenians. But if you make haste to give them a naval battle, I fear lest your fleets receiving damage may prove also very prejudicial to your land-forces." (Ibid. viii. 68.) Certainly Herodotus wanted nothing but verses to make Artemisia another Sibyl, so exactly prophesying of things to come. Therefore Xerxes also delivered his sons to her to be carried to Ephesus for he had (it seems) forgot to bring women with him from Susa, if indeed the children wanted a train of female attendants.

But it is not our design to search into the lies of Herodotus; we only make inquiry into those which he invented to detract from the glory of others. He says: "It is reported by the Athenians that Adimantus,

captain of the Corinthians, when the enemies were now ready to
join battle, was struck with such fear and astonishment that he fled;
not thrusting his ship backward by the stern, or leisurely retreating
through those that were engaged, but openly hoisting up his sails, and
turning the heads of all his vessels. And about the farther part of the
Salaminian coast, he was met by a pinnace, out of which one spake
thus to him: Thou indeed, Adimantus, fliest, having betrayed the Grecians; yet they overcome, and according to their desires have the better of their enemies." (Herodotus, viii. 94.) This pinnace was certainly
let down from heaven. For what should hinder him from erecting a
tragical machine, who by his boasting excelled the tragedians in all
other things? Adimantus then crediting him (he adds) "returned to
the fleet, when the business was already done." "This report," says he,
"is believed by the Athenians; but the Corinthians deny it, and say,
they were the first at the sea-fight, for which they have the testimony
of all the other Greeks." Such is this man in many other places. He
spreads different calumnies and accusations of different men, that he
may not fail of making some one appear altogether wicked. And it has
succeeded well with him in this place; for if the calumny is believed,
the Corinthians–if it is not, the Athenians–are rendered infamous.
But in reality the Athenians did not belie the Corinthians, but he hath
belied them both. Certainly Thucydides, bringing in an Athenian
ambassador contesting with a Corinthian at Sparta, and gloriously
boasting of many things about the Persian war and the sea-fight at
Salamis, charges not the Corinthians with any crime of treachery or
leaving their station. Nor was it likely the Athenians should object
any such thing against Corinth, when they saw her engraven in the
third place after the Lacedaemonians and themselves on those spoils
which, being taken from the barbarians, were consecrated to the
gods. And in Salamis they had permitted them to bury the dead near
the city, as being men who had behaved themselves gallantly, and to
write over them this elegy:–

> *Well-watered Corinth, stranger, was our home;*
> *Salamis, Ajax's isle, is now our grave;*
> *Here Medes and Persians and Phoenician ships*
> *We fought and routed, sacred Greece to save.*

And their honorary sepulchre at the Isthmus has on it this epitaph:–

> *When Greece upon the point of danger stood,*
> *We fell, defending her with our life-blood.*

Moreover, on the offerings of Diodorus, one of the Corinthian sea-
captains, reserved in the temple of Latona, there is this inscription:–

> *Diodorus's seamen to Latona sent*
> *These arms, of hostile Medes the monument*

And as for Adimantus himself, against whom Herodotus frequently inveighs,–saying, that he was the only captain who went about to fly from Artemisium, and would not stay the fight,–behold in how great honor he is:–

> *Here Adimantus rests: the same was he,*
> *Whose counsels won for Greece the crown of liberty.*

For neither is it probable, that such honor would have been shown to a coward and a traitor after his decease; nor would he have dared to give his daughters the names of Nausinica, Acrothinius, and Alexibia, and his son that of Aristeas, if he had not performed some illustrious and memorable action in that fight. Nor is it credible that Herodotus was ignorant of that which could not be unknown even to the meanest Carian, that the Corinthian women alone made that glorious and divine prayer, by which they besought the Goddess Venus to inspire their husbands with a love of fighting against the barbarians. For it was a thing divulged abroad, concerning which Simonides made an epigram to be inscribed on the brazen image set up in that temple of Venus which is said to have been founded by Medea, when she desired the goddess, as some affirm, to deliver her from loving her husband Jason, or, as others say, to free him from loving Thetis. The tenor of the epigram follows:–

> *For those who, fighting on their country's side,*
> *Opposed th' imperial Mede's advancing tide,*
> *We, votaresses, to Cythera pray'd;*
> *Th' indulgent power vouchsafed her timely aid,*
> *And kept the citadel of Hellas free*
> *From rude assaults of Persia's archery.*

These things he should rather have written and recorded, than have inserted Aminocles's killing of his son.

After he had abundantly satisfied himself with the accusations brought against Themistocles,–of whom he says that, unknown to the other captains, he incessantly robbed and spoiled the islands,–(Herodotus, viii. 112.) he at length openly takes away the crown of victory from the Athenians, and sets it on the head of the Aeginetans, writing thus: "The Greeks having sent the first-fruits of their spoils to Delphi, asked in general of the god, whether he had a sufficient part of the booty and were contented with it. He answered, that he had enough of all the other Greeks, but not of the Aeginetans for he expected a donary of them, as having won the greatest honor in the battle at Salamis." (Ibid. viii. 122.) See here how he attributes not his fictions to the Scythians, to the Persians, or to the Egyptians, as Aesop did his to the ravens and apes; but using the very person of the Pythian Apollo, he takes from Athens the chief honor of the battle at Salamis. And the second place in honor being given to Themistocles at the Isthmus by all the other captains,–every one of which attributed to himself the first degree of valor, but give the next to Themistocles,–and the judgment not coming to a determination, when he should have reprehended the ambition of the captains, he said, that all the Greeks weighed anchor from thence through envy, not being willing to give the chief honor of the victory to Themistocles. (Ibid. viii. 123, 124.)

In his ninth and last book, having nothing left to vent his malice on but the Lacedaemonians and their glorious action against the barbarians at Plataea, he writes, that the Spartans at first feared lest the Athenians should suffer themselves to be persuaded by Mardonius to forsake the other Greeks; but that now, the Isthmus being fortified, they, supposing all to be safe at Peloponnesus, slighted the rest, feasting and making merry at home, and deluding and delaying the Athenian ambassadors. (Herodotus, ix. 8. See also viii. 141.) How then did there go forth from Sparta to Plataea a thousand and five men, having every one of them with him seven Helots? Or how came it that, exposing themselves to so many dangers, they vanquished and overthrew so many thousand barbarians? Hear now his probable cause of it. "It happened," says he, "that there was then at Sparta a certain stranger of Tegea, named Chileus, who had some friends amongst the Ephori, between whom and him there was mutual hospitality. He then persuaded them to send forth the army, telling them that the fortification on the Isthmus, by which they had fenced in Peloponnesus, would be of no avail if the Athenians joined themselves with Mardonius." (Ibid. ix. 9.) This counsel then drew Pausanias with his army to Plataea; but if any private business had kept that Chileus at Tegea, Greece had never been victorious.

Again, not knowing what to do with the Athenians, he tosses to and fro that city, sometimes extolling it, and sometimes debasing it. He says that, contending for the second place with the Tegeatans they made mention of the Heraclidae, alleged their acts against the Amazons, and the sepulchres of the Peloponnesians that died under the walls of Cadmea, and at last brought down their discourse to the battle of Marathon, saying, however, that they would be satisfied with the command of the left wing. (Ibid. ix. 26, 27.) A little after, he says, Pausanias and the Spartans yielded them the first place, desiring them to fight in the right wing against the Persians and give them the left, who excused themselves as not skilled in fighting against the barbarians. (Ibid. ix. 46.) Now it is a ridiculous thing, to be unwilling to fight against an enemy unless one has been used to him. But he says farther, that the other Greeks being led by their captains to encamp in another place, as soon as they were moved, the horse fled with joy towards Plataea, and in their flight came as far as Juno's temple. (Ibid. ix. 52.) In which place indeed he charges them all in general with disobedience, cowardice, and treason. At last he says, that only the Lacedaemonians and the Tegeates fought with the barbarians, and the Athenians with the Thebans; equally defrauding all the other cities of their part in the honor of the victory, whilst he affirms that none of them joined in the fight, but that all of them, sitting still hard by in their arms, betrayed and forsook those who fought for them; that the Phliasians and Megarians indeed, when they heard Pausanias had got the better, came in later, and falling on the Theban horse, were all cut off; that the Corinthians were not at the battle, and that after the victory, by hastening on over the hills, they escaped the Theban cavalry. (See the account of the battle of Plataea, Herodotus, ix, 59-70.) For the Thebans, after the barbarians were overthrown, going before with their horse, affectionately assisted them in their flight; to return them thanks (forsooth) for the marks they had stigmatized them with at Thermopylae! Now what rank the Corinthians had in the fight at Plataea against the barbarians, and how they performed their duty, you may hear from Simonides in these verses:

> *I' th' midst were men, in warlike feats excelling,*
> *Who Ephyre full of springs, inhabited,*
> *And who in Corinth, Glaucus' city, dwelling,*
> *Great praise by their great valor merited;*
> *Of which they to perpetuate the fame,*
> *To th' gods of well-wrought gold did offerings frame.*

For he wrote not these things, as one that taught at Corinth or that made verses in honor of the city, but only as recording these actions in elegiac verses. But Herodotus, whilst he desires to prevent that objection by which those might convince him of lying who should ask, Whence then are so many mounts, tombs, and monuments of the dead, at which the Plataeans, even to this day, celebrate funeral solemnities in the presence of the Greeks?–has charged, unless I am mistaken, a fouler crime than that of treason on their posterity. For these are his words: "As for the other sepulchres that are seen in Plataea, I have heard that their successors, being ashamed of their progenitors' absence from this battle, erected every man a monument for posterity's sake." (Herodotus, ix. 85.) Of this treacherous deserting the battle Herodotus was the only man that ever heard. For if any Greeks withdrew themselves from the battle, they must have deceived Pausanias, Aristides, the Lacedaemonians, and the Athenians. Neither yet did the Athenians exclude the Aeginetans who were their adversaries from the inscription, nor convince the Corinthians of having fled from Salamis before the victory, Greece bearing witness to the contrary. Indeed Cleadas, a Plataean, ten years after the Persian war, to gratify, as Herodotus says, the Aeginetans, erected a mount bearing their name. Now came it then to pass that the Athenians and Lacedaemonians, who were so jealous of each other that they were presently after the war ready to go together by the ears about the setting up a trophy, did not yet repel those Greeks who fled in a fear from the battle from having a share in the honor of those that behaved themselves valiantly, but inscribed their names on the trophies and colossuses, and granted them part of the spoils? Lastly they set up an altar, on which was engraven this epigram:

> *The Greeks, by valor having put to flight*
> *The Persians and preserved their country's right,*
> *Erected here this altar which you see,*
> *To Jove, preserver of their liberty.*

Did Cleadas, O Herodotus, or some other, write this also, to oblige the cities by flattery? What need had they then to employ fruitless labor in digging up the earth, to make tombs and erect monuments for posterity's sake, when they saw their glory consecrated in the most illustrious and greatest donaries? Pausanias, indeed, when he was aspiring to the tyranny, set up this inscription in Delphi:–

> *Pausanias, of Greeks the general*
> *When he the Medes in fight had overthrown,*
> *Offered to Phoebus a memorial*
> *Of victory, this monumental stone.*

In which he gave the glory to the Greeks, whose general he professed himself to be. Yet the Greeks not enduring but utterly misliking it, the Lacedaemonians, sending to Delphi, caused this to be cut out, and the names of the cities, as it was fit, to be engraven instead of it. Now how is it possible that the Greeks should have been offended that there was no mention made of them in the inscription, if they had been conscious to themselves of deserting the fight? or that the Lacedaemonians would have erased the name of their leader and general, to insert deserters and such as withdrew themselves from the common danger? For it would have been a great indignity, that Sophanes, Aeimnestus, and all the rest who showed their valor in that fight, should calmly suffer even the Cythnians and Melians to be inscribed on the trophies; and that Herodotus, attributing that fight only to three cities, should raze all the rest out of those and other sacred monuments and donaries.

There having been then four fights with the barbarians; he says, that the Greeks fled from Artemisium; that, whilst their king and general exposed himself to danger at Thermopylae, the Lacedaemonians sat negligent at home, celebrating the Olympian and Carnean feasts; and discoursing of the action at Salamis, he uses more words about Artemisia than he does in his whole narrative of the naval battle. Lastly, he says, that the Greeks sat still at Plataea, knowing no more of the fight, till it was over, than if it had been a skirmish between mice and frogs (like that which Pigres, Artemisia's fellow countryman, merrily and scoffingly related in a poem), and it had been agreed to fight silently, lest they should be heard by others; and that the Lacedaemonians excelled not the barbarians in valor, but only got the better, as fighting against naked and unarmed men. To wit, when Xerxes himself was present, the barbarians were with much difficulty compelled by scourges to fight with the Greeks; but at Plataea, having taken other resolutions, as Herodotus says, "they were no way inferior in courage and strength; but their garments being without armor was prejudicial to them, since being naked they fought against a completely armed enemy." What then is there left great and memorable to the Grecians of those fights, if the Lacedaemonians fought with unarmed men, and the other Greeks, though present, were ignorant of the battle; if empty monuments are set up everywhere, and tripods and altars full of lying inscriptions are placed before the gods; if, lastly, Herodotus only knows the truth, and all others that give any account of the Greeks have been deceived by the fame of those glorious actions, as the effect of an admirable prowess? But he is an acute writer, his style is pleasant, there is a certain grace, force, and elegancy in his narrations; and he has, like a musician, elaborated his discourse, though not knowingly, still clearly and elegantly. These things delight, please, and affect all men. But as in roses we must beware of the venomous flies called cantharides; so must we take heed of the calumnies and envy lying hid under smooth and well-couched phrases and expressions, lest we imprudently entertain absurd and false opinions of the most excellent and greatest cities and men of Greece.

READ THE TOP 40 ROYAL CLASSICS

20,000 Leagues Under the Sea BY JULES VERNE
A Christmas Carol BY CHARLES DICKENS
A Tale of Two Cities BY JULES VERNE
Aesop's Fables BY AESOP
Alice in Wonderland BY LEWIS CARROLL
Anna Karenina BY LEO TOLSTOY
Candide BY VOLTAIRE
Crime and Punishment BY FYODOR DOSTOEVSKY
Don Quixote BY MIGUEL DE CERVANTES
Dracula BY BRAM STOKER
Frankenstein BY MARY SHELLEY
Great Expectations BY CHARLES DICKENS
Jane Eyre BY CHARLOTTE BRONTË
Les Misérables BY VICTOR HUGO
Meditations BY MARCUS AURELIUS
Moby Dick BY HERMAN MELVILLE
Plato: Five Dialogues BY PLATO
Pride & Prejudice BY JANE AUSTEN
The Adventures of Sherlock Holmes BY A. CONAN DOYLE
The Adventures of Tom Sawyer BY MARK TWAIN
The Art of War BY SUN TZU
The Count of Monte Cristo BY ALEXANDRE DUMAS
The Iliad BY HOMER
The Importance of Being Earnest BY OSCAR WILDE
The Odyssey BY HOMER
The Origin of Species BY CHARLES DARWIN
The Prince BY NICCOLÒ MACHIAVELLI
The Prophet BY KAHLIL GIBRAN
The Republic BY PLATO
The Tale of Peter Rabbit BY BEATRIX POTTER
The Three Musketeers BY ALEXANDRE DUMAS
The Time Machine BY H. G. WELLS
The Wealth of Nations BY ADAM SMITH
The Wind in the Willows BY KENNETH GRAHAME
The Wizard of Oz BY L. FRANK BAUM
This Side of Paradise BY F. SCOTT FITZGERALD
Treasure Island BY ROBERT LOUIS STEVENSON
Ulysses BY JAMES JOYCE
War and Peace BY LEO TOLSTOY
Wuthering Heights BY EMILY BRONTË